TEACHER'S ANNOTATED EDITION

# HOUSING
# DECISIONS

**Evelyn L. Lewis, Ed.D.**
Professor Emeritus, Home Economics
Northern Arizona University
Flagstaff, Arizona

**Carolyn S. Turner, Ph.D., CFCS**
Professor, Housing Research and Associate Dean for Research
North Carolina Agricultural and Technical State University
Greensboro, North Carolina

Teaching Strategies written by

**Linda G. Smock, CFCS**
Educational Consultant and Writer
Largo, Florida

Publisher
**The Goodheart-Willcox Company, Inc.**
Tinley Park, Illinois

International Standard Book Number 1-59070-141-0

2 3 4 5 6 7 8 9 10   04   09 08 07 06 05 04 03

# CONTENTS

# HOUSING DECISIONS

## Student Text

**Examines housing needs and choices, design basics, and career opportunities in the wide-ranging housing and interior design fields.**

- **Key Terms** introduce new terminology.
- **Objectives** set realistic learning goals for students.
- **Charts and Illustrations** clarify topics presented in the lesson.
- **Chapter Summaries** reinforce key concepts.
- **To Review** questions help students recall important information.
- **In Your Community** activities encourage students to seek answers from resources in the area and apply concepts to situations in their own communities.
- **To Think About** provides exercises that involve the higher-order thinking skills of analysis, synthesis, and evaluation.
- **Using Technology** presents activities that involve using the Internet, computer software programs, a camera, or a PowerPoint® presentation.

43

CHAPTER 2
## Influences on Housing

*To Know*

agrarian
density
tenement houses
row houses
architect
substandard
census
tract houses
new town
new urbanism
subdivision
culture
hogan
demographics
baby boomers
disability
dual-income family
telecommuting
Sunbelt
environment
climate
topography
dysfunctional
resources
housing market
gross domestic product (GDP)
technology
high tech
computer-aided drafting and design (CADD)
building codes
zoning regulation
infrastructure
Habitat for Humanity

James F. Parnell

*Objectives*

After studying this chapter, you will be able to
- relate historical events to housing.
- describe various cultures and housing characteristics.
- determine the relationship between societal changes and housing.
- analyze concerns about environmental aspects of housing.
- relate the effects of economy and housing on each other.
- summarize the impact of technology on housing.
- identify the role of government in housing decisions.

---

## Page 40

### Summary

People interact with their housing. Their housing affects them, and they affect their housing. Housing helps satisfy people's physical and psychological needs and can help them move toward self-actualization. Beauty, self-expression, and creativity are other needs that can be met through housing.

Each person chooses a lifestyle, which is reflected in his or her housing. Needs and personal priorities are closely related. However, the needs and personal priorities of people and living units vary as they move through the life cycles.

Housing affects the quality of life for both individuals and society. The study of human ecology can help improve housing and the quality of life for society.

### To Review

1. The word *housing* refers to the dwelling and what is within and _____ it.
2. Housing is your _____.
   A. near environment
   B. total environment
3. List three physical needs people have.
4. Four psychological needs that people have are _____, _____, _____, and _____.
5. How is a person's personal-priority system formed?
6. Give an example of how housing can help you meet each of the following needs:
   A. security
   B. creativity
   C. self-expression
7. Describe five ways to achieve privacy.
8. Explain how space and privacy are related.
9. Given the chance, how would you change your housing to better meet your need for self-actualization?
10. People who share the same living quarters are _____.
11. Provide an example of an extended family that is not a stepfamily.
12. List the four stages of the individual life cycle.
13. Give an example of the way housing needs change as a family moves from one stage of the life cycle to another.
14. Explain how a couple in the beginning stage of the family life cycle differs from a couple in the aging stage.

---

## Page 41

### In Your Community

1. Identify 10 households in your community that you know well. For each, identify the type of household it is. Also, write a one-sentence description of each member, identifying sex, approximate age, and relationship to the family.
2. Consider your household members and examine your home's interior space. In the last five years, has the size of your household changed? If so, how? Has the change resulted in more or less space per person? Do you have more or less personal privacy today compared to five years ago? Forecast your household's need for space five years from now. What possible changes in the household may occur in the next five years that will increase the amount of space per person? that will decrease the space per person?
3. Interview an older person to describe changes in his or her housing over the years. Ask how the person's lifestyle and housing affect each other. If possible, tape-record the interview and share it with the class.
4. Does your community have homeless people? Investigate what the town (city) and local charitable organizations are doing to handle this problem. What is being done to prevent it? Summarize your findings in a one-page report.
5. Obtain permission to rearrange furniture in a part of your house to provide more privacy. Report your actions and results to the class.

### To Think About

1. Suppose a family's lifestyle involves some members using their home to do work for their job. What changes might have to be made to the interior of the home if one or more family members begin (or already are) working at home?
2. List in order of importance the needs and personal priorities that are met by your housing.
3. Describe how the use of a spare bedroom may change depending on whether the living unit includes the following: small children, teenagers, people with hobbies, a person working at home, or retirees.

### Using Technology

1. Use the Internet to research cliff dwellings. Determine who built them and why they were built. Find out how many different sites containing cliff dwellings exist in Colorado. How many

---

## Page 32

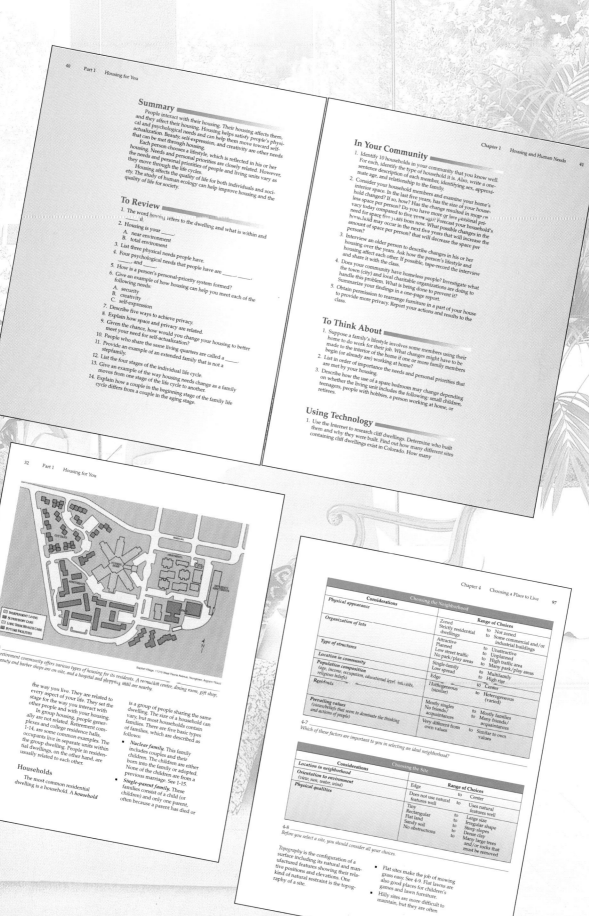

Legend: INDEPENDENT LIVING · SUPERVISED CARE · LONG-TERM HEALTH CARE · FUTURE FACILITIES

1-13
This retirement community offers various types of housing for its residents. A recreation center, dining room, gift shop, and beauty and barber shops are on-site, and a hospital and shopping mall are nearby.

Baptist Village, 11315 West Peoria Avenue, Youngtown, Arizona 85363

the way you live. They are related to every aspect of your life. They set the stage for the way you interact with other people and with your housing.

In group housing, people generally are not related. Retirement complexes and college residence halls, 1-14, are some common examples. The occupants live in separate units within the group dwelling. People in residential dwellings, on the other hand, are usually related to each other.

### Households

The most common residential dwelling is a household. A *household* is a group of people sharing the same dwelling. The size of a household can vary, but most households contain families. There are five basic types of families, which are described as follows:

- *Nuclear family.* This family includes couples and their children. The children are either born into the family or adopted. None of the children are from a previous marriage. See 1-15.
- *Single-parent family.* These families consist of a child (or children) and only one parent, often because a parent has died or

---

## Page 97

**Choosing the Neighborhood**

| Considerations | Range of Choices | | |
|---|---|---|---|
| **Physical appearance** | | | |
| Organization of lots | Zoned | to | Not zoned |
| | Strictly residential dwellings | to | Some commercial and/or industrial buildings |
| Type of structures | Attractive | to | Unattractive |
| | Planned | to | Unplanned |
| Location in community | Low street traffic | to | High traffic area |
| | No park/play areas | to | Many park/play areas |
| **Population composition** (age, income, occupation, educational level, interests, religious beliefs) | Single-family | to | Multifamily |
| | Low spread | to | High rise |
| | Edge | to | Center |
| Residents | Homogeneous (similar) | to | Heterogeneous (varied) |
| **Prevailing values** (views/beliefs that seem to dominate the thinking and actions of people) | Mostly singles | to | Mostly families |
| | No friends/acquaintances | to | Many friends/acquaintances |
| | Very different from own values | to | Similar to own values |

4-7
Which of these factors are important to you in selecting an ideal neighborhood?

**Choosing the Site**

| Considerations | Range of Choices | | |
|---|---|---|---|
| Location in neighborhood | Edge | to | Center |
| Orientation to environment (view, sun, water, wind) | Does not use natural features well | to | Uses natural features well |
| **Physical qualities** | Tiny | to | Large size |
| | Rectangular | to | Irregular shape |
| | Flat land | to | Steep slopes |
| | Sandy soil | to | Dense clay |
| | No obstructions | to | Many large trees and/or rocks that must be removed |

4-8
Before you select a site, you should consider all your choices.

Topography is the configuration of a surface including its natural and manufactured features showing their relative positions and elevations. One kind of natural restraint is the topography of a site.

- Flat sites make the job of mowing grass easy. See 4-9. Flat lawns are also good places for children's games and lawn furniture.
- Hilly sites are more difficult to maintain, but they are often

# HOUSING DECISIONS

## Teacher's Annotated Edition

**Provides diverse strategies to stimulate student learning and coordinates supplemental teaching materials.**

**Teaching Elements** pack the side and bottom margins to help you present and reinforce chapter content.

- **Activity** exercises promote student retention of chapter concepts. Many focus on a specific curriculum area, such as *Writing Activity* or *Math Activity.*

- **Discuss** items reinforce learning through class dialogue and brainstorming. Answers identified in the lesson appear in parentheses.

- **Enrich** activities challenge students to enhance their knowledge through role-playing, researching, debating, surveying, and actively listening to guest presenters.

- **Example** items illustrate important points in the chapter material.

- **Note** items include statistics, facts, or historical references to spark student interest.

- **Reflect** questions pose issues of a more personal nature for students to consider quietly and mentally evaluate for their own lives.

- **Resource** materials for students to use from the *Student Activity Guide* or *Teacher's Resources* are keyed to chapter topics.

- **Vocabulary** activities reinforce key terms through defining, comparing, using in sentences, and using the glossary.

**Answer Keys** facilitate review and assessment.

**Web Sites** relevant to the lesson appear in margin notes throughout the text. A chapter-by-chapter listing is also included in the Introduction here and in the *Teacher's Resources*.

**Portfolio Project** at the end of each chapter prompts students to apply lesson concepts while incorporating personal expression and interpretation.

**National Standards Correlation** identifies the knowledge presented in the text that students in family and consumer sciences need to know and the skills they should be able to demonstrate.

**Suggestions for using these resources are found in the Introduction of the *Teacher's Resources*.**

# HOUSING DECISIONS

## Teacher's Resources

**Add variety to your lessons with suggestions offered in three practical formats: easy-to-use soft cover; convenient CD, and three-ring binder separated by chapter tabs within a secure carrying portfolio.**

**Student Learning Experiences** prepared for each chapter include bulletin board ideas, introductory activities, and teaching strategies to promote learning through various approaches.

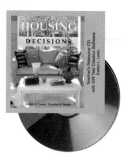

**Reproducible Masters** provide ready-to-use student activity sheets, black line overheads, and chapter tests.

**Color transparencies** add visual appeal to your lesson plans.

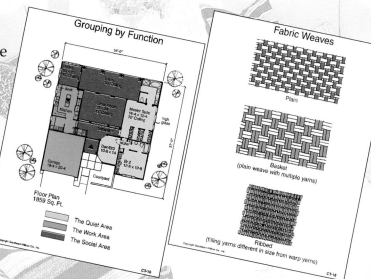

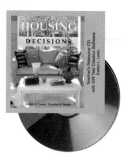

## Teacher's Resource CD with G-W Test Creation Software

A quick and convenient access to all the resources in the portfolio!

This exciting new ancillary puts all the contents of the *Teacher's Resource Portfolio* plus the *G-W Test Creation software* on one CD-ROM. Everything you'll need for planning lessons and creating tests is only a few keystrokes away. Print off just what you need.

### Features of G-W Test Creation Software:
- 25 percent more questions beyond those found in the printed tests.
- Create customized tests using any chapters or chapter questions; alter questions; add your own questions to the database.
- Test questions exist in a variety of formats—true/false, multiple choice, matching, and essay.
- Available in Windows.

# HOUSING DECISIONS
## Student Activity Guide

**Helps learners prepare to make future housing decisions with assurance and competence.**

**Activities and Exercises** encourage students to review and apply what they learn, often by using the higher-order thinking skills.

**Suggestions for using these resources are found in the Introduction of the *Teacher's Resources*.**

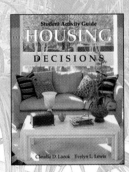

Student Activity Guide
HOUSING
DECISIONS

Claudia D. Lazok   Evelyn L. Lewis

---

Activity B
Chapter 3

**Decision Groupings**

Name
Date
Period

Read the following paragraph. Then diagram a possible chain decision and a possible central-satellite decision based on the information provided. (You may make your own assumptions about any information that is not provided. Both decisions may be based on the same or different assumptions.)

The Benson family always uses the municipal pool in town for summertime swimming. The Bensons don't want to stop summer swimming, so they must decide on an alternative. They have many options. They could join a private pool in the area for about three times the cost of the city municipal pool. They could use the municipal pool in the next city at a slightly higher cost, but more time would be spent traveling to and from the pool. The Bensons could buy a pool for their backyard. The initial cost could be very high depending on the type of pool purchased. However, money would be saved in pool memberships, and the pool would be very convenient.

The Bensons might decide on the following chain of decisions:

The Bensons might decide on the following group of central-satellite decisions:

22   Chapter 3   Using Decision-Making Skills

---

Activity B
Chapter 12

**The Principle of Rhythm**

Name
Date
Period

Write the type of rhythm illustrated by each of the window treatments shown below. Briefly explain each type of rhythm.

1.

2.

3.

4.

5.

82   Chapter 12   Using the Principles of Design

# Introduction

*Housing Decisions* explores a topic that affects all students—their home environments. The text addresses the psychological, physiological, and sociological needs of individuals in relation to housing as well as ways they can meet those needs by enhancing their surroundings. *Housing Decisions* is appropriate for basic courses in housing, environmental design, and interior design. The topics presented are planned to help students learn the following:

- recognizing the many factors that influence housing

- using sound decision-making skills to acquire housing throughout the life cycle

- recognizing basic architectural and furniture styles

- understanding current construction methods and materials

- knowing principles of good design and how to apply them to indoor and outdoor living spaces

- selecting and arranging furniture and accessories to meet household needs and priorities

- understanding the many factors to consider when choosing appliances

- managing a safe and secure home

- practicing consumer rights and responsibilities related to housing

*Housing Decisions* also acquaints students with careers in housing and ways to prepare for career success. The text includes career material on how to develop workplace skills and make informed career decisions. Many jobs available in the vast housing industry are discussed to expose students to the wide range of career opportunities available.

## Strategies for Successful Teaching

By using a variety of teaching strategies, you can make *Housing Decisions'* subject matter exciting and relevant for your students. Many suggestions for planning classroom activities appear in the teaching supplements that accompany this text. As you plan your lessons, you might also want to keep the following points in mind.

### Helping Your Students Develop Critical Thinking Skills

As today's students leave their classrooms behind, they will face a world of complexity and change. They are likely to work in several career areas and hold many different jobs. Providing young people with a base of knowledge consisting only of facts, principles, and procedures is not enough. Students must also be prepared to solve complex problems, make difficult decisions, and assess ethical implications. In other words, students must be able to use critical thinking skills, the higher-order thinking skills that Benjamin Bloom listed as follows:

- analysis—breaking down material into its component parts so its organizational structure may be understood

- synthesis—putting parts together to form a new whole

- evaluation—judging the value of material for a given purpose

Just as importantly, students must be able to use reflective thinking to decide what to believe and do. According to Robert Ennis, students should be able to do the following:

- Define and clarify problems, issues, conclusions, reasons, and assumptions.

- Judge the credibility, relevance, and consistency of information.
- Infer or solve problems and draw reasonable conclusions.

To think critically, students must possess knowledge that goes beyond simply memorizing or recalling information. Critical thinking requires individuals to use common sense and experience, apply their knowledge, and recognize the controversies surrounding an issue.

Critical thinking also requires creative thinking to construct all the reasonable alternatives, possible consequences, influencing factors, and supporting arguments. Unusual ideas are valued and perspectives outside the obvious are sought.

The teaching of critical thinking does not require exotic and highly unusual classroom approaches. Complex thought processes can be incorporated in the most ordinary and basic activities such as reading, writing, and listening, if these activities are carefully planned and well executed.

Help your students develop their analytical and judgmental skills by going beyond what they see on the surface. Rather than allowing students to blindly accept what they read or hear, encourage them to examine ideas in ways that show respect for others' opinions and different perspectives. Encourage students to think about points raised by others. Ask them to evaluate how new ideas relate to their attitudes about various subjects.

Debate is an excellent way to thoroughly explore an issue. You may want to divide the class into two groups, each examining an opposing side. You can also have students explore an issue from all sides in small groups. With both methods, representatives can be chosen to summarize the key thoughts expressed within each group.

## Helping Students Develop Decision-Making Skills

An important aspect in the development of critical thinking skills is learning how to solve problems and make decisions. Important decisions lie ahead for your students, particularly related to their future education and career choices. Chapters 23 and 24 of *Housing Decisions* will help students prepare for career success.

Case studies can help students evaluate situations in which they are not directly involved. They encourage students to recognize the variety of ways certain problems can be solved. Simulation games and role-plays allow students to practice solving problems and making decisions in non-threatening circumstances. Role-playing allows students to examine others' feelings as well as their own. It can help them learn effective ways to react or cope when confronted with similar situations in real life.

## Using Cooperative Learning

The use of cooperative learning groups in your classroom will give students an opportunity to practice teamwork skills, which are highly valued in the community and the workplace. During cooperative learning activities, students learn interpersonal and small-group skills that will help them function as part of a team. These skills include leadership, decision making, trust building, communication, and conflict management.

When planning for cooperative learning, you will have a particular goal or task in mind. First, specify the objectives for the lesson. Then, match small groups of learners based on the task and assign each person a role. Group members should be selected to include a mix of abilities and talents so opportunities for students to learn from one another exist. As groups work together over time, individuals' roles should rotate so everyone has an opportunity to practice and develop different skills.

The success of the group is measured not only in terms of group outcome, but also in terms of the successful performance of each member in his or her role. Interdependence is a basic component of any cooperative learning group. Students understand that one person cannot succeed unless everyone does. The value of each group member is affirmed as learners work toward the group's goal.

You will also need to monitor the effectiveness of the groups, intervening as necessary to provide task assistance or help with interpersonal or group skills. Finally, evaluate the group's achievement and help members discuss how well they collaborated.

## Helping Students Recognize and Value Diversity

Your students will be entering a rapidly changing workplace—not only in matters pertaining to technology, but also in the diverse nature of its workforce. The majority of the new entrants to the workforce are women, minorities, and immigrants, all representing many different views and experiences. The workforce is aging, too, as over half the people in the workplace are between the ages of 35 and 54. Because of these trends, young workers must learn how to interact effectively with a variety of people who are unlike them.

The appreciation and understanding of diversity is an ongoing process. The earlier and more frequently young people are exposed to diversity, the more quickly they can develop skills to bridge cultural differences. If your students are exposed to various cultures within your classroom, the process of understanding cultural differences has already begun. This is the best preparation for success in a diverse society. In addition, teachers find the following strategies for teaching diversity helpful:

- Actively promote a spirit of openness, consideration, respect, and tolerance in the classroom.

- Use a variety of teaching styles and assessment strategies.

- Use cooperative learning activities whenever possible, making sure group roles are rotated so everyone has leadership opportunities.

- When grouping students, have each group's composition as diverse as possible with regard to gender, race, and nationality. If groups present information to the class, make sure all members have a speaking part.

- Make sure one group's opinions are not over-represented during class discussions. Seek opinions of under-represented groups or individuals if necessary.

- If a student makes a sexist, racist, or other comment that is likely to be offensive, ask the student to rephrase the comment in a manner that will not offend other members of the class. Remind students that offensive statements and behavior are inappropriate in the classroom.

- If a difficult classroom situation arises involving a diversity issue, ask for a time-out and have everyone write down his or her thoughts and opinions about the incident. This helps to calm the class down and allows you time to plan a response.

- Arrange for guest speakers who represent diversity in gender, race, and ethnicity, even though the topic does not relate to diversity.

- Have students change seats occasionally throughout the course and introduce themselves to their new "neighbors" so they become acquainted with all their classmates.

- Several times during the course, ask students to make anonymous, written evaluations of the class. Have them report any problems that may not be obvious.

## Teaching Learners of Varying Abilities

The students in your classroom will represent a wide range of ability levels and needs. Special needs students in your classes will require unique teaching strategies. On the other hand, gifted students must not be overlooked. You will be challenged to adapt daily lessons to meet the needs of all of your students in the same classroom setting. The chart that follows provides descriptions of several ability levels of students you may find in your classes as well as strategies and techniques to keep in mind as you work with them.

## Using Assessment Techniques

Various forms of assessment are used with students to fully evaluate their achievements. Written tests have traditionally been used to evaluate performance. This method of evaluation is good to use when assessing knowledge and comprehension. Other methods of assessment are preferable for measuring the achievement of the higher-level skills of application, analysis, synthesis, and evaluation. The text includes the following:

- A *To Review* section follows each chapter's summary to evaluate students' recall of key concepts.

| Learning Disabled* | Mentally Disabled* | Behaviorally Emotionally Disabled* |
|---|---|---|
| **Description** | | |
| Students with learning disabilities (LD) have neurological disorders that interfere with their ability to store, process, or produce information, creating a "gap" between ability and performance. These students are generally of average or above-average intelligence. Examples of learning disabilities are distractibility, spatial problems, and reading comprehension problems. | The mentally disabled student has subaverage general intellectual functioning that exists with deficits in adaptive behavior. These students are slower than others their age in using memory effectively, associating and classifying information, reasoning, and making judgments. | These students exhibit undesirable behaviors or emotions that may, over time, adversely affect educational performance. Their inability to learn cannot be explained by intellectual, social, or health factors. They may be inattentive, withdrawn, timid, restless, defiant, impatient, unhappy, fearful, unreflective, lack initiative, have negative feelings and actions, and blame others. |
| **Teaching Strategies** | | |
| <ul><li>Assist students in getting organized.</li><li>Give short oral directions.</li><li>Use drill exercises.</li><li>Give prompt cues during student performance.</li><li>Let students with poor writing skills use a computer.</li><li>Break assignments into small segments and assign only one segment at a time.</li><li>Demonstrate skills and have students model them.</li><li>Give prompt feedback.</li><li>Use continuous assessment to mark students' daily progress.</li><li>Prepare materials at varying levels of ability.</li><li>Shorten the number of items on exercises, tests, and quizzes.</li><li>Provide more hands-on activities.</li></ul> | <ul><li>Use concrete examples to introduce concepts.</li><li>Make learning activities consistent.</li><li>Use repetition and drills spread over time.</li><li>Provide work folders for daily assignments.</li><li>Use behavior management techniques, such as behavior modification, in the area of adaptive behavior.</li><li>Encourage students to function independently.</li><li>Give students extra time to both ask and answer questions while giving hints to answers.</li><li>Avoid doing much walking around while talking to MD students as this is distracting for them.</li><li>Give simple directions and read them over with students.</li><li>Use objective test items and hands-on activities because students generally have poor writing skills and difficulty with sentence structure and spelling.</li></ul> | <ul><li>Call students' names or ask them questions when you see their attention wandering.</li><li>Call on students randomly rather than in a predictable sequence.</li><li>Move around the room frequently.</li><li>Improve students' self-esteem by giving them tasks they can perform well, increasing the number of successful achievement experiences.</li><li>Decrease the length of time for each activity.</li><li>Use hands-on activities instead of using words and abstract symbols.</li><li>Decrease the size of the group so each student can actively participate.</li><li>Make verbal instructions clear, short, and to the point.</li></ul> |

*We appreciate the assistance of Dr. Debra O. Parker, North Carolina Central University, with this section.

| Academically Gifted | Limited English Proficiency | Physically Disabled |
|---|---|---|
| **Description** | | |
| Academically gifted students are capable of high performance as a result of general intellectual ability, specific academic aptitude, and/or creative or productive thinking. Such students have a vast fund of general knowledge and high levels of vocabulary, memory, abstract word knowledge, and abstract reasoning. | For many of these students, English is generally a second language. Such students may be academically quite capable, but they lack the language skills needed to reason and comprehend abstract concepts in English. | Includes individuals who are orthopedically impaired, visually impaired, speech-impaired, deaf, hard-of-hearing, hearing-impaired, and health-impaired (cystic fibrosis, epilepsy). Strategies will depend on the specific disability. |
| **Teaching Strategies** | | |
| <ul><li>Provide ample opportunities for creative behavior.</li><li>Make assignments that call for original work, independent learning, critical thinking, problem solving, and experimentation.</li><li>Show appreciation for creative efforts.</li><li>Respect unusual questions, ideas, and solutions these students provide.</li><li>Encourage students to test their ideas.</li><li>Provide opportunities and give credit for self-initiated learning.</li><li>Avoid overly detailed supervision and too much reliance on prescribed curricula.</li><li>Allow time for reflection.</li><li>Resist immediate and constant evaluation. This causes students to be afraid to use their creativity.</li><li>Avoid comparisons with other students, which applies subtle pressure to conform.</li></ul> | <ul><li>Use a slow but natural rate of speech, speak clearly, use shorter sentences, and repeat concepts in several ways.</li><li>Act out questions using gestures with hands, arms, and the whole body. Use demonstrations and pantomime. Ask questions that can be answered by a physical movement such as pointing, nodding, or manipulation of materials.</li><li>When possible, use pictures, photos, and charts.</li><li>Write key terms on the chalkboard. As they are used, point to the terms.</li><li>Corrections should be limited and appropriate. Do not correct grammar or usage errors in front of the class, causing embarrassment.</li><li>Give honest praise and positive feedback through your voice tones and visual articulation whenever possible.</li><li>Encourage students to use language to communicate, allowing them to use their native language to ask/answer questions when they are unable to do so in English.</li><li>Integrate students' cultural background into class discussions.</li><li>Use cooperative learning where students have opportunities to practice expressing ideas without risking language errors in front of the entire class.</li></ul> | <ul><li>Seat visually and hearing-impaired students near the front of the classroom. Speak clearly and say out loud what you are writing on the chalkboard.</li><li>In lab settings, in order to reduce the risk of injury, ask students about any conditions that could affect their ability to learn or perform.</li><li>Rearrange lab equipment or the classroom and make modifications as needed to accommodate any special need.</li><li>Investigate assistive technology devices that can improve students' functional capabilities.</li><li>Discuss solutions or modifications with the student who has experience with overcoming his or her disability and may have suggestions you may not have considered.</li><li>Let the student know when classroom modifications are being made and allow him or her to test them out before class.</li><li>Ask advice from special education teachers, the school nurse, or physical therapist.</li><li>Plan field trips that can include all students.</li></ul> |

- Activities listed afterward, under *In Your Community*, *To Think About*, and *Technology Applications*, provide opportunities to assess your students' abilities to use critical thinking, problem solving, and application.
- *Portfolio Project* concludes each chapter, requiring creativity, personal interpretation, and synthesis of the lesson concepts. Many of these projects provide an informal type of career-connecting activity.

The *Teacher's Resources* contain the two following ways to assess learning:

- An objective test for each chapter appears in the *Teacher's Resource Guide/Portfolio/CD*.
- A tool to create customized tests exists in the *Teacher's Resource CD with G-W Test Creation Software*.

## Performance Assessment

When you assign students some of the projects appearing at the end of each chapter, a different form of assessing mastery or achievement is required. One method that teachers successfully use is a rubric. A rubric consists of a set of criteria that includes specific descriptors or standards used for determining performance scores for students. A point value is given for each set of descriptors, leading to a range of possible points to be assigned, usually from 1 to 5. The criteria can also be weighted. This method of assessment reduces the guesswork involved in grading, which leads to fair and consistent scoring. The standards clearly indicate to students the various levels of mastery of a task. Students are even able to assess their own achievement based on the criteria.

When using rubrics, students should see the criteria at the beginning of the assignment. Then they can focus their effort on what needs to be done to reach a certain performance or quality level. They have a clear understanding of your expectations of achievement.

Though you will want to design many of your own rubrics, several generic versions are included in the front section of the *Housing Decisions* teachings resources (the *Guide*, *Portfolio*, and *CD*). The rubrics are designed to assess the following:

- *Individual Participation*
- *Individual Reports*
- *Group Participation*

These rubrics allow you to assess a student's performance and arrive at a performance score. Students can see what levels they have surpassed and what levels they can still strive to reach.

## Portfolios

Another type of performance assessment frequently used by teachers is the student portfolio. A portfolio consists of a selection of materials that students assemble to document their performance over a period of time. The purpose of the portfolio determines the type of items it should contain. Portfolios basically serve two purposes—to gauge student progress or demonstrate employability.

For portfolios developed to gauge student progress in a course, items should demonstrate problem-solving and critical-thinking skills. A self-assessment summary report should be included that explains what has been accomplished, what has been learned, what strengths the student has gained, and which areas need improvement.

Items chosen for the portfolio are discussed with the teacher in light of educational goals and outcomes. When portfolios are evaluated for a grade, students should be given a portfolio rubric to follow and guidance on how creativity will affect their grade. Portfolios should remain the property of students when they leave the course.

For a job portfolio, items should provide evidence of employability and academic skills. These portfolios are appropriate for displaying at job interviews. Students select their best work samples to showcase their achievements. Some items appropriate for job portfolios are as follows:

- work samples (including photographs, assessments, and so forth) that show mastery of specific skills
- writing samples that show communication skills
- resume
- letters of recommendation that document specific career-related skills

- certificates of completion
- awards and recognition

Portfolio assessment is only one of several evaluation methods teachers can use, but it is a powerful tool for both students and teachers. It encourages students to make a thorough self-reflection and self-assessment. Traditional evaluation methods of tests, quizzes, and reports have their place in measuring the achievement of some course objectives, but portfolios and other assessment tools should also be used to fairly gauge the realization of other desired outcomes.

## Using Other Resources

Learning in your class can be reinforced and expanded by exposing your students to a variety of viewpoints. Information may be obtained through various government offices, trade and professional organizations, and consumer publications. Local sources of information might include cooperative extension offices.

The Internet serves as a vast source of information relating to topics students will study in your classroom. You will want to encourage students to utilize this technology, but emphasize that not all information on the Internet is reliable. Coach students to verify information by checking multiple sources.

The following list includes sources of information and materials that may be useful to you and your students. The first half identifies resources relevant to specific chapters, while the last half lists resources for the general study of housing and interiors. Please note that phone numbers and Web site information may have changed since publication.

# Chapter-by-Chapter Resources

## Chapter 1 Housing and Human Needs

### Americans with Disabilities Act (ADA)
usdoj.gov/crt/ada/adahom1.htm

Explains ADA requirements and has a question-and-answer section.

### Center for Universal Design
ncsu.edu/ncsu/design/cud

Contains easy-to-understand visuals and descriptions of principles of universal design.

### Great Buildings Collection
greatbuildings.com

Excellent resource for obtaining a broad perspective of architecture worldwide.

### National Coalition for the Homeless
nationalhomeless.org

Helpful fact sheets, personal experiences, advocacy information, legislation, and other issues related to homelessness.

### F. Schumacher & Co., Waverly Products ON LINE Lifestyle Quiz
waverly.com

Provides a quiz that relates fabric selections to the identified lifestyle. Select *How to Decorate*, then *Lifestyle*.

### Universal Designers and Consultants, Inc.
universaldesign.com

Has newsletter, magazine, and a good list of related sites regarding universal design.

## Chapter 2 Influences on Housing

### Environmental Protection Agency
epa.gov

Resource on environmental issues, laws, consumer tips, and background information.

### Habitat for Humanity
habitat.org

Humanitarian effort to build housing for people who otherwise would not be able to afford it.

### National American Indian Housing Council
naihc.indian.com

Provides information on culturally appropriate housing and related sites.

### Native American Technology and Art
nativetech.org

Describes the cultural differences of various Native American groups.

**U. S. Census Bureau**

census.gov

Has Census statistics and discussions of demographic trends.

**U.S. Department of Energy**

eren.doe.gov

Covers all aspects of energy conservation.

**U. S. Department of Housing and Urban Development**

hud.gov

Reference site for federal housing laws and programs.

**U. S. Government**

usa.gov

Reference for federal laws and agencies.

# Chapter 3  Using Decision-Making Skills

**Consumer World**

consumerworld.org

Has links to consumer resources in many areas including house and home. Contains information to compare appliances and other consumer products.

**Mind Tools**

mindtools.com

Contains decision-making and time-management resources.

# Chapter 4  Choosing a Place to Live

**Apartment Renter's Resource**

aptrentersresource.com

Comprehensive source for quick and easy answers about renting.

**Government National Mortgage Association (Ginnie Mae)**

ginniemae.gov

Provides data on all aspects of the home-buying process. Also, search *Buy vs. Rent* for information on financial and other factors to consider before buying a home.

**National Council on Economic Education (NCEE)**

econedlink.org/lessons

Provides information for teaching various lessons on economics, including buying versus renting a home.

**HomeRoute Online Real Estate Services**

homes101.net

Several online tests for understanding the facts in buying and selling a house. Can locate available housing for city, county, and state geographic areas according to price ranges.

**Monster.com, TMP Worldwide**

monstermoving.com

Information about relocation resources and goods needed to successfully manage all stages of the moving process.

**U.S. Dept. of Housing and Urban Development**

hud.gov/renting/index.cfm

Offers the Renter's Kit, a primer for those preparing to rent.

**Texas Apartment Association**

taa.org

Tips on renting versus owning.

# Chapter 5  Acquiring Housing

**Apartment Rental Service**

forrent.com

National service to locate apartment by geographical location. Can enter city and state.

**Ameriquest Mortgage**

ameriquestmortgage.com

Quick and easy tool to calculate monthly mortgage payments. (Enter loan amount, interest rate, and length of mortgage). Good source to have students compare impact of interest rates.

**eHow, Inc.**

ehow.com

Site for how to do just about everything. Also, an excellent site for locating an apartment.

**National Association of Home Realtors**

realtor.com

Source for locating realtors in various areas as well as single-family houses and apartments by location and price. Has numerous articles about home buying.

# Chapter 6  The Evolution of Exteriors

**American Architectural Foundation**

archfoundation.org

Resource for research information and educational materials on the importance of architecture in current designs.

**American Institute of Architects**
aia.org

Source for current trends in architecture.

*Architecture Week* **Magazine**
architectureweek.com

A source for current housing trends and information on design, technical, and cultural issues.

**Benjamin Moore & Co.**
benjaminmoore.com

Listing of architectural styles with brief descriptions and sketches. (Go to *homeowner index*.).

**Frank Lloyd Wright Resource Website**
cypgrp.com/flw

This site includes an extensive photo list of Frank Lloyd Wright houses.

**Great Buildings Collection, Artifice, Inc.**
greatbuildings.com

Excellent source for exterior period housing designs.

**The National Park Service Historic American Buildings Survey/Historic American Engineering Record**
cr.nps.gov/habshaer

Good reference for historical buildings, criteria for selection, and photos.

# Chapter 7  Understanding House Plans

**Broderbund LLC**
broderbund.com

Creator of the popular *3D Home Architect*® software program.

**ePlans.com House Plans Superstore**
eplans.com

Extensive site for examining house plans, renderings, and virtual tours of new homes.

**Family Education Network, Inc.**
teachervision.com

Easy lesson plans for understanding floor plans. Designed especially for teachers to use in the classroom. (Search *floor plans*.)

**The COOL House Plans Company**
coolhouseplans.com

Contains hundreds of house plans, categorized by styles and sizes.

**The House Designers**
thehousedesigners.com

Offers floor plans, exterior views from all sides, and some renderings of rooms in various plans.

# Chapter 8  House Construction

**Building Products, A to Z**
ebuild.com

Resources for residential building products.

**Cellulose Insulation Manufacturers Association**
cellulose.org

Graphic presentation of cellulose information and installation.

**Composting Toilets**
envirolet.com/enwatsel.html

Description and photos of self-contained waterless toilet.

**Home Building Industry Reference Information**
builderonline.com

Has variety of information pertinent to the home building industry including trends, news, special reports, building products and house plans. Good place to browse.

**Homeowner Problems**
lakesidepress.com/dreams

Actual cases of homeowner problems with builders and defects in new construction.

**House Construction Course**
www.howstuffworks.com/house.htm

Excellent photos and descriptions of how houses are constructed.

# Chapter 9  The Systems Within

**Building Energy Codes, U.S. Dept. of Energy**
energycodes.gov

A resource for tools to facilitate energy code training, compliance, development, adoption, implementation, and enforcement.

**Faucet Direct, Inc.**
faucetdirect.com

Extensive display of plumbing fixtures.

**Handyman USA LLC—Recommended R Values for the USA and Canada**
handymanwire.com

Displays a national map of zones and a chart specifying recommended R values for insulation. (Go to *Attics*, then *R Values*.)

**Honeywell Corporation**
honeywell.com

Contains solutions for automation and security systems.

**Kohler Co.**
kohler.com

Shows extensive product line for kitchen and bath fixtures.

**Truebro**
www.truebro.com

Provides lavatories that satisfy the Americans with Disabilities Act.

# Chapter 10 Elements of Design

**About, Inc., A PRIMEDIA Company**
interiordec.about.com/cs/designprinciples

Information about using the principles of design for interior decorating.

**Virtual Library Museums**
icom.org/vlmp

Listing of museum sites, many having virtual tours.

# Chapter 11 Using Color Effectively

**Color Matters, J.L. Morton**
colormatters.com

Good source for reviewing the importance of color and how people react to different colors.

**Color Theory Online**
members.cox.net/mrsparker2/intro.htm

Extensive online interactive activities including puzzles, games, and PowerPoint® presentation that can be downloaded.

**River City Graphics Design**
home.att.net/~gary-weirich/ioctheory.html

Interesting site on color theory with a section on the impact of color.

**The Sherwin-Williams Company**
sherwin.com

Excellent site for studying color groupings.

# Chapter 12 Using the Principles of Design

**Gefen Productions**
thehome.com

Good source for quick and easy reference to new home products and trends.

**HomeDecorating.com**
decorating-your-home.com

Source for planning an office and handling many other do-it-yourself projects.

# Chapter 13 Textiles in Today's Homes

**Fibersource: American Fiber Manufacturers Association**
fibersource.com

Excellent resource on fabric definitions, statistics, and general industry information.

**Fiber World Classroom, American Fiber Manufacturers Association**
fiberworld.com

General reference for fiber products, common uses, care/maintenance, and fiber history.

**Upholstery Fabric Online**
upholstery-fabric.com

Shows examples of different types of upholstery materials for home furnishings.

# Chapter 14 Creating Interior Backgrounds

**Armstrong World Industries**
armstrongfloors.com

Good visuals of up-to-date flooring materials.

**Ceramic Tile Institute of America**
thetiledoctor.com

Has tile glossary and explanation of how tile is made.

**Consentino Group**
silestone.com

Explanation and visual display of engineered quartz used in countertops.

**Florida Tile Industries, Inc.**
floridatile.com

Good source for ceramic tile product information, installation designs, and visuals.

**Interior Acoustical Products**
silentsource.com

Good source to locate acoustical items on the market for interior walls, ceilings, and floors.

**The Home Depot, Inc.**
homedepot.com

Source of product and consumer information on home improvement materials and services.

*Note: Phone numbers and Web site addresses throughout the text may have changed since publication.

**Wilsonart International—Products For Surfaces In The Home (countertops, cabinets, fixtures, floors)**
wilsonart.com

Includes a full line of flooring products as well as laminate and solid surface materials for countertops.

## Chapter 15 Furniture Styles and Construction

**American Furniture Manufacturers Association**
afma4u.org

Visuals of furniture styles and good glossary of furniture styles and terms.

**Domain**
domain-home.com

Simple, quick online quiz for determining decorating style.

**Gefen Productions**
thehome.com/woodfurn.html

Lists common furniture construction types on the market and includes a furniture buying guide.

**Iowa State University**
iastate.edu

Excellent source for fabric flammability questions. (Search the keyword *flammability*.)

## Chapter 16 Arranging and Selecting Furniture

*Better Homes and Gardens* **Magazine**
bhg.com

Provides downloadable software for arranging a room.

**Decorating Alternatives**
decoratingalternatives.com

Excellent photos on redesign of space achieved partially by rearranging furniture.

**Ethan Allen Furniture**
ethanallen.com

Uses good visuals to show an extensive line of furniture and fabrics.

**PowerHomeBiz.com LLC**
powerhomebiz.com/vol12/furniture.htm

Includes tips on buying all types of furniture including home office furniture.

## Chapter 17 Addressing Windows, Lighting, and Accessories

**American Lighting Association**
americanlightingassoc.com

Information on how to choose lighting for the house.

**Andersen Corporation**
andersenwindows.com

Contains product photos of an extensive variety of windows.

**Efficient Windows Collaborative, U.S. Dept. of Energy**
efficientwindows.org/selection.html

Excellent guide for selecting energy-efficient windows and learning how they are made.

**International Association of Lighting Designers**
iald.org

Consumer information on working with a lighting designer and the importance of doing so.

**Lowe's Home Improvement Warehouse**
lowes.com

Has full line of lighting products and helpful consumer information.

**North Carolina State University Cooperative Extension**
ces.ncsu.edu/depts/fcs

Offers publications and web links on many housing topics including accessories.

## Chapter 18 Selecting Household Appliances

*Appliance* **Magazine**
appliance.com

Up-to-date information from the industry on new product lines and appliance features.

**Association of Home Appliance Manufacturers**
aham.org

Statistics on appliances and the appliance industry.

**University of Kentucky Cooperative Extension**
ca.uky.edu/fcs/homeappliances

Good source for current issues, new technology, professional organizations, listing of brand names, and related web sites.

**U.S. Environmental Protection Agency**
energystar.gov

Description of Energy Star products and the criteria for the designation.

### Websites of Appliance Manufacturers

Individual companies provide available products as well as helpful information on shopping and selection. A number of these companies are listed here:

Amana: amana.com

Frigidaire: frigidaire.com

General Electric: geappliances.com

Jennair: jennair.com

Kenmore: sears.com

Kitchen Aid: kitchenaid.com

Maytag: maytag.com

Sub-Zero: subzero.com

Whirlpool: whirlpool.com

## Chapter 19 The Outdoor Living Space and Environment

### American Society of Landscape Architects

asla.org

Contains information about working with landscape architects. Also has consumer publications about landscaping.

### iVillage, Inc.

ivillage.com/home

Contains diverse information on gardening topics as well as other home decorating subjects.

### *Southern Living* Magazine

southernliving.com

Many articles on gardening and design of outdoor space.

## Chapter 20 Keeping Your Home Safe and Secure

### Building Science Corporation

buildingscience.com

Articles on preventing and treating mold in housing.

### Gefen Productions

thehome.com/wincov.html

Lists ways to make window treatments safe for children.

### Healthy Home Institute

hhinst.com

Has indoor air quality information including asthma triggers and an audit to analyze home moisture problems.

### National Lead Information Center, U.S. Dept. of Housing and Urban Development

hud.gov/offices/lead/outreach/nlic.pdf

Provides consumer information about existing laws and regulations regarding the prevention of lead poisoning in housing.

### National Safety Council

nsc.org

Contains consumer information on health safety legislation regarding housing, including lead-based paint.

### North Carolina State University Cooperative Extension

ces.ncsu.edu/depts/fcs

Numerous articles, fact sheets, and related resources on health issues in the home. (Go to the *Housing* link.)

### U. S. Environmental Protection Agency

epa.gov

Information on air quality, pollution prevention, and environmental concerns. Students can locate environmental issues by neighborhood. Has section on resources for teachers.

## Chapter 21 Maintaining Your Home

### Bob Vila Show

bobvila.com

Has extensive information on home improvement projects, gardening, energy conservation, and water conservation.

### DoItYourself, Inc.

doityourself.com

Offers helpful information on home repair and many other home-related projects.

### Gefen Productions

thehome.com/harfloor.html

Guide to maintaining hardwood floors.

### North Carolina State University Cooperative Extension

ces.ncsu.edu/depts/fcs

Preventive maintenance guide and general references on home repair.

### This Old House Online

thisoldhouse.com

Excellent source for renovating and remodeling old homes. Covers all aspects of home and garden with visual materials and references.

---

*Note: Phone numbers and Web site addresses throughout the text may have changed since publication.

# Chapter 22  Housing for Today and Tomorrow

## Biosphere 2
bio2.edu

The largest ecosystem on earth, an affiliate of Columbia University, with virtual tours inside the center and many photos.

## *Electronic House* Magazine
electronichouse.com

Lists new home automation products.

## Florida Solar Energy Center, University of Central Florida
fsec.ucf.edu

Provides research on solar applications and numerous consumer publications.

## North Carolina State University Solar Center
ncsc.ncsu.edu

Source for information on solar applications in residences. Has solar demonstration house and extensive consumer information sources.

## Southface Energy Institute
southface.org

Source for information on sustainable housing.

## The Massachusetts Institute of Technology Home of the Future
architecture.mit.edu/house_n/web/intro/intro.htm

Research house focused on how the home and its related technologies, products, and services should evolve to meet the challenges of the future.

# Chapter 23  Careers in Housing

## American Institute of Architects
aia.org

Professional organization that offers new information and addresses member needs. Has descriptive ethics section.

## American Society of Interior Designers
asid.org

Has search features to find information about interior design careers and presents guidelines on beginning a business.

## American Society of Landscape Architects
asla.org

Site has information for landscapers and general public. Publications are of particular interest.

## Foundation for Interior Design Education Research
fider.org

Listing of accredited post-secondary and university programs in interior design.

## National Society of Professional Engineers
nspe.org

Professional organization for engineers. Contains requirements for licensure.

# Chapter 24  Preparing for Career Success

## America's Career InfoNet
acinet.org

Excellent source of information on job and wage trends, career preparation, and available jobs. Links to America's Job Bank.

## CareerBuilder LLC
careerbuilder.com

Provides students an opportunity to search for jobs by geographic location. Students can also post their resumes.

## Job Shadowing
jobshadow.org

Helpful guidelines for establishing shadowing arrangements. Sponsored by Monster.com and News Corporation.

## TMP Worldwide
monster.com

Online search tool for jobs around the country and the world. Also offers resume-writing and career-building assistance

## Southeastern Oklahoma State University Career Office
job-interview-questions.com

Contains a list of actual interview questions, from simple to difficult, with sample answers.

# Additional Resources for Housing and Interiors

## Publications

*Architectural Digest*
condenet.com/mags/
archdigest

*Better Homes and Gardens*
bhg.com

*Consumer Reports*
consumerreports.org

*Fine Homebuilding*
taunton.com/finehomebuilding/
index.asp

*Home Magazine*
homemag.com

*House and Garden*
condenet.com/mags/hg/

*Interior Design*
interiordesign.net

*Journal of Family and Consumer Sciences*
aafcs.org

*What's New in Family and Consumer Sciences*
whats-new-mag.com/

## Trade and Professional Organizations

*Air-Conditioning and Refrigeration Institute*
(703) 524-8800
ari.org

*Aluminum Association*
(202) 862-5100
aluminum.org

*American Architectural Manufacturers Association*
(847) 303-5664
aamanet.org

*American Association of Family and Consumer Sciences (AAFCS)*
(703) 706-4600
aafcs.org

*American Concrete Institute*
(248) 848-3700
aci-int.org

*American Design Drafting Association*
(803) 771-0008
adda.org

*American Fiber Manufacturers Association, Inc.*
(202) 296-6508
fibersource.com

*American Gas Association*
(202) 824-7000
aga.org

*American Hardware Manufacturers Association*
(847) 605-1025
ahma.org

*American Lighting Association*
(800) 274-4483
americanlightingassoc.com

*American Plastics Council*
(800) 2-HELP-90
plasticsinfo.org

*American Plywood Association*
(235) 565-6600
apawood.org

*American Printed Fabrics Council*
(212) 695-2254

*American Society for Testing and Materials (ASTM)*
(610) 832-9585
astm.org

*American Society of Furniture Designers*
(910) 576-1273
asfd.com

*American Society of Interior Designers*
(202) 546-3480
asid.org

*American Textile Manufacturers Institute, Inc.*
(202) 862-0518
atmi.org

*American Wool Council*
(303) 771-3500
americanwool.org

*Architectural Woodwork Institute*
(703) 733-0600
awinet.org

*Association for Career and Technical Education*
(800) 826-9972
acteonline.org

*Association of Home Appliance Manufacturers*
(202) 872-5955
aham.org

*Barrier Free Environments Inc.*
(919) 839-6380

*California Redwood Association*
(888) 225-7339
calredwood.org

*National Council of Better Business Bureaus, Inc.*
(703) 276-0100
bbb.org

*Craft Yarn Council of America*
(704) 824-7838
craftyarncouncil.com

*Crafted with Pride in the USA Council, Inc.*
(202) 775-0658
craftedwithpride.org

*ETR Associates*
(831) 438-4060
etr.org

*International Association of Lighting Designers*
(312) 527-3677
iald.org

*International Fabricare Institute*
(800) 638-2621
ifi.org

*International Technology Education Association*
(703) 860-2100
iteawww.org

*Kitchen Cabinet Manufacturers Association*
(703) 264-1690
kcma.org

*Note: Phone numbers and Web site addresses throughout the text may have changed since publication.

*Manufactured Housing Institute*
(703) 558-0400
manufacturedhousing.org

*National Association of Home Builders*
(800) 386-5242
nahb.com

*National Association of the Remodeling Industry*
(800) 611-6274
nari.org

*National Cotton Council of America*
(901) 274-9030
cotton.org

*National Foundation for Consumer Credit*
(800) 388-2227
nfcc.org

*National Fraud Information Center/Internet Fraud Watch*
(800) 876-7060
fraud.org

*National Institute for Consumer Education*
(734) 487-2292
nice.emich.edu

*Plumbing, Heating, and Cooling Information Bureau*
(312) 372-7331

*Sustainable Buildings Industries Council*
(202) 628-7400
sbicouncil.org

*The Soap and Detergent Association*
(202) 347-2900
sdahq.org

# Corporate Resources

*Alcoa Building Products*
(800) 962-6973
alcoahomes.com

*Alcoa Vinyl Windows*
(800) 238-1866

*American Olean Tile Co.*
(215) 855-1111
americanolean.com

*Andersen Windows*
(651) 264-5150
andersenwindows.com

*AristOKraft*
(717) 359-4131
aristokraft.com

*Armstrong World Industries Inc.*
(800) 233-3823
armstrongfloors.com

*BASF Corp.*
(704) 423-2000
basf.com

*Benjamin Moore & Co.*
(800) 344-0400
benjaminmoore.com

*Brown Jordan International*
(800) 473-4252
brownjordan.com

*Bruce Hardwood Floors*
(214) 887-2000
bruce.com

*Burlington Industries Inc.*
(333) 379-2000
burlington.com

*Carrier Air Conditioning Co.*
(800) 227-7437
carrier.utc.com

*Clorox Co.*
(800) 292-2200
clorox.com

*Colgate-Palmolive Co.*
(800) 468-6502
colgate.com

*Congoleum Corp.*
(800) 274-3266
congoleum.com

*Cotton Inc.*
(212) 413-8300
cottoninc.com

*Delta Faucets Co.*
(800) 345-3358
deltafaucet.com

*Dow Chemical USA*
(989) 636-5955
dow.com

*Dupont Fibers*
(800) 441-7515
dupont.com

*Ethan Allen Inc.*
(888) EAHELP1
ethanallen.com

*F. Schumacher& Co.*
(800) 988-7775
fschumacher.com/

*Faultless Starch/Bon Ami Co.*
(816) 472-4987
bonami.com

*Georgia-Pacific Corp.*
(800) 284-5347
gp.com

*Hoover Co.*
(800) 944-9200
hoover.com

*Hunter Douglas*
(800) 366-4327
hunterdouglasgroup.com

*Kirsch*
(800) 817-6344
kirsch.com

*Kohler Co.*
(800) 456-4537
kohler.com

*KraftMaid Cabinetry*
(888) 562-7744
kraftmaid.com

*Lane Furniture*
(804) 369-5641
lanefurniture.com

*Laufen International*
(800) 331-3651
laufen.com

*Lennox Industries Inc.*
(972) 497-5000
davelennox.com

*Levolor Home Fashion*
(800) 538-6567
lexmark.com

*Masco Corp.*
(313) 274-7400
masco.com

*Mannington Mills, Inc.*
(800) 356-6787
mannington.com

*Marvin Windows*
marvin.com

*Mills Pride*
(800) 441-0337
millspride.com

*Minwax/Sherwin-Williams*
(800) 526-0495
minwax.com

*Nu Tone Inc.*
(513) 527-5231
nutone.com

*Owens-Corning Fiberglas Corp.*
(800) 438-0465
owenscorning.com

*Peachtree Doors*
(888) 888-3814
peach99.com

*Peerless*
(800) 438-6673
peerless-faucet.com

*Pella Windows and Doors*
(641) 628-6376
pella.com

*Pendleton Woolen Mills*
(800) 760-4844
pendleton-usa.com

*Pfaff American Sales Corp.*
(201) 262-7211
pfaffusa.com

*Philips Lighting Co.*
(800) 555-0050
lighting.Philips.com/nam

*Pozzi Wood Windows*
(800) 547-6880
pozzi.com

*Proctor & Gamble Co.*
(513) 945-8787
pg.com

*Prudential Property & Casualty Co.*
(800) 437-5556

*Rubbermaid*
(330) 264-6464, ext. 2502
rubbermaid.com

*Sherwin-Williams Co.*
(800) 474-3794
sherwin-williams.com

*Stanley Hardware (Division of the Stanley Works)*
(800) 622-4393

*Velux-America Inc.*
(800)-88-VELUX
velux-america.com

*Whirlpool Corp.*
(800) 253-1301
whirlpool.com

*Wood-Mode Inc.*
(717) 374-2711
wood-mode.com

# Government Agencies and Allied Organizations

## Sources of General Information

The Consumer Information Center (CIC) publishes the free *Consumer Information Catalog*, which lists more than 200 free and low-cost government booklets on a wide variety of consumer topics. Copies of the catalog can be obtained by contacting the Web address *www.pueblo.gsa.gov*, writing to *Consumer Information Catalog*, Pueblo, CO 81009, or calling (719) 948-4000.

The Federal Information Center (FIC), which is administered by the General Services Administration (GSA), can help you find information about United States government agencies, services, and programs. The FIC can also tell you which office to contact for help with problems. You can contact the FIC online or by calling (800) 688-9889.

## Federal Offices, Hot Lines, and Databases

**Consumer Product Safety Commission**
(800) 628-2772 (Product Safety Hotline)
cpsc.gov

**Consumer Resource Handbook**
pueblo.gsa.gov

**Department of Energy**
(800) 342-5363
energy.com
*Office of Energy Efficiency and Renewable Energy*
(800) 363-3732
eren.doe.gov

**Department of Health and Human Services**
(877) 696-6775
dhhs.gov
*National Center for Injury Prevention & Control*
(770) 448-1506
cdc.gov/ncipc
*National Institute on Aging*
(800) 222-2225
nih.gov/hia

**Department of Housing and Urban Development**
(202) 708-1112
hud.gov
*Office of Fair Housing and Equal Opportunity*
(800) 669-9777
hud.gov

**Department of Labor**
(866) 4USA-DOL
dol.gov
*Bureau of Labor Statistics*
bls.gov
*Dictionary of Occupational Titles*
wave.net/upg/immigration/dot_index.html
*Occupational Information Network (O*NET)*
online.onetcenter.org
*Occupational Outlook Handbook*
bls.gov/oco/
*Occupational Safety and Health Administration*
(202) 693-1999
osha.gov
*Online Career Center*
(800) 666-7837
occ.com/occ

**Federal Trade Commission**
202-326-2222
ftc.gov
*Cybershopping*
pueblo.gsa.gov/

**Government Printing Office**
Publications Office
(202) 512-1800
gpo.gov

**Small Business Administration**
(800) 827-5722
sba.gov

# Marketing Your Program

Your housing and design program can become one of the most important course offerings in your school. You cover material that every student and teacher can use to advantage so it pays to make the student body, faculty, and community aware of your program. With good public relations, you can increase your enrollment, gain support from administrators and other teachers, and achieve recognition in the community. Following are some ways to market your program:

- **Create visibility.** It is important to let people know what is going on in your program. Ways to do this include announcements of projects and activities at faculty meetings and in school bulletins or newspapers, displays in school showcases or on bulletin boards, and articles and press releases in school and community newspapers. "Talk up" your program with administrators, other teachers, and students. Invite them to visit your classes.

- **Interact with other subject matter areas.** You can strengthen your program and contribute to other disciplines by cooperating with other teachers. For example, you can work with the math teacher to present housing-related activities that involve math skills or the English teacher to practice effective writing. The more interaction you can generate, the more you promote your class.

- **Contribute to the educational objectives of the school.** If your school follows stated educational objectives and strives to strengthen specific skills, include these overall goals in your teaching. For example, if students need special help in developing verbal or writing skills, select projects and assignments that will help them in these areas. Show administrators examples of work that indicate student improvement in needed skills.

- **Serve as a resource center.** Occupational information is of practical use and interest to almost everyone. You can sell your program by making your department a resource center of materials related to career exploration and employment skills. Invite faculty members, students, and parents to tap into the wealth of work-related information available in your classroom.

- **Generate involvement and activity in the community.** You are teaching concepts students can apply in their everyday lives. You can involve students in community life and bring the community into your classroom through field trips, interviews with business-people and community leaders, surveys, and presentations from guest speakers. You may be able to establish cooperative projects between the school and community organizations around a variety of topics.

- **Connect with parents.** If you can get them involved, parents may be your best allies in teaching topics related to family decisions regarding housing. Let parents know when their children have done good work. Moms and dads have had experiences related to many of the issues you discuss in class. Call on them to share individually or as part of a panel addressing a specific topic. Parents can be a rich source of real-life experience. Keep them informed about classroom activities and invite them to participate, as they are able.

- **Establish a student sales staff.** Enthusiastic students will be your best salespeople. Encourage them to tell their parents and friends what they are learning in your classes. You might create bulletin boards or write letters to parents that focus on what students are learning in your classes. Ask students to put together a newsletter highlighting their work-related experiences. Students could write a column from your department for the school paper.

# Goodheart-Willcox Welcomes Your Comments

We welcome your comments or suggestions regarding *Housing Decisions* and its ancillaries as we are continually striving to publish better educational materials. Please send any comments you may have to the editor by visiting our Web site at **g-w.com** or writing to:

Editorial Department
Goodheart-Willcox Publisher
18604 West Creek Drive
Tinley Park, IL 60477-6243

# Correlation of National Standards for Housing, Interiors, and Furnishings with *Housing Decisions*

In planning your program, you may want to use the chart shown here. It correlates the Family and Consumer Sciences Education National Standards with the content of *Housing Decisions*. The chart lists the competencies for each content standard within the "Housing, Interiors, and Furnishings" area. Also listed are the text topics that relate to each competency and the chapters in which they are found (with numbers shown in bold).

After studying the content of this text, students will be able to achieve the following comprehensive standard:

**11.0 Integrate knowledge, skills, and practices required for careers in housing, interiors, and furnishings.**

| Content Standard 11.1 Analyze career paths within the housing, interiors, and furnishings industry. | |
|---|---|
| **Competencies** | **Text Concepts** |
| **11.1.1** Determine the roles and functions of individuals engaged in housing, interiors, and furnishings careers. | **5:** A place to buy <br> **23:** Who provides housing? career clusters; career opportunities in housing; effect of technology on housing careers; career levels |
| **11.1.2** Explore opportunities for employment and entrepreneurial endeavors. | **23:** Career opportunities in housing; housing careers in planning, engineering, and design; housing careers in construction; housing careers in sales and service; entrepreneurial careers in housing and design; housing careers in allied fields; effect of technology on housing careers |
| **11.1.3** Examine education and training requirements and opportunities for career paths in housing, interiors, and furnishings. | **23:** Career opportunities in housing; housing careers in planning, engineering, and design; housing careers in construction; housing careers in sales and service; housing careers in allied fields; effect of technology on housing careers <br> **24:** Setting career goals; finding a job |
| **11.1.4** Examine the impact of housing, interiors, and furnishings occupations on local, state, national, and global economies. | **1:** Housing and the quality of life; quality of life for society; human ecology <br> **2:** How housing affects the economy <br> **23:** Who provides housing? |

*(continued)*

## Content Standard 11.2  Evaluate housing decisions in relation to available resources and options.

| Competencies | Text Concepts |
|---|---|
| **11.2.1** Determine the principles and elements of design. | **10:** Design characteristics; elements of design; line; form; space; mass; texture<br>**11:** Understanding color; the color wheel; color harmonies<br>**12:** The principles of design; proportion and scale; balance; emphasis; rhythm |
| **11.2.2** Determine the psychological impact the principles and elements of design have on the individual. | **11:** Using color harmonies<br>**12:** Goals of design; harmony with unity and variety; beauty; sensory design<br>**17:** The properties of light; functions of lighting |
| **11.2.3** Determine the effects the principles and elements of design have on aesthetics and function. | **11:** Using color harmonies; choosing the right colors; using color correctly<br>**12:** Goals of design; function and appropriateness; sensory design<br>**17:** The properties of light; lighting for visual comfort; lighting for safety; lighting for beauty |

## Content Standard 11.3  Evaluate the use of housing and interior furnishings and products in meeting specific design needs.

| Competencies | Text Concepts |
|---|---|
| **11.3.1** Research product information including but not limited to floor coverings, wall coverings, textiles, window treatments, furniture, lighting fixtures, kitchen and bath fixtures and equipment, accessories, and building materials. | **8:** Materials used for exterior construction; windows and doors<br>**9:** Plumbing systems; heating systems; cooling systems<br>**13:** Understanding fibers, yarns, and fabrics; textiles for home use; textiles for floor treatments; textiles for upholstered furniture; textiles for window treatments; textiles for kitchen, bath, and bed<br>**14:** Floor treatments; wall treatment.<br>**15:** Evaluating furniture construction; wood in furniture<br>**17:** Window treatments; choosing accessories<br>**18:** Appliance considerations; choosing kitchen appliances; choosing laundry appliances |
| **11.3.2** Select manufacturers, products, and materials considering care, maintenance, safety, and environmental issues. | **9:** Conserving energy<br>**13:** Textiles for home use; appearance; durability; maintenance; comfort; ease of construction<br>**14:** Planning your background treatments; planning your floors; planning your walls; planning your countertops |

## Content Standard 11.3 *(cont.)*

| Competencies | Text Concepts |
|---|---|
|  | **16:** Selecting furniture<br>**18:** Choosing kitchen appliances; choosing laundry appliances; choosing climate-control appliances; choosing other appliances<br>**21:** Resources for home care |
| **11.3.3** Review measuring, estimating, ordering, purchasing, and pricing skills. | (The competencies for this content standard are applicable for more advanced texts.) |
| **11.3.4** Appraise various interior furnishings, appliances, and equipment which provide cost and quality choices for clients. | **14:** Planning your background treatments; planning your floors; planning your walls; planning your countertops<br>**16:** Selecting furniture; prioritizing furniture needs; determining how much you can afford; identifying your lifestyle; identifying your furniture style; determining your design preferences; stretching your furniture dollars; using multipurpose furniture; reusing furniture; creating the eclectic look<br>**17:** Choosing accessories<br>**18:** Appliance considerations; purchase price; energy cost; features; size; safety; quality; consumer satisfaction |

## Content Standard 11.4 Demonstrate computer-aided drafting design, blueprint reading, and space planning skills required for the housing, interiors, and furnishings industry.

| Competencies | Text Concepts |
|---|---|
| **11.4.1** Read information provided on blueprints. | **7:** Architectural drawings for a house; prints of architectural drawings; views for architectural drawings |
| **11.4.2** Examine floor plans for efficiency and safety in areas including but not limited to zones, traffic patterns, storage, electrical, and mechanical systems. | **7:** The space within; grouping by function; traffic patterns; survey the storage space<br>**9:** Electrical systems; gas as an energy source; plumbing systems; heating systems; cooling systems<br>**21:** Meeting storage needs; organize for storage; space savers |
| **11.4.3** Draw an interior space to scale using correct architecture symbols and drafting skills. | **7:** Architectural drawings for a house; prints of architectural drawings; views of architectural drawings<br>**16:** Developing a scale floor plan |
| **11.4.4** Arrange furniture placement with reference to principles of design, traffic flow, activity, and existing architectural features. | **7:** The space within; grouping by function; traffic patterns; survey the storage space<br>**16:** Arranging furniture; developing a scale floor plan; factors to consider when arranging furniture |

*(continued)*

## Content Standard 11.4 *(cont.)*

| Competencies | Text Concepts |
|---|---|
| **11.4.5** Utilize applicable building codes, universal guidelines, and regulations in space planning. | **4:** Zoning regulations and other restrictions; natural restraints; legal restraints; housing for special needs; considerations for senior citizens; considerations for people with disabilities; considerations for families with children<br>**19:** Completing a scaled plan<br>**20:** Equipping a home for people with disabilities; universal design; features for special needs |
| **11.4.6** Create floor plans using computer design software. | **2:** High tech<br>**8:** Computer applications in construction<br>**16:** Developing a scale floor plan; computer-aided drafting and design (CADD) |

## Content Standard 11.5 Analyze influences on architectural and furniture design and development.

| Competencies | Text Concepts |
|---|---|
| **11.5.1** Explore features of furnishings that are characteristic of various historical periods. | **15:** Choosing furniture styles; traditional furniture styles; twentieth century furniture styles; late twentieth century styles; twenty-first century furniture styles; antiques, collectibles, and reproductions |
| **11.5.2** Consider how prosperity, mass production, and technology are related to the various periods. | **2:** Housing during the 1700s and 1800s; housing in the 1900s; finding affordable housing; planning for leisure time; working at home; a mobile society; early technology; industrialization<br>**6:** Traditional houses; modern houses; contemporary houses<br>**15:** Traditional furniture styles; twentieth century furniture styles; late twentieth century styles; twenty-first century furniture styles; antiques, collectibles, and reproductions |
| **11.5.3** Examine the development of architectural styles throughout history. | **2:** Historical influences on housing; cultural influences on housing; societal influences on housing; environmental influences on housing; economic influences on housing; technological influences on housing; governmental influences on housing<br>**6:** Traditional houses; modern houses; contemporary houses |
| **11.5.4** Compare historical architectural details to current housing and interior design trends. | **6:** Contemporary houses; solar houses; earth-sheltered houses; housing trends<br>**15:** Twentieth century furniture styles; contemporary; traditional; casual; country; eclectic |

| Content Standard 11.5 *(cont.)* | |
|---|---|
| **Competencies** | **Text Concepts** |
| | **16:** Determining your design preferences; creating the eclectic look |
| | **20:** Equipping a home for people with disabilities; universal design; features for special needs |
| | **22:** Innovative solutions in housing; universal design; green buildings; planned communities; new living spaces |
| **11.5.5** Consider future trends in architectural and furniture design and development. | **6:** Contemporary houses; solar houses; earth-sheltered houses; housing trends |
| | **9:** Electricity in the house; energy conservation through computer power |
| | **15:** Twenty-first century furniture styles; wood in furniture; plastic, metal, rattan, wicker, bamboo, and glass furniture |
| | **22:** Recent developments in housing; automated houses; housing concerns; sources of energy; conserving energy; a clean environment; solving environmental concerns |

**Content Standard 11.6** Evaluate clients' needs, goals, and resources in creating design plans for housing, interiors, and furnishings.

| **Competencies** | **Text Concepts** |
|---|---|
| **11.6.1** Assess human needs, safety, space, and technology as they relate to housing and interior design goals. | **1:** People and their housing; meeting needs through housing; personal priorities; housing needs vary; personal quality of life |
| | **2:** Societal influences on housing; technological influences on housing; environmental protection |
| | **20:** A safe home; a secure home; equipping a home for people with disabilities |
| | **21:** Keeping the home clean and well-maintained; meeting storage needs; redecorating; remodeling |
| **11.6.2** Assess community, family, and financial resources needed to achieve clients' housing and interior goals. | **1:** Housing needs vary; households; life cycles; life cycles and housing needs; quality of life for society |
| | **4:** Location; housing for special needs; considerations for senior citizens; considerations for people with disabilities; considerations for families with children |
| | **5:** Acquiring a place to live; to rent or to buy? a place to rent; a place to buy; condominium ownership; cooperative ownership |

*(continued)*

| Content Standard 11.6 *(cont.)* | |
| --- | --- |
| **Competencies** | **Text Concepts** |
| **11.6.3** Assess a variety of available resources for housing and interior design. | **2:** Legislation<br>**3:** Resources for housing decisions; human resources; nonhuman resources; the decision-making process<br>**13:** Textile laws<br>**16:** Information sources<br>**21:** Resources for home care |
| **11.6.4** Critique design plans that address clients' needs, goals, and resources. | **1:** Personal priorities; roles; lifestyle; housing needs vary; personal quality of life<br>**3:** The decision-making process<br>**7:** The space within; grouping by function; traffic patterns; survey the storage space; housing modifications for people with physical disabilities<br>**14:** Planning your background treatments; planning your floor; planning your walls; planning your countertops<br>**16:** Developing a scale floor plan; factors to consider when arranging furniture |

**Content Standard 11.7**  Demonstrate design ideas through visual presentation.

(The competencies for this content standard are applicable for more advanced texts.)

**Content Standard 11.8**  Demonstrate general procedures for business profitability and career success.

(The competencies for this content standard are applicable for more advanced texts.)

# HOUSING
# DECISIONS

**Evelyn L. Lewis, Ed.D.**
Professor Emeritus, Home Economics
Northern Arizona University
Flagstaff, Arizona

**Carolyn S. Turner, Ph.D., CFCS**
Professor, Housing Research and Associate Dean for Research
North Carolina Agricultural and Technical State University
Greensboro, North Carolina

Publisher
**The Goodheart-Willcox Company, Inc.**
Tinley Park, Illinois

2

Library of Congress Cataloging-in-Publication Data

Turner, Carolyn S.
    Housing decisions / Evelyn L. Lewis, Carolyn S. Turner.
        p. cm.
    ISBN 1-59070-140-2
    1. House construction 2. Dwellings—Purchasing. 3. Architecture, Domestic. I. Title.

TH4808 .T87 2003
643'.12—dc21
                                                                2002029737

Photo Credits:
Cover—Kreiss Collection. 1-800-KREISS-1.  WWW.KREISS.COM
Page 238—Ethan Allen, Inc.
Page 428—Weather Shield Windows & Doors
Page 510—Weather Shield Windows & Doors

# INTRODUCTION

*Housing Decisions* is designed to encourage a broad understanding and appreciation of the housing and interior design fields. Topics will lead you through the many issues faced when selecting and personalizing a home. Various housing and design options are presented to help you recognize the wide variety of choices available for addressing different needs and life situations.

Included are hundreds of photos showing design ideas that can be adapted to fit various homes. The visuals are provided to help demonstrate and clarify text information. Charts and illustrations are also used to explain important facts and present examples.

For students interested in a housing or interior design career, the last two chapters of *Housing Decisions* describe the many related career opportunities available and ways to prepare for them.

# ABOUT THE AUTHORS

**Dr. Evelyn L. Lewis** retired from 37 years of teaching in primary, secondary, and higher education. She developed curricula for the Arizona Department of Education and prepared training programs for Coconino County career education. Lewis also served Flagstaff's Habitat for Humanity as a volunteer.

**Dr. Carolyn S. Turner** teaches housing and resource management at the college level. She also conducts research on housing for populations with special needs, residential energy efficiency, and renewable energy applications. Turner served on the board of directors as a national officer of the American Association of Family and Consumer Sciences. She was past president of the American Association of Housing Educators and the North Carolina Association of Family and Consumer Sciences. Turner has also served on the States Energy Advisory Board for the U.S. Department of Energy.

## Contributing Authors

*Judith Brinkley-Berry*, ASID, Judith Brinkley-Berry Interior Design, Atlanta, GA, and Hilton Head Island, SC. Professional member, American Society of Interior Designers; design associate, National Trust for Historic Preservation; affiliate member, American Society of Landscape Architects; and retired secondary school educator.

*Clair S. Hill*, Professor, Construction Management, College of Engineering and Technology, Northern Arizona University, Flagstaff, AZ

*Susan Sherman Differding*, Hoffman Estates, IL

*L. Annah Abbot*, Windsor, VT

## Reviewers for This Edition

*Dr. Jorge H. Atiles*, Assistant Professor and Extension Housing Specialist, Department of Housing and Consumer Sciences, University of Georgia, Athens, GA; *Warren L. Beck*, Textile Consultant, McCormick, SC; *Hank Cunningham*, Cunningham & Company / Mortgage Bankers, Greensboro, NC; *Dr. JoAnn Emmel*, Assistant Professor, Department of Apparel, Housing and Resource Management, Virginia Polytechnic and State University, Blacksburg, VA; *Rhonda Enoch*, Greensboro Housing Counseling Service, Greensboro, NC; *Margaret Faison*, Yost & Little Realty Inc., Greensboro, NC; *Tom Faris*, Grayco Building Center, Hilton Head Island, SC; *Dr. Marihelen Glass*, Landscape Architecture, North Carolina Agricultural and Technical State University; Greensboro, NC; *Dr. Morton B. Gulak*, Associate Professor of Urban Studies and Planning, Virginia Commonwealth University, Richmond, VA; *Rob Harrison*, Landscape Architect, The Long Cane Group, Atlanta, GA; *Kathleen Levy Hoppe*, Instructor of Art, St. Christopher's School, Richmond, VA; *Arnie Katz*, Advanced Energy Corporation, Raleigh, NC; *Drew Plott*, Dodgson Interiors, Hilton Head Island, SC; *Suzanne Sharp*, Stone Works, Inc., Hilton Head Island, SC; *Ellis Smith*, Sandcastle Constructors, LLC, Hilton Head Island, SC; *Susan Stone*, Advanced Kitchen Designs, Hilton Head Island, SC; *Ken Szymanski*, Executive Director, Apartment Association of North Carolina, Charlotte, NC; *Dr. Jane E. Walker*, Associate Professor, Department of Human Environment and Family Sciences, North Carolina Agricultural and Technical State University, Greensboro, NC; *Leslie Young*, Center for Universal Design, North Carolina State University, Raleigh, NC

# BRIEF CONTENTS

# CONTENTS

# Part 2   Making Housing Choices
## Chapter 3   Using Decision-Making Skills   76

## Chapter 4   Choosing a Place to Live   90

## Part 4    The Inside Story

### Chapter 10    Elements of Design    240

### Chapter 11    Using Color Effectively    253

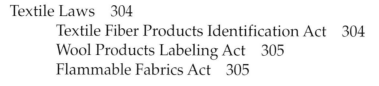

## Chapter 17   Addressing Windows, Lighting, and Accessories   379

## Chapter 18   Selecting Household Appliances   402

## Part 5    A Safe and Attractive Environment

### Chapter 19    The Outdoor Living Space and Environment    430

## Chapter 20    Keeping Your Home Safe and Secure    456

## Chapter 21    Maintaining Your Home    481

# Part 6    Progress in Housing

# PART 1
# Housing for You

# CHAPTER 1
# Housing and Human Needs

## To Know

housing
near environment
needs
physical needs
archeologist
adobe
yurt
psychological needs
esteem
self-esteem
self-actualization
beauty
self-expression
creativity
personal priorities
family
roles
lifestyle
household
nuclear family
single-parent family
stepfamily
extended family
single-person household
life cycle
quality of life
human ecology

Silestone® Photo courtesy of Cosentino USA

## Objectives

After studying this chapter, you will be able to

- explain how you interact with your housing.
- show how you move toward self-actualization through housing.
- explain how your housing helps you satisfy your needs and personal priorities.
- describe how housing needs change with the life cycle.
- compare housing needs with various lifestyles.
- determine how housing affects the quality of life.
- explain human ecology.

**Resource:** *Getting Acquainted Through Housing,* reproducible master I-A, TR. Students become acquainted with each other and various aspects of housing.

**Discuss:** Read the chapter objectives. Which topics belong in the category of *facts you already know*? Which topics belong in the category of *facts you need to learn*?

**Note:** Web sites such as *findarticles.com* will help you find relevant information for almost any topic in this text.

Housing, good or poor, has a deep and lasting effect on all people. Winston Churchill once said, "We shape our buildings, and then they shape us." This is especially true of the buildings in which people live. First, people find shelter to satisfy their needs, and then this shelter affects the way they feel and behave.

*Housing*, as the word is used in this text, means any dwelling that provides shelter. It refers to what is within and near the shelter, such as furnishings, neighborhood, and community. The relationship between people and their housing will be considered throughout this text.

## People and Their Housing

Housing is your **near environment**, a small and distinct part of the total environment in which you live. Housing includes your dwelling place, the furnishing in the space, your neighborhood, and your immediate community. Your *total environment* includes all your interactions with people and buildings as well as different geographical areas outside your dwelling place, neighborhood, and local community. Although housing is just one part of your total environment, it is a very important part. It has a great effect on how you live and develop as a person.

Whether you live alone or with others, you interact with your housing. Housing affects your actions, and in turn, your actions affect your housing. For example, if you live in a small apartment, you will not be able to host large parties. You will not have enough room, and your neighbors might complain about the noise.

However, if you want to host large parties, you might choose to live in a large house that is set apart from other houses.

Interaction with housing can also be seen on a smaller scale. Suppose a room in your house is decorated with many fragile and expensive accessories. This would give you a feeling of formality and elegance. You would not want to exercise in this room. However, if exercise is important to your lifestyle, you could furnish the room differently. You could adapt your housing to match your way of life.

## Meeting Needs through Housing

Your well-being is affected by everything around you. Your near environment, in the form of housing, helps you meet your needs. *Needs* are the basic requirements that people must have filled in order to live. All people have physical, psychological, and other needs. They share the need for shelter in which to eat, sleep, and carry on daily living activities.

A director of a shelter for the homeless observed that human needs were arranged in the following order: soup, soap, salvation. When people came to him for help, their basic needs had not yet been satisfied. They were hungry and could think only of food. Once they had eaten, their next concern was to be comfortable. Only when their most basic needs were met could they think of their psychological needs.

Psychologist Abraham Maslow prioritized human needs as shown in 1-1. According to Maslow, as each type of need is met, you progress up the pyramid to the next level. Your basic physical needs must be met first.

**Resource:** *Housing for You*, transparency master I-B, TR. Students review the topics they will cover in Chapter 1.

**Resource:** *Who Lives in Your Home?* reproducible master 1-1, TR. Students have an adult complete a housing survey and discuss results in class.

**Resource:** *Maslow's Hierarchy*, color transparency CT-1, TR. Students review and discuss Maslow's hierarchy of human needs.

**Vocabulary:** Create a word web by writing the term *housing* in the center and descriptions of housing around it.

**Note:** Be aware that homeless students may be in your class. Provide them with safe alternatives to assignments that may cause embarrassment or awkwardness.

**Vocabulary:** Look up the meanings of the terms *near* and *environment*. Put the meanings together into a sentence. Compare what you wrote to the definition in the dictionary or glossary.

**Reflect:** Defend the comment made by the director of a homeless shelter, that "human needs are arranged in the following order: soup, soap, salvation."

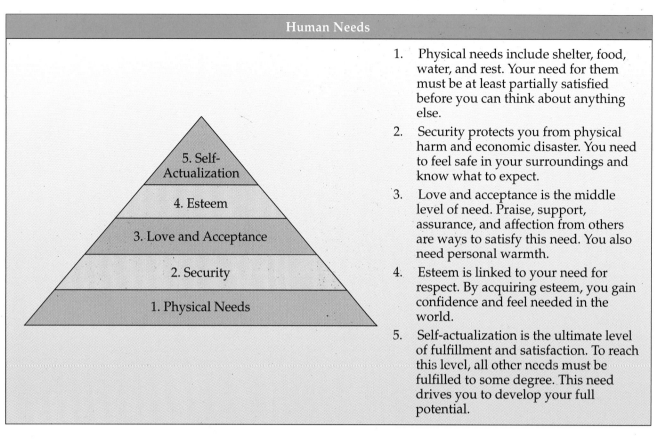

**Human Needs**

1. Physical needs include shelter, food, water, and rest. Your need for them must be at least partially satisfied before you can think about anything else.

2. Security protects you from physical harm and economic disaster. You need to feel safe in your surroundings and know what to expect.

3. Love and acceptance is the middle level of need. Praise, support, assurance, and affection from others are ways to satisfy this need. You also need personal warmth.

4. Esteem is linked to your need for respect. By acquiring esteem, you gain confidence and feel needed in the world.

5. Self-actualization is the ultimate level of fulfillment and satisfaction. To reach this level, all other needs must be fulfilled to some degree. This need drives you to develop your full potential.

1-1 _____
*Physical needs are the most basic needs and, therefore, the first step of the pyramid.*

When they are satisfied, you can think about other needs, such as security, love, esteem, and self-actualization.

## Physical Needs

*Physical needs* are the most basic human needs. They have priority over other needs because they are essential for survival. Physical needs include shelter, food, water, and rest. They are sometimes called basic needs or primary needs.

### Shelter

The need for shelter and protection from the weather has always been met by a dwelling of some type. This we know from the findings of archeologists. *Archeologists* are social scientists who study ancient cultures by unearthing dwelling places of past civilizations. Archeological findings reveal how ancient structures were made and used, and how they met the need for shelter—a basic or universal need.

The earliest dwellings were in natural settings, such as caves and overhanging cliffs. See 1-2A and 1-2B. Later, crude dwellings were built from materials that were readily available. The Pueblo Native Americans used *adobe*, which is building material made of sun-dried earth and straw. They also used rafters made from native materials. The thick walls and flat roofs, as shown in 1-2C, provided shelter from the hot climate. Apache Native Americans built houses from tree branches. See 1-2D. Their houses

A

B

W.H. Troxell

C

D

Western Ways Features

1-2

*The Qumran Caves (A) are located near the Dead Sea. You can see the entrances to caves that were used for shelter by shepherds over 2,000 years ago. The large cliff dwelling called Montezuma Castle (B) is located in central Arizona. It gave shelter to Native American farmers who lived there probably over 1,000 years ago. Adobe (C) is still used in housing today to help keep houses cool in warm climates. The housing of the Apache (D) is a clue to their way of life. Their summer house is being constructed, while their sturdier house in the background is occupied during winters.*

**Discuss:** In what other classes have you studied Maslow's Theory of Human needs? Why do you think it is discussed in other classes?

**Enrich:** Working in small groups, create a model of a cave dwelling used by Native Americans 1,000 years ago, demonstrating their living, dining, and sleeping quarters.

**Reflect:** Compare living in a tent to living in a cave or cliff dwelling.

offered protection from the scorching sun, while cooling breezes circulate through the branches.

Some tribes throughout the world called *nomads* periodically move their residences depending on weather, available farmland, and other factors. Today nomadic tribes in Kazakstan, Central Asia, still use tents or huts such as the yurt pictured in 1-3. A *yurt* is a portable hut made of several layers of felt covered with canvas. These huts are used in summer as the people move to more fertile areas. The occupants live in permanent huts with thick walls in the winter to stay warm in severely cold temperatures, which stay below 0°F for long periods.

### Food and Water

In the past, people located their housing near sources of food and water. They stored food and a small supply of water in their dwellings while they prepared and ate their food outside.

Today, areas within dwellings are set aside for storing, preparing, and eating food. See 1-4. However, people still like to prepare food and eat outside. Some houses are designed with this in mind. Food preparation areas are sometimes located in enclosed patios to make outside eating easier.

## Psychological Needs

Once the basic physical needs are met, people strive to meet the psychological needs, which are higher on Maslow's pyramid of human needs. *Psychological needs* are needs related to the mind and feelings that must be met in order to live a satisfying life.

1-3

*A yurt is a portable hut made of several layers of felt covered with canvas. It can be taken down in about 20 minutes and folded to fit on the back of a camel or horse.*

Acorn Structures, Inc.

1-4

*Today's modern kitchen has developed from a simple area for stockpiling food and water to a comfortable room for storing and preparing food and eating meals.*

## Security

Housing provides security from the outside world. It offers protection from physical danger and the unknown. It helps you feel safe and protected. Living in a dwelling that is well built and located in an area free from crime can help you feel secure.

## Love and Acceptance

Housing affects your feelings of being loved and accepted. If you have your own bedroom or private place, you know that others care about you. They have accepted you as a person who has needs. When you are assigned household chores, it is because you have been accepted as part of a group.

## Esteem

You need to feel *esteem*, or the respect, admiration, and high regard of others. Your housing tells other people something about you and can help you gain esteem. A house that is clean, neat, and attractive will gain the approval and respect of others.

You also need self-esteem. *Self-esteem* is awareness and appreciation of your own worth. When you have

**Vocabulary:** Look up the word *esteem*. Can self-esteem ever be low? Why?

**Reflect:** How would you rate your self-esteem? What types of activities or accomplishments tend to increase your personal self-esteem?

**Discuss:** What messages do Figures 1-3 and 1-4 convey regarding the housing differences among diverse cultures in the world?
**Discuss:** What does a modern kitchen, such as that shown in Figure 1-4, reveal about the lifestyle of the home's occupants? What

does a big-city apartment with a tiny kitchen and no cooking appliances indicate about the occupants?
**Reflect:** How does the kitchen of your home compare to the kitchen of your grandparents? Why are there differences?

John Running

1-5

*As this son gives his mother a table that he made, both of them gain self-esteem.*

Brown Jordan International Company, Designs by Rich Frinier

1-6

*Beauty in a room can help you feel happy, content, and peaceful.*

self-esteem, you think well of yourself and are satisfied with your own role and skills. See 1-5. Living in a pleasant, satisfying home can help you gain self-esteem.

### Self-Actualization

When you meet the need for *self-actualization*, you have developed to your full potential as a person. You have become the best you can be, and you are doing what you do best. If your talent is sports, you will be trying to increase your strength, stamina, and athletic skills. If your talent is building furniture, each piece will be better built than the previous one.

For self-actualizing people, housing is more than a place to live. It is the place where each person can progress toward becoming what he or she is capable of being. Striving toward self-actualization is often a lifelong process.

## Other Needs Met through Housing

Recognizing the levels of human needs as described by Maslow can help you understand how important needs are in relation to housing. Beauty, self-expression, and creativity are also important needs. They can be achieved through your housing decisions.

### Beauty

*Beauty* is the quality or qualities that give pleasure to the senses. Your concept of beauty is unique. What is beautiful to you may not be beautiful to someone else. In fact, the same objects may not appear beautiful to you as you mature. An appreciation of beauty develops over time as exposure to it increases. Beautiful surroundings, such as that in 1-6, can make you feel content and relaxed.

**Discuss:** Give examples of times when housing may hinder a person from becoming all he or she is capable of becoming.

**Reflect:** Create a Venn diagram comparing self-esteem to self-actualization. Draw overlapping circles, writing the qualities they share in the overlap. In the outer parts of the circles, write the

qualities about them that differ. Use one side for self-esteem and the other for self-actualization, labeling each.

**Discuss:** Does the culture in which a person is raised affect his or her ideas of beauty? How has your culture influenced your ideas of beauty?

### Self-Expression

Showing your true personality and taste is called self-expression. *Self-expression* is evident when you choose colors to decorate your house. Those colors are often a clue to your personality. For instance, if you have an outgoing, vibrant personality, you might show it by using bright, bold colors inside your house. If you have a quiet, subdued personality, you might show it by using pale, soft colors. See 1-7. Furnishings can also help you express yourself.

### Creativity

*Creativity* is the ability to create imaginatively. It can be described as combining two or more things or ideas into a new whole that has beauty or value. You show creativity when you express your ideas to others.

Your housing provides opportunities for you to express your creativity. Primitive people exhibited creativity when they painted pictures on the walls of their cave dwellings. Today, people still use painting to express their creativity. Likewise, some people enjoy gardening and working with flowers. They express their creativity by designing beautiful gardens or making floral arrangements to display around the house. See 1-8.

# Factors Affecting Housing Choices

There are many factors that influence choices in housing. These include personal priorities, family relationships, space needs, costs, roles, and lifestyle.

## Personal Priorities

*Personal priorities* are strong beliefs or ideas about what is

© Spiegel 1998

1-7

*Quiet, mild-mannered people often show their personalities by decorating with soft, pale colors.*

important. They can be views, events, people, places, or objects you prize highly. When you choose something freely and take action on that choice, you are acting on a personal priority. This gives meaning to your life and enhances your growth.

All the personal priorities you hold, such as family, friendship, money, status, religion, and independence, form your personal-priority system. Your personal-priority system is different from anyone else's. You form your personal-priority system as a result of the experiences you have. The people you know and the activities in which you participate all influence your personal-priority system.

Whenever you decide between two or more choices, you use your personal-priority system. The choice you make depends on which items

Laufen International

1-8

*A person who enjoys gardening created this space to arrange fresh-cut flowers and wash homegrown vegetables.*

you desire most. Suppose you had a choice between sharing an apartment with a friend or living alone. If you were not bound by economics, your decision would depend on how highly you value privacy versus interactions with others.

If you share a home with others, you will find that some of your personal priorities are different from theirs. Therefore, the personal priorities that household members have in common will control the thinking and actions of the group. Shared personal priorities will influence your housing decisions.

### How Needs and Personal Priorities Relate

Your needs and personal priorities are closely related. For example, you

need a place to sleep. A cot can satisfy this need. However, the cot may not meet your priority for comfort. If you have a choice, your personal priority for comfort may cause you to choose a bed with a mattress instead of the cot.

You may also need space in your bedroom for activities other than sleeping. Therefore, your personal priorities will determine whether you choose a large or small bed for the room. While the large bed may provide more comfort, the smaller bed will use less floor space. Some people may want to devote a corner of a bedroom to a play area, desk, or exercise equipment. See 1-9.

## Space

People have spatial needs. While too much space can make people feel lonely, they need a certain amount of space around them to avoid feeling crowded. They create invisible boundaries around themselves. Others can sense those boundaries and, therefore, know whether they have permission to enter.

Hobbies and activities can influence the need for space. For example, people who like to garden need space for a garden. People who enjoy spending time with friends need space for entertaining.

The way space is used also influences the amount that is needed. In places where space cannot be added or removed, the right furnishings can make the space seem larger or smaller. For example, reducing the number of furniture pieces in a crowded room can make it more spacious and airy. Likewise, by adding furniture, a large room can become warm and cozy.

### Privacy

People need privacy to maintain good mental health. Sometimes they need to be completely alone, where others cannot see or hear what they are doing. Sometimes, too, they want to avoid seeing and hearing what others are doing. They may want to think, daydream, create, read, or study without being disturbed. See 1-10.

Since the need for privacy varies among people, it can be satisfied in a number of ways. One of the most extreme ways is to live alone in a dwelling that is set apart from other dwellings. Another way is to have a private room or some other private place where people can enter only when invited.

Some people may not have the opportunity to live alone or have their own private place. However, they can still meet their need for privacy. Doing a task alone, such as mowing the lawn or driving a car, provides some privacy. A chair that is set apart from other furnishings in a room can create a sense of privacy. Also, solitary activities that require concentration, such as woodworking or piano playing, can free people from interacting with others. Even the sound of a TV or music playing gives some degree of privacy. It isolates a person from sounds made by others.

### Family Relationships

If people believe the well-being of their family is important, they will consider this factor when making housing decisions. Decisions in families that value relationships are made to benefit all family members, not just some. A *family* is two or more people living together who are related by birth, marriage, or adoption.

When concern for family relationships is an important personal priority, several areas of the house can be designed for group living. A great room may be used for family activities. A large eat-in kitchen may be

Ethan Allen, Inc.

1-9 _____

*This bunk bed takes less floor space than twin beds and allows part of the room to be used for other activities.*

desired so family members can cook and eat together. Families may also have an outside area for group recreation, as in 1-11.

## Costs

For most people, the cost of housing is an important factor in making housing decisions. Whether people rent or buy housing, it costs money. Additional expenses include the furnishings and equipment that go into a house plus the bills for repair and maintenance. Utilities, such as electricity, gas, and water, also cost money.

When money is very limited, people choose dwellings that provide just

Ethan Allen, Inc.

1-10

*This area provides privacy for a child to play or study.*

1-11

*Having a yard or nearby park provides opportunities for family interaction.*

enough space for their needs. They buy only the furnishings and equipment they can afford. They save money by conserving energy, as in turning off lights in empty rooms and setting thermostats at moderate temperatures. They can also maintain their houses well since maintenance bills nearly always cost less than repair and replacement costs. These owners do their own house repairs whenever possible.

## Roles

*Roles* are patterns of behavior that people display in their homes, the workplace, and their communities. Usually each person has more than one role. An adult female, for example, may have the roles of a wife, mother, teacher, and hospital volunteer. An adult male may be a husband, father, grandfather, carpenter, and neighborhood soccer coach. You currently balance the roles of a student and son (or daughter). Perhaps you also are a brother (or sister) and even a part-time worker.

The roles people have can affect the type of housing they choose and the way the housing is used. To fulfill the role of student, a home needs a quiet area for studying. If young children live there, space is needed for playing with toys and each other. People involved in sports and hobbies need room for their supplies and equipment.

The role of a wage earner can also impact housing choices. A lawyer may work from home, needing an office for working and a seating area for greeting clients. A professional seamstress needs space for storing supplies, cutting fabric, and sewing garments, as well as space for clients trying on and modeling their finished outfits. People whose work involves entertaining at home have other requirements that must be addressed before the housing meets their needs. Ideally, housing should meet the needs of all its members in all their roles. See 1-12.

## Lifestyle

A *lifestyle* is a living pattern or way of life. Together, all the various roles of the occupants make up the lifestyle of the residence. How you live influences the type of housing you choose to enhance your way of life.

When thinking of lifestyles and their influences on housing choices, consider everyday activities in the home. The following questions can help identify activities related to lifestyle: Are members involved with hobbies that need space, such as furniture refinishing or indoor gardening? What type of entertaining, if any, occurs at home—both inside and outside? Do any adults work from the home and need a high-tech office? Are the occupants retired, traveling frequently, and not spending much time at home?

The answers to these and other related lifestyle questions determine the type of housing selected. For example, people who love the outdoors seek housing with a view of nature or a private patio or garden. Those who spend little time at home often prefer a maintenance-free residence close to major thoroughfares so they can travel quickly to their various commitments. Retirees may choose a retirement community as shown in 1-13, which has a convenient central dining room plus on-site recreation and grooming services.

Income also influences lifestyle. Higher incomes allow people to spend more money on their homes. Consider the example of those who enjoy swimming. They can use a local recreation

Ethan Allen, Inc.

1-12

*A home office is becoming a common feature of many residences since greater numbers of people are working from their homes.*

center to enjoy their favorite form of exercise, but if they can afford it, many install a pool at home. Depending on their income, a new pool may be installed above-ground, in-ground, or perhaps indoors as part of a new wing built onto the home. Income greatly affects the degree to which comforts and conveniences are added to a home to address the occupants' lifestyle.

## Housing Needs Vary

On almost a daily basis, you can be sure of change. Life situations and circumstances cause change and affect

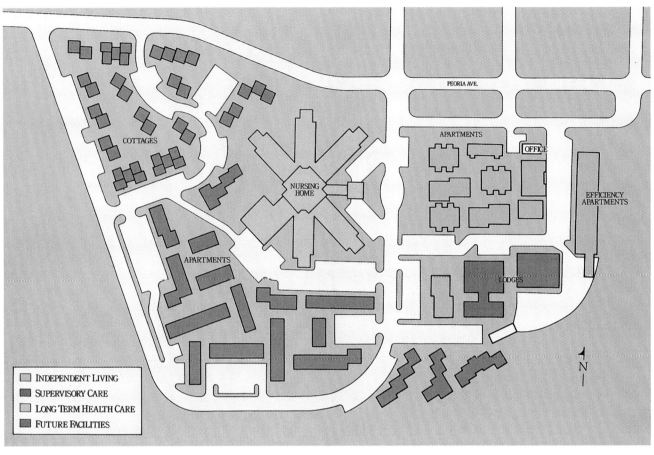

Baptist Village, 11315 West Peoria Avenue, Youngtown, Arizona 85363

1-13 ————————————————————————————————————

*This retirement community offers various types of housing for its residents. A recreation center, dining room, gift shop, and beauty and barber shops are on-site, and a hospital and shopping mall are nearby.*

**Resource:** *Types of Households*, color transparency CT-2, TR. Review the various types of household composition possible.

**Resource:** *Households*, Activity E, SAG. Students draw or mount two cartoon examples of households and describe how the characters fit each household depicted.

the way you live. They are related to every aspect of your life. They set the stage for the way you interact with other people and with your housing.

In group housing, people generally are not related. Retirement complexes and college residence halls, 1-14, are some common examples. The occupants live in separate units within the group dwelling. People in residential dwellings, on the other hand, are usually related to each other.

## Households

The most common residential dwelling is a household. A *household*

is a group of people sharing the same dwelling. The size of a household can vary, but most households contain families. There are five basic types of families, which are described as follows:

- *Nuclear family.* This family includes couples and their children. The children are either born into the family or adopted. None of the children are from a previous marriage. See 1-15.

- *Single-parent family.* These families consist of a child (or children) and only one parent, often because a parent has died or

**Activity:** Create illustrations of "stick people" to show each of the six basic types of households (the five family structures plus the single-person household).

**Enrich:** Attend a presentation by an activity director from a retirement center or nursing home who describes life in a retirement community. Be prepared to ask questions. Summarize in one paragraph what you learn.

left home. Other single-parent families consist of a never-married adult with one or more children.

- *Stepfamily.* This family consists of parents, one or both of whom have been married before. The family also includes one or more children from a previous marriage.
- *Childless family.* These families consist of a husband and wife who have not had children. For some couples this is a temporary condition, delaying the arrival of children until their finances improve. For others, it is a permanent condition. The couple is unable to have children or chooses to remain childless, for whatever reason.

University of North Carolina at Greensboro

1-14

*A residence hall offers group housing to students pursuing an education.*

1-15

*The nuclear family is the first image that comes to mind when people picture a typical family.*

**Reflect:** Which type of household best describes your current situation? Of which household type do you anticipate being a member 10 years from now?

**Activity:** Draw six columns on a sheet of paper and label each a different household type. Then, think of people you know and write their names in the column that identifies their particular household type. Continue until you have at least one name for each column.

**Discuss:** What are some advantages of college students living in dorms or other housing designed for group living?

■ *Extended family.* There are two basic types of extended families, which are formed by adding one or more relatives to a household already identified. One type consists of several generations of a family, such as children, parents, and grandparents. Variations can include aunts, uncles, or cousins as well as their children. See 1-16. The second type of extended family consists of members from the same generation, such as brothers, sisters, and cousins.

The smallest household is a *single-person household*, which consists of one person living alone in the dwelling. That person may be someone who has never married or whose marriage has ended because of the loss of a spouse through death, desertion, or divorce.

Throughout this text, you will see how your household affects your housing decisions. In turn, you will also learn how the decisions you make concerning your housing affect your household.

## Life Cycles

Life cycles are another way to view your housing needs. A *life cycle* is a series of stages through which an individual or family passes during its lifetime. In each stage, you have new opportunities and face new challenges. You develop new needs and priorities. These changes are related to your housing.

### Individual Life Cycle

Each person follows a pattern of development called an individual life cycle. It is divided according to age groups into the following four stages:

■ infancy
■ childhood

**Extended Family**

Husband and Wife and Their Second Child

Wife's Sister

First Child and Spouse

Grandchild

Child of Wife's Sister

Child of Wife's Sister

1-16
*Some families are extended in more than one direction.*

■ youth
■ adulthood

Each stage can be divided into substages, as in 1-17. In what stage do you belong? Do you have brothers or sisters in other stages?

### Family Life Cycle

Just as you have a place in an individual life cycle, your family has its place in the family life cycle. A family life cycle has six stages. See 1-18. In addition, one or more substages may exist within each stage.

■ The *beginning stage* is the early period of the marriage when the couple is without children. The husband and wife make adjustments to married life and to each other. See 1-19.

■ The *childbearing stage* is the time when the family is growing. It includes the childbearing periods and the years of caring for preschoolers.

■ The *parenting stage* occurs when the children are in school. This stage includes the years of caring for school-age children and teenagers.

| Individual Life Cycle | | | |
|---|---|---|---|
| **Infancy Stage** | **Childhood Stage** | **Youth Stage** | **Adulthood Stage** |
|  | | | |
| • Newborn, birth to 1 month old<br>• Infant, 1 month to 1 year old | • Early childhood, 1 to 6 years old<br>• Middle childhood, 6 to 8 years old<br>• Late childhood, 9 to 12 years old | • Preteen<br>• Early teen<br>• Middle teen<br>• Late teen | • Young adult<br>• Mature adult<br>• Aging adult |

1-17 _____

*This chart divides the individual life cycle into substages.*

| Family Life Cycle | | |
|---|---|---|
| **Beginning Stage** | **Childbearing Stage** | **Parenting Stage** |
| • Married couple without children | • Couple with child(ren) up to 2½ years old<br>• Couple with child(ren) 2½ to 6 years old | • Couple with child(ren) 6 to 13 years old<br>• Couple with child(ren) 13 to 20 years old |
| **Launching Stage** | **Midyears Stage** | **Aging Stage** |
| • Couple with child(ren) leaving home<br>• Couple with child(ren) living away from home | • Couple before retirement but after all children have left home | • Couple during retirement until death of both spouses |

1-18 _____

*The family life cycle includes both stages and substages.*

**Resource:** *Family Stages,* Activity G, SAG. Each student interviews one or two members of a family to learn about the family's current housing needs and predict how those needs might change in the future.

**Reflect:** Based on the lifespan of members of your family tree, how long are you likely to live? What will your housing needs be in each decade of your life?

**Writing Activity:** Watch a television program from a comedy series. Then, write a description of the household it shows and the stage of the family life cycle that is reflected.

Courtesy of Trina Olson Photography

1-19

*These newlyweds are entering the beginning stage of their own family's life cycle.*

- The *launching stage* is the time when the children become adults and leave their parents' house. They may leave to go to college, take a job, or get married.

- The *midyears stage* is the time between when the children leave home and the parents retire. When all the children have left home, the couple is again alone.

- The *aging stage* begins with retirement. Usually, at some point in this stage, one spouse lives alone after the death of the other. As people live longer, the length of this stage increases.

In some cases, the family fits the description of two life cycle stages. For example, when a family has both a preschool child and a school-age child, the family is in overlapping stages. Other families may have gaps between the stages or substages. An example is a family in which the mother is pregnant and the children are teenagers.

## Life Cycles and Housing Needs

As you move from one stage or substage of a life cycle to another, your housing needs change. Therefore, you should consider what stage or substage of the life cycles you are in as you plan your housing. If you think about both your present and future needs, your housing can help you live the kind of life you desire.

One example of a need that changes as a person moves through the life cycles is the need for space. During the infancy stage, a baby takes no more space than a small crib. As that baby grows, he or she needs more sleeping space. From the childhood stage through the youth stage, youngsters often sleep in twin or bunk beds. See 1-20. Finally as adults,

Ethan Allen, Inc.

1-20

*When a child outgrows a crib, he or she may sleep in a trundle bed. This also provides space for playmates to spend the night.*

people prefer more spacious beds that provide greater comfort.

The need for space also changes throughout a family's life cycle. A young married couple in the beginning stage may not need very much space. However, once they enter the child-bearing stage, their need for space will increase. During this stage, the number, ages, sexes, and activities of their children will affect their space needs.

As families add new members, additional space is required. See 1-21. As each member grows, he or she requires even more space. Teenagers need space for studying and entertaining friends. They also need space to store sports equipment, computer equipment, clothes, and personal belongings.

When family members are launched, they take many of their belongings with them. This leaves more space for the rest of the family. When all the children have been launched, parents enter the midyears stage and may feel they have too much space. At this time some couples desire a change of scenery. They may want a smaller home that presents fewer demands.

Other couples, however, prefer to stay in their present homes. They may not want to leave behind the memories

**Discuss:** Do you know anyone who moved into a big home, only to realize later that it was too big? What did the person do?

**Enrich:** Think about your extended family and create a family tree. Choose one branch and write a description of the ideal housing for those members.

1-21
*With the addition of children comes the need for additional bedrooms, perhaps more bathrooms, and more space in commonly used areas such as the kitchen.*

**Reading Activity:** Research the newspaper to find articles about families in each of the six stages of the family life cycle. Are any facing housing challenges? If so, write or draw a description of the housing that would best meet their needs.

**Enrich:** Help to organize a panel discussion with adults from the various stages of the family life cycle. Be prepared to ask questions about the adjustments they made as they left one stage and entered the next. Summarize in one paragraph what you learn.

1-22

*This formal dining room reflects the lifestyle of the people who live in this house.*

Bruce® Hardwood Floors, coastal woodlands in natural maple

1-23

*The priorities of the people who live in this home are obvious in the*

linked to their family's home. They may also want to have plenty of room when their children and grandchildren come to visit.

# Housing and the Quality of Life

*Quality of life* is the degree of satisfaction obtained from life. Housing is considered "good" when it provides people with satisfying surroundings that can improve their quality of life.

## Personal Quality of Life

Quality of life is important to you as an individual. Just as you are unique, your concept of the quality of life is unique. See 1-22. Your idea of an improved quality of life may not appeal to someone else. Your housing environment helps you meet your needs and personal priorities. It also adds satisfaction to your life and, therefore, improves the quality of your life.

Quality of life is also important to the other members of your household. Your household, whether it is your family or some other group, is one part of your life situation. The members play a part in shaping your attitudes and personal priorities. In turn, the combined needs and personal priorities of the members determine the type of housing environment in which you live. See 1-23. If all the members are concerned about the well being of the group as a whole, the quality of life for everyone will be enhanced.

## Quality of Life for Society

The future of a society depends on individuals and groups who work to make life better for everyone. Some of the work is social in nature. That means groups of people must cooperate to reach a common goal. See 1-24. The goal is to improve the quality of life for society. All people cannot make equal contributions toward any given goal. One example is the plight of people who are homeless. They do not have the resources to secure housing for themselves. Therefore, groups of people work together to see that housing is available for the homeless.

People must also work together and use their resources of time, money, and energy to maintain and support beautiful surroundings. Examples of such surroundings are well-kept buildings and natural land-scapes. These surroundings satisfy the needs and desires of many people in society.

## Human Ecology

*Human ecology*, the study of people and their environment, is the focus of considerable research. People are concerned about the problems caused by pollutants entering streams, lakes, and underground water supplies. Generating electricity and burning fuel for heat and power add harmful elements to the air.

Instead of wishing for the good old days to return, people must move forward to find solutions for today's

Patrick Bonz/Habitat for Humanity® International

1-24

*Due to the efforts of community volunteers, a family was able to move out of the deteriorating house and into the newly constructed one.*

problems. Noise and air pollution, traffic congestion, and the waste of natural resources are just some of these problems. Solving them will improve housing and the quality of life for society.

**Discuss:** Why is a better quality of life for everyone in a society an important goal?
**Vocabulary:** Use the term *human ecology* in a sentence to demonstrate understanding.

**Resource:** *Human Needs and Housing Crossword Puzzle*, Activity H, SAG. Students fill in the crossword puzzle to review important concepts and terms.

# Summary

People interact with their housing. Their housing affects them, and they affect their housing. Housing helps satisfy people's physical and psychological needs and can help them move toward self-actualization. Beauty, self-expression, and creativity are other needs that can be met through housing.

Each person chooses a lifestyle, which is reflected in his or her housing. Needs and personal priorities are closely related. However, the needs and personal priorities of people and living units vary as they move through the life cycles.

Housing affects the quality of life for both individuals and society. The study of human ecology can help improve housing and the quality of life for society.

## Answer Key

1. near
2. A
3. (List three:) shelter, food, water, rest
4. security, love / acceptance, esteem, and self-actualization
5. as a result of past experiences, people known, and activities
6. (Student response. See pages 25-27.)
7. (List five:) living alone, having a private room, having a private space in a room, doing solitary activities, doing activities that require concentration, setting a chair apart from the other furnishings, using a sound to drown out all other sounds
8. (Student response. See pages 28-29.)
9. (Student response.)
10. household
11. several generations living together, such as grandparents, parents, and children; members of the same generation living together, such as brothers and sisters
12. infancy, childhood, youth, and adulthood
13. (Student response. See pages 36-37.)
14. In the beginning stage, the couple is establishing a home and a new life with each other. In the aging stage, the couple has an established home and home life, and probably a family, but eventually one spouse will be alone after the death of the other.

# To Review

1. The word *housing* refers to the dwelling and what is within and _____ it.
2. Housing is your _____.
   A. near environment
   B. total enviroment
3. List three physical needs people have.
4. Four psychological needs that people have are _____, _____, _____, and _____.
5. How is a person's personal-priority system formed?
6. Give an example of how housing can help you meet each of the following needs:
   A. security
   B. creativity
   C. self-expression
7. Describe five ways to achieve privacy.
8. Explain how space and privacy are related.
9. Given the chance, how would you change your housing to better meet your need for self-actualization?
10. People who share the same living quarters are called a _____.
11. Provide an example of an extended family that is not a stepfamily.
12. List the four stages of the individual life cycle.
13. Give an example of the way housing needs change as a family moves from one stage of the life cycle to another.
14. Explain how a couple in the beginning stage of the family life cycle differs from a couple in the aging stage.

**Writing Activity:** Write each letter of the alphabet on separate lines of a sheet of paper and work independently to write one term from the chapter that begins with each alphabet letter. (After three minutes, pairs of students confer to fill in any blank lines. If blanks still remain, discuss with the class some possible choices.)

**Activity:** Working in pairs, write brief answers to the chapter objectives phrased as questions. (Pairs then pair to form teams, exchanging information with other teams until each student has a comprehensive list of answers.)

# In Your Community

1. Identify 10 households in your community that you know well. For each, identify the type of household it is. Also, write a one-sentence description of each member, identifying sex, approximate age, and relationship to the family.

2. Consider your household members and examine your home's interior space. In the last five years, has the size of your household changed? If so, how? Has the change resulted in more or less space per person? Do you have more or less personal privacy today compared to five years ago? Forecast your household's need for space five years from now. What possible changes in the household may occur in the next five years that will increase the amount of space per person? that will decrease the space per person?

3. Interview an older person to describe changes in his or her housing over the years. Ask how the person's lifestyle and housing affect each other. If possible, tape-record the interview and share it with the class.

4. Does your community have homeless people? Investigate what the town (city) and local charitable organizations are doing to handle this problem. What is being done to prevent it? Summarize your findings in a one-page report.

5. Obtain permission to rearrange furniture in a part of your house to provide more privacy. Report your actions and results to the class.

# To Think About

1. Suppose a family's lifestyle involves some members using their home to do work for their job. What changes might have to be made to the interior of the home if one or more family members begin (or already are) working at home?

2. List in order of importance the needs and personal priorities that are met by your housing.

3. Describe how the use of a spare bedroom may change depending on whether the living unit includes the following: small children, teenagers, people with hobbies, a person working at home, or retirees.

# Using Technology

1. Use the Internet to research cliff dwellings. Determine who built them and why they were built. Find out how many different sites containing cliff dwellings exist in Colorado. How many

Note: For researching cliff dwellings, have students explore *greatbuildings.com*.

Note: For researching homelessness, have students explore *nationalhomeless.org*.

households do these cliff villages contain? Why did the people build their homes in the cliffs? Present a brief report to the class.

2. Imagine a full day in the life of a homeless person. Look for a Web site that tries to convey that experience and examine the information it provides. What facts about homeless people surprise you? How many youth are homeless? How does home-lessness affect their learning? Look for facts about homeless youth and make a printout of a fact that surprised you. Report it to the class.

3. Using a camera, find examples of housing that address a household's psychological needs. Take separate pictures to demonstrate examples of housing that meet the following four needs: security, love/acceptance, esteem, and self-actualization. Prepare an simple, inexpensive scrapbook to display your collection to the class.

**Portfolio Project:** Create a storyboard that reflects housing appropriate for a family progress-ing through the six stages of the family life cycle. Use magazine pictures, drawings, and other illustrations to depict the stages. Assume the following:

- In the beginning stage, the couple lives on one spouse's earnings while the earnings of the other spouse go toward savings and paying off college loans.
- In the childbearing stage, the family has one full-time wage earner working outside the home, one part-time wage earner working from the home, and two children under age four.
- In the parenting stage, the family has enough money to make a down payment on a moderately priced home, the wage earner working from home now works full-time, and all members are very active in sports.
- In the launching stage, one child marries and the other leaves for college.
- In the midyears stage, the couple frequently entertains children and grandchildren on weekends and travels as much as possible.
- In the aging stage, one spouse lives alone after the death of the other.

# CHAPTER 2
# Influences on Housing

## To Know

agrarian
density
tenement houses
row houses
architect
substandard
census
tract houses
new town
new urbanism
subdivision
culture
hogan
demographics
baby boomers
disability
dual-income family
telecommuting
Sunbelt
environment
climate
topography
dysfunctional
resources
housing market
gross domestic product (GDP)
technology
high tech
computer-aided drafting and design
    (CADD)
building codes
zoning regulation
infrastructure
Habitat for Humanity

James F. Parnell

## Objectives

After studying this chapter, you will be able to

- relate historical events to housing.
- describe various cultures and housing characteristics.
- determine the relationship between societal changes and housing.
- analyze concerns about environmental aspects of housing.
- relate the effects of economy and housing on each other.
- summarize the impact of technology on housing.
- identify the role of government in housing decisions.

**Resource:** *Housing for You*, transparency master overlay I-C, TR. Students look back at the topics covered in Chapter 1 by first reviewing transparency master I-B. Then, with the addition of the overlay, they explore the topics they will cover in Chapter 2.

**Resource:** *Influences on Housing*, color transparency CT-4, TR. Students are introduced to the chapter's concepts.

**Resource:** *Housing in My Community*, Activity A, SAG. Students pose questions to an invited city planner or local historian about growth in the community and write a summary of the speaker's comments.

**Discuss:** What do you think were some reasons that convinced the early settlers to build their housing in group settlements?

**Enrich:** Check the local historical society to determine the earliest types of housing that existed in your community. Do nearby communities date back to earlier times? Have one or more homes been preserved for viewing? Visit these houses and talk with the society's director about how the original occupants lived.

**Discuss:** What factors affected how Native American housing was constructed? *(available materials, climate, permanent versus temporary structures based on the lifestyle of the people)*

Housing changes according to the needs and desires of those who occupy it. Housing also changes because of outside influences such as historical, cultural, societal, environmental, economic, technological, and governmental influences.

# Historical Influences on Housing

The story of housing in the United States began before the first European settlers established the colonies. There is a sharp contrast between the houses of today and those of early North America.

## Early Shelter

Early humans lived in caves that provided a degree of safety and protection from the weather and wild animals. These caves helped people meet the basic need for shelter—a place to sleep and rest.

Another form of early shelter was a dugout, which is a large hole dug in the earth. Dugouts were warm in cold weather and cool in warm weather. Sometimes a dome-shaped covering was added to the dugout to make it roomier. The covering was often made of animal skins, mud and bark, or mud and branches.

### Housing of Native Americans

Early Native Americans, who were known as cliff dwellers, often used a crude rock overhang or cliff for housing. The overhangs were modified for housing by adding an enclosure. The enclosure gave warmth, privacy, and security to the cliff dwellers. Living in cliffs gave cliff dwellers the advantage of being able to see great distances, which added to their security.

Native Americans occupied North America before European settlers began to arrive. The materials used for their housing depended on what was available in the section of the country in which they lived. Some lived in huts that were constructed with a framework of poles and coverings of thatch, hides, or mud placed over the poles. Others lived in tepees and wigwams. Some Native Americans lived in permanent dwellings constructed of adobe. See 2-1 for the different types of Native American dwellings and where they were located.

### Housing of the Colonists

The first shelters used by the European settlers were copied after Native American dwellings. Other houses were built of sod. Dirt floors were common.

The early colonists built their own houses. Sometimes they built them with the help of many neighbors, an event called a *house raising*. Since many people helped with the work, a house could be built in a short amount of time. The quality of these early dwellings was limited due to the lack of skills, tools, and materials.

After the colonists became settled, they attempted to copy the houses in their homeland. However, the styles had to be adapted to the materials available. Some housing styles of the Old Country were not well-suited to the climate of the new land and consequently were not copied. For instance, the thatched roof, commonly used in England, was not suited to the cold New England climate. See 2-2.

The abundance of trees in the eastern forests made the log cabin convenient to build. It is believed that the first *log cabins* were built about 1640 by

**Discuss:** Other than Native Americans, do any Americans today live in caves or dugouts? Have you heard any wartime experiences from soldiers who lived in such shelters?

**Social Studies Activity:** Name five historical figures, politicians, or other famous Americans associated with a log cabin.

## Native American Housing

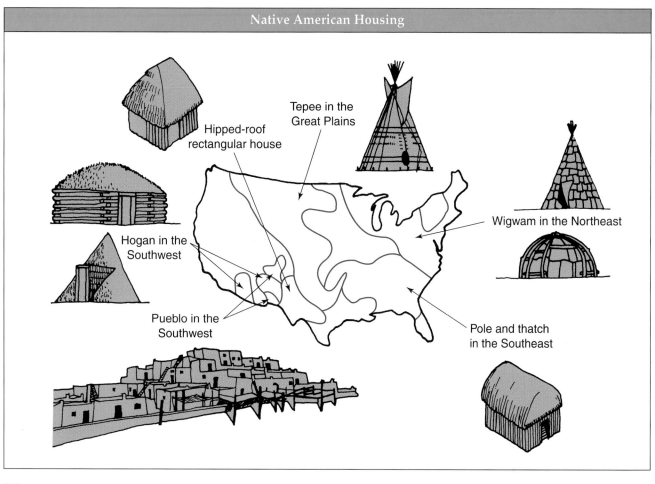

Hipped-roof rectangular house

Tepee in the Great Plains

Wigwam in the Northeast

Hogan in the Southwest

Pueblo in the Southwest

Pole and thatch in the Southeast

2-1

*Early Native Americans lived in housing that varied according to the region in which they were located.*

Swedish and Finnish colonists. They began as one-room structures with fireplaces for heating and cooking. See 2-3. The chimneys were located on the outside of the cabins.

Later, the log cabin was built in a variety of styles. Rooms were often added as families grew larger. Some log cabins were built with three rooms—an entryway, kitchen, and sleeping room. Others were two stories tall. The kitchens in these log cabins were large, so food could be both processed and prepared in the house. Sleeping rooms were small and sometimes located in a loft. If a small log cabin was replaced by a larger

dwelling, the small cabin was sometimes used for storage.

The log cabin spread from the Northeast into the South and onto the western frontier. It became a symbol of the early United States.

Most housing in early settlements could be found in group settings. The houses were placed close together for security reasons. The houses were generally square or rectangular. Many had one or two rooms and a fireplace. When other rooms were added around the main room, it became known as the *great room.*

As the country became settled, more people with building skills

**Note:** If the map in Figure 2-1 were extended to show Alaska, igloos would be added. In Hawaii, thatched-roof housing was typical.

**Math Activity:** Research the square footage of living areas within cliff dwellings. Compare the average amount of private space used per person in a cliff dwelling to that of the per-person space used by a couple in a 900-square-foot-apartment. *(Compare per-person living* *space in cliff dwellings to the apartment's space of 450 square feet per person to find the answer.)*

**Discuss:** How does housing in a high rise compare to the housing of cliff dwellers?

2-2

*The thatched roof, which is not appropriate for cold climates, is very common in warmer climates.*

Fern Mountain Historic Homestead

2-3

*A typical log cabin looked similar to this.*

arrived. They helped build houses and taught others their skills. When logs were cut into lumber, it became a common building material. Other houses also appeared that were built of stone or brick.

## Housing during the 1700s and 1800s

Throughout the 1700s and 1800s, many people moved west and settled on large plots of land. They lived on their land in a variety of dwellings. Farmhouses ranged in design and construction from sod houses to log cabins to ranch houses. At the same time, large plantation houses were being built in the South, as shown in 2-4.

In the late 1700s, most settlers who had come to North America were *agrarian*, or people who earned their living from the land. By 1890, the rural population had decreased as a result of the Industrial Revolution. People began to move to the cities along with immigrants looking for jobs. The birth rate also increased and the cities grew. This increased the demand for housing in the urban areas.

### Urban Housing

The housing in cities was built close together and crowded with inhabitants, causing a high density. *Density* is the number of people in a given area. Most houses were frame houses that varied in design. A number of *tenement houses*, or early apartments, were constructed before housing regulations existed. The first tenement houses appeared in New York City around 1840 to house immigrants. Most were built on a city lot, 25 by 100 feet. A typical tenement house was a five-story building, measuring 25 by 25 feet. Next to each dwelling was another 25-foot-square building.

**Math Activity:** Since the typical size of a log cabin in early settlements was 200 to 300 square feet, how many of these housing structures would fit inside your classroom? *(Multiply the classroom's length by its width to find its total square footage. Then, divide that by 250 square feet to find the answer.)*

**Social Studies Activity:** Create a timeline showing the development of housing during the 1700s and 1800s.

**Vocabulary:** Pair the words *agrarian* and *density* in one sentence using each correctly.

The typical tenement house consisted of as many as 116 two-room apartments. The outdoor toilets were located on the land between the buildings. Conditions were very poor and the landlords earned the title of *slumlords.*

By 1890, government regulations required that each room in a new tenement house have a window. Each apartment was to have running water and a kitchen sink. Community toilets were to be located in the stairway area connecting the floors.

The first row houses were built in the 1820s. **Row houses** are a continuous group of dwellings connected by common sidewalls. Many of them were built to house factory workers. See 2-5. Two-story row houses sometimes housed as many as six families at a time.

Eventually, row houses with fewer common walls evolved into dwellings for one family. Two-family dwellings, called *duplexes*, were built. Multifamily housing was built for four or six families.

The tenement houses and row houses were forerunners of modern apartments. Some apartments first appeared during the housing shortage caused by the Industrial Revolution. At the same time, mansions were being built for the well-to-do. See 2-6.

## Changes in Housing

Many changes were taking place in housing and the housing industry in the 1700s and 1800s. There were new inventions, machinery, and technology.

Wood- and coal-burning stoves appeared in houses. Steam-heating systems were installed. Oil and gas lamps replaced candles. Iceboxes were available. Water supplies, plumbing, and sanitation facilities were improved. Some houses had indoor toilets and bathtubs. However, only

Madewood Plantation, Louisiana Office of Tourism

2-4 ——————————————

*Plantation houses were common dwellings for large landowners of the South.*

Historic Pullman Foundation

2-5 ——————————————

*Many employees of The Pullman Palace Car Company lived in these rowhouses in the late 1800s.*

W. Metzen/H. Armstrong Roberts

2-6 _____

*Mansions, such as the Vanderbilt Mansion shown here, were often
built for wealthy businesspeople in the late 1800s.*

**Internet Activity:** Find
the Web sites for homes
such as Biltmore Estate
and the Vanderbilt
Mansion. Find out what
made them so special for
their era.

people with high incomes could afford
to take advantage of these new developments. Rural areas were slow to
adopt the improvements.

Machinery, craftspeople, and
architects were all important in the
housing industry. An *architect* is a
person who designs buildings and
supervises their construction. They got
ideas from designs used in buildings
in other countries. Machinery helped
the buildings go up rapidly. People
skilled in various crafts contributed
high-quality work. No single housing
style dominated the scene.

## Housing in the 1900s

During the early 1900s, the number of immigrants to the United States
increased dramatically and many

moved to the cities. A housing boom
in the early 1900s began to meet this
need for housing.

Then, during World War I, almost
no housing was built, except by the
federal government. This caused a
housing shortage. House ownership
declined. Housing was overcrowded.
There was a shortage of materials and,
as a result, structures fell into disre-
pair. After World War I, about one-
third of the population was living in
substandard housing. *Substandard*
means the houses are not up to the
standards that are best for people.
Only a half-hearted housing reform
was taking place.

By the time the Great Depression
began in 1929, more than half the U.S.
population lived in cities. However,
the building of houses had slowed
down. People of all income levels had
to struggle to meet their own housing
needs. Private enterprise as well as the
government soon saw the need for
housing reform and began to lay the
foundation.

The first census of housing in the
United States was taken in 1940. A
*census* is an official count of the population by the government. The census
supported what the people knew—the
housing needs of people at all income
levels had not been met. The impact of
the increased population, World War I,
and the Great Depression had left
housing conditions in a neglected
state.

### New Solutions to Housing Shortages

In response to housing shortages,
factory-produced units emerged as a
major type of American housing.
Depending on the type, units were
produced to various levels of completion and delivered to a housing site.
The advantage of factory-built housing involved the savings in cost as
well as in construction time.

**Social Studies Activity:** Add the important housing events of the
1900s to the timeline created earlier in this chapter.

**Discuss:** Do housing shortages exist in parts of the world today? If
so, where? How are the shortages being addressed?

Houses that are conventionally built on-site generally take more time to complete because building is often prolonged by weather-related delays and coordination of the many different tradespeople. When housing is built in a factory, usually on an assembly line, it is more coordinated and takes less time to complete. Some units are completely finished in the factory, while some come in parts that need to be put together. All involve a certain amount of labor when being placed on the site. These housing types are described more fully in Chapter 4, "Choosing a Place to Live."

Factory-built housing units helped with the housing shortage by serving as year-round housing for many people, including defense workers, factory employees, and military personnel. Housing units on wheels provided an affordable solution for home ownership since the cost was considerably less than a conventional house built from a foundation at a housing site. Today, manufactured housing is one of the fastest growing types of affordable housing in the United States. See 2-7.

Following World War II, housing construction resumed. *Tract houses*, which are groups of similarly designed houses built on a tract of land, appeared. They were moderate in size and built to meet the needs of the moderate-income family. The owners of tract houses today have adapted them to fit their needs.

### Steps to Improve Housing

Several new housing ideas were developed to improve housing. Two of these were new towns and subdivisions. A *new town* is an urban development consisting of a small to midsize city with a broad range of housing and planned industrial, commercial, and recreational facilities. See 2-8. It covers up to 6,000 acres. The number of residents ranges from 10,000 to 60,000. The industrial facilities provide opportunities for employment. A new town is designed to appeal to people of all ages, economic

Schult Homes

2-7

*Some manufactured homes must be moved in sections and joined on-site.*

RESTON
MASTERPLAN

Single Family

Townhomes

Apartments/Condominiums

Parks/Open Space/Tennis/Pools

Community Use/Schools/Churches/
   Child Care

Lakes

Town Center District

Town Center Urban Core
   Office/Retail/Hotels/Residential

Business and R & D

Village Centers/Convenience Retail

Courtesy of Reston Land Corporation

2-8

*A master plan was used when developing the planned community of Reston, Virginia.*

levels, races, educational backgrounds, and religious beliefs.

The idea for new towns dates back to the early 1900s, but it was 1960 before the idea started to gain attention. New towns were planned communities, not accidental developments. They were created to promote the orderly growth of areas with fast-growth potential. By the early 1970s, about 15 new towns were started. The idea continued and by 1990, 60 new towns were in progress in the United States.

Since the early 1990s a new version of new town, called new urbanism, gained popularity. *New urbanism* refers to towns that encourage pedestrian traffic, are more in harmony with the environment, and are sustainable. *Sustainable* means producing most of the energy needed and/or using minimum natural resources. In communities built on the new urbanism concept, everything is within walking distance. These developments are mixed-use, which means shops, offices, apartments, and single-family homes are included in one planned area.

A *subdivision* is a smaller version of the new town concept. In a subdivision, the density and types of buildings are controlled. Subdivisions are often created from undeveloped land by private investors called *developers.* Developers must obtain permission to create a subdivision from local government officials, who must consider many factors. One such factor is the impact the new subdivision will have on the amount of traffic it will add to area roads. Other considerations include the potential overcrowding of schools and excess strain on government services such as police and fire protection, a fresh-water supply, waste pick-up, and sewage treatment.

A well-thought-out design for a subdivision could include recreational facilities such as a pool, tennis courts, basketball courts, hiking trails, bike paths, and man-made lakes for boating and fishing. New roads are included in the plan and possibly a new school, too. A well-designed subdivision may also include easy access to shopping centers and medical offices.

Adequate housing for everyone has never fully been achieved in the United States and remains one of the nation's greatest challenges. See 2-9. Ideally, the housing supply will

**Discuss:** Study the plan of Figure 2-8. Compare it to your community. Was your community planned or did it just evolve? In which type of community would you prefer to live? Explain your choice.

**Vocabulary:** Identify the similarities and differences between a new town and a subdivision.

Habitat for Humanity® International

2-9

*The housing in the foreground did not meet building code requirements so volunteers constructed a new home nearby that did.*

someday meet the needs of the diverse U.S. population. This includes older people, people with disabilities, singles, first-time homeowners, and people of all cultures, races, and income levels.

# Cultural Influences on Housing

The beliefs, social customs, and traits of a group of people form their *culture*. A group's culture influences its housing, and the housing becomes part of the culture. The following examples illustrate how housing influences culture.

The Navajo, a Native American tribe of the North American Southwest, lived in a *hogan*, which was a building made of logs and mud. The windows faced west and a single

door faced east. The placement of the door had religious significance. The Navajo believed that the door must face east so the spirit guardians could enter. The tradition exists today, even though the type of housing for many Navajos has changed. Housing built by the Crow, a Native American tribe of the Northwest, also have doors facing east.

The Native American tribes in North America had cultures that equated the environment with their religious beliefs. They typically viewed the land and water as common property to be respected and used wisely by everyone. Then, European settlers arrived in North America with contrasting views. They saw the opportunity for private ownership of the land and water.

Before regions in the South and Southwest became states, they were

**Reflect:** How many subdivisions are in your city or town? When were they built? Are new ones under construction? Are there any new towns in your area?

**Reflect:** Are you willing to welcome new students to school who speak a different language or come from a different cultural experience? What are some ways that you can help do this?

**Reflect:** How has the cultural background of your family affected your home? Write an entry in your journal describing this.

**Writing Activity:** Work in pairs to search for a picture of a house with the exterior design features of the Spanish mission shown in Figure 2-10 and write a paragraph describing the key Spanish features.

settled by the Spanish. The Spanish built missions with whitewashed walls and red-tiled roofs. The style of the Spanish missions greatly influenced the local architecture. In the early 1900s, there was a revival of Hispanic heritage, including architecture. The old missions were preserved and early Spanish architecture was copied in houses and other buildings. See 2-10. Today the Hispanic influence can be found in architecture throughout the South and Southwest as well as across the nation.

When the Pilgrims arrived at Plymouth Rock in the winter of 1620, they needed shelter immediately. They duplicated the housing of the Native Americans. After the winter was over, they began to duplicate the English cottages of their homeland. They used wood, which was abundantly available and the traditional building material of their homeland. The first cottages were often crude and made of timber. They had dirt floors, few windows, and chimneys built of sticks and heavy clay. As better materials and skills became available, the cottages were built to more resemble the cottages in England.

As other cultures came to North America from Europe, they also contributed their styles of housing to the American landscape. As mentioned earlier, the Swedish log cabin became a popular form of housing. The Dutch Colonial, Pennsylvania Dutch (German) Colonial, French Normandy, and Italianate housing styles are other examples of European influences on American housing. (These will be examined later in Chapter 6, "The Evolution of Exteriors.")

Throughout history, houses have been strong indicators of culture. Heritage as well as traditional skills and materials are reflected in housing. As cultures change, the changes are evident in the housing.

## New Immigrants

Each year, the United States welcomes thousands of legal immigrants from all over the world. Now, as in the past, these immigrants bring their dreams and expectations for a better life as they adapt to their new home. Finding housing that reflects their cultural preferences and personal priorities is part of that dream.

Many immigrants, for example, are members of large extended families that need housing to have extra space for sleeping quarters. An Asian family may want housing that incorporates Feng Shui elements in its architecture. *Feng Shui* is a design philosophy that uses space planning and design to attract good fortune and prosperity to its occupants. Other

San Xavier Del Bac Mission, Arizona Office of Tourism

2-10 _____

*Spanish missions, such as this one, influence architecture even today.*

**Discuss:** What are some architectural features or styles of housing in America that were influenced by the occupants' religious beliefs? (*a front-facing door in Native American housing linked to the belief that the entry of spirit guardians required it; and whitewashed walls and red tile roofs of Spanish style homes patterned after the designs of* the local Spanish missions central to the lives of the people)

**Reading Activity:** Check out a library book such as Laura Ingalls Wilder's *Little House in the Big Woods* to study the housing of rural families before the twentieth century. Compare the description to rural housing today.

immigrants may want to have a large yard where they can grow a vegetable or fruit garden, just as they did in their homeland.

Low wages and limited knowledge of the English language often serve as barriers to finding decent, safe, and affordable housing. Too many new immigrants live in conditions that are substandard and unsafe, and jeopardize their families' desires for a better life. To help find suitable housing that reflects their culture in a way that meets housing codes and regulations, new immigrants need simple housing information provided in their own language.

Not all immigrants fall into the category of low-paid laborers, however. Many new immigrants are skilled workers, professionals, and workers with advanced degrees or exceptional abilities. Even the majority of low-paid immigrants are eventually able to improve their living conditions and save enough money to buy a home. Acquiring a home, personalizing it, and becoming a part of a community is a desire shared by foreign-born and native-born citizens alike. See 2-11.

# Societal Influences on Housing

Signs of societal change are everywhere. They can be seen in the growth of the cities and the movement of people to new jobs and locations. They can be seen in relationships and lifestyles. Many of these changes affect housing.

## Household Size

The U. S. Census Bureau collects data to provide information on *demographics*, which are statistical facts about the human population.

2-11
*About 67 percent of foreign-born citizens are homeowners, which is about the same percent of U.S.-born citizens who own homes.*

Demographic information helps society plan for future needs and understand trends that affect those needs. Demographic information includes characteristics of individuals such as age, income, race, gender, and the relationship of people living in the household.

One important social change that has influenced housing is the average number of people living in a household. Since the first U.S. Census was taken in 1790, the average number has gradually decreased. This first census showed that most households had between three and seven members. In 1900, the majority had two to five members. The 2000 U.S. census shows that only one or two people lived in most households today.

## Household Composition

The decrease in the number of household members is not the only change evident in households. Their composition has also changed. In 1940, for example, married couples headed 75 percent of all households, and 7 percent were single-person households. By 2000, the number of single-person households had increased dramatically, accounting for almost 26 percent of the total. Households headed by married couples, on the other hand, had decreased to 53 percent.

In the past, married couples were more likely than single people to own their own homes. However, this has changed, due in part to an increase in the number of singles. The 2000 U.S. census counted 81 million single people over 19 years of age. That represents an increase of more than 15 million singles in 10 years. The increase is due to many reasons, such as the tendency to postpone marriage until careers are established and the steady increase in the nation's divorce rate.

Some singles choose to live with roommates and share housing costs, while others prefer to live alone. See 2-12. Many singles are renters and live in apartments. Others own houses, condominiums, cooperatives, or townhouses.

Some singles live with their parents. Never-married singles or single-

again adults may return to live with their parents after living on their own for a while. The combined living arrangement may last for a short or extended period, and sometimes their children accompany them.

## An Older Population

The continual aging of the population is another change in society that affects housing. The median age of the U.S. population is 35.3 years, reflecting the ever-growing number of people in higher age categories. Median means the arithmetic average.

According to the 2000 U.S. census, the two age categories showing the fastest growth were 50-to-54-year-olds and 45-to-49-year-olds. They grew at nearly 55 percent and 45 percent, respectively. Their members are part of the large segment of the adult population referred to as *baby boomers*. They get their name from the period after World War II called the *baby boom*, which includes births from 1946 through 1964. Since this group is so large, the housing they will need as they become senior citizens is expected to place high demands on society.

Already the housing needs of senior citizens are large and growing. According to the 2000 U.S. census, 35 million people were age 65 or older, accounting for 12 percent of the population. The majority of elderly persons live with a spouse. Among those who live alone, most are women.

Housing needs for older people differ from those of the general population. Many older people lose some of their physical abilities as they age. They may have a partial loss of hearing or sight. They may be more sensitive to heat and cold. They may no longer be able to use stairs. Many older people live in housing that presents limits or

2-12

*Singles who want extra space to pursue a hobby or a business may prefer to live alone rather than share housing with a roommate.*

barriers to taking full advantage of their homes. See 2-13. Housing that is adapted or designed to fit the needs of older people helps them live in their homes longer, thus remaining independent.

As a result of the aging population, housing and related services for the elderly have become a national concern. Retirement centers, assisted living arrangements, and personal health assistance will need to expand to meet the changing population demands.

## People with Disabilities

Many people have physical, sensory, or mental disabilities that limit

2-13

*Compact, one-story houses are ideal for senior citizens.*

**Reflect:** Do you know singles who live alone in order to pursue a hobby or business, as is shown in Figure 2-12? What hobbies and businesses do they pursue?

**Writing Activity:** Write a story for children about adapting a home for an elderly person with special needs.

their activities. A *disability* is an impairment or limit to a person's ability. These may interfere with a person's ability to walk, lift, hear, or see, for example. Their physical limitations may be temporary or permanent. As a result, they have special housing needs. Their housing must allow them to carry out day-to-day activities with as little restriction as possible.

When housing limits a person's activities, consideration must be given to how housing can be built or adapted to meet specific needs. Guidelines will be discussed further in Chapter 4, "Choosing a Place to Live"; Chapter 20, "Keeping Your House Safe and Secure"; and Chapter 22, "Housing for Today and Tomorrow."

## Finding Affordable Housing

Many people live in inadequate housing. They may live on social security or welfare benefits, which provide minimum resources. Some become

homeless as a result of unemployment and loss of income.

Inadequate housing has many effects on society. Substandard dwellings become overcrowded, which results in a lack of privacy and increased family conflict. It also contributes to the spread of disease.

The middle-income group is the largest in the United States. Most jobs provide middle-income salaries, and most houses and furniture are designed for middle-income families. However, today's middle-income individuals and families sometimes have difficulty buying houses. This is because they have excess debt (usually credit card payments) and incomes that are not rising as fast as housing costs. Usually, too, they have not saved enough money for a down payment.

In the recent past, families were advised to spend no more than two and one-half times their annual income to purchase a house. Today, the average house in the United States is more costly. The average family spends at least one-third of its income on housing. Some of those who purchase houses may pay up to four times their annual income for an average house. These increases in the cost of housing make single-family homes unaffordable to many.

Since the housing costs have risen faster than income, middle-income families must decide how to balance their housing and lifestyle needs. Instead of buying a single-family house, for example, they may choose to buy a condominium, cooperative, or townhouse, or simply rent an apartment. See 2-14.

### Changing Roles

Today, many women are working outside the home. Some are working to support themselves. Others are working to support their families,

2-14

*Many families today choose to live in low-maintenance apartments such as these.*

which might include children or older parents. Many women own their own houses.

When both adults in a nuclear family are employed outside the home, they have a *dual-income family*. This common situation has become necessary for many families because income has not kept up with the cost of living. While dual-income families may have more income, they may have less time for household tasks. They may desire more convenient housing and timesaving devices.

## Planning for Leisure Time

People today are spending more time at various types of work, juggling their jobs, home responsibilities, child care, and sometimes parent care. Too often, no time is left for relaxation and recreation. Consequently, many individuals and families must make time for leisure and use that time wisely.

How you choose to use your leisure time affects your housing decisions. Most people choose housing with low-maintenance requirements so less time is needed for upkeep. On the other hand, many enjoy decorating or fixing up their homes, and view these as leisure or recreational activities.

Some people specifically choose housing that provides opportunities for leisure activities. The house may have a special room, such as an exercise or hobby area. It may be near a golf course, tennis court, or swimming pool. A large backyard may be the place a homeowner wants to spend leisure time with family and friends. See 2-15.

## Working at Home

Due to technological and other changes in the workplace, the number of people working from their homes is increasing. These individuals may have their own business in their home or may be an employee working as a telecommuter. *Telecommuting* is working at home or another site through an electronic link to a central office's computer.

The use of the home as the workplace requires creating a work area that is both functional and convenient. This has implications for the design or redesign of the home environment. How to design a workspace that successfully meets the specific needs of a

Acorn Structures, Inc.

2-15 _____

*This large swimming pool is an inviting leisure space.*

telecommuter is discussed further in Chapter 7, "Understanding House Plans," and several following chapters.

Working at home not only presents challenges for designing the workspace but also for dealing with distractions that interfere with the work routine. Persons working at home need to develop strategies to deal effectively with difficulties that may arise in family relationships, completion of household tasks, and focusing their job requirements.

## A Mobile Society

In a mobile society, people often travel from one location to another. The average vehicle owner travels 15,000 miles a year. Some travel with their portable dwellings, as in 2-16. The average household moves every four years, which can exceed 17 moves in a lifetime.

Sometimes people move to change from renting to homeownership or vice versa. The main reason for so much movement is to relocate for

2-16
*Many people use motorized recreational vehicles as a home for traveling around the country.*

employment reasons. Other reasons for moving include retirement, a better climate, the desire for larger (or smaller) housing, or the preference for a quieter (or livelier) neighborhood.

Population shifts in the United States are the result of a mobile society. Before 1970, there was a slow, continuing westward movement. People also moved toward large bodies of water such as the oceans, Great Lakes, and Gulf of Mexico. Then, after 1970, people began moving to the Sunbelt. The *Sunbelt* includes the southern and southwestern regions of the United States.

# Environmental Influences on Housing

Your *environment* is the total of all conditions, objects, places, and people that are around you. People adapt to their environments in the housing they design and build. They are also able to manipulate their environments through their housing decisions.

## The Natural Environment

The *natural environment* is provided by nature. Land, water, trees, and solar energy are elements of the natural environment. The natural environment also includes *climate,* which is the combination of weather conditions in a region over a period of years as shown by temperature, wind velocity, and precipitation. The altitude and distribution of the land and water help produce the climate.

Shelter varies according to the climate in which it is located. For instance, in areas where it snows or rains often, roofs are sloped to shed snow and rain. In warm, dry areas, roofs may be flat and accessible so people can sleep on the cooler rooftops at night. In cold regions, houses may have smaller doors and fewer windows.

While people want protection from nature, they do not want to be closed off from it. Large windows can frame views of the outdoors while providing protection from the elements. On mild days, patios, swimming pools, and decks provide great opportunities for outdoor living. See 2-17.

A region's *topography*, or lay of the land, and its climate influence the location and design of dwellings. Houses that are designed and located to harmonize with the natural setting and climate are more likely to be efficient.

During the 1950s, integrating houses with the natural environment was explored. Architects designed houses to fit various natural environments. One of the most influential architects concerned with the environment was Frank Lloyd Wright. He broke away from traditional housing designs, saying people should have the courage to follow nature. He used natural settings and many native building materials. See 2-18. Wright positioned houses to take advantage of natural sunlight and prevailing breezes. He also located them so they had a great deal of privacy. Much of today's housing is designed to take advantage of the natural environment.

## The Constructed Environment

The *constructed environment* includes the natural environment after it has been changed by human effort. A constructed environment is created when a dwelling is built, landscaped, and heated and/or cooled to control the indoor climate.

Together, natural and constructed environments can provide pleasing

2-17
*A new deck gives this family a chance to spend time together outdoors in beautiful surroundings.*

Courtesy of The Frank Lloyd Wright Foundation

2-18
*Frank Lloyd Wright designed this building to visually blend into its hillside environment.*

Weather Shield Windows & Doors

2-19

*The people who live in this beach house have easy access to the ocean plus a beautiful view.*

surroundings. Highways through the mountains make the beautiful scenery accessible to people. Dwellings located along beaches allow people to enjoy a view of the ocean, as in 2-19.

## The Behavioral Environment

Housing creates an environment for people to interact with one another. This interaction is called the *behavioral environment*. Human qualities, such as intelligence, talent, and energy, are part of this environment. Feelings, such as happiness,

loneliness, love, and anger, are another part of it.

The behavioral environment overlaps with the natural and constructed environments. It is found wherever people interact—in child care centers, schools, shopping centers, neighborhoods, and houses.

Housing fosters social behavior. It may restrict certain types of behavior and permit others. Housing is more than a response to the physical environment. It is a setting for the development of the members of the household.

A positive behavioral environment is desired. However, sometimes an individual or family is *dysfunctional*. This means the behavioral environment produces a negative effect on household members. For instance, drug addiction, alcoholism, and violence cause households to become dysfunctional. Substandard housing can be the cause of negative behavior and result in a dysfunctional family, while attractive housing often contributes to more positive behavior. See 2-20.

## Interaction of the Environments

Each type of environment affects the other two, causing a chain reaction. One example is a community that has no open space. Houses in this community are built close together, covering most of the land. No land is set aside to preserve part of the natural environment.

The behavioral environment in this community is full of conflict because the constructed and natural environments are not satisfying to the residents. People are simply too crowded. They do not have the space they need or the natural beauty they want. Because their environments are not controlled, all their needs and wants cannot be met. Individuals in such an environment cannot move toward self-actualization.

# Economic Influences on Housing

The economic influences on housing involve the production and consumption of goods and services related to housing. These influences include the interaction among consumers, businesses, and government in meeting housing needs.

People make economic decisions every day. Their decisions concern how they use their resources to meet their goals. *Resources* are objects, qualities, and personal strengths that can be used to reach a goal. One resource people have is money, or purchasing power. They will need that resource to achieve the goal of paying for housing.

Houses are expensive and costs keep rising. According to the National Association of Realtors, the median price of existing homes was $52,200 in 1980. By 1990, the median price rose to $95,500. In 2000, the median price of an existing home was $139,000. The cost had risen almost three times over that 20-year period.

## How Housing Affects the Economy

One way to measure the economy is to determine the number of families that can afford to buy a median-priced home in their area. High mortgage rates and high unemployment affect the ability of households to purchase housing. According to the U. S. Census Bureau, 52 percent of the total population in 1984 could afford to purchase median-priced homes in their area. By 1995, only 48 percent could afford to buy them.

2-20

*Many of a person's fondest memories are often linked to the social experiences he or she enjoyed at home.*

Another measure of the economy is the number of *housing starts*, or new houses being built, in a given year. In an average year, the housing starts should number around two million, which would meet the demand for new housing. When the economy is up, that number may be reached. When the economy is down, the number of housing starts may fall short of expectations.

Resource: *Housing and the Economy,* Activity D, SAG. Students brainstorm and list all of the jobs involved in building, selling, and decorating a home.

Reflect: What economic decisions did your family make during the last week?

Vocabulary: Explain the meaning of the term *housing starts* by relating it to the demand for new housing.

Internet Activity: Check the Census Bureau's Web site at *census.gov* to get the reported number of housing starts for the last four months. What do these numbers indicate about the economy?

## How the Economy Affects Housing

The economy affects, and is affected by, the production of houses. Many nationally produced goods and services are related to the housing industry. Employment goes up and down in relation to the condition of the housing industry. See 2-21. The housing industry employs planners, developers, builders, material suppliers, trades people, and financial experts. There are millions of enterprises involved in this industry.

The housing industry depends on the housing market. The *housing market* is the transfer of dwellings from the producers to the consumers. The strength of the housing market depends on supply and demand. This is the number of existing houses versus the number needed by the population. The housing market changes considerably from year to year since it follows the general pattern of economic prosperity and decline. War, recession, depression, inflation, and economic uncertainty all negatively impact the housing market.

Housing is traditionally the first major sector of the economy to rebound after an economic slump. Growth in the housing industry has a positive impact on the *gross domestic product (GDP)*, which is the value of all goods and services produced within a country during a given time period. See 2-22. The GDP is the most accurate indicator of the health of a nation's economy.

Mortgage interest rates and tax advantages affect growth in the housing industry. Interest rates on home mortgages and inflation seem to increase at the same time. When mortgage rates are low, demand for housing is so high that enough housing may not be available to meet the demand. When rates are high, fewer households invest in new housing.

The federal tax advantages to owning a house include the opportunity to deduct mortgage interest and real estate taxes from your taxable income. Also, homeowners are not required to pay taxes on any profits they make from selling their homes, provided they meet a few easy conditions. Finally, those who move because of a job change may have yet another tax advantage.

# Technological Influences on Housing

*Technology* is the practical application of knowledge. Knowledge of tools, materials, and processes allows

Lowden, Lowden & Co.

2-21
*Construction workers have plenty of employment opportunities when demand for housing is strong.*

people to adapt to their environment. Technology changes over time as new and better ways of meeting human needs are discovered.

## Early Technology

Technology began with the early cave dwellers. Caves met the housing needs of the day because they were dry and secure, and maintained a moderate temperature. However, caves were in short supply and often located far from food and water.

When people evolved from hunting and gathering food to farming, living in caves became less desirable. People then used technology to build dwellings. They constructed their houses with naturally occurring materials, such as logs, sticks, bark, rocks, leaves, grass, mud, and snow. These houses were temporary, lasting only two or three years. They were quickly abandoned if the household wanted to move or better housing became available. The main shortcoming of these dwellings was the quality of materials used, not the design.

Over time, technology improved natural materials and new techniques replaced the old. Logs were made into wood planks and stones were chipped into blocks. Animal hides became coverings for windows and doors. Later bricks, tiles, pipes, glass, and cement were developed.

## Industrialization

The Industrial Revolution had a dramatic technological impact on housing. Goods were mass-produced and the railroad system moved them efficiently. Farmers and factories used the railroads to ship their products, which included housing materials. Prefabricated houses became popular because they could be shipped in

Ethan Allen, Inc.

2-22

*A boom in housing construction translates into increased sales of furniture, appliances, carpeting, and other items for new homes.*

sections. Sears, Roebuck & Company shipped 110,000 mail-order houses in a 40-year period.

Industrialization changed housing in many ways. Today, many parts of houses, such as doors and windows already in frames, come from the factory ready to install. Factory-produced climate-control units, such as heat pumps, air conditioners, and furnaces, have replaced fireplaces and simple fans. Labor-intensive tasks once done by humans are now accomplished by laborsaving devices, such as electric saws and automatic clothes washers.

**Resource:** *Filling a House with High Tech,* Activity E, SAG. Students mount pictures of high-toch produoto in tho space provided and explain how the products can improve the quality of housing.

**Social Studies Activity:** Find out when the Industrial Revolution began. Check with the historical society in your community to find out whether homes were built in your community in the early years of the Industrial Revolution. If so, visit one that is open to the public, and write a report on the level of technology used in it.

**Enrich:** Find information about the housing kits that were once sold through the Sears catalog. What did they include? How much did they cost? How was the kit delivered? What did the buyer need to do to transform the kit into livable housing? Find out where one such home exists today.

The pace of change is increasing faster than ever, fueled by nonstop scientific discoveries. Change is occurring so rapidly that sometimes equipment becomes outdated before it is fully utilized.

## High Tech

Technology, also called *high tech*, has a big and growing influence on housing decisions. Homes now may include media rooms or home theaters complete with large screens and high-tech sound systems, 2-23. Home computers are used extensively for connecting to the Internet and for creating reports. Computers can even be used to select and locate housing through virtual tours of homes on the Web.

Computer technology is the basis for many of the high-tech items found throughout the house. You probably do not even think about the simple computer systems you use, such as a touch-tone telephone or touch-pad microwave oven. Computer technology is the reason they operate as they do, and this is true for many other household items. Computerized systems, for example, allow central control of energy management, entertaining, and security systems, and promote convenience in living. See 2-24.

Many energy-saving and other features on today's appliances result from technology advances. Ranges now have safety locks to protect children and others from unauthorized use. Voice-activated commands assist blind individuals in using appliances. The

Photo courtesy of Scott Moody. System by Audio/Video Architects, Hilton Head Island, S.C.

2-23 _____

*More and more homes are being designed to include media rooms and home theaters.*

Photo courtesy of GE Plastics

2-24

*By touching a button, interior windows can change from clear to translucent through the use of a crystal polyester film material.*

future may allow the homeowner to order groceries from a flat-panel computer on the refrigerator door. Appliances may soon be Web-connected to the appliance manufacturer, who can diagnose any problems that may arise.

Advances in technology continue to improve building design, assembly systems, and construction materials. For example, treated materials such as wood shingles and asphalt are now made to last at least a half century. Today's factory-built housing offers higher quality materials in manufactured and modular housing, too.

Many architects and interior designers use *computer-aided drafting and design (CADD)*, which is software and hardware that creates designs with a computer. CADD is used to develop housing interiors and house plans. With CADD, plans can quickly be adjusted to conserve materials and improve a building's structure and energy efficiency. Adjustments based on client needs and desires can easily be made. Consumer versions of CADD are also available for individuals who wish to use their computers to explore possible home modifications or decorating plans. See 2-25.

While technology is used to solve some problems, it sometimes causes others. One example is a freeway system in a large city that helps people drive quickly and easily between home and work. However, with increased traffic, pollution often develops and decreases air quality.

## Governmental Influences on Housing

Government at all levels—federal, state, and local—influences housing decisions. This influence began early in U.S. history and continues today.

2-25

*Several brands of computer software in the consumer market can simplify house planning and design.*

## Legislation

Laws regulating housing began during colonial times. Some laws prohibited the building of houses on the village green, which was often set aside for government and church buildings. Other laws helped control the spread of fire between adjacent houses. Fireplaces used to cook food and provide heat were often inferior. They caught fire easily and soon the whole house burned. The fire would often spread to other dwellings, and sometimes a single fire would wipe out a whole settlement. In 1649, the British ordered that houses be built of brick or stone and the roofs be made of slate or tile to help prevent the spread of fire.

Over the years, the government has played an increasingly stronger role in safeguarding people and their housing. In the late 1800s, Congress began enacting laws and allocating money for housing. Laws were also introduced at the turn of the twentieth century to control the use of land, prevent overcrowding, and encourage beautification.

Since the 1930s, the federal Government has stepped up its efforts to improve housing conditions in the United States. Efforts were made to rebuild the slum areas. The Housing Act of 1934 created the Federal

**Activity:** Select a piece of legislation from Appendix A ("Housing and Related Legislation"), research it further, and provide a report, explaining the impact it has made.

**Social Studies / Science Activity:** Contact your state's department of natural resources to learn which programs protect native habitat and natural resources, thus preventing homes from being built in certain locations. Are any areas near you off-limits to development? Report your findings.

Housing Administration (FHA), an agency that still exists today. With the passage of the Housing Act of 1937, the public-housing program was created with the objective of providing decent, sanitary housing for low-income families.

Subsequent legislation continued to provide housing programs for low-income families and older citizens. Even more tract houses were built and numerous apartments and town-houses appeared on the scene. In 1965, the *U.S. Department of Housing and Urban Development (HUD)* was formed. This is a cabinet-level, policy-making body whose mission is to promote a decent, safe, and sanitary home, and suitable living environment for every American.

Congress continues to pass housing legislation and allocate money for housing programs. See Appendix A, "Housing and Related Legislation" for a summary of important national laws that have affected housing.

States also pass laws related to housing and are required to conform to federal legislation. More and more responsibility for regulating housing is being delegated to the states.

City or county governments may establish local housing-related ordinances. These regulations must conform to both federal and state laws. Most local housing legislation falls into one of the following categories:

- standards for quality construction
- control of land and density
- funding for housing
- housing for people in need
- environmental protection

### Housing Standards

Much of the housing legislation sets minimum standards of quality for various areas. Standards are set for land use and dwelling construction. They are also set to control density and separate residences from industry. Other standards are set to protect human health.

Standards include building codes. *Building codes* establish minimum standards for materials and construction methods. There are codes for plumbing, heating, ventilation, and electrical systems. See 2-26. Placement of stairways and exits are also included in the codes. The codes are used to assure healthy, safe, and sanitary conditions. Some standards also have to do with appearance. They indicate roof styles or maximum height. Codes are formulated and enforced by local and state governments. The latest edition

2-26

*Building codes require qualified electricians to install the electrical systems. The same is true for the heating, cooling, and plumbing systems.*

Discuss: How does your community deal with people who become homeless? Why is it unwise to allow the homeless to take shelter wherever they may find it?

Reflect: Think about the realty signs in your neighborhood. Do any of them indicate zoning regulations, such as the word *Commercial* in Figure 2-27?

of the *Uniform Building Code* is the most widely adopted model building code in the world. It sets minimum standards for building construction.

Some housing codes determine the use, occupancy, and maintenance of buildings. One reason is to prevent overcrowding. Another is to guarantee that major alterations made to a dwelling meet required standards. These codes may not be well-enforced in some communities, sometimes because of too few inspection officials. Also, some people resist inspections that will result in exposure of their code breaking, which often involves a fine and/or penalties.

A *zoning regulation* is a government requirement that controls land use. It specifies the type of buildings and activities that are permitted in a certain area. An area may be zoned for residential, commercial, or industrial use. In a residential zone, only residential dwellings can be built. In a commercial zone, only stores and office buildings can be built. See 2-27. In an industrial zone, only factories and other industrial businesses can be

built. Sometimes within a residential area, only one type of dwelling is permitted. The location of manufactured housing and multifamily dwellings are usually restricted to specific areas. Sometimes, the minimum size of dwellings to be built is specified.

Density is also controlled through zoning. Density control reduces the risk of fire and keeps traffic and pollution manageable. It also restricts excessive noise and lighting. Lot size and the placement of a building on a lot are also indicated.

Government controls at all levels tend to increase the cost of housing. However, building and zoning controls are intended to serve the best interests of the public.

## Funding for Housing

Funding is another example of government involvement in housing. Several government agencies are charged with buying and selling home mortgages. The government assures some loans, which means it stands behind the lender if homeowners do not meet their obligations. The government helps special groups—such as older people, people with disabilities, veterans, low-income families, and first-time homeowners—acquire funding. Most of these financial organizations are a part of HUD.

### Housing for People in Need

Various forms of government assistance are available to help people who cannot afford housing. HUD provides rent supplements to low-income families and individuals, and builds public housing for those unable to fully pay for satisfactory housing. The federal government also gives support to private programs created to help the homeless.

Seaboard Properties, Hilton Head Island, S.C.

2-27

*The land under this sign is zoned for commercial purposes only.*

Enrich: Attend a presentation by a building construction teacher who discusses the Uniform Building Code and other codes that must be followed when building homes in your community. Be prepared to ask questions. Summarize in one paragraph what you learn.

Enrich: Attend a meeting of a local zoning board and observe a discussion over a zoning issue. Explain the board's proposal and describe your reaction to it? Do you feel more changes in zoning laws should occur in your community? If so, elaborate.

Local governments may donate existing houses that need rehabilitation or may assist with the infrastructure, see 2-28. *Infrastructure* is the underlying foundation or basic framework. In housing, the term often refers to the sewer, water, gas, and electrical lines that must be laid to make the housing liveable.

In recent years, the number of homeless people has increased dramatically. It is estimated there are between 500,000 and seven million homeless people in the United States. Over 40 percent of them are members of families with children. About 25 percent are war veterans. Many are newly and temporarily homeless, having suddenly lost a job or the ability to work. Others are chronically homeless, having accepted their homeless condition as a way of life.

People who become homeless do not fit any one description. However, all people experiencing homelessness have basic needs, including adequate incomes, affordable housing, and health care. Some homeless people may need special services such as mental health or drug abuse treatment to be housed adequately. All their needs must be met to prevent and end homelessness.

Many people have benefited from government housing assistance. However, there never seems to be enough assistance to accommodate everyone who needs it. Since government assistance cannot meet the total housing-assistance needs in American society, various community partnerships have formed to help meet the housing needs of limited-resource families.

An important example is *Habitat for Humanity*. This is a partnership formed to help eliminate homelessness and substandard housing, not only in the United States, but also in other countries. Habitat for Humanity

Habitat for Humanity® International

2-28
*Before a nonprofit group can build a home for a family, the local government must first "set the stage" by running utilities and improving the street.*

relies on volunteers for a number of tasks, including the providing of labor to actually build the houses. See 2-29. The future homeowners must make a generous hands-on donation of labor or similar resources, called "sweat equity," to help produce their own housing. They make a down payment and reduced monthly payments. The money goes into a revolving fund to help others obtain housing through the program. Hundreds of volunteers from civic clubs, religious groups, professional organizations, student groups, and institutions have joined together to build housing structures as well as a true sense of community.

## Environmental Protection

Concern for the environment has led to a number of environmental protection laws. In addition, government agencies such as the U.S. Environmental Protection Agency (EPA) and the U.S. Consumer Product

**Note:** The Web site for the U.S. Department of Housing and Urban Development (HUD) is *hud.gov*. It provides a wealth of housing information.

**Discuss:** What in America today can be compared to the house raisings that were common among early settlers in the colonies?

**Example:** People who contribute "sweat equity" to obtain housing through Habitat for Humanity spend time doing carpentry, painting, clean-up, and any other tasks they are able to handle.

**Research Activity:** Compare the cost of housing today to the cost of housing 20 years ago. Begin by searching the Department of Labor's consumer price index (CPI) to determine how much the CPI for housing expenses has increased in 20 years. What are some factors that have caused the increase?

2-29

*These college students spent their spring break as volunteers building new homes for families without adequate housing.*

Safety Commission (CPSC) were created to foster a positive natural environment. They support research and provide information to consumers so the housing environment, as well as the total environment, will be safe and protected. The agencies have hot lines to assist consumers with problems concerning the environment.

The job of the *Environmental Protection Agency (EPA)* is to safeguard the natural environment, including the air, water, and land upon which life depends. Consequently, the agency focuses on the natural environment as well as the quality of air and water within housing. EPA also assists with voluntary pollution prevention programs and energy conservation methods.

The *Consumer Product Safety Commission (CPSC)* has jurisdiction over more than 15,000 consumer products used in and around the constructed environment. The agency's focus is to save lives and keep families safe by reducing the risk of injuries and deaths associated with consumer products. The CPSC has the authority to recall unsafe products or require their repair. The agency also investigates product complaints linked to injuries and deaths and issues safety guidelines and consumer education.

**Internet Activity:** Search the Web sites of the Environmental Protection Agency (EPA) and the Consumer Product Safety Commission (CPSC) to determine what issues are high priorities with these agencies.

**Vocabulary:** Demonstrate an understanding of the term *environmental protection* by using it correctly in a sentence.

# Summary

Many forces work together to influence housing. Some forces, such as history, culture, and society, involve people. Other forces, such as the environment, economy, technology, and government, involve conditions. All are interrelated.

The cultural development of housing in North America occurred when settlers arrived from all over the world to join the Native Americans. They brought their unique cultures with them, which influenced their housing.

Historical events such as the Industrial Revolution, Great Depression, and World Wars I and II impacted how people were housed. Societal events such as changes in household needs, wants, and lifestyles affected housing designs.

The Industrial Revolution, population increases, and economic crises all caused housing shortages. To ease the shortages, technology and government were used to help develop new solutions for affordable housing.

Housing is a part of the constructed, natural, and behavioral environments. Each type of environment impacts the other two. The government passes legislation that establishes building standards, zoning regulations, and environmental protection. It makes sure all three environments work well together and provides funding for affordable housing for many people.

# To Review

1. List three types of early Native American dwellings.
2. Describe the housing of the first European settlers.
3. Why is the log cabin the symbol of the early United States?
4. What was the main cause of the population shift from rural to urban areas in the late 1700s?
5. List two housing problems created by the population shift.
6. Describe the differences between tenement and row houses.
7. Name three historical events that resulted in substandard housing.
8. Explain the principles of new urbanism.
9. Give an example of how culture influenced housing.
10. Name three factors regarding households that can influence housing.
11. Give two reasons many older people have special housing needs.
12. Why are many middle-income families choosing to live in apartments, condominiums, cooperatives, or townhouses instead of single-family houses?
13. How can leisure time affect housing decisions?

14. The average household moves every _____ years.
15. After the natural environment has been changed by human effort, it is called the _____ _____.
16. What effect does housing growth have on the GDP?
17. What determines the strength of the housing industry?
18. List two ways that CADD is used to improve housing.
19. Describe two responsibilities of HUD.

## In Your Community

1. Identify a local problem that involves the environment. Research how this problem could be solved and which government agencies could help you.
2. Identify a style of housing discussed in this chapter that appears in your community. Research the housing style and determine its country of origin. Then, write a short essay describing how the style has influenced housing in the United States.
3. Interview older members of your community about what housing was like when they were growing up. Where did they grow up? Ask them how housing has changed and improved over time. Share your findings with the class.
4. Walk around your neighborhood and look for ways people have altered the natural environment for housing purposes. Report your findings to the class.
5. Obtain brochures from different housing developers and house builders. List the advantages they give for the types of houses they promote. Explain how the advantages are related to the natural, constructed, and behavioral environments.

## To Think About

1. Not all people have incomes sufficient to meet their housing needs adequately. In your opinion, should all, part, or none of their housing costs be paid (subsidized) by government sources? If the government is involved, what selection process should be used to determine who is eligible to receive assistance?
2. What could happen to housing if building regulations were suddenly eliminated, allowing anything to be built in any way? In what instances (if any) could the resulting housing be better? In what instances could it be worse?
3. Working with two or three classmates, predict what new technology will be used in houses in 20 years. List your ideas with as much detail as possible and share them with the class.

# Using Technology

1. Search the Internet for new technologies in housing. Choose one that interests you and determine the following: What are the benefits (advantages) of using the technology? What are some possible problems with using this technology? In your opinion, is the technology likely to be used in almost all houses? Why or why not?

2. Identify the harmful health effects that lead-based paint poses to humans. Contact the National Safety Council or the U.S. Consumer Product Safety Commission for your research. Determine where it is generally found and how it can be removed safely. What groups of people are identified as most affected by lead-based paint? Use your computer to create an informative news bulletin or brochure.

3. Choose a topic from the chapter and use images to show how the topic has influenced housing. Obtain the images by printing them off the Internet or taking pictures with a digital camera. Add appropriate captions to the photos. Possible topics include: household composition, life expectancy, government influences, and technological advances.

**Note:** For researching new technologies in housing, have students explore *newtechnologyhome.com*.

**Note:** For researching lead-based paint, have students explore *nsc.org/library/facts.htm*.

**Portfolio Project:** Using a black and white map of your community, color code it by zoning regulations. Take a second map and color code it to create an ideal zoning plan. What changes do you believe are needed? How would they benefit the community? Write a persuasive essay on why you would make the zoning changes you propose.

# PART 2
# Making Housing Choices

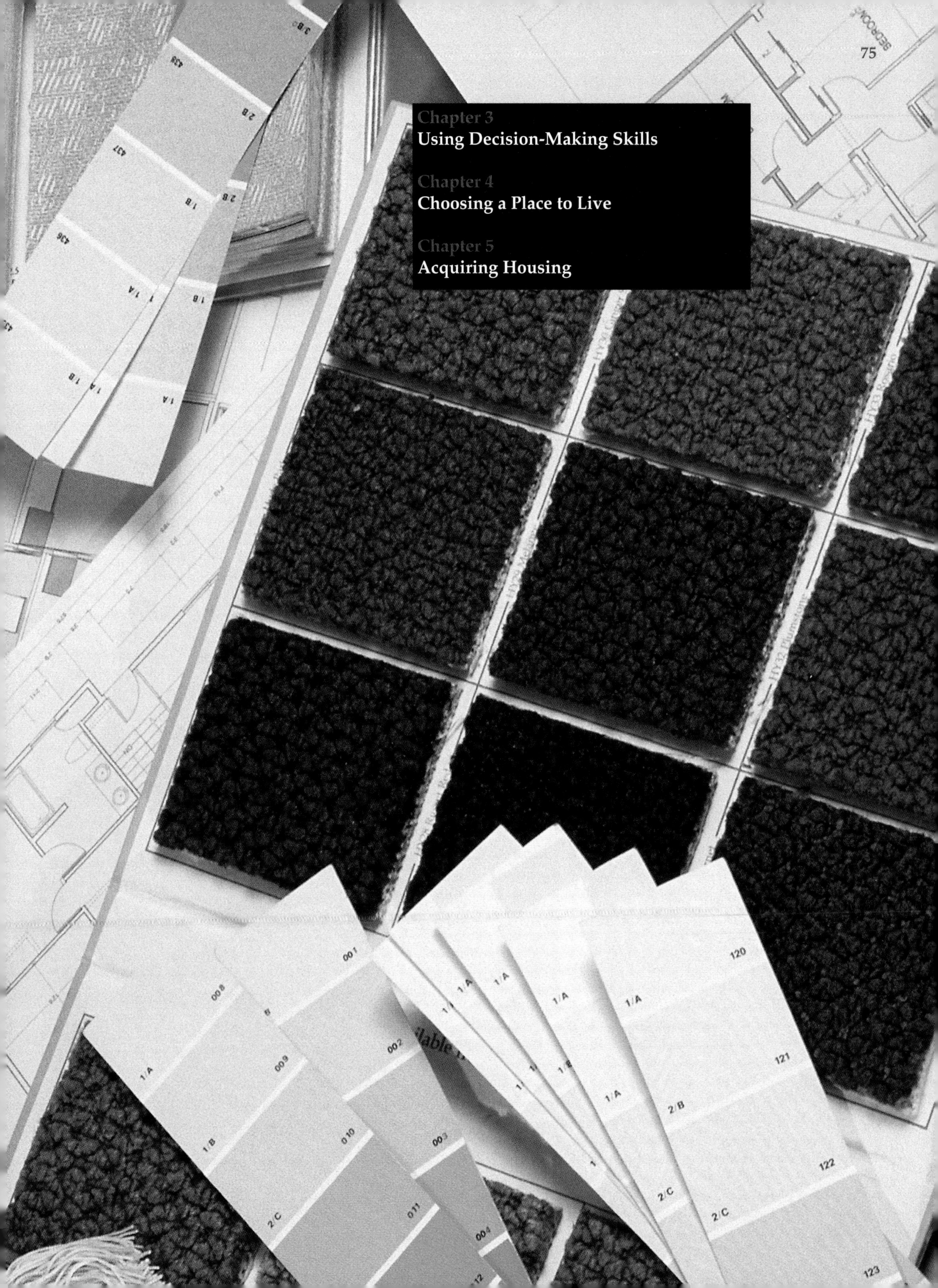

# CHAPTER 3
# Using Decision-Making Skills

## To Know

rational decision
spur-of-the-moment decision
habitual behavior
central-satellite decision
chain decision
human resources
nonhuman resources
implement

Ethan Allen, Inc.

## Objectives

After studying this chapter, you will be able to

- define the different types of decisions.
- list your human and nonhuman resources.
- explain the steps of the decision-making process
- demonstrate how to make wise decisions.

In the first two chapters of this textbook, you read that many decisions affect housing. These decisions are related to your needs, personal priorities, life situations, lifestyle, and environmental and governmental influences. Since these factors are constantly changing, you continually face making new decisions. By making these decisions wisely, you and other members of your household will have the chance to grow and develop to full potential. It is important to develop good decision-making skills so you are able to enhance your life and your housing. These skills will also be necessary in any career path you choose to follow.

# Types of Decisions

All decisions are not alike. Learning to recognize the different types of decisions will help you develop decision-making skills.

Decisions can be classified into two groups. See 3-1. One group consists of those decisions that vary according to the thought and care used in making them. The other group of decisions consists of interrelated decisions and is based on their relationship to other decisions.

## Decisions Made with Thought and Care

The three types of decisions grouped according to the amount of thought and care used are as follows: rational, spur-of-the-moment, and habitual.

Suppose you have your own bedroom and you want to place an upholstered chair in it. If you shop until you find a chair that looks good with what you already have in your room, you would be making a rational decision. A *rational decision* is one based on reasoning. However, if you buy the first chair that appeals to you without thinking about how it would look in

**Resource:** *Decisions,* transparency master II-B, TR. Students sort examples of housing-related decisions from miscellaneous decisions.

**Resource:** *Types of Decisions,* transparency master 3-1, TR. Students review and give examples of each type of decision presented in the text.

**Reflect:** Consider the decisions you made today. What was your first? the latest?

| Types of Decisions | |
|---|---|
| **Based on the Degree of Thought Involved** | |
| *Rational decisions* | Choices are made only after looking at problems carefully. Consequences are considered. |
| *Spur-of-the moment decisions* | Choices are made hurriedly, with little thought given to possible outcomes. |
| *Habitual behavior* | An action results instinctively. Decisions are involved only when new situations arise. |
| **Based on Relationships** | |
| *Central-satellite decisions* | A major decision is surrounded by related but independent decisions. |
| *Chain decisions* | One decision creates other choices that must be made to complete the action. |

3-1

*Decisions are classified by the amount of thought devoted to them or by their relationships to other decisions.*

**Vocabulary:** In a paragraph, compare and contrast the three types of decisions: rational, spur-of-the-moment, and habitual.

**Activity:** List at least 10 decisions you remember making and discuss with a partner the decision-making process you used for each. Did you make some decisions out of habit? some very deliberately and carefully? some hastily and without much forethought? Should you have thought more carefully about any spur-of-the-moment decisions?

your room, your decision would be a spur-of-the-moment one. A *spur-of-the-moment decision* is one that is made quickly, with little thought of the possible consequences.

*Habitual behavior,* on the other hand, is an action that is done as a matter of routine without thought. It does not call for you to make a decision unless there is a new factor in the situation. For instance, turning on the faucet in your bathroom is a habit. You do not need to make a decision unless water fails to flow from the faucet.

## Interrelated Decisions

Central-satellite decisions and chain decisions are examples of decisions that can be described according to their relationship to other decisions.

### Central-Satellite Decisions

A *central-satellite decision* is a group of decisions consisting of a major decision that is surrounded by related but independent decisions. The concept of central-satellite decisions is illustrated in 3-2.

### Chain Decisions

A *chain decision* is a sequence of decisions in which one decision triggers others. All decisions in the chain must be made to complete an action. See 3-3 for a diagram of a chain decision related to housing.

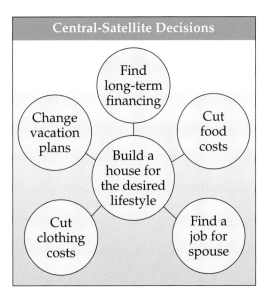

3-2

*The central decision is to build a house; the others are satellite decisions. They are related to the central decision, but they are not dependent on it.*

One example of making interrelated decisions is described in the following housing-related case. Suppose a homeowner needs to decide what to do about the many patches of dead grass in the yard. Right after the grass was planted, the backyard looked very attractive. Now children and pets use the yard constantly as a playground. Neighborhood children walking back and forth to school also use a part of it as a path. This heavy traffic is preventing the grass from growing.

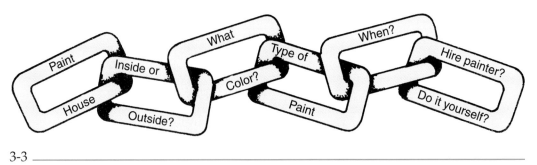

3-3

*In chain decisions, additional decisions are needed to complete the action of the first decision.*

Suppose the owner decides to keep the grass and protect it from heavy use. In this case, the decision to keep the grass becomes a central decision. Satellite decisions are needed. Perhaps play activities should be moved to a patio since they are better suited to hard-surface areas. See 3-4. Other activities could be moved to another part of the yard. Traffic barriers could be established or areas that receive high traffic could be converted to natural areas. Stepping stones could be added to the landscape plan. Careful placement of lawn furniture, shrubs, or flowers could force people to walk around the grassy area instead of through it.

On the other hand, the owner may choose to remove the grass and replace it with a hardier variety instead. The new variety would withstand the traffic and still look attractive. It would also require less care.

The decision to replace the dead grass is the first decision in a chain. The second link is deciding which variety of grass to plant. The next decision is to determine where you will buy the grass. Other links include deciding whether you will plant it yourself or have someone else do it, when to plant it, and how to pay for it. Each of these decisions must be made before the grass can be replaced.

# Resources for Housing Decisions

As you learned in Chapter 2, "Influences on Housing," resources are material objects, qualities, or personal strengths that can be used to reach a goal. You need resources to carry out any type of decision you make. Resources are available to you in many forms.

3-4 _____

*Using the patio for fun and games was a satellite decision to the central decision of throwing a neighborhood party.*

## Human Resources

*Human resources* are resources that are available from people. They include ability, knowledge, attitude, energy, and health. See 3-5.

You may have many resources that help you make housing decisions. For instance, if you have the ability to make house repairs, you have skill as a human resource. If you are willing to learn how to make house repairs, you have intelligence as a human resource. When these resources are developed and used, decisions can be made and results can be achieved.

If you are a person with a high energy level, you may spend time after school and on weekends doing extra projects to improve your housing. If you have a low energy level, you may choose to hire someone to do what is needed to keep your house in shape.

If you have good health, that resource will enable you to use other human resources to an advantage. For example, when you are healthy, you are likely to be motivated to use your knowledge and skills. You might

**Discuss:** What is likely to happen when decisions are made without thinking them through?

**Reflect:** Have you studied decision-making skills in other classes? What steps were emphasized for working on group decisions? How do you think your past decision-making experiences will apply to the information in this chapter?

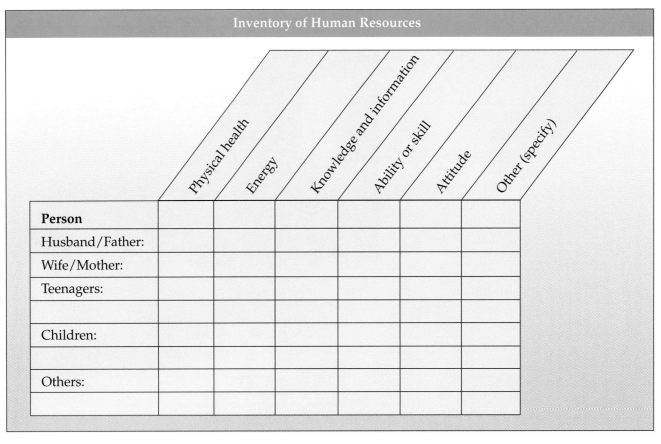

**Inventory of Human Resources**

| Person | Physical health | Energy | Knowledge and information | Ability or skill | Attitude | Other (specify) |
|---|---|---|---|---|---|---|
| Husband/Father: | | | | | | |
| Wife/Mother: | | | | | | |
| Teenagers: | | | | | | |
| | | | | | | |
| Children: | | | | | | |
| | | | | | | |
| Others: | | | | | | |
| | | | | | | |

3-5

*Make an inventory of the human resources in your household by preparing a chart similar to this. Rate members on a scale of 1 to 5, the highest rating.*

decide to remodel your kitchen. If you have poor health, you are likely to postpone the project or hire someone to do it for you.

## Nonhuman Resources

*Nonhuman resources* are resources that are not directly supplied by people. They include money, property, time, and community resources. These are shown in 3-6.

### Money

Consider how the nonhuman resource of money is used in housing. Everyone has some housing expenses. Money is needed to buy or rent a place to live. Additional money is needed for furnishings, equipment, utilities, and repairs. You must decide what you can afford to spend for these items. That amount will be determined by factors such as the following:

- income
- savings
- lifestyle
- possessions

### Property

The property you acquire and the way you use it are related to your housing decisions. Property resources include such items as land, buildings, and furnishings. The housing you can afford is partly determined by choices you have made and property already

Cliff Snider

3-6 _____

*Books, land, buildings, money, and tools are examples of nonhuman resources.*

in your possession. Perhaps you are willing to live in a less expensive apartment so you can have new furniture. If you choose a more expensive apartment, the furniture or some other housing feature may need to wait. You may decide to reupholster or repair older furniture rather than replace it.

## Time

Time is also a nonhuman resource. How you use time is what counts most. You have 24 hours a day, 365 days a year, just as everyone else has. Time is the only resource all people have in equal amounts. Other resources come in different quantities for different people.

## Community Resources

Community resources are often taken for granted, but they can play an important part in your housing decisions. You may base the decision of where you will live on the quality of the community resources available. For example, you may want to have a good public library in your community. This will help you do your homework, prepare for a career, and even find a job. You can also use library resources for recreation.

A city park with a playground and a picnic area is another community resource. If you know that a park is nearby, you may choose housing with a yard smaller than originally planned.

Some community schools and recreation departments offer special classes for self-improvement. By taking advantage of these classes, you can learn such skills as furniture refinishing, upholstering, remodeling, and house maintenance.

Other community resources include hospitals, fire stations, police departments, shopping centers, and sports facilities. See 3-7. What community resources are available where you live?

**Reflect:** Study Figure 3-6. What other nonhuman resources are used to maintain your home environment?
**Activity:** Think about the community resources available to residents and list them. Consider parks, recreational areas, educational institutions, hospitals, shopping centers, police and fire departments, and other public facilities.

**Discuss:** Why do you think some people regard time as a human resource?
**Discuss:** Why do some people seem to have "time on their hands" while others never have enough time to complete all their tasks? What can be done to help people avoid "running out of time"?

**Enrich:** Interview two homeowners to determine how much time they spend taking care of their homes. Also, interview two renters or condominium owners on the same matter. Compare the interview findings. How will this knowledge influence decisions you make?

3-7 _____

*A community library is an invaluable learning and entertainment resource.*

## Using Resources

You will have different quantities of resources at different times in your life. For instance, today you may have more energy than you will 30 years from now. On the other hand, in the future you may have more money to spend than you have now.

Some people are short of both money and energy. To make their resources meet their needs, they must know how to use their knowledge and abilities to save money and energy.

You can choose which resources to spend and which to save. Suppose that you own a house that needs painting. You could paint it yourself. This would take a lot of time that you may prefer spending in some other way. You may decide to hire someone else to paint the house, such as a professional painter or experienced friend.

Some of your human resources decrease as you use them, namely time and energy. Others increase with use, such as your abilities and knowledge. You will seldom use only one resource at a time since all are closely related. To develop a new skill, you will need a good attitude, knowledge, energy, health, and time.

# The Decision-Making Process

To make a wise decision, you must first understand the question, problem, or issue involved. Knowing that, you can then reach a satisfactory answer or solution by following the steps in the decision-making process. See 3-8.

## Steps in Decision Making

The first step in the decision-making process involves *problem identification*. It focuses on defining the question or challenge accurately. This is the most important step. If the real issue is not properly identified, all the work that follows may be in vain.

The second step involves *exploring possible answers or solutions*. You look for various ways to address the issue and list each possible option. While exploring your options, you would answer the following questions:

- What is the likely outcome of each possible approach?
- Will any approach provide lasting satisfaction to those involved?
- Do other decisions need to be made first?

| Steps in the Decision-Making Process |
| --- |
| 1. Identify the challenge. |
| 2. List possible solutions. |
| 3. Make a decision. |
| 4. Take action. |
| 5. Evaluate results. |

3-8 _____

*Following these steps carefully will help you make good decisions.*

During the second step, you must also examine your resources since they will affect which decisions you can make. Suppose you plan a backyard get-together with friends. If storms arrive, you must have the resource of sufficient indoor space to use. Without it, you do not have all the resources you need for the get-together.

Sometimes you cannot consider an option because of limitations imposed by others. Suppose a student decides to use the money earned mowing lawns to buy a pet rabbit. However, if her family will not allow a pet rabbit at home, she cannot make that decision. She must reconsider her options and make a different decision.

The third step involves *making a decision by choosing which of the recommendations on your list is best*. If one option does not clearly stand out as the best choice, you probably need to repeat one or both of the earlier steps. Then, the best option should be clear. See 3-9.

**Resource:** *Decision Making,* Activity E, SAG. Students solve a housing problem by using the decision-making steps and evaluate their decision.
**Reflect:** What purchases have you made in the last month? Before making the purchases, did you follow the steps in the decision-making process?

3-9 _____

*Shopping for items to fill a specific need forces you to go through the steps of the decision-making process.*

**Economics Activity:** Using an economics textbook, search for the decision-making steps it recommends. Make a compare-and-contrast table of the two by folding a sheet of paper vertically in half to create two columns. List the five decision-making steps from your text on the left and, on the right, the steps listed in the economics text. Use a highlighting marker on any step that differs significantly. If there are differences, explain some possible reasons.

3-10

*This couple is carefully deciding what option will be best for their family.*

The fourth step involves *taking action to implement your decision*. *Implement* means to put thoughts into action. You will need to devise an action plan so that your decision is fully implemented. Before taking action, you will need to plan exactly *what to do* as well as *when, where, how,* and *with whom* to do it.

The fifth step is to *evaluate the results of your decision*. Did everything go as planned? Was the problem or challenge satisfactorily addressed? Did something totally unexpected occur? If so, you may need to plan a new course of action or repeat part or all of the decision-making process.

That last step will *provide ideas on how to improve your decision making next time*. If you are not pleased with the results, ask yourself the following questions: Did I define the problem clearly? Did I think of all possible alternatives? Did I implement my decision in the most desirable way? How could I have made a better decision in this case? How could I have implemented the decision with a better plan of action? See 3-10.

## Going through the Steps

One way to learn about the decision-making process is to consider a housing-related problem and think through the steps needed to make a decision about it. For example, imagine that your grandmother in Maine is coming to spend a winter at your family's home in Arizona. She needs to spend the winter in a milder climate and cannot afford to pay rent.

As a result of this visit, the housing needs and desires of every family member is likely to change. How will the family's new needs and personal priorities be met? How will your grandmother's needs and personal priorities be met? These questions can be answered by going through the decision-making steps.

### Step One: Identify the Challenge.

State the basic question or problem. In this case, the question is as follows: Where in your family's house will grandmother stay so that the needs and personal priorities of the new, larger household are addressed?

## Step Two: List Possible Solutions.

Look for ways to solve the problem or answer the challenge. You need to find a comfortable place in your home for grandmother while making sure the others remain comfortable, too. Suppose all the options available to your family are as follows:

- Have grandmother use the living room sofa.

- Turn the storeroom into a new bedroom, move all the stored items elsewhere, and buy new furniture and bedding.

- Let grandmother use someone's room for the winter and have that person crowd into another member's room.

- Give her the combination office/guest room and move the computer and file cabinet to a corner of the living room.

The first option might work if grandmother's stay were only for a weekend. However, family life would be completely disrupted if the living room became someone's bedroom for an entire winter. The second option needs the purchase of furniture and bedding—requiring money that the family does not have. The third option would make life uncomfortable for the members who would need to vacate one bedroom and crowd into another. The fourth option seems the best choice for grandmother's comfort as well as the comfort of others. Can you think of other options?

Grandmother's living arrangements should be discussed thoroughly with all family members. Everyone who could be affected by the decision should be able to provide his or her input. In this case, Steps 2 and 3 need input from everyone who would be affected, which is every household member.

## Step Three: Make a Decision.

Suppose your family decides that grandmother will occupy the guest room. While this option is not perfect, it causes the fewest problems. For example, family members can keep their own rooms. They will not be disrupted if grandmother wakes and sleeps around a different schedule. Also, family members will still have access to the computer.

## Step Four: Take Action.

Turning the idea into a reality will require the cooperation of all family members. Perhaps the whole family would spend a week with grandmother, help her pack, and drive her to Arizona. Maybe just one or two family members would handle these tasks. Perhaps relatives living in Maine could help grandmother pack and arrange her travel.

In Arizona, everyone would need to make small adjustments to blend another person into the family routine. This is the only way to achieve greater satisfaction for all.

## Step Five: Evaluate the Results.

A major change, such as adding a relative to the household, cannot be evaluated in a day or two. After a week, the family would be able to judge whether everything is proceeding as planned. If everyone wants grandmother to stay when spring arrives, that would mean the visit was more successful than planned. See 3-11.

Going through the decision-making process takes time and thought. It helps you make rational and wise decisions. The decisions related to grandmother's move—such as when she will move, how she will

**Discuss:** In the example of grandmother staying for the winter, what factors should be considered in the evaluation?

**Reflect:** Do you ever postpone making certain decisions because they seem too hard or difficult to handle? What tends to happen in such cases?

**Enrich:** Interview a business executive to find out what decision-making steps she or he uses in business to reach major decisions. Would the executive recommend adding any substeps or additional steps to the five key steps listed?

**Activity:** What would be the central-satellite decisions to make if the family chooses to expand their living space by adding a room and bathroom to the house? *(where to add the room, how to finance it, who to design the house addition, who to get to implement the design plans and do the construction, who to assign to the new space—grandmother or another family member, what furnishings to buy for the new space, how to pay for them, what final details to add to grandmother's room to make her comfortable)*

3-11
*Having an older relative move into the house can be a pleasant experience for all when possible problems are expressed and addressed before the move.*

**Discuss:** In the example of grandmother staying for the winter, can you think of other options for finding a place for her stay?

**Reflect:** Think about the decisions you have made today. Will they have long-range results? How will you feel five years from now about the decisions you make this year? What one or two decisions may be the most important for the long term?

move, and what items she will bring— are rational and chain decisions.

The decisions made by your family can also be classified as central-satellite decisions. The central decision is that grandmother is coming to stay with the family for the winter. The other decisions are satellite decisions.

When choosing housing, there are many different types of decisions to make. For example, you will need to decide the location, method of financing, type of house, and interior and exterior design. The skills learned in this chapter will help you make these decisions.

# Summary

There are three types of decisions that are grouped according to the amount of thought or care used. They are rational, spur-of-the moment, and habitual. Other types of decisions, such as central-satellite and chain decisions, are grouped according to the relationships between decisions.

You use resources in your decision making. Human resources, such as ability, knowledge, attitude, energy, and health, are factors in making decisions. Nonhuman resources, such as money, property, time, and community resources, also affect decisions.

If you follow the logical steps of the decision-making process, you are more likely to make wise decisions. The problems or challenges will be identified as well as possible alternatives. You will not know if you have made the best decision until after you evaluate results.

**Resource:** *Resources and Decisions,* Activity F, SAG. Students complete statements about decision-making skills by filling in the blanks.

# To Review

1. A _____ decision is one that is made after thinking carefully about a problem or goal.
2. True or false. A spur-of-the-moment decision is only used in unimportant matters.
3. True or false. Closing the door as you leave your house is a habitual behavior.
4. When one decision requires other decisions to carry it out, it is called a _____.
    A. central-satellite decision
    B. chain decision
    C. satellite decision
5. List five community resources.
6. What one resource is the same for everyone?
7. Name three resources that people possess in different quantities during their lives.
8. True or false. You can choose which resources to spend and which to save.
9. Identify the five basic steps in the decision-making process.

**Answer Key:**
1. rational
2. false
3. true
4. B
5. (List five:) libraries, parks, recreation departments, schools, hospitals, fire stations, police departments, shopping centers, sports facilities
6. time
7. (List three:) ability, knowledge, energy, health, money, property
8. true
9. Identify the challenge. List possible solutions. Make a decision. Take action. Evaluate results.

# In Your Community

1. Take a pro or con position on the following statement: rational decisions give more satisfaction than spur-of-the-moment decisions. Prepare to defend your position in a debate with a

**Reflect:** Review the chapter objectives. Do you still need to review or research some topics to get the information you feel you need? If so, what topics?

**Activity:** Working with another student, alternate talking for 30 seconds apiece about what the chapter covered. Together, write a summary of the concepts in the chapter.

classmate having the opposing view. Use common examples seen in the community to support your position.

2. Divide a sheet of paper into three columns. Label the first column *Decision*, the second column *Type of Decision*, and the third column *Degree of Satisfaction*. In the first column, list three housing decisions that have been made by members of your household. In the second column, identify whether the decision was *rational*, *spur-of-the-moment*, or *habitual behavior*. In the last column, write + + if a great deal of satisfaction resulted from the decision, + if some satisfaction resulted, and – if no satisfaction resulted.

3. Read the classified ads to learn current purchasing and rental costs of housing in the area. Share your findings with the class.

## To Think About

1. Evaluate a recent decision that you made in terms of the success of its outcome. What could have been done differently to yield more successful results. What lesson did you learn that will help you improve future decision making?

2. Read the following case study and complete the suggested activities. Andy and Noelle are both students at a community college. They plan to be married in June. Both have part-time jobs, will continue in school after the wedding, and graduate after another year. Andy plans to work in an auto repair and welding shop. Noelle wants to continue her job in the college library. In four or five years, they plan to start a family. They want two children. Noelle likes music and wants a piano. Andy likes to fish and play golf.

   A. Identify a major housing decision this couple will face.
   B. What resources will be available to them? What are the alternatives they may consider? What are the possible outcomes of each alternative? What other related decisions will they need to make?
   C. Which alternative would you choose as a solution? Give reasons for your choice.

## Using Technology

1. Join two or three students to write and present a skit showing how some resources are decreased while others are increased at the same time. Videotape the script. Play the tape for the class by first giving a brief introduction. Then, answer any questions your classmates have afterward.

2. Select a favorite TV series and videotape one of the shows. Listen carefully to the plot and note all the decisions made by the characters in the program. Then, analyze each decision made and label the behavior *rational, spur-of-the-moment,* or *habitual.*

3. Search for a Web site that allows you to select an apartment to rent in your area or in a city that interests you. Consider your college or career plans for the year after high school and search for housing in that area. What type of apartment would you need? Select an apartment that appeals to you and determine what it costs. How does its cost compare to similar apartments in the area? Make a print-out of the information you find.

**Note:** For researching apartments, have students explore *realtor.com.*

**Portfolio Project:** Working with a partner, recommend a decision to a family trying to decide how to address the need for more space. The couple has two sons and are expecting a daughter. The family lives in a three-bedroom house with two bathrooms. One bedroom is quite large and is currently being used by the parents. They also have a one-car garage, basically used for storage, plus a small kitchen and separate living room. The house has a small, screened porch that may be converted into a bedroom. The yard is small, but an additional room could be built onto the corner of the house where the children currently play. (The couple could probably get a $20,000 loan for the remodeling job.) Follow the steps of the decision-making process as you develop a recommendation to address this family's space dilemma.

# CHAPTER 4

# Choosing a Place to Live

## To Know

region
community
neighborhood
physical neighborhood
planned neighborhood
site
landscaping
orientation
minimum property standards (MPS)
public zone
service zone
private zone
house
home
multifamily house
cooperative
condominium
con-ops
single-family house
attached houses
freestanding houses
contractor
owner-built housing
factory-built housing
site-built house
modular housing
manufactured housing
mobile homes
panelized housing
precut housing
kit house
universal design
assisted-living facility
graduated-care facility
reverse mortgage
Fair Housing Act
bill of lading

U-Haul International

## Objectives

After studying this chapter, you will be able to

■ describe different regions in which people live.

■ list factors people consider when choosing a community or neighborhood.

■ describe different types of housing.

■ identify decisions involved in choosing a site and house.

■ determine special needs to consider when choosing housing.

■ compare the different ways to move.

**Vocabulary:** Select 10 terms from the vocabulary list that are unknown or very unfamiliar. List them on a piece of paper, writing one term on every third or fourth line. When you reach each term in the text, write its definition and use it in a sentence.

Y ou will have many decisions to make when finding a place to live. Some of those decisions will concern the location and type of dwelling to choose. Other decisions will concern any adaptations you must make to the housing for special needs. Finally, you will need to make decisions regarding the various moving options possible.

# Location

When choosing a place to live, you will need to carefully consider the following about the location:

- the region or area of the world, country, or state
- the community—country, suburb, or city
- neighborhood or section of the community
- composition of the population
- the site or lot within the neighborhood

## Region

A *region* is a specific part of the world, country, or state in which you live. The reasons for choosing to live in a certain region vary. You may like the scenery. Perhaps the climate is important to you. See 4-1. You may want to be close to family members or friends. Employment may also lead you to a certain region. Jobs are usually easier to find in regions with large cities.

Several items to consider when choosing a region are listed in 4-2. Which would describe your ideal region?

## Community

A region is divided into communities. A *community* may be a large city, small village, or rural area.

Cities are high-density areas. Many people live close together. If you enjoy living in close proximity to other people, you are a *contact person*. You may enjoy an urban lifestyle.

A                    B                    C

4-1 _____

*Some people choose a place to live that is close to the sports activities they enjoy. For example, they may prefer living where they can spend most of the year (A) swimming, (B) hiking, or (C) snow skiing.*

| Choosing a Region | | | |
|---|---|---|---|
| **Considerations** | **Range of Choices** | | |
| *General climate* | Hot | to | Cold |
| | Dry | to | Wet/humid |
| | Constant temperature | to | Varying temperature |
| *Topography* (*mountains, lakes, prairies, and so forth*) | Flat | to | Mountainous |
| | Desert | to | Forest |
| | Low altitude | to | High altitude |
| *Cost of living* | Low | to | High |

4-2 _____

*These are some of the choices that will influence your selection of a region in which to live.*

Vocabulary: Use the words *region*, *community*, and *neighborhood* in sentences to demonstrate understanding.
Reflect: What services could be added to improve your community?

Rural areas and the outskirts of towns and cities are low-density areas. If you enjoy a less populated area and reduced contact with other people, you are a *noncontact* person. You may prefer a more secluded community.

Some communities are designed for specific groups of people. For instance, retirement communities are built especially for retired people. University communities are planned for large groups of students and professors. Some communities are developed by businesses for employees and their families.

Before choosing a community, you should consider more than just its size and social aspects. The number and type of services offered in a community should also be studied. For instance, what stores are in the community? Does the school have a reputation for high academic standards? Does your religious group have a meeting place? Are there good medical facilities? Will you have adequate fire and police protection? Are resources available for self-improvement? What recreational facilities are offered? Are jobs easy to find? If some of these services are not available in the community, how far away are they? What type of public transportation is offered?

The chart in 4-3 can serve as a guide for evaluating a community. Which factors apply to your present community? Which would you want in your ideal community?

## Neighborhood

While regions are divided into communities, communities are divided into neighborhoods. A *neighborhood* consists of a group of houses and people. The buildings in any one neighborhood are usually similar in age, design, and cost. The people in a neighborhood usually have some similarities, too.

### Physical Neighborhood

The *physical neighborhood* is determined by the way the land and buildings are used. Some neighborhoods are all residential, with homes occupied by people. Commercial neighborhoods include stores and businesses. A shopping center is a kind of commercial neighborhood. Industrial neighborhoods include businesses, factories, warehouses, and industrial plants.

Some neighborhoods combine residential, commercial, and industrial buildings. For instance, when houses

Discuss: Describe the climate of your area. What type of climate do you prefer? How might your housing options change if you lived in your preferred climate?

Discuss: What are the characteristics of the region in which you live? What other types of regions are in your state or a neighboring state? Consider Figure 4-2 as you answer the questions.

| Choosing a Community | | | |
|---|---|---|---|
| **Considerations** | **Range of Choices** | | |
| *Type* | Rural<br>Residential | to<br>to | Urban/suburban<br>Industrial/commercial |
| *Size* | Farm<br>Village/town | to<br>to | Ranch<br>City/metropolis |
| *Population density* | Uncrowded | to | Crowded |
| *Cost of living* | Low | to | High |
| *Employment opportunities* | Few<br>Little variety<br>Low-paying<br>Seasonal | to<br>to<br>to<br>to | Many<br>Varied<br>High-paying<br>Steady |
| *Public facilities and services*<br>*(educational, recreational, medical, religious,*<br>*transportation, police and fire protection, shopping)* | Few | to | Many |

4-3 _____

*When you look for the ideal community, these factors are considered.*

surround a local grocery, the neighborhood is a combination of residential and commercial buildings.

## Zoning Regulations and Other Restrictions

*Zoning regulations* control land use in certain areas, as you read in Chapter 2, "Influences on Housing." A neighborhood may be zoned for residential, commercial, or industrial use, or a combination of uses.

Housing *developers* subdivide land and make improvements such as streets and street lighting before building structures. They can set additional limits called restrictions. These restrictions may control the design of the buildings that can be constructed. They may also limit the kind and number of animals that can be kept in a neighborhood. In 4-4, you can see a set of restrictions drawn up for a subdivision.

A *planned neighborhood* is usually in a zoned area with restrictions. In a planned neighborhood, the size and layout of individual lots are determined before dwellings are built. This creates the shape of the neighborhood. Three ways to arrange lots are shown in 4-5.

All houses built in a planned neighborhood must fit into the overall plan. Some planned neighborhoods have single-family houses. Some have only apartment buildings. Others are designed to include more than one type of housing with the types grouped together.

The quality of construction and the type of design are sometimes controlled in a planned neighborhood. This assures the residents the neighborhood will not deteriorate because of poor quality materials or workmanship.

Many planned neighborhoods include recreational facilities. Parks and playgrounds are built in locations that are convenient to the people living in the neighborhood, 4-6. Clubhouses are often built as places for meetings and social activities.

**Resource:** *Your Community Zoning Rules*, Activity A, SAG. Students listen to a presentation by a local government representative about zoning rules in the community and answer worksheet questions about what they heard.
**Vocabulary:** Compare and contrast *zoning regulations* and *restrictions* by using both terms in a sentence.
**Discuss:** When restrictions are not followed, how do you suppose violators are handled?

**Discuss:** What do you feel are the advantages of a neighborhood having characteristics of both residential and commercial neighborhoods? What are the disadvantages?
**Reflect:** Are you considering moving to another community after you graduate from high school? If so, study Figure 4-3 and determine the type of community that will become your new home.

**Enrich:** Check your city or town's Web site for zoning rules or visit your city hall to get a copy. What interesting facts do you find? Discuss these with your classmates.

## Declaration of Restrictions for Swiss Manor Subdivision

1. All of said lots in Swiss Manor Subdivision shall be known and designated as residential lots and shall not be used for any business purposes whatsoever.

2. No structure whatsoever other than one private dwelling, together with a private garage or carport for not more than three cars, shall be erected, placed, or allowed to remain on any of the lots.

3. No dwelling house shall be erected which contains less than 1,200 feet of livable space, exclusive of attached garage, porches, patios, and breezeways. No residence shall be built which exceeds the height of $2\frac{1}{2}$ stories or 30 feet from the curb level. All structures on said lots shall be of new construction and no building shall be moved from any other location onto any of said lots.

4. There shall be no trailer houses or homes built around or incorporating trailer homes. All camper trailers, campers, or boats shall be stored behind the dwelling house or within the garage.

5. There shall be no unused automobiles, machinery, or equipment allowed on theses premises outside of enclosed garages. All driveways or parking areas used for parking vehicles shall be constructed of concrete.

6. All clotheslines, equipment, service yards, woodpiles, or storage piles shall be kept screened by adequate planting or fencing to conceal them from views of neighboring lots or streets. All rubbish, trash, or garbage shall be removed from the lots and shall not be allowed to accumulate thereon. All yards shall be kept mowed and all weeds shall be cut. Garbage and refuse containers may be brought to the street not more than 12 hours before collection time and must be removed within 12 hours after collection time.

7. No animals, livestock, or poultry of any kind shall be raised, bred, or kept on any lot, except for dogs, cats, and other household pets that may be kept, provided they are not kept, bred, or maintained for commercial purposes, and so long as applicable laws on restraining or controlling animals are observed.

8. No lot may be subdivided or a portion sold unless it becomes a part of the adjacent property.

9. No solid wall, hedge, or fence over $2\frac{1}{2}$ feet high shall be constructed or maintained past the front wall line of the house. No side or rear fence shall be constructed more than 6 feet in height.

10. All utility lines must be brought underground to the dwelling house.

11. No structure shall be built nearer than 25 feet to the front property line. No living areas shall be located nearer than 10 percent of the lot width to any side property line. No carport or garage closer than 5 feet.

12. No billboards, signs, or advertising devices, except for suitable "For Sale" or "For Rent" signs shall be maintained.

13. Before construction of the initial structure of any building, the plans, specifications, and materials must be approved by the Developer or its successor.

14. Construction of the homes must be started within one year after purchase of the lot and must be complete within one year after commencement of construction.

15. No property owner shall in any way divert the drainage so that it encroaches upon a neighbor's property.

16. These declarations shall constitute covenants to run with the land, as provided by law, and shall be biding on all parties and persons claiming under them, and are for the benefit of and shall be limitations upon all future owners in said Swiss Manor Subdivision.

4-4

*This is a typical list of restrictions for a subdivision. Its purpose is to assure all owners maintain a similar style of living.*

**Enrich:** Secure a copy of restrictions from a community in your area. Compare it to the restrictions listed in Figure 4-4.

**Reflect:** Could you live with the rules listed on this page? If not, why? What options do people have who do not like to live with such restrictions?

**Writing Activity:** Identify by number each restriction listed in Figure 4-4 that applies to your neighborhood. Explain how these restrictions affect your neighborhood. (If none of the restrictions apply, select one that you wish would apply to your neighborhood and explain how it would affect your neighborhood.)

4-5

*There are several ways to arrange lots, including (A) the traditional "gridiron" arrangement, with all lots the same size and shape; (B) the contour arrangement, with the shape of streets and lots adding variety and interest to the neighborhood; and (C) the cluster layout, with houses placed together in groups to discourage traffic from nonresidents.*

## Population Composition

The type of people in any neighborhood may be quite varied. When this happens, the neighborhood is *heterogeneous*. If the residents are very similar to each other, the neighborhood is *homogeneous*. Some neighborhoods or whole communities have residents of similar age, ethnic background, income level, or occupation.

**Reflect:** Compare your neighborhood to the three patterns shown in Figure 4-5. Which does yours resemble? What are the advantages of this type of layout?

**Discuss:** Which of the lot arrangements in Figure 4-5 creates the neighborhood with the highest density? (*A*) Which creates the lowest density? (*C*)

4-6
*Playgrounds are a part of many planned neighborhoods.*

These patterns occur in both rural and urban settings.

Another factor associated with the people in a neighborhood is population density. A low-density neighborhood has more space for each individual than a high-density neighborhood. Smaller houses, smaller lots, and more people in less space create high-density neighborhoods.

Apartment buildings and manufactured-housing parks also fit in the high-density category.

Which kind of neighborhood would you choose? What are your reasons for making that choice? The factors listed in 4-7 can help you make a decision.

## Site

A location within a neighborhood is called a site, or lot. A *site* is the piece of land on which the dwelling is built. It extends to the property lines.

Each site has its own characteristics—size, shape, contour (hills and curves), and soil type. What kind of site would be your ideal? Would you like to have your house on a hill or on flat land? What kind of view would you like? Would you like to be close to your neighbors, or would you prefer to have more privacy? These characteristics should be considered before you choose a site for your house. See 4-8.

If you are buying a house that someone else built, or if you are renting an apartment, you should look carefully at the placement of the house on the site. It will have a great effect on your near environment. It will determine the views, the amount of sunlight, and the amount of protection from wind you will have.

If you are building a house, you can choose the site and the type of house you want. You can place the house where you want it on the site. This gives you the chance to make the house and site work together to form a satisfying near environment for you.

When you plan your site, you will encounter restraints, or obstacles. Some will be natural restraints. Others will be legal restraints.

### Natural Restraints

Natural restraints are those that come from nature. To gain the maximum advantage from the site, it is important to consider the topography.

| Choosing the Neighborhood | | |
|---|---|---|
| **Considerations** | **Range of Choices** | |
| *Physical appearance* | Zoned | to Not zoned |
| | Strictly residential dwellings | to Some commercial and/or industrial buildings |
| *Organization of lots* | Attractive | to Unattractive |
| | Planned | to Unplanned |
| | Low street traffic | to High traffic area |
| | No park/play areas | to Many park/play areas |
| *Type of structures* | Single-family | to Multifamily |
| | Low spread | to High rise |
| *Location in community* | Edge | to Center |
| *Population composition* (age, income, occupation, educational level, interests, religious beliefs) | Homogeneous (similar) | to Heterogeneous (varied) |
| *Residents* | Mostly singles | to Mostly families |
| | No friends/ acquaintances | to Many friends/ acquaintances |
| *Prevailing values* (views/beliefs that seem to dominate the thinking and actions of people) | Very different from own values | to Similar to own values |

4-7 _____

*Which of these factors are important to you in selecting an ideal neighborhood?*

| Choosing the Site | | |
|---|---|---|
| **Considerations** | **Range of Choices** | |
| *Location in neighborhood* | Edge | to Center |
| *Orientation to environment* (view, sun, water, wind) | Does not use natural features well | to Uses natural features well |
| *Physical qualities* | Tiny | to Large size |
| | Rectangular | to Irregular shape |
| | Flat land | to Steep slopes |
| | Sandy soil | to Dense clay |
| | No obstructions | to Many large trees and/or rocks that must be removed |

4-8 _____

*Before you select a site, you should consider all your choices.*

*Topography* is the configuration of a surface including its natural and manufactured features showing their relative positions and elevations. One kind of natural restraint is the topography of a site.

- Flat sites make the job of mowing grass easy. See 4-9. Flat lawns are also good places for children's games and lawn furniture.
- Hilly sites are more difficult to maintain, but they are often

**Resource:** *Housing Location*, Activity C, SAG. Students design and evaluate a site and neighborhood for a house.

**Discuss:** Consider the range of neighborhood choices listed in Figure 4-7. How might these factors affect housing costs?

**Vocabulary:** Use the word *topography* correctly in a written sentence.

**Discuss:** After studying Figure 4-8, describe the factors characteristic of the most expensive lot on which to build housing. *(in center of neighborhood, uses natural features well, large size, irregular shape, steep slopes, dense clay, trees and rocks that must be moved)*

4-9

*The topography of this site is very flat, which makes yard maintenance easy.*

Weather Shield Windows & Doors

4-10

*In this landscape plan, brick and stone were used to create terraces and to take advantage of the lot.*

attractive. Some houses, such as split-level houses, look best on hilly sites.

■ Sites with extremely steep slopes have some disadvantages. A house built at the top of a slope may be difficult to reach, especially in icy weather. Also, soil may wash away and cause land erosion.

*Landscaping* is altering the topography and adding decorative plantings to change the appearance of a site. See 4-10. For instance, small hills can be built to make the site more attractive. You will learn more about landscaping in Chapter 19, "The Outdoor Living Space and Environment."

Soil and water can be natural restraints. Soil conditions affect both the site and the house. Poorly drained soil freezes and expands. This can cause sidewalks and driveways to crack and bulge. Plants have difficulty growing in shallow or nonporous topsoil. High water levels can cause swampy yards, wet basements, and poor plant growth.

Orientation can be a restraint or an advantage. *Orientation* is placing a structure on a site in consideration of the location of the sun, prevailing winds, water sources, and scenic view. Houses with southern and western exposures receive more sunlight than houses with northern and eastern exposures. In colder regions, houses are often built with large amounts of glass on the south and west sides of the dwelling. The glass allows sunlight to bring light and warmth into the dwellings.

Because of the earth's changing position in relation to the sun, more sunlight reaches the earth during the summer. See 4-11. Therefore, houses may need protection from the intense summer sun. Trees shade some houses. Built-in features, such as roof overhangs, can also provide shade. The width of the overhang on a roof

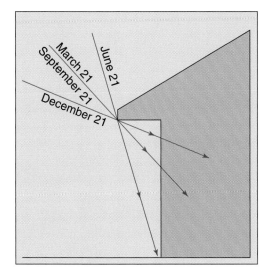

**4-11** _____

*The sun shines on the south side of a house at different angles depending on the time of the year. By knowing this, architects can plan proper roof overhangs.*

affects the amount of sunlight that enters a building. Wider overhangs block out more sunlight.

Orientation to the wind is another natural restraint. Houses can be located so they are protected from strong winds. Windbreaks are used to provide some of this protection. Trees and shrubs are natural windbreaks. Walls and stone or wood fences are also windbreaks. A garage placed on the north side of a house will usually eliminate drafts from cold winter winds and reduce heating costs in the house.

In most regions, the general direction of the wind is linked to the season of the year. This should be taken into consideration when planning for protection from the wind. The illustration in 4-12 shows a house that is well oriented to both the sun and wind.

**Science Activity:** Look at the roof overhang on the south side of your house or school. Compare it to the drawing in Figure 4-11. In a similar drawing that you prepare, show where the sun hits the building in the middle of the day.

**Discuss:** Does your school have natural restraints from the wind? If so, what are they? If not, how does the wind affect the microenvironment of your school?

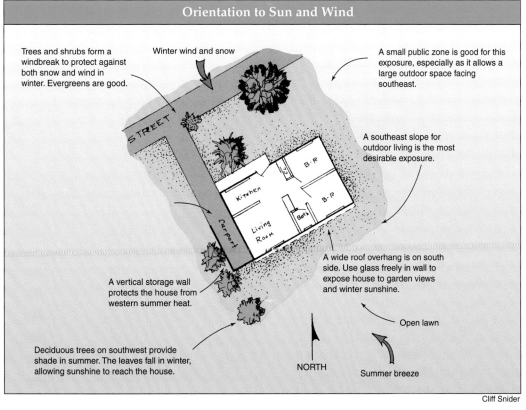

### Orientation to Sun and Wind

Trees and shrubs form a windbreak to protect against both snow and wind in winter. Evergreens are good.

Winter wind and snow

A small public zone is good for this exposure, especially as it allows a large outdoor space facing southeast.

A southeast slope for outdoor living is the most desirable exposure.

A vertical storage wall protects the house from western summer heat.

A wide roof overhang is on south side. Use glass freely in wall to expose house to garden views and winter sunshine.

Open lawn

Deciduous trees on southwest provide shade in summer. The leaves fall in winter, allowing sunshine to reach the house.

NORTH

Summer breeze

STREET

Kitchen    B·R

Living Room    Bath    B·R

Carport

Cliff Snider

**4-12** _____

*Orientation to sun and wind are important factors to consider when deciding the ideal location for a dwelling on a site.*

**Math Activity:** Find an average size lot in your community and determine its dimensions. In percentage terms, how much greater or smaller is it compared to the square footage of a 130-by-65-foot lot?

*(Compare the square footage of your lot to 8,450 square feet to find the answer.)*

Orientation to scenery is also a consideration. A pleasant view is desirable, but it is not always provided by nature. If necessary, you can create a nice view through landscaping. Landscapers use gardens, shrubs, trees, and decorative elements to change the scenery.

## Legal Restraints

Federal, state, or local laws establish the legal restraints that affect a site. They are set for your protection. ***Minimum property standards (MPS)*** are standards set by the Federal Housing Administration (FHA) that regulate the size of lots. MPS vary according to the shape and location of a site. In some cases, the minimum size of a lot is 65 feet wide and 130 feet long. Look at 4-13 to see a plan for a lot that meets these MPS.

The local government or the developer may set higher standards than the MPS. State and local authorities also establish limits and standards for the quality of construction, water supplies, and disposal of wastes. Do you have a housing authority office in your community? If so, what legal restraints does it enforce?

## Zones Within the Site

The part of the site that is not the actual dwelling is divided into three zones—public zone, service zone, and private zone.

The ***public zone*** is the part of the site that can be seen from the street or road. It is usually in front of the house. If the house is on a corner lot, the public zone is L-shaped. It includes the front and side of the lot closest to the street. Since the public zone is seen more often than any other part of the site, people want to make it attractive. See 4-14. It is seldom used for activities.

If the house is as far forward on the lot as the law permits, the public

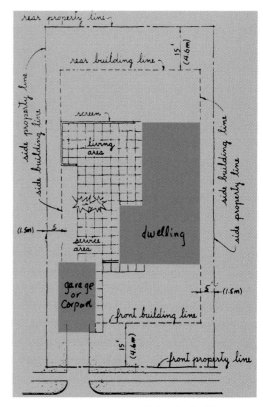

Federal Housing Administration

4-13
*This plan meets the MPS for a rectangular lot in the middle of a block.*

4-14
*Various items were used to make this public zone attractive.*

zone is small. Many people want small public zones because they are easier to maintain.

The *service zone* is the part of the site that is used for necessary activities. It includes sidewalks, driveways, and storage areas for such items as trash, tools, lawn equipment, firewood, and cars. Others can usually see at least part of the service zone, as in 4-15. However, many people choose to have as much of it screened from view as possible.

In this zone, convenience is most important. The service area should be directly connected to the indoor service area, which includes the kitchen and laundry area. It is important for the service zone to be accessible from the street since deliveries are usually made in the service zone.

The *private zone* is the part of the site hidden from public view. It provides space for recreation and relaxation. See 4-16. Private zones can be separated from public zones by using shrubs, hedges, screens, fences, or walls.

Some households want a large private zone. They may want a place for yard accessories, such as outdoor furniture and barbecue equipment, yard games or a swimming pool, as in 4-17. Other households prefer a small private zone that requires little upkeep.

**Discuss:** What types of items are commonly found in a service zone that homeowners wouldn't want to place in the public zone? (*trash, tools, lawn equipment, firewood*)
**Activity:** List the activities you enjoy with friends that are appropriate for a home's private zone.

4-15
*Sidewalks and driveways are parts of the service zone that can be seen by others. The garage door is hidden from view by being located on the side of the house.*

**Vocabulary:** Create a Venn diagram comparing the service zone to the private zone. Draw overlapping circles, writing the qualities the zones share in the overlap. In the outer parts of the circles, write the different qualities they possess. Use one side per zone and label each side with the appropriate zone's name.

**Writing Activity:** Create a one-paragraph summary of the three zones within a site (to be selected by the teacher).
**Discuss:** After viewing Figure 4-15, consider how the service zone of this house might be used for private activities.

4-16
*This private zone provides a secluded area for people to relax.*

Some want all the available space inside the house and do not want an outdoor private zone.

In 4-18 you can see how a house is placed on the site to provide all three zones—public, service, and private.

# Types of Housing

After choosing a region, community, neighborhood, and site, your next decision is to choose a form of housing. A *house* is any building that serves as living quarters for one or more families. A *home*, on the other hand, is any place a person lives. The two major groups of houses are multi-family and single-family. Within each group are several variations.

## Multifamily Houses

A *multifamily house* is a structure that provides housing for more than one household. Each household within the dwelling has its own distinct living quarters.

Today, lifestyles are changing, and the demand for multifamily housing is increasing. In the past, single people, young married couples, and retired people were the primary residents of this type of housing. Now, others are turning to multifamily housing, too.

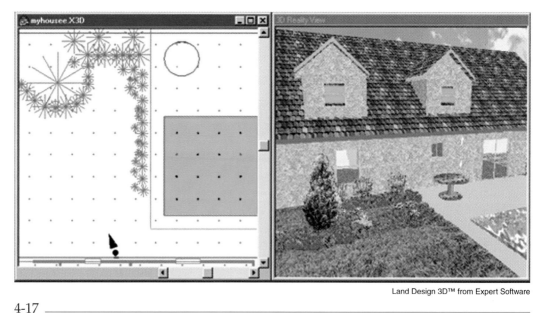

Land Design 3D™ from Expert Software

4-17
*This plan, showing a swimming pool in the private zone, was created using a computer program.*

| | Private |
| | Service |
| | Public |

Home Planners, Inc.

4-18

*The house shown at the top has a huge private zone. Examine the plan to see how the sizes of the public and service zones compare.*

**Discuss:** Rank the three zones shown in Figure 4-18 from largest to smallest. (*private, public, service*) What might such a large private zone indicate?

**Note:** Web sites such as *dreamhomesource.com/* allow students to view a variety of single-family house designs to identify private,

public, and service zones. Multifamily and single-family dwellings are also shown.

**Activity:** Create a drawing of your home, indicating the public, private, and service zones.

Cityfront Place, photographer David Clifton

4-19

*Cityfront Place is a series of high-rise buildings in Chicago where several hundred families live.*

4-20

*Low-spread apartment buildings require larger lots per household than high-rise buildings.*

This type of housing is usually less costly and easier to maintain than single-family houses.

Some multifamily housing is in *high-rise buildings*, 4-19. Others are in low-rise buildings as shown in 4-20. Those in *low-rise* buildings may be *duplexes* (two households), *triplex* (three households), or *quadraplexes* (four households).

## Rentals

Rental apartments range from garden apartments to penthouses. *Penthouses* are suites located at the top of apartment buildings. *Garden apartments* are one-story units with landscaped grounds. Rentals also vary in the number and type of facilities offered. An *efficiency apartment* has one main room, a small kitchen area, and a bathroom. Many apartment buildings have laundry appliances, tennis courts, and swimming pools available to residents. Some large, high-rise buildings are like small cities. They include business offices, stores, recreational facilities, and parking space.

## Cooperative Units

The word **cooperative** refers to a type of ownership in which people buy shares of stock in a nonprofit housing corporation. These shares entitle them to occupy a unit in the cooperative building. Therefore, when people move into a cooperative unit, or co-op, they "buy" their apartment by purchasing shares in the corporation. If a resident wants a larger unit, he or she purchases more stock. Residents have an absolute right to occupy the unit for as long as the stock is owned.

Although residents do not own their units, they own an undivided interest in the entire property. They have a voice in how the corporation is run and even get the chance to select their neighbors. When people want to buy shares in the corporation and move into the building, the members of the corporation vote on admitting them.

An advantage of living in a co-op is neighbors meet regularly and work together to create a pleasant housing environment for all residents. A disadvantage is that anyone who disagrees with the majority on an issue must accept and live with the decision.

### Condominium Units

A *condominium* is a type of ownership where the buyer owns individual living space and also has an undivided interest in the common areas and facilities of the multiunit project. In comparison to co-ops, buyers purchase condominium units as separate dwellings. At the same time, the buyers receive a portion of the common areas. They share the ownership of the site, parking areas, recreational facilities, hallways, and lobbies with the other condominium owners.

Although condominium owners own their units, they must answer to the desires of the entire group of owners for certain items. For instance, the appearance of the outside of their units and their yards may be under the control of the group's management.

Some experimentation is occurring with *con-ops*, which are a blend of condominium and cooperative units. In con-ops the buyers own their individual living spaces, just like condominium ownership. However, ownership of the common areas and facilities are cooperative ownership.

The terms *cooperative* and *condominium* refer to a type of ownership, not a building design. When you look at a multifamily dwelling, you cannot tell if it is a rental, cooperative, or condominium. See 4-21.

## Single-Family Houses

In spite of the rising trend for multifamily dwellings, the *single-family house* is still popular. It is designed to house one family. Single-family houses can be rented or owned.

### Attached Houses

Some single-family houses are *attached houses*. They are designed for one household but share a common wall with the houses on each side. End units, however, have only one shared wall. Townhouses and *row houses* are names for these houses. A *townhouse* is a unit that has at least two floors.

Usually, entire sidewalls of houses are shared, but there are variations. The designs of the attached dwellings are often alike.

The owners of an attached, single-family house possess the dwelling itself and the land on which it is located. They have their own entrance and yard area.

Copyright, Kavanagh Homes

4-21

*This multi-family unit could be rentals, co-ops, or condos. There is no way to know by looking at exteriors.*

## Freestanding Houses

When single-family houses stand alone, not connected to another unit, they are called *freestanding houses*. They vary in size, design, color, features, and cost.

The most individualistic type of house is *custom-designed* and *custom-built* by an architect and a contractor. This kind of house is a dream house. It is often expensive and takes a long time to plan and build.

When custom-designing a house, an architect considers the needs, personal priorities, and life situations of the household. He or she then designs a house to "fit" that household's needs and desires.

A *contractor* is a person who contracts, or agrees, to supply certain materials or do certain work for a specific fee. With a custom-built house, a contractor arranges for all the tradespeople to do their various jobs efficiently and on schedule. He or she builds the house according to the architect's plans and owner's wishes.

Some houses are custom-built from stock plans. In these cases, people go to a contractor and look at house plans. They choose the plan they want and the contractor builds a house for them on their site. They also incorporate any adjustments or individualized treatments the owner desires. For example, the owner may want larger windows located in different locations than the plan indicates. See 4-22.

*Owner-built housing* is for people with lots of spare time, energy, and building skills. This type of house can be less expensive than a custom-built house. There is less investment in money and more investment in other resources, such as time and energy. Sometimes a contractor is hired to construct the house shell while the owner does the interior work. In other cases, the owner builds the entire house, often with volunteer help from friends. Building codes usually require some parts of the project to be handled by qualified experts, such as an electrician and plumber.

On the other hand, developers sometimes build entire neighborhoods at once, creating *tract houses*. The houses are built before they are sold. One or two sets of plans are repeated throughout the development to save money. Because few variations are made, the houses lack individuality. However, they are less expensive to buy than custom-built houses.

*Factory-built housing* is housing constructed in a plant and moved to a site. Some units are fully finished in the plant, while others arrive in parts that are joined at the site, 4-23. All involve some labor when being placed on the lot. The advantages of factory-built housing are decreased cost and/or completion time in making a home available. You often cannot tell a site-built house from a factory-built

4-22

*This home's exterior looks like the stock plan, but many changes were made to the inside. The kitchen area was doubled and an office was added to the first floor.*

house. A *site-built house* is built on a lot, piece by piece on a foundation, using few factory-built structural components. Five types of factory-built housing are used today:

- modular
- manufactured/mobile
- panelized
- precut
- kit

*Modular housing* is factory-built in a coordinated series of modules. The wall, floor, ceiling, and roof panels are combined in boxes (or modules) complete with windows, doors, plumbing, and wiring before delivery to the site. When the modules arrive at the housing site, they are placed on the foundation and joined together. These housing units are built to meet local building codes and standards.

Both *manufactured housing* and *mobile homes* are single-family dwellings that are completely built in a factory. The completed housing units are moved by attached wheels to a lot or housing site. Units built before 1976 are called mobile homes, while those built later are called manufactured housing. Early units first appeared as travel trailers in the 1920s and 1930s, and evolved into house trailers in the 1930s and 1940s.

Manufactured houses are built to federal standards called the HUD Code because the U.S. Department of Housing and Urban Development (HUD) administers it. A manufactured or mobile home is one solution to affordable home ownership since cost is considerably below that for a conventional, site-built house. See 4-24.

Manufactured housing is available in many sizes. Smaller homes come in single units called single-sectional housing. Larger homes come in two or more units, either double-sectional or multi-sectional, that are joined at the

Oakwood Homes Corporation

4-23

*The site selected for this manufactured housing provides for a beautiful night view of the city.*

Oakwood Homes Corporation

4-24

*When in place and landscaped, a manufactured home is difficult to distinguish from a site-built home.*

site. Because these housing units are pulled across highways to their sites, their length and width are limited by transportation requirements.

Although manufactured houses and mobile homes have wheels and can be moved, less than five percent are ever moved from their original sites. Each state has laws that must be followed when moving one of these homes. Some local governments have

**Discuss:** Study the photo in Figure 4-24. Why is it difficult to determine if this is a site-built or factory-built house? Does anything "give it away"?

**Activity:** Use Web sites such as *jimwalterhomes.com/* and *palmharbor.com/index2.asp* to compare factory-built housing and modular housing. Consider size, financing options, and price.

**Enrich:** Visit a manufactured-housing factory to observe how automation can shorten and improve the homebuilding process. Be prepared to ask questions. Summarize in one paragraph what you learn.

passed additional rules, such as zoning regulations that prohibit the placement of these homes in certain areas.

The owners can move single-sectional homes as long as all laws are followed. Larger homes must be moved in parts from the factory to the site. A company specializing in moving manufactured or mobile homes handles the job. Once joined together, double-sectional and multi-sectional units are usually fixed permanently to their sites.

*Panelized housing* involves panels of walls, floors, ceilings, or roofs that can be ordered separately and are assembled at the housing site. The units are usually complete with windows, doors, plumbing, and wiring.

*Precut housing* refers to housing components that are cut to exact size in the plant and delivered to the building site. Lumber, finish materials, and other components are then assembled by a crew at the site. See 4-25.

A *kit house* is a type of factory-built housing. Kit houses are shipped to the site in unassembled parts or as a finished shell from the factory. The

interior is then completed according to the buyer's wishes.

A kit house is less costly than most other types of factory-built housing. The total cost is influenced by several factors such as the size and style of the house. Another cost factor is the delivery cost, which is based on the distance from the factory to the site. Finally, the cost of a kit house is influenced by whether all the materials and labor for the house are purchased with the kit or separately.

## More Decisions

Other items to consider when choosing a dwelling include the house's condition (if it is not new), price, size, design, and appearance on the site. The chart in 4-26 can guide you as you make decisions about a house.

# Housing for Special Needs

In the 1980s, housing became a much-discussed issue. Government officials, builders, housing developers, and the general public expressed a growing need for safe, decent, affordable housing for everyone. Groups of people with special requirements were the focus. They included senior citizens, people of all ages who have disabilities, and households with children. Today, housing designs are addressing their special needs.

## Considerations for Senior Citizens

Many people look forward to retirement. They may plan to enjoy activities they could not pursue much in the past, such as golfing, fishing,

Velux-America, Inc.

4-25

*Many modern-day log homes are precut housing.*

| Choosing the Dwelling | | |
|---|---|---|
| **Considerations** | **Range of Choices** | |
| *Type of ownership* | Rental   to | Buyer (cooperative, condominium, or private dwelling) |
| *Type of dwelling* | Low spread   to<br>Multifamily   to<br>Old   to | High rise<br>Single family<br>Newly built<br>• Owner-built versus contractor-built<br>• Stock plans versus custom design<br>• Site-built versus factory-built (modular, manufactured/mobile, panelized, precut, or kit housing) |
| *Landscaping* | Dwelling looks out of place   to<br>No landscaping   to | Site harmonizes with dwelling<br>Attractive use of landscaping elements |
| *Size of outside zones* (public, service, and private) | Small   to | Large |
| *Structural quality* | Substandard/ deteriorated quality   to | High quality |
| *Size of dwelling* | Cramped   to | Spacious |
| *Price* | Affordable   to | Expensive |

4-26

*Many options are possible when choosing a home.*

traveling, or volunteering. Their retirement plans will likely affect their housing decisions. They may want housing that requires less maintenance or that will be secure while they are away. The situations vary with each retiree, as do their housing choices.

As people age, their energy levels often decrease. Perhaps their health declines and they find their houses difficult to maintain. This makes it hard for older people who prefer to "age in place," or stay in their present houses. They need housing that permits easy cleanup and requires little maintenance.

One option for aging individuals is adding universal design features into their homes. **Universal design** is the concept of making houses easier for everyone to use. The goal is to make housing more accessible to even those without physical impairments.

With universal design, older people can remain independent even when aging reduces their mobility. For example, adding a no-step entrance with a wider doorway and nonslip floors are universal design changes that would benefit everyone. However, they would especially benefit a person with a broken leg using

**Discuss:** Give examples of housing features that benefit people with special needs. *(no-step entrance, wider doorway, nonslip floors)*

**Reflect:** Think about senior citizens you know. What special housing needs do they have now or are likely to have in the future?
**Writing Activity:** Consider the term *universal design*. In a brief paragraph, explain how the term clearly indicates who the intended beneficiary of the design is. (*The design is intended to benefit*

*everyone since the term means "a concept of making houses easier for everyone to use.")*
**Writing Activity:** Write a case study showing wise decision making for selecting housing, using the information in Figure 4-26.

crutches. Even more so, the changes would benefit those in wheelchairs or with permanent impairment from old age. Universal design is discussed more fully in Chapter 20, "Keeping Your Home Safe and Secure," and Chapter 22, "Housing for Today and Tomorrow."

Some senior citizens find that living in their old neighborhoods is no longer convenient. They may be far from shopping areas and community centers where they can be with people their age. If they have difficulty driving, they may not want to leave home often. This can lead to loneliness, especially if they live alone.

When older people can no longer live alone due to loneliness or health problems, they usually change

housing. They may become a part of another household. They may live with a son, daughter, or someone who can help care for them.

They may choose to become part of larger group quarters, such as a senior living community. They may instead choose a retirement home or an assisted-living facility, 4-27. An *assisted-living facility* serves those who need daily living assistance but not constant care. Prepared meals, laundry service, and household cleanup are the most common services provided.

Another option for older people is to move to a life care community. Many are *graduated-care facilities.* These are facilities in which the residents move from individual apartments to a nursing home unit as needed. Facilities that are well designed and administered offer comfortable living.

For older people who choose to live on their own, the cost of house ownership is high. However, they may find they are "house rich and cash poor" because their savings went to acquire their houses. With time, their houses may become run down. When income is limited, older people may not have money for maintenance, repairs, utilities, or taxes. In this case, they would not have extra money to adapt their houses to meet their special needs.

Measures have been taken to assist older people. Some states allow reverse mortgages. A *reverse mortgage* enables older people to convert the money tied up in their houses into income. They receive a monthly payment as long as they live in the dwelling. When they no longer live in the house, the mortgage company assumes ownership of the dwelling. Reverse mortgages can help older homeowners stay in their houses.

Chambrel at Roswell, Georgia, an Oxford Senior Living Community

4-27 ⎯⎯⎯⎯⎯⎯⎯⎯⎯⎯⎯⎯⎯⎯⎯⎯⎯⎯⎯⎯⎯⎯⎯⎯⎯

*Senior-living communities often include assisted-living facilities.*

## Considerations for People with Disabilities

There are many people with disabilities in the United States. They include children, senior citizens, and adults who work and live on their own or with their families. The types of disabilities vary. Some people have a vision or hearing loss. Many have difficulty moving and must use wheelchairs, crutches, or walkers. Others may have learning or developmental disabilities.

People with disabilities need housing to meet their needs. They may be unable to live independently in housing built in the past. Appropriate housing can assist people who have disabilities with their daily living. For example, the bathroom in 4-28 has been adapted to meet the needs of a person in a wheelchair.

The *Fair Housing Act* of 1988 gives people with disabilities greater freedom to choose a place to live that meets their needs. The Act forbids discrimination in housing and requires multiunits to be accessible to people with disabilities. The law requires accessible entrances, wider doors, and easier installation of grab bars around toilets and bathtubs. Although the law does not address every aspect of making multiunits fully accessible, definite improvements were made. As a result, the law helps provide housing that is safer and easier for everyone to use. (See "Appendix A, Housing and Related Legislation" for additional information.)

If you or a member of your household has a disability, these factors should be considered.

- Choose a ground-level dwelling.
- Look for at least a 5-foot by 5-foot level entryway or landing that will permit entry doors to be opened easily.
- Look for wide interior doorways and hallways.
- Provide good lighting for people with low vision.
- Install audio and visual smoke detectors.
- Choose housing along or near public transportation lines.
- Choose housing near shopping areas.

When people with disabilities have housing that meets their needs, they can live more independently. If you should build a home someday, you can incorporate features of universal design to extend the house's usage for all conditions of life. See Chapter 22 for a full description of these features.

**Discuss:** Study the photo in Figure 4-28. Explain why people with physical disabilities need more maneuvering space than others.

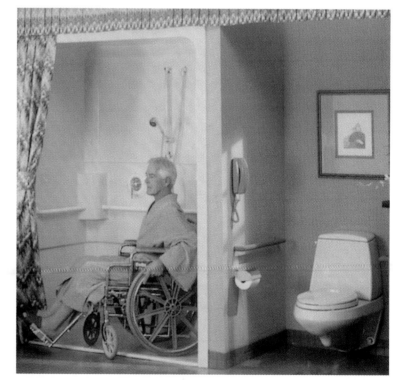

Photo courtesy of Kohler Company

4-28 _____

*The smooth floor, space around and under the sink and toilet, and the wide, level shower opening make this bathroom accessible to everyone in the household.*

**Enrich:** Visit a residence designed for people with special needs. Consider Goodwill facilities, nursing homes, and similar housing. Look for adaptations that address the special needs of the residents.

**Activity:** Using the Internet, look up the Fair Housing Act (*hud.gov/fhe/fheact.html*) and write a one-page summary. **Note:** The Web site *uniteddesign.com* provides several designs that incorporate universal design.

Resource: *Moving Checklist*, reproducible master 4-4, TR. Students review a checklist of actions to take before and during a move.
Discuss: What are some of the things you would expect to find in a "child friendly" home or neighborhood?

## Considerations for Families with Children

Children develop physically, mentally, emotionally, and socially. No matter how old they are, they need to live in a safe and healthy housing environment that promotes positive development.

A housing choice that fits the needs and desires of a couple without children may not be satisfactory when a child arrives. Children need room to grow as they learn to crawl and walk. As they grow older, they need additional space for activities. See 4-29. An outdoor play area that is protected from street traffic is desirable. This gives children a place to move around and play safely.

The community in which children grow can influence their development. When choosing a place to live, look for communities and neighborhoods that will foster healthy growth and development. Look for good schools, safe neighborhoods, park programs, and recreational facilities.

Often children have pets, which also require special considerations. If you rent a house, you may find that neither children nor pets are wanted. However, antidiscrimination laws prevent landlords from refusing to rent apartments to families with children. The same is not true for pets.

# Moving to a New Home

Sometimes a household moves from one house to another within the same neighborhood or community. Short moves may be expected as a

Kate Shenberger Interiors, Flossmoor, Illinois

4-29
*The playhouse gives this little girl her own special place to grow and develop.*

Discuss: What parts of your home's interior and exterior environment have been used as play areas?

Reflect: What do you anticipate will be included in the next section, "Moving to a New Home"? Confer with a partner to compare thoughts.

family ends one stage of its life cycle and enters another. Changes in lifestyle, occupation, socioeconomic status, or other life situations also cause people to move.

A long-distance move is a bigger job and has a greater emotional impact than a move across town. Relocating family and possessions is likely to cause stress. The amount of stress can be reduced if you take the right steps before moving day.

No matter how far you are moving, it is a good idea to get rid of household items you no longer need or want. People often find they have paid to move items that are discarded shortly after the move. You may consider selling, and then later replacing, heavy items such as old refrigerators that add to moving costs. If you decide to sell and replace goods, consider renting them at your new home. This gives you a chance to look around for the best deals.

Another way to eliminate the amount of belongings you move is to have a yard or garage sale. You can also give unwanted items to charity or recycle them. Items given to charity are good for an income tax deduction if you get a receipt.

Moving expenses may also qualify as an income tax deduction. If you move because of a job change or transfer and live at least 50 miles farther from work, you may qualify. You must be working full time and make the move within one year of the time you began the new job.

Use the moving expense checklist in 4-30 to be sure you have all the records you need to claim a tax deduction. Be sure you have the correct forms from the Internal Revenue Service (IRS) to claim your deductions.

Once you have decided to move, you need to decide how to do it. You have two alternatives: moving yourself or hiring a moving company.

| Moving Expense Checklist |
|---|

The following records pertaining to your move should be kept in one place.

*House-hunting trip receipts*
- ❏ transportation costs, including air, bus, and train fares, and automobile expenses
- ❏ meals
- ❏ lodgings

*Residence replacement records*
- ❏ advertising expense
- ❏ real estate commissions
- ❏ attorney fees
- ❏ mortgage expenses, including title fees and costs, points, and escrow fees
- ❏ state transfer taxes
- ❏ appraisal fees
- ❏ lease settlement costs

*Mover's documents*
- ❏ bill of lading
- ❏ inventory
- ❏ packing and unpacking certificates
- ❏ weight certificates

*Receipts for temporary quarters*
- ❏ meals
- ❏ lodgings

4-30
*A moving-expense checklist helps when you move. Some items may be tax deductible.*

## Moving Yourself

About two-thirds of all moves are do-it-yourself efforts. If you do not own a truck or trailer, you can rent one and move yourself. There are many good reasons for tackling the job yourself. First the cost is about one-third that of a professional mover. Second, you can move on your own schedule. Third, you and your goods arrive at the same time.

On the other hand, realize what you save in money will cost you in time and energy. You will do all the packing, loading, unloading, and unpacking yourself. Family and friends can help if the move is only a short distance. They can also help with packing and loading for a long move.

Before you begin the process of moving, you need to plan ahead. You need to make arrangements with a rental firm early to assure the equipment you need is available when you need it. Also, before you reserve a truck or trailer, you will need to estimate the amount of items to be moved. This will help you choose the correct-size truck or trailer. The rental firm can help you with this. You can also rent supplies, such as furniture pads and dollies, or purchase moving cartons and other materials.

As you rent moving equipment, check on liability and damage insurance for it. Find out the cost of insuring your belongings. Sometimes your homeowner's or renter's policy covers your goods. If not, you may buy supplemental insurance to cover them. Get a written estimate from the insurance company and ask if there will be additional charges.

You can begin packing early. As you pack, take an inventory of your household items. An inventory will help you check the arrival of your belongings at your new house. It will also provide information you may need to collect insurance if any of your goods are damaged or lost. See 4-31. If this seems like too much to do, consider the money you will save by moving yourself.

## Hiring a Moving Company

If you choose to hire a moving company, you will also need to plan ahead for the move. The checklist in 4-32 is a good one to use regardless of the moving method you choose.

Thousands of U.S. moving companies exist, but about 15 do most of the business, especially for interstate moves. To decide which one to hire,

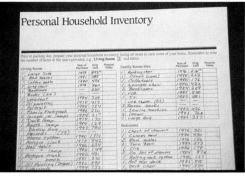

United Van Lines

4-31
*An inventory of household items, similar to this, is good to have when you unpack.*

you can ask your friends, neighbors, or business associates who have moved recently about a dependable carrier. The relocation manager of your company and a reliable real estate agent can also be valuable resources. Choose only licensed movers and obtain at least three written estimates to compare.

After you have chosen a moving company, you need to ask about insurance. Be sure to read the fine print and ask about additional costs. Also, ask about discounted moves, which offer a lower cost for moving during the nonpeak season. Most people move between May 15 and September 30—the peak season. If you move during a nonpeak season, be sure the cost is the only item that would change.

The next step is deciding how much, if any, of the packing and unpacking you will do. The cost of the packing boxes and the service of packing and unpacking are not included in the actual moving expense. However, the extra cost can be worth it. See 4-33. Packing takes time and it can be hard work. Also, if an item you packed yourself is damaged in the move, it will be harder to file a claim with the moving company. It is a good idea to photograph expensive pieces to prove their condition and value.

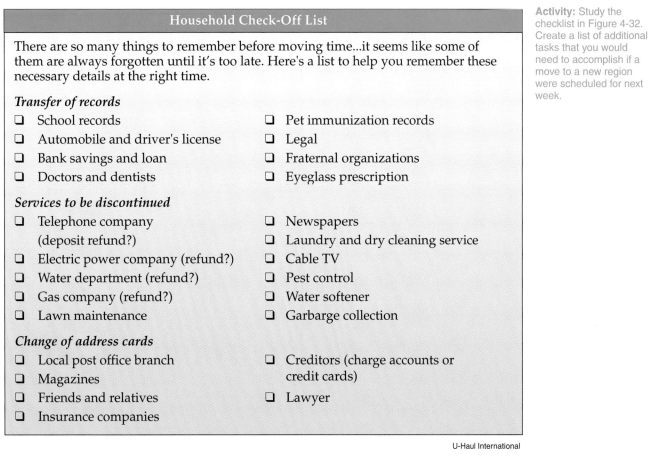

**Household Check-Off List**

There are so many things to remember before moving time...it seems like some of them are always forgotten until it's too late. Here's a list to help you remember these necessary details at the right time.

*Transfer of records*

- ❑ School records
- ❑ Automobile and driver's license
- ❑ Bank savings and loan
- ❑ Doctors and dentists

- ❑ Pet immunization records
- ❑ Legal
- ❑ Fraternal organizations
- ❑ Eyeglass prescription

*Services to be discontinued*

- ❑ Telephone company (deposit refund?)
- ❑ Electric power company (refund?)
- ❑ Water department (refund?)
- ❑ Gas company (refund?)
- ❑ Lawn maintenance

- ❑ Newspapers
- ❑ Laundry and dry cleaning service
- ❑ Cable TV
- ❑ Pest control
- ❑ Water softener
- ❑ Garbarge collection

*Change of address cards*

- ❑ Local post office branch
- ❑ Magazines
- ❑ Friends and relatives
- ❑ Insurance companies

- ❑ Creditors (charge accounts or credit cards)
- ❑ Lawyer

U-Haul International

4-32 _____

*Checklists can guide you through the steps you need to take when moving.*

When you are moving with children, special considerations need to be made. Moving may be traumatic for them. It is helpful to involve children in the move as much as possible. See 4-34. Tell them about the move early and let them decide what to pack. Give them a floor plan of their new bedrooms so they can have fun deciding where to put their furniture.

It is best to move when it is most convenient for all family members. For instance, children usually do not like to change schools, especially during the school year. When the children arrive at their new schools, make the change as easy as possible by having their records already there.

When the moving van arrives at the new house, be sure the dwelling is

United Van Lines

4-33 _____

*Many people find it worth the expense to hire professionals to pack their household items.*

4-34

*Children adjust better to the move when they are involved.*

ready for occupancy. Clean or paint ahead of time since both are difficult to do in a house filled with moving cartons. Decide how you want your furniture arranged and supervise its placement. Be sure items that were taken apart are reassembled.

As your belongings are unloaded from the van, check for damaged or missing items. List any of these items on the driver's copy and your copy of the ***bill of lading***, which is a receipt listing the goods shipped.

If you file a claim for damaged or missing items, first list the lost items. Then, make a list of damaged items and estimate the cost to repair them. Interstate movers are required by law to acknowledge and respond to your claim.

Moving can be difficult. Therefore, it is important to weigh the advantages and disadvantages of the different ways to move. This will help you decide whether to move yourself or hire a moving company.

# Summary

When choosing a place to live, you need to examine its location. Considerations include the region, neighborhood, site, and zone within the site. You also need to consider the restraints, natural and legal, of the location.

There are many different housing choices. Multifamily houses include apartments, cooperatives, and condominiums. Single-family houses may be attached or freestanding. They can also be owner-built, built by contractors or developers, or a type of factory-built housing. You can either rent or buy housing.

If an older person or someone with a disability is part of your household, you will need to consider his or her special needs when making housing decisions. If there are children, their needs must also be considered. You want to choose housing that promotes their development.

After you have chosen a place to live, you must decide how to move to it. The move may be short or cross-country. You can move your own belongings or hire a moving company. Both options have advantages and disadvantages. After you have made your decision, there are certain steps you need to take to ensure a smooth move.

**Resource:** *Places to Live*, Activity G, SAG. Students complete the statements about finding a place to live.

# To Review

1. List the five major factors regarding location that must be decided when considering housing.

2. Give three reasons for living in a certain region.

3. Regions are divided into communities, which are divided into _____.

4. Neighborhoods in which all buildings are occupied by households are called _____.
   A. residential
   B. commercial
   C. industrial

5. List two natural restraints that affect sites.

6. The legal restraints that affect sites involve _____ laws.
   A. local and state
   B. state
   C. state and federal
   D. local, state, and federal

7. Explain how the FHA relates to the MPS.

8. Name and describe the three zones within a site.

9. What are the ownership differences among rentals, cooperative units, and condominium units?

**Answer Key**

1. region, community, neighborhood, population composition, and site

2. (List three:) scenery, climate, family, friends, employment, cost of living, topography

3. neighborhoods

4. A

5. (List two:) topography, soil conditions, water levels, orientation to sun, orientation to wind, orientation to scenery

6. D

7. FHA, the Federal Housing Administration, establishes minimum property standards (MPS).

8. The public zone is part of the site that can be seen from the street. The service zone includes sidewalks, driveways, and storage areas. The private zone is hidden from public view and used for recreation and relaxation.

9. rental units—landlords; cooperative units—a corporation whose stockholders are usually the occupants; condominium units—the individual occupants

**Writing Activity:** Students write each letter of the alphabet on separate lines of a sheet of paper and work independently to write one term from the chapter that begins with each alphabet letter. After three minutes, pairs of students confer to fill in any blank lines. If blanks still remain, discuss with the class some possible choices.

10. An attached house is one that _____.
    A. shares at least part of a common wall with an adjacent dwelling
    B. is connected to two or more dwellings
    C. is attached to a foundation that is anchored to the ground
11. An architect _____ the dwelling and the contractor _____ it.
12. How does a tract house differ from a house custom-built from stock plans?
13. Name the five types of factory-built houses.
14. Identify three groups of people who have special housing needs.
15. List the advantages of moving yourself versus hiring a professional mover.

## In Your Community

1. Visit a house that is for sale. List the features that need to be adapted for a person with a disability.
2. At your public library, look up the zoning regulations and building codes of your community. Find out what the requirements are for local housing.
3. Contact a local or a nearby Chamber of Commerce office and obtain the literature it provides to new or prospective area residents. What features of the area would appeal to different types of residents, such as senior citizens, families with children, and single persons?

## To Think About

1. When moving from one place to another, one way to save money is to have friends help you move. Would you accept the risk of possible damage to furniture or the new home due to accidents caused by your friends? What could you do to help prevent any damage?
2. One trend in housing is to build the total housing or various parts in a factory and move them to the housing site. Do you think this trend will continue? Do you think it will ever be predominant? Why or why not?

## Using Technology

1. Search the Internet to locate at least two moving companies that serve the local area. What services do they provide? How are the costs calculated? Make a chart showing the services provided

and the costs per company. Enter the data into a table created with a word processing program to share with your class. Which company would you choose and why?

Note: For researching regions and communities, have students explore *realtor.com*.

2. Choose a region beyond your community where you would enjoy living. Locate the Web site for the area's chamber of commerce and find out more about the community. What would be the advantages and disadvantages of living there?

3. Research the Internet for information and write a report about one of the following topics:
   - housing for senior citizens
   - housing for people (either adults or children) with disabilities
   - housing for children

4. Survey 10 people in your community and ask what they like about living there. Also find out what they dislike. Select individuals of both sexes and different ages to get a range of responses. Using a computer, create a chart or spreadsheet to display the information to your class. Keep the identities of the surveyed individuals confidential.

5. Using a computer-assisted design software package, draw a dwelling on a site showing the three zones within the site.

**Portfolio Project:** Imagine you are preparing to move into an apartment near your new job or college. Create a list of tasks you will need to do for a successful move. Write a diary describing what you plan to do each day until settled into the new apartment.

CHAPTER 5

# Acquiring Housing

## To Know

process
down payment
cost
wants
credit cards
interest
installment buying
finance charge
security deposit
lease
landlord
renter
lessor
lessee
assign
sublet
breach of contract
eviction
equity
foreclosure
gross income
bid
closed
inspector
appraiser
Internet
virtual reality
agreement of sale
earnest money
abstract of title
mortgage
conventional mortgage
FHA-insured mortgage
VA-guaranteed mortgage
adjustable rate mortgage
renegotiable rate mortgage
closing costs
title
deed
declaration of ownership

## Objectives

After studying this chapter, you will be able to

- determine the advantages and disadvantages of renting and buying houses.
- contrast the impact of needs and wants on housing costs.
- list several items to check before signing a lease.
- explain the steps in buying a house.
- define legal and financial terms related to acquiring housing.
- describe what to examine when buying condominium or cooperative units.

Atsome time, you will need to decide how to spend money for housing. You will need to use rational decision making to choose between renting and purchasing a house as well as to make other related choices. Your choices will depend on your lifestyle, stage of the life cycle, and other life situations.

## Acquiring a Place to Live

People make many decisions in the process of acquiring a place to live. *Process* is the method used to accomplish a task. These decisions are part of a process beginning with the decision to rent or buy housing, followed by a determination of how to pay for the housing choice. Additional decisions are required later for operating the unit as well as replacing and adapting it through time. See 5-1.

In thinking about the process of acquiring housing, can you describe how your family acquired the housing in which you live? Was it purchased or rented? If purchased, was it new or pre-owned? Was the housing built for a previous owner or for your family?

After choosing to either rent or buy, additional decisions in the process are needed to operate and maintain the housing. You need to make arrangements to have the water, electricity, and/or gas turned on. You need to arrange to have your belongings moved to your house. You also need to repair or replace parts of the dwelling from time to time. It may involve something as simple as replacing a worn seal in a leaky water faucet or as complex as adding a second floor.

You will need to decide how to pay for these housing expenses. You can pay for them in the following ways:

- Pay the full amount now with cash, a check, a transfer of funds from another account, or by debit card. (A *debit card* looks like a credit card but immediately releases money from your account.)
- Postpone payment by using a credit card.
- Pay part of the total now, or a *down payment*, to secure a purchase. (The remainder is then paid in regular installments.)

| The Process of Acquisition | | |
|---|---|---|
| **Considerations** | | **Range of Choices** |
| *Possessing* | Own | Buy<br>Build<br>Own to rent |
| | Rent | Privately owned<br>Publicly owned<br>Company owned |
| *Financing* | Cash | Currency<br>Check |
| | Terms | Short term<br>Long term |
| | Sources | Current income<br>Savings<br>Private loans<br>Commercial loans<br>Governmental<br> loans |
| *Operating* | | Furnish<br>Maintain<br>Repair |
| *Replacing* | | Sell<br>Trade<br>Abandon |
| *Adapting* | | Remodel<br>Refinish<br>Redecorate |

5-1 _____
*When acquiring housing, you will want to consider all available choices.*

**Resource:** *Making Housing Choices,* transparency master overlay II-D, TR. Students look back at the topics covered in Chapters 1-4 by reviewing transparency master II-A and overlay II-C. Then, with the addition of the overlay, they explore the topics they will cover in Chapter 5.

**Resource:** *Hunting for Housing,* reproducible master 5-1, TR. Students use the worksheet to analyze real estate ads.

**Activity:** Create a survey form by using questions in the second paragraph under "Process." Use the form to interview at least five adults. Report your results to the class by displaying the data in a table.

**Discuss:** Why is using a debit card on a purchase like paying with cash? (*It releases money immediately from an account.*)

**Activity:** List the key terms on the left side of a sheet of paper, writing one term on every other line. Write the definition of each term upon seeing it defined in the text (shown in bold italics).

**Note:** Before making a down payment, make sure it is refundable if you should change your plans for any reason.

**Reflect:** Study the chart in Figure 5-1. When you move from home, what process of acquisition do you anticipate using? Why?

# Human and Nonhuman Costs

When considering housing costs, it is important to recognize the many factors that affect them. *Cost* is the amount of human and nonhuman resources used to achieve something. The money you spend for rent or mortgage payments, utilities, and home maintenance is part of your housing costs. The other resources you must spend, such as time, energy, and skills, are other forms of housing costs.

For example, consider what is involved in adding plumbing to a house. First, you need to pay for materials. Additional costs would involve the time and energy you would spend installing the new plumbing. On the other hand, you may not have the necessary skill to do it yourself, or cannot spend the time and energy needed. In such cases, you would need to pay for the labor of an expert. See 5-2.

5-2 _____

*This new homeowner had the time and energy to paint her home. She decided to use these resources rather than money resources to hire a professional painter.*

Usually the cost of materials for a house is far lower than the human costs involved. Human costs can involve planning the work, ordering materials, and delivering them plus handling their installation, maintenance, and repair.

# Needs, Wants, and Housing Costs

When considering the costs associated with acquiring housing, it is important to know the difference between your housing needs and wants. Needs are basic necessities, while *wants* are things you would like to have. Wants almost always cost more than needs. Sometimes people have wants that cost far more than they can afford on their current income.

An example is a couple of first-time homebuyers who want the home of their dreams. In reality, they only need adequate shelter that protects them from the elements. As they search for housing, they will likely find that what they want is not what they can afford. They must examine their priorities and identify which of their preferences they can afford.

# Costs Involved in Method of Paying

When you pay cash for an item, such as a lamp, you know its exact cost. However, when you pay by check, debit card, or automatic transfer of funds, you may have some banking costs. Some banks charge for checks and for providing various banking services.

Sometimes a *credit card* is used for a purchase. A credit card is an extension of money to the cardholder based on an agreement to repay. The cost of using a credit card varies.

Some charge an annual fee, while others are free. If you make only the minimum payment by the bill's deadline, interest will be added to the rest of the amount you owe. *Interest* is the price paid for the use of someone else's money. The credit card company is required by law to tell you exactly how much interest you will be charged. You can avoid paying interest by paying the entire amount of the bill by the due date. To determine the cost of a credit card, ask the following questions:

- How much is the annual fee?
- What is the interest rate?
- Do interest charges begin at the time of purchase?

*Installment buying* is the process of buying something by making a series of payments during a given length of time. See 5-3. Installment buying costs more to use than most other methods. This is because a person, company, or bank is *financing*, or providing credit, to you. They have paid your bill and are willing to wait for you to pay them back. Therefore, in addition to the original cost of the merchandise, you must pay extra for the privilege of using their money.

This extra amount is called a *finance charge.* It includes the interest as well as any other service. The finance charge is stated as an annual percentage rate of the amount borrowed. You can pay back the money you borrow over a short or long period of time. The longer you take, the more interest you will pay. Most houses are purchased with *long-term financing.* You can take as long as 30 years to pay back the money you borrow for a house. However, with long-term financing, the total interest you

**Enrich:** Debate whether using a credit card is a wise way to make purchases. Take a "pro" position, citing common examples; or a "con" position, arguing that credit card use poses too many risks.
**Discuss:** What are the advantages of paying back a loan over a short period of time versus a longer period? (*saves money in interest payments*)

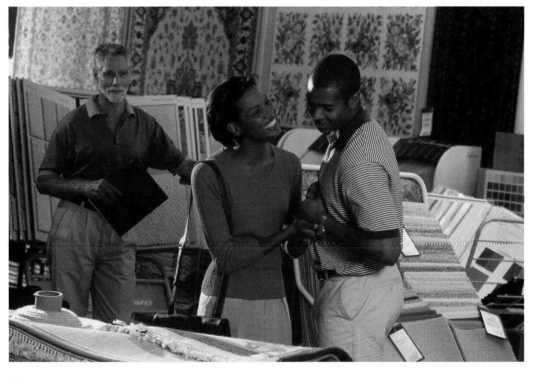

5-3

*Whenever you consider spreading the cost of a purchase over time, find out what the extra charges are.*

**Math Activity:** Calculate how much a $100 bookcase will cost when put onto a credit card at 18% interest and paid within a year? (*$118*) How much will the bookcase cost if the $25 annual fee for the card is totaled into the amount? (*$143*)
**Enrich:** Investigate various credit cards to determine answers to the following questions: Which credit card companies allow a grace period before interest and fees are applied? Which have no annual fee? Which charge the lowest rates on unpaid balances? Which offer additional bonuses, such as frequent-flier miles? Identify a credit card that you would recommend and explain why.

Resource: *A Place to Rent*, Activity A, SAG. Outside of class time, students visit an apartment and evaluate it according to the renter's checklist and landlord questions.

Enrich: Invite a speaker from a credit counseling agency or organization to speak about the cost and problems of excessive use of credit.

Activity: Before reviewing Figure 5-4, work within a team to create a list of advantages and disadvantages of renting versus purchasing a home.

eventually pay will far exceed the cost of the dwelling itself.

It is important to know all the costs associated with any housing consideration and figure them into the purchase decision. For instance, it may be better to wait to buy a lamp with cash rather than pay extra for credit card costs. On the other hand, few people could ever afford to buy a house if they had to save all the money needed to make a cash purchase. For them, paying some extra interest each month is the only way to afford such a costly purchase.

## To Rent or to Buy?

The first decision in selecting housing is whether to rent or buy. There are advantages and disadvantages to both. Some of the major considerations in renting versus buying are outlined in 5-4. All these considerations will become clearer as you read the chapter.

## A Place to Rent

About one-third of all people in the United States rent their housing. The majority of these are single people, young married couples, and senior citizens. Many are people who have very mobile lifestyles.

Renters usually pay for their housing in monthly installments. When they first move into a building, the owner or building manager usually requests a security deposit in addition to the first month's rent. The *security deposit* is a payment that ensures the owner against financial loss caused by the renter. For example, the renter may damage the property or fail to pay the rent. The amount of the security deposit commonly includes one month's rent and may include an additional amount.

| Renting versus Buying | |
|---|---|
| *Advantages of Renting* | *Disadvantages of Renting* |
| Generally costs less than buying. | No tax benefit. |
| Total housing costs are clearer. | No investment in or from property. |
| You can usually move more easily. | No equity in building. |
| Little responsibility for maintenance. | Rent payment can increase frequently. |
| No responsibility for repairs. | Possibility of eviction. |
| *Advantages of Buying* | *Disadvantages of Buying* |
| Greater stability. | You are responsible for property taxes, maintenance, and repairs. |
| Usually a good investment. | Possibility of foreclosure. |
| Your equity builds. | In foreclosure, loss of all equity. |
| First home oftens leads to better home. | Monthly housing usually costs more. |
| Great individuality in decor. | Your cash is tied up. |
| Greater choice in space arrangement. | You usually can't sell a home quickly. |
| Greater sense of security. | You have less mobility than renting. |
| Oftens fufills the American dream. | Payment on some types of mortgages can increase. |

Reprinted with permission by the copyright owner, BOECKH, a division of Thomson Publishing Corporation, Stamford, CT

5-4 _____

*When deciding where to live, you need to consider the advantages and disadvantages of both renting and buying.*

Enrich: Find out what happens to mortgage holders when they fall behind on payments and report your findings to the class. Based on the information you learn, what advice would you give to future owners of home mortgage loans?

Math Activity: Check ads, Web sites, and other sources to find out the average security deposit on apartments in the area where you plan to live after graduation. Create a bar graph showing the variation in the dollar amounts reported by class members.

Being a renter has a number of advantages. Renters are free to move as they desire. They do not need to worry about the value of property going up or down or about buying and selling. They have a clear idea of what housing will cost them. There are no hidden costs, like repairing a roof, that often come with ownership. Since renters do not own the dwelling, they do not need to budget some money for maintenance and repairs. These are the responsibilities of the building's owner.

Any type of housing can be rented, but the most common are multifamily dwellings. Renters usually occupy duplexes, triplexes, and apartment buildings. Single-family houses can also be rented as well as condominiums and vacation houses.

As a renter, examine a rental unit closely before you move into it. It is helpful to use a checklist like the one in 5-5. Ask the owner of the unit the following questions:

- What is the rent per month? How and when is it to be paid?
- Is a security deposit required? If so, how much is it? Under what conditions will it be returned?
- Does the lease say rent can be increased if real estate taxes or other expenses to the lessor are raised?
- What are the expenses/fees besides rent? (These may include utilities, storage space, parking space, air conditioning, master TV antenna connections, use of recreational areas, installation of special appliances, and late rent payments.)
- How are deliveries of packages handled?
- Is loud noise prohibited at certain hours?

Be sure that each question is answered and you are happy with the answers. You want your housing to bring you satisfaction, not frustration.

## The Written Lease

Rental agreements can be on a month-to-month basis or for a specific length of time, such as one year. An oral agreement is possible, but a written lease is the preferred agreement between renter and owner. See 5-6. A *lease* is a legal document spelling out the conditions of the rental agreement. It lists the rights and responsibilities of both the property owner, usually called the *landlord*, and the *renter*, who agrees to pay rent for a place to live. Other names for landlord and renter are *lessor* and *lessee*, respectively.

Always read a written lease carefully. It should include the following:

- address and specific apartment number
- date signed
- signatures of renter(s) and landlord
- date of occupation and length of lease
- cost of rent plus directions for when and where to pay it
- statement on lease renewal  (Is it automatic? See 5-7.)
- allotment of specific responsibilities, such as shoveling snow, cutting the lawn, or painting the walls
- entry clause allowing the landlord to enter the apartment for specific reasons (with notice) or in an emergency
- statement indicating who is responsible for waste pick-up and for paying utilities such as water, electricity, and gas

**Discuss:** Have you lived in an apartment (or condominium) as well as a single-family house? Based on your experience, what are the major differences between the two forms of housing?

**Discuss:** When reviewing an apartment for rent, would it be wise to take a list of the items a lease should include? Explain your answer.

## Apartment Renters' Checklist

*Laundry facilities*
___ How many washers and dryers are available?
  (A good ratio is one washer and dryer for every ten apartments.)
___ Are washers and dryers in good working order?

*Building lobby*
___ Is the lobby clean and well lit?
___ Is the main entrance locked so only residents can enter?
___ Is a security guard provided? If so, what hours?

*Entrance, exit, and halls*
___ Are elevators provided? If so, are they in good working order?
___ Are the stairs soundly constructed and well lit?
___ Are fire exits provided?
___ Is there a fire alarm or other warning system?
___ Are halls clean, well lit, and soundly constructed?

*Bathroom(s)*
___ Do all plumbing fixtures work? Are they clean?
___ Does the hot water supply seem adequate?
___ Do floors and walls around fixtures seem damp, rotted, or moldy?

*Kitchen*
___ Is the sink working and clean? Does it have drain stoppers?
___ Is there an exhaust fan above the range?
___ Is the refrigerator working properly? Does it have
  a separate freezer compartment?
___ If there is a dishwasher, does it work properly?

*Air conditioning*
___ Is the building centrally air conditioned or are
  separate units present for each apartment?
___ Does the air conditioning unit work properly?

*Heating*
___ What type of heat is provided (gas, electric)?
___ Does the heating system work properly?
___ Is there a fireplace? If so, are there smoke stains or any
  other signs that it has not worked properly?

*Wiring*
___ Are there enough electrical outlets?
  (There should be at least three to a room.)
___ Do all switches and outlets work?
___ Are there enough circuits in the fuse box or circuit breaker panel
  to handle all of your electrical equipment?

*(continued)*

5-5 _____
*Check apartments carefully as you search for a place to rent.*

**Reflect:** How many electrical outlets are in your room at home? Are there enough?

**Discuss:** Why do you think at least three electrical outlets are recommended?

## Apartment Renters' Checklist

*Lighting*
___ Are there enough fixtures for adequate light?
Are the fixtures in good working order?
___ Does the apartment get a good amount of natural light from windows?

*Windows*
___ Are any windows broken or difficult to open and close?
___ Are windows arranged to provide good ventilation?
___ Are screens provided?
___ Are there drafts around the window frame?
___ In high-rise buildings, does the landlord arrange for the outside
    of the windows to be cleaned? If so, how often?

*Floors*
___ Are floors clean and free of gouges?
___ Do floors have any water stains indicating previous leaks?

*Ceilings*
___ Are ceilings clean and free of cracks and peeling?
___ Are there any water stains indicating previous leaks?

*Walls*
___ Are walls clean and free of cracks and peeling?
___ Does the paint run or smear when rubbed with a damp cloth?

*Soundproofing*
___ When you thump the walls, do they seem hollow or solid?
___ Can you hear neighbors downstairs, upstairs, or on either side of you?

*Telephone*
___ Are phone jacks already installed?
___ Are phone jacks in convenient locations?

*Television*
___ Is an outside antenna connection provided?
___ Is a cable TV connection provided?

*Storage space*
___ Is there adequate closet space?
___ Are there enough kitchen and bathroom cabinets?
___ Is additional storage space provided for tenants?

*Outdoor play space*
___ Are outdoor facilities provided? If so, are the facilities well maintained?

5-5 _____
*(continued)*

**Discuss:** What steps would you take if an affordable apartment you wanted had dirty carpeting and cracks in the walls and ceilings?
**Enrich:** Invite an apartment manager to review the checklist and recommend other questions that potential renters should consider.

**Discuss:** Which apartment in a building is likely to be one of the quietest? Why?

# APARTMENT LEASE
## UNFURNISHED

| DATE OF LEASE | TERM OF LEASE | | MONTHLY RENT | SECURITY DEPOSIT * |
|---|---|---|---|---|
| | BEGINNING | ENDING | | |
| | | | | |

*IF NONE, WRITE "NONE". Paragraph 2 of this Lease then INAPPLICABLE.*

**LESSEE**

NAME •

APT. NO. •

ADDRESS OF •
PREMISES

**LESSOR**

NAME •

BUSINESS •
ADDRESS

In consideration of the mutual covenants and agreements herein stated, Lessor hereby leases to Lessee and Lessee hereby leases from Lessor for a private dwelling the apartment designated above (the "Premises"), together with the appurtenances thereto, for the above Term.

ADDITIONAL COVENANTS AND AGREEMENTS *(if any)*

## LEASE COVENANTS AND AGREEMENTS

**RENT**

1. Lessee shall pay Lessor or Lessor's agent as rent for the Premises the sum stated above, monthly in advance, until termination of this lease, at Lessor's address stated above or such other address as Lessor may designate in writing.

**SECURITY DEPOSIT**

2. Lessee has deposited with Lessor the Security Deposit stated above for the performance of all covenants and agreements of Lessee hereunder. Lessor may apply all or any portion thereof in payment of any amounts due Lessor from Lessee, and upon Lessor's demand Lessee shall in such case during the term of the lease promptly deposit with Lessor such additional amounts as may then be required to bring the Security Deposit up to the full amount stated above. Upon termination of the lease and full performance of all matters and payment of all amounts due by Lessee, so much of the Security Deposit as remains unapplied shall be returned to Lessee. This deposit does not bear interest unless and except as required by law. Where all or a portion of the Security Deposit is applied by Lessor as compensation for property damage, Lessor when and as required by law shall provide to Lessee an itemized statement of such damage and of the estimated or actual cost of repairing same.

**CONDITION OF PREMISES; REDELIVERY TO LESSOR**

3. Lessee has examined and knows the condition of Premises and has received the same in good order and repair except as herein otherwise specified, and no representations as to the condition or repair thereof have been made by Lessor or his agent prior to, or at the execution of this lease, that are not herein expressed or endorsed hereon; and upon the termination of this lease in any way, Lessee will immediately yield up Premises to Lessor in as good condition as when the same were entered upon by Lessee, ordinary wear and tear only excepted, and shall then return all keys to Lessor.

**LIMITATION OF LIABILITY**

4. Except as provided by Illinois statute, Lessor shall not be liable for any damage occasioned by failure to keep Premises in repair, and shall not be liable for any damage done or occasioned by or from plumbing, gas, water, steam or other pipes, or sewerage, or the bursting, leaking or running of any cistern, tank, wash-stand, water-closet or waste-pipe, in, above, upon or about said building or Premises, nor for damage occasioned by water, snow or ice being upon or coming through the roof, sky-light, trap-door or otherwise, nor for damages to Lessee or others claiming through Lessee for any loss or damage of or to property wherever located in or about said building or Premises, nor for any damage arising from acts or neglect of co-tenants or other occupants of the same building, or of any owners or occupants of adjacent or contiguous property.

5-6

*Responsibilities of the lessor and the lessee are clearly stated in the lease.*

**Resource:** *The Written Lease*, Activity B, SAG. Students answer questions about the lease shown in Figure 5-6 of the text.

**Activity:** Use three blank transparency sheets and a marker to underline confusing phrases in the lease in Figure 5-6. Work as a team with three or four classmates to research Web sites such as hud.gov/consum.cfm or talk with representatives of a local renters association to learn what the phrases mean. Create a glossary of terms and definitions to report to the class.

**Enrich:** Participate in a presentation by a guest apartment owner or manager who discusses the importance of an individual understanding a lease before signing it. What happens when a person tries to break or not fulfill a lease contract? Summarize in one paragraph what you learn.

**USE;
SUBLET;
ASSIGNMENT**

5. Lessee will not allow Premises to be used for any purpose that will increase the rate of insurance thereon, nor for any purpose other than that hereinbefore specified, nor to be occupied in whole or in part by any other persons, and will not sublet the same, nor any part thereof, nor assign this lease, without in each case the written consent of the Lessor first had, and will not permit any transfer, by operation of law, of the interest in Premises acquired through this lease, and will not permit Premises to be used for any unlawful purpose, or purpose that will injure the reputation of the same or of the building of which they are part or disturb the tenants of such building or the neighborhood.

**USE AND
REPAIR**

6. Lessee will take good care of the apartment demised and the fixtures therein, and will commit and suffer no waste therein; no changes or alterations of the Premises shall be made, nor partitions erected, nor walls papered, nor locks on doors installed or changed, without the consent in writing of Lessor; Lessee will make all repairs required to the walls, ceilings, paint, plastering, plumbing work, pipes and fixtures belonging to Premises, whenever damage or injury to the same shall have resulted from misuse or neglect; no furniture filled or to be filled wholly or partially with liquids shall be placed in the Premises without the consent in writing of Lessor; the Premises shall not be used as a "boarding" or "lodging" house, nor for a school, nor to give instructions in music, dancing or singing, and none of the rooms shall be offered for lease by placing notices on any door, window or wall of the building, nor by advertising the same directly or indirectly, in any newspaper or otherwise, nor shall any signs be exhibited on or at any windows or exterior portions of the Premises or of the building without the consent in writing of Lessor; there shall be no lounging, sitting upon, or unnecessary tarrying in or upon the front steps, the sidewalk, railing, stairways, halls, landing or other public places of the said building by Lessee, members of the family or other persons connected with the occupancy of Premises; no provisions, milk, ice, marketing, groceries, furniture, packages or merchandise shall be taken into the Premises through the front door of said building except where there is no rear or service entrance; cooking shall be done only in the kitchen and in no event on porches or other exterior appurtenances; Lessee, and those occupying under Lessee, shall not interfere with the heating apparatus, or with the lights, electricity, gas, water or other utilities of said building which are not within the apartment hereby demised, nor with the control of any of the public portions of said building; use of any master television antenna hookup shall be strictly in accordance with regulations of Lessor or Lessor's agent; Lessee and those occupying under Lessee shall comply with and conform to all reasonable rules and regulations that Lessor or Lessor's agent may make for the protection of the building or the general welfare and the comfort of the occupants thereof, and shall also comply with and conform to all applicable laws and governmental rules and regulations affecting the Premises and the use and occupancy thereof.

**ACCESS**

7. Lessee will allow Lessor free access to the Premises at all reasonable hours for the purpose of examining or exhibiting the same, or to make any needful repairs on the Premises which Lessor may deem fit to make; also Lessee will allow Lessor to have placed upon the Premises, at all times, notice of "For Sale" and "To Rent", and will not interfere with the same.

**RIGHT TO
RELET**

8. If Lessee shall abandon or vacate the Premises, the same may be re-let by Lessor for such rent and upon such terms as Lessor may see fit; and if a sufficient sum shall not thus be realized, after paying the expenses of such reletting and collecting, to satisfy the rent hereby reserved, Lessee agrees to satisfy and pay all deficiency.

**HOLDING
OVER**

9. If the Lessee retains possession of the Premises or any part thereof after the termination of the term by lapse of time or otherwise, then the Lessor may at Lessor's option within thirty days after the termination of the term serve written notice upon Lessee that such holding over constitutes either (a) renewal of this lease for one year, and from year to year thereafter, at double the rental specified under Section 1 for such period, or (b) creation of a month to month tenancy, upon the terms of this lease except at double the monthly rental specified under Section 1, or (c) creation of a tenancy at sufferance, at a rental of _____ dollars per day for the time Lessee remains in possession. If no such written notice is served then a tenancy at sufferance with rental as stated at (c) shall have been created, and in such case if specific per diem rental shall not have been inserted herein at (c), such per diem rental shall be one-fifteenth of the monthly rental specified under Section 1 of this lease. Lessee shall also pay to Lessor all damages sustained by Lessor resulting from retention of possession by Lessee.

**RESTRICTIONS
ON USE**

10. Lessee will not permit anything to be thrown out of the windows, or down the courts or light shafts in said building; nothing shall be hung from the outside of the windows or placed on the outside window sills of any window in the building; no parrot, dog or other animal shall be kept within or about said apartment; the front halls and stairways and the back porches shall not be used for the storage of carriages, furniture or other articles.

**WATER AND
HEAT**

11. The provisions of subsection (a) only hereof shall be applicable and shall form a part of this lease unless this lease is made on an unheated basis and that fact is so indicated on the first page of this lease, in which case the provisions of subsection (b) only hereof shall be applicable and form a part of this lease.

(a) Lessor will supply hot and cold water to the Premises for the use of Lessee at all faucets and fixtures provided by Lessor therefor. Lessor will also supply heat, by means of the heating system and fixtures provided by Lessor, in reasonable amounts and at reasonable hours, when necessary, from October 1 to April 30, or otherwise as required by applicable municipal ordinance. Lessor shall not be liable or responsible to Lessee for failure to furnish water or heat when such failure shall result from causes beyond Lessor's control, nor during periods when the water and heating systems in the building or any portion thereof are under repair.

(b) Lessor will supply cold water to the Premises for the use of Lessee at all faucets and fixtures provided by Lessor therefor. Lessor shall not be liable or responsible to Lessee for failure to furnish water when such failure shall result from causes beyond Lessor's control, nor during periods when the water system in the building or any portion thereof is under repair. All water heating and all heating of the Premises shall be at the sole expense of Lessee. Any equipment provided by Lessee therefor shall comply with applicable municipal ordinances.

**STORE ROOM**

12. Lessor shall not be liable for any loss or damage of or to any property placed in any store room or any storage place in the building, such store room or storage place being furnished gratuitously and not as part of the obligations of this lease.

5-6

*(continued)*

**Reflect:** What safety issues need to be addressed in an apartment lease?

**Discuss:** Do you think apartment managers in college towns are likely to have different lease agreements than those available in urban residential areas? Explain your view.

**FORCIBLE DETAINER**

13. If default be made in the payment above reserved or any part thereof, or in any of the covenants or agreements herein contained, to be kept by Lessee, it shall be lawful for Lessor or his legal representatives, at his or their election, to declare said term ended, to re-enter the Premises or any part thereof and to expel, remove or put out the Lessee or any other person or persons occupying the same, using such force as he may deem necessary in so doing, and again to repossess and enjoy the Premises as in his first estate; and in order to enforce a forfeiture of this lease for default in any of its conditions it shall not be necessary to make demand or to serve notice on Lessee and Lessee hereby expressly waives all right to any demand or notice from Lessor of his election to declare this lease at an end on declaring it so to be; but the fact of the non-performance of any of the covenants of this lease shall in itself, at the election of Lessor, without notice or demand constitute a forfeiture of said lease, and at any and all times, after such default, the Lessee shall be deemed guilty of a forcible detainer of the Premises.

**CONFESSION OF JUDGMENT**

14. Lessee hereby irrevocably constitutes any attorney of any court of record of this state to enter Lessee's appearance in such court, waive process and service thereof, and confess judgment from time to time, for any rent which may be due to Lessor or his assignees by the terms of this lease, with costs and reasonable attorney's fees, and to waive all errors and right of appeal from said judgment and to file a consent in writing that a proper writ of execution may be issued immediately.

**RENT AFTER NOTICE OR SUIT**

15. It is further agreed, by the parties hereto, that after the service of notice, or the commencement of a suit or after final judgment for possession of the Premises, Lessor may receive and collect any rent due, and the payment of said rent shall not waive or affect said notice, said suit, or said judgment.

**PAYMENT OF COSTS**

16. Lessee will pay and discharge all reasonable costs, attorney's fees and expenses that shall be made and incurred by Lessor in enforcing the covenants and agreements of this lease.

**RIGHTS CUMULATIVE**

17. The rights and remedies of Lessor under this lease are cumulative. The exercise or use of any one or more thereof shall not bar Lessor from exercise or use of any other right or remedy provided herein or otherwise provided by law, nor shall exercise nor use of any right or remedy by Lessor waive any other right or remedy.

**FIRE AND CASUALTY**

18. In case the Premises shall be rendered untenantable during the term of this lease by fire or other casualty, Lessor at his option may terminate the lease or repair the Premises within 60 days thereafter. If Lessor elects to repair, this lease shall remain in effect provided such repairs are completed within said time. If Lessor shall not have repaired the Premises within said time, then at the end of such time the term hereby created shall terminate. If this lease is terminated by reason of fire or casualty as herein specified, rent shall be apportioned and paid to the day of such fire or other casualty.

**PLURALS; SUCCESSORS**

19. The words "Lessor" and "Lessee" wherever herein occurring and used shall be construed to mean "Lessors" and "Lessees" in case more than one person constitutes either party to this lease; and all the covenants and agreements herein contained shall be binding upon, and inure to, their respective successors, heirs, executors, administrators and assigns and be exercised by his or their attorney or agent.

**SEVERABILITY**

20. If any clause, phrase, provision or portion of this lease or the application thereof to any person or circumstance shall be invalid or unenforceable under applicable law, such event shall not affect, impair or render invalid or unenforceable the remainder of this lease nor any other clause, phrase, provision or portion hereof, nor shall it affect the application of any clause, phrase, provision or portion hereof to other persons or circumstances.

WITNESS the hands and seals of the parties hereto, as of the Date of Lease stated above.

LESSEE:                                                            LESSOR:

_____ (seal)    _____ (seal)

_____ (seal)    _____ (seal)

**ASSIGNMENT BY LESSOR**

On this _____ , _____ , for value received, Lessor hereby transfers, assigns and sets over to

_____ . all right, title and interest in and to the above lease and the rent thereby reserved.

except rent due and payable prior to _____ , _____ .

_____ (seal)

_____ (seal)

**GUARANTEE**

On this _____ , _____ , in consideration of Ten Dollars ($10.00) and other good and valuable consideration, the receipt and sufficiency of which is hereby acknowledged, the undersigned Guarantor hereby guarantees the payment of rent and performance by Lessee, Lessee's heirs, executors, administrators, successors or assigns of all covenants and agrements of the above lease.

_____ (seal)

_____ (seal)

5-6
*(continued)*

**Discuss:** Why do you think both the lessor and lessee need to sign a lease? (*because it states the rights and responsibilities of both the owner and renter and thereby holds both accountable*)

**Discuss:** Why do you need to give written notice to the lessor when there are major repairs that need to be made? (*It is required by the lease. If repairs are not made, you will have grounds for breach of contract.*)

---

**Notice to Terminate Tenancy***

To:  Name _____

     Address _____

     City _____ State _____


You are hereby notified that I (we) shall be terminating my (our) tenancy of –

Apartment _____ at _____ Street _____

State of _____ on _____ day of _____ , 20 _____

Dated: _____ , 20 _____ .

                                          Name _____

                                          Address _____

                                          City _____ State _____

* This form may be used by tenant as a 30 day notice to landlord to terminate month-to-month tenancy, or to give landlord 30 day notice prior to end of term created by rental agreement. It is also suggested that you retain a fully executed, and conformed copy of this notice, and on your copy, make a note of the name on whom same was served, and date and time of service.

---

5-7

*In some cases, the landlord automatically renews the lease if you do not give a written notice that you will move when the lease expires. Once renewed, the lease binds you to its terms for the stated period of time.*

- security deposit statement noting the amount of deposit, the conditions that must be met before it is returned, and when it will be returned

- clause stating the final inspection of the premises will be made in the renter's presence

- clause stating the lease cannot be changed without the written approval of both landlord and renter

- clause on assigning and subletting (which is explained in the next section)

If the renter does not like one or more of the provisions in the lease, he or she should try to have them removed from the lease. Similarly, if additional provisions are desired in the lease, the renter should request to have them written and added to the original lease. Such provisions might include necessary repairs, additional furniture,

**Discuss:** Study Figure 5-7. Why is it important to be aware of the fact that renters are often obliged to sign a document at the time they sign their leases that triggers an automatic renewal? (*The contract binds the renter to the terms of the lease for an additional period.*)

**Enrich:** Search the Web for sites such as *hud.gov/consum.cfm* to determine more about leases, special restrictions, and the definition of important terms. Make a list of helpful Web sites to share with the class.

or the installation of appliances. A specific date should be included by which time all changes are to be made. Signatures of both parties should be obtained.

Leases vary greatly. Some of them include restrictions about guests, pets, excessive noise, and the installation of extra locks. See 5-8. Be sure you are aware of any special restrictions in a lease before you sign it.

Sometimes the words in a lease are hard to understand. Assistance for renters is often available from a renter's association in the community or state. A member of the renter's association will be glad to explain the unfamiliar terms. Do not sign a lease until you understand everything in it.

## Assigning or Subletting a Lease

If you have signed a lease, but you wish to move out early, you have the following three options:

- Continue rent payments until the lease expires.
- Assign the lease.
- Sublet the lease.

To *assign* the lease, you transfer the entire unexpired portion of the lease to someone else. After the assignment is transacted, you can no longer be held responsible for the lease.

To *sublet* the lease, you transfer part interest in the property to someone else. For instance, you could turn over your apartment to another person

5-8 _____

*Apartment residents can maintain good relations with their neighbors by discouraging gatherings of friends from getting too noisy.*

for a period of time. Both you and the other person would be held responsible to the landlord for all terms of the lease.

## Responsibilities and Rights in Rental Housing

Both landlords and renters have responsibilities and rights in the rental relationship. These responsibilities arc stated in the lease agreement. Two legal consequences can occur when the responsibilities of the lease are violated—breach of contract and eviction.

### Breach of Contract

Landlords and renters are sometimes unable to fulfill promises. When this happens there is a **breach of contract.** This is a legal term for failure to meet all terms of a contract or agreement. If you cannot keep your agreement, you should try to work it out with your landlord. You should be aware that a lawsuit can be filed against you for breach of contract. Responding to lawsuits is costly and time-consuming.

The most common breach of contract on the part of the renter is failure to pay rent. For example, if you lose your job, you may not be able to pay the rent on schedule. You will need to make arrangements with your landlord, if possible, to allow for a late rent payment.

A landlord may also be guilty of breach of contract. If there is failure to provide water or a means of heating your dwelling, the contract has been violated. Major repairs are usually the responsibility of the owner. If such repairs are needed, you should give written notice to your landlord. If the repairs are not made, you will have grounds for breach of contract.

### Eviction

If a renter fails to live up to his or her responsibilities, he or she can be evicted. *Eviction* is a legal procedure that forces a renter to leave the property before the rental agreement expires. Landlords may begin a court action leading to eviction only after a renter fails to live up to his or her responsibilities.

The eviction process varies from state to state. However, nearly all states require that the renter receives a warning before he or she can be evicted. The warning is a written legal notice.

## Renter's Insurance

As a renter, you need to have insurance to protect against the loss of your personal property due to theft, fire, or other causes. Renter's insurance can be obtained at a reasonable price. It provides a sense of security in event of loss of personal property.

# A Place to Buy

About two-thirds of the people in the United States own their own houses. Instead of renting, they prefer to stay in one place for several years and buy a house. House ownership has many advantages. It provides a sense of freedom. For example, homeowners know they have a place to live. They are not likely to be evicted, unless they fall behind in their mortgage payments. Also, they can make decisions about their housing and do not need to depend on another person such as an apartment owner.

Financial advantages also exist with house ownership. A house can be a hedge against inflation, which means it probably will increase in

**Resource:** *Buying or Renting,* Activity C, SAG. Students analyze two ads for available housing—one for sale and one for rent—and list the advantages and disadvantages of each.
**Vocabulary:** What are synonyms for *breach* and *contract*? Use these words to create a definition for *breach of contract.*

**Enrich:** Attend a presentation by a manager of a local apartment complex who speaks to the class on the responsibilities of both lessees and lessors. Be prepared to ask questions. Summarize in one paragraph what you learn.

**Social Studies Activity:** Research the eviction process and explain each step. If possible, find out what the annual eviction rate is in your area and how consistent it has been over the last decade.

value at a higher rate than the rate of inflation. People who pay rent must make higher payments for the same housing as inflation rises. Houses tend to increase in value over time. See 5-9.

As the value of your house increases, and you make payments on the principle of the mortgage, you build up equity. *Equity* is the money value of a house beyond what is owed on the house. Renters are not able to build equity in their housing. Homeowners can gain from equity if they sell or refinance their houses.

House ownership also gives a tax advantage. The federal government permits deductions for annual real estate taxes on a house and the interest paid on the mortgage. Some states allow these deductions, too.

Although there are many attractions to home ownership, it is not for everyone. Buying a house is a complex, time-consuming, and costly process that brings many ongoing responsibilities.

One possible drawback to home ownership is the potential strain on

finances. Usually, you can expect to pay more for your housing than you did for rent, at least for the first several years. Even if your mortgage payments are less than you paid previously in rent, you must pay property taxes, homeowner's insurance, utilities, and maintenance expenses.

Another possible drawback to home ownership is foreclosure on the home. *Foreclosure* is a legal proceeding in which a lending firm takes possession of the property. This occurs when the borrower fails to make monthly mortgage payments on a timely basis or does not fulfill the agreements related to the mortgage. A foreclosure means that the agency that lent the money to buy the home may take the property and sell it. Foreclosure is discussed more fully later in the chapter.

Homeowners tend to have less mobility than renters. The owner of a house cannot simply move away and stop paying the mortgage. He or she must fulfill the terms of the mortgage contract and pay all real estate taxes. These responsibilities continue until a new owner buys the property. If a person is expecting a transfer within the next year or two, this might not be a good time to buy a house.

Handling maintenance and repairs is a necessary part of owning a single-family house. Some homeowners prefer to avoid maintenance requirements, such as mowing the grass, by owning a condominium. Condominium owners pay a monthly fee for routine upkeep of the entire property.

When someone decides to seek home ownership, a number of people, agencies, and organizations are available to assist them. Each of the many participants in the home buying process offers different services. See 5-10 for a listing of the primary

| Estimating House Value | | | | |
|---|---|---|---|---|
| *If your home was built in:* | and the original cost was: | | | |
| | $60,000 | $80,000 | $100,000 | $120,000 |
| | the approximate cost to rebuild in 1998 was: | | | |
| 1970 | $255,300 | $340,400 | $425,500 | $510,600 |
| 1975 | 171,300 | 228,400 | 285,400 | 342,500 |
| 1980 | 116,600 | 155,400 | 194,300 | 233,200 |
| 1985 | 85,600 | 114,100 | 142,600 | 171,100 |
| 1990 | 75,000 | 100,100 | 125,100 | 150,100 |

Reprinted with permission by United Guaranty Residential Insurance Company, Greensboro, NC

5-9

*The dollar value of a house tends to increase over time.*

participants and services provided. If you decide to buy a house, you will work with these professionals on your journey to home ownership.

## The Right Price

Buying the right house is not a simple task. You want a house that makes you feel comfortable and happy. However, it must also be one that you can afford.

Being able to afford home ownership begins with an assessment of your income, the size of your savings account, and the debts you have. Most people do not have the cash to buy a house outright and must borrow a substantial amount of money. The ultimate decision about your ability to

Discuss: Why do you think so many people are involved in the home buying process, as shown in Figure 5-10?

| Who's Who in the Home Buying Process | |
|---|---|
| **Title** | **Description of Service** |
| *Real estate professional* | A person licensed to negotiate and transact the sale of real estate. |
| *Hazard insurance representative* | A person who provides hazard insurance to protect the homeowner and the lender against physical damage to a property. This insurance may cover fire, wind, vandalism, or other hazards. |
| *Lender or mortgagee* | The person or institution that lends mortgage money using the property as security for payment of the debt. |
| *Borrower or mortgagor* | A person who borrows money to buy a home, pledging to repay the money with interest and to maintain hazard insurance on the property. |
| *Mortgage insurer* | An institution that insures the lender against loss in case the borrower does not repay the loan. |
| *Loan servicer* | The person or institution that actually collects payments for the loan. A mortgage may be serviced by someone other than the original lender. |
| *Professional home inspector* | The property or mechanical inspector who examines the home for structural defects, such as problems with the roof, wiring, plumbing, or heating and cooling systems. A termite inspector is usually required to evaluate the home for insect damage. |
| *Property appraiser* | A real estate professional, qualified and certified to evaluate a property and assign a market value. Lenders typically require a professional appraisal of the property before approving a mortgage loan. |
| *Attorney* | A person legally appointed or empowered to act for another individual, giving legal advice to clients and representing them in court. The attorney, or lawyer, makes arrangements for the title search, funds disbursement, and arranges the legal tranfer of ownership. |
| *City, county, state, and federal support program representatives* | Special programs for first-time buyers differ from one community to the next. Your local Housing and Urban Development (HUD) office, a federal agency, is a good place to start the search for programs in your area. Some states have a housing finance agency that offers assistance with the down payment and extra tax credits, and most cities and counties have special housing programs. |

5-10
*A number of persons providing various services are involved in the home buying process.*

**Enrich:** Participate in organizing a panel discussion of recent homebuyers. Which of the services shown in Figure 5-10 did each use? Were other professionals who are not listed also used? What were the costs of these services? Summarize in a paragraph what you learn.

**Research Activity:** Find out what your state requires before a person can claim to be a real estate professional. After a person is licensed to sell real estate, what duties and responsibilities are required of that person? Can a real estate agent represent both the seller of a property as well as a prospective buyer? How are real estate professionals paid?

buy a house will be made by the financial institutions.

Moneylenders want to deal with responsible borrowers who will pay them back. They carefully screen applicants to avoid future home foreclosures. They will determine how much house you can afford while you meet your other financial obligations. They will examine how high your monthly house payments can go and, therefore, how much they can safely lend you.

There are three general guidelines for determining the price range of a house you can afford. One is a general rule for estimating house affordability. The other two are used by lending agencies to determine how much income can go toward a house purchase. These guidelines provide a fairly clear picture of what house price is best for you. They are explained in the next two sections.

## Estimating What You Can Afford

One way to quickly determine the price range you can afford in buying a home is to use a simple rule. Multiply two-and-one-half times your annual *gross income,* or income before deductions. This provides a general idea of the maximum price of a house you can afford. If you have an annual income of $40,000, for example, you should be able to afford up to $100,000 for a place to live.

Remember, though, this rule for measuring house affordability provides just a "ballpark" figure. A banker must take into account the other debts and responsibilities the buyer has that may make it difficult for repayment of the loan. Consequently, a person with many debts may not be approved for a loan to acquire housing valued at two-and-one-half times his or her gross income.

## Estimating How Much Money You Can Borrow

The buyer must make a down payment that cannot be part of the loan. This usually is at least 5 percent of the cost of the home, but may vary depending on the requirement of the loan obtained. Obtaining a loan from a lending institution then pays the unpaid balance.

Your earnings and your existing debt will determine the size of the loan that can be obtained. To qualify for a loan, two lender guidelines, or ratios, must be met.

**Housing-to-Income Ratio.** Your monthly housing costs should total no more than 28 percent of your gross monthly income. These housing costs include the mortgage payment, property taxes, insurance, utilities (such as gas, water, and electricity), repairs, maintenance, and a cooperative or condominium fee, if applicable. The housing-to-income ratio is expressed as follows:

$$\frac{\text{Housing costs}}{\text{Gross Income}} = 28\% \text{ or less}$$

**Debt-to-Income Ratio.** The second guideline compares total monthly debt to total monthly income. Your monthly housing costs plus other long-term debts should total no more than 36 percent of your monthly gross income. *Long-term debts* are those debts that will take 10 or more months to repay. The debt-to-income ratio is expressed as follows:

$$\frac{\text{Housing costs + Debts}}{\text{Gross Income}} = 36\% \text{ or less}$$

Both of these ratios must be met for a buyer to be eligible for a loan. These ratios may vary slightly with the specific type of loan obtained. Other factors also enter into the decision to receive a loan to buy housing. A major factor is the credit history of the potential buyer.

The *credit history* of person is kept by a central agency and includes the past payment record as well as a profile of outstanding debts. The credit history gives a bank and other lending agencies some information on whether the person is likely to repay the loan. People are considered "high risk" if their credit history indicates frequent late payments and high debt. An individual can contact a credit bureau to obtain a copy of his or her record and correct errors, if any should appear. There may be a charge for obtaining a copy of the credit history.

## To Build or to Buy?

Once you have decided how much you can afford to spend for a house, you will want to decide whether to build one or buy one already built.

### Building a House

If you choose to build a house, you will need to buy a lot and then build the house. This involves four steps, accomplished in the following order:

1. Choose a region, community, neighborhood, and site. Finding the right location may take weeks or months.

2. Find a house plan you like that fits the site and your lifestyle. The plan may be custom-designed by an architect or chosen from stock plans.

3. Select the contractor. Check the reputation and character of each contractor you are considering by obtaining a list of references of recently completed jobs. Let each one examine your plans, the list of materials for the house, and their type and quality of the materials. See 5-11. When you have narrowed your choices to a few

contractors, you should ask each for a *bid*, or what each would charge to construct the house. The bid should include the cost for both materials and labor. You also need to find out when work can be started and how long the job will take. Ask about the method and time of payments. Builders or contractors generally get paid by installments once the work is in progress.

4. Obtain enough money to pay for the house. If you do not have enough cash, you must borrow more money. When you apply for a loan, you must provide the appraised value of the dwelling. This can be estimated using the information given in your plans. The first loan will be for construction of the house. After the house is finished, you can receive a long-term loan.

### Buying a New House

If you want a new house, but do not want to build it, you can buy a

5-11

*A contractor can help you choose the best materials for your house.*

Reflect: If your family did not build the home you currently live in, what changes would you recommend to make the home more suitable to your family? Explain your recommendations.

Discuss: Do you know anyone who found expensive problems in a house that were not noticeable when the house was purchased? If so, what did the problems involve?

recently built home. See 5-12. This process requires much less time than buying a lot and having a house built on it.

If a reputable builder builds the house, the workmanship will be guaranteed for a period of time, usually one to two years after completion. Some top builders guarantee their work for 5 to 10 years. Be sure to get the guarantee in writing for your protection.

Buying a new house has some unique advantages. One is that you can move in as soon as the deal is *closed*, or when all legal and financial matters have been settled. Another advantage is you can see the finished product before you buy. If you are a person who cannot visualize a finished house by studying the plans, you may prefer a new house already built.

### Buying a Pre-Owned House

For various reasons, many buyers choose previously occupied houses. The same amount of space usually costs less in a pre-owned house rather

than a new one. Often you can see how previous owners made use of the space. See 5-13. When you look at furnished rooms, you can get a better idea of how much usable space exists. This can help you visualize how your furniture will fit into the same space. Another bonus is that taxes in established communities are not likely to increase as rapidly as those in new areas.

Also, some items that usually do not come with a new house may be included with a pre-owned one. The previous owner usually leaves the window coverings and their hardware. The carpeting may also be left in the dwelling. The lot may have mature trees and shrubs. Fences, walls, and screens may have been added. These are costly in time, money, and effort if you add them yourself.

While you may find that some pre-owned houses are bargains, others are not. No house is perfect. You need to know the flaws before you buy. If you do not find out about the shortcomings until after you move in, it can be a shock. The shock becomes greater when you realize how much they cost to fix.

Before you sign a contract agreeing to buy a pre-owned house, you should check carefully. Look for serious defects, such as the following:

- A cracked foundation indicates that the house will probably sag or shift, which will weaken the structure.

- Rotten or sagging roofs, walls, or supports are signs of major construction defects or poor care. All are costly to repair.

- Insect damage may be serious enough to require major repairs. It may also mean defects exist that are not visible to the inexperienced observer.

5-12 _____

*Sometimes contractors build houses that are ready for sale.*

Enrich: Find a new housing development in your area that includes model homes. Tour the homes to see what features are included in the various models, the construction options available, and their prices.

Discuss: Do you prefer seeing rooms empty or already furnished when touring homes for sale? Do furnished models help you estimate how well your possessions will fit the space? Explain.

Less serious conditions can be repaired if you want to spend the time, money, and effort. Perhaps a window is broken, the roof needs repair, or the structure needs painting. Walls, ceilings, or floors may show slight damage, or the electrical wiring may be inadequate. The yard may appear shabby, needing major landscaping work.

To learn about any shortcomings ahead of time, you should have the house inspected. An *inspector* will judge the construction and present condition of the house. You should also have the house appraised before you buy it. The *appraiser* will give you an expert estimate of the quality and value of the property.

## Shopping for a Place to Buy

When you know what type of house you can afford and want, it is time to go shopping. You can locate a home through real estate firms, the Internet, and the real estate section of newspapers. Also, you can learn about homes for sale through word of mouth. Finally, you can ride through neighborhoods looking for sale signs. Each of these shopping methods is discussed more fully.

### Real Estate Firm

Real estate firms are in the business of selling land and buildings. They often advertise properties in free shopping guides and in the real estate section of newspapers, as in 5-14. More properties are listed in the real estate agent's catalog. Home seekers can learn about all the houses for sale through a *multiple listing service*. This service provides a combined list of all area houses listed for sale by real estate firms.

Oakwood Homes Corporation

5-13 _____

*A house may be easier to sell if shown with furnishings in place. This helps potential buyers imagine how their furniture will look in it.*

| Tom Hendrickson Real Estate |
| :---: |

**121 E. Main Street**
**OPEN HOUSE**
**Saturday and Sunday**
**May 22-23, 1-4 p.m.**
**$169,900**

Remodeled, updated, and delightful! 4-bedroom brick ranch with fireplace, 2 baths, utility room, 2 1/2 car garage, and large deck off master bedroom. Great layout. Quiet location plus a bonus—160-ft. lake frontage on South Lake. Get your fishing pole ready! Take Rt. 50 to Western. Turn west at 3rd Street, north at Walnut, east at Main Street. Signs are posted.

5-14 _____

*Advertisements in local newspapers can help you find real estate firms.*

Real estate agents can give you information about the community and neighborhood that you are considering. They can screen out places that would not appeal to you. Sometimes they can help you get financing.

Real estate agents charge a commission, or fee, for their services. The commission will range from 5 percent to 10 percent of the selling price. The seller usually pays the real estate fee. However, the price of the house may be raised to cover this cost.

### Internet Shopping

Houses for sale are also advertised on special TV programs and on the Internet. The *Internet* is the network linking thousands of computers from government agencies, businesses, educational institutions, groups, and individuals.

Internet home-shopping guides can include floor plans plus inside and outside shots of housing for sale. The viewer can search for real estate by specifying the number of bedrooms, the geographic area, and the price range sought. Prospective buyers can use this information to narrow down choices before spending the time to actually visit different units. See 5-15.

A service offered on some Internet sites is a *virtual tour*. The term comes

Apple Computer

5-15

*Searching real estate sites on the Internet can save house-hunting time and expenses.*

from the computer concept of *virtual reality*, which means experiencing a computer-generated image so completely that it seems real. Internet users can log onto selected sites and see 360-degree views or "walk" through each room.

Online services are available to help shoppers determine what they can afford and where to get a home loan. Some mortgage lenders offer home loans online. Home-finder sites provide additional information to buyers, such as the property tax rates for various areas as well as the location of schools.

### Newspapers

In addition to listings in newspapers by real estate firms, you may find homes that are for sale by the owner. This means that you buy directly from the owner. This also means that the price of the house is not inflated to cover the fees the seller must pay to a real estate agent.

However, you need to have a great deal of time and knowledge to shop on your own. If you do not have a knowledge of real estate deals, the mistakes you might make could be much more costly than any money you might save.

### Word-of-Mouth Publicity

When shopping for a house, you should not totally rely on real estate agents. Tell friends and acquaintances that you are looking for a home to buy. They may know about certain houses that you would like. They may even know some houses that will be offered for sale in the near future.

### *For Sale* Signs

Driving or walking past houses you like is a good way to become more familiar with a neighborhood in general. You may find a model house on display. You may also find places with *For Sale* signs that you overlooked in real estate ads. See 5-16. You may possibly find houses that are not advertised anywhere else.

As you look at houses and talk with people, keep a written record about each dwelling. Note the price and the location. Get the name and address of the owner. Write down the features of each house-number and size of the rooms, size of the lot, condition of the structure, and your reactions to it.

**Discuss:** What are some reasons for keeping a written record of homes or apartments that you visit?

5-16
*A real estate sign advertises that a house is for sale. A* sold *sign may be added while the sales transaction is being finalized.*

**Internet Activity:** Find a Web site that provides a virtual tour of a house for sale, preferably in your area. Share the Web address with your classmates. Discuss what computer-related real estate options might be available in 10 to 15 years.

**Writing Activity:** Write a description of a home viewed on a virtual tour, including details about one or more rooms. Describe the family that might choose to purchase and live in the home.

# Steps in Buying a House

After you find a house you want and agree to pay the listed price, you must settle many legal and financial matters. This is the point at which a lawyer's advice is needed in most cases. See 5-17. The long process begins with an agreement of sale.

### Agreement of Sale

When a buyer agrees to buy and a seller agrees to sell, they both sign a contract called an ***agreement of sale.*** The agreement of sale states all specific terms and conditions of the sale. This can also be called a *contract of purchase, purchase agreement,* or *sales agreement.* The agreement of sale is a legal document. Read all of the fine print before signing it.

The agreement of sale should include a detailed description of the real estate and its legal location. The total purchase price, the amount of the down payment, and the possession date of property should also be included. The agreement of sale should state that the sale will be complete only if the seller has clear title to the property.

Any specific terms and conditions of the sale should be spelled out in writing. For instance, an owner may agree to leave the draperies, carpeting, range, and refrigerator in the house. Each of these items should be listed in the agreement of sale. This way, the buyer knows exactly what he or she is buying. Other specific terms that should be explained are how the payment of property taxes will be divided and who bears the risk of loss to the property. Loss may occur as a result of fire, wind, and other disasters while the deal is being completed.

5-17
*Experts recommend homebuyers seek the advice of a lawyer before signing any papers.*

## Earnest Money

*Earnest money* is a deposit the potential buyer pays to show that he or she is serious about buying the house. The money is held in trust until the closing of the deal. When the deal goes through, the earnest money is applied toward the payment of the total price. If the buyer cannot get a loan, the money is refunded. The buyer may lose the earnest money if he or she backs out of the agreement.

## Abstract of Title

Before a buyer buys a house, he or she must be sure the seller is the legal owner. A lawyer or title insurance company reviews an *abstract of title*, which is a copy of all public records concerning the property. The abstract reveals the true legal owner and any debts that are held on the property. This is important since the buyer becomes responsible for any such debts when he or she becomes the owner of the property. Often, the buyer purchases title insurance for protection against financial loss caused by errors in the abstract of title.

## Survey

A professional survey is often required. This assures the lender of the home loan that the building is actually located on the land identified in the legal description.

## Securing a Mortgage

A *mortgage* is a pledge of property that a borrower gives to a lender as security for the payment of a debt. The lender is usually a bank, savings bank, or mortgage banker. The seller may also be the lender.

For years, the standard home mortgage was a long-term, fixed-rate loan. This means that the mortgage was usually written for 20 to 30 years with the interest rate and monthly payments constant. The three common fixed-rate mortgages are conventional, FHA-insured, and VA-guaranteed.

- A *conventional mortgage* is a two-party contract between a borrower and a lending firm. The government does not insure this type of mortgage.

- *FHA-insured mortgages* are three-party contracts that involve the borrower, a lending firm, and the Federal Housing Administration (FHA). This government agency is part of the U.S. Department of Housing and Urban Development (HUD). FHA does not make loans, but it insures the lender against the borrower's possible default. Anyone can apply for an FHA-insured loan by going to an approved lending institution. Compared to conventional loans, FHA-insured loans can often be secured with a smaller down payment.

- *VA-guaranteed mortgages* generally cost less than the other types of common, fixed-rate mortgages. They are three-party loans involving the borrower who is a veteran of the U.S. Armed Forces, a lending firm, and the Veterans Administration (VA). Veterans may apply for a VA-guaranteed loan at a lending institution. Their applications will be submitted to a VA office. Congress sets eligibility requirements. The VA does not require a down payment, but the lender may. The size of the down payment and the length of the repayment period are decided by the veteran and the lender.

Although conventional, FHA-insured, and VA-guaranteed

**Discuss:** Why is title insurance so important to homebuyers? (*It protects property buyers against financial loss caused by errors in the abstract of title, that is, against errors caused by buying property from someone who does not legally own it.*)

**Enrich:** Attend a presentation by a mortgage broker who explains all the different types of mortgages offered in your community. Be prepared to ask questions. Summarize in one paragraph what you learn.

**Interview Activity:** Find the Web site for Habitat for Humanity, and contact a representative to discuss the repayment options arranged for homeowners in the program.

mortgages are still popular, several alternative mortgages have come into existence. These alternatives keep lenders and borrowers from having to finance long-term mortgages at fixed interest rates. Lenders want greater flexibility, so they can keep up with changes in interest rates. Borrowers want affordable mortgages. Two plans, the adjustable rate mortgage and the renegotiable rate mortgage, provide alternatives.

- With an *adjustable rate mortgage*, the interest rate is adjusted up or down periodically according to a national interest rate index. Depending on interest rate changes, monthly payments may increase or decrease. However, some of these mortgages have rate caps. This means the interest rate will never exceed a certain rate regardless of the national interest rate index.

- In a *renegotiable rate mortgage*, sometimes called a *rollover mortgage*, the interest rate and monthly payments are fixed for a stated length of time. When this length of time expires, interest rates are reviewed and may be changed according to the current rate of interest. If the current interest rate is below the original one, monthly payments will decrease. If the current interest rate is higher, monthly payments will increase.

Other creative house financing plans are presented in 5-18. One type of creative financing is available to limited-income, first-time homebuyers who are involved in a homebuyer education and counseling program. Program counselors help these buyers secure financing after they attend buyer education classes, reduce personal debts, and maintain a good credit rating.

| Creative Home Financing | |
|---|---|
| **Type** | **Description** |
| *Balloon mortgage* | Monthly payments based on a fixed interest rate, usually short term. Payments may cover interest only, with principal due in full at term's end. |
| *Shared appreciation mortgage* | Below-market interest rate and lower monthly payments in exchange for a share of profits on a specified date or when property is sold. |
| *Assumable mortgage* | Buyer takes over seller's original, below-market interest rate mortgage. |
| *Land contract* | Seller retains original mortgage. No transfer of title until loan is fully paid. Equal monthly payments based on below-market interest rate with unpaid principal due at loan's end. |
| *Rent with option* | Renter pays an option fee for the right to purchase property at specified time and agreed-upon price. Rent may or may not be applied to sales price. |
| *Secondary financing* | Financing secured by the buyer to reduce the amount of funds required for down payment and/or closing costs. |

5-18

*Many creative house-financing plans are now available to meet the varying needs of buyers and sellers.*

**Vocabulary:** Explain a mortgage by answering the following questions: What is it? What five types are generally available to consumers? What are the advantages of a mortgage?

**Writing Activity:** Check local newspapers or banks to find out what types of mortgages are being advertised in your area. Write a paragraph to discuss your findings.

House financing alternatives vary from state to state and lender to lender. Research all the options to find the method of financing that is best for you.

## Foreclosure

Suppose you secure a mortgage and buy a house. It will probably be the largest purchase you ever make. You agree to make monthly payments for many years, usually decades. What would happen if you lost your job or became ill and could not make your mortgage payments?

Legally, the lender could foreclose your mortgage and take possession of the property. To recover the money you borrowed but cannot repay, the lender could then sell the property.

It is extremely important to notify your lender about problems that prevent you from making payments on time. If possible, make a personal visit to the lender to try to agree on an alternative payment plan until your situation improves. The possibility of losing your home is at stake. You may ask for an extension of time. Know your financial situation and be prepared to answer these questions:

- Why did you miss your payments?
- From where are you currently getting income?
- When will you begin payments again?
- When can you pay the payments you missed?

## Closing Costs

Before a real estate sale is final, fees and charges for settling the legal and financial matters must be paid. They are called *closing costs*. These closing costs can amount to several thousand dollars. The buyers should ask for an estimate of the cost and be sure to have enough money to pay for them. They can be paid by cash or check. Closing costs may include the following items:

- recording fees for the deed and mortgage
- attorney's fee or fee to a title company
- abstract of title and title insurance
- appraisal
- survey charge
- escrow fees. These are funds paid to an escrow agent to hold until a specified event occurs. After the event has occurred, the funds are released to designated people. In practice, this often means that when the homeowner makes mortgage payments, he or she pays an additional sum that is placed in a trust fund. This extra money is used to pay other expenses, such as taxes, insurance premiums, and special assessments.
- points. This refers to a type of interest paid to offset interest lost by the lender. One point equals one percent of the mortgage loan.
- origination fee. This fee is paid to the lender for processing the loan. It usually is one percent of the mortgage loan.
- miscellaneous fees. Other costs include flood insurance, termite inspection, a credit report, tax services, the underwriter's charge, and application fees.

The seller also has some closing costs. They may include the real estate commission and his or her share of the year's taxes, insurance, and any special assessments. The buyer and seller each pays the taxes, insurance, and special assessments for the portion of the year they own the property. The

**Enrich:** Research the foreclosure rate for the last 10 years. Is any specific pattern apparent? Does the foreclosure rate have any relationship to the health of the U.S. economy? Explain your findings.

**Vocabulary:** Review the items listed under "Closing Costs." List any you do not understand. Talk to a realtor or go to a Web site for a further explanation of each. Write a definition in your own words.

**Internet Activity:** Find an online mortgage lender and determine which of the fees commonly charged as "closing costs" are eliminated with an online purchase. Is the savings substantial enough to persuade you to consider obtaining a home mortgage through the

Internet? Find out what percentage of homes is financed through mortgages obtained on the Internet?

**Discuss:** After viewing a site such as *turbo-search.net*, discuss whether closing costs are always disclosed at the beginning of a transaction.

seller's closing costs may actually be higher than those of the buyer, but the price of the house may be raised to cover them.

### Title and Deed

When the sale is closed, the title is passed to the new owner. The *title* is a document that gives proof of the rights of ownership and possession of particular property. The legal document by which the title is transferred from one person to another is called a *deed.* The deed describes the property being sold. It is signed and witnessed according to the laws of the state where the property is located.

Several types of deeds are used to transfer property. A *general warranty deed*, 5-19, transfers the title of the

**WARRANTY DEED**
Statutory (ILLINOIS)

(Individual to Individual)

(The Above Space For Recorder's Use Only)

THE GRANTOR _____

of the _____ of _____ County of _____ State of _____
for and in consideration of _____ DOLLARS, in hand paid,

CONVEY ___ and WARRANT ___ to _____

of the _____ of _____ County of _____ State of _____
the following described Real Estate situated in the County of _____ in the State of Illinois, to wit:

hereby releasing and waiving all rights under and by virtue of the Homestead Exemption Laws of the State of Illinois.

DATED this _____ day of _____ ____

_____ (Seal)    _____ (Seal)

PLEASE
PRINT OR
TYPE NAME(S)
BELOW
SIGNATURE(S)                 _____ (Seal)    _____ (Seal)

State of Illinois, County of _____ ss.    I, the undersigned, a Notary Public in and for said County, in the State aforesaid, DO HEREBY CERTIFY that _____

personally known to me to be the same person___ whose name_____
IMPRESS    subscribed to the foregoing instrument, appeared before me this day in person,
SEAL    and acknowledged that ___ h___ signed, sealed and delivered the said instrument
HERE    as_____ free and voluntary act, for the uses and purposes therein set forth, including the release and waiver of the right of homestead.

Given under my hand and official seal, this_____ day of _____

Commission expires _____ ____ _____
                                                                          NOTARY PUBLIC

ADDRESS OF PROPERTY:

MAIL TO: { (Name) (Address)    THE ABOVE ADDRESS IS FOR STATISTICAL PURPOSES ONLY AND IS NOT A PART OF THIS DEED.
SEND SUBSEQUENT TAX BILLS TO:
(City, State and Zip)    (Name)

OR    RECORDER'S OFFICE BOX NO _____    (Address)

AFFIX "RIDERS" OR REVENUE STAMPS HERE

5-19
*A general warranty deed transfers the title of the property to the new owners and guarantees the title is clear of any claims.*

property to the buyer. It guarantees that the title is clear of any claims against it. If any mortgage, tax, or title claims are made against the property, the buyer may hold the seller liable for them. This type of deed offers the greatest legal protection to the buyer.

A *special warranty deed* also transfers the title to the buyer. However, it guarantees that during the time the seller held the title to the property, the seller did nothing that would, or will in the future, impair the buyer's title.

A *quitclaim deed* transfers whatever interest the seller has in the property. By accepting such a deed, the buyer assumes all legal and financial risks for the property.

### Insurance

A house is a big financial undertaking. Homeowners insurance or property insurance can help protect the homeowner's investment. Most mortgage holders require the house buyer to protect the house from loss with insurance against fire and other hazards. Several types of coverage are available. See 5-20.

### Refinancing

At some point after you purchase a house, you may decide to refinance your mortgage. The main reasons people refinance are to lower monthly payments or to take advantage of lower interest rates. Other reasons for refinancing include making house improvements and paying for expenses, such as college tuition.

You may need to lower monthly payments because you are having trouble meeting present payments. Using the equity in your house may allow you to get a loan with smaller payments that are spread over a longer period of time. Even though your payments are lower, refinancing

for this reason probably won't save you money. Many times, it costs you more in the long run. In an emergency, however, refinancing can be an alternative to foreclosure.

You can refinance to save money if the current interest rate drops one percent or more below your rate. If you decide to refinance for this reason, shop for the best deal. Start with the institution carrying your present mortgage. By staying with them you may eliminate some costs, such as closing costs. Another institution would need to charge these fees. If you plan to live in the house long enough, refinancing can be worthwhile. Before making a decision about refinancing, get the answers to the following questions:

- Is there a prepayment penalty? Will paying the old mortgage early cost more?
- Is a title search, appraisal, survey, or inspection required? How much will they cost?
- Are there other costs?
- Who pays the recording and escrow fees?
- How much will monthly payments change?
- How many months will it take to recover the cost of refinancing?

# Condominium Ownership

Buying a condominium unit is similar to buying any other house. You will need to choose a location you like and a unit you can afford. You must decide between a new and pre-owned unit. You will probably work with either a real estate agent or developer. You will sign an agreement of sale,

| Homeowner's Insurance Policy | |
|---|---|
| **Basic Coverage** | |
| *Fire and extended coverage hazards* | • Lightening and fire, including fire department charges<br>• Sudden smoke damage from faulty heating or cooking unit<br>• Wind, tornado, and hail<br>• Explosion, riot<br>• Damage by aircraft<br>• Damage to insured person's property by another' vehicle |
| *Theft, vandalism, and glass coverage* | • Vandalism<br>• Theft, burglary, robbery<br>• Breakage of glass, constituting part of a building |
| *Comprehensive family liability insurance* | • Claims for injuries to guests, tradesmen, and others<br>• Claims for damage to property of others<br>• All costs of the suit whether you are liable or not<br>• Medical expenses of persons injured, liable or not<br>• Damage to property of others, liable or not |
| **Additional Types of Coverage** | |
| *General* | • Unrestricted explosion, including heating system rupture<br>• Damage by own cars<br>• Broad smoke damage<br>• Falling object from outside source<br>• Weight of ice, snow, or sleet<br>• Collapse<br>• Water escape from heating or plumbing systems<br>• Hot water heater loss by rupture, cracking, and so forth<br>• Freezing of plumbing or heating systems<br>• Electrical injury except tubes, transistors, and so forth |
| *Broad theft coverage (optional)* | • Theft of boats even when unattended<br>• Theft of cars even when unattended |

Cumis Insurance Society, Inc.

5-20

*The basic coverage offered in this homeowner's insurance policy is shown in the main part of the house. Additional types of coverage are shown in the "chimney."*

make a down payment, secure a mortgage, pay closing costs, and sign a deed.

Condominium owners have the same financial advantages conventional homeowners have. They are investing in real estate and can take advantage of certain income tax deductions. They also build equity in their property.

**Enrich:** Attend a presentation by an insurance agent who discusses the insurance options available for homeowners. Be prepared to ask questions. Summarize in one paragraph what you learn.

**Art Activity:** Draw symbols depicting the various types of insurance described in Figure 5-20.

Condominium units are usually less expensive to build than freestanding, single-family houses. However, because of the extras you buy, the price may be high. Extras may include access to recreational facilities such as a clubhouse, swimming pool, and tennis courts, as shown in 5-21.

You will want to approach the purchase of a condominium unit carefully. First, be sure to read the *declaration of ownership.* It contains the conditions and restrictions of the sale, ownership, and use of the property within a particular group of condominium units. Check to see that you can sell your unit at any time and that you are liable for only the mortgage and taxes for your unit. Then, find out who has control of the management of the units.

Finally, get a detailed breakdown of your monthly payments. Besides mortgage payments and taxes, you must pay utilities, insurance, and maintenance fees. Maintenance fees are used for the repair and maintenance of the common areas of the condominium. See 5-22. They vary widely and are usually subject to change. Check to see that the fee seems reasonable.

# Cooperative Ownership

Buying a cooperative unit is different from buying a house. The first step, finding a unit, may be the most difficult one. Although the concept of

**Discuss:** What is the purpose of condominium maintenance fees? (*to pay for upkeep of the common areas*)

5-21 _____
*A tennis court may be part of the common-use area when a condominium unit is the buyer's choice.*

**Discuss:** What is a *common area* of a condominium? *(an area that can be used by all members, such as a clubhouse, swimming pool, and tennis courts)*

**Activity:** Study the expenses involved in maintaining a home, such as the yard and housing exterior, by talking to someone who pays these bills. Find out what some common bills average and what to budget monthly for these items.

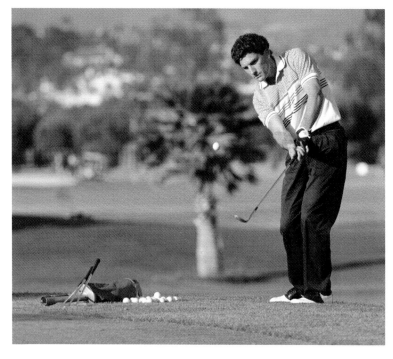

5-22

*Whether you use them or not, common areas in condominium complexes involve upkeep expenses that are paid by all condo owners in the complex. The fee is usually monthly.*

**Vocabulary:** Write sentences or a series of paragraphs using at least 10 of the chapter's "To Know" terms.

cooperative dwellings is growing in popularity, relatively few exist today.

The legal and financial aspects of cooperative housing are unique. When a corporation buys an entire building, or a lot to begin a cooperative housing project, it secures a mortgage on the property. When you move into a cooperative building, you cannot get a mortgage. This is because you are buying stock, not real estate. In many cases, you will need to pay the full price of the stock in cash. However, you will not pay closing costs, since you are dealing directly with the corporation.

The tax advantages of living in a cooperative unit are different from those for other types of house ownership. In a cooperative situation, the corporation owns the building. It pays real estate taxes and makes the mortgage payments. As a stockholder, you can deduct from your income tax a certain portion of what the corporation pays in real estate taxes and mortgage interest.

When you live in a cooperative dwelling, you will pay a monthly fee. This money is used for maintenance and taxes. It is also used to make the corporation's mortgage payments on the property. If some residents were to fail to pay this for any length of time, the corporation might be unable to make mortgage payments and, therefore, face the possibility of foreclosure. Because of this risk, check the financial stability of the corporation before you buy any stock.

**Discuss:** How does ownership of a cooperative unit differ from ownership of a single-family dwelling or condominium? (*With a cooperative unit, you purchase stock, not the actual dwelling.*)

**Activity:** Create a crossword puzzle of recreational options provided by various condominiums and cooperatives. Use software you have or a Web site such as *webgamestogo.com/creat_fs.htm.*

# Summary

When acquiring a house there are various processes and costs involved. You must determine how much you will spend and how you will finance your house.

You may decide to rent your housing. Any type of dwelling can be rented, but the most common types are multifamily dwellings. Carefully inspect the dwelling you choose before you sign a lease. It is also important to know about assigning or subletting, breach of contract, and eviction.

If you decide to buy, it is important to know how much you can spend. There are several methods to help you determine this. Then, decide which you want to do: have a house built, buy a new house already built, or buy a pre-owned house.

Once you have decided what type of house you want, shop for one that is right for you. You may use a real estate agent or shop on your own. After you have found the house, follow the correct steps for purchasing a house. This includes securing a mortgage and paying the closing costs. If you should need to refinance your house, you will need to go through many of the same steps again.

Instead of buying a single-family dwelling, you may choose to buy a condominium unit or shares in a cooperative. When choosing a condominium unit, carefully read the declaration of ownership and understand what maintenance fees are required. When choosing a cooperative unit, understand the unique legal and financial aspects of the corporation and make sure it is financially stable.

**Resource:** *Housing Selection,* reproducible master 5-4, TR. Students work in small groups to list the pros and cons of each housing choice and share their responses with the class.

**Resource:** *The Details of Acquiring Housing,* Activity F, SAG. Students complete statements about housing by filling in the blanks.

# To Review

1. List four advantages of renting a house.

2. Name eight items a written lease should include.

3. True or false. When you sublet your apartment, you are no longer responsible for it.

4. If a renter fails to pay rent, the landlord could sue him or her for _____.

5. What is a general way to determine the cost of a house that a person or family can afford?

6. As the new owner of a mortgaged house, decide which of the following items should be considered when figuring your monthly housing costs.

   A. income tax
   B. mortgage loan payments
   C. house insurance payments
   D. heating bill
   E. car payments
   F. real estate taxes
   G. maintenance allowance

**Answer Key**

1. (List four:) less expensive than buying, more freedom to move, no worry about property's value or buying and selling concerns, clear idea of total housing costs, no responsibility for repairs, no expenses for home improvements

2. (List eight. See pages 125 and 131.)

3. false

4. breach of contract

5. multiply annual gross income by 2 ½

6. B, C, D, F, G

**Activity:** Working with another student, alternate talking for 30 seconds apiece about what the chapter covered. Together, write a summary of the concepts in the chapter.

7. An appraiser will tell you _____.
   A. the houses available for sale
   B. if your mortgage is accepted or rejected
   C. how much a particular house is worth
8. Name five items included in an agreement of sale.
9. Why should the buyer of a house purchase title insurance?
10. Give one characteristic each of a fixed-rate, adjustable rate, and negotiable rate mortgage.
11. List two reasons for refinancing.
12. How are the terms *title* and *deed* related?
13. When you purchase a condominium, you buy _____.
    A. stock in a corporation
    B. your individual unit
    C. your individual unit and an undivided interest in all common areas

# In Your Community

1. Visit an apartment building and ask the landlord for a copy of the lease used. Does it include all the important points listed in this chapter? Does it include any additional restrictions?
2. Find a classified ad in your local newspaper offering a house for sale. Investigate the monthly cost of buying it using three different types of loans.
3. Ask the manager of a condominium complex for a copy of the declaration of ownership for the units. Examine it closely. Explain to the class the advantages and disadvantages of condominium ownership.

# To Think About

1. Suppose someone broke into your apartment and stole your computer and an expensive CD player you borrowed from a friend. If you had renter's insurance, what do you think you could you recover in costs from the theft? What could you recover without insurance?
2. When home inspectors evaluate a home that is about to be purchased, perhaps there are problems in the foundation, heating system, or windows. Do you think the new owner should fix the items? Why or why not?

# Using Technology

1. Check out available houses on the Internet by searching *real estate*. Select a geographic area, number of bedrooms, and a price range on a home-finder Web site. How many choices did you find? What types of information can be learned about an individual house?

2. Take a virtual tour of a home offered on the Internet. Are these tours realistic? Would shopping online help you make a decision about where to look for a place to live?

**Note:** For researching virtual tours of homes, have students explore *realtor.com*.

3. Using information from class and other sources, develop a chart showing the advantages and disadvantages of buying each of the following types of housing:

   A. pre-owned house
   B. newly built house ready for occupancy
   C. new house yet to be custom-built

4. Using a word processing program, develop a chart showing the information you gathered and share it with your class.

5. Find a mortgage calculator on the Internet and enter a house purchase, down payment amount, and an interest rate. Then enter a higher interest rate and determine the monthly payment cost. Determine what happens to the monthly payment when the interest rate is increased. Is it better to have a low interest rate or a high interest rate in terms of being able to pay for the home?

**Note:** For researching interest rates, have students explore *realtor.com*.

**Portfolio Project:** Develop a plan for selecting and renting an apartment. Include guidelines for conducting a search, reviewing your housing options, reviewing your housing rights and responsibilities, and examining the required contracts.

PART 3

# From the Ground Up

Chapter 6
**The Evolution of Exteriors**

Chapter 7
**Understanding House Plans**

Chapter 8
**House Construction**

Chapter 9
**The Systems Within**

C H A P T E R   6

# The Evolution of Exteriors

## To Know

Native Americans
Traditional
Folk
Classic
Spanish
stucco
asymmetrical
Scandinavian
log cabin
gable roof
German
pent roof
Early English
Tidewater South
New England
Cape Cod
symmetrical
saltbox
garrison
Dutch Colonial
gambrel roof
French Normandy
French Plantation
French Manor
Mansard roof
French Provincial
Georgian
hip roof
Federal
Greek Revival
Southern Colonial
Victorian
Modern style
Prairie style
International style
bungalow
ranch
Contemporary style
solar energy
earth-sheltered

Pozzi Wood Windows®

## Objectives

After studying this chapter, you will be able to

- identify Traditional (both folk and classic), Modern, and Contemporary exterior house styles.
- discuss the background of housing styles and current trends.

Housing in North America began with the *Native Americans*, who are also known as American Indians. They developed a wide variety of housing styles prior to the arrival of foreign explorers and settlers. The styles included hogans, pueblos, teepees, wigwams, pole-and-thatch structures, and others. When settlers arrived in North America, they brought with them the styles that existed in their homelands. Over time, these styles evolved into new types of housing that have become known as traditional styles.

# Traditional Houses

*Traditional* houses reflect the experiences and traditions of past eras. These designs have adapted and changed over time to meet the needs of their inhabitants. Many house designs used today actually were created in the past. Each style has distinct characteristics that set it apart from the others.

The two categories of Traditional style design are Folk and Classic. *Folk* is a style originating from the common experiences of a group of people. *Classic* is a style that represents the authentic repetition of architecture with enduring excellence.

## Traditional Folk Houses

The styles of traditional folk houses varied from region to region. In some cold areas such as the Midwest, houses had to withstand heavy snowfalls. In warm climates such as the Southeast, orientation to the cooling breeze was important. In windy locations such as the coastal Northeast, housing needed to withstand heavy gusts.

Besides the effects of climate and geographical location, traditional folk housing was based on the ethnic experiences and lifestyles of the inhabitants. These housing styles were also shaped by the natural resources available to construct them. Styles described as Native American, Spanish, Scandinavian, German, Early English, Dutch, and French are types of traditional folk houses.

### Native American

The many different styles of Native American housing have influenced today's housing. Early settlers sometimes copied the eight-sided mud and log hogans of the Navajo or the wood frame structures of the Seminole. Refer back to Figure 2-1 in Chapter 2, "Influences on Housing," to see widely varied styles of Native American housing.

The Pueblo in New Mexico still live in apartment-type adobe dwellings. See 6-1. The basic design used in these adobe dwellings is

David Muench

6-1

*The Pueblo live in these adobe dwellings.*

**Resource:** *From the Ground Up*, transparency master III-A, TR. Students look back at the topics covered in Chapters 1-5 and look ahead to the topics they will cover in Chapter 6.
**Note:** An assortment of housing photos or drawings will be very helpful for teaching this chapter. Have an assistant clip them from old magazines or books.
**Example:** Figure 2-1 is on page 45.
**Enrich:** Investigate the process of constructing a home of adobe. Make a presentation to the class, using visuals to clarify the process.

**Vocabulary:** Pick one term from the vocabulary list, write it on the board, and link it to one of the chapter objectives. (Note: Successive students should repeat the process until the only terms left pose difficulty to all students.)

**Activity:** Quickly sketch a drawing of your favorite style of housing or find a photo in a magazine. As you go through this chapter, compare it to the drawings and photos in the lesson. Identify exterior features of the design you prefer.

**Writing Activity:** Write a paragraph describing the characteristics that make the photo in Figure 6-2 a traditional Spanish style house.

copied in housing throughout the country, especially the Southwest. Pueblo housing is characterized by boxlike construction, flat roofs, and projecting roof beams.

## Spanish

A large portion of what is now the southwestern United States was under Spanish, then Mexican, control from the seventeenth to the mid-nineteenth century. Spanish Texas gained its

6-2

*This house includes many of the traits of the traditional Spanish style house.*

Fern Mountain Historic Homestead

6-3

*The original log cabins looked very similar to this one.*

independence from Mexico in 1836, and Florida was under mostly Spanish control from 1565 to 1821.

The *Spanish* style developed in these areas where the climate was warm. Early Spanish style was characterized by one-story structures with flat or low-pitched red tile roofs. The houses were masonry construction of adobe brick or stone covered in stucco. *Stucco* is a type of plaster applied to the exterior walls of a house.

The overall design of Spanish style housing is *asymmetrical*. This means that one side of the center point is different from the other. A Spanish-style house is pictured in 6-2. Specific features include courtyards, enclosed patios, wrought iron exterior decor, and arch-shaped windows and doors. This style of housing is still widely used today in the Southwest.

## Scandinavian

Immigrants from Sweden, Finland, Norway, and Denmark were known as *Scandinavians*. They brought to North America the log cabin, which originated in Europe. The *log cabin* originally was a one-room house made from bulky pieces of unshaped lumber. It was a popular style for the North American frontier, where timber was a readily available resource for a building material.

Typical log cabins were built of unfinished logs as small, one-story rectangular buildings with few windows and gable roofs. *Gable roofs* come to a high point in the center and slope on both sides. See 6-3. Log cabins are still popular today in many areas as either a primary residence or as a second home used for vacations. Many companies specializing in manufactured log cabins offer a wide range of floor plans and price ranges. They meet the need that many homeowners have for a rustic or simpler lifestyle.

**Discuss:** Why do you think the log cabin has evolved into the modern log homes that are popular today?

**Vocabulary:** Sketch a drawing that shows the meaning of the term *asymmetrical*.

## German

The majority of early *German* settlers, who traveled from the region called Germany today, arrived in North America in the late seventeenth century. They primarily settled in what is now southeastern Pennsylvania. They built large, durable homes of wood and fieldstone for warmth. The houses were constructed to have gable roofs. See 6-4. Some also had small roof ledges between the first and second floors called *pent roofs*.

## Early English

An architectural style built by English settlers in North America beginning in the early 1600s is *Early English*. Several distinct housing styles evolved from this traditional folk style. They include the styles known as Tidewater South and New England. New England styles include Cape Cod, saltbox, and garrison.

### Tidewater South

Tidewater areas are low-lying coastal lands. *Tidewater South* is an architectural style built by early English settlers in the southern coastal

regions of what is now the United States. The first English settlement in North America was established in 1607 in Jamestown, Virginia.

The earliest homes built in this Southern tidewater area were simple, one-room wooden buildings with a wood or stone chimney at one end. As families grew, house additions were built. The first addition was another room, often built as large as the first. It was added next to the wall with the chimney. See 6-5. Many rural farmhouses throughout the South had similar plans. Covered porches were also added to these simple plans to increase the amount of living area and shelter it from the hot sun.

### New England

The region of North America known as *New England* now includes the states of Maine, New Hampshire, Vermont, Massachusetts, Connecticut, and Rhode Island. Early seventeenth century English settlers in northern New England commonly built two-story houses. They were constructed

Pennsylvania Dutch Convention and Visitors Bureau

6-4

*Germans who settled in Pennsylvania built houses similar to this.*

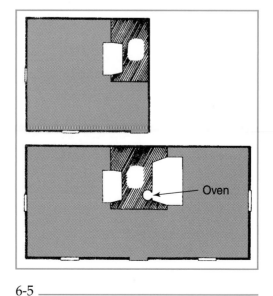

— Oven

6-5

*Colonists made their houses larger by adding a room on the other side of the chimney.*

Clois Kicklighter

6-6

*The Cape Cod is a one-and-a-half-story house with a gable roof and central entrance.*

Western Wood Products Association

6-7

*A saltbox house has narrow wood siding and windows without shutters.*

of heavy timber frames covered with boards and shingles. Some one-story houses were also built. As a family grew, rooms were added to the basic plan. This is how the Cape Cod house design was created.

■ **Cape Cod.** The *Cape Cod* is a small, symmetrical, one-and-one-half story house with a gable roof. A design is **symmetrical** when identical objects are arranged on both sides of a center point, as shown in 6-6. The Cape Cod style has a central entrance and a central chimney with several fireplaces. The eave line of the roof is just above the first floor windows. The windows usually have shutters.

Usually the loft area of the Cape Cod is expanded and made into finished bedrooms. Openings are then cut in the roof for dormers. *Dormers* are structures that project through a sloping roof and contain a window in the second story. They add light and air to the second story.

■ **Saltbox.** Another style home built by the English settlers in the New England area was the saltbox house. The **saltbox** is a variation of the Cape Cod. See 6-7. Adding a lean-to section to the back of the house created it. The name *saltbox* comes from the shape of the boxes that were used at the time to store salt.

Saltbox houses are two or two-and-one-half stories high and usually constructed of wood. They have steep gable roofs that extend down to the first floor in the rear. A large central chimney and large windows with small panes of glass are other typical features.

■ **Garrison.** A later design built by the English settlers in New England was the **garrison** house, which is named after early garrisons, or forts. Like the old forts, they have an overhanging second story. See 6-8. The overhang allows extra space on the second floor without widening the foundation. It also has a supporting effect, which prevents the second-story floor from sagging in the middle. This supporting effect is created when beams extending out from the first floor support the second floor. The farther the beams extend out, the greater is the support in the center.

The overhang is always on the front of the house and sometimes extends to the sides and rear. Carved drops or pendants below the overhang provide ornamentation. Other characteristics of the garrison house are symmetrical design, a steep gable roof, and windows that have small panes of glass.

### Dutch

Dutch settlers founded settlements in North America as early as 1614 in what is now known as Albany, New York. A later settlement began in 1626 in New Amsterdam, which became New York City. The first Dutch houses were one-story structures of brick in urban areas, or stone in rural areas. One of the most important characteristics was the front door, which was divided in half horizontally. This style became known as the *Dutch door.* However, it was the later design by the Dutch that left their mark on architecture.

The later style is known as Dutch Colonial. Houses of this style were often built of fieldstone or brick, sometimes wood, in New York and Delaware. The Dutch did not bring this style from their homeland, but created it after settling in this country. *Dutch Colonial* is a housing style with a gambrel roof. A *gambrel roof* has

Massachusetts Office of Travel & Tourism

6-8

*This garrison style house, which was originally owned by Paul Revere, features an overhanging second story.*

eaves that flare outward. Sometimes the flared portion extends over an open porch, which is known as the *Dutch kick.* Other characteristics of the Dutch Colonial are dormers, a central entrance, an off-center chimney, and windows with small panes. See 6-9.

### French

During the colonial period, French settlements formed in the 1700s along the St. Lawrence River, Great Lakes, and Mississippi River. Early French homes were the **French Normandy** style, which was brought to North America by the Huguenots. These were one-story structures with many narrow door and window openings. The roofs were steeply pitched and either hipped or side-gabled. The walls were stucco, which was usually applied over a half-timbered frame. Porches were added in settlements located in warmer regions. Also, houses in the South were constructed on posts one story above ground. This

Discuss: Name the Traditional Folk housing styles that are Early English styles. (*Tidewater South and the New England styles of Cape Cod, saltbox, and garrison*)

Vocabulary: What is a synonym for *garrison*? (*fort*) Identify the key feature of this housing style. (*overhanging second story*)

Discuss: Describe the walls of the early French Normandy style of housing that was built around major waterways in central and northeastern U.S. regions. (*Stucco was usually applied over a half-timbered frame.*)

Discuss: Describe the unique feature of the French Normandy style of housing commonly built in humid southern areas. (*Homes were built on posts one-story above ground to protect against humidity and floods.*)

H. Armstrong Roberts

6-9

*This new home has features used in original Dutch Colonial homes such as a gambrel roof that flares at the bottom and dormer windows.*

Pennsylvania Historical and Museum Commission

6-10

*French Manor houses are noted for their stately appearance and Mansard roofs.*

Discuss: Name the Traditional Folk housing styles that are French styles. (*French Normandy, French Plantation, Louisiana French, French Manor, and French Provincial*)

provided better air circulation in the humid environment and protected the house from floods. The Southern adaptation of this design is known as the *French Plantation* house.

A distinctive style evolved in New Orleans known as the *Louisiana French* style. The most outstanding characteristics of this style include balconies with elaborate ironwork railings and white stucco walls. The structures are built on a raised brick or stone basement to protect the houses in the case of a flood.

Even after Louisiana became the eighteenth state in the Union in 1812, the French influence continued to impact American architecture in many ways. One example is the *French Manor.* These are symmetrical homes with wings on each side and a Mansard roof on the main part of the house. See 6-10. A *Mansard roof* is a variation of the gambrel roof. It was designed by a French architect named Mansard. When used on detached single-family dwellings, the roof continues all around the house. Dormers often project from the steeply pitched part of the roof. When used on commercial buildings, the Mansard roof may be used only on one or two sides.

French influence is also seen in the house style called *French Provincial*. This style was introduced to New Orleans and became popular all over the country. It has a delicate, dignified appearance and is usually symmetrical. The windows are a dominant part of the design. The tops of the windows break into the eave line. A French Provincial house can be as tall as two-and-a-half stories. See 6-11.

## Classic Traditional Houses

As the early settlements flourished and colonies and states were formed,

Discuss: What are the differences in the gambrel roof pictured in Figure 6-9 and the Mansard roof of Figure 6-11? (*The gambrel roof is more rounded, comes to an obvious center ridge, and slopes on two sides of the house. The Mansard roof is boxier, appears flat on top, and slopes on all four sides of the house.*)

prosperity brought change and improvement to housing. The quality of building materials improved and the growth of trade brought new information to the settlers. Architects and house plans from Europe became available. Classic traditional homes include the following styles: Georgian, Federal, Greek Revival, Southern Colonial, and Victorian.

## Georgian

The Georgian style was adapted from English architecture. It is called Georgian because it was popular during the era when Kings George I, II, and III ruled England.

*Georgian* houses have simple exterior lines, dignified appearances, and symmetry. They have windows with small panes of glass and either gable or *hip roofs*, which are roofs with sloping ends and sides. Hip roofs are sometimes topped by a flat area with a *balustrade*, or railing. This area is called a captain's or widow's walk. Georgian houses usually have a tall chimney at each end of the roof, and most have some ornamentation under the eaves. See 6-12.

As the style developed, it became more elaborate. Additional ornamentation was given to doors and windows. The style also changed according to the region in which it was built. Wood was used in New England, and stone in the Mid-Atlantic region. In the South, brick was used and a wing was added to each side of the main house.

## Federal

Following the American Revolution, Federal style architecture became popular. A house built in the *Federal* style has a boxlike shape, is symmetrical, and at least two stories high. The roof is flat and surrounded

Camerique

6-11

*French Provincial houses are usually symmetrical with a formal appearance.*

Photograph by Thomas A. Heinz, Copyright 1993

6-12

*Georgian houses have simple, dignified lines with ornamentation often found under the eaves.*

by a balustrade. Sometimes a small portico is added to the main entrance. A *portico* is an open space covered with a roof that is supported by columns. Federal-style houses also have *pediments*, which are architectural rooflike decorations that are usually found over a portico, window, or door. See 6-13. The pediments can be segmental or triangular. See 6-14.

## Greek Revival

Another style of classic traditional design is called *Greek Revival*. It developed during a period when the architectural elements found in ancient Greek architecture were carefully duplicated.

6-13
*This building was built with a balustrade, portico, and pediments.*

The main characteristic of the Greek Revival style is a two-story portico. The portico is supported by Greek columns and has a large triangular pediment. See 6-15. Houses of this style are large and impressive. Some government buildings are designed in the Greek Revival style.

## Southern Colonial

An offshoot of the Greek Revival style is the Southern Colonial. The *Southern Colonial* is a large, two- or three-story frame house of symmetrical design. See 6-16. Two-story columns extend across the entire front, covered by an extension of the roof. The roof style is hip or gable. Dormers, shutters, and a belvedere are often included. A *belvedere* is a small room on the roof of a house used as a lookout.

## Victorian

Following the Civil War, the *Victorian* house style became popular. It is named after Queen Victoria of England. The main feature of this housing style is an abundance of decorative trim. Other characteristics are high porches, steep gable roofs, tall windows, high ceilings, dark stairways, long halls, and a *turret*, which is a small tower. This style came to be associated with the haunted houses of horror movies.

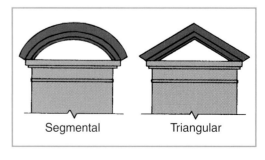

Segmental    Triangular

6-14
*Pediments are used over doors and windows to add interest to a design.*

As the style developed, owners tried to outdo one another in the amount of decorative trim on their houses. Quantity became more important than quality. Scrolls and other decorative trim made from wood appeared under eaves and around windows and doors. This came to be known as *gingerbread*. See 6-17.

# Modern Houses

The housing designs developed in the United States from the early 1900s into the 1960s are classified as the *Modern style*. Compared to the other housing styles discussed so far, these are quite new. Modern styles include the Prairie style, the International style, and the bungalow, ranch, and split-level. All are very popular and will probably continue to be used in the future.

## Prairie Style

Frank Lloyd Wright, who is one of the most noted architects of modern times, designed the Prairie style house. Wright is considered the greatest figure in modern American architecture. He designed a series of Prairie style houses between 1900 and 1910 that were very different from the traditional architecture built before this period. See 6-18.

*Prairie style* houses have strong horizontal lines. Wright liked to create the illusion that the house had actually evolved from the site. To accomplish this, he had the homes constructed with wood, stone, and materials found in the natural environment. The colors used were all earth tones.

Previous architectural styles had used walls to divide interior space into boxlike rooms. Wright reduced the number of walls to allow one room to

Photograph by Thomas A. Heinz, Copyright 1993

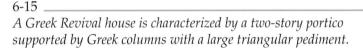
6-15
*A Greek Revival house is characterized by a two-story portico supported by Greek columns with a large triangular pediment.*

Oak Alley Plantation, Louisiana Office of Tourism
6-16
*The design of this Southern Colonial evolved from the Greek Revival style.*

flow into another. In addition, the interior space visually flows outdoors through porches, terraces, and windows. His flexible use of space greatly influenced the design work of European architects.

**Discuss:** When were the Modern style house designs created? (*in the twentieth century*)

**Note:** For more information on Frank Lloyd Wright, check the Web at cypgrp.com/flw/.
**Discuss:** What are some influences Frank Lloyd Wright left on American architecture? (*outdoor/indoor spaces that flow together, no boxlike rooms, addition of porches and terraces, an exterior design that blends well with the natural surroundings, and a use of materials found in nature*)
**Enrich:** Research Prairie style architecture and the remaining homes that most exemplify it. Where are they located? Find out what influences shaped Wright's development of the style.

Kindra Clineff, Massachusetts Office of Travel & Tourism

6-17 —————————————————

*Excessive ornamentation called gingerbread is found on Victorian houses.*

## International Style

The most dramatic architectural style during the Modern movement was the *International style.* It is a style of architecture and furniture design that began in the 1900s, influenced strongly by Bauhaus. Bauhaus was the German state school of design that merged art and technology. It focused on emphasizing the simplicity of design and eliminating unnecessary elements.

International style is a blend of ideas from four leading architects of the early twentieth century:

- Frank Lloyd Wright
- Walter Gropius, a famous German architect and founder of the Bauhaus School
- Ludwig Mies van der Rohe, another famous German architect and director of the Bauhaus School
- Le Corbusier, a famous French architect

Geometric shapes and large expanses of glass windows were the foremost features of U.S. houses built in the International style. Many of these houses were constructed of reinforced white concrete. Flat roofs with

Larry G. Morris

6-18 —————————————————

*The many porches, terraces, and windows of this house designed by Frank Lloyd Wright are characteristic of the Prairie style.*

**Discuss:** Note the gingerbread trim in Figure 6-17. What do you think this type of trim does to the cost of a home? Explain.

**Enrich:** Research the artistic contributions of Walter Gropius, Ludwig Mies van der Rohe, or Le Corbusier to International style housing. Provide pictures that show examples of the architect's work and display his unique contributions.

American Plywood Association

6-19 _____

*This home is an example of the International style of architecture.*

garden areas were also common. The exteriors of the houses had little or no ornamentation. See 6-19.

## Bungalow

A *bungalow* is a small, one-story house with a low-pitched roof and front, covered porch. Sometimes the porch is enclosed. The bungalow is usually made of wood or brick. The shingled roof extends beyond the walls. Windows are set high so furniture can be placed beneath them. See 6-20. The California Bungalow is similar in design but larger.

## Ranch

A *ranch* house is a one-story structure that may have a basement. It has a low-pitched roof with a wide

Virginia Crossno

6-20 _____

*Bungalows typically have low-pitched roofs and covered porches.*

Discuss: If building a home for yourself, would you add a basement? Explain why or why not. For what type of homes do you think basements are most appropriate?

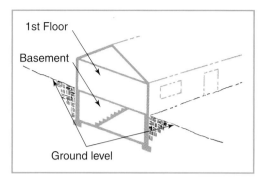

6-21

*Some ranch houses have basements that are entirely underground.*

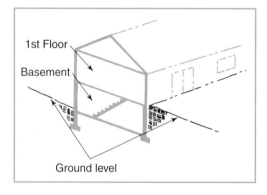

6-22

*Ranch-style houses began in the West on farms and ranches where space was plentiful. Now they are found in many communities.*

6-23

*Part of the basement of a hillside ranch is aboveground level.*

overhang. Large windows and sliding glass doors that open onto a patio are common. See 6-21. The use of building materials and energy-saving features vary according to each region. For instance, light-colored siding and paint are used to reflect the heat in warm climates. Brick is another common exterior siding choice.

The ranch style began in the West. The informal lifestyle, large plots of land, and generally warm climate made the ranch style ideal for the region. See 6-22. Ranch style homes have since become popular throughout the country.

Ranch houses vary considerably in size. Small ranch houses may be relatively inexpensive to build, while larger sizes can be expensive. This is due to the large foundations and costly roof areas. Larger ranch style houses are less energy efficient than more compact house plans.

One-story ranch houses are easy to maneuver through and maintain. Such structures are regaining popularity as seniors seek homes with all rooms on one level in an effort to eliminate climbing stairs. One-story ranch houses are also a good choice for incorporating universal design.

There are many variations of the ranch style. One is the *hillside ranch*. As its name implies, the house is built on a hill. It has a basement that is partly exposed, as shown in 6-23. Depending on the layout of the lot, the exposed part may be anything from a living area to a garage.

Another variation is the *raised ranch,* or split-entry. It is like a ranch, except the upper half of the basement is aboveground. See 6-24. This allows light to enter the basement through windows. The basement living area can be very pleasant if it is well-insulated and waterproof. A disadvantage is that stairs must be climbed to get

Vocabulary: Define a *ranch house* and the characteristics of two variations—the *hillside ranch* and the *raised ranch.*

Discuss: Why are raised ranches and split-levels difficult for many people to use? (*In many cases, the occupants cannot go from one room to another without climbing or descending stairs.*)

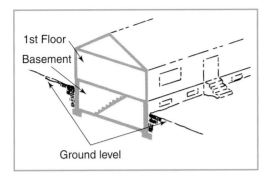

6-24 _____
*Since the top part of the basement of a raised ranch is aboveground, the basement can be used as a living space.*

anywhere in the house. This can be a problem for small children, people with disabilities, and older people.

## Split-Level

A split-level house has either three or four levels. The levels can be arranged in many ways, as shown in 6-25. The split-level was developed for sloping lots, although it is occasionally built on flat lots. See 6-26.

One advantage of a split-level house is that traffic into the social, quiet, and service areas can be separated easily. Also, there are few stairs to climb to get from one level to another. On the other hand, getting from one level to another always requires climbing stairs. Again, the stairs may present a problem for individuals who are less physically agile.

# Contemporary Houses

*Contemporary styles* are the current or latest house designs being constructed today. Many of the styles reflect design features from the traditional styles, both folk and classic. In some cases, current contemporary designs actually combine design

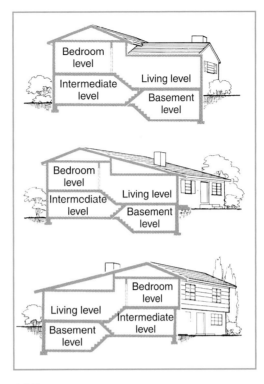

6-25 _____
*Changing the arrangement of levels in a split-level house also changes its outside appearance.*

6-26 _____
*Split-level houses are designed to adapt to sloped sites.*

elements from several traditional architectural styles.

Some contemporary housing designs may seem surprising or even controversial when compared to the traditional styles of the past. See 6-27. Other contemporary houses may combine both traditional and modern elements in their plan. Because of this, contemporary houses are not as easy to classify and describe as are the purely traditional or purely modern styles. Contemporary designs may also vary widely from one to another in shape, materials used, and details. Many convey a custom or distinctive one-of-a-kind design. The exterior may be brick, siding, stucco, stone, or concrete.

Roof styles used in contemporary houses can also vary widely. Study 6-28 to see the variety of roof styles available. While most of these styles are used in traditional houses, they can also be used in unique ways for contemporary housing. See 6-29.

Although contemporary houses do not easily fit into categories, there are two distinct types that do. They are solar houses and earth-sheltered houses.

## Solar Houses

*Solar energy* is energy derived from the sun. Today, many houses are being designed to use solar energy. They can use either active solar heating systems or passive solar heating systems. See 6-30.

Houses with *active solar* heating systems use special equipment, such as panels installed in the roof of the building, to capture the sun's energy. Then, fans and pumps move heated air or liquid from the panels to a storage area or wherever heat is needed.

*Passive solar* heating systems have no working parts. Instead, they include any design or construction material that makes maximum use of the sun for heating. A house with a passive solar system might include large areas of windows on the southern side of the house. Cement-pipe columns or dark-colored walls may be used to absorb heat from the sun and gradually transfer it inside.

## Earth-Sheltered Houses

Another type of contemporary housing is earth-sheltered housing. *Earth-sheltered* houses are partially covered with soil. They are energy-efficient since the soil is a natural insulation and helps protect the house from the elements and climate extremes. See 6-31. Some earth-sheltered houses are designed to be partly underground. Other dwellings are built into a hill or have soil compacted against the sides of the building.

A number of earth-sheltered houses are powered in part by solar energy. They may be designed with active or passive solar heating systems or both.

Weather Shield Windows & Doors

**6-27**

*This contemporary house combines the classic element of columns with a surprise custom-design feature resembling a lighthouse.*

## Roof Styles

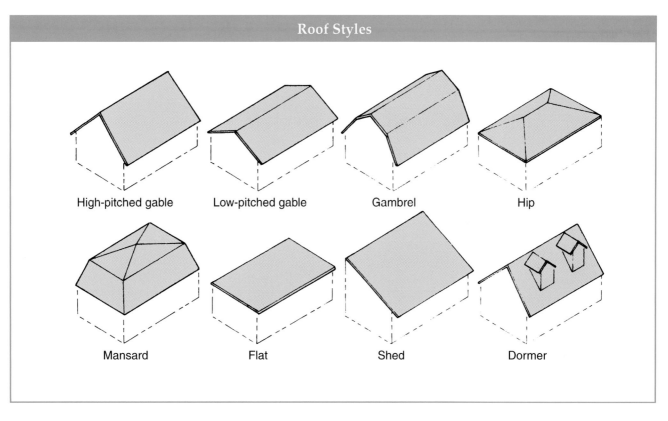

High-pitched gable        Low-pitched gable        Gambrel        Hip

Mansard        Flat        Shed        Dormer

6-28

*Roof styles have a great effect on the exterior design of buildings.*

Weather Shield Windows & Doors

6-29

*How many roof styles can you identify in this contemporary home?*

**Activity:** Working in small teams, solve puzzles made from Figure 6-28. Cut a copy of the chart apart, placing the eight illustrations into an envelope and their names into another. Give both envelopes to another team. Take the envelopes that your team receives, sort the strips, and match roof styles and correct names.

**Activity:** Search magazines, the Internet, and other sources to find photos of earth-sheltered houses. Identify any solar heating systems they may have.

**Enrich:** Investigate the requirements for building earth-sheltered homes. What building materials and processes must be used for construction to prevent deterioration of the structure? Is there a limit to how much earth can be used as insulation or a covering? How much lower are the heating and air-conditioning costs of earth-sheltered homes?

6-30

*This house has both active and passive solar heating systems.*

Concept 2000, Hermann J. Fraunhoffer

6-31

*This earth-sheltered house is partially covered with soil. The soil helps insulate it from the desert heat.*

# Housing Trends

In Chapter 22, "Housing for Today and Tomorrow," you will study the trends destined to shape the future of housing.

Another trend in housing is actually a step back in time. Nationally, there is a growing concern for restoring and preserving older buildings and houses. Increasingly, various agencies, local governments, and private organizations are identifying properties that represent architectural value and importance. One such group is the *National Trust for Historical Preservation.* This group identifies such structures and grants them landmark status. Once landmarked, these buildings cannot be destroyed or significantly altered.

Restoration work must follow careful guidelines to insure that materials, colors, and designs are true to their original era of the building's construction. In this way, a society preserves the best of its past for future generations to experience.

**Discuss:** In your own words, explain the importance of restoring and preserving architecturally significant homes.
**Internet Activity:** Research the National Trust for Historical Preservation and its mission. What has it accomplished? How did this group form and how long has it operated? Has the group been involved in any sites in or near your community?
**Reflect:** Which of the houses described in this chapter are most typical of your community?

# Summary

There is a wide variety of exterior housing styles in the United States. They evolved from the housing styles of the Native Americans and of the settlers, many of whom brought styles from their homelands.

Traditional folk styles include those from the Native Americans, Spanish, Scandinavians, Dutch, Germans, French, and English. During colonial times, other styles unique to this country began to evolve. They include the Cape Cod, saltbox, and garrison styles. Later, the classic traditional styles of Georgian, Federal, Greek Revival, Southern Colonial, and Victorian were developed.

During the twentieth century, modern and contemporary housing was designed to fit and take advantage of the environment and changing lifestyles. Modern houses include the Prairie Style, the International Style, the bungalow, the ranch and its variations, and different versions of the split-level.

Contemporary housing covers the styles of homes that are currently being built today. Two categories of contemporary design are the solar house and the earth-sheltered house. Contemporary homes may use traditional or modern styles, or be a unique, distinctive one-of-a-kind design.

What does the future hold for housing? Styles will continue to evolve to meet changing trends and lifestyles. In addition, outstanding examples of past architectural styles are being saved from demolition.

# To Review

1. Red tile roofs, enclosed patios, and arch-shaped windows and doors are characteristics of which style of housing?
   A. Native American
   B. Spanish
   C. Dutch Colonial
   D. French Provincial

2. The log cabin was brought to North America by _____ immigrants.

3. Which house style began as a one-room dwelling?
   A. Spanish
   B. French Provincial
   C. Cape Cod
   D. Southern Colonial

4. An overhanging second story is a characteristic of what house style?

5. Which housing style was named after an era when three similarly-named kings ruled England?

**Answer Key**
1. B
2. Scandinavian
3. C
4. garrison
5. Georgian

6. an open space covered with a roof that is supported by columns

7. (List four:) abundance of decorative trim (gingerbread), high porches, steep gable roofs, tall windows, turrets, high ceilings, dark stairways, long halls

8. Frank Lloyd Wright

9. (List one of each:) advantages—easy to maintain, easy to walk through, informal, many variations, few or no stairs; disadvantages—uses much space, expensive to build, not as energy efficient as more compact homes

10. sloped

11. D

12. Contemporary

13. to preserve the best of a society's past architecture for future generations to experience

6. Describe a portico.

7. List four characteristics of a Victorian house.

8. Who designed the Prairie style house?

9. Name one advantage and one disadvantage of the ranch house.

10. What kind of lot is best suited to the split-level house style?

11. Which of the following words best describes contemporary housing designs?

　A. steel
　B. rectangular
　C. three levels
　D. unique

12. Solar and earth-sheltered houses are two energy-efficient examples of the _____ housing style.

13. Why is there growing concern to restore and preserve older buildings?

# In Your Community

1. Tour one of the oldest residential areas of your community. What styles of architecture do you see? Examine the historical records of your community to find out when it was first settled. Who were the earliest inhabitants? Summarize your findings in a report to the class.

2. Examine the classified ads from your local newspaper, either in print or online. Using the information and pictures in the ads, compile a listing of the prices of different styles of homes that are currently on the market. Note the styles that are mentioned and how they are described. Analyze your information to see if you can identify a trend. Are the older homes more expensive because of historical significance? Are certain styles of homes priced below the market average? Is there a style of house that reflects the greatest value?

3. Research your community (or a nearby community) to determine if any buildings have been designated as historical buildings. To find this information, search the Web site for the Library of Congress. Share your research with the class.

# To Think About

1. Imagine you are an architect designing housing in the year 2020. Create an exterior design that you think would reflect future design trends. Does your design relate to any previous historical styles or time periods? What elements of exterior design, if any, do you think are classic and will be repeated in the future? How does your design relate to changes of lifestyle for future generations?

2. Imagine you and your family were among the early settlers in North America. Pick one of the styles of Folk architecture and write a story that describes the lifestyle you and your family would have experienced living in the house. Think in terms of cooking, sleeping, bathing, working, learning, enjoying recreation, and conducting other aspects of daily life. You may wish to illustrate your story. Share your story with the class.

# Using Technology

1. Using the Internet, research the architecture designed by Frank Lloyd Wright. Write a one-page report on how he influenced housing and architecture. Include pictures of his work that represent his particular style. Determine where your class would need to travel to find the closest example of a building designed by Wright.

   **Note:** For researching Frank Lloyd Wright, have students explore *cypgrp.com/flw*.

2. Research a specific architectural house style on the Internet. Obtain pictures as well as background information beyond that presented in the chapter. Use a computer to develop a poster for the classroom that clearly shows and describes the housing style.

   **Note:** For researching housing styles, have students explore *greatbuildings.com* and *benjaminmoore.com*.

3. Tour your community and take pictures with a digital or regular camera of as many different house exteriors as you can find. Identify the styles and historical periods that they represent. Share your pictures with the class and make a report on your findings.

**Portfolio Project:** Pretend you are a contractor preparing a pamphlet that has photos, drawings, and descriptions of styles of houses your company builds. Determine the styles of homes that your business will offer. If the styles are part of a planned housing development or subdivision, also describe it. Provide pictures (drawings and photos) and a brief description of the type of housing you offer to the public.

# CHAPTER 7
# Understanding House Plans

## To Know

architectural drawings
specifications
print
alphabet of lines
symbols
plan view
floor plan
exterior elevations
elevation view
section view
detail view
rendering
model
quiet area
multipurpose room
work area
work triangle
social area
alcove
traffic patterns
built-in storage
common-use storage

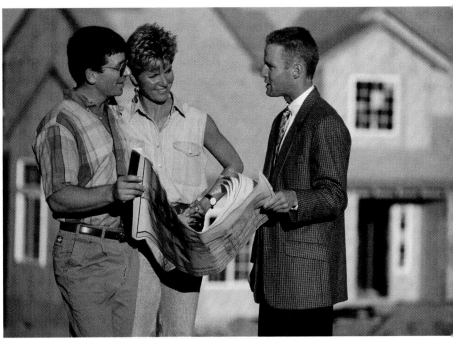

© Kavanagh Homes

## Objectives

After studying this chapter, you will be able to

- interpret architectural drawings.
- describe how computers can assist in understanding house plans.
- organize space by grouping rooms according to function.
- plan safe and convenient traffic patterns.
- evaluate storage needs and space.
- list ways to modify housing for people with physical disabilities.

**Resource:** *From the Ground Up*, transparency master overlay III-B, TR. Students look back at the topics covered in Chapters 1-6 by reviewing transparency master III-A. Then, with the addition of the overlay, they explore the topics they will cover in Chapter 7.

**Reading/Writing Activity:** Change the objectives into questions and list them on the left side of a piece of paper. On the right, answer the questions as you read the chapter.

The design and construction of a house involves many people working together. These people include the owner, architect, designer, contractor, banker, and various tradespeople. These people and many others form the design and construction team. Members of the team communicate through house plans. If you are buying or building a house, it is important that you, as a member of the team, be able to interpret the house plans.

## Architectural Drawings for a House

An important part of house plans is architectural drawings. *Architectural drawings* contain information about the size, shape, and location of all parts of the house. See 7-1. This universal language of the construction industry uses lines, symbols, views, and notes to convey ideas. To insure that everyone understands architectural drawings, standard rules of drafting determine the types of lines, symbols, and views, and the location of dimensions. These rules give meaning to each set of architectural drawings.

Architectural drawings are drawn in proportion to actual size. For instance, if a drawing is *half size*, it is one-half as large as the actual object. When an architectural drawing is either smaller or larger than the actual object, it is *drawn to scale*. Drawings for a house are normally drawn at a scale of ¼" = 1'. This means that one-foot measures on the house equal one-fourth inch in the drawing. This scale can also be written as ¼" = 12", 1" = 48", or ¹⁄₄₈ *size*. The scale for each drawing is indicated in a footnote.

Not all information about a house can be conveyed by architectural drawings. For example, it would be difficult to show texture or represent paint color on the drawings. However, wall texture and paint color are important parts of the finished house.

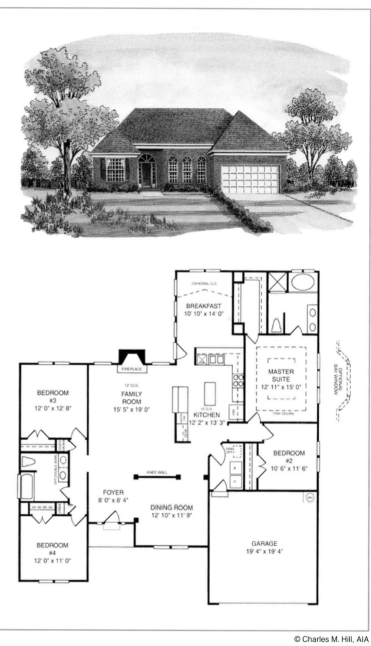

© Charles M. Hill, AIA

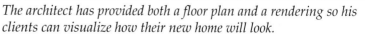

7-1

*The architect has provided both a floor plan and a rendering so his clients can visualize how their new home will look.*

Therefore, some information for the design and construction is prepared in written form called specifications or *specs*. The **specifications** tell the types and quality of materials to be used and give directions for their use.

## Prints of Architectural Drawings

Drafters in architects 'or contractors' offices using drafting machines and instruments made most architectural drawings in the past. Today, *computer-aided drafting and design (CADD)* drawings are used.

When the drafter completes a set of architectural drawings, copies must be made for all members of the construction team. A **print** is a copy of a drawing. In the past, a reproduction of a drawing consisted of white lines on a dark blue background. Consequently, the term *blueprint* was used.

Today the drawings can be reproduced by the *diazo process*, which creates prints that have dark lines on a light background. Engineering copiers, which are similar to office photocopiers, handle the heavier and much larger sheets of paper used for these drawings.

### Alphabet of Lines

To understand the architectural drawings, you must first understand the lines used on the drawings. Seven different lines, called the **alphabet of lines**, are commonly used on architectural drawings. They allow the drafter to communicate ideas clearly and accurately.

These lines vary in thickness or weight. They may be solid or a combination of dashes and breaks. The following examples are illustrated in 7-2:

- *Phantom lines* show alternate positions, repeated details, and paths of motion.

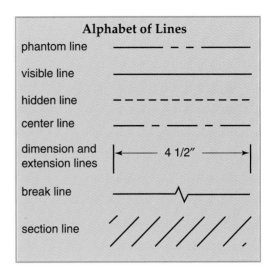

7-2

*The alphabet of lines are basic lines that are used in all architectural drawings.*

- *Visible lines* show the outline of the building and walls.
- *Hidden lines* show edges of surfaces that are not visible in a specific view of the house.
- *Center lines* show the center of an arc or circle.
- *Dimension and extension lines* show the extent and direction of measurements. *Dimension lines* show the size and location of the dimension. *Extension lines* show the termination points of a dimension.
- *Break lines* show the object continues on, but the complete view is not shown.
- *Section lines* show a feature that has been sectioned. These lines are often called crosshatch lines.

### Symbols

Many features of a house cannot be drawn exactly as the finished product. Therefore, standard symbols are used on the drawings. **Symbols** represent plumbing and electrical fixtures, doors, windows, and other common objects in a house. Drafters use templates to trace symbols. CADD programs insert symbols to represent common objects. Notes on the drawings give additional explanation for symbols. In 7-3, you can see several common symbols.

- *Door and window symbols* show the type of door or window and the direction each opens.
- *Mechanical symbols* indicate plumbing, heating, and air-conditioning fixtures used on a plan.
- *Electrical symbols* on a drawing include switches, receptacles, light fixtures, and appliances. Hidden lines drawn between switches, fixtures, and receptacles indicate wiring.

# Views for Architectural Drawings

Architectural drawings of a house usually include different types of views. Among these are *plan views*, *elevation views*, and views of *sections* and *details*. Imagine the house enclosed in a large glass box. Each view is projected toward its viewing surface on the glass box, and then brought into position as though unfolding the sides of the box.

## Plan Views

Views taken from the top of the imaginary glass box are called **plan views.** The *site plan, floor plan, foundation plan*, and *roof plan* are all plan views. The **floor plan** is the most important drawing on a set of house plans. It is a simplified drawing that shows the size

**Resource:** *Interpreting Floor Plan Symbols*, reproducible master 7-1, TR. Students work individually or in groups to identify floor plan symbols.

**Resource:** *Interpreting Electrical Symbols*, transparency master overlay 7-2, TR. With this overlay superimposed on *Interpreting Floor Plan Symbols*, transparency master 7-1, students identify the symbols shown. Discuss how symbols vary slightly on different plans.

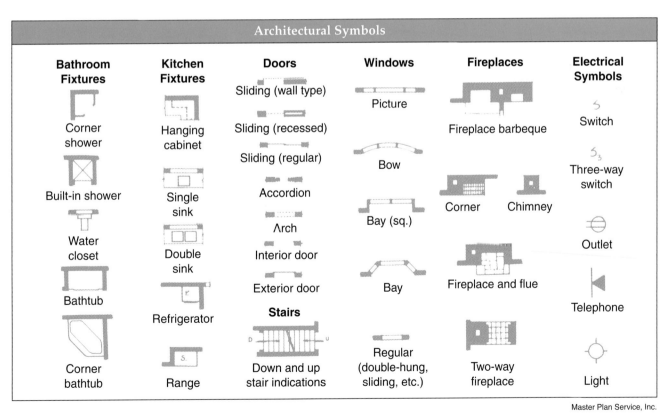

## Architectural Symbols

**Bathroom Fixtures**
- Corner shower
- Built-in shower
- Water closet
- Bathtub
- Corner bathtub

**Kitchen Fixtures**
- Hanging cabinet
- Single sink
- Double sink
- Refrigerator
- Range

**Doors**
- Sliding (wall type)
- Sliding (recessed)
- Sliding (regular)
- Accordion
- Arch
- Interior door
- Exterior door

**Stairs**
- Down and up stair indications

**Windows**
- Picture
- Bow
- Bay (sq.)
- Bay
- Regular (double-hung, sliding, etc.)

**Fireplaces**
- Fireplace barbeque
- Corner
- Chimney
- Fireplace and flue
- Two-way fireplace

**Electrical Symbols**
- Switch
- Three-way switch
- Outlet
- Telephone
- Light

Master Plan Service, Inc.

7-3

*These symbols are used on drawings to represent objects in the house.*

**Enrich:** Attend a presentation by the school's assistant principal in charge of facilities who discusses the school building's architectural drawings and specifications. Identify as many symbols as possible. Summarize in one paragraph what you learn.

**Activity:** Create a reference card of the symbols in Figure 7-3 for the following uses: to serve as a study aid and to help develop portfolio ideas.

and arrangement of rooms, hallways, doors, windows, and storage areas on one floor of a home. In 7-4 you can see the symbols used in the floor plan.

## Elevation Views

Architectural drawings that show the outside views of the house are called *exterior elevations*. A set of drawings usually includes four elevations showing all four sides of the house. If the building is simple, there may be only the front elevation and one side elevation.

An *elevation view* shows the finished exterior appearance of a given side of the house. Height dimensions are usually shown on elevations. Elevation views help people visualize the completed house. By studying both the floor plan and the elevation views, you can envision the completed structure. See 7-5.

## Section Views and Detail Views

To show how individual structural parts of the house fit together, section and detail views are used. For instance, the drafter may want to show the inside of the house. When a view is taken from an imaginary cut through a part of a house, such as a wall, it is called a *section view*. See the example in 7-6. (Notice that 7-4, 7-5, and 7-6 are various views of the same house. Figure 7-6 views an interior slice of Figure 7-5 at the line marked *B-B*.)

A *detail view* is usually an enlargement of some construction feature. The detail drawing often uses a larger scale than other drawings. It shows the details of a small part of the house. See 7-7 for a house and garage detail.

## Renderings and Models

To help clients better visualize a finished house, architectural firms frequently produce a rendering. A *rendering* is a drawing with color to show a realistic view of the completed house. Refer back to the top of 7-1.

A model may also be developed to show all sides of the new house. A *model* is a three-dimensional miniature of a design. It can be viewed from different angles and in various lighting conditions to get more realistic views of the house.

Producing renderings and models by hand is very costly in terms of time and materials. It also requires considerable artistic skill. Usually landscaping plans and other aspects of the completed house are also incorporated into these views.

Today, architects have a choice in producing renderings and models. Depending on the requirements of the project, they may use CADD. The computer creates very realistic views of the house under various lighting conditions. See 7-8. Accuracy and timesavings are the biggest advantages of using computers to create housing views.

**Floor Plan**
1859 Sq.Ft.

Bloodgood Sharp Buster Architects & Planners, Inc.

**7-4**

*Understanding an architectural drawing is a matter of knowing what the symbols mean.*

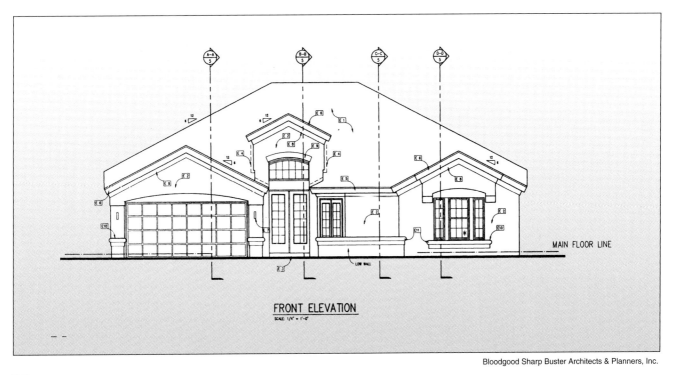

FRONT ELEVATION
SCALE 1/4" = 1'-0"

Bloodgood Sharp Buster Architects & Planners, Inc.

7-5

*The main feature of this house is the great room in the center.*

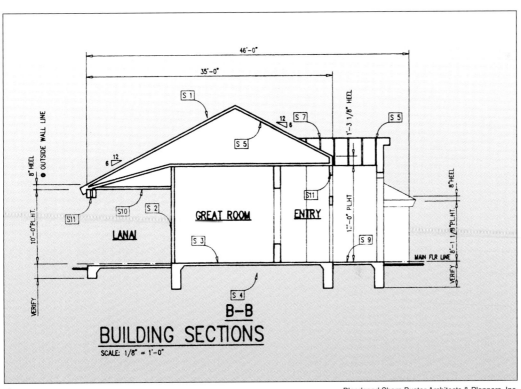

BUILDING SECTIONS
SCALE: 1/8" = 1'-0"

Bloodgood Sharp Buster Architects & Planners, Inc.

**Resource:** *Detailed Floor Plan,* reproducible master 7-3, TR. Students work in small groups to identify the scale used, the lines from the alphabet of lines, and the location of windows and doors of this detailed version of Figure 7-4.

**Resource:** *Front Elevation Rendering,* reproducible master 7-4, TR. Students compare this rendering to the elevation view it depicts, which is Figure 7-5 in the text.

**Note:** Figures 7-4, 7-5, and 7-6 are various views of the same house.

7-6

*This section view shows that the ceiling in the great room is higher than the lanai's ceiling.*

**Activity:** Study Figures 7-4, 7-5, and 7-6. Lay a blank transparency over them to highlight the great room in each figure. On a separate sheet of paper, create a detail view of the great room, using a ¼" = 1' scale.

**Research / Writing Activity:** Research the term *spatial intelligence* to learn about the special aptitude that gifted architects possess. Explain what it is. Name a famous architect who demonstrated it and identify an example of his or her work that clearly illustrates the aptitude.

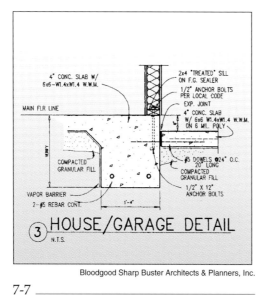

Bloodgood Sharp Buster Architects & Planners, Inc.

7-7

*This detail view shows how the outside wall is fastened to the garage floor.*

3D Home Architect Deluxe from Broderbund Software, Inc.

7-8

*This cross section elevation of a house was created by using computer-aided drafting and design (CADD).*

Some architectural firms use CADD to allow the client to view the structure from many different angles before finalizing the plan. The customer can "walk through" the space

and determine if the building's layout meets expectations. If not, adjustments can easily be made to the plan, and different versions of the plan can be produced quickly. CADD brings the plan to life for the client. It also helps architects and builders avoid costly mistakes and verify that the final design meets client expectations.

# The Space Within

Once you understand the drawings for the house, you need to consider the space within. The way space is divided within the house is one of the most basic concerns in housing.

When planning how to use the space within a house, consideration must be given to the activities, habits, lifestyles, and life situations of the occupants. Then, the interior space is divided into areas according to the intended use of each. Space divisions should satisfy the needs and preferences of the occupants.

## Grouping by Function

As you look at floor plans, you will notice that certain rooms of a house are usually located next to one another. This is because certain rooms are used for similar purposes, or *functions*. Grouping rooms together by function is an efficient way to organize space. Most of the space within a house is divided into three areas: a *quiet area, work area*, and *social area*.

### The Quiet Area

The **quiet area** in most houses consists of bedrooms and bathrooms. See 7-9. These rooms provide space for sleeping, resting, grooming, and dressing. The quiet area of a house offers the best setting for rest and relaxation.

**7-9**

*The shaded area of this floor plan represents the quiet area.*

It is usually a comfortable and private place.

Since sleep and rest are basic needs, they should be among the first to be considered when planning the use of space. In some homes, each person has a separate room. In other homes, this is not possible or desirable. The important goal is to ensure the comfort of each person and put his or her spatial needs ahead of group needs.

Dressing and grooming are other activities that take place in the quiet area. They require privacy and space for storing clothes and grooming supplies. Both bedrooms and bathrooms help fulfill these spatial needs. See 7-10.

**Activity:** Estimate the percentage of the house shown in Figure 7-9 that is used for quiet space.

Photo courtesy of Kohler Co.

**7-10**

*This bathroom is part of the quiet area of the house.*

**Discuss:** Have you ever heard people complain about a home's layout? What common complaints have you heard?

**Reflect:** What percentage of your house is used for quiet space? Is any of the quiet space actually multipurpose?

**Reflect:** Is your bedroom predominantly for quiet or for multipurpose uses? For what activities do you use it?

Some bedrooms may provide space for other activities, such as reading, studying, watching TV, listening to music, and working on hobbies. When this is true, the rooms are called *multipurpose rooms*. They are used during active periods of the day as well as sleeping hours.

© Charles M. Hill, AIA

7-11

*The shaded kitchen and utility room represent the work area.*

Photo courtesy of Kohler Co.

7-12

*This combination utility, mud, and gardening room is part of the work area of the house.*

## The Work Area

Some rooms in a home are set aside as the work area, 7-11. The *work area* includes all parts of the house needed to maintain and service the other areas. Sometimes the work area overlaps with the service zone outside the house. Rooms in the work area vary from house to house. The kitchen, laundry area, utility room, and garage are generally part of the work area. See 7-12. A workshop, home office, or sewing room may also be included.

If your lifestyle requires a home office, you will need to include this space in the work area of your home. When planning office space, the first step is to determine its purpose. Is it for occasional use, such as paying bills and organizing household documents? Will the home office be used frequently, maybe by children doing homework or adults bringing work home from the office? Will the office be used daily, perhaps by a household member working from home or telecommuting? Knowing how the home office will be used helps to determine its location.

The actual space available in the dwelling also affects the location of a home office. Some home offices are planned for a corner of the kitchen or in an alcove. For daily use, a home office generally requires much more space, such as a separate room. However, few households can afford to give that much space to a home office. Instead, most home offices are planned for a spare bedroom, the basement, or attic space. See 7-13.

After the workspace for the home office is determined on the floor plan, attention can later turn to the next steps. These include selecting and arranging furniture, securing the lighting, and getting the necessary equipment. (Refer to the following chapters for more information: Chapter 16, "Arranging and Selecting Furniture"; Chapter 17,

"Addressing Windows, Lighting, and Accessories"; and Chapter 18, "Selecting Household Appliances."

In most homes, the kitchen is used more often than any other room in the work area. It has the following three primary areas of activity:

■ food preparation and storage center

■ cleanup center

■ cooking and serving center

The imaginary line that connects these three centers forms a *work triangle*. Anyone preparing a meal in a kitchen will walk along the lines of the triangle several times before the meal is ready. In a well-designed kitchen, the total length of all sides of the work triangle does not exceed 22 feet. Six basic kitchen designs are shown in 7-14.

Ethan Allen, Inc.

7-13

*This home office has a sofa bed so the room can also be used as a guest room.*

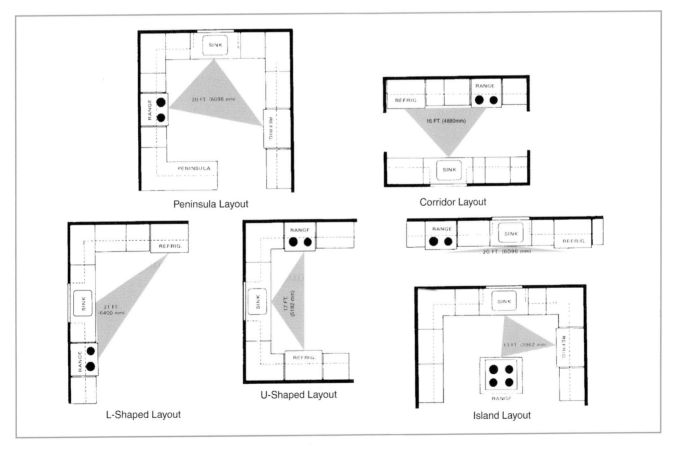

7-14

*The distance around the work triangle in each of these kitchen designs is less than 22 feet.*

**Reflect:** Which of the kitchen layouts in Figure 7-14 best reflects your home's kitchen area?

**Activity:** Make a sketch of the kitchen in your home. Sit and observe as a member of your family prepares a meal. Mark each of their trips back and forth between the food preparation area, cleanup center, and cooking and/or serving center. Does it create a triangle?

Measure the distance for a complete path to each of the centers and back to the starting point.

**Discuss:** Why is it important to keep a work triangle under 22-feet long? (*to prevent the cook from becoming too tired, to save time, and to utilize space well*)

**Reflect:** Do you prefer open space or separate rooms for a home's social area?

**Discuss:** Study Figure 7-15. What other social space might this house have that is not shown?

## The Social Area

Members of a household spend much of their time in the social area of the house. The *social area* provides space for daily living, entertaining, and recreation. It includes entrances, dining rooms, living rooms, and family rooms. See 7-15.

An entry or entrance is a place where guests are identified and greeted. It is here that outerwear is removed and placed in nearby coat closets. Entries also help direct the movement of people throughout the house. If a dwelling has more than one entrance, each may have a slightly different purpose. However, each is still part of the social area.

Some houses have separate dining rooms. They can be used for eating meals and entertaining guests. If a dining room is not used regularly, the cost of having a separate dining room may be too great. In that case, household members may prefer to eat close to where the food is prepared. This can be in the kitchen at a special

counter or a separate table. During mild weather, household members often enjoy eating outdoors. When special events are on TV, many families like to eat meals in the family room or living room.

Living rooms provide space for family activities as well as for entertaining guests. If a dwelling has both a living room and a family room, the family room is often more casual. It is usually used for recreational activities as well as relaxation. See 7-16.

### Separating Areas and Rooms

The quiet, work, and social areas can be separated in several ways. One way is to locate different areas on different ends or levels of the house. For instance, the quiet area may be upstairs, while the social and work areas are on the ground floor.

Hallways are another way to separate areas. Besides physically separating areas, hall space also acts as a buffer zone for noise. A hallway between the quiet and social areas makes it possible for some people to rest or sleep, while others are entertaining guests, dining, or watching TV. Hallways near work areas help reduce the volume of noise from appliances and tools that reaches the quiet and social areas.

Hallways range from 36 inches to 42 inches wide. A 36-inch width is used for very short halls. A 40-inch width is the most common width used. A 42-inch width is used for very long halls or halls where wheelchairs are used regularly.

Walls usually separate individual rooms. However, some dwellings have large open areas that are divided into separate areas. *Alcoves*, which are small recessed sections of a room, and balconies are sometimes used. Screens, freestanding storage units, and careful

© Charles M. Hill, AIA

7-15 _____

*The shaded portion represents the social area.*

**Discuss:** What is the difference between a living room and family room? (*The family room is often more casual and used for recreational activities and relaxation.*)

**Enrich:** Attend a presentation by an architect or construction contractor who discusses different layouts of homes and options.

Be prepared to ask questions. Summarize in one paragraph what you learn.

**Discuss:** What can be used to separate rooms or housing areas? (*walls, halls, closets, furniture*)

arrangement of furniture can also be used to separate space according to function. Even when there are no walls dividing a room, you can see that the room is designed for different activities.

An advantage of not separating areas with walls is a large, open area where people can enjoy more than one activity at a time. For instance, the kitchen may be open to the family room or living room. The open space allows those preparing food to take part in other activities, such as conversing with family members or entertaining guests.

## Traffic Patterns

Have you ever been in a traffic jam after leaving a football game or concert? Often the police relieve the congestion by directing traffic and creating alternate routes.

Traffic planning also helps reduce or prevent congestion throughout a house. When space is organized well, people can move easily within a room, from room to room, or to the outdoors. The paths they follow are called *traffic patterns*.

Traffic patterns require enough space for people to move about freely. However, it is wasteful to use more space than is needed. As a rule, traffic patterns should be about 40 inches wide.

Traffic patterns should be designed so people can move throughout a house without disturbing other activities. For example, major traffic patterns should avoid the quiet area of a home so it can remain quiet. Work areas are unsafe if people frequently walk through them. To avoid accidents, traffic patterns should lead to work areas, but not through them. Also, traffic patterns should not be located through social areas, since

Ethan Allen, Inc.

7-16

*This casual living and dining room are part of the social area of the home.*

conversation, study, and TV viewing can be interrupted.

The easiest way to evaluate traffic patterns is to study floor plans. Look at the examples in 7-17. See if the following guidelines for safe and convenient traffic patterns have been followed. Traffic patterns should

- be convenient and direct.

- provide adequate space without wasting it.

- provide easy access from the entrances to other parts of the house.

**Discuss:** How are traffic jams in homes similar to traffic jams in schools and in street traffic?

**Reflect:** Where are the traffic jams in your home? What could be done to make those areas safer?

**Activity:** Create a scale floor plan of your home and mark the traffic patterns. Using the information in the text, indicate the steps that could be taken to improve the traffic flow in your home.

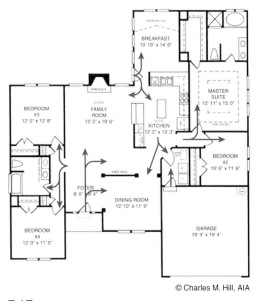

© Charles M. Hill, AIA

7-17

*The open floor plan of this home permits traffic to flow smoothly in many directions.*

- separate traffic to the work area from traffic to the quiet and social areas.
- avoid cutting through the middle of rooms.
- avoid interfering with a good furniture arrangement or interrupting activities within a room.

- avoid interfering with privacy in areas of the house where privacy is expected.
- avoid cutting through a kitchen, work area, or any other hazardous area.
- give the kitchen easy access to all areas of the home.
- provide a direct access from the service entrance to a cleanup area.
- provide access from a service entrance to the quiet area without going through the social area.
- provide direct access from utility area to the outside service zone.

## Space for Doors

Outside doors and doors between rooms also help determine the flow of traffic. Other doors within a room may conceal storage. It is important that the space in front of these doors remain free. Blocked doors will stop traffic and cut off access to stored items.

Not only should the space immediately in front of doors be free, but there should also be space for doors to swing and stand open. In 7-18, you can see the amount of space that is needed for different types of doors to

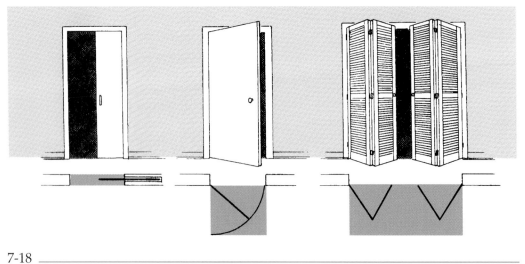

7-18

*The colored areas show the amount of space that must be kept clear around each type of door.*

swing open. People also need space to go through the doors or to use storage areas.

## Survey the Storage Space

It is important to have plenty of storage space scattered throughout a house. When looking at house plans, look at what storage space is available. Make sure there is enough space to store all your belongings. Check to see if the storage space is located in convenient places. If you plan to use some rooms for more than one activity, make sure they have the storage space you need. For instance, you may plan to use the dining room as both a study area and a place to eat. Therefore, you will need space to store paper, pens, and reference books as well as dishes and table linens.

Looking at floor plans can help you evaluate the storage space of a home. A floor plan, such as the one in 7-19, shows the location of built-in storage units. ***Built-in storage*** cannot be sold, replaced, or moved like pieces of furniture. A section view would show the number of shelves and drawers in the storage unit. Floor plans also show how much floor space is available for additional storage, such as shelves and bookcases.

### Planning for Storage

If you plan to build a house or have one built for you, you will need to plan for storage. First, you need to determine the storage needs of each member of your household. Then you need to plan for ***common-use storage***, which is storage used by all who live in a house. It includes the storage near the entrance where outerwear is kept and storage for food, tools, and other items that are shared.

You can add to the amount of built-in storage available in a dwelling with storage units and storage furniture. Storage furniture includes desks, chests, and dressers. Another type is shown in 7-20. Storage furniture can

© Charles M. Hill, AIA

7-19 _____

*This floor plan shows the location of closets, a pantry, and kitchen cabinets, which are all forms of built-in storage.*

Hold Everything

7-20 _____

*Armoires can be used in addition to built-in storage to hold household items.*

be moved to other locations in the house and taken with you when you leave.

Built-in storage, storage units, and storage furniture also have advantages. You cannot take built-in storage with you when you move, so you will not have the cost of moving it. Also, a home increases in value if it includes built-in storage. Portable storage units, as in 7-21, can be moved to other locations in the house as storage needs change. Also, you can keep portable storage units when you move, although some may need to be disassembled.

## Evaluating the Floor Plan

When considering a floor plan on paper, on a computer screen, or by walking through a home, evaluate the layout carefully. Ask yourself the questions in 7-22. By answering these

Hold Everything

7-21

*These storage shelves can be easily disassembled and taken with you if you move.*

questions, you can identify any areas that may present future problems.

No floor plan is perfect for everyone so your ideal plan may present problems to someone else. Problems in a floor plan can be solved by making changes to the construction of the space or by *adapting the space*. When you adapt a space, you use it for something other than the original purpose. Sometimes, too, problems in a floor plan may be solved by using interior design treatments.

## Housing Modifications for People with Physical Disabilities

Housing should provide convenience, safety, and accessibility for all members of the household. This includes people with physical disabilities.

Houses for people with physical disabilities can be attractive and affordable. It is estimated that by spending only two percent above the base cost on a new house, it can be made barrier free. Also, the exterior and interior of existing houses can be modified at a reasonable cost to meet the needs of people with physical disabilities. For example, the kitchen in 7-23 was modified to make the cooking and cleanup areas more accessible to household members with limited reach. (Also see Chapter 23, "Housing for Today and Tomorrow," for a discussion of universal design features that make living space more usable for all.)

### Exteriors

The exteriors of houses for people with physical disabilities should be as safe and accessible as possible. When building or choosing a house, keep the following points in mind:

## Evaluating a Floor Plan

Answering "yes" to the following question indicates a well-designed floor plan. Any "no" answers may indicate a need to modify the floor plan.

- Would all members of your household have enough space to satisfy their needs?
- Are rooms grouped according to function?
- Are quiet areas away from public view and traffic?
- If a multipurpose room exists, can it be used for all the intended purposes?
- Are eating areas close to the kitchen?
- Is space provided for entertaining as well as day-to-day living?
- Are the entrances conveniently locate?
- Are the traffic patterns safe and convenient?
- Is storage adequate and convenient?
- Is the house free of barriers?

**Note:** The Web site *design.ncsu.edu/cud/* provides useful information on universal design as well as house and apartment designs.

7-22 ──────────────
*Can you think of other questions you would ask yourself when evaluating a floor plan?*

- Lots should be flat for easy access.
- Entrance should face south, so ice and snow on sidewalks and the driveway will melt faster.
- Sidewalks, driveways, and garage floors should have nonskid surfaces, such as textured asphalt or concrete. (Oil and debris should be kept off these surfaces.)
- Driveways and garages should be wide enough to park cars and to move in and around wheelchairs.
- Garage door openers that automatically light garages should be used.
- Ramps with handrails should be installed for easy access to the house.
- Sidewalks, ramps, and entries must be wide enough for wheelchairs to move easily. To allow for enough room on each side of a wheelchair, sidewalks should be 4 or 5 feet wide and entries should be 3 feet wide.

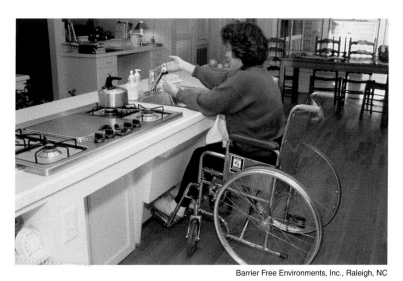

Barrier Free Environments, Inc., Raleigh, NC

7-23 ──────────────
*Instead of installing storage cabinets under this sink and cooktop, the space was left open to accommodate a wheelchair.*

- Thresholds should be as level as possible to prevent stumbling.
- Push-button or automatically operated doors should be considered, since they are the easiest to use.

**Activity:** Evaluate your home by answering the questions in Figure 7-22. Imagine that you are evaluating the home from the perspective of a person who is seeing the home for the first time. Take into account all the needs of the members who make up your family. Based on your evaluation, does the floor plan fit your family's current needs or not? Explain.

**Activity:** Create a survey form that lists the important points for keeping housing exteriors accessible to people with physical disabilities. Use the form to evaluate your home. How many of the 11 points does your home pass?

7-24

*Pull-out storage is convenient for everyone, especially people with disabilities.*

**Activity:** Create a survey form that lists the 13 points for keeping housing interiors accessible to people with physical disabilities. Use the form to evaluate your home. How many of the points does your home pass?

- Doors should be equipped with levers or handles, which are easier to grasp and turn than conventional knobs.
- Outdoor and entry areas should be well lit.

## Interiors

Since people spend most of their time inside, safety and accessibility are important. Keep the following points in mind when choosing housing that eliminates barriers for people with physical disabilities:

- Stairs should have steady handrails, thin enough to grip securely.
- Floors and stairs should be covered with wood or hard-surface coverings for easy mobility. If carpet is used, it should have a low pile.
- Floor plans should allow for use of a walker or wheelchair.
- Open traffic lanes should lead directly to specific areas.
- Halls should be at least 4 feet wide to permit a wheelchair to turn into a room.
- There should be enough turn-around space within rooms for wheelchairs.
- Doors should be at least 3 feet wide. Doors that swing both ways or fold are easier to use.
- Storage space, equipment, appliances, electrical receptacles, and switches should be installed within easy reach.
- Pullout trays and drawers, as shown in 7-24, are easier to use than traditional shelves.
- Lavatories and toilets should be mounted on the wall for easy access.
- Showers or bathtubs should have doors for easy access.
- Handles should be easy to grasp and use.
- A home elevator or stairway lift should be installed if the person's living quarters are on more than one level of the house.

If a house cannot be modified to make life easier for a person with physical disabilities, a decision must be made. Can that person live there comfortably, or should another house be found? This is an important question to answer and should include input from all members of the household.

**Reflect:** Review the chapter objectives. Do you still need to review or research some topics to get the information you feel you need? If so, what topics?

**Writing Activity:** Before reading the summary, write your own summary of the chapter. Then, compare the text's summary to what you wrote.

# Summary

Architectural drawings contain information about the size, shape, and location of all parts of the house. They are drawn to scale. Then prints are made, accompanied by specifications. To understand architectural drawings, it helps to be familiar with the special lines and symbols used. Architectural drawings usually include several views of the house.

After the drawings are evaluated, the actual space within a house needs to be considered. Rooms are usually grouped by function. Space is divided into three different areas—for quiet, work, and socializing. Levels, hallways, walls, screens, freestanding storage units, and furniture arrangements separate these areas.

Planned traffic patterns help reduce and prevent traffic congestion and provide enough space for opening doors. Organizing space to provide plenty of storage is also important. This can be done with built-in storage, storage units, and storage furniture.

The exterior and interior space of a house sometimes needs to be modified to meet the needs of a member of the household who has a physical disability. If a house is convenient, safe, and accessible for people with physical disabilities, it will meet the needs of any occupant.

**Resource:** *Understanding Plans for a House*, Activity E, SAG. Students decide what chapter terms are missing from several sentences and fill in the blanks with the missing terms.

# To Review

1. What does an architectural drawing contain?

2. If the scale of a drawing is 1" = 1'-0", identify three more ways this scale can be written.

3. You would not find _____ in an architectural drawing.
   A. dimensions for the garage
   B. location of built-in storage
   C. location of furniture in a room
   D. room sizes and locations

4. A _____ _____ shows the arrangement of rooms, halls, and doors on one floor of a house.

5. Answer the following questions by examining Figure 7-4:
   A. How many windows are in the house?
   B. Where is the furnace located?
   C. The house has approximately how many square feet?
   D. The house has how many bathrooms?
   E. What type of layout exists in the kitchen?

6. The space in a house can be divided into three areas according to function. Name them.

7. In a well-designed kitchen, what is the maximum length around a work triangle?

**Answer Key**

1. information about the size, shape, and location of all parts of the house
2. ¼" = 3", 1" = 12", 1⁄12
3. C
4. floor plan
5. A. 10 windows
   B. in the closet nearest the front entry
   C. 1,859
   D. two
   E. island
6. quiet, work, and social
7. 22 feet

8. (List two:) separate areas; act as a buffer zone for noise; provide privacy

9. (List five. See page 186.)

10. (List one of each:) built-in storage—is shown in house plans, does not need to be moved, increases house value; storage furniture—can be moved to other locations in the house, can be moved to other houses, is relatively inexpensive

11. (List two. See pages 190-192.)

12. (List three. See page 192.)

8. Identify two functions of hallways.

9. List five guidelines for good traffic patterns.

10. Name one advantage of each: built-in storage and storage furniture.

11. Give two examples of how housing exteriors can be modified for people with physical disabilities.

12. Describe three features of a house interior that is free of barriers to people with physical disabilities.

## In Your Community

1. Visit a model home in a new subdivision or housing complex nearby and do the following:
   A. Walk through the home and answer the questions in Chart 7-22.
   B. Compare the impression of the house you get from studying the floor plan to the actual experience of being in the house. Were some aspects of the house not conveyed clearly in the floor plan?
   C. Identify aspects of the floor plan that you would like to change.

2. Try to locate either an apartment or home that has features specifically designed for people who need a walker or wheelchair to get around. Describe these features. What other features would make the housing more usable to these occupants?

## To Think About

1. Suppose you check the traffic patterns in a home you plan to buy and see potential problems between the private and public areas. Otherwise, the house is very pleasing and convenient to use. Would you buy the house with the idea of changing the traffic patterns later, or would you keep looking for a better floor plan? Give the reasons for your choice.

2. Housing should be adaptable to meet the needs of changes in life circumstances and family life cycles. Imagine having a home with flexible features such as movable walls and adjustable kitchen countertops. Do you think this is a good idea? Why or why not?

# Using Technology

1. Locate a floor plan on the Internet that you like and print a copy. Use the floor plan to do each of the following:

   A. Shade the quiet, social, and work areas with different-colored pencils. Determine if the areas are divided appropriately and justify your decision.

   B. Trace the traffic patterns, and check them with the guidelines listed in this chapter. Explain if they are safe and convenient.

   C. Identify which storage is for individual use and which is for common use.

   D. Indicate how the living space could be modified for people with physical disabilities, if this became necessary.

2. Use a computer-assisted design program to draw a floor plan that includes three bedrooms, one bathroom, a kitchen, dining room, and living room. Evaluate it according to the questions in Chart 7-22. Make changes in the plan as needed to improve the design. Print a copy of the plan and present your design decisions to the class.

3. Using a desktop publishing program, develop a brochure that shows safety issues in housing plans. Develop a list of safety considerations for adults and children in the following areas of a floor plan: the home's entrances, traffic patterns in kitchens, and placement of interior doors.

**Note:** For researching safety issues of housing plans, have students explore *realtor.com.*

**Portfolio Project:** Using one of the house exteriors from the pamphlet or flyer developed for the portfolio in Chapter 6, create an interior floor plan that includes built-in storage. Apply the symbols and lines discussed in this chapter.

C H A P T E R   8

# House Construction

## To Know

foundation
footing
concrete
foundation wall
frost line
sill plate
anchor bolt
joist
girder
subflooring
stud
header
rafter
ridge
truss rafter
masonry
siding
brick
natural stone
veneer wall
bond
shingle
flashing
gutter
downspout

Photograph courtesy of Judy M. Beck, Unireal Construction Company, McCormick, SC

## Objectives

After studying this chapter, you will be able to

- describe how a house is constructed.
- list the parts of the foundation and frame of a house.
- list the advantages and disadvantages of different types of materials used for exterior construction.
- list basic types of windows used in houses.
- distinguish between different types of doors.
- explain how computer applications can assist the house construction process.

**Resource:** *From the Ground Up,* transparency master overlay III-C, TR. Students look back at the topics covered in Chapters 1-7 by reviewing transparency master III-A with overlay III-B. Then, with the addition of overlay III-C, they explore the topics they will cover in Chapter 8.

**Vocabulary:** While reading through the chapter, create a crossword puzzle using the vocabulary words.

**Writing Activity:** Read the chapter objectives and state in your own words, in writing, what the purpose of this chapter is.

When buying a pre-owned house or building a new one, it is helpful to understand how housing is constructed. By being familiar with housing construction, you will be able to make good decisions when selecting a place to live. Poor decisions, on the other hand, can result in poor investments and/or expensive repair costs.

# The Foundation and the Frame

The foundation and frame are the basic structure of the house. Understanding how they are constructed is the first step in making an informed housing decision. When building a house, you will be able to observe the construction and make sure it is done correctly. When buying a pre-owned house, you may be able to inspect the foundation and frame for defects and needed repairs.

## The Foundation

The *foundation* is the underlying base of the house. There are three types of foundation construction. Houses may be constructed with a basement, a crawl space with a pier foundation, or a slab on grade foundation. The foundation consists of foundation walls and the footing. The very bottom of the foundation is called the *footing*. See 8-1. Footings are usually made from *concrete.* This is a hard building material made by combining cement, sand, and gravel with water.

The footings must be reinforced for added strength with a system of horizontal steel rods, called *rebar*. The concrete and steel footing should be strong enough to support the rest of the foundation and the house it will

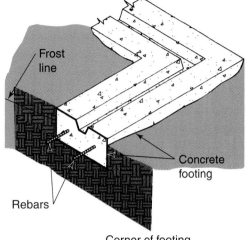

Frost line

Concrete footing

Rebars

Corner of footing

Resource: *Footing and Foundation,* transparency master 8-1, TR. Students examine the details of the footing and foundation, and point out the anchor bolts, sill sealer, sill plate, footing, and foundation wall.

Discuss: What are the three types of foundation construction? (*a basement, a crawl space with a pier foundation, or a slab on grade foundation*)

8-1
*The footing is a wide concrete base that supports the foundation and the rest of the house.*

support. The footings need to be the correct width and thickness to support the weight of the foundation and house.

*Foundation walls* support the load of the house between the footing and the floor. They form an enclosure for basements or crawl spaces. Foundation walls are commonly made from concrete or concrete block. Some may be constructed from pressure-treated timber. The thickness of the foundation wall varies from 6 to 10 inches. Wall thickness and requirements for reinforcements are normally controlled by local building codes.

Footings should be placed on undisturbed, compacted soil below the frost line. The *frost line* is the depth to which frost penetrates soil in the area. If the footing is placed above the frost line, the soil under it would freeze and expand. This expansion causes the foundation to crack until the soil is compact again. It also causes cracks to appear in the foundation wall. In extreme cases, cracks will appear on inside walls. This cracking

Vocabulary: Demonstrate an understanding of the terms *foundation* and *footing* by using both in one sentence.

Activity: Estimate the depth of the frost line in your area. Then, call a local weather reporter or contractor to learn how deep the frost line is.

and settling will continue for years, and the cracks will continue to expand and lengthen. The local building code may specify how deep the foundation must be, based on soil conditions and the depth to which the ground freezes.

Most foundations settle evenly as the house adjusts to the ground. The foundation and walls may show hairline cracks, which are cracks less than ⅛-inch wide. Cracks greater than ⅛-inch are considered excessive. The builder is required to surface patch these cracks.

Stress cracks differ from hairline cracks and are signs of possible structural problems. They are usually wider at one end than the other. Stress cracks can be caused when the footing has settled more at one point, and the foundation is being pulled apart from underneath. They can also indicate that one side of the house is settling more than the other.

How stress cracks are corrected depends on the extent of the damage and usually requires leveling the house and reinforcing the footing. This is a costly procedure. Unless the purchase price of the house is low enough to cover the cost of this problem, the prospective buyer should not purchase this type of house.

When looking at a pre-owned house, make sure that the foundation walls are straight and square at the corners. They should not have major stress cracks.

A house built with a slab on grade foundation has no basement or crawl space. See 8-2. This type of construction is particularly used when building ranch style homes. The earth beneath the slab must be very hard and compact. Before the slab is poured, the ground at the site must first be graded or leveled. The contractor then spreads a filler, which is usually stone. A thin plastic sheet, called a *moisture barrier*, is then spread across the filler. Parts of the heating and plumbing systems are actually put in place before the slab is poured. Concrete is poured over the moisture barrier, forming a slab that is about 4 inches thick. The slab has a turned-down footing that totals approximately 16 inches in depth. The concrete slab is reinforced with rebar to strengthen it and discourage cracking.

## The Frame

The frame of the house is the skeleton around which the rest of the house is built. It consists of joists, studs, and rafters fastened together to support the house and its contents. See 8-3. When assembled and covered with sheet materials, they form floors, walls, and roof surfaces.

### Floor Frame

After the foundation walls are completed, the floor frame is built. First, a sill sealer and sometimes a termite shield are placed on top the walls. Next, the first piece of lumber, called a

© Kavanagh Homes

8-2

*This brick ranch style house is built on a slab on grade foundation.*

8-3 _____

*The framing members of the house provide the skeletal structure.*

*Vocabulary:* Define the terms *joist* and *girder* as they pertain to the construction of a floor frame.

*sill plate*, is installed. The sill plates support the outside walls of the house. They are bolted to the foundation wall with *anchor bolts*. The spacing between the anchor bolts may be specified by local building codes to meet uplift requirements to withstand tornadoes and hurricanes. Anchor bolts are set into the concrete of the foundation walls before the concrete hardens.

If the foundation wall is made from concrete block, the top two cores in the blocks are first filled with a sand and cement mixture called grout. Then, the 16-inch anchor bolts are embedded into the grout to bolt down the sillplate.

The floor frame is built on top of the sill plate or on top of wall frames when a second or third floor is desired. It consists of joists, girders, and subflooring. *Joists* are lightweight horizontal support members. Header

joists and rim joists form the perimeter of the floor framing. The ends of the floor joists are nailed to the header joists at 16- to 24-inch intervals. They are supported by a wood or steel girder. A *girder* is a large horizontal member in the floor that takes the load of joists. It supports the load of the floor joists and the weight of the floor or roof above it. The girder is built from three wooden planks nailed together. A girder which provides intermediate support for joists creates an interior support wall called a bearing wall.

Subflooring covers the floor framing members. *Subflooring* is a covering of plywood sheets nailed directly to the floor joists. The better the floor frame is constructed, the less likely it is to develop problems. Problems with floor frames leveling are usually indicated by squeaky floors. Because

**Math / Writing Activity:** Explain in writing how you would use the following math skills—addition, subtraction, measuring, multiplication, and division—to construct a floor and wall frame.

**Discuss:** What does a squeaky floor usually signal? (*poor floor construction*)

normal vibrations over a period of time may loosen the subflooring, some houses develop floor squeaks, especially in heavy traffic areas. Refer to 8-4 to see the components of a floor frame and wall frame.

### Wall Frame

The wall frame is built on top of the floor frame. It is made from 2-inch by 4-inch or 2-inch by 6-inch vertical framing members called *studs* and horizontal pieces called plates. Wall frames have a single *sole plate* on the bottom and a double *top plate* that supports the ceiling joists and roof members. Exterior and interior walls are generally built flat on the subfloor and then raised and nailed into position on the floor frame.

*Headers* are small, built-up beams that carry the load of the structure over door and window openings. For a 6-inch-thick outside wall, headers are made from 2-inch by 10-inch lumber

on edge with a piece of ½-inch plywood between them. This forms a header that is 3½-inches thick.

See Chapter 14, "Creating Interior Backgrounds," for a discussion of options for finishing interior walls. Cracks, waves, or buckles in these walls indicate that the wood frame has shifted or the wall covering was not installed correctly. Also, moisture from a leaky roof can be detected as a stain on the wall covering. Any such area should be corrected as soon as possible to prevent the growth of mold in the structure.

An alternative to traditional wood wall framing for the exterior walls of houses is the use of *autoclaved aerated concrete (ACC)*. This system has been used in Europe for many years and has gained acceptance in the U.S. market. In ACC masonry block construction, sand, lime, cement, water, and an expansion agent are mixed together. The mixture is cast into a mold, cut into blocks, and cured under pressure and heat for 8 to 12 hours at the manufacturing plant. The finished blocks are then assembled at the job site to create the framing system of the house. The result is an ultra lightweight concrete building material that is energy efficient, very strong, sound absorbent, and not harmful to the environment.

ACC masonry block construction has many advantages over traditional wood framing. Because it is noncombustible, homeowners can reduce the cost of their homeowner's insurance. Also, it is not susceptible to termite or insect attack. In addition, it is a low-maintenance product and cannot rot as wood does. You can expect to see more homes in the future use this material.

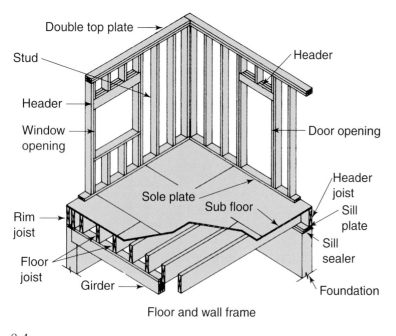

Double top plate
Stud
Header
Window opening
Rim joist
Floor joist
Girder
Header
Door opening
Sole plate
Sub floor
Header joist
Sill plate
Sill sealer
Foundation
Floor and wall frame

8-4
*The floor and wall framing consists of joists, studs, girders, plates, headers, and subflooring.*

### Roof Frame

The roof frame consists of a series of beams, called *rafters*, that support the weight of the roof. They extend from the exterior walls to the ridge. See 8-5. The *ridge* is the horizontal line at which the two slopes of the roof meet. It is the highest point of the roof frame.

In modern houses, most roof framing is done with truss rafters. A *truss rafter* is a group of members forming a rigid triangular framework for the roof. They are assembled at a factory and delivered to the job site. Then, they are attached directly to the double top plate. Truss rafters usually span the distance between exterior walls.

As you evaluate the frame of the house, remember to look for stress cracks and hairline cracks. If you notice a sagging ceiling, it could indicate that the wrong size or type of lumber was used. New houses will not show problems until they have settled. Pre-owned houses have had time to settle and probably will not crack further unless remodeling or more construction takes place.

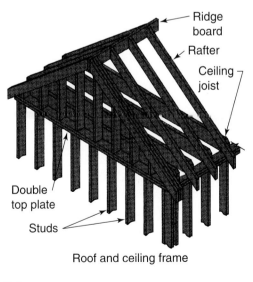

Roof and ceiling frame

8-5 _____

*The roof and ceiling framing consists of plates, joists, rafters, and the ridge board.*

# Materials Used for Exterior Construction

**Resource:** *Construction Materials,* Activity A, SAG. Students identify the advantages and disadvantages of various construction materials.

After the foundation and frame are built, the exterior walls and the roof coverings are added. The materials used for exterior construction vary. The first layer applied is called the sheathing. It may be wood, fiberboard, or plywood that is nailed to the studs. The sheathing is then usually covered with a waterproof paper called *building paper* or with a thin plastic sheet called *house wrap.*

Next, the siding is applied. The most common types of siding are wood, aluminum, vinyl, pressed wood (OSB or fiberboard), or fiber-cement siding. Masonry materials, such as brick, concrete block, stucco, and natural stone are also used. *Masonry* is a hard building material. The materials selected depend on their availability in the area, the cost of the materials, and the preference of the homeowners. Siding materials present different advantages and challenges.

## Wood Siding

*Siding* is the material forming the exposed surface of outside walls of a house. It is applied in strips, as shown in 8-6. Wood is a common material used. Wood siding is milled from cedar, redwood, pine, and cypress. It is suitable for a wide variety of exterior styles.

Wood has some distinct advantages as a siding material. It has a relatively low cost and is an excellent nonconductor of heat. It is also easy to cut and assemble. The ease of working with and fastening wood together with simple tools provides flexibility without extensive redesigning. Wood does, however, expand and contract with changes in temperature or humidity.

**Discuss:** What is the most common material used to make exterior siding? (*wood*) What trees are used to make it? (*cedar, redwood, pine, and cypress*)

**Enrich:** Visit a store that carries exterior sidings. View each and report a salesperson's descriptions of the advantages and disadvantages of each.

8-6

*Wood siding is being applied to the side of this new house.*

It must be checked routinely to be certain that it has not been damaged by rot or invaded by termites or other pests. Another disadvantage of wood is the maintenance cost of frequent painting or staining. Some parts of the country have climates that require painting every four years. However, periodic painting does give homeowners the flexibility of changing house colors as they see fit.

When inspecting the exterior siding of a house, look for putty marks covered with paint. This may indicate that the siding was applied poorly or repaired. Also, a house that has siding covered up with putty and paint may have other problems that have been disguised.

Plywood cedar siding is another type of wood siding. It can be applied horizontally or vertically. It covers large areas and saves installation time. Plywood siding must also be painted or stained, then sealed. It is also susceptible to termite damage and climatic changes.

## Manufactured Siding

Siding is also made from materials such as aluminum, vinyl, pressed wood and fiber-cement products. These different materials have varying advantages and disadvantages.

The advantages of *aluminum siding* are its durability and lack of need for repainting. It often has weather- and corrosion-resistant finishes. However, it does dent, as often occurs in hail storms, and may conduct electricity.

*Vinyl siding* is also durable and does not conduct electricity. It can expand and contract with changes in the temperature and humidity. Like aluminum, it does not require painting. However, it, too, will show dents.

Pressed wood siding is referred to as *oriented strand board (OSB)* or primed fiberboard. OSB is constructed by layering wood chips and fiber in a cross hatch pattern. Fiber board has similar construction but uses longer strands of fiber. Both products are easy to paint, but cannot be stained. They are less expensive than plywood siding. Special surface treatments are available, such as brushed, texture-embossed, and V-grooves.

*Fiber cement siding* is made from a calcium-silicate material that is evenly dispersed with reinforcing fibers. It is dimensionally stable, and resists moisture, mold and mildew development, and pests. It will not burn and has a zero smoke-development rating. It is less expensive than brick, but has all the benefits. Fiber cement siding can be ordered with a factory primed finish. It does require painting, but holds paint two to three times longer than wood.

## Masonry Siding

To construct the entire exterior wall, sometimes brick, clay tile, concrete block, natural stone, or stucco are used. As discussed in Chapter 6, "The Evolution of Exteriors," stucco is a type of plaster. See 8-7. *Brick* is a block molded from moist clay and hardened with heat. *Natural stone* is hardened earth or mineral matter.

Sometimes a brick veneer wall is used to create the look of a masonry wall. A *veneer wall* is a nonsupporting wall tied to the wall frame that is covered with wallboard. Thin sheet-metal ties are used to hold the veneer wall to the wallboard. Masonry veneer walls are used in many areas of the country.

Masonry products have distinct advantages. The products are strong, durable, and usually inexpensive to maintain. Also, they generally last a long time. The disadvantage of masonry products is the initial cost. They are usually hand-laid, which is one reason for their expense.

Masonry materials are available in a wide range of sizes, colors, and textures to produce different architectural effects. Other interesting effects can be created by the *bond*, or the way that masonry units are arranged together in a pattern. By varying the bonds and the depth and shape between units, additional depth dimensions and shadows can be added to the masonry wall.

When you examine a masonry house, you need to look for cracks or bows in the walls. Hairline cracks in the joints are only normal expansion cracks. However, larger cracks can break bricks as they continue up or down the wall.

## Roofing Materials

Common roofing materials include asphalt, fiberglass, vinyl, wood, tile,

Authentic Builders, Buddy Delozier, President, Hilton Head Island, SC

8-7 _____

*Stucco homes have gained in popularity in the last decade.*

slate, concrete, and metal. These materials provide color and texture that make the exterior of the house more attractive. However, they must also provide a protective, watertight covering to keep out rain and snow. If the roof leaks, the structure of the house and its contents can be damaged.

Most houses have sloping roofs that are covered with shingles. *Shingles* are thin pieces of material for laying in overlapping rows on roofs. Asphalt shingles are the most common roofing material. In warmer regions shingles which combine asphalt and fiberglass are used to help keep the house cooler. Asphalt shingles range in price from inexpensive to more costly depending on the composition, warranty, and quality of the product. See 8-8. Vinyl shingles are similar to asphalt shingles and come in a variety of textures and colors.

Wood shingles as well as *shakes*, which are a thicker shingle, are more

**Enrich:** Check builders in the community to find out how much more it would cost to use a masonry product instead of aluminum siding on an entire house. Check costs for brick and stone. Check the price of using the products only on the front elevation and the bottom half of the remaining elevations.

**Vocabulary:** Look up the meaning of *veneer*. Explain how knowing that term's meaning helps a person understand the meaning of the term *veneer wall*.

**Activity:** Survey 20 homes in your neighborhood and record the dominant material used as the exterior covering on the front and sides of the home. (Note: More than one type of material may be used.) Report the different materials evident and the number of homes using each.

Enrich: Find out what it would cost to replace a roof on your home. Get an estimate based on replacing the type of material currently used. Also, find out the price for upgrading to a top-quality version of the given material.

Photography courtesy of Judy M. Beck, Unireal Construction Company, McCormick, SC

8-8

*Many roofs are covered with asphalt shingles. Note the waterproof building paper wrapping the structure.*

8-9

*Roof tiles weigh about ten pounds each. This heavy load requires stronger rafters and other framing members to support the total weight of the roof.*

expensive than asphalt shingles. They should be treated with fire-retardant and decay-resistant chemicals. Shingles and shakes are popular because of their natural colors. They are most often used where cedar, redwood, and cypress trees grow.

In parts of the country with hot sun and little snowfall, clay or fiberglass tile, slate, and concrete roofing materials are often used. These materials are heavy and require proper roof design and structure to support the extra weight. Also, they are expensive. See 8-9. Clay or fiberglass tile, slate, and concrete roofing are very durable and will last the lifetime of the house.

Metal is also used as a roofing material. Aluminum and tin-plated steel are used in sheet form. Copper may be used on an entire roof or as an accent to a small area. The price of a metal roof varies depending on the quality. They are more expensive than asphalt and vinyl shingles, but not as expensive as tile.

Most roofing materials are applied in the same manner. First, the roof frame is covered with sheathing, which is a sheet material such as plywood. Then the sheathing is covered with a heavy building paper or roofing felt. This process will help keep out a limited amount of rain. Then, starting at the bottom of the roof, a starter strip of shingles is applied. The rest of the roof should be shingled in straight lines. When a shingled roof is finished it should have a uniform appearance in the pattern of application.

When inspecting an existing roof, it is important to ask for reasons for every roof repair. You can tell if it has been patched instead of reroofed by looking for a change in the color of the shingles. Problems that caused the patching usually resurface at a later date. In addition, it is important to pay close attention to the materials used for

Discuss: What types of materials are used for roofing? (*shingles made of wood, asphalt, fiberglass, or vinyl; sheets of aluminum, tin-plated steel, or copper; tiles of clay or fiberglass; slate; concrete*)

Enrich: Research sod roofs and where they are used. Why are they used instead of other types of materials? Approximately how much does a sod roof weigh? What are the benefits of a sod roof? the drawbacks?

flashing and their installation. *Flashing* is a sheet metal used in waterproofing the roof. It is used in valleys that exist in the line of the roof or where a chimney meets the roof. If the flashing is a substandard material or installed incorrectly, leaks can occur.

Special attention must also be given to inspecting flat areas of the roof. These areas should be covered with a buildup of asphalt or a heavy rubber sheeting. If the sheeting is used, it should have few or no seams. Such flat areas on a roof must be inspected carefully as they are very prone to leaks.

The remaining components of a roof system are the gutters and downspouts. A *gutter* is a horizontal open trough located under the perimeter of the roof to channel water away. A *downspout* is a vertical pipe that connects the gutter system to the ground to carry rainwater away from the house's foundation. Gutters and downspouts are constructed of aluminum or vinyl. The color is baked onto aluminum, but exists throughout vinyl. Both give the same advantage of not having to be painted. Aluminum has one additional advantage in that it can actually be extruded on site for a seamless installation.

# Windows and Doors

When people first built dwellings, a window was an opening that provided ventilation. A door was an opening for entry and security. In the past, windows and doors did not fit houses well and allowed heat to escape from houses. They also provided very little insulation. Over time, many new types of windows and doors were developed. They were built to prevent air from escaping and to provide better insulation. See 8-10.

Today a wide range of styles, shapes, and special options are available for both windows and doors.

## Windows

Windows have many uses in a house. From the interior, they provide natural light, air circulation, and a view. They can also serve as a point of emphasis in a room or as a part of the background. On the exterior, their size, shape, and placement affect the appearance of the house. In addition, some windows have built-in features or special coatings that conserve energy and prevent heat transference.

Weather Shield Windows & Doors

8-10

*The installer is checking to be sure the rough opening is the correct size for the window installation.*

**Discuss:** What roof areas should receive special attention in inspections? Why? (*flat areas because they are very prone to leaks*)

**Reflect:** How do you think it would feel to live in a house without windows? Imagine living in a cave. What problems do you think would develop as a result?

**Reflect:** What is your preference—swinging or sliding windows? What types of windows predominate in your home?

**Activity:** Draw the floor plan of your bedroom showing furniture placement and the elevations of walls containing doors and/or windows. Determine how you would like to change the door and window placement and/or design. Explain the changes in a brief paragraph and display them in a new set of floor plans and elevations.

Also, high-impact glass in the panes add protection from breakage by flying objects during storms or high winds. These windows are more costly because of the additional features. However, certain regions of the country, such as coastal areas, are adopting building codes that require these windows in new construction.

Windows have many parts. These parts include the frame, pane, sash, sill, and apron. See 8-11. The frame is the perimeter of the window which fits into the window opening and is nailed into place. The sash holds the glass and swings or slides open. Each sash may be divided into small sections by

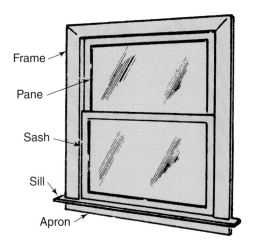

8-11

*The five main parts of a window are the frame, sash, pane, sill, and apron.*

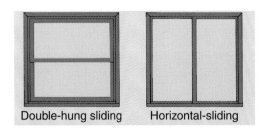

Double-hung sliding    Horizontal-sliding

8-12

*In double-hung windows, both sashes are operable. One sash is operable in two-sash, horizontal-sliding windows.*

wooden dividers called *muntins* and *bars*. These muntins and bars divide the glass in the pane into sections. Originally, window frames were made from either wood or aluminum. Today, as a result of strict local and national energy codes, new energy-efficient materials are used, such as vinyl and wood covered with aluminum or vinyl.

There are three basic types of windows: sliding, swinging, and fixed windows. All other window styles are based on these three. The type you choose for a house depends on the exterior style of the house, building codes, and personal preference. A traditional design, such as a Southern Colonial or French Provincial, looks best with a sliding window with muntins and bars. A contemporary house may feature large expanses of fixed windows.

### Sliding Windows

Sliding windows can operate either vertically or horizontally, as shown in 8-12. A *double-hung window* is a vertical sliding window, as shown in 8-13. It provides an opening of about one-half the size of the window.

*Horizontal-sliding* windows have two or three sashes. Two-sash windows have one sash that slides and the other that stays fixed. On a three-sash window, the center sash is fixed and the two outside sashes slide toward the center. Screens are mounted on the outside.

### Swinging Windows

There are four types of swinging windows. They are casement, awning, hopper, and jalousie windows. See 8-14. *Casement* windows open and close with a crank and swing outward. Usually the entire window area can be opened for ventilation. See 8-15.

**Enrich:** Research the most energy-efficient types of windows available. What should consumers look for when shopping for such windows? What material is used to make the window frame? Are any special coatings on the pane? What ratings signify a highly energy-efficient window?

Weather Shield Windows & Doors

8-13 ───────────────
*The windows in this kitchen are double-hung sliding.*

Awning windows swing outward at the bottom and are hinged at the top. This provides protection from rain. A similar window is the *hopper window*. It is hinged at the bottom to allow the top of the sash to swing inward.

*Jalousie windows* are a series of horizontal, adjustable glass slats fastened into a metal frame. They open and close with a crank and are used where ventilation is needed. Screens and storm windows are located on the interior.

## Fixed Windows

Fixed windows admit light and provide a view. However, they do not open. They come in many shapes and sizes, including rectangular, oval, half-round, round, and arched. See 8-16. Glass blocks are fixed windows that can be used to provide light while preserving visual privacy. See 8-17.

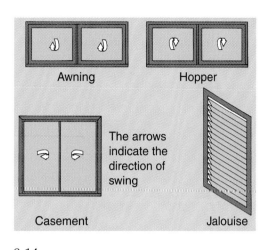

**Reflect:** Visualize the windows in your home. Are they fixed, sliding, or swinging? How many of each type exist?

8-14 ───────────────
*Awning, hopper, casement, and jalousie windows swing out to provide excellent ventilation.*

Weather Shield Windows & Doors

8-15 ───────────────
*These kitchen windows are casement style. Notice the decorative Gothic trim.*

**Research:** Find out what questions consumers should ask to get quality screens with their windows. What varieties are available? Do screens automatically come with windows?

**Activity:** Ask the older members of your family what storm windows are. When and how were they used?

**Writing Activity:** Write a paragraph describing how the fixed window unit in Figure 8-16 could be altered and become a combination window that would allow air circulation without jeopardizing the dramatic focal point in the room.

Pozzi Wood Windows®

8-16

*This fixed window unit creates a dramatic focal point in the room.*

Wood-Mode, Inc.

8-17

*Glass-block windows admit light but provide privacy.*

## Combination Windows

Fixed windows used with other types of windows are called *combination windows*. For example, hopper windows are often used above a fixed window. A large fixed window can have a casement window on either side.

A *bay window* is a combination window that projects outward from the exterior wall of the house. It often has a large fixed window in the center and double-hung windows on both sides.

### Skylights and Clerestory Windows

Skylights and clerestory windows are used to let light into areas that get little or no natural light. They can also be used to add additional light to give a room an airy appearance. See 8-18. *Skylights* are normally located in the ceiling or roof. They are usually square or rectangular and come in various sizes. *Clerestory windows* are placed high on a wall. They can be standard or custom-made windows.

## Doors

Doors provide access, protection, safety, and privacy. They also provide a barrier against sound, extreme temperatures, and light. Exterior doors are made from wood or wood covered with metal or vinyl. Interior doors are made from wood, metal, or wood covered with vinyl.

Doors are often classified by their method of operation. See 8-19. *Swinging doors* operate on hinges and usually swing open in one direction. Enough room needs to be left for the door to swing open and close. *Sliding doors* are set on a track and are opened or closed by gliding on the track. A *folding door* folds when open into a

**Vocabulary:** Use the terms *skylights* and *clerestory* in one sentence to demonstrate understanding.
**Math Activity:** Assume that glass blocks cost $5 each, installation materials cost $27, and sales tax is 7%. Also, assume that the installer of the new window is charging an installation fee of $4 per block.
How much would it cost to install the glass block window in Figure 8-17? (*$197.19*)
**Discuss:** What purposes do doors play? (*access; protection; safety; privacy; barrier against sound, extreme temperatures, and light*)

multisection stack. Doors are also classified by their method of construction and assembly, as shown in 8-20.

## Stile and Rail Doors

Stile and rail doors consist of stiles (solid vertical members), rails (solid horizontal members), and panels (space between stiles and rails). The panels may be decorative or glass. They may be raised or flat. Raised panels are cut from solid wood, and flat panels are usually cut from plywood. There is an unlimited number of panel combinations.

## Flush Doors

These doors are made by covering a framework core with wood or other material, such as metal or vinyl. There are two basic types of cores—solid and hollow. A *solid-core door* consists of tightly fitted blocks of wood covered with veneer. Sometimes particleboard is used as the core. These doors are heavy and are used mainly for exterior doors and for interior doors where sound control is a consideration. A *hollow-core door* has a heavier outside frame combined with wood strips, stiff cardboard, or paper honeycomb as the core. This type of door is lightweight and is used mainly as an interior door.

## Framed-Glass Doors

These are stile and rail doors with glass panels. The glass may be single pane or insulating glass. *French doors* are framed-glass doors with the glass divided with muntins into small sections. French doors are usually installed in pairs, as shown in 8-21. Sliding glass doors are another example of a framed-glass door. They often take the place of windows in small or medium-sized houses.

Velux-America, Inc.

8-18

*The half-round clerestory window and skylights play an important part in the interior design of this house.*

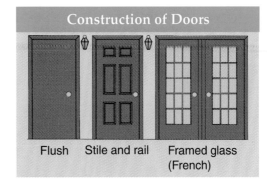

Operation of Doors

Swinging    Folding    Sliding

8-19

*Doors operate in three different ways—by swinging, folding, or sliding.*

**Vocabulary:** Discuss the differences that exist in operating a swinging, folding, and sliding door.
**Enrich:** Have a law enforcement officer speak about safety issues and how to increase safety with doors and windows.

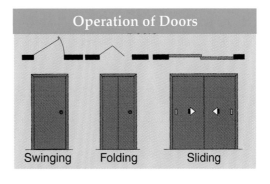

Construction of Doors

Flush    Stile and rail    Framed glass (French)

8-20

*Doors can be constructed in many different ways, including these three methods.*

**Activity:** Working from memory, make a written list of all the doors in your home. Double-check your list later at home and include any that were forgotten. (Remember to count closet doors.) Identify the type, style, and size of each.

**Discuss:** Why do you think hollow-core doors are usually used on the interior rather than exterior of a house?

8-21

*This dramatic combination of French doors with fixed glass window units creates both a division and a transition between spaces.*

8-22

*The builder of this house used special windows with insulated glass. The roof was engineered to withstand heavy snow.*

# Computer Applications in Construction

More and more, architects, engineers, building contractors, and interior designers are using the computer to assist them with decisions related to house construction. Computer applications usually speed the process of designing houses and help to assure the accuracy of the designs. Another advantage of using a computer is the realistic view it provides of the final product—the house. Since most people cannot visualize from architectural plans how a finished house will look, seeing a lifelike picture can avoid disappointed clients.

House designers use the computer in three basic ways. One way is to analyze the strength and appropriateness of planned materials. They also use a computer to select construction components and manage the building process.

## Analyzing Components of Construction

The designer of a house must assure the structural integrity of the design. For instance, the steep roof on the mountain home in Figure 8-22 was designed to prevent the build-up of snow. Besides providing the support needed under normal conditions, the house was also designed to withstand heavy snowfalls of several feet at a time.

A computer can analyze the planned materials and structural supports. It can also examine the stress these materials will undergo as a result of conditions in the geographic area, such as high heat and humidity. Computer programs allow the designer to "test" various designs and materials to

**Activity:** Before reading "Computer Applications in Construction," anticipate how you think computers are being used. Prepare a written list.
**Discuss:** If you were building a home, would you want it to be analyzed by a computer? Explain your answer.

**Reflect:** Does your home have any problems that might have been prevented with the use of a computer? What are they?

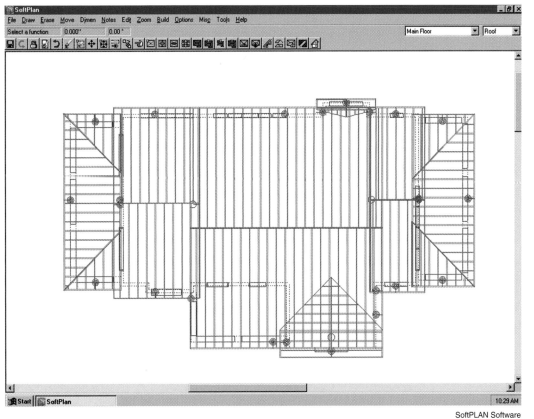

SoftPLAN Software

8-23

*This image clearly shows the structural parts of the frame. The designer can identify and solve problems before construction begins.*

assure the safety and effectiveness of the structure before it is built. See 8-23 for an example of using a computer to analyze structural components.

## Selecting Components of Construction

Housing components that are available in a wide variety of choices, such as windows, are best selected with the help of a computer. Housing designers and builders, for example, can view various window options and different placement combinations by using special CD-ROMs. A *CD-ROM* is a compact disk containing information that can be displayed on a computer monitor.

Often CD-ROMs provide product photos, price charts, sizing charts, design templates, and order forms. Window companies, cabinet manufacturers, and providers of other construction components make CD-ROMs available. You can also obtain information about these companies by going online to their Web sites.

## Managing the Construction

Computers are used to assist the designer and builder in developing plans that identify the sequence of steps required to construct the house. Also, computers are used to develop a timetable for the project so the house can be completed on time and cost-effectively.

# Summary

Understanding how houses are constructed helps house buyers make good decisions. The foundation and the frame are the basic structure of the house. The foundation supports the frame structure above it. It needs to be constructed correctly to prevent uneven settling.

Once the foundation and frame are built, the exterior walls and the roof are added. A variety of materials are used.

Windows and doors complete the basic construction of the house. The three main types of windows are sliding, swinging, and fixed. Other windows are variations of these three types or combinations of them.

Doors are classified by their method of operation—swinging, sliding, or folding. They are also classified by the method of construction used to make them. With the help of the computer, designers and builders can work more efficiently.

# To Review

1. Why do footings need to be placed on undisturbed, compact soil below the frost line?
2. What structural problems might cause stress cracks?
3. List the three main parts of the frame that work together to support the house and its contents.
4. List three advantages of wood siding.
5. List the advantages and disadvantages of each of the four types of manufactured siding discussed in the chapter.
6. List five types of roofing materials.
7. For each of the following, identify what type of window it is: fixed, sliding, or swinging.
   A. jalousie
   B. double-hung
   C. awning
   D. half-round
   E. horizontal-sliding
   F. casement
   G. hopper
8. How is an interior door constructed differently from an exterior door?
9. What is the difference between a solid-core and hollow-core door?
10. List three benefits of computer applications in construction.

**Language Arts Activity:** Working in pairs, students discuss what they learned from this chapter, using as many "To Know" terms as possible. The ground rules are: one declarative sentence is spoken at a time, partners take turns speaking, and key terms cannot be used in questions.

**Writing Activity:** Students write each letter of the alphabet on separate lines of a sheet of paper and work independently to write one term from the chapter that begins with each alphabet letter. After three minutes, pairs of students confer to fill in any blank lines. If blanks still remain, discuss with the class some possible choices.

# In Your Community

1. Observe a house under construction and identify as many of the structural components discussed in this chapter as you can. If possible, take photographs of the house under construction. Make a report to your class on your findings.

2. Make a list of the sizes of the doors and windows in one room of your house. Take this list to a building supply company and obtain costs for replacing these windows and doors with energy-efficient units. Compare the costs of two manufacturers. Also find out the labor cost for installing them. Share your findings with the class.

3. Invite a contractor to make a presentation to your class concerning his or her work. Request that he or she bring slides or pictures of newly constructed homes as well as a house at various stages of construction. Ask what are the favorite and least favorite parts of his or her work.

# To Think About

1. Imagine you are a contractor hired by a family to build their new home. The house plan they have selected contains a total of 1,800 square feet of heated space. Your clients want a rough estimate of how much it would cost to build this plan before they proceed with contract discussion. How would you determine this? Contact a number of builders in your community, and ask them what the building costs currently are per square foot of space. Find the average and multiply it by 1,800 square feet. What is your estimate?

2. Contact your state's attorney general for information about problems with new home construction or remodeling that homeowners report. Also, check the cautionary information to homeowners that office provides. Use the information to write a list of briefly-stated steps to help homeowners avoid potential problems when building or remodeling.

3. Imagine you are hired by the local government to fill the position of building inspector. Develop a house evaluation form that will help you inspect buildings for problems. Share your results with the class.

# Using Technology

1. Determine if your school has housing design software similar to what is used in the housing industry. If so, explore the program(s) and determine how the software can assist a builder. Print out a drawing from the computer and present it to your class.

2. Search the Internet for a major window manufacturer. Copy photos of the various window styles, shapes, and special options. Print out the photos and make a poster of your findings. Share the poster with your class.

3. Search the Internet using the term *house construction* to find a site containing photos of houses under construction. Identify the various stages of house construction. What stages did you not find?

**Note:** For researching window manufacturers, have students explore *andersenwindows.com* and *pella.com*.

**Note:** For researching stages of housing construction, have students explore *howstuffworks.com/house.htm* and *pgmillard.dyndns.org/gallery/*.

**Portfolio Project:** Using one of the homes you used in your pamphlet from Chapter 6, draw the foundation and frame of the house, labeling each part. Select the types of windows and doors you would suggest for it. Include drawings, magazine pictures, or photos from sales brochures to illustrate your selections.

# CHAPTER 9

# The Systems Within

## To Know

system
electricity
electric current
conductor
circuit
ampere (amp)
voltage
watts
fossil fuel
conduit
service drop
meter
service entrance panel
overcurrent protection devices
fuse
circuit breaker
septic tank
soil stack
trap
composting toilet
HVAC
forced warm-air system
duct
thermostat
hydronic heating systems
electric radiant-heating systems
central heat-pump system
fireplace insert
insulation
R-value
weather stripping

Peerless

## Objectives

After studying this chapter, you will be able to

■ describe the parts of the electrical system.
■ tell how natural gas and propane gas reach gas-burning appliances.
■ explain the functions of the two main parts of the plumbing system.
■ list the different types of heating systems.
■ explain how a cooling system works.
■ determine ways to conserve energy in the house.

Almost every house has systems within it to make it physically comfortable. A *system* is an interacting or interdependent group of items forming a unified whole. The systems in a house are usually called mechanical systems. They control the interior temperature and relative humidity, and provide electricity, gas, and water to the house.

Basic housing considerations regarding the interior systems may include the following questions: Will I have gas or electric appliances, or both? How can I make the house more energy efficient? How much insulation do I really need? What window type is best for the climate? What new technology is used in today's houses? These questions will be easier to answer after studying this chapter.

# Electrical Systems

Almost all houses in the United States have electrical power. Electricity provides energy for lighting and the operation of appliances. It also powers the operation of most of the systems within the house. See 9-1.

Around your house, perhaps you've noticed words like *watts, volts,* or *amperes (amps)* on electrical appliances or even lightbulbs. Understanding basic electricity will help you understand these terms and how the electrical system functions.

## Electrical Terms

*Electricity* is the movement of electrons along a conductor. Another name for electricity is *electric current*. The *conductor* allows the flow of

KraftMaid Cabinetry

9-1

*Electricity provides the capacity to watch TV in a well-lighted room.*

electricity and is usually a wire. This movement takes place at about the speed of light. The electrons follow a path from the source of the electricity to the device and back to the source. This is called a *circuit*. The circuit is composed of a delivery wire and a return wire.

The greater the number of electrons passing a given point in a circuit, the greater the current is. The measure of the amount of electricity passing through a conductor per unit of time is the *ampere (amp)*. A 100-watt lightbulb requires a current of almost one ampere to make it work properly.

*Voltage* is a measure of the pressure used to push the electrical current along a conductor. This pressure is present in wiring circuits whether electricity is being used or not. The greater the voltage is, the higher the current.

The electrical utility company delivers electricity to your house at a voltage that will operate your lights, electrical appliances, and other electrical equipment. Lights and most small appliances require 110 volts. Larger appliances such as the kitchen range, refrigerator, water heater, and furnace require 220 volts.

The amount of electrical power used is measured in *watts*. Watts tell consumers how much electrical power will be used when a device is being operated. For example, one watt of power is used when one ampere lights a 100-watt lightbulb in a circuit with a force of one volt. This can be shown in the following equation:
watts = amperes × volts.

## Electrical Power Generation

Electrical power comes from a variety of sources. Power plants usually generate electrical current by converting the energy from falling water, atomic fission, or burning fossil fuels into electricity. A *fossil fuel* is a fuel formed in the earth from plant or animal remains. Fossil fuels include natural gas, propane, gasoline, coal, charcoal, and wood. These energy sources are often burned to produce steam that turns turbines in generators to produce electricity.

Electricity is transmitted from the power plant at high voltages in wires held high by steel towers. When the electricity reaches the community, a transformer reduces the voltage and increases the current. The electricity is then distributed throughout a neighborhood in wires on poles or buried underground in a conduit. A *conduit* is a metal or plastic pipe that surrounds and protects the wires.

Before the electricity reaches your house, another transformer lowers the voltage even further. A three-wire line from the transformer provides both 110 and 220 voltages for the house.

## Electricity in the House

At the house, the electric company installs a service drop. A *service drop* is the connecting wires from the pole transformer to the point of entry to the house. See 9-2. Wires can also be run underground to the house through a *service lateral*. In both instances, the three wires are run to the electric meter for the house. The *meter* monitors electrical usage in the house. A power company representative periodically checks the meter to determine how much power has been used. In some locations, the power company uses computerized technology to read the meter from a central office.

The *service entrance panel* is a large metal box that receives power from the electric company's service drop or service lateral. It divides the power into individual circuits. These

Resource: *Electricity in the House*, transparency master 9-1, TR. Discuss having electric lines installed underground versus aboveground, identifying advantages and disadvantages of each.
Vocabulary: Describe electricity by using the following terms: *ampere (amp)*, *voltage*, and *watts*.
Discuss: What happens after your home loses electrical power during a storm? How does life at your house change?
Activity: In your home, find the service entrance panel and determine how to restore the electricity if a circuit is broken.

Discuss: Have you heard people voice concerns about the safety of living or going to school near an electric power generator? Do you feel that generating electricity may endanger human health?
Research Activity: Find out as much as you can about the history of electricity. When was it discovered, how, and by whom? Who were the earliest users? Who produced it and how was it sold? When did electrical wiring begin appearing in homes? When did it become common in America?
Internet Activity: Visit the Web site of your local electric company and a different company that services a community nearly the size of yours. Compare their electricity rates.

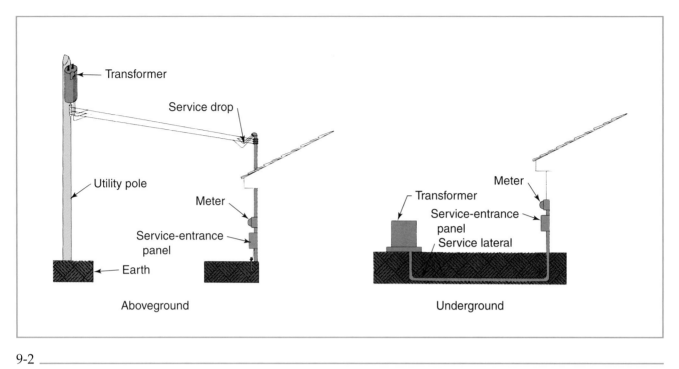

9-2

*Electricity travels from the power plant to your house through conductors that carry the electric current.*

**Vocabulary:** Compare the terms *fuse* and *circuit breaker*.

**Enrich:** Visit a model home and notice where the outlets are placed, how many exist per room, and where the service entrance panel is.

circuits are needed to provide electricity to each room or combination of rooms in the house. See 9-3. Each circuit is protected by an **overcurrent protection device** that stops the excessive flow of electrical current in the circuit. This situation occurs when too much current is being drawn.

Two types of overcurrent protective devices exist: a fuse and a circuit breaker. A **fuse** is a device used to open an electric current when an overload occurs. A **circuit breaker** is a switch that automatically interrupts an electrical current in an abnormal condition. If trouble develops on one circuit, only that circuit will be out of operation when the fuse blows or circuit breaker trips. Fuses were used mainly in older houses, while circuit breakers are in newer houses.

Electricians install the wiring inside the house from the service entrance panel to the points where electrical power is needed. Wiring is installed while the wall framing is

open and accessible. An electrical code authority is required to inspect the wiring installation while it is still visible.

Deciding where to place electrical outlets and other electrical connections requires advance planning of each room's use. The electrician will need to know where specific items go, such as the range, refrigerator, furnace, and water heater. Knowing where furniture will be placed is very useful, too. Furniture placement helps determine where connections for phones, TVs, and computers go. As a general guideline, each room should have at least three outlets. Also, no point along the base of a wall should be more than 6 feet from an outlet.

With greater use of computers, electronic communications, and home automation, homes need integrated wiring schemes to be able to use the new, electricity-dependent technologies. In the case of existing homes, rewiring or additional wiring is

**Enrich:** Attend a presentation by a speaker from the local electric company. Request an explanation of an electric bill. Summarize in one paragraph what you learn.

**Writing Activity:** Write a list of safety precautions for a young child who is learning about electricity.

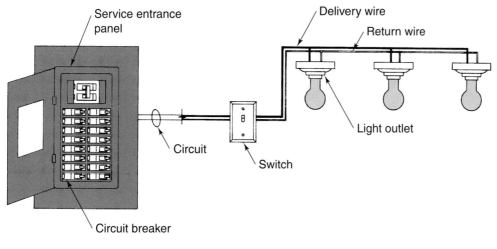

**Vocabulary:** Explain in your own words what the term *integrated wiring* means.

9-3

*A circuit carries electricity from the service entrance panel to the electrical devices in your home.*

needed. Often both options are expensive. However, in new or remodeled homes, installation of the integrated wiring can easily occur during the construction process. This is an affordable way to prepare for current and future electrical needs.

The new *integrated wiring* should include coaxial cabling and telephone connections that are threaded through a central plastic pipe extending vertically to all floors. The purpose of wiring in this manner is to integrate, or join, all the systems in the home. This integration offers occupants additional convenience in home entertainment, safety, communications, and management.

- For entertainment options, the occupant can program from one location the same video and audio selections throughout the house. Although TVs and other entertainment systems will be integrated, they can also be operated separately.

- Safety is enhanced because occupants can view visitors on TV before answering the door. Likewise, strangers near the house can be monitored. Smoke detectors can also be controlled and monitored for exit strategies in event of smoke or fire.

- Improved communication of information results as family members send messages to all computers and monitors in the home. The home computer can also link to a variety of home services, including banking and shopping.

- Integrated wiring makes installation and repair of home systems easier. For appliance maintenance, a manufacturer can monitor the equipment through the computer to alert the owner of what steps to take for a repair. The computer lets occupants control and monitor activities and systems in the home, including lighting and room temperatures.

# Gas as an Energy Source

Many houses use gas as an additional source of energy. It is a popular fuel for cooking, heating water, and

**Activity:** Make a one-column list of all the items in your home that use electricity. Draw lines to connect the items that can be linked through integrated wiring. For each linked item, write a one-sentence description of the special benefits that occupants gain as a result of the special wiring.

**Discuss:** Do you use gas or electricity at home to cook? Have you ever cooked on an appliance that uses another type of fuel? What was your reaction?

heating the air. Gas fuels include natural gas, which is piped from a gas main to your house, and liquid propane gas, which is delivered in pressurized tanks to your house.

## Natural Gas

Natural gas is taken from wells in the ground. From the gas fields, high-pressure pumps force the gas through large pipelines to communities. See 9-4. Then, the pressure is reduced, and the gas is distributed throughout the community in pipes called *gas mains*. To furnish gas to your house, the gas company taps the main and lays an underground pipe to your house. A gas meter is placed where the line enters your house. Like an electric meter, it records the amount of fuel used.

In the house, the plumber installs branch lines to all gas-burning appliances. Black pipe and fittings are

used for the branch lines. A pipe-thread compound, which prevents the leakage of natural gas, is used on all fittings. The system must be checked for leaks before it is used.

## Liquid Propane Gas

Propane is a colorless, odorless gas. It is used as fuel by houses that normally do not have access to a natural gas line. Propane is produced at oil refineries from natural gas, crude oil, or oil refinery gases. Gas supply companies then deliver the liquid propane gas (LPG) in tanker trucks to each house as needed. LPG must be stored in large, pressurized metal tanks on concrete pads near the house, but not next to it.

A tank is then connected to the gas line of the house. LPG has about twice the heating value of natural gas per cubic foot. However, with the delivery cost and storage requirements, it is normally more expensive than natural gas.

# Plumbing Systems

The plumbing system in a house provides water to the house and removes waterborne waste from it. (The gas lines already discussed are also considered part of the plumbing system.) A water supply system provides sufficient hot and cold water so fixtures and appliances can function properly. A wastewater removal system removes waste and used water, depositing them into a sewer line or private septic tank.

## Water Supply System

Water is supplied under pressure to your house from a community water main or a private well or system. It enters the house through a pipe

9-4
*Natural gas is transported in large pipes to communities where it is distributed to houses through gas mains.*

called the *building main*. Inside the house, the water may pass through a water softener, filter, or another treatment device. It then flows to separate cold and hot water mains. The hot water main starts at the water heater. Hot and cold water-branch lines travel throughout the house to each fixture or appliance that needs water.

Piping for the water supply system is located in the floor, walls, or ceiling of a house. Water lines are usually made of ½- or ¾-inch-diameter pipes of copper, plastic, or galvanized steel. See 9-5. Local codes may restrict the use of certain types of pipe. The lines are usually under a pressure of 45 to 60 pounds per square inch (psi).

A shutoff valve is installed in the building main next to the water meter and on each branch line next to the fixture or appliance. Shutoff valves make it possible to repair separate parts of the system without shutting off the water for the entire house. A leak in the main water line requires closing the valve at the meter.

## Wastewater Removal System

In the house, waterborne waste comes mainly from bathrooms, kitchens, and laundry areas. Since it tends to decompose quickly, the waste needs to be removed before it causes odors or becomes hazardous to human health.

Waste disposal pipes are completely separate from the water supply system. They are much larger than water supply lines and are not pressurized. These are also shown in 9-5. Instead, they rely on gravity to remove waste. The number and type of plumbing fixtures that discharge into the line determine the size of wastewater piping. Piping such as plastic, cast iron, copper, and brass alloy are used. Local codes specify the

Lowden, Lowden and Co.

9-5

*The small metal pipes are the hot and cold water lines. The large white pipes are the waste disposal pipe and soil stack.*

types and sizes of pipes required in the area.

As the wastewater leaves the house, it moves either to the community sewer lines or a private septic tank. When connected to a community sewer line, wastewater goes through a treatment system. Then, it usually is recycled and used for industrial and irrigation purposes.

When community sewer lines are unavailable, homes use septic tanks to dispose of wastewater. A *septic tank* is an underground tank that decomposes waste through the action of bacteria. The wastewater flows into the tank where bacteria dissolve much of what settles to the bottom. The liquid wastewater at the top of the tank flows into a system of perforated underground pipes called a *leach bed*. There, wastewater is dispersed into the soil.

Gases that result from a wastewater removal system must also be removed. A *soil stack* is a vertical pipe that extends through the roof to vent gases outdoors. The pipe also channels the water and waste to drain down and away from the house. Every house has at least one soil stack for each toilet.

Each plumbing fixture has a *trap*, which is a device that catches and holds a quantity of water. This pocket of water prevents the sewage gases from backing into the house. Traps are installed at each fixture unless the fixture has a built-in trap, as in a toilet.

Sometimes in remote cabins or isolated cottages, a water source and sewage system for an installed toilet are not available. Installing a toilet in places such as basements, workshops, and garages may also be difficult. In these cases, one option is a composting toilet. A *composting toilet* is a self-contained, stand-alone toilet. These units require no water or external plumbing. The system operates like a garden compost pile, transforming waste into a stable end product.

Photo courtesy of Kohler Co.

9-6

*The surfaces of plumbing fixtures are extremely durable and stain resistant.*

## Plumbing Fixtures

A plumbing fixture is a device that is connected to the plumbing system. Plumbing fixtures include kitchen sinks, lavatories, toilets, and bathtubs. Modern plumbing fixtures are made from a variety of materials. They include enameled cast iron, enameled steel, stainless steel, fiberglass, and plastics. These materials are chosen because they are durable, corrosion-resistant, nonabsorbent, and have smooth, easy-to-clean surfaces. See 9-6.

A kitchen sink is a flat-bottomed plumbing fixture used for food preparation and cleanup. Sinks are available in a large variety of sizes and shapes. The most common is the double-compartment sink installed in a cabinet countertop. See 9-7.

A *lavatory* is a plumbing fixture designed for washing hands and faces. It is commonly found in bathrooms. Lavatories come in a variety of colors, sizes, and shapes. They are available in wall-hung, countertop, and pedestal models.

A toilet is a water-flushed plumbing fixture designed to receive human waste. Toilets are usually made of a ceramic material called porcelain. They are installed directly on the floor or suspended from the wall.

A bathtub is a fixed tub designed to hold water for bathing. It comes in a variety of shapes, but the most common is rectangular. Most tubs have showerheads installed overhead. In addition, separate showering units are available.

# Heating Systems

A house may be heated with one of four conventional heating systems. They are forced warm-air, hydronic, electric radiant, and central heat-pump systems. Houses can also be heated by nonconventional heating systems, such as solar heat, fireplaces, and stoves. A common term used to refer to systems that condition the living space for thermal comfort is *HVAC*. This refers to heating, ventilating and air-conditioning systems.

## Conventional Heating Systems

Electricity, gas, oil, or coal are used to fuel conventional heating systems. However, coal is rarely used in newly built houses. The choice of which energy source to use is based on availability and the cost of fuel and operation. Environmental concerns also influence the choice of fuels.

### Forced Warm-Air System

In the *forced warm-air system*, the air is heated by a furnace and delivered to the rooms through supply ducts. A *duct* is a large round tube or rectangular boxlike structure that delivers heated (and air-conditioned) air to distant rooms or spaces. Ducts are located beneath floors and along ceilings. See 9-8. They connect the heating (or cooling) system to vents in or near the floor. The heating unit is a tall, sometimes thin, upright appliance, but ducts require a large expanse of surface area.

Gas, oil, or electricity is used to heat the air in the furnace. A blower moves the heated air through the supply ducts to the living quarters. A separate set of ducts, called the cold-air return, carries the cool air from each room back to the furnace. This periodic movement of warm air into cold spaces continues until rooms are heated to the desired temperature.

The indoor temperature is controlled in the living area with a

Photo courtesy of Kohler Co.

9-7 ———————————————————
*Kitchen sinks can be plain or quite fancy, as this beautiful design shows.*

9-8 ———————————————————
*In a forced warm-air system, supply ducts are located under the floor and in the attic.*

**Research Activity:** Before the advent of gas and electrical heating, how were homes heated? What was the incidence of house fires then? Explain the term *open flame* and describe the precautions that were taken.

**Discuss:** Are there any buildings in your area with exposed heat supply ducts similar to that shown in Figure 9-8?

**Reflect:** What is the method of heating used in your school? in your home?

thermostat that is wired to the furnace. A *thermostat* is a device for regulating room temperature. Furnace filters trap dust to prevent blowing it throughout the house. Forced warm-air systems are very common because they are economical and easy to install. However, some people dislike the sound and feel of the rapid air movement they cause.

### Hydronic Heating System

Circulating hot water systems are called *hydronic heating systems*. Water is heated in a boiler to a preset temperature, usually 180°F to 210°F.

When the water reaches the proper temperature, it is pumped through pipes to radiators, as shown in 9-9. As the water cools, it returns to the boiler for reheating. Radiators are located throughout the living areas, usually along the outside walls to reduce cold air drafts and increase comfort.

Hot water may also be circulated through copper or plastic tubing embedded in a concrete floor, wood floor, or plaster ceiling. The tubing is laid in a coil or grid pattern. The heat then radiates from the floor or ceiling into the room. This system is often used in mild climates. It may also be used as a backup heating system.

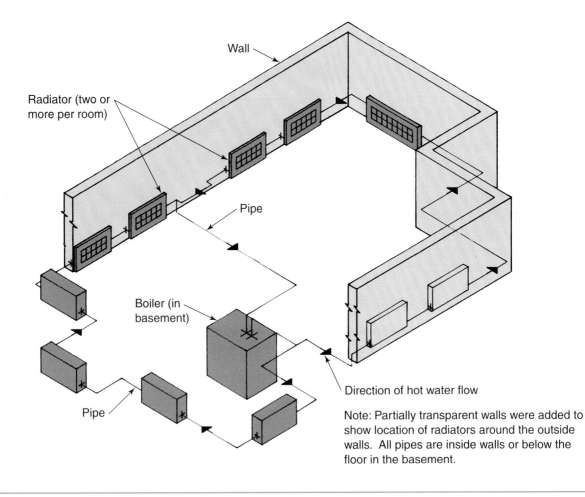

Wall

Radiator (two or more per room)

Pipe

Boiler (in basement)

Pipe

Direction of hot water flow

Note: Partially transparent walls were added to show location of radiators around the outside walls. All pipes are inside walls or below the floor in the basement.

9-9

*Hot water is pumped from the boiler to the radiators in individual rooms. Cool water is returned to the boiler for reheating.*

**Note:** The Web site *spnwsupply.com* has information on hydronic heating systems.

**Enrich:** Tour the boiler room or other heating facility in the school. Listen to an explanation of how the heating system works from the assistant principal for facilities or a school plant operator. Summarize in one paragraph what you learn.

Hydronic heating is a quiet, clean, and efficient type of system that does not create drafts. However, it takes longer to raise a room's temperature to the desired level. Also, if installed in a concrete floor that cracks for any reason, repairs are costly. Hydronic heating systems normally don't provide for cooling, air filtration, humidification, or dehumidification.

### Electric Radiant-Heating System

*Electric radiant-heating systems* use resistance wiring to produce heat in the wire. The wire is placed in the ceiling, floor, or baseboards. The heat moves from the wiring through the air molecules since heat travels from hot to cooler objects. Individual thermostats control the temperature in each room.

This type of heating system allows complete freedom in furniture and drapery placement. No air is introduced, no radiators are used, and air movement from the system is almost nonexistent. Disadvantages of the electric radiant-heating system include the high cost of electrical energy and the installation costs. This type of system should be installed when the house is built.

### Central Heat-Pump System

A *central heat-pump system* is an electric refrigeration unit used to either heat or cool the house. It removes heat from the outside air or ground in cold weather. In warm weather, it removes heat from the air in the house. The heat pump consists of liquid refrigerant, a compressor, and heat exchangers. A fan circulates the heated or cooled air through the house. See 9-10.

A central heat pump system is most efficient in areas with moderate to mild winter climates, where temperatures

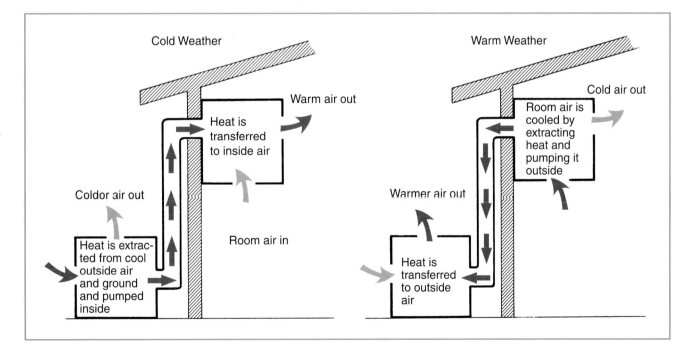

9-10

*In cold weather, the heat pump absorbs heat from the air and ground outside and pumps it inside. In warm weather, the heat pump absorbs heat from the air inside the house and pumps it outside.*

Resource: *Solar Heating Systems,* color transparency CT-12, TR. Students are introduced to the concept of using solar energy in homes for heat.

Vocabulary: Compare *active* and *passive systems* of solar heating.

Reflect: Other than heating a home, in what ways is solar energy used?

stay above 20°F. It usually costs more than other heating systems. However, it costs less than buying both a heating system and an air-conditioning unit.

## Solar Heating Systems

Solar heating systems use energy from the sun to provide heating and sometimes hot water for a house. A house that uses a solar heating system often has a backup heating system such as a stove to compensate for long periods of cloudy weather. The two main types of solar heating systems are active and passive. Both systems consist of a collector and a storage area.

### Active Systems

Active systems have solar collector panels on the roof of the house. This type of system requires pumps, fans, or other devices to move the heat from the collectors to a storage area or the space requiring heat.

### Passive Systems

Passive systems have no solar panels. Instead, they rely on the construction materials to collect and store the sun's heat. Windows, doorways, greenhouses, or skylights act as solar collectors. Walls and floors made from masonry materials such as concrete, concrete block, brick, stone, and adobe absorb the heat and act as the storage areas. Water-storage walls or tanks also store heat effectively.

## Fireplaces and Stoves

Fireplaces and stoves are used as heat sources as well as focal points. They differ from models of the past because they are safer, cleaner, and more efficient. However, wood-burning fireplaces and stoves still require

firewood that must be cut, split, and stacked. Moving wood indoors can leave debris on the floor. Also, after prolonged use, most stoves and fireplaces produce a light film of smoke in the room.

### Fireplaces

Fireplaces need to be carefully designed and built to operate correctly and prevent heat loss when not in use. Most fireplaces today are built with a single opening, or *face*, in the front. Some are also built with two or three openings. Metal, freestanding fireplaces are often used in contemporary houses.

Traditional fireplaces are made from masonry, while newer models are often made from metal. Metal fireplaces may be covered with brick or other materials so they look like solid masonry. Many of these new units are wood burning. However, some use electricity or gas to give the appearance of a log fire.

A fireplace consists of a hearth, firebox, damper, smoke shelf, chimney, and flue. See 9-11. The hearth is the flat area where the fire is built, and the apron is in front of the fire area. The firebox is the combustion chamber. It is lined with firebrick, which is made from fire-resistant clay. A damper is a metal device that closes off the airflow when the fireplace is not in use. The smoke shelf is where the smoke collects before going up the chimney. The smoke shelf also prevents outside air currents from forcing smoke back into the room. The flue carries smoke outdoors and creates a draft for the fire. The flue is lined with special tiles or metal liners that resist high temperatures. The chimney pipes the smoke out of the house. See 9-12.

A ***fireplace insert*** is a metal device that fits into an existing fireplace and

Note: Solar heating systems appropriate for various zip codes can be found on the Web at *servicemagic.com.*

Discuss: What moods or feelings are often associated with fireplaces? Explain your answer.

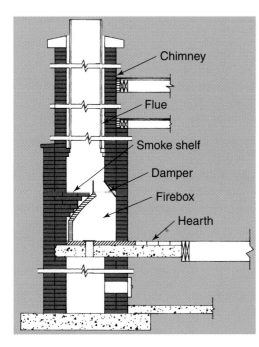

9-11
*Each part of the fireplace plays an important role in the efficient burning of wood and removal of smoke.*

Florida Tile Industries, Inc.

9-12
*This beautiful fireplace design was created by using quality wall and decorative tile. Note the coordinating tile floor treatment.*

attaches to the chimney liner. The fireplace may be made of masonry or factory-built. Fireplace inserts are used to transform a drafty fireplace into a more energy-efficient heat source. The insert draws the room's air into the fireplace, circulates it around a heat exchange, and returns it to the room. Heat-detecting sensors on the insert automatically shut off the blower when the room reaches a desired temperature. This can reduce heating costs since fireplaces with inserts normally have efficiency ratings near 70 percent. Fireplaces without inserts have an efficiency rating of 15 to 35 percent.

## Stoves

Stoves usually produce more heat than fireplaces. They use coal or wood to generate heat. There are two main types of stoves. *Radiant stoves* produce heat that radiates through the room to cooler objects. The surfaces of these stoves are extremely hot. Flammable materials must be kept away from them.

In *circulating stoves*, the main fire area is separated from the outside of the stove by a compartment. Air circulates into and out of the compartment, transferring heat into the room. Sometimes a fan helps the air move through the compartment. A thermostat controls the level of heat entering the room. These stoves are safer than radiant stoves because they produce less smoke and their exposed surfaces are cooler.

Stoves are more efficient and clean burning because of standards established by the U.S. Environmental Protection Agency (EPA). One standard limits the amount of smoke released per hour through the chimney. Another requires stoves to produce more heat per unit of fuel used.

These two standards help to assure a cleaner and safer environment.

Another type of stove is the *pellet stove*. See 9-13. It is designed to burn waste wood or other organic materials. The waste materials are compressed into pellets resembling rabbit food. One ton of pellets generates about 17 million British thermal units (Btu) of heat. A wood-burning stove generates about 8 to 10 million Btu per cord of firewood. Usually, only a handful of pellets are burned at a time. This results in high combustion efficiency, which means less ash and no visible smoke. Instead of the conventional chimney, a vent is required.

Vermont Castings

9-13 ————————————————
*A pellet stove is a highly efficient and functional heating unit.*

# Cooling Systems

Cooling systems provide cool, clean, moisture-free air during hot, humid weather. A central air conditioner is the most frequent cooling system used in houses. Room air conditioners are also used for cooling certain rooms.

The most common cooling system is the compressor-cycle system. It uses a compressed refrigerant to absorb heat, which cools the air. The refrigerant absorbs heat as it passes through the evaporator coil and changes from a liquid to a gas. The gas passes through a compressor, where it is pressurized. The hot, pressurized gas passes through the condenser coil, where it gives up heat and changes back to a liquid. Moving through the liquid line, it passes through a metering device into the evaporator coil to begin the cycle again. See 9-14.

When a room is cooled, moisture in the air condenses on the fins of the condenser and is drained away. This process dehumidifies the air and increases the comfort level. The cooler air is moved to various parts of the living space through a system of ducts. A blower or air handler usually moves the air through the heating system's ducts.

In a central air-conditioning system, the compressor and the condenser unit are placed outside the building while the air handler is located inside the house. In a room air conditioner, all components are contained in one unit. A part of this unit extends outside through a window or wall opening.

# Conserving Energy

About one-fifth of all the energy used in this country is used in housing so efforts to improve the

**Writing Activity:** Write a one-sentence summary of Figure 9-14.

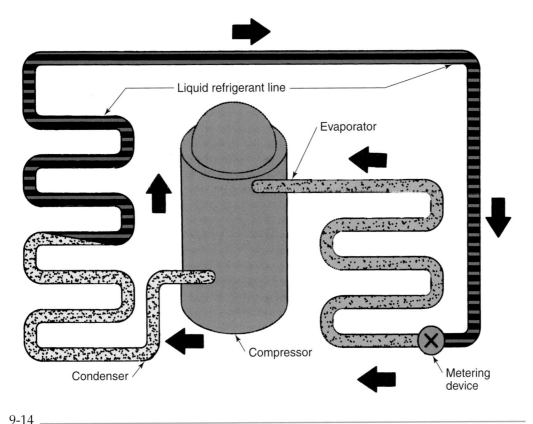

9-14

*This diagram shows the path the refrigerant takes as it moves through the compressor-cycle system.*

energy-efficient construction of houses are underway. The stated goal of the U.S. Department of Energy (DOE) is to reduce energy consumption in houses by 30 to 50 percent. This applies to both new and existing houses. Building code authorities are promoting the inclusion of energy codes in state building codes to accomplish this goal. The National Association of Home Builders (NAHB) is cooperating in the effort.

In addition, a new program jointly offered by the EPA and DOE informs consumers of the most energy efficient housing, materials, and appliances on the market. This program is called Energy Star. The greatest energy savings can be achieved by choosing items with the Energy Star seal. (Chapter 18, "Selecting Household Appliances," discusses the Energy Star program in greater detail.)

Controlling room temperature through heating and cooling systems accounts for most of the energy used in a home. Heating water is the next greatest energy user. Together, space conditioning and hot water systems account for over two-thirds of the energy used in homes.

There are many ways to use less energy at home and thus reduce energy bills. Several recommendations appear in Appendix B, "Energy Savers: Tips on Saving Energy and Money at Home." However, a major focus of saving energy should be improving the air-tightness of the building and installing energy-efficient equipment. The remainder of this chapter examines ways to save energy with insulation, energy-efficient windows and doors, and computerized energy management.

**Enrich:** Evaluate a newspaper or magazine article about energy conservation. Examine the author's statements for facts, assumptions, opinions, and motivation for writing the article.

**Discuss:** What has your state done to conserve energy and encourage families to conserve energy? Why is energy conservation a concern of legislators?

# Insulation

One of the best ways to conserve energy is by surrounding the living space with proper insulation during house construction. **Insulation** is material used to restrict the flow of air between a house's interior and the outdoors. Insulation has millions of tiny air pockets that resist the flow of heat through it. Insulation materials keep heated air indoors in winter and outdoors in summer. How well a material insulates is measured by its **R-value**. The larger the R-value, the more resistant the material is to the movement of heat. See 9-15.

Insulation is made from a variety of materials that differ in efficiency, quality, and safety. These materials include fibrous glass, rock wool, cellulose, urethane, and polystyrene. Insulation is available in blanket, board, and loose-fill forms. Each has different uses and shapes and meets different requirements.

*Blanket insulation* comes in long rolls, or *batts*, which are shorter rolls usually 4 to 8 feet long. Both rolls and batts come in 16- to 24-inch widths and in various thicknesses. The thicker the insulation is, the shorter the roll. Blanket insulation is commonly used in attics, floors, walls, and around pipes and ducts. See 9-16.

*Board insulation* is made from rigid foamed plastics. It is available in sheets ½-inch to 4 inches thick. It is usually 2 by 4 feet or 4 by 8 feet in size. Board insulation is higher in R-value per inch of thickness than other forms of insulation. However, board insulation also tends to be more expensive. It is used between concrete and earth, around foundation walls, and on one side of the footing. It is also used on the outside of studs as sheathing.

*Loose fill* is used in spaces where other types of insulation are difficult to install. It may also be used in attics, inside frame walls, in cores of concrete block, and as filler between other types of insulation. It comes in bags and may be poured or blown into place, 9-17.

| R-Values | Batts or Blankets (thickness in inches) | | Loose Fill (Poured In) (thickness in inches) | | |
|---|---|---|---|---|---|
| | Glass fiber | Rock wool | Glass fiber | Rock wool | Cellulosic fiber |
| R-11 | 3.5-4 | 3 | 5 | 4 | 3 |
| R-13 | 4 | 4.5 | 6 | 4.5 | 3.5 |
| R-19 | 6-6.5 | 5.25 | 8-9 | 6-7 | 5 |
| R-22 | 6.5 | 6 | 10 | 7-8 | 6 |
| R-26 | 8 | 8.5 | 12 | 9 | 7-7.5 |
| R-30 | 9.5-10.5 | 9 | 13-14 | 10-11 | 8 |
| R-33 | 11 | 10 | 15 | 11-12 | 9 |
| R-38 | 12-13 | 10.5 | 17-18 | 13-14 | 10-11 |

Table title: Common Insulation Materials

9-15 _____
*This chart compares the R-values of different thicknesses of common insulating materials.*

Installing more insulation usually slows the escaping of heated air in winter and cooled air in summer. This helps to lower energy use, which lowers heating and cooling bills. Some areas of the country need insulation to combat intensely hot summers, extremely cold winters, or a mix of both.

Both heating and air conditioning contribute to the recommended R-values shown in Figure 9-18. These figures reflect national, state, and local recommendations. To use the information, look at the map and find the zone that covers your area. Then, read the various R-values shown for that zone to determine your insulation needs.

Having insulation of the proper R-value is very important for promoting energy efficiency and occupant comfort. Equally important is the proper installation of insulation. Consumers should use skillful installers from companies with a reputation for doing high-quality work.

## Targeted Air Sealing

A major way to control energy use in a residence is to block conditioned air from leaving the living area. The top of the building should receive first priority, followed by the bottom of the building. Attention should be given to any leakage from the ducts in forced warm-air heating systems. A special test can help identify air leakage from heating ducts. See 9-19. Walls, windows, and doors should be targeted last. Then appropriate strategy and design can be developed to reduce energy loss.

## Windows and Doors

Heat loss around windows and doors and through glass panes is an energy problem. Adding weather

Discuss: Is clothing ever used as insulation for our bodies? Give examples.

Lowden, Lowden and Co.

9-16
*Blanket insulation is used here to insulate a wall.*

U.S. Green Fiber, Cocoon Insulation

9-17
*Here, recycled cellulose insulation is being blown into the attic area. It is excellent for sound control, fire protection, and energy savings.*

Enrich: Visit a home supply store and study the different types of insulation available. Ask questions about the R-value and about methods of installation. Summarize your findings in a written report.

Enrich: Invite a guest speaker from the local electric company to explain the importance of using good insulation and sealing places where air may escape.

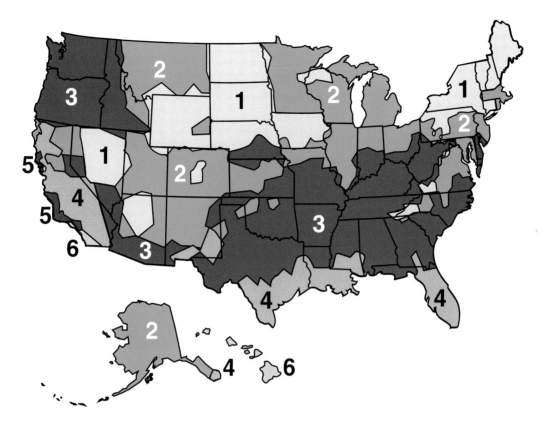

| Recommended R-Values for Zones | | | | | | | | | | | | |
|---|---|---|---|---|---|---|---|---|---|---|---|---|
| | | | | | Ceiling | | | | | | Basement | |
| Zone | Gas | Heat Pump | Oil | Electric Furnace | Attic | Cathedral | Wall | Floor | Crawl Space | Slab Edge | Interior | Exterior |
| 1 | X | X | X | | 49 | 38 | 18 | 25 | 19 | 8 | 11 | 10 |
| 1 | | | | X | 49 | 60 | 28 | 25 | 19 | 8 | 19 | 15 |
| 2 | X | X | X | | 49 | 38 | 18 | 25 | 19 | 8 | 11 | 10 |
| 2 | | | | X | 49 | 38 | 22 | 25 | 19 | 8 | 19 | 15 |
| 3 | X | X | X | X | 49 | 38 | 18 | 25 | 19 | 8 | 11 | 10 |
| 4 | X | X | X | | 38 | 38 | 13 | 13 | 19 | 4 | 11 | 4 |
| 4 | | | | X | 49 | 38 | 18 | 25 | 19 | 8 | 11 | 10 |
| 5 | X | | | | 38 | 30 | 13 | 11 | 13 | 4 | 11 | 4 |
| 5 | | X | X | | 38 | 38 | 13 | 13 | 19 | 4 | 11 | 4 |
| 5 | | | | X | 49 | 38 | 18 | 25 | 19 | 8 | 11 | 10 |
| 6 | X | | | | 22 | 22 | 11 | 11 | 11 | none | 11 | 4 |
| 6 | | X | X | | 38 | 30 | 13 | 11 | 13 | 4 | 11 | 4 |
| 6 | | | | X | 49 | 38 | 18 | 25 | 19 | 8 | 11 | 10 |

9-18

*The different heating zones in the states are numbered 1 to 6. The chart shows the R-values recommended for house insulation in each zone.*

**Discuss:** Looking at the map on this page, in what zone is your community? What are the recommend R-values for attic and wall insulation in homes using gas for heating? in homes using electricity? Why is there a wide difference between the R-values recommended for walls versus attics?

**Enrich:** Evaluate brochures for new housing construction to determine R-value being used by local builders. Develop a chart that presents your findings

**Reflect:** What steps has your family taken to conserve energy? Have these efforts helped to lower the electric bill? Discuss this with your family.

Advanced Energy, Raleigh, North Carolina

9-19 _____

*Trained heating and cooling technicians use a blower-door test to check air leakage in a home.*

Weather Shield Windows & Doors

9-20 _____

*This remodeling contractor selected quality windows that provide energy efficiency and reduce the harmful effects of ultraviolet rays on interior furnishings.*

stripping to windows and doors helps prevent drafts and heat transfer. *Weather stripping* is a strip of material that covers the edges of a window or door to prevent moisture and air from entering the house.

Another way to conserve energy is to install storm windows over single-pane glass windows. The air space between the windows acts as an insulator.

Windows that have double or triple the insulation value of single-pane windows are available. Window ratings assist the consumer in evaluating the expected energy performance of specific types of windows.

Many types of energy-efficient windows contain two or three gas-filled insulating chambers that block almost all the sun's ultraviolet rays. They provide more daylight with less winter heat loss and less summer heat gain. Very energy-efficient windows are available, including low-emission glass (low-e) and other window technologies. See 9-20. Consumers can also

add a film to windows to control excessive heat transfer and damaging rays. Frequent exposure to sun rays can fade and/or weaken fibers and wood finishes.

The need for energy efficiency is not limited to windows. Sliding patio doors feature the same double- and triple-pane window systems. Door construction has evolved so that many attractive doors are also extremely durable and energy-efficient.

## Energy Conservation Through Computer Power

An inexpensive device for controlling heating and cooling levels is a programmable thermostat, which uses a computer chip. You can set programmable units to automatically adjust temperatures around your personal schedule—a comfortable setting when you're home and an energy-saving setting when you're away. Most climate controls can be set to change temperatures four times during a

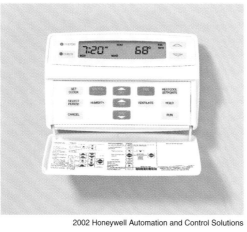

2002 Honeywell Automation and Control Solutions

9-21

*Besides regulating the home's heat and air conditioning, this comfort-control center manages the fans, air cleaner, humidifier, and fresh air ventilator.*

24-hour period—when you wake, leave for work, return home, and go to bed. A programmable thermostat is inexpensive and generally pays for itself in a short period of time.

More powerful comfort controls resemble a thermostat, but do so much more. The controls can reduce energy use 20 to 40 percent by monitoring items that operate electronically. See 9-21. The items that can be regulated include appliances as well as communications, HVAC, and electronic equipment. Computerized controls can manage the lighting, interior climate, and maintenance systems in the following ways:

- Turn lights on and off automatically as people enter and leave rooms.
- Roll shades up and down automatically to admit sun or block cold air.
- Adjust heating, ventilation, and air-conditioning systems to outdoor weather conditions.
- Adjust the interior temperature according to activities in the house.

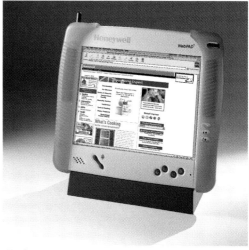

WebPAD is a registered trademark of National Semiconductor Corporation

9-22

*This unit allows a homeowner to control a home's lighting system, security system, heating, air conditioning, home electronics, and appliances from any location that has access to the Internet.*

- Report maintenance and equipment problems automatically so total climate comfort and maximum use of equipment are maintained.
- Monitor the climate-control system for dirty filters so the efficiency of this system can be maximized.

An example of computerized housing management is the Smart House. For an explanation and illustration of circuits in a Smart House, see Chapter 22, "Housing for Today and Tomorrow."

The most advanced comfort-control centers provide all the features discussed previously with additional conveniences. Occupants can regulate their home's system from anywhere inside or outside the building. Since the control system links wirelessly to the Internet, homeowners can make adjustments to their settings from anywhere they can access the Internet. See 9-22.

# Summary

The systems within a house provide electricity, gas, and water to the house to make it more comfortable. As you choose or evaluate systems for your house, you will have several options.

Electricity provides energy for operating lights, appliances, and most of the systems within the house. Understanding the basic electrical terms—conductor, electric current, circuit, ampere, voltage, and watt—and how electricity works will help you use electricity wisely.

Gas is another source of energy for the home. It can be in the form of natural gas, which reaches the house from a gas main. Liquid propane gas, which is delivered to the house in pressurized tanks, is another option.

The plumbing system brings water to and through the house via the water supply system. Waterborne waste is removed from the house through the wastewater removal system.

The four types of conventional heating systems used to heat houses are the forced warm-air, hydronic, electric radiant, and central heat-pump systems. Nonconventional heating systems include solar heat, fireplaces, and stoves. Central air conditioners and room air conditioners are used to provide cool, clean, dehumidified air during hot, humid weather.

When choosing systems for your house, look for those designed to conserve energy. Use the proper insulation to keep the house warm in cold weather and cool in warm weather. Energy-efficient windows and doors also provide insulation. Computer systems can help conserve energy in your home by controlling lighting and interior climate, and by maintaining the systems.

**Resource:** *Systems Savvy*, Activity D, SAG. Students match terms from the chapter with the identifying phrases.
**Writing Activity:** Make a list of 10 important concepts you learned from this chapter. Write one- or two-sentence summaries of each.

# To Review

1. Define *electricity*.
2. Which appliances require 220 volts of electricity?
3. Why are gas lines checked before they are used?
4. True or false. Hot and cold water supply lines rely on gravity to move the water.
5. True or false. The water supply system is separate from the wastewater system in the house.
6. List advantages and disadvantages of the four types of conventional heating systems.
7. Why might someone choose a radiant-heating system instead of a forced warm-air heating system?
8. Describe a fireplace, wood stove, and pellet stove. Explain which you would choose for a new house.

**Answer Key**

1. the movement of electrons along a conductor
2. large appliances such as a range, refrigerator, water heater, and furnace
3. for gas leaks
4. false
5. true
6. (Student response. See pages 223-225.)
7. has little air movement, no noise, and no ducts
8. A fireplace is an open chamber in which wood burns (or gas or electricity give the appearance of a wood fire) and smoke exits through the chimney. A wood-burning stove is a closed chamber that produces heat by burning wood. A pellet stove is similar to a wood-burning stove, but it creates more heat by burning pellets of compressed organic material.

9. refrigerant
10. board
11. by managing the systems that use energy

9. The most common type of air-conditioning system uses a compressed _____ to absorb heat from the air.

10. The best insulation to use under a concrete floor is _____ insulation.

11. How can a personal computer help conserve energy in a house?

## In Your Community

1. Determine the type of overcurrent protection devices you have in your house and where they are located. Determine what to do when a fuse blows or a circuit breaker trips.

2. Locate the water shutoff valves for each water-using fixture in your house.

3. Look through newspapers and magazines to find ads for windows and doors that claim to be energy efficient. Display the ads on a bulletin board for others to compare.

4. Research the cost of installing a computer system to conserve energy use by the systems in a house. Report your findings to the class.

5. Call the local office of the Cooperative Extension Service to determine if their office can complete a blower door test on a residence. If so, ask them if you can see a demonstration on a home. Write a report on what you observe and learn from the demonstration. If they do not do this type of testing, determine if they know what local agency or company can do this. If possible, schedule a demonstration, and write a report on what you observe and learn from it.

## To Think About

1. Suppose you joined a team to design the mechanical systems on a space station, including HVAC, plumbing, and power systems. What types of systems do you think would be necessary? What new types of technologies would be needed to make life in outer space comfortable, convenient, and energy efficient?

2. Suppose you bought a house with an elaborate computerized program to manage its systems. Make a list of what home systems you would like to control with the computer. What would be the advantages of using a computerized system? What problems might occur when using a computer, and what could be done to combat them?

3. To what extent do you believe this country can stop using foreign oil in 10 years and totally rely on domestic sources instead? What new or expanded energy sources are needed for such independence? How can these energy sources be developed?

# Using Technology

1. Survey your classmates to determine all the types of heating systems used in their homes. Create a computer spreadsheet to chart the systems and the numbers used. Which types of heating systems are used most frequently? Which, if any, are not used? Summarize your results in a paragraph and share it with your classmates.

2. New technologies for use in the home are always under development and in the media. Search the Internet for five examples of equipment or computer programs that relate to this chapter. Obtain photos if available. Using a desktop publishing program, develop a brochure to share with your classmates. Analyze what needs the new technologies meet in a home?

**Note:** For researching new technologies in housing, have students explore *newtechnologyhome.com.*

3. The composting toilet is one option for homes located in remote areas. Search the Internet for information on this option. Using a desktop publishing program, develop a handout including photos and a description of how this works. Share the handout with your classmates. What is your initial reaction to this type of waste management? What questions do you have that are not answered in the information provided by companies selling these toilets?

**Note:** For researching composting toilets, have students explore *cityfarmer.org/comptoilet64.html.*

**Portfolio Project:** Continue working on the home you chose for Chapter 8's portfolio project by creating plans for its electrical, gas, plumbing, heating, and cooling systems.

# PART 4

# The Inside Story

# CHAPTER 10
# Elements of Design

## To Know

visual imagery
design
function
construction
aesthetics
line
horizontal lines
vertical lines
diagonal lines
curved line
form
realistic form
abstract form
geometric form
free form
space
mass
high mass
low mass
texture
tactile texture
visual texture

Ethan Allen, Inc.

## Objectives

After studying this chapter, you will be able to

- list the three characteristics of design.
- describe the different types of lines and explain their effects.
- demonstrate the different types of form.
- explain how space is used in design.
- identify high mass and low mass.
- describe tactile texture and visual texture.

Communication takes place in many ways. It can be verbal or nonverbal. Verbal forms of communication include expressing yourself by talking, writing a letter, or singing a song. Nonverbal communication includes using sign language or body language such as a smile, a grimace, a shrug of the shoulders, or making a "high five" sign. In order for people to understand each other, they must understand the language. For example, the sender and the receiver must both know the sign for "high five" and its meaning.

*Visual imagery* is a type of *nonverbal communication*. It is the language of sight. When you see an item of clothing, a piece of furniture, or an unusual object, you see a visual image. This image communicates a feeling to you. Look at 10-1 and 10-2. Each room's visual image communicates a certain personality or mood. This visual image is based on design. Understanding and creating good design requires knowing design characteristics and the elements of design.

The word *design* has many meanings. To a fashion designer, it refers to the specific pattern in a fabric or a garment. A printer sees design as the way letters and pictures are arranged in a layout. Interior designers refer to **design** as the entire process used to develop a specific project. The project might be an object, room, or building. Design also refers to the product or result of the process.

**Vocabulary:** Look up *design* in the dictionary and select the meaning most appropriate to interior design. Use the term correctly in a sentence.

Ethan Allen, Inc.

10-1

*What does this room communicate to you?*

**Activity:** Write a paragraph describing the visual imagery you perceive in an article of clothing or small piece of furniture brought to class by the teacher.

Ethan Allen, Inc.

10-2

*How does the visual image of this room differ from that in Figure 10-1?*

**Discuss:** Compare Figures 10-1 and 10-2. What different messages are communicated by their respective visual imageries?

# Design Characteristics

Design has three characteristics: function, construction, and aesthetics. All are used as guidelines in creating and evaluating any design.

The first characteristic is *function*, or how a design works. A design's function includes usefulness, convenience, and organization. Good design makes a product or room better or easier to use. It considers the needs of people using the item. Good functional design also accommodates the ages, sizes, and physical abilities of the users. Successful functional design provides easy access for all people and eliminates barriers.

The second characteristic of design is *construction*. Construction includes materials and structure. *Materials* are the different kinds of fabrics, woods, metals, plastics, or stones used to build a product or room. Appropriate materials need to be chosen to support the room's function. When selecting materials, consider design function, quality, initial cost, maintenance, and long-term costs such as repair and replacement. Materials also need to meet industry standards, government codes, and regulations.

*Structure* refers to how the materials are assembled. Products need to be safe, durable, and well made. Like materials, structures must meet industry standards, government codes, and regulations.

The third characteristic of design is beauty, or *aesthetics*, which is a pleasing appearance or effect. Beauty is difficult to define because each person has his or her own personal taste. However, good aesthetic design is pleasing to many people. It may communicate a message or stimulate an emotion, such as exciting or relaxing, humorous or serious. See 10-3. Personalized design reflects the aesthetics a person wants to express in a room.

Function, construction, and aesthetics all must be considered to create a successful design. For example, a room that is aesthetically pleasing but does not function well and is poorly constructed is not good design.

# Elements of Design

Successful designers use tools to create designs. These tools are called the elements of design. They include line, form, space, mass, texture, and

Permission granted by Hunter Douglas, Inc. to use copyrighted designs. Designs © Hunter Douglas, Inc.

10-3

*This room's pleasing appearance communicates a feeling of relaxation.*

color. However, because color involves a detailed discussion, it will be covered in a separate chapter. (See Chapter 11, "Using Color Effectively.") All the elements of design are needed to describe, plan, and evaluate your housing.

## Line

A *line* is the most basic element of design. It is created when two dots are connected. Lines form the edges or outlines of objects and areas. They also show direction and cause the eyes to move from one point to another. For example, a line can cause you to look from objects on one end of a shelf to objects at the other end.

### Types of Lines

The two major types of lines are straight and curved lines. The different types of lines create different emotional responses.

Straight lines can be horizontal, vertical, or diagonal. *Horizontal lines* are parallel to the ground. See 10-4. They often direct your eyes across. Horizontal lines communicate feelings of relaxation, calmness, and restfulness. For example, horizontal lines are associated with sunsets on the horizon, which suggests the end of a day and time for rest. This is the same feeling you get when sleeping in a horizontal position.

Horizontal lines are found in many home furnishings. They can be seen in fireplace mantels, bookcases, long sofas, shelving, or fabrics or wallpaper that decorates the room.

*Vertical lines* are perpendicular to the ground. They cause your eyes to move up and down. This movement suggests height, strength, dignity, and stability.

In 10-5, notice how the columns visually communicate height. This is

Resource: *Lines,* Activity B, SAG. Students follow instructions to create lines and answer related questions.
**Discuss:** What are the elements of design? (*line, form, space, mass, texture, color*)

Photo courtesy of Andersen Windows, Inc.

10-4 _____

*Horizontal lines can make a room feel more relaxing and informal.*

Lexington Homes

10-5 _____

*These columns give the front of this house the feeling of height, strength, dignity, and stability.*

**Discuss:** What role does line play in aesthetics? (*forms edges or outlines of objects and areas, shows direction, and causes the eyes to move from one point to another*)

**Vocabulary:** Explain what is meant by *horizontal line* and *vertical line.*
**Discuss:** What type of lines predominate in Figures 10-3, 10-4, and 10-5?

because the vertical lines direct your eyes upward. A feeling of strength is also communicated since the columns support the *pediment*, which is an architectural rooflike decoration found over the door. Because the columns stand straight and tall, they communicate dignity. Vertical lines that rest on the ground convey stability.

Vertical lines appear in many home furnishings. Look for vertical lines in window treatments, striped wallpaper, and decorative trims that carry your eyes upward. Grandfather clocks, highboys, armoires, tall mirrors, and most picture frames also have vertical lines.

Lines that angle between horizontal and vertical lines are called *diagonal lines*. They communicate different levels of activity, ranging from a low- to high-level of energy. See 10-6. The level depends upon the degree of the angle and total number of angles. For example, the symbol for a bolt of lighting has several sharp diagonal lines.

Ethan Allen, Inc.

10-6 _____

*The diagonal lines in these candlesticks create interest and movement.*

This symbol communicates action, excitement, and sometimes agitation. Use of diagonal furniture placement in floor plans not only brings movement, interest, and excitement, but can also enhance conversational areas.

In home furnishings, diagonal lines create a feeling of transition from one level to another. They appear in roof lines, cathedral ceilings, staircases, lampshades, and various fabrics and paintings.

Curved lines are the second major type of line. A *curved line* is a part of a circle. If you completely extend and connect a perfectly curved line, it becomes a circle. The curved line may also extend to form an oval. Curved lines can also take a free-form shape and range from slightly to very curvy.

The different degrees of curves in lines communicate different ideas. Generally, curved lines seem softer than straight lines. A circle or oval reflects organization, eternity, and uniformity. Slightly curved, free-form lines have a natural and flowing movement. They communicate softness, freedom, and openness. See 10-7.

### Using Lines in Housing Decisions

Applying different types of lines to specific decorating situations can result in different effects. For example, a space can appear larger, smaller, calmer, or busier just by using different types of lines. Repeating straight lines or curved lines can create a strong, intense statement. To create a more relaxed look, combine various types of lines.

Observe the use of various straight, diagonal, and curved lines in 10-8. The vertical lines in the wall treatment and the lamps draw the eyes upward. Horizontal lines in the wall treatment and the table make the space appear wider. Diagonal lines in the table and lamp bases create a gradual transition

Ethan Allen, Inc.

10-7 _____

*The curved lines of these containers convey a calm, organized feeling. The curved lines in their decorative patterns are flowing and active.*

from the floor to the ceiling. Finally, curved lines in the mirror and pottery help soften the many straight lines in the room.

## Form

*Form* is the physical shape of objects. It outlines the edges of a three-dimensional object and contains volume and mass. Form also has height, width, and depth.

### Types of Form

There are four different types of form: realistic, abstract, geometric, and free form. When a form looks very much like the real thing, it has *realistic form*. Realistic form communicates a lifelike, traditional, and familiar feeling, 10-9. For example, a common chair has realistic form because of its specific form. It is easily recognized as a chair.

*Abstract form* rearranges or stylizes a recognizable object. The abstract item has traits that look like the real

Ethan Allen, Inc.

10-8 _____

*Combining horizontal, vertical, diagonal, and curved lines can be very pleasing to the eyes.*

item, but altered. Abstract form communicates a contemporary, changing, creative, and artistic feeling.

*Geometric form* uses squares, rectangles, circles, and other geometric figures to create form. It communicates organization, order, planning, and a tailored look. Geometric forms are found in home furnishings, such as square tables, round lampshades, and various shapes of pillows.

Resource: *Form*, Activity C, SAG. Students find or draw pictures illustrating four types of form and list the guidelines for using form in design.

**Note:** Repetition, as shown in Figures 10-6, 10-7, and 10-8, is a type of rhythm, which is a principle of design discussed in Chapter 12.
**Reflect:** Do you think a room needs a variety of lines to be pleasing?

**Writing / Math Activity:** Imagine you have $5.00 to buy words, each costing 10¢ no matter how long or short. Write a summary of the section on "Form," using no more than $5.00.

Laufen International

10-9

*The pictures of fruit on this ceramic tile kitchen wall is an example of realistic form.*

Southface Energy Institute, Atlanta, Georgia

10-10

*The related square forms used in this bath create a pleasing look.*

*Free form* is random and flowing. It is found in nature—in plants, stones, and wood. It does not have geometric design. Free form communicates a sense of freedom. Free form is untraditional, unfamiliar, and different from realistic form.

### Using Form in Housing Decisions

There are three guidelines to follow to help use form wisely in housing design.

- *Form follows function.*
- *Related forms are more agreeable than unrelated forms.*
- *A gradual change in form smoothly directs the eyes.*

Regarding the first guideline, the function of an object should be considered first in the design process. Then the form should be chosen. For instance, chairs for a family room should have a form that lets people sit comfortably and relax. If chairs had seats that slanted to one side or legs that were too tall, they would not be comfortable. The unusual form would not function well as a chair.

According to the second guideline, your eyes feel comfortable looking at similar forms. For instance, square forms dominate in 10-10 and are used throughout this room to give it a crisp, organized look.

The third guideline means seeing an abrupt change in form or too many different forms together may be unpleasant and confusing. When forms change, your eyes have to work harder to follow the different shapes. However, sometimes a change in form can cause excitement.

## Space

*Space* refers to the area around a form such as the area around a table. It also refers to the area inside a form,

**Activity:** Look around the classroom and identify objects of realistic form, abstract form, geometric form, and free form.

**Discuss:** What are the three guidelines for using the design element of form well? (*Form follows function. Related forms are more*

*agreeable than unrelated forms. A gradual change in form smoothly directs the eyes.*)

**Discuss:** What are two factors to consider when working with the design element of space? (*size and arrangement*)

such as the area inside a room. When discussing space, two closely related factors need to be considered: the size of the space and its arrangement.

## Size of the Space

The size of interior space is often defined by its height, length, and width. The size affects who will use the space and how they will use it. For example, a bedroom that is 10 by 12 feet is probably too small for two teenagers who each need a bed, dresser, desk, and chair. However, the same size bedroom is adequate for two small children who only need beds and one shared dresser.

The size of a space can also communicate positive or negative feelings. For example, a large space can communicate feelings of openness, grandeur, or freedom. See 10-11. However, a large space such as a sports arena may make you feel small, lost, or overwhelmed.

Small spaces can make you feel cozy, intimate, or comfortable. If more people and furnishings are added to a small room, it might feel very crowded.

## Arrangement of the Space

When using space in design, you first need to evaluate the space and decide what design effect you want to achieve. You can achieve various effects by arranging the space differently. For example, you can arrange space to make large spaces look smaller and small spaces look larger.

To open and expand spaces, you can expand window area, use mirrors, or remove walls. See 10-12. To create the feeling of cozy quarters, the space can be divided into separate areas. This can be done by using area rugs, clustering furniture, or even building a kitchen island. You must be careful, however, because poor divisions of space can create an unorganized or confused feeling.

Weather Shield Windows & Doors

10-11 —————————————————————————
*This cathedral ceiling creates an open and visually expanding space.*

Ethan Allen, Inc.

10-12 —————————————————————————
*The half-wall and columns create a cozy setting in this open, expansive space.*

**Math Activity:** Working with a partner, determine the amount of space in the classroom in terms of cubic feet.
**Discuss:** How do you feel when you are in a very large room that is sparsely furnished? How do you feel in a room too full of furniture? How does the design element of space contribute to these feelings?

**Discuss:** What has the designer done to create small, intimate spaces in the great room shown in Figure 10-11?

# Mass

*Mass* is the amount of pattern or objects in a space. It also refers to how crowded or empty a space appears. A space can have high mass or low mass.

## High Mass

*High mass* refers to a space that is visually crowded. A lot of pattern or lines are found in a high-mass fabric design. A room with high mass has many items in it and may look congested. High-mass rooms may reflect a full, crowded, or cluttered feeling. See 10-13. The impression communicated by high mass may include formality and weightiness.

## Low Mass

*Low mass* refers to a space that is simple and sparse. It is the opposite of high mass. Only the essential furnishings are used in a low-mass design. It communicates clean and airy feelings. The traditional design styles called *Minimalism* and *Shaker* reflect low mass. The room in 10-14 is an example.

## Using Mass in Housing Decisions

Either high mass or low mass can be used to create a strong design statement. Blending high and low mass can create variety in a room design. For example, placing a low-mass design above a high-mass design creates a very open feeling in the room. The two extremes may complement each other.

# Texture

*Texture* refers to the way a surface feels or appears to feel. There are two kinds of texture: tactile and visual texture.

Ethan Allen, Inc.

10-13
*The use of high mass evident in the patterned fabric, wallcovering, and dark, heavy furniture gives this room a formal feeling.*

Photo by Paul Rocheleau, Shaker Hancock Village

10-14
*The plain lines and lack of ornamentation give this Shaker room a sparse but airy feeling.*

## Tactile Texture

*Tactile texture* is how the surface feels to the touch. You can see and feel tactile texture. For example, think of yourself standing next to a stone wall. You can see the ridges and crevices in the stone with your eyes, and you can feel its coolness and roughness with your hand. A stone wall has tactile texture.

There are many tactile textures used in design. For instance, a surface might feel bumpy, rough, soft, smooth, grainy, porous, or hard. When selecting items for the home, you should consider the way they feel. For example, some fabrics may be too rough and uncomfortable to use in upholstery.

### Visual texture

*Visual texture* is texture that you see, but cannot feel. It can be found in scenic wallpaper or fabric patterns as well as in pictures. For instance, in a photograph of a stone fireplace, you can visually see the texture. However, you cannot feel any coolness and roughness, as you do with actual stone. Instead, you only feel the smoothness of the photo.

### Using Texture in Housing Decisions

You can use specific textures to communicate different feelings in a room. For example, rough surfaces, such as textured plaster or paint treatments, can create a more casual feeling. Smooth surfaces, such as glass, polished wood, or brass, may communicate an elegant feeling. Polished stone or marble can communicate both elegance and strength. Terms used to describe the roughness or smoothness of texture are *nubby, crinkled, quilted, ribbed, uneven,* and *even.* Terms that describe the hardness and softness of texture include *rigid, crisp, harsh, flexible,* and *limp.*

Ethan Allen, Inc.

**10-15** _____
*The wide range of textures used in this room create both variety and interest.*

The use of textures can affect the visual size of a room. Heavy or rough textures absorb more light than smooth textures. They do not reflect light throughout the room, so the room looks smaller. On the other hand, smooth surfaces make small rooms look larger. The light reflects off the smooth surface, creating the illusion of a larger space.

You can create variety by using both visual and tactile textures. When more than one texture is used in a room, the room looks more interesting. See 10-15. However, too many kinds of texture in one room may be confusing.

**Activity:** Analyze Figure 10-15 and identify elements that contribute to the room's tactile texture.
**Discuss:** What may be the result of using too many different textures in a room? (*a confusing or busy look*)

Resource: *Elements of Design*, color transparency CT-13, TR. Students discuss how the elements of design can transform a room. (Show how adding each element of design changes the image from a one-dimensional line to a three-dimensional form with mass and texture.)

# Summary

Visual imagery is the language of sight. It communicates different feelings. Understanding visual imagery is based on knowing the design characteristics and elements of design.

The three characteristics of design—function, construction, and aesthetics—are used as guidelines in creating and evaluating design. The tools used to create good design are color, line, form, space, mass, and texture.

Using different types of straight and curved lines can create different emotions in a room. They can be used together in different combinations to create various effects. The four types of form and the three guidelines for using form can inspire countless design ideas. When using space, the area inside and around a form, you need to consider its size and arrangement. You can use high mass or low mass to create a strong design statement. You can also use both types together to create variety in a room. Tactile and visual texture can be used to communicate different feelings, affect the visual size, and create variety.

## Answer Key

1. the language of sight
2. function
3. Horizontal lines communicate relaxation, calmness, and restfulness. Vertical lines communicate height, strength, dignity, and stability. Diagonal lines communicate activity ranging from little energy to chaos.
4. A. realistic
   B. free form
   C. geometric
   D. abstract
5. Form follows function; related forms are more agreeable than unrelated forms; and gradual change in form can direct the eyes smoothly.
6. It is more comfortable and less confusing to the eyes.
7. area rugs, furniture arrangement, kitchen island
8. Form contains both.
9. high
10. Tactile texture is how a surface actually feels, and visual texture is how it appears to feel by the way it looks.

# To Review

1. What is meant by the term *visual imagery*?
2. Which characteristic of design is concerned with how a design works?
3. List the three types of straight lines and a feeling each communicates.
4. Identify the type of form described by each of the following:
   A. lifelike, normal, and traditional
   B. random and flowing
   C. organized, ordered, planned, and tailored
   D. rearranged or stylized
5. List three guidelines for using form in design.
6. Why are related forms more agreeable than several unrelated forms?
7. What can be done to divide space and create smaller areas?
8. How are space and mass related to form?
9. A floral print fabric has _____ mass.
10. How does tactile texture differ from visual texture?

**Reflect:** Review the chapter objectives. Do you still need to review or research some topics to get the information you feel you need? If so, what topics?

**Enrich:** Visit a model home and identify examples of each element of design. Summarize your findings in writing.

# In Your Community

1. Choose a room in your school and evaluate how each element of design is used. On a sheet of paper, rate each element based on the following scale: *1 = very poor, 3 = average,* and *5 = very good.* Total the score and share your evaluation with your classmates.

2. Obtain a free brochure from a local real estate company serving your community. Find four pictures of rooms, each illustrating several design elements discussed in the chapter. Mount the pictures on separate sheets of paper and label the design element shown in each.

3. Refer to a beautiful room that you have visited in the area. Write a short report on how each element of design was used in the room.

4. Choose a word that describes a texture. Write the word in the middle of a large sheet of heavy cardboard or construction paper. Create a collage by mounting items found in the area—such as pieces of fabric, wood, or stone—as well as pictures representing the word.

# To Think About

1. Imagine your are a professional architect who is hired by your community to design a new building for the city's art collection. The design must incorporate examples of as many different lines as possible. Try to include horizontal, vertical, diagonal, and curved, including circular, oval, curvy, and complex free-form. Have fun sketching the interior and exterior of a building that meets these requirements.

2. Imagine you are a professional interior designer, hired by your local school board to evaluate your school environment as it relates to form and function. Select any room in the school and analyze whether form follows function. List the items in the room that address the room's function and make a separate list of items that address form. What recommendations would you make to improve both the form and function of the space?

# Using Technology

1. Search the term *interior design* on the Internet and find a site that provides useful ideas. What interior design techniques are recommended for changing the perception of a room's size and space? What design choices can make a room appear smaller? appear larger? Print out copies of the design examples to show the class, and identify the product or service offered by the manufacturer sponsoring the Web site.

**Note:** For researching interior design techniques, have students explore *waverly.com.*

2. Create a PowerPoint® presentation or an overhead presentation to display the various types of line, form, and mass in interior design. Select pictures of well-designed rooms from magazines or the Internet. Label the designs accordingly.

3. Select a favorite photo in the text outside this chapter and identify how the room's line, form, mass, space, and texture convey good interior design. Develop a five-minute audio presentation by recording your comments on a tape recorder. Identify the photo you selected, and play your recording for the class.

**Portfolio Project:** Create a notebook or storyboard of pictures of beautiful interiors, each describing the elements of design contained within. Label each element of design.

# CHAPTER 11
# Using Color Effectively

## To Know

color
color spectrum
color wheel
primary colors
secondary colors
intermediate colors
hue
value
tint
shade
intensity
complement
pigment
warm colors
cool colors
color harmony
monochromatic color harmony
analogous color harmony
complementary color harmony
split-complementary color harmony
double-complementary color harmony
triadic color harmony
neutral color harmonies
color scheme

Ethan Allen, Inc.

## Objectives

After studying this chapter, you will be able to

- explain the meaning of different colors.
- understand how color influences human behavior.
- describe the relationships between colors on the color wheel.
- give examples of color harmonies.
- plan pleasing color harmonies.

Resource:
*Psychological Effects of Color*, Activity A, SAG. Students describe how the listed colors make them feel and evaluate their color preferences for interiors.
**Discuss:** Do you agree or disagree with this sentence from the first paragraph: *Color is probably the most important element of design.* Explain your opinion.

In the previous chapter, you learned about the elements of design—line, form, space, mass, and texture. In this chapter, you will learn about another element of design—color. Color is probably the most important element of design. Deciding what color to use is usually the first decision made when decorating a room. It is one of the first things others notice about your housing. Color sets the mood in a room and leaves a lasting impression with most people.

# Understanding Color

*Color* is an element or property of light. It can help you create certain

Permission granted by F. Schumacher & Co. to use copyrighted photographs.
Designs and photograph © F. Schumacher & Co.

11-1 ⎯⎯⎯⎯⎯⎯⎯⎯⎯⎯⎯⎯⎯⎯⎯⎯⎯⎯⎯⎯

*The combination of colors used in this child's room creates a cheerful space.*

moods in your home by communicating excitement, calmness, mystery, or other sensations and emotions. When you understand the effects of color, you can use it to make your personal living space attractive and satisfying. See 11-1.

Each color has certain psychological effects on people. For instance, red is associated with power, danger, fire, strength, and passion. It is bold, aggressive, exciting, and warm. It demands attention. Red can make you feel energetic. However, too much red in a room can be overpowering.

Orange is hopeful, cheerful, warm, and less aggressive than red. It expresses courage and hospitality. It can make a room feel energetic and friendly.

Yellow is friendly, happy, and warm. It is associated with sympathy, sunlight, prosperity, cowardice, and wisdom. Yellow rooms are cheerful, light, and airy. However, pure yellow draws attention due to its brightness, so care should be taken to avoid applying it in large amounts.

Green is the color of nature. Consequently, it is refreshing, friendly, cool, and peaceful. It is also associated with hope, good luck, and envy. Green mixes well with other colors and looks especially good next to white.

Blue is cool, quiet, and reserved. It is associated with tranquility, serenity, and formality. Blue can be soothing and peaceful. It looks especially pleasing when used with white. However, too much blue in a room can be depressing.

Violet is a royal color. It is dignified and dramatic. It works well with most other colors.

Black is sophisticated and mysterious. It is associated with wisdom, evil, and death. Small amounts of black help to give a room a crisp appearance. When used in large quantities, however, black may be oppressive.

**Reflect:** Study the photo of Figure 11-1. How would you feel in a room decorated with the variety of colors used here? Why? How do you think a child would feel?

**Discuss:** Do you feel the fashion industry should use the real names of colors to describe clothing and cosmetics, or continue using fanciful names such as "siesta" and "passion"?

White is fresh, peaceful, and pure. It is associated with youth, innocence, and faith. Like black, small amounts of white make rooms look crisper and livelier.

People feel most comfortable when they are surrounded by colors that reflect their personalities. For instance, outgoing people might choose bright red or yellow for the main color in a room. Shy people might feel awkward in a red room. Instead, they might prefer a room that is decorated with a soft blue or green.

When making color decisions for your home, the preferences of each family member should be considered. No single color will satisfy everyone. However, the social area of the home should be decorated to make all members feel as comfortable as possible. Individual color preferences can be used in the personalized sleeping areas and other private work or play spaces.

## The Color Spectrum

The *color spectrum* is the full range of all existing colors. Spectral colors are produced by a beam of white light as it passes through a prism. Although unlimited in number, more than 10 million colors have been identified in the color spectrum. Each distinct color is derived from a few basic colors. The rainbow in 11-2 is the ideal example in nature of how sunlight can be separated into a continuous band of colors called a *spectrum*. In the case of a rainbow, the raindrops themselves serve as tiny prisms separating the light.

The variety of colors possible in nature is virtually limitless. Paint manufacturers have translated the spectrum into several hundreds of different paint colors. See 11-3.

11-2

*The water droplets in a rainbow separate light into its many colors.*

11-3

*This fan of different paint colors represents a portion of the many colors that exist in nature.*

**Science Activity:** Borrow a prism from the science department. Experiment with dividing light into its component colors.

**Discuss:** Why do you think a person feels most comfortable when surrounded by colors that reflect his or her personality?

**Discuss:** What are the dominant colors in the school's interior? What are the dominant colors of the sports teams? Why do you think these colors were chosen?

# The Color Wheel

Color relationships are easy to understand when a few basic principles are learned. The standard color wheel is the tool used to best illustrate these principles. The *color wheel*, 11-4, is the most commonly used tool to understand the basis of all color relationships. It is made of three concentric rings: an outer, middle, and inner ring. The middle ring of the color wheel consists of three types of colors: primary, secondary, and intermediate.

Yellow, red, and blue are the *primary colors*. They are the basic colors and cannot be created by mixing other colors. However, by mixing, lightening, or darkening the primary colors, all other colors can be made.

Orange, green, and violet are the *secondary colors*. Mixing equal amounts of two primary colors produces these colors. Orange is a mixture of red and yellow. Green is a mixture of yellow and blue. Violet is a mixture of blue and red. Look again at the color wheel. Notice each secondary color is located halfway between the two primary colors used to make it.

The other colors in the middle ring of the color wheel—yellow-green, blue-green, blue-violet, red-violet, red-orange, and yellow-orange—are the *intermediate colors*. They are sometimes called *tertiary colors*, which means the third level. They are named after the two colors used to make them—a primary color and a secondary color. Note that their names always have the primary color listed first.

## Color Characteristics

Each color has three characteristics: hue, value, and intensity. Various tools are used to illustrate these characteristics. The color wheel shows hues and some values. Separate scales are used to show color values more completely as well as color intensity.

### Hue

A *hue*, or color name, is the one characteristic that makes a color unique. It is what makes red different from blue and green different from yellow. It is the specific, individual nature of each color.

### Value

The *value* of a hue is the relative lightness or darkness of a hue. The normal values of hues are shown in the middle ring of the color wheel. The normal values of some hues are lighter than the normal values of others. For instance, yellow has the lightest normal value of any color in the middle ring of the wheel. As you move away from yellow on the color wheel, the normal values of hues become darker. Violet has the darkest normal value.

The value of a hue is made lighter by adding white. This addition of white to a hue produces a *tint*. For instance, pink is a tint of red. It is made by adding white to red. Adding white to blue creates baby blue, a tint of blue. Tints are shown in the innermost ring of the color wheel. For lighter tints, more white is added.

The value of a hue can be made darker by adding black. This addition of black to a hue produces a *shade*. For instance, maroon is a shade of red. It is made by adding black to red. Navy blue is a shade of blue and is created by adding black to blue. For darker shades, more black is added. Shades are shown in the outer ring of the color wheel. Refer again to the color

Outer ring = shades of hues
Middle ring = normal values of hues
Inner circle = tints of hues

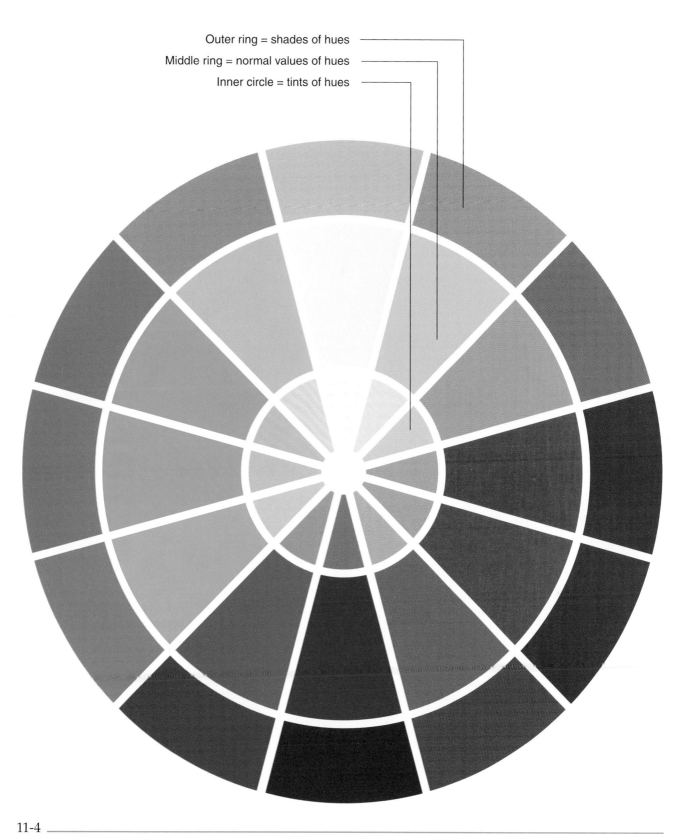

11-4
*The arrangement in a color wheel provides a basis for all color relationships.*

**Enrich:** Attend a presentation by a color analyst from the home decorating, fashion, or cosmetics industry to learn about the importance of color and successful color selection. Summarize in one paragraph what you learn.

**Reflect:** Look around the room at the various colors and note the array of values of each.

**Resource:** *Tints and Shades*, Activity C, SAG. Students create a value scale of tints and shades from two colors from the color wheel.

**Resource:** *Value Grid*, reproducible master 11-1, TR. Students select three primary or secondary colors from the same medium and fill the squares with the proper hues and intensities to complete the grid.

wheel to identify the normal value of hues, tints, and shades.

A *value scale* is pictured in 11-5. The left column shows the range of tints obtained by adding greater amounts of white to the blue color. The right column shows the range of shades obtained by adding greater amounts of black to the blue.

### Intensity

*Intensity* refers to the brightness or dullness of a hue. The normal intensity of each hue is shown on the middle ring of the color wheel.

One way to dull a hue, or lower its intensity, is to add some of its complement. The *complement* of a hue is the hue opposite it on the color wheel. For instance, blue is the complement of orange. To lower the intensity of orange, you add varying amounts of blue, as shown in 11-6. To lower the intensity of red, you add small amounts of its complement, green. Examples of high-intensity colors include hot pink and fire-engine red. Smoky blue and rust are examples of low-intensity colors.

## Neutrals

Although neutrals are not really colors, they are usually classified as colors when discussing design. Black, white, and gray are neutrals. Black is the combination of all colors when it exists as a pigment. A *pigment* is a coloring agent used in paint and printed materials. In contrast to black, white used as a pigment has no color. Gray is a combination of black and white. Brown and its tints and shades are also considered neutrals. Combining equal amounts of complementary colors forms a brown color.

By adding a neutral color to a hue, the value of the hue is changed to either a tint or a shade. This makes the

11-5
*Values for the color blue, ranging from tints to shades, are shown on this value scale.*

11-6
*Adding blue to orange reduces the intensity of orange, making it a duller color.*

**Discuss:** What impact do you think color has on attitudes? Where would you expect to see very intense colors?

**Art Activity:** Using tempura paints, create various values and intensities of a color.

**Discuss:** How do you make a color less intense? (*by adding its complement to make it duller*)

hue less intense. When any of these changes are made, the hue is neutralized. Neutralized hues blend better with other colors.

## Warm and Cool Colors

Colors can be classified as either warm or cool. Although the actual temperature may be the same throughout an entire home, some rooms may seem cooler or warmer due to the colors used in decorating.

*Warm colors* include yellow, orange, red, and the colors near them on the color wheel. Red is considered the warmest. They are called warm colors because they remind us of fire and the sun.

Warm colors are called the *advancing colors*. Warm-colored objects appear closer to you. Warm-colored walls look closer together. So, a room painted red, yellow, or orange appears smaller than it really is.

Warm colors attract your attention. They can make you feel happy, energetic, and full of excitement. Research has shown the color red actually stimulates the nervous system and can increase blood pressure, heartbeats, and breathing rate. Many advertisements use warm colors to make you notice them. Restaurants use warm colors to increase your appetite. Locker rooms use them to generate excitement. Warm colors in homes make household members feel lively and cheerful. An overuse of warm colors, however, may make you feel nervous or tense, especially if they are full-intensity colors.

*Cool colors* are found opposite the warm colors on the color wheel. These include blue, green, violet, and the colors near them. They are called cool colors since they remind you of water, grass, and trees.

Cool colors are called the *receding colors*. They make objects seem smaller and walls seem farther away than they really are. A small room decorated in cool colors can appear larger than it actually is.

Cool colors are quiet and restful. They are often used in hospitals to help patients feel calm and relaxed. They are also popular for bedrooms. However, if cool colors are overused, they may make people feel depressed.

Warm and cool colors create different moods that make people feel differently. See 11-7. For example, workers in an office complained their lunchroom was always cold. When the employer changed the light blue room to orange, the complaints stopped even though the temperature never changed.

# Color Harmonies

The surest and easiest way to achieve success when using color is to follow one of the standard color harmonies. A *color harmony* is a pleasing combination of colors based on their respective positions on the color wheel. There are seven basic color harmonies: monochromatic, analogous, complementary, split-complementary, triadic, double-complementary, and neutral. Established color harmonies bring colors together in combinations that are very satisfying to the eyes.

## Monochromatic Color Harmony

A *monochromatic color harmony* is the simplest color harmony. It uses a single hue from the standard color wheel. The hue selected for the monochromatic color harmony in 11-8 is green.

Variation is achieved by changing the value and/or intensity of the hue. Accents of neutral colors can be used to add interest to the color scheme.

**Discuss:** If you wanted a very large room to feel cozier, what would be a good color choice for its walls? Why? (*Any of the warm colors because they create a feeling of advancing, which makes the walls appear closer.*)

**Reflect:** Is there a room in your school, home, or some other place you frequent that always makes you feel cold? What color is the room? Is it possible that a change in color could help you feel warmer?

A

Ethan Allen, Inc.

B

Ethan Allen, Inc.

11-7 _____

*By comparing these two living rooms, you can sense the warmth created by the use of yellow and red (A) and the feeling of coolness generated by the use of green and blue (B).*

**Discuss:** Study the photos of Figure 11-7. Why do you think color makes so much difference in the feel of temperature in a room?

**Discuss:** What role do neutral colors play in the monochromatic color harmony of Figure 11-8?

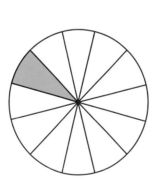

Ethan Allen, Inc.

11-8 _____

*Green is the basis for this monochromatic color harmony.*

**Reflect:** Think about the color combinations you wear most often. Why do you like these colors together?

**Enrich:** Attend a presentation by a paint manufacturer's representative who discusses the importance of selecting colors for interiors. Be prepared to ask questions. Summarize in one paragraph what you learn.

Using a monochromatic color harmony can make a room appear larger. It can also unify the furnishings and accessories used in the space.

## Analogous Color Harmony

Selecting related hues from the standard color wheel creates an *analogous color harmony*. These are hues that are next to each other on the color wheel. In an analogous color harmony, usually three to five hues are used. Since they are related, they blend together well. One color seems to merge into another. An example of an analogous color harmony is shown in 11-9.

An analogous color harmony will look best if you choose one color as the dominant color and use smaller amounts of the others to add interest and variety. You may also want to use a tiny amount of an unrelated color as an accent.

## Complementary Color Harmony

Selecting two colors that are positioned directly opposite each other on the standard color wheel creates a *complementary color harmony*. Complementary colors are sometimes called contrasting colors because they make each other look brighter and more intense. When blue is used next to orange, the blue looks bluer, and the orange looks stronger. A complementary color harmony can make a room look bright and dramatic.

Although such a sharp contrast is fine for some rooms, most rooms look better if the contrast is lessened. Varying the values and intensities of the colors can do this. See 11-10. Also, the colors can be used in varied amounts. The more one color is allowed to dominate the other, the less the contrast is noticed.

## Split-Complementary Color Harmony

A *split-complementary color harmony* is made when one hue is used with the two hues adjacent to its complement. For example, if blue is the first hue chosen, you would look directly across the color wheel to find orange, its

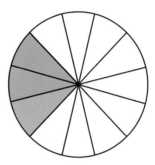

© Spiegel 1998

11-9

*An analogous color harmony using green, blue-green, and blue gives this room a fresh appearance.*

**Discuss:** What could be done in the room in Figure 11-8 to create a complementary color harmony? (*adding pink or red*)

**Activity:** Create a brochure showing all of the color harmonies by using magazine pictures or fabric swatches as examples.

Ethan Allen, Inc.

11-10 _____
*Shades of green and red are used in this country-style bedroom to create a complementary color harmony.*

complement. You would then select the colors on both sides of orange to establish your split-complementary color harmony. The resulting color harmony uses blue, yellow-orange, and red-orange. See 11-11. With this color selection, blue would most likely be used as the dominant color, while yellow-orange and red-orange provide lively contrast.

## Double-Complementary Color Harmony

Selecting two colors and their complements from the standard color wheel

creates a ***double-complementary color harmony***. In this way, four colors are used to create the color harmony. One example of a double-complementary color harmony results by pairing red and green with violet and yellow, as shown in 11-12. Any combination of pairs may be used as long as each pair is composed of complementary colors.

## Triadic Color Harmony

A ***triadic color harmony*** uses any three colors that are equally distant from each other on the standard color wheel. For example, yellow, blue, and red—the primary colors—form a triadic color harmony. See 11-13. The secondary colors—green, orange, and violet—also create a triadic color harmony. The two other possible color combinations are: yellow-orange, red-violet, and blue-green; or red-orange, blue-violet, and yellow-green. Care and skill are needed to achieve pleasing triadic harmonies. Changing values and intensities can lessen the sharp contrasts.

## Neutral Color Harmony

Although black and white are not hues on the standard color wheel, they are the basis for ***neutral color harmonies***.

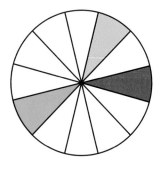

11-11 _____
*A split-complementary color harmony uses a main color with the colors on both sides of its complement.*

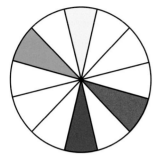

**Reflect:** Try to imagine a family room decorated in a double-complementary color harmony such as pictured in Figure 11-12. How would it feel? Why are many family rooms decorated in monochromatic, analogous, or neutral color harmonies?

**Activity:** Ask students to bring examples of a single color harmony to class tomorrow. (Examples may consist of the outfits they wear or an item they bring, such as scarves or pictures.) On the next day, students display their items as the class identifies the color harmonies shown.

**Reflect:** Picture the uniforms of sports teams that you follow. What are the color harmonies of their uniforms?

11-12

*A double-complementary color harmony is made of two sets of complementary color schemes.*

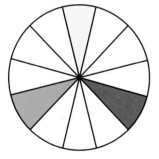

11-13

*Triadic color harmonies are often used in children's bedrooms.*

Combinations of black, white, and gray create neutral color harmonies. Brown, tan, and beige can also be used. Small amounts of other colors are sometimes added to neutral color schemes to give the room more interest. See 11-14.

# Using Color Harmonies

Now that you have learned about color and the color harmonies, you can begin to use this information to create your personal color scheme for your home. A *color scheme* is the combina-

tion of colors selected for the design of a room or house. When designing a room, you choose colors that you like seeing together. The chosen colors probably look good together because they conform to an established color harmony.

A well-planned color scheme will use color harmonies to blend and unify the design of the home as you transition from one room to another. By following important guidelines, you can create a color scheme that will enhance your near environment and increase the enjoyment of your home. See 11-15.

## Choosing the Right Colors

The color harmonies you choose for the color scheme of your home depend on several factors. They include what mood or style you want, the lifestyle of the family members, the items in the room, and the room's location.

### Moods and Styles

You can create a variety of moods in a room through the use of color. For example, you may want a room to feel restful, or you may want it to appear exciting. Choosing cool colors that have similar values will create a restful mood in the room, such as in 11-16. Choosing warm colors with contrasting values will make the room feel exciting.

You can also choose colors that will create a certain style in a room. Different styles, such as southwestern or country, often suggest the use of specific colors. You can use these colors in different color harmonies to achieve the style you want.

In a southwestern-style room, for example, you may choose warm desert colors, such as rust, sunset orange, brick, and sand. See 11-17. In a country-style room, you may choose

Ethan Allen, Inc.

11-14

*Small amounts of accent colors in the accessories add interest to this soothing neutral color scheme.*

11-15

*The color scheme for this bedroom was inspired by colors found in nature.*

**Discuss:** When families do not have adequate funds to completely color-harmonize their home, what might they do to change an unharmonious interior into a "pulled together" look?

low-intensity shades of reds, blues, oranges, and yellows.

## Lifestyles

Some people have active lifestyles while others lead quieter lives. The colors you choose depend on the lifestyles of household members. For instance, with small children, consideration should be given to darker colors and shades that do not show dirt easily. On the other hand, a household of adults may choose lighter colors for the walls and upholstery since upkeep is less of a concern.

**Activity:** Create a checklist to use as a reference when choosing colors for a room.

**Reflect:** Think about the lifestyle of your family. How does it affect the colors used in your home? Do you have younger siblings or older grandparents in the home? Does their presence influence color choices?

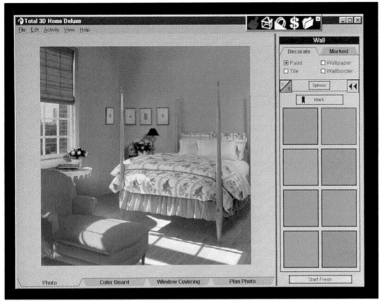

11-16 _____

*By using a CADD program, you can test how a paint color will look in a room to see the warmth or coolness created.*

11-17 _____

*A southwestern look is created in this room through the use of rust, brown, black, and gold colors.*

The colors you choose for each room also depend upon how they are used. Primary and secondary colors of normal intensity are fine for a child's room, such as in 11-18. If the same hues were used in an adult's bedroom, however, softer tints at lower-intensity levels would probably be preferred.

### Items in the Room

Another way to choose color harmonies is to consider the items that will be used in the room. For instance, you may have an area rug, couch, or favorite picture planned for the room. To create a color scheme around any of these items, you need to select one color used in the object. This color becomes the base or main color. After choosing the base color, you can use your knowledge of color harmonies, values, and intensities to pick colors to go with it. See 11-19.

You also need to consider the type of lighting used in the room. The colors

11-18 _____

*Primary and secondary colors are used in this child's room to give it a feeling of fun and excitement.*

**Discuss:** After studying the CADD picture of Figure 11-16, what would you anticipate was used as the inspiration piece from which all colors were selected?

**Discuss:** Why do you think adults prefer lower intensity colors while children prefer higher intensity colors?

**Enrich:** Visit a furniture store to view the groupings of furniture and identify the color harmonies used with each.

you select must work well for you during both day and night. This means viewing the intended colors during daylight hours in natural light and at night when they are influenced by artificial light. You should always make your final color selections in the actual room where they will be used. Many disasters have occurred when a paint color selected in a retail store under fluorescent light was then applied in a room with natural and incandescent lighting. Tungsten-halogen incandescent lighting renders the best color. See Chapter 17, "Addressing Windows, Lighting, and Accessories," for a discussion of types of lighting.

Most homes have some combination of natural, incandescent, and fluorescent lighting. Incandescent lighting can bring dullness to some colors and fluorescent lighting can completely distort color. Incandescent lighting generally makes colors appear warmer. Fluorescent lighting makes colors appear warmer or cooler depending on the color of the lightbulb or tube. See 11-20. In general, most fluorescent lighting will make colors appear cooler compared to incandescent lighting. Halogen lighting renders the truest presentation of colors.

Ethan Allen, Inc.

11-19

*A neutral base color and harmony were selected for this room as a backdrop for the existing art collection.*

### Location of the room

The direction the room faces—north, south, east, or west—must be taken into consideration when choosing the base color and color harmony. If a bedroom is located on the north side of a house, the subdued light of the northern exposure may make colors

**Discuss:** Determine the type of lighting present in your classroom after studying the chart in Figure 11-20. How are colors affected by it?

| Color and Artificial Lighting | | | | | |
|---|---|---|---|---|---|
| **Type of Artificial Lighting** | **Yellow** | **Orange** | **Red** | **Blue** | **Green** |
| *Standard incandescent* | Warms | Strengthens | Enriches | Dulls | Darkens |
| *Tungsten-halogen incandescent* | Warms | Strengthens | Enriches | Dulls slightly | Darkens slightly |
| *Deluxe cool-white fluorescent* | Enriches and intensifies | Close to true hue | Warms | Enriches | Brightens |
| *Deluxe warm-white fluorescent* | Brightens | Strengthens | Enriches | Darkens and enriches | Enriches |

11-20

*Colors change when viewed under different types of artificial light.*

appear cooler. To make the room appear warmer, you could choose a color harmony that uses warm colors. A southern exposure receives the most sunlight and generally makes colors appear bright and warm. Sometimes cool colors are preferred for rooms with southern exposures. See 11-21.

It cannot be assumed, however, the quality of light entering a room from a specific direction is always the same. The light entering a bedroom with a northern exposure will be changed significantly, for example, if it is reflected off a bright white house next door. Also, a room with a southern exposure will not be sunny if a covered porch overhangs the windows and doors. Even the light that filters through trees outside a window can change the quality of sunlight entering the room. Consequently, the best rule of thumb is to view a color sample in the actual room at different times of day and night so all lighting factors can be examined.

When considering location, you also need to think about the colors used in adjoining rooms. The new colors you choose should blend with those used in adjoining rooms. In general, color should not change abruptly from room to room. Instead it should make a gradual transition from one space to another.

If a dining room is located next to the living room, the same base color could be used in both rooms. You could use an analogous color harmony with yellow as the base color of the color scheme in both rooms. In the living room you could select yellow to be the dominant color with the other analogous hues playing secondary roles. Then you could use the same analogous color harmony in the dining room but expand the harmony from three to five hues and add interest by changing the tints or shades of the hues selected. You could also choose to have yellow play a less dominant role in the dining room than it did in the living room. A color in the split-complementary color harmony with yellow could be introduced as an accent to add excitement to the room. Since yellow is the base color of all the harmonies used in both rooms, it provides a smooth transition.

There is an exception to the rule of blending colors in adjoining rooms. In homes using contemporary design, the walls of adjoining rooms may intentionally have different, bold colors. Special care, however, must be devoted to applying the basic rules of color harmonies so the abrupt transitions result in good design.

Bruce® Hardwood Floors, bayport strip in spice

11-21

*Cool colors were chosen to decorate this sunny bedroom with a southern exposure. These colors keep this room looking light and airy.*

## Using Color Correctly

As you work with color, the following guidelines will help you use color well:

- Colors seem to gain intensity when they are applied to large areas. Because of this, a color selected from a paint chip may appear too intense or dark when painted on all four walls of a room. When using paint chips, it is advisable to choose a color several tints lighter than the color actually desired for the room.

- Using contrasting colors draws attention. For example, a white sofa against a dark wall will draw more attention than a white sofa against a white wall. See 11-22.

While you may want to avoid a totally neutralized room, you should remember too many strong contrasts in a room can be confusing and tiring.

- Color harmonies look better when one color, the base color, dominates. Your dominant color should cover about two-thirds of the room area. When you use equal amounts of two or more colors in a room, your eyes become confused, and your color selection appears cluttered.

- When choosing colors for large areas, such as walls and floors, select low-intensity colors. If you use high-intensity colors in large amounts, they can become

**Discuss:** How does color help to create a focal point in the room shown in Figure 11-22?

Ethan Allen, Inc.

11-22 _____

*The contrast of the blue desk against the light wall draws more attention than the placement of the white sofa against the same wall.*

**Activity:** Using the guidelines in the text, create a checklist that would help people use color correctly.

**Internet Activity:** Visit several Web sites, such as those of paint manufacturers and interior design magazines, to identify the current color trends for housing. Report your findings to the class.

**Discuss:** If a home's interior uses color in a way that reflects the members' preferences and lifestyles, should the occupants be concerned about incorporating color trends?

Lexington Furniture Industries

11-23 _____

*The cabinetry and wicker seating use the same green color, but the texture of the chairs make the room look darker.*

overpowering. Instead, high-intensity colors should be used in small amounts as accent colors in accessories or small pieces of furniture.

- Textured surfaces make colors appear dark. This is because the light strikes the surface at different angles, making the item appear to have greater depth. See 11-23. When you are trying to match fabrics, it is important to have samples of the fabrics you are matching. For example, if you are matching drapery fabric to a carpet, make sure you have samples of the carpet with you.

- If a room is very large, choose colors that will make it look smaller. Shades, high-intensity colors, and warm hues that have advancing qualities make a room appear smaller.

- If a room is small, choose colors that will make the room appear larger. Tints, low-intensity colors, and cool hues that have receding qualities make a room look larger.

Choosing the right colors, creating color harmonies, and following the color guidelines is important. This will help you make color work well for you and your home.

**Enrich:** Research the colors associated with housing interiors and exteriors during a specific period in U.S. history. Describe the colors used inside and outside a fashionable home.

**Reflect:** How does the color of this classroom affect the feeling of size?

# Summary

Color is one of the most important elements of design. It can create and communicate different moods. Color has it own physiological and psychological effects on people.

The basis of all color relationships is the color wheel. Colors in the middle ring of the color wheel are primary, secondary, or intermediate colors. Color has three characteristics—hue, value and intensity. The cool colors are located on one side of the wheel, and the warm colors are on the other.

When colors are used together in a pleasing manner, color harmonies are created. They may be monochromatic, analogous, complementary, split-complementary, double-complementary, triadic, or neutral. Neutral colors are black, white, gray, tan, beige, and brown.

When choosing a color harmony for your personal color scheme, you first choose the right colors for your home and lifestyle. Then, following certain guidelines will coordinate the colors you select into good design.

**Activity:** Working with another student, alternate talking for 30 seconds apiece about what the chapter covered. Together, write a summary of the concepts in the chapter.

**Writing Activity:** Students write each letter of the alphabet on separate lines of a sheet of paper and work independently to write one term from the chapter that begins with each alphabet letter. After three minutes, pairs of students confer to fill in any blank lines. If blanks still remain, discuss with the class some possible choices.

# To Review

1. What moods are created by each of these colors: red, green, and violet?
2. List the secondary colors and explain what primary colors are used to make each.
3. Which color name is listed first in the name of an intermediate color?
4. Explain the difference between value and intensity of color.
5. Describe how to neutralize a hue.
6. _____ colors include yellow and red; _____ colors include green and blue.
7. Give an example of each of the seven color harmonies.
8. True or false. Darker shades of colors do not show soil as readily as lighter tints.
9. _____-intensity colors should be used for large areas.

**Answer Key**

1. Red conveys power, danger, strength, excitement, and boldness. Green conveys nature, peace, friendliness, and coolness. Violet conveys royalty, dignity, and drama.
2. orange—yellow and red; green—yellow and blue; violet—red and blue
3. primary color
4. Value is the lightness or darkness. Intensity is the brightness or dullness.
5. by adding white, gray, or black
6. warm; cool
7. (Student response. See pages 259-264.)
8. true
9. low

# In Your Community

1. Visit a model home and observe the use of color. Record your observations. Did the colors match your preferences? Did the colors reflect current trends? Make a brief report to the class.
2. Write a brief report on the color scheme of your bedroom. Which of the colors used is your favorite? How long has your room had this appearance? What color scheme did you have before? If you could redecorate next week, what colors would you select? What do you think your color preferences reveal about your personality?

3. Identify a home or business in the community whose exterior has a pleasing combination of colors. Name the colors used. Also, identify a building's exterior that represents the opposite of *pleasing* to you. What colors are used? Which colors would you change if you had the job of updating the look of the building on a budget?

## To Think About

1. Imagine you are a professional color consultant who has been hired to help select the room colors for a new community center in your neighborhood. Based on your knowledge of the psychological effect color has on people, what colors would you use in each of the following spaces?
   - children's recreation room
   - reading room for senior citizens
   - hospitality room with a snack bar
   - small nature museum room
   - room for drama and theatrical rehearsals

2. No two people perceive color in exactly the same way and indeed some people are unable to distinguish between certain colors at all. How could these behaviors pose an obstacle to an interior designer's presentation to a committee in charge of finalizing selections for new corporate offices? What techniques could the designer use to overcome objections?

## Using Technology

Note: For researching color schemes, have students explore *housebeautiful.com*.

1. Take pictures of 10 rooms that display good interior design. (Perhaps some are in your home or in historical homes that you have visited.) For each room, identify the type of color harmony that predominates. Also, analyze possible reasons for the color harmonies selected, given the purpose of each room. Which room represents your color preference?

Note: For researching color trends, have students explore *benjaminmoore.com*.

2. Search the Internet for current color trends in residential design. What are the newest colors being presented? What cultural influences, elements of nature, or other factors are inspiring the new color trends? Which of the new color trends appeal most to you personally?

3. Using CADD or a popular interior design software program, create two small rooms of the same dimensions. Cover the walls of one room with light, dull, cool colors. Cover the walls of the other room with dark, bright, warm colors. Which room looks larger?

**Portfolio Project:** Continue the notebook or storyboard started in Chapter 10. Add color as a design element and provide samples of all the color harmonies, labeling the colors used.

# CHAPTER 12
# Using the Principles of Design

## To Know

proportion
golden rectangle
golden mean
golden section
scale
visual weight
balance
formal balance
informal balance
emphasis
rhythm
repetition
gradation
radiation
opposition
transition
harmony
unity
sensory design

Permission granted by F. Schumacher & Co. to use copyrighted photographs. Designs and photograph © F. Schumacher & Co. Taken from WILLIAMSBURG Timeless Traditions Collection

## Objectives

After studying this chapter, you will be able to

- determine how proportion and scale are related to objects.
- give examples of formal and informal balance.
- explain how emphasis creates a focal point.
- list the different types of rhythm.
- describe the goals of design.
- give examples of sensory design.

**Resource:** *The Inside Story*, transparency master IV-A, TR. Students look back at the topics covered in Chapters 1-11 and review the final "design" topic they will cover in Chapter 12.

**Vocabulary:** Write 10 to15 words from the vocabulary list on the board. Have students review the chapter objectives, relating them to as many of the words as possible.

In the previous two chapters, you learned about the elements of design. When the elements of design are applied using the principles of design, you can achieve the goals of design. This chapter will tell you how to use this process to create well-designed rooms.

# The Principles of Design

The principles of design are guidelines for working with the elements of design. When you understand the principles of design, you can use the elements of design successfully. The principles of design are proportion and scale, balance, emphasis, and rhythm.

## Proportion and Scale

Proportion and scale are closely related but different. They both describe size, shape, and amount. They are both concerned with the relationships of objects and parts of objects.

### Proportion

*Proportion* is the relationship of parts of the same object, or the relationship between different objects in the same group. It is an important consideration when selecting and positioning furniture and accessories in a room. For example, proportion is a consideration when choosing a shade for a lamp. The lamp base and the lampshade need to be in proportion to each other (parts of the same object). Proportion is also a consideration when choosing the surface on which to place the lamp. The lamp and table need to be in proportion to each other (different objects in the same group). The accessories that surround the lamp are also considered. The accessories must be in proper proportion to both the lamp and the table (different objects in the same group).

Proportion can also be described as the ratio of one part to another part or of one part to the whole. Ratios such as 2:3, 3:5, and 5:8 are more effective than ratios of 1:1 or 1:2. For instance, a rectangle has more pleasing proportions than a square. These ratios also apply to rooms, furniture, and accessories. See 12-1.

The Greeks were masters of the use of proportion. They developed guidelines that have been used for centuries. Study 12-2 as you read about the Greek guidelines for developing pleasing proportions:

- The *golden rectangle* has sides in a ratio of 2:3. The short sides are two-thirds the length of the long sides. One example of the golden rectangle is the Parthenon in Athens. The golden rectangle is frequently found in good design.

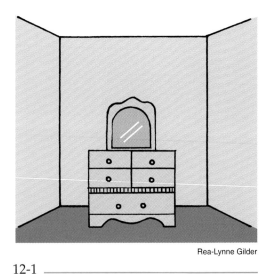

Rea-Lynne Gilder

12-1

*Good proportion is important in furnishing a room.*

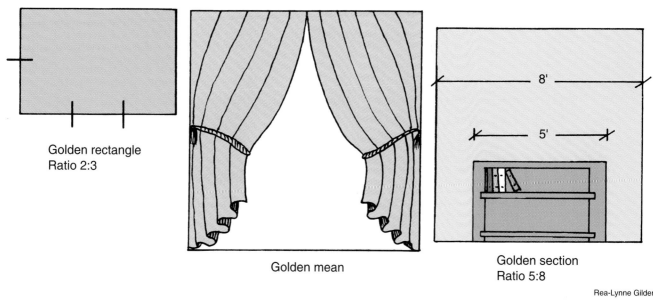

Golden rectangle
Ratio 2:3

Golden mean

Golden section
Ratio 5:8

Rea-Lynne Gilder

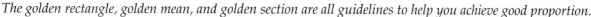

12-2

*The golden rectangle, golden mean, and golden section are all guidelines to help you achieve good proportion.*

You can find many examples of the golden rectangle in houses and their furnishings.

- The *golden mean* is the division of a line midway between one-half and one-third of its length. This unequal division is more pleasing visually than an equal division or a division at a point that is less than one-third of the line's length. The golden mean is often applied when planning wall arrangements, tying draperies, and hanging pictures.

- The *golden section* is the division of a line or form in such a way that the ratio of the smaller section to the larger section is equal to the ratio of the larger section to the whole. This relationship is based on the progression of the numbers *1, 2, 3, 5, 8, 13, 21,* and so forth. Notice that the number *3* and each number following is the sum of the two previous numbers.

When using the golden section to help you plan, you will find that the ratio of 2:3 is about the same ratio as 3:5 and other similar ratios. Using the concept of the golden section can help you develop more pleasing proportions in your designs.

Most people do not actually measure proportions. They can tell by looking at a rug on a floor if it is in the proper proportion. Likewise, they can tell if a bed or sofa visually "fits" its room. People tend to develop an awareness or *sense of proportion* based on their own visual perceptions.

### Scale

*Scale* refers to the relative size of an object in relation to other objects. For example, a chair is a small piece of furniture in comparison to a bed. A twin bed is small in comparison to a king-size bed. However, the twin bed is still larger than the chair.

When furnishings are scaled to the space they occupy, they are visually pleasing. For example, large rooms require large-scale furnishings. A king-size bed is appropriate in a

**Math Activity:** After studying Figure 12-2, create your own examples of applying the golden rectangle, golden mean, and golden section.

**Math Activity:** Draw a ratio of 2:3 and one of 3:5. How do they differ?

**Math Activity:** Teach an elementary school child the meaning of *ratio* and help him or her find examples.

**Vocabulary:** Explain the difference between the meanings of *proportion* and *scale*.

large bedroom. However, it might seem too large for a small room. Small rooms require small-scale furniture.

The furnishings within a room should be in scale with one another. For example, a large sofa requires a large coffee table. A small sofa would not go well with a large coffee table.

Furnishings also need to be in scale to the people using them. A large person will feel more comfortable in a chair of substantial size. Likewise, a child will feel more comfortable in a chair that is scaled to his or her size. See 12-3.

Another aspect of scale is visual weight. *Visual weight* is the perception that an object weighs more or less than it really does. For example, a wooden chair and an upholstered chair may have the same dimensions. However, the upholstered chair will look larger and heavier than the wooden chair. Thick lines, bold colors, coarse textures, and large patterns add to visual weight.

When decorating a small room, choose furniture that has light visual weight. This will prevent the furniture from making the room look crowded. Likewise, choose accessories that are in scale to the furniture. In a small room, it is wise to "think small" in regard to furniture and accessories.

## Balance

*Balance* implies equilibrium among parts of a design. It is a perception of the way arrangements are seen. When there is balance, there is a sense of equal weight on both sides of a center point. See 12-4. There is not a visual pull in one direction more than the other. Balance can be either formal or informal. Both types of balance can be used in the same room or space.

In *formal balance*, identical objects are arranged on both sides of a center

© Spiegel 1998

12-3

*The reduced scale of these furnishings and sofa provide greater comfort and accessibility for the children.*

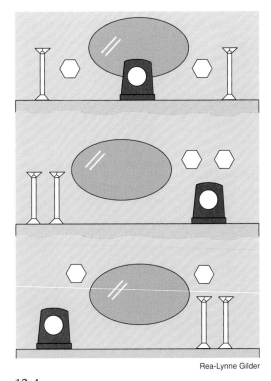

Rea-Lynne Gilder

12-4

*The same accessories can be arranged in many different ways to create balance.*

point. Formal balance is also called symmetrical balance. This type of balance is often used in elegant and formal rooms, 12-5. It is especially appropriate for traditional decorating styles. It can also be used in exterior design. Formal balance is easy to achieve and makes people feel comfortable because of its orderliness.

In *informal balance*, different but equivalent objects are arranged to the sides of a center point. Informal balance is also called asymmetrical balance. Although the sides are not alike, neither side overpowers the other. A feeling of equilibrium is created.

Informal balance can be achieved in various ways. In order to balance a heavy object and a light object, the heavier object must be placed closer to the center line than the light object. Several smaller objects can balance a single, large one. If objects are the same size but of unequal distance from you, the object closest to you will appear larger.

An object that has visual weight can also balance a single, large object. Color, texture, and form all create visual weight, 12-6. Bold, warm colors will appear heavier than subdued, cool colors. Decorations added to an object give it visual weight. Typically, large objects appear heavier than small objects.

Balance is a very important principle to follow when arranging accessories and furnishings. The furnishings on each half of a wall or opposite walls should balance with each other. Likewise, the accessories chosen for display on a table or in a bookcase should also balance with each other. The type of balance used helps determine the mood of a room. Formal balance creates an air of formality. Informal balance creates a casual atmosphere. In 12-7, the wood columns and entry lights on both sides of the front door create formal balance.

Weather Shield Windows & Doors

12-5

*The symmetry created in this stairway is an excellent example of formal balance.*

Ethan Allen, Inc.

12-6

*The arrangement of these accessories is an example of informal balance.*

**Vocabulary:** Compare and contrast *formal* and *informal* balance.
**Discuss:** What aspects of the classroom reflect informal balance? Do any reflect formal balance? If no, how could formal balance be achieved?

**Discuss:** When applied to furniture arrangement, how do the two types of balance affect the mood of a room? (*Formal balance creates an air of formality, while informal balance creates a casual atmosphere.*)

**Activity:** Using magazines, find pictures of formal and informal balance. Label them and use some as examples on a bulletin board.

Also in 12-7, the arrangement of furniture and accessories illustrate informal balance.

## Emphasis

*Emphasis* creates a center of interest or focal point in a room. It is the feature that is seen first and repeatedly draws attention. Every well-designed room has a focal point. With one area of emphasis, the eyes are immediately drawn to that point when you enter a room. This gives a feeling of stability and unity to the room. When planning a focal point, keep the following guidelines in mind:

- The focal point should be worthy of the attention it will receive.

- The focal point should dominate the room, but not overpower it or the design.

- No features should compete with the focal point. Otherwise, confusion will result.

Architectural features, such as picture windows and fireplaces, can provide a focal point for a room. On the other hand, you can create a focal point through the use or special placement of various items. These include furniture groupings, colorful rugs, striking works of art, mirrors, shelves of books or other collections. See 12-8. Unusual accessories and objects, or their placement in a room, can also serve as focal points. For example, a beautiful piece of antique furniture in a contemporary setting is eye-catching. Likewise, the inclusion of contemporary sculpture as an accessory in a very traditional setting could create a prominent focal point. Special lighting cast upon a significant object can also create a focal point.

Bruce® Hardwood Floors, meridian stone in sedona and creme

12-7 _____

*Both formal and informal balance are represented by the placement of furnishings and accessories in this space.*

© Spiegel 1998

12-8 _____

*The focal point of this room was created by the placement of striking artwork over the fireplace.*

The focal point gives order and direction to a room. Everything else in the setting should relate to it through color, texture, proportion, scale, and theme.

Color is usually the first aspect of a focal point to catch one's attention. Carrying it throughout the room in accessories, window treatments, and upholstery fabric can further emphasize the color. The texture of the focal point can be emphasized throughout the room in similar ways.

The size of the point of interest should be in proportion and scale to the room and its furnishings. A massive focal point will be too large for a small room. However, a large room or a room with a cathedral ceiling demands a focal point that will not be dwarfed by the room size.

How a room will be used determines the theme of the room. The focal point should set the stage for the furnishings. For example, a living room will be used for socializing. If the fireplace is the focal point, comfortable seating that permits socializing should be grouped around the fireplace.

## Rhythm

*Rhythm* smoothly leads the eyes from one area to another in a design. Rhythm results when an element of design forms an organized pattern. For example, a continuous line found in window and door frames produces rhythm. Rhythm can be achieved through repetition, gradation, radiation, opposition, and transition.

All types of rhythm are based on some repetition. Rhythm by *repetition* is created when an element of design—such as color, line, form, or texture—is repeated. Repetition is one of the easiest ways to achieve rhythm in a design. For instance, a dominant color

can be repeated throughout a room. Lines that are repeated in shelves of a bookcase create rhythm. See 12-9. Repetition of form is found when rectangular end tables and a rectangular coffee table are used in the same setting. Texture may be repeated in fabrics used in draperies and upholstery.

*Gradation* is the type of rhythm created by a gradual increase or decrease of similar elements of design. The eyes travel through the levels of progression. For example, color value can change from dark to light or from light to dark. Lines can vary from thick to thin in a design. Objects that have the same form can increase or decrease in size. See 12-10. Textures can range from smooth to rough.

In rhythm by *radiation*, lines flow outward from a central point, as in a

Weather Shield Windows & Doors

12-9

*The repeated use of line in this stairway creates rhythm by repetition.*

Resource: *Rhythm in Design*, color transparency, CT-17, TR. Students are introduced to the types of rhythm in design and find examples in the classroom.

Discuss: Explain the difference between a focal point dominating a space versus overpowering it. Give an example.

Note: Web sites such as *southernliving.com/homes* and *hgtv.com* often have features to help people apply the principles of design.

**Resource:** *The Principle of Rhythm*, Activity B, SAG. Students label and write a brief explanation of the type of rhythm used in each window.
**Discuss:** Name the five ways rhythm can be achieved in interior design. (*by repetition, gradation, radiation, opposition, and transition*)

Rea-Lynne Gilder

12-10

*These nesting tables are a good example of rhythm by gradation. The eyes move from the largest table to the smallest.*

wagon wheel. See 12-11. Sunburst designs are examples of rhythm by radiation. In home furnishings,

radiation can usually be found in accessories. For example, a flower arrangement or a cushion may have radiating lines. A window that forms a half-circle with a sunburst design is a good example of rhythm by radiation.

In rhythm by *opposition*, lines meet to form right angles. Rhythm by opposition is often found in the construction of a room as well as in the furnishings. It can be found at the corners of windowpanes, picture frames, fireplaces, tables, and other furniture. Rhythm by opposition also exists in floor treatments, as in 12-12. It can also be created in simple ways as you accessorize and decorate. For instance, a row of books may be held in place by three books lying on their sides. The three books form a right angle to the other books on the shelf.

Rhythm by *transition* is created when curved lines carry the eyes from

Crate & Barrel

12-11

*The lines in the backs and seats of these chairs show rhythm by radiation.*

Ethan Allen, Inc.

12-12

*The corners of the block pattern used in this floor treatment create rhythm by opposition.*

**Vocabulary:** Does the term *rhythm* have the same meaning in design as it does in music? (*Yes, in both cases the word refers to an organized pattern.*)

**Enrich:** Attend a presentation by an art, music, or drama teacher who discusses the importance of harmony, rhythm, and emphasis in his or her field. Be prepared to ask questions. Summarize in one paragraph what you learn.

one part of an object or room to another part. See 12-13. Transition leads the eyes in, through, and over an object until they have seen the whole object. Curved lines are found in architectural features and in furnishings. An arched window will lead your eyes from one side to the other. A drapery swag will draw your attention from one part of the drapery to another.

# Goals of Design

As you work with the elements and principles of design, you need to keep in mind the goals of design. The goals of design are function and appropriateness, harmony with unity and variety, and beauty. These goals help make sure that your design works together as a whole. The use, convenience, and satisfaction of household should also be considered as you work to achieve the goals of design.

## Function and Appropriateness

Function and appropriateness are closely related. If furnishings serve their various functions, they are considered appropriate. Rooms and furnishings within the rooms have functions that are determined by the people who live there. When furnishings provide service, comfort, and pleasure with minimum care, they are considered functional and appropriate. There are three guidelines to follow when thinking about function and appropriateness in the home.

- Furnishings should be appropriate for the function of the dwelling. For example, formal dining room furniture is not appropriate for a vacation cabin.

Bruce® Hardwood Floors, natural reflections in cherry with gunstock accents. The New American Home 1996, Photography by Robert Muir

12-13
*These curved arches are an example of rhythm by transition. They lead the eyes up to the second floor of this home.*

- Furnishings should be appropriate for each room. For instance, a living room is not an appropriate place for a refrigerator.
- The form of furnishings should be appropriate for their function. Their designs should adapt to the structure of the human body. Their arrangements should meet the needs to reach, stand, sit, and move within a room.

Above all, your home should be appropriate and functional for all members of the household. It should fit the personalities, lifestyles, needs, and wants of those who live there.

Vocabulary: What are some other words that use *harmony* as their root? What connotations do they all have?

Discuss: When striving for harmony with unity, explain the importance of adding variety. (*It prevents monotony.*)

Activity: Using items in the classroom, create two vignettes—one that illustrates harmony and one that does not.

# Harmony with Unity and Variety

*Harmony* is an agreement among the parts. It is created when the elements of design are effectively used according to the principles of design. One idea is used and carried throughout the design.

Harmony in design can be compared to the beautiful sounds of an orchestra in concert. The instruments or "elements" are in tune, so the resulting sound is harmonious. The total effect is more important than any of the parts.

Harmony results when there is unity among the elements. *Unity* occurs when all parts of a design are related by one design idea. When unity is present in a design, you see the room as a whole—not as separate pieces. See 12-14. Unity is achieved by repeating similar elements of design. For example, the furnishings and accessories in a room may all be square or rectangular. This ties the room together.

It would be monotonous, however, for the room to have only square and rectangular furnishings and accessories. By adding a few circular or triangular accessories, variety can be created. Unity with some variety makes a design more interesting. See 12-15. Without variety, the limitations on the elements and principles of design can result in a boring, lifeless room.

While some variety is needed, too much variety can cause confusion. Variation is like seasoning in food. The right amount of a seasoning makes the food tasty. Too little or too much may make it unacceptable. Consequently, the goal of good design is unity with some variation.

When working to achieve harmony, let only one type of each element of design dominate. For example, one color should dominate. This color can be the base color of your color harmony. Smaller amounts of a coordinating color can be used as an accent. This will assure harmony and unity with variety in the design. The overall appearance of a room will be pleasing. If several colors are used in equal amounts, the room may be a confusing combination of parts.

## Beauty

In addition to being a characteristic of design, beauty is also a goal of design. Each person has a unique concept of beauty. However, the word beauty is generally used to describe well-designed and pleasing objects.

The elements and principles of design have been developed as a result of studying objects that most people consider beautiful. If elements of design are arranged according to the principles of design, the result will appear beautiful to most people. The separate elements enhance one

Ethan Allen, Inc.

12-14

*When the elements and principles of design are used effectively, a harmonious room such as this is created.*

Activity: Identify the elements and principles of design that have been used in Figure 12-14.

Reflect: Think about various classrooms in your school. Do some appear harmonious while others do not? What makes the difference?

Vocabulary: What perceptions of the word *beauty* did you have prior to reading this chapter? If they have changed since reading this chapter, explain how.

Unity

Unity with variety

Rea-Lynne Gilder

12-15 ———————————————————————————————

*Using unity with variety in a design creates additional interest.*

another and heighten the overall effect of beauty. Beauty gives a house, its furnishings, and its surroundings a distinction. Although beauty is not the only goal in planning and furnishing a home, it is what makes the visual appearance memorable.

## Sensory Design

Good design responds to all sensory needs and serves people of all ages, sizes, and physical capabilities. Design that considers the senses enriches the total environment. *Sensory design* is the application of design that affects the senses of sight, hearing, smell, and touch. It is used to make housing more accessible and functional for people with disabilities as well as those without disabilities.

Most types of design affect the sense of sight. People can tell if they like a design by how it looks. With housing design, however, the other senses need to be considered, too. Using specific materials in construction and design can control the noise levels in a room. For instance, hard and smooth surfaces make sounds louder. Rough and soft surfaces absorb sound, which creates a quiet atmosphere. See 12-16. As you design

Ethan Allen, Inc.

12-16 ———————————————————————————————

*This dining room uses an area rug to absorb sound.*

**Writing Activity:** Write a paragraph explaining why adding variety to unity is more appealing than simply displaying unity. Use Figure 12-15 for reference.

**Activity:** Find magazine pictures of examples of rooms or interior settings that you consider beautiful. Discuss why with a partner.

**Enrich:** Research what various Presidents and First Ladies regarded as beautiful as they designed, decorated, or redecorated various rooms in the White House.

Discuss: Why is fabric used for sound absorption? In what typical places is it used for this purpose?

Discuss: What are some ways that restaurants use sensory design to create a pleasing atmosphere for dining?

Ethan Allen, Inc.                Ethan Allen, Inc.

12-17

*Placing fresh flowers and fruit in these accessories enhances the sensory design of the room.*

a room, think about what kinds of sounds you want to hear in the room. Then think about the kinds of materials you need to include in your design to create this atmosphere.

The smell of a room can evoke feelings and emotions. Fresh flowers placed in a room may provide a fragrance that many associate with elegance. A lemon scent used in cleaners can create the impression of freshness. Pine reminds people of the outdoors. Candles, herbs, and spices used as accessories in design can create certain atmospheres in a room. See 12-17.

The sense of touch also affects your response to design. The texture of various materials used in design can communicate specific feelings. Marble is cold and hard, silk can be soft, and wood can be rough or smooth. People who are visually impaired rely on their sense of touch to direct them. For example, Braille used in elevators helps them identify specific floors.

The temperature of a room also affects design. As explained in Chapter 11, "Using Color Effectively," the choice of colors used in a room can convey either warmth or coolness. Also, people are sensitive to actual temperature changes, which can affect their comfort level. Heating and cooling systems are used to keep a room comfortable.

Enrich: Attend a presentation by a teacher from the visually impaired program to learn about the importance of touch to students who use Braille. Summarize in a paragraph what you learn.

Activity: Find two examples of interiors in magazines that show warm colors predominating. Also, find two examples with cool colors.

Explain in a paragraph how the room colors demonstrate sensory design.

Reflect: Review the chapter objectives. Do you still need to review or research some topics to get the information you need? If so, what topics?

# Summary

The elements of design are applied by using design principles. The principles of design are proportion and scale, balance, emphasis, and rhythm.

Proportion and scale are both used to describe size, shape, and amount. They are also concerned with the relationships of objects and parts of objects. Guidelines for using proportion are the golden rectangle, the golden mean, and the golden section. Visual weight, an aspect of scale, is a perception that an object weighs more or less than it really does.

Balance can be formal or informal. It is a perception that both sides of an imaginary centerline are equal. Balance can be attained through the arrangement of objects and the use of color, texture, and form.

Emphasis creates a focal point in a design. The focal point gives order and direction to a setting.

Rhythm leads the eyes from one area to another in several ways. The design may be repeated. Gradation may be used to gradually increase or decrease similar elements. Lines may flow outward from a central point or meet to form right angles. Curved lines may carry the eyes from one part of an object to another.

The goals of design can be achieved when the elements and principles of design are used together well. The goals of design are function and appropriateness, harmony with unity and variety, and beauty. Sensory design incorporates the senses into design.

**Resource:** *Using the Principles of Design*, Activity C, SAG. Students describe how the principles of design are used in the room illustrated.

**Resource:** *Design in Reverse*, Activity D, SAG. Students write questions for the answers given. Students form small groups and ask group members their questions.

# To Review

1. True or false. A sofa with an adjacent coffee table is more pleasing in a 1:2 ratio than in a 2:3 ratio.
2. Large-scale furnishings need _____-scale accessories.
3. Define formal balance and informal balance. Sketch an example of each.
4. How can emphasis be used to create a focal point? Give an example.
5. List the five kinds of rhythm.
6. How are the design goals of function and appropriateness related?
7. What can be done to avoid monotony in a harmonious design?
8. What is the relationship between beauty and the elements and principles of design?
9. Give an example of how sensory design can benefit you.

**Answer Key**

1. false
2. large
3. Formal balance is the symmetrical arrangement of identical objects on both sides of a center point, while informal balance is arrangement of different but equivalent objects on both sides. (The sketch is a student response.)
4. by using color, size, proportion, scale, or theme (The example is a student response.)
5. repetition, gradation, radiation, opposition, transition
6. Function is purpose, whereas appropriateness is suitability. If an object fits its function, it will be appropriate.
7. using variety
8. The elements and principles of design have been developed as a result of studying what people consider beautiful.
9. (Student response.)

## In Your Community

1. Visit a furnished model home. If one is not nearby, visit a local furniture store that displays room settings and select your favorites for the following: a living room, dining room, and bedroom. Identify how the principles of design are represented in the home (or room displays). List the principles and explain how they are represented. Does the home (or room displays) meet the goals of design? Give examples of how each goal is or is not met. Share your findings with the class.

2. Interview someone in your community who has a special need or physical disability. Determine ways that good housing design can enhance the quality of his or her life. What elements of sensory design could be used to make the home more accessible and increase the enjoyment of the space?

3. Look around your school and identify where the golden rectangle, golden mean, and golden section are used. If they are not used, make suggestions where they could be applied. Write a one-page paper on your observations.

## To Think About

1. Imagine that you rent an apartment on your own and need to design your living room, which currently is empty. Consider your lifestyle and personal preferences. What would you select for the focal point of this room? What other accessories would you include in the room to complement the focal point? Then, consider a focal point for your family's current living room. What would you recommend? Remember to consider the personal preferences and lifestyles of all household members.

2. What would you do if you bought a furnishing or accessory that you later found had offensive sounds, aromas, or textures? For example, suppose you take the following new purchases home, only to discover "problems"—a clock that ticks too loud, pottery with an unpleasant smell, or a chair with upholstery that scratches. When trying to return the items, how would you explain the "problem" to the store manager? Do you think he or she would understand and refund your money? Why or why not?

# Using Technology

1. Working within a team of three or four classmates, assemble a variety of room accessories such as books, bookends, plants, clocks, pictures, photographs, baskets, sculptures, and vases. Create an area in your classroom for display, such as a long desk or bookshelf. Take turns arranging the accessories in different ways to give examples of both formal and informal balance. Take photos of each design with a digital camera. Identify how the principles of proportion, scale, balance, emphasis, and rhythm are displayed in each photo. Discuss what you notice about the visual weight of the accessories as you change their position in each arrangement. Record your observations on paper and share them with your teammates.

2. Using a computer-assisted design software program, design a wall, against which is placed a chest or large piece of storage furniture (as is used in a dining room or bedroom). Create five different designs and make a printout of each. Ask your classmates to vote for their favorite design and explain the reason for their choice. Was the vote unanimous? How can you explain the differences?

**Portfolio Project:** Create a typed, one-page checklist that includes the elements and principles of design with a brief summary of each. (Be sure to review Chapters 10-11 to include all the information necessary.) Laminate the sheet for use in future projects.

C H A P T E R   13

# Textiles in Today's Homes

## To Know

textiles
fiber
cellulosic natural fiber
protein natural fiber
resiliency
manufactured fiber
generic name
trade name
yarn
blend
combination yarn
weaving
warp yarn
grain
weft yarn
wale
float
nap
knitting
tanned
bonded
structural design
applied design
finishes
tufted
needlepunching
upholstery
comforter
flammable

Ethan Allen, Inc.

## Objectives

After studying this chapter, you will be able to

- distinguish between natural fibers and manufactured fibers.
- list characteristics of various fibers.
- describe the fabric construction processes.
- identify appropriate textiles for various household uses.
- explain the benefits of textile laws.

**Resource:** *The Inside Story,* transparency master IV-A, TR. Students look back at the topics covered in Chapters 1-12 and review the new "textile" topics they will cover in Chapter 13.

**Vocabulary:** Students review the chapter objectives and relate them to as many of the words as possible.

**Discuss:** What do you already know regarding these objectives? What do you need to know? How will the objectives help you?

*T*extiles are any products made from fibers, including fabrics. You come in contact with a variety of textiles in your home every day. Your clothes are made from textiles and so are many other products. They include carpets, rugs, upholstery, curtains, tablecloths, towels, and sheets.

You need to choose textile products carefully when decorating and furnishing your house. It is important to understand the characteristics of the many fibers and fabrics used in textiles. You also need to know how to maintain and care for them.

# Understanding Fibers, Yarns, and Fabrics

To understand how to use and care for textiles properly, you need to know how they are made. Textiles begin as fibers. These are made into yarns, which are made into fabrics.

## Fibers

*Fibers* are the raw materials from which fabric is made. They are long, thin, and hairlike. Fibers are obtained from either natural or manufactured sources.

### Natural Fibers

Natural fibers come from plant or animal sources. They are divided into cellulosic natural fibers or protein natural fibers.

*Cellulosic natural fibers* come from the cellulose in plants. They are usually highly absorbent, launder well, and are seldom damaged by insects. However, they burn easily and can be stained by mildew. Also, prolonged exposure to sunlight can cause yellowing. The fibers are low in elasticity and may wrinkle easily. Specific traits and uses of some cellulosic natural fibers are listed in 13-1.

*Protein natural fibers* come from animal sources. They burn slowly and have good elasticity. They also have

| Cellulosic Natural Fibers | | | | |
|---|---|---|---|---|
| **Fiber** | **Source** | **Characteristics** | **Uses** | |
| *Cotton* | Cotton plant | Absorbent<br>Strong<br>Dyes well<br>Shrinks in hot water | Sheets<br>Bedspreads/Comforters<br>Rugs | Towels<br>Upholstery<br>Draperies |
| *Flax (Linen is the fabric name)* | Flax plant | Strong<br>Wears well | Tablecloths<br>Upholstery<br>Bedspreads/Comforters | Kitchen towels<br>Draperies |
| *Ramie* | China grass | Dyes well<br>High gloss or shine<br>Shrinks | Table linens | |
| *Kapok* | Kapok tree | Light<br>Soft<br>Not washable | Pillows and pad filling | |

13-1
*Cellulosic natural fibers come from a variety of plant sources.*

*resiliency*, an ability to return to the original size and shape. Care must be taken in cleaning them, however, and they often need to be dry-cleaned. Characteristics and uses of some natural protein fibers are listed in 13-2.

### Manufactured Fibers

*Manufactured fibers* are made from wood cellulose, oil products, and other chemicals. They are classified as cellulosic and noncellulosic fibers. Each fiber is given a *generic name*, which describes a group of fibers with similar chemical compositions. *Trade names* are used by companies to identify the specific fibers they develop. Another term for *manufactured fiber* is *synthetic fiber.*

Each manufactured fiber has its own characteristics. However, all manufactured fibers have some traits in common. For example, they generally launder well and are mothproof. They are nonallergenic, which means you are not likely to develop an allergy to them. Some common manufactured fibers and their traits and uses are listed in 13-3.

## Yarns

Fibers are spun or twisted into yarns, 13-4. *Yarns* are made from fiber staples (short fibers) and filaments (long, continuous fibers). A yarn may be made from a single type of fiber like wool or nylon. It can also be made from two or more different fibers, such as cotton and polyester. When two or more types of fibers are combined to make yarn, it is called a *blend*. Blends bring out the good qualities of the fibers and minimize the less favorable characteristics. When two or more different yarns are combined, they create a *combination yarn*.

## Fabric Construction

Fabric traits are determined by the type, amount, and size of fibers and how they are used to make yarns. How fabrics are constructed is also important. The methods include weaving, knitting, felting, or bonding.

### Woven Fabrics

Many fabrics used in the home are woven. See 13-5. *Weaving* is the

| Protein Natural Fibers | | | | |
|---|---|---|---|---|
| **Fiber** | **Source** | **Characteristics** | **Uses** | |
| *Silk* | Silkworm cocoon | Strong<br>Absorbent<br>Dyes well<br>Lustrous<br>Water spots easily<br>Poor resistance to prolonged exposure to sunlight | Draperies<br>Lampshades | Wall hangings<br>Upholstery |
| *Wool* | Hair of sheep | Absorbent<br>Wrinkle resistant<br>Not moth resistant<br>Shrinks | Rugs<br>Curtains<br>Blankets | Draperies<br>Upholstery |

13-2

*Protein natural fibers are strong and absorbent.*

| Manufactured Fibers | | | |
|---|---|---|---|
| Generic Name (Some Trade Names) | Type | Characteristics | Uses |
| **Acetate** Celebrate Chromspun Estron | Cellulosic | Drapes well Dyes easily Weak Heat sensitive Poor abrasion resistance | Bedspreads Draperies Upholstery Sheers |
| **Acrylic** Acrilan Creslan Orlon | Noncellulosic | Warm Lightweight Resists wrinkles Low absorbency Heat sensitive | Blankets Carpets Draperies Rugs Upholstery |
| **Glass** Fiberglas Fiber glass | Noncellulosic | Strong Resists sun fading Nonabsorbent | Curtains Draperies Insulation |
| **Lyocell** Tencell Lenzingly Lyocell | Cellulosic | Stronger than other cellulosic fibers Absorbent Drapes well Soft Wrinkle resistant | Bedding Draperies Slipcovers Upholstery |
| **Metallic** Lame Lurex Chromoflex | Noncellulosic | Resists shrinking Durable Nonabsorbent Increases fabric stiffness | Draperies Rugs Tablecloths Upholstery |
| **Modacrylic** SEF | Noncellulosic | Warm Dyes easily Resists flames and wrinkling Weak Nonabsorbent Heat sensitive | Blankets Carpeting Curtains Draperies Rugs |
| **Nylon** Anso Captiva Supplex | Noncellulosic | Strong Resistant to chemical damage and abrasion Does not stretch, shrink, or absorb water Creates static electricity | Carpets Curtains Draperies Slipcovers Tablecloths Upholstery |
| **Olefin** Essera Herculon Marvess | Noncellulosic | Lightweight Strong Resistant to abrasion Heat sensitive Nonabsorbent | Carpet backs Carpeting Slipcovers Upholstery |
| **Polyester** Dacron Fortrel Kodel | Noncellulosic | Strong Resistant to abrasion, creases, and shrinkage Holds its shape Low absorbency Heat sensitive | Bedding Carpeting Curtains Draperies Rugs Tablecloths Upholstery |
| **Rayon** Beau-Grip Zantrel | Cellulosic | Highly absorbent Soft Dyes easily Drapes well Weak | Bedding Draperies Slipcovers Tablecloths Upholstery |

13-3

*Each manufactured fiber has its own unique traits.*

**Research:** Find out when manufactured fibers were created? When was the first manufactured fiber developed? What was it? When did manufactured fibers become popular? Summarize your findings in a brief oral presentation.

**Enrich:** Students research *microfiber*, a term used to describe the fiber content of many clothes today. What is the term's definition? How does it compare to other fibers?

interlacing of two sets of yarns at right angles. The **warp yarns** run the lengthwise direction and form the

National Cotton Council of America

13-4 ———————————————

*Cotton fibers are twisted and pulled into small strands to make fine yarns.*

Ethan Allen, Inc.

13-5 ———————————————

*Many woven fabrics are used in this room. They are found in the sofa, chair, and ottoman upholstery, as well as in the window treatment and pillows.*

lengthwise grain. **Grain** is the direction threads run in a woven fabric. Extra warp yarns form the selvage, which is the lengthwise woven edge of the fabric. The **weft yarns** are the filling yarns that run in the crosswise direction. They form the crosswise grain.

Woven fabrics are made from three basic weaves. They are the plain weave, twill weave, and satin weave. Each weave varies according to how the yarns are crossed or interlaced. All other weaves are variations on these three basic weaves. See 13-6.

The *plain weave* is the simplest weave. The weft yarn goes over and under each warp yarn. A variation of the plain weave is the *basket weave*. Two or more weft yarns are interlaced with two or more warp yarns. The *rib weave* is another variation of the plain weave. Coarser weft yarns are combined with regular warp yarns to give a corded effect.

In the *twill weave*, the warp or weft yarn passes over two or more yarns. Each succeeding pass begins one yarn above or below the last one. The result is a **wale**, which is a diagonal rib or cord pattern.

A twill weave can be even or uneven. When the weft yarns go over and under the same number of warp yarns, an even twill weave is created. When the number of the weft yarns and the warp yarns are not the same, an uneven twill weave is created. Twill weave fabrics are stronger than plain weave fabrics. They also tend to show soil less quickly.

The *satin weave* has long **floats**, or segments of yarn on the surface of the fabric. Either the warp yarns or weft yarns float over four or more opposite yarns, then go under one. Each successive float begins two yarns away from the beginning of the last one. The satin weave is smooth and slippery. It drapes well and is good for linings.

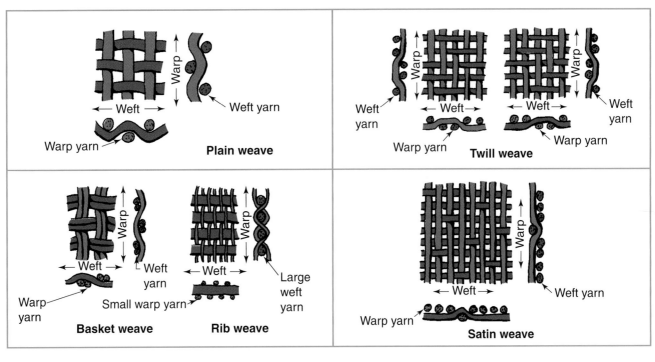

13-6
*Each weave is constructed differently. This gives each type of fabric a different look and feel.*

However, it is less durable than the other basic weaves.

The *pile weave* is a variation of the plain and twill weaves. Pile fabrics have yarn loops or cut yarns that stand away from the base of the fabric. In 13-7, you can compare a plain weave, loop-pile weave, and a cut-pile weave. Examples of pile weave fabrics are velvet, velveteen, corduroy, terry cloth, and frieze.

Pile fabrics have a **nap**, which is a layer of fiber ends that stand up from the surface of the fabric. The nap appears different when you view it from varying directions. It is important the nap runs in the same direction throughout a product. For example, if you make draperies that have two or more panels, the nap of the pile fabric needs to run in the same direction on all of the panels.

Two other weaves used for home furnishings are the jacquard weave and leno weave. The jacquard weave is used for damask, tapestry, and brocade, 13-8. The leno weave, 13-9, is used for curtains and thermal blankets. In addition, you will find the dobby weave, which is characterized by having small geometric shapes such as diamonds or squares woven into the fabric. The dobby weave is used primarily for upholstery fabric, but also is used for some draperies.

**Activity:** Using a magnifying glass, look at two fabrics and draw what you see. Label each. Compare your drawings to Figure 13-6.

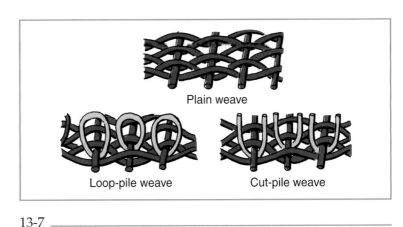

13-7
*A pile weave fabric has additional yarn covering the surface.*

Ethan Allen, Inc.

13-8 _____
*The tapestry fabric used on this sofa is an example of a jacquard weave.*

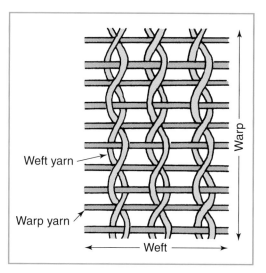

13-9 _____
*The leno weave is loosely woven and has open spaces.*

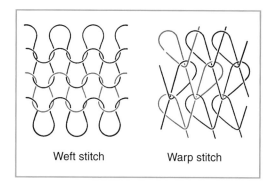

Weft stitch          Warp stitch

13-10 _____
*Knitted fabrics vary according to yarn size, yarn texture, and loop construction. The weft stitch allows more stretch than the warp stitch.*

### Knitted Fabrics

*Knitting* is the looping of yarns together. The size of the loops and how close together they are varies, as well as the way the loops are joined. See 13-10. Depending on whether one or two needles are used, knits can be single or double knits.

Weft knits are either circular or flat. They produce single knits, double knits, jersey, rib knits, and jacquard. Warp knits are flat. They are generally tighter, flatter, and less elastic than weft knits.

Knitted fabrics are mainly used in home fabrics as backing for other fabrics. This is because they lack the stability and body needed for many home textiles. However, they are increasingly being used for upholstery.

### Other Types of Fabrics

There are other fabrics used in the home that are not woven or knitted.

They are constructed in a variety of ways.

Nonwoven fabrics are made by joining fibers together using adhesives, heat fusion, or entanglement of fibers. During these processes, the masses of fibers interlock and hold together. Felt and fusible interfacing are examples of nonwoven fabrics. Nonwoven fabrics are generally not as strong as woven or knitted fabrics, and they do not have as much stretch.

Vinyl and other plastic materials are not made from fibers. Instead, they are thin, nonwoven sheets. These sheets can be finished to look like woven fabrics or leather. Vinyl is usually backed with a knit fabric to give it stability and strength.

Leather is sometimes classified as a nonwoven fabric. When it is *tanned*, or treated with a special acid called tannin, it becomes soft and resists stains, fading, and cracking. Since it is strong and durable, it is sometimes used in the home.

In *bonded* nonwoven fabrics, two layers of fabric are permanently joined together with an adhesive. Heat is used to set the bond. Often a face fabric is bonded to a lining. At other times, the face fabric is bonded to synthetic foam.

## Fabric Modifications

Fabrics can be modified to improve their appearance, feel, performance, and durability. These changes can be made through design, dye, and finishes.

### Design

Designs in fabrics may be structural or applied. *Structural designs* are made by varying the yarns while the fabric is either woven or knitted. The size, texture, and placement of the yarns all affect the final pattern. *Applied designs* are printed onto the surface of the fabric. They can be seen distinctly only on one side of the fabric.

### Dye

Dyes give color to fabric. There are three main methods of dyeing fabric, depending on when color is added. Color may be applied to the fibers, the yarn, or the fabric.

When you add color to the fibers, it is called *stock dyeing*. It is done before the fibers are spun into yarn. The dyeing is uniform and long lasting. Adding color to the yarn is one of the oldest methods. It is done before the yarns are made into fabric. This method is widely used and color absorption is good. The easiest and least expensive method is adding color to the fabric. It is called *piece dyeing* and usually a single color is used.

### Finishes

The appearance, feel, and performance of fabrics can be improved with *finishes*. These are applied only to the fabric, not to the fiber or yarn. Manufacturers are able to produce many finishes for fabrics. See 13-11 for a description of common finishes used and the wide variety of benefits they provide.

# Textiles for Home Use

The fabrics used in the home are called household textiles. The textiles you choose will depend on where and how they will be used. You need to consider the appearance, durability, maintenance, and comfort of the fabric. You should also think about the ease of working with the fabric and the cost. Using what you have learned about fabric types and construction will help you make these decisions.

| Basic Textile Features | |
|---|---|
| *Antistatic* | Prevents buildup of static electricity |
| *Bleaching* | Whitens natural fabric from the mill |
| *Crease resistance* | Prevents fabric from wrinkling |
| *Flame resistance* | Prevents fabric from burning easily |
| *Moth resistance* | Discourages moths and carpet beetles from attacking wool fibers |
| *Napping* | Produces a raised surface by lifting fiber ends |
| *Permanent press (durable press)* | Prevents fabric from wrinkling |
| *Preshrunk* | Prevents fabric from shrinking more than a small amount |
| *Sizing* | Provides extra body and weight to fabric through a solution of starch |
| *Soil release* | Makes stain removal easy |
| *Stain resistance (soil resistance)* | Makes fibers less absorbent so stain removal is easier |
| *Waterproof* | Prevents water from soaking into the fabric |
| *Water repellent* | Resists water but does not make fabric waterproof |

13-11

*Finishes can be applied to fabrics to improve their appearance, durability, maintenance, and comfort.*

## Appearance

Appearance is the overall visual effect. For instance, a fabric may appear soft or stiff. It may also appear bulky or sheer, light or dark, rough or smooth, bright or dull. Fabrics can make a room appear elegant or relaxed. See the two examples in 13-12.

## Durability

Durability is the capacity to be long-lasting under normal conditions. You want fabrics to last as long as possible to avoid the costs of replacing them. Fabrics that receive heavy use need to withstand wear. Tightly

woven fabrics or fabrics with bulky yarns have the most durability.

## Maintenance

Maintenance is the care needed to keep fabrics clean and looking their best. Proper cleaning techniques—dry cleaning or laundering—should be used. You need to follow instructions to ensure good results. You also need to consider the cost of maintaining fabrics. Textiles that can be laundered at home can help you avoid the high costs of dry cleaning. Most textiles have suggested care instructions.

## Comfort

You want fabric that makes you feel comfortable. Comfort is a psychological consideration and is different for each person. A fabric can give you visual comfort if you like its appearance. It can give you physical comfort if it is soft or pleasant to the touch.

## Ease of Construction

If you are going to sew some of the textiles yourself, you need to consider the ease with which the fabric can be managed. Heavy, closely-woven fabrics are harder to handle than lightweight, loosely-woven fabrics. On the other hand, loosely woven-fabrics tend to catch on objects. Also, stitching is more difficult to see on dark fabric than light fabric.

## Cost

Cost is always an important consideration, but do not base your decision on cost alone. You will want to buy the best fabric for its use. A good-quality fabric at a high price may be more economical in the long run than buying a low-quality fabric inexpensively.

Crate & Barrel

A

Ethan Allen, Inc.

B

**13-12**

*Fabrics can convey different moods, as demonstrated by different collections of pillows. The atmosphere can range from cheerful and relaxed (A) to formal (B).*

Also, keep in mind the costs of installation, maintenance, and replacement besides the initial price.

Evaluate fabrics based on these important factors before you make a purchase.

# Textiles for Floor Treatments

Buying carpets and rugs for your house is a major purchase. There are many different construction methods, textures, fibers, and finishes from which to choose. In order to make a good decision, it is important to know what choices are available.

## Construction Methods

There are several methods used to construct carpets and rugs, including weaving, tufting, and needlepunching. See 13-13. Each of these methods combines the pile yarn, which is the part you walk on, with the backing material, which is the part that holds the yarn together.

Woven carpets and rugs are made on a loom. The pile yarns and the backing are interwoven. Axminster, velvet, and Wilton are the three main types of weaves used to make woven carpets and rugs. Only about two percent of today's carpeting is woven.

*Tufted* carpets and rugs are made by looping the yarn into the backing material and securing it to the backing

Resource: *Construction Methods for Carpets and Rugs*, reproducible master 13-1, TR. Students label the methods of carpet construction and answer related questions.

**Art Activity:** Using plastic weave and knitting yarn, make samples of tufted, woven, and needlepunched rugs.

**Enrich:** Create a list of carpet-related questions concerning fibers, weaves, and so forth. Visit a carpet store to view carpets of various construction methods and ask questions.

**Enrich:** Attend a demonstration of rug making by an art teacher or local artisan. Summarize in one paragraph what you learn.

**Discuss:** What is the meaning of *density* as it relates to carpet construction? (*the number of tufts or yarns per square inch*)
**Activity:** Collect samples of carpets with five different piles. Identify and label each.

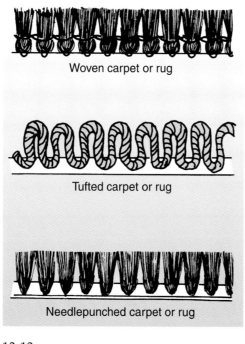

Woven carpet or rug

Tufted carpet or rug

Needlepunched carpet or rug

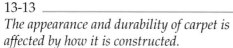

13-13

*The appearance and durability of carpet is affected by how it is constructed.*

and a second backing with an adhesive. Tufting is easy to do and is less expensive than weaving.

*Needlepunching* is the process of interlocking fibers by using felting needles. The process produces a flat carpet that resembles felt. It is mainly used for indoor/outdoor carpets and rugs.

## Textures

Carpet texture is called *pile*. Different textures are created in carpets and rugs when the yarn is cut, left uncut, twisted, untwisted, or cut in different lengths. The five types of pile that result are called cut, level loop, multilevel loop, cut and loop, and shag. Level loop pile wears the best. Multilevel loop pile results when there is a combination of cut and looped yarns.

Texture can also be achieved by twisting the pile yarns. At other times, flecks of color are added and the appearance of texture results. The thickness of the yarn affects the texture, too. The thicker the yarn, the more plush the carpet. Density refers to the number of tufts or yarns per square inch. Carpets with a high density look better and are more durable.

## Fiber Content

Fiber content greatly affects the quality of rugs and carpets. Wool, nylon, acrylic, rayon, olefin, and cotton are the major fibers used for carpets and rugs. Each has unique traits that affect the carpeting.

Wool is an ideal fiber for carpets and rugs because it is very resilient. It is also durable and resistant to soil and stains. Wool, however, is expensive. Therefore, wool is used only for luxury carpets and rugs.

Nylon is the most-used fiber for carpets and rugs today. It is very durable, resilient, and soil resistant, but oily stains are difficult to remove. Nylon is less costly than wool.

Acrylic looks like wool. It also has good resilience, durability, and soil-resistance like wool. See 13-14. However, oily stains are difficult to remove. Acrylic costs less than wool but more than nylon.

Rayon carpets and rugs are attractive, but not very practical. They are low in resilience, durability, and soil resistance. Rayon rugs are, however, low in price and used when quality is not an important factor. Scatter rugs and inexpensive room-size rugs are sometimes made of rayon.

Olefin is sometimes used for kitchen, bathroom, and outdoor carpets. It is very durable and resistant to soil and stains. Olefin is also fairly resilient. Prices for olefin carpets range from medium to low.

**Enrich:** Visit a historical house in your area. Study the rugs and carpets. Are they original? Have they been repaired? What construction and fibers were used?

**Note:** The Web site *carpet-rug.com/* provides information on fibers, finishes, care, and construction of rugs and carpets.

Cotton rugs are attractive and durable, but low in resilience and soil resistance. Prices vary according to the type of cotton, but are generally low. Cotton is used mostly for washable scatter rugs, such as rugs used in bathrooms and kitchens.

## Finishes

The application of finishes to carpets and rugs is mainly for functional reasons. For example, an antistatic finish reduces static buildup. A flame-resistant finish prevents the fabric from burning easily. Stain-resistant and soil-release finishes make carpet care easier.

# Textiles for Upholstered Furniture

Upholstered furniture is fully or partially covered with fabric, 13-15. **Upholstery** is the fabric, padding, or other material used to make a soft covering for furniture. When you choose upholstery fabric, you need to consider where and how the furniture will be used.

For furniture that will receive constant wear, choose fabric that is durable, stain-resistant, and easy to clean. Wool, mohair, and manufactured fibers such as nylon and acrylic are very durable. They are often available in blends.

By knowing the fabric content, you will know how well the fabric will clean and withstand wear. These and other factors are determined by the fibers used in producing the fabric and the finishes applied to it.

Fabrics used for upholstery are chosen according to their use in formal and informal settings. Formal rooms have an elegant appearance. The fabrics most often used include plain or

© Spiegel 1998

13-14

*This acrylic area rug is constructed with high-density tufts to give it the appearance of an animal's coat.*

Ethan Allen, Inc.

13-15

*The chairs in this room are partially upholstered, while the sofa is completely upholstered.*

**Resource:** *Textiles for Upholstered Furniture,* reproducible master 13-2, TR. Students mount a picture of upholstered furniture and answer related questions.

**Enrich:** Research the finishes used on upholstery fabrics and find out how long they last. Do they degrade with time, frequent traffic, or exposure to moisture or sunlight? Summarize your findings in chart form.

**Resource:** *Fabrics for Window Treatments*, Activity D, SAG. Students mount a fabric swatch, sketch a window treatment appropriate for it, and answer questions.
**Activity:** Create a collage of fabrics used for formal and informal upholstery. Create a second collage for formal and informal window treatments. Label the fabrics in each.

Ethan Allen, Inc.

13-16

*You can add an accent to a simple piece of upholstered furniture by draping a paisley throw across it or adding a contrasting pillow.*

Ethan Allen, Inc.

13-17

*This sheer fabric selected for this window treatment softly filters the light entering the room.*

textured satins, damask, velvet, velveteen, brocade, faille, mohair, or matelassé. These fabrics can be made of silk or a blend of natural and manufactured fibers. See 13-16.

In informal or casual settings, patterns can range from a very small print to a large scenic design. You can use a wide variety of fabrics, including chintz, polished cotton, gingham, sailcloth, burlap, denim, poplin, or corduroy.

# Textiles for Window Treatments

Fabric is often used for draperies and curtains. When making your selections, you need to consider the purpose and style of the room. You also need to consider the colors and patterns used throughout the room. Finally, the cost of the fabric and its care are other factors to consider.

## Purpose and Style of Rooms

A window covering can regulate the natural light that enters a room. Sheer fabrics will filter the light. They will give you a feeling of privacy in the daytime. You will be able to see out, but others will not be able to see into the room. However, sheers do not provide privacy at night. See 13-17.

When closed, opaque window treatments will not allow you to see out. They can shut out light and provide privacy both day and night. This is an important consideration when choosing fabrics for some rooms, such as bedrooms. Opaque fabrics are usually heavy and thick. Lighter-weight fabrics may not give the privacy you desire.

As you choose window treatments, you need to consider the styles of the rooms in which they are used.

**Discuss:** Why is the window treatment in Figure 13-17 not appropriate for a bedroom, bathroom, or kitchen?

**Reflect:** Do fabrics provide privacy in your room at home, or are blinds or shades used for that purpose instead?

In work or informal areas, denim, poplin, and other casual fabrics are good choices. In more formal settings, you may use damask, antique satin, or similar fabrics.

## Colors and Patterns

The fabric colors and patterns in window treatments should match or complement the furnishings in the room, as in 13-18.

You may choose a dominant color for your window treatments. It could be a color that is in the upholstery or carpet. When choosing patterns, select large patterns for large rooms and small prints for small rooms.

## Cost and Care

You can buy ready-made or made-to-order window treatments. Also, you can purchase fabric and make them yourself. However, it is important to remember that more fabric and detail used in the window treatments will cost more.

You also should consider the cost of caring for window treatments. Most draperies and some curtains need to be dry-cleaned, which can be expensive. Other window treatments are made from fabrics that can be washed at home. However, if they are very large, they will need to be laundered professionally.

# Textiles for Kitchen, Bath, and Bed

Textiles used in the kitchen, bathroom, and bedroom are called linens, although few are actually made of linen today. You need to consider their appearance, durability, and care requirements.

Ethan Allen, Inc.

13-18
*The colors and patterns in this window treatment complement the other fabrics and furnishings in the room.*

## Kitchen

The main linens used in the kitchen or dining room are table coverings and towels.

### Table Coverings

Table coverings include tablecloths, place mats, and napkins. See 13-19. Silence cloths that go under the tablecloths to reduce noise are also considered a table covering.

Thinking about how the table coverings will be used will help you choose the best type. Is the table covering intended for use everyday or only for special occasions? Is it planned for a formal dining room or a breakfast nook? Knowing answers to these basic questions will help you select an appropriate fabric.

Linen was the preferred fabric for table coverings, but it requires ironing. Most people today are more interested in easy care fabrics. Many table coverings

**Discuss:** Why do you think "spring cleaning" is a tradition in many homes throughout the country?

**Math Activity:** Survey local dry cleaners to determine what they charge for cleaning curtains and draperies. Create a bar graph showing the price variation.

**Reflect:** Does your family practice "spring cleaning"? What items are usually cleaned?

Spiegel, Inc.

13-19

*Tablecloths and napkins often coordinate with the tableware.*

are available in fabrics that require little or no ironing and have soil-release finishes.

### Towels

Kitchen towels include dishcloths, dish towels, and lint-free towels, which are used for drying glass. Kitchen towels are usually made of linen or cotton. Linen is good for lint-free towels because it does not have a nap and dries more quickly than cotton. Ideally, towels should absorb water quickly and easily, provide durability, and look attractive. All the towels you choose should possess those qualities in that order. They also should be easy to launder.

Towels are available in a variety of colors and patterns. Some have

borders and woven designs. Any additional decoration, such as special borders or monograms, will increase the cost of towels. This, however, does not make them better-quality towels.

## Bathroom

Household linens used in the bathroom include towels, bath mats, and shower curtains.

### Towels

Bathroom towels come in several sizes. These include a bath sheet (extra large), a bath towel (large), a hand towel (medium), and a washcloth (small). Sometimes even smaller towels, called guest towels or fingertip towels, are available. Bath towels often come in sets.

Many towels are made of cotton terry cloth because it is absorbent. Also, the loops absorb moisture well. Sometimes the cotton is blended with polyester. The polyester decreases drying time, adds strength, and reduces shrinkage. The more closely woven the fabric is, the more durable and absorbent it is. Velour terry cloth is also used. It has a cut pile on one side of the towel, which gives it a velvetlike appearance.

### Bath Mats

Some bath mats are made of a material resembling towels but heavier. Others are tufted and have latex backing to keep them from slipping. Still others are made of yarn sewn onto a backing. You may see bath mats made from braided fabrics. Fibers used to make bath rugs include cotton, rayon, and various blends. They often have colors that match or coordinate with the bath towels.

## Shower Curtains

Shower curtains are used to prevent water from spraying outside the shower area. They are made from plastic or fabric that is treated with a waterproof finish. They have a wide variety of colors and patterns. Often they coordinate with bath towels, bath mats, wallpaper, and window treatments. See 13-20.

## Bedroom

Linens used in the bedroom are called bedding. Bedding includes sheets, pillowcases, blankets, bedspreads, comforters, as well as accessories such as shams, pillows, and dust ruffles.

### Bed Linens

Bed linens include sheets and pillowcases, which are usually available in matching sets. The sheets may be flat or fitted. A flat sheet can be used as the top or bottom sheet. A fitted sheet, on the other hand, snugly fits the shape of the mattress and functions only as a bottom sheet. Sheets and pillowcases are available in various sizes to fit the different bed sizes. These range from crib and twin beds to standard, queen, and king sizes. Also, sheets designed to fit waterbeds are available.

Sheets and pillowcases are usually made of cotton or a cotton/polyester blend. Cotton sheets are more absorbent, but polyester decreases wrinkling. Sometimes sheets are made from acetate or nylon. Cotton sheets are usually made from percale, muslin, or flannel. Percale is a high-quality, lightweight, plain-weave cotton fabric. Muslin is also a plain-weave cotton fabric that ranges from lightweight to heavyweight. Flannel has a napped surface that provides extra warmth.

Photograph courtesy of Waverly

13-20

*The fabric used in this shower curtain coordinates with the wallpaper and other fabrics in the room.*

When you purchase sheets and pillowcases, look at the thread count. The higher the thread count is, the more closely woven is the fabric. Lower-count sheets are lower in price. Fine percale sheets may have a thread count of 200 to 300, while less expensive muslin sheets may have a count of only 112 to 180.

Also, you need to be concerned about the washability of sheets and pillowcases. Since they will be washed often, they need to be colorfast and durable.

**Activity:** Working with a partner, list the different fabrics visible in Figure 13-20.

**Activity.** Find the standard measurements of bed sizes for twin, standard, queen, and king sizes.

**Activity:** Use muslin or other inexpensive material to test different brands of water repellant. Apply them to the fabric, following manufacturer's directions. Test which is most effective. Write a summary of recommendations based on the results.

**Vocabulary:** Create a Venn diagram comparing percale sheets to muslin sheets. Draw overlapping circles, placing the qualities they share in the overlap. In the outer parts of the circles, place the qualities about them that differ. Use one side for percale sheets and the other for muslin sheets, labeling each.

## Blankets, Bedspreads, and Comforters

These items come in weights suitable for different seasons of the year. In certain climates and air-conditioned homes, blankets are used all year. Light cotton or rayon blankets are ideal for summer. They are easy to launder and less expensive than heavy blankets. Wool, acrylic, or a combination are good for cold winter nights. Thermal blankets made using the leno weave are often a good choice. The open spaces in the weave form pockets that trap air and serve as insulation. Again, comfort, attractiveness, and durability are considerations in choosing blankets.

Bedspreads are usually purchased for their attractiveness. They come in a variety of fabrics. You can make a satisfying choice if you know your fabrics.

While some bedspreads are washable, many need to be dry-cleaned.

In addition to your bedspread being attractive, it should be the correct size for the bed. It should also harmonize with the other furnishings in the room. Matching bedspread, window treatment, and sheet sets are available.

Filled bed coverings called *comforters* are often used as bedspreads. They are chosen for their attractiveness and warmth. The covering makes a comforter attractive. See 13-21. Comforter coverings made from rayon, acetate, and silk often appear luxurious. Comforter covers made from sateen, polished cotton, and challis are not as luxurious appearing. However, they are more durable, yet very attractive.

The filling is what makes the comforter warm. The warmest comforters are filled with wool or down. Down is the soft, fine feathers from ducks or geese. Down is light and resilient, but quite expensive. As a result, lower-quality feathers are sometimes used instead. Other fillings used in comforters include polyester or cotton and kapok, which tend to mat or clump.

# Textile Laws

There are many laws in the United States that regulate textiles. They were passed to inform and protect the consumer from false labeling and advertising. See 13-22. Three major textile acts that apply to household textiles are summarized here.

## Textile Fiber Products Identification Act

According to this law, fibers in a textile product must be labeled in

© Spiegel 1998

13-21
*The comforter and its coordinating pillows, dust ruffles, and sheets make this bed very attractive.*

order of predominance by weight. If the fibers are less than five percent of the fabric, they can be listed as "other fiber or fibers." Natural and manufactured fibers are listed by their generic names. Trade names can also be used. The information must be attached to the product. However, certain items, such as already installed upholstery fabrics, mattress materials, and carpet backings are exempt.

## Wool Products Labeling Act

This law requires all products containing any quantity of wool to include a label identifying the kind and amount of wool used. Wool products must be labeled as one of the following types:

- Wool—wool fiber that has never been manufactured into a product or used by a consumer.
- Recycled wool—wool fiber made from a woven or felted wool product that may have been used by a consumer. (Felted wool consists of wool fibers held together by moisture, heat, pressure, and chemicals.)

Products made from wool must have labels identifying the percentage of each type of wool used. The name of the manufacturer is also required. Imported wool must be labeled with

Ethan Allen, Inc.

13-22 _____

*As you shop, read labels to learn what fibers and finishes are used in the various fabrics.*

the name of the country where it was processed and manufactured.

## Flammable Fabrics Act

This law prohibits the sale of *flammable* fabrics, which are fabrics that burn quickly. The *Flammable Fabrics Act* covers fabrics in textile products used in the home, such as carpets, rugs, mattresses, mattress pads, blankets, draperies, and upholstery. Many new flame-resistant finishes have been developed as a result of this law.

**Vocabulary:** Look up the terms *felt*, *felting*, and *felted* to name some common examples of felted wool.

**Internet Activity:** Research the Flammable Fabrics Act and the issues and concerns that caused the passage of this law.

**Reflect:** Do you anticipate future laws being written for textiles? If so, what might be some of the issues they address?

**Resource:** *Textile Review*, Activity E, SAG. Students use the clues to fill in the crossword puzzle.

# Summary

Fibers come from plant and animal sources, wood cellulose, oil products, and other chemicals. Each fiber has its own traits. You can make wise fabric choices by understanding fiber traits and the ways used to construct fabrics. Fabrics can be woven, knitted, felted, tanned, or bonded. Other factors to consider when choosing fabrics are the design, color, and finishes.

Some textiles are used for floor treatments, upholstery, and window treatments. Other textiles are used as various types of linens in the kitchen, bathroom, and bedroom. The function and placement of the textiles are important. You need to consider how the fabrics will look with other furnishings in the room. Durability, maintenance, comfort, ease of use, and cost are other factors to consider.

Various textile laws inform and protect the consumer. Some laws require specific labeling information on textiles. Labels can help you wisely choose household textiles.

## Answer Key

1. (Student response. See Figures 13-1 and 13-2.)
2. (Student response. See Figure 13-3.)
3. Natural fibers come from plant and animal sources whereas manufactured products come from wood cellulose, oil products, and other chemicals.
4. Fibers (staple and filament) are the beginning of fabrics. They are made into yarns that are woven or knitted to make fabrics.
5. Weaving is the interlacing of two sets of yarns at right angles. Knitting is the looping of yarns together with the use of needles.
6. by joining two layers of fabric together with an adhesive
7. installation, maintenance, replacement
8. Woven carpets are made with a loom on which the pile yarns and backing are interwoven. Tufted carpets are made by looping the yarns into the backing material and securing them with an adhesive and second backing.
9. (List three:) wool, nylon, and acrylic—indoor carpeting; rayon and cotton—scatter rugs; olefin—outdoor and kitchen carpeting
10. (List three:) where and how the furniture will be used, cleanability, maintenance requirements, cost, appearance, fiber content, types of finishes
11. Curtains, drapes
12. false
13. terry cloth, because of its absorbent quality
14. (Student response. See pages 304-305.)

# To Review

1. Name two natural cellulosic fibers and two natural protein fibers.
2. List five manufactured fibers and give two characteristics of each.
3. What is the difference between natural and manufactured fibers?
4. How do fibers and yarns differ?
5. Explain the difference between weaving and knitting.
6. How are bonded fabrics made?
7. Besides the initial price, what three costs are important to consider before buying textiles for home use.
8. Describe the weaving and tufting processes used in carpet construction.
9. Name three fibers and the type of carpet or rug made from each.
10. List three factors to consider when choosing upholstery fabrics.
11. _____ and _____ are the most common types of window treatments that use textiles.
12. True or false. Closely woven fabrics are less opaque than loosely woven fabrics.
13. What type of fabric is usually used to make bathroom towels? Why?
14. Choose a textile law and explain how it protects consumers.

**Discuss:** Students make a list of 10 important concepts learned from this chapter, writing one- or two-sentence summaries of each.

**Language Arts Activity:** Working in pairs, students discuss what they learned from this chapter, using as many "To Know" terms as possible. Ground rules are: one declarative sentence is spoken at a time, partners take turns speaking, and key terms cannot be used in questions.

# In Your Community

1. Go to a department or linens store and locate fabric items to decorate an imaginary kitchen, bathroom, or bedroom. Carefully take notes on each item. Later in class, summarize your selections and review the factors you considered when making the selections.

2. Choose five textile products from one room of your house. Read any labels found on them. Note on paper the information required by law that appears on each. Share your findings with the class.

3. Using retail catalogs or information from local stores, find and list descriptions of the fiber content, cost, and care required for fabrics suitable for one of the following:
   A. upholstery
   B. window treatment
   C. bedroom linens

# To Think About

1. The U.S. Government has created many laws to inform consumers and protect them from such dangers as fabrics that burn too quickly. If you were shopping one weekend at a neighbor's yard sale, would you feel comfortable buying blankets or draperies that no longer had labels showing fiber content and flammability ratings? Would the money you could save by purchasing these items represent a good bargain to you? Explain your reasons for either making or not making such a purchase.

2. Imagine you and your college roommate want a new carpet as an area rug for your dormitory room. You are on a limited budget and you want to buy a rug that will be durable, affordable, resilient, and soil resistant. To accomplish these goals, would you buy a carpet that is woven or tufted? What kind of density would you look for in the carpet? What would be your most likely choice of fiber content? Which finishes would you want?

# Using Technology

1. Search the Internet to research which countries are the largest suppliers of various natural and manufactured fibers. How many metric tons were produced globally of the 10 most commonly used fibers in today's homes? For what percentage of fiber production is the United States responsible? Present your findings to the class.

**Note:** For researching suppliers of natural and manufactured fibers, have students explore *fiberworld.com*.

2. Develop a PowerPoint® or overhead presentation that summarizes what fibers were used in textiles for everyday home use in the early history of the country or of your state. Research the type of household textiles commonly owned and the fiber content of each. What were some of the drawbacks of the fibers used before modern fibers and finishes were developed?

3. Using images on the Web or taken with a digital camera, create a consumer bulletin that explains the important points consumers should know before buying carpeting. Have the class critique the usefulness of your consumer information.

**Portfolio Project:** Create a vignette of fabrics you would like to use in the bedroom of your future dorm or apartment. Label each, identifying its fiber content, finishes, and proposed use.

# CHAPTER 14
# Creating Interior Backgrounds

## To Know

floor treatment
flooring materials
tile
ceramic tile
floor coverings
soft floor covering
resilient floor covering
laminate
cork
gypsum wallboard
plastic wallboard
paneling
synthetic
plaster
wall treatment
paint
faux finish
stenciling
wallpaper
ceiling treatment
acoustical
countertop
solid surface
engineered quartz
butcher block

Permission granted by F. Schumacher & Co. to use copyrighted photographs.
Designs and photograph © F. Schumacher & Co.

## Objectives

After studying this chapter, you will be able to

- compare floor treatments.
- describe several wall materials and wall treatments.
- explain how ceiling treatments serve as interior backgrounds.
- recognize the choices available for countertops.
- demonstrate how to plan satisfying interior backgrounds.

**Resource:** *The Inside Story,* transparency master overlay IV-B, TR. Students look back at the topics covered in Chapters 1-13 by reviewing transparency master IV-A. Then, with the addition of overlay IV-B, they explore the topics they will cover in Chapter 14.

**Reading / Writing Activity:** Change the chapter objectives into questions and list them on the left side of a piece of paper. As you read the chapter, write the answers on the right half of the paper.

**Discuss:** Read the chapter objectives. Which topics belong in the category of *facts you already know*? Which topics belong in the category of *facts you need to learn*?

Resource: *Floor Treatments*, Activity A, SAG. Students determine the best floor coverings for the situations listed. They mount pictures and complete the information on the form.

Discuss: Name the interior backgrounds of a room. (*flooring, walls, and ceilings*)

Floors, walls, and ceilings create interior backgrounds for furnishings and accessories in rooms. They also hide construction details and provide insulation. How they are treated helps to determine the total look of the room and create a desired mood.

# Floor Treatments

The floor treatment is usually the first background that is planned in a room. *Floor treatments* consist of flooring materials and floor coverings. There are many types of flooring materials and floor coverings from which to choose. However, before you choose a floor treatment, you should consider its appearance, comfort, durability, cost, and maintenance.

Bruce® Hardwood Floors, northshore oak in butterscotch

14-1 _____

*This hardwood floor adds warmth and beauty to the room.*

## Flooring Materials

*Flooring materials* are materials that are used as the top surface of a floor. They do not include the subflooring, but they are structurally part of the floor and are fairly permanent. Common flooring materials include wood, tile, concrete, and brick.

### Wood

Wood has always been a popular flooring material. It looks good with all styles of furniture. It offers beauty and warmth to a room, as shown in 14-1. Wood has some resilience and is durable, but can be scratched and dented. The cost of wood flooring is moderate to high, depending on the type and quality of wood chosen. Hardwoods are typically more expensive than softwoods. Oak, hard maple, beech, birch, hickory, mahogany, cherry, and teak are common hardwoods used for floors. Oak is the most common because of its beauty, warmth, and durability. Hard maple is also common because it is smooth, strong, and hard.

Southern yellow pine, Douglas fir, hemlock, and larch are common softwoods used for floors. Redwood, cedar, cypress, and eastern white pine are used where they are readily available. There are two different kinds of wood floor installations. They include unfinished solid wood and prefinished engineered wood flooring.

When installing unfinished solid wood floors, they must be given enough time to adjust to the house environment. Wood that is unfinished will expand and contract during fluctuations in humidity and temperature. The floor finishing process requires multiple steps of repeated sanding and staining. The last step involves sealing the floor surface with a protective coating.

Reflect: What is the most common flooring material used in homes in your area?

Discuss: What types of flooring material is used throughout your school?

Activity: Research the differences between hardwood and softwood. How did the two basic categories of wood get their names? List each of the different woods used for flooring materials in this country and identify its classification.

An alternative to a solid wood floor is a floor made of engineered wood, available in many styles and finishes. These floors are prefinished at the factory and, therefore, already sanded and stained. Engineered wood floors can be installed over concrete and wooden subfloors. Solid wood floors, however, require a plywood underlayment when installed over concrete. Engineered wood floors are constructed to withstand moisture. They have more stability than solid wood and will expand and contract less with seasonal changes in the environment.

The most common method of installing engineered wood floors is to nail down thin strips of wood that are tongue-and-grooved to keep them close together. This is called *strip flooring*. If wider widths of wood are used, the floor is called *plank flooring*. Another style of wood flooring is *parquet flooring*. Decorative patterns, such as alternate plank and parquetry, 14-2, can be created to add interest to a wood floor.

Wood finishes of polyurethane, plastic, wax, and oil make the task of maintaining wood floors easy. They protect the wood from moisture, stains, and wear. If properly maintained, a quality wood floor can last the lifetime of the house.

### Tile

*Tile* is a flat piece of fired clay or natural stone that is available in a wide range of sizes, colors, finishes, and patterns. Tile feels cool to the touch and is therefore more popular in Sunbelt areas than in colder climates. The primary tile choices for residential use are ceramic, porcelain, natural stone, and quarry. Because of the amount of labor required for installation, tile can be expensive to install.

Bruce® Hardwood Floors, oakmont in auburn

14-2
*The use of parquet in this foyer adds interest to the entrance.*

### Ceramic Tile

*Ceramic tile* is a flat piece of fired clay coated with a protective glaze. High-quality ceramic tile is harder, more durable, and more expensive than ceramic tile of lesser quality. Ceramic tile is a durable choice for a floor treatment, but quality and cost can vary considerably.

Glazed ceramic tile is water- and stain-resistant, which makes it easy to maintain. To further protect the floor, you can seal the grout to make it resistant to stains, too. *Grout* is the cementlike substance that fills the spaces between the tiles. Ceramic tile can be kept clean by mopping with soapy water.

**Discuss:** Is the parquet pictured in Figure 14-2 a floor covering or a flooring material? (*flooring material*)

**Note:** Web sites such as *ceramic-tile.com/* and *infotile.com* provide additional information on tile.

**Discuss:** Why do you think many older homes have hardwood floors, while many newer homes do not?

**Discuss:** Which type of wood floors expand and contract least with seasonal change? (*engineered wood floors*)

Florida Tile Industries, Inc.

14-3

*Tile is being used more in rooms throughout the entire house.*

In the past, ceramic tile was most often used in bathrooms and entryways. However, with current design trends, ceramic tile can be used for flooring throughout the house. See 14-3. Ceramic can be produced in almost any color, pattern, or finish. Recent advances in computer imaging and glazing techniques have enabled ceramic tile to resemble natural stone and marble.

### Porcelain Tile

Porcelain tile is the highest quality ceramic tile made. The tile has a white or light clay-colored body that is fired at a very high temperature. The result is a very strong and durable product. Because of its strength, porcelain tile withstands freezing temperatures and can therefore be used indoors and outdoors. However, tiles with a smooth, high-gloss surface should not be used outside, as they would become very slippery when wet.

The color of a porcelain tile often penetrates the tile's entire thickness.

In contrast, the color of a ceramic tile is only on the surface. Porcelain tile is more expensive than ceramic tile.

### Quarry Tile

Quarry tile is available in black and a range of golds, beiges, reds, browns, and grays. It is made from terra-cotta that has been mixed and *fired*, or baked at a high temperature. Quarry tile is very strong and durable. It resists grease, chemicals, moisture, and changes in temperature. The shapes and textures of quarry tile vary, and it can be glazed or unglazed. Glazed quarry tile is easily cleaned with soapy water. Unglazed tile may need a protective sealer applied to make it as easy to clean as glazed tile.

## Natural Stone

Natural stone floors are beautiful and durable, but are usually costly to purchase and install. Stone comes in a variety of types, sizes, and qualities. Five types of stone, commonly available in the following colors, are very popular for home use:

- limestone—taupe, white, light and dark brown, and gray; with gold or light green veins
- travertine—usually cream or beige
- granite—almost any color
- marble—almost any color
- slate—usually gray, gold, or green

Stones may be used in their natural shapes or cut into geometric shapes. Attractive designs are achieved by mixing different types and shapes of stone together. The texture of stone tile may be rough or polished. Polished stone creates a formal appearance, while rough stone has a more rustic and informal look.

Stone floors are fairly easy to maintain by mopping with a solution of white vinegar and water. A sealer protects them from grease, oil, and household stains. Stone floors can be used throughout the house including entryways, kitchens, living and dining rooms, and bathrooms.

### Concrete

Concrete can have a smooth or textured surface. A smooth surface can be used as a finished floor. Color can be added in powder form when mixing concrete, or finished concrete can be painted with a special paint.

Concrete is extremely sturdy and durable, but uncomfortable to stand on for long periods. It is often used for entryways, basements, patios, and garages. Indoor concrete floors need to be waxed for easy maintenance. Concrete floors are relatively inexpensive because they do not require subflooring.

### Brick

Brick floors are beautiful, durable, and costly. They look best in informal settings. Bricks come in many sizes, colors, and textures, and can be used in a wide variety of patterns. The care of brick floors is similar to that of stone floors.

## Floor Coverings

*Floor coverings* are surfaces placed over the structural floor. Although they may be attached to the floor, they are not part of the structure. Floor coverings last several years and are expensive. However, they are not as expensive as flooring materials and can be changed more often. Floor coverings include soft floor coverings, 14-4, and resilient floor coverings.

### Soft Floor Coverings

Carpets and rugs are types of *soft floor coverings*. They are floor

Wear-Dated Carpet

**14-4**
*Wall-to-wall carpeting is an example of a soft floor covering.*

treatments made from manufactured or natural fibers. Manufactured fibers include nylon and olefin, while natural fibers include wool, cotton, sisal, and seagrass. Carpets and rugs insulate cold floors, provide sound control and walking comfort, and add color and texture to a room. They vary in their methods of construction as well as their textures and finishes. (Refer to Chapter 13, "Textiles in Today's Homes.")

Soft floor coverings can cover the entire floor or portions of it. Classified by how much floor they cover, common soft floor coverings are wall-to-wall carpeting, room-size rugs, and area rugs.

*Wall-to-wall carpeting* covers an entire floor, making rooms appear large and luxurious. It can hide any damage or faults in the surface of the floor. Wall-to-wall carpeting is maintained by routine vacuuming. Stains can be removed by applying an appropriate cleaning product. As time passes, the carpet will show wear and dirt in areas of highest traffic. A thorough cleaning can be done by scheduling a professional cleaning service or by renting the proper equipment and following manufacturer's care directions.

A *room-size rug* exposes a small border of floor. It can show off a beautiful wood floor while keeping the warmth and comfort of the soft floor covering. See 14-5. You would maintain a room-size rug in the same way you maintain a wall-to-wall carpet. One disadvantage of having a room size rug is that separate cleaning procedures are needed for the rug and the adjacent floor.

*Area rugs* vary in size, but they are not as large as a room-size rug. Area rugs are used to define areas of a room, add interest, and even serve as a focal point. They can be moved from one furniture grouping to another to create a new look. See 14-6. Area rugs are maintained with routine vacuuming and spot-stain removal. One big advantage of area rugs is they are portable. They can move with the household and be sent out for professional cleaning.

Padding is used under carpeting and rugs to lessen wear and increase resilience. It also adds luxury and warmth. Padding is made of hair, jute, sponge, or foam rubber. Different types of carpeting require specific products be used for padding. Always check the carpet or rug manufacturer's recommendations when buying your padding.

## Resilient Floor Coverings

**Resilient floor coverings** are floor treatments that are generally nonabsorbent, durable, easy to maintain, and fairly inexpensive. They provide some cushioning for walking comfort and noise control. Vinyl floor coverings, laminate floor coverings, and cork tile are types of resilient floor coverings. They are available in a wide range of colors and patterns and can be used in any decorating scheme.

*Vinyl floor coverings*, 14-7, are available in many colors, patterns, and textures. The quality of the flooring varies with the cost. Vinyl floor coverings are resistant to wear and stains, but abrasion can damage the surface. They are available in either tile or sheet form. Little or no waxing is needed. Some sheet vinyl is made with a layer of vinyl foam on the bottom. The result is a floor with good walking comfort and sound absorption.

*Solid vinyl floor coverings* are growing in popularity. They are a higher quality than sheet vinyl. With solid vinyl, the flooring is made totally of vinyl as opposed to sheet vinyl, which only has vinyl as the top layer. Solid

© Spiegel 1998

14-5 _____

*A room-size rug provides comfort without covering the beauty of the floor beneath.*

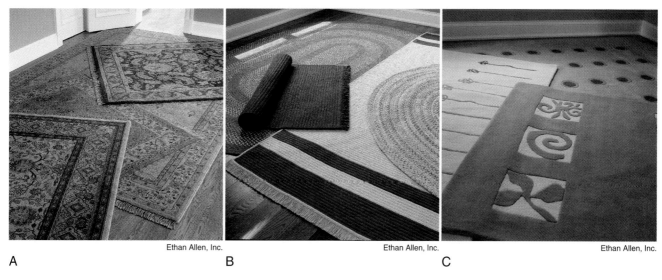

Ethan Allen, Inc.    Ethan Allen, Inc.    Ethan Allen, Inc.

A                                    B                                    C

14-6

*These area rugs are examples of three different design styles: Traditional (A), Country (B), and Modern or Contemporary style (C).*

vinyl flooring products are available in many striking colors, styles, and patterns. These floors may have the appearance of fine hardwood, elegant stone, marble, slate, granite, or a geometric pattern. They are available in planks, tiles, blocks, or squares. These different shapes and patterns can be combined in the same floor to provide an endless opportunity for creative custom designs.

Laminate floors vary in quality depending on their construction. A *laminate* is a product made by uniting one or more different layers, usually a decorative surface to a sturdy core. The best laminate floors have four layers of materials that are fused under intense heat and pressure. This process creates a single unit with a decorative surface and a sturdy core. The layers consist of a moisture-guard backing, a core of high-density material for structure, the pattern design, and a wear- and stain-resistant finish. The final product is resistant to traffic, stains, and fading. See 14-8. Laminate floors are easy to clean, comfortable

© Armstrong World Industries

14-7

*This vinyl floor covering is attractive and easy to keep clean.*

Bruce® Laminate Floors, country kitchen in cherry

14-8 ————————————————————
*Laminate floors are beautiful yet durable enough for high-traffic areas. The use of an area rug defines the dining area.*

for walking, and good at sound absorption. They are not, however, as resilient and durable as quality solid vinyl flooring.

*Cork tile* must be covered with a protective coating in order to be water resistant, durable, and easy to maintain. If this coating is not applied, cork wears rapidly, dents easily, is difficult to maintain, and can be damaged by grease stains. Without the protective coating, cork cannot be classified as a resilient floor covering. Cork is rich in appearance and is good for walking comfort and sound control. *Cork* is the woody bark tissue of a plant.

# Walls

Walls make up the largest surface area of a room. They provide protection from the outdoors and reduce the amount of noise entering a room. They hide pipes, wiring, and insulation. They also divide space within a dwelling and provide privacy.

## Wall Construction

How walls are constructed is an important factor to consider when planning backgrounds. A variety of materials can be used to construct interior walls. They include gypsum wallboard, plastic wallboard, paneling, plaster, and masonry. The materials used in wall construction will help determine what type of treatment to use. (Wall treatments will be discussed in the next section.)

### Gypsum Wallboard

*Gypsum wallboard*, also known as *drywall* and *sheet rock*, is the most common building material used for interior walls and ceilings. It comes in 4-foot by 8-foot panels. Joints are taped, hidden by a fast-drying compound, and sanded. Then, paint, wallpaper, or fabric is used to cover the smooth surface.

### Plastic Wallboard

*Plastic wallboard* is a building material with a durable decorative finish that is used for interior walls. It comes in both enamel and plastic laminate finishes, which make it easy to maintain. It is used primarily in bathrooms and kitchens.

### Paneling

*Paneling* is a building material that is usually made of plywood but can be produced from a synthetic material. A *synthetic* is a manufactured material made to imitate or replace another. Paneling comes in many different colors and textures, and is commonly available in 4-foot by 8-foot panels. It can be applied directly to the wall frame. However, a more substantial wall installation is achieved when it is applied over gypsum board. Paneling is appropriate for almost any room. See 14-9.

### Plaster

*Plaster* is a paste used for coating walls and ceilings that hardens as it dries. Plastered surfaces can be either smooth or rough. They are usually covered with paint. Applying plaster requires special skills and equipment, so it costs more than most other types of walls. It is seldom used except in older homes and commercial buildings.

### Masonry

Masonry walls can serve as both the exterior and interior walls. *Cement blocks* are a commonly used form of masonry. Sometimes they are painted. Since cement blocks are large, they belong in large rooms decorated with large pieces of furniture, rough textures, and bold colors.

*Brick* or *stone* may form entire walls, primarily decorative walls and fireplace walls, as in 14-10. They are beautiful and durable, and they require little or no upkeep. However, they are costly to install. Both brick and stone are often used in informal settings.

Some of the materials used in wall construction can also serve as the wall treatment. For example, paneling, bricks, and stones do not need additional treatment. They can be used in their original state.

## Wall Treatments

A *wall treatment* is a covering, such as paint or wallpaper, applied to

Photo courtesy of Andersen Windows, Inc.

14-9 _____
*Paneling is used to give this contemporary room a feeling of warmth.*

Masco Corporation/Scholz Design Architects

14-10 _____
*A brick wall is an attractive background for an informal room.*

**Discuss:** What are the basic choices for interior wall construction? (*gypsum wallboard, plastic wallboard, paneling, plaster, and masonry*)
**Activity:** Look through pictures of interiors in magazines to find examples of wall construction other than painted gypsum wallboard.

**Discuss:** With what room of a house do you usually associate a brick or stone wall? (*family rooms*) With what rooms do you usually associate plastic wallboard? (*kitchens and bathrooms*)

© Spiegel 1998

14-11
*Paint has been used to give this room a cheerful, light, and airy appearance.*

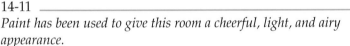

expensive way to cover wall surfaces and change the look of a room. See 14-11. The types commonly used for interior walls are water-based paints, either vinyl or acrylic latex, and oil-based paint. Water-based paint is easy to apply and dries quickly. Oil-based paint is thinner and takes longer to dry. Also, it is much harder to clean the paint equipment when you use an oil-based paint.

Paints vary in how glossy or shiny their surfaces look. *Enamel paints* have the most gloss. They give a protective and decorative finish to kitchen and bathroom walls, wood trim, windowsills, radiators, masonry, and heating pipes.

*Semigloss paints* have less gloss and are slightly less durable than enamel paints. They can be used in most of the same places as enamel paints.

Paints with a *satin* or *eggshell finish* have a slight sheen and are usually used on walls. They are slightly less durable than semigloss paints.

*Flat wall paints* have no gloss. They give a soft finish to walls and ceilings. They should not be used for windowsills or kitchen or bathroom walls and woodwork. Flat paints are usually the least expensive and the most difficult to clean.

When you choose paint, choose a color that is slightly lighter than the color you want. When color is applied to walls, it appears stronger and darker than the color on the paint chip sample in the store because you see so much of it. Textured paints give walls a rough surface. They can be used to cover cracks or irregularities in walls and ceilings. Refer to the directions on the label before applying paint. Paint can also be applied to minimize the appearance of other designs.

When you finish painting a room, paint one side of an index card. On the reverse side, write the brand name and

an interior wall. Common wall treatments are paint, wallpaper, fabric, cork, ceramic tile, mirrors, glass, and reflective metals. Applying these wall treatments varies from easy to difficult. Some treatments are inexpensive while others are high in cost.

As you choose a wall treatment for a room, keep in mind that it should harmonize with the floor and ceiling. It should add to the general mood of the room. Most of all, it should reflect the personalities of the people who use the room.

## Paint

*Paint* is a mixture of pigment and liquid that thinly coats and covers a surface. It is the fastest and least

color name of the paint. If you ever need to match it, you will have the necessary information. The painted index card can also be used to help you select coordinating window treatments, floor treatments, or furniture.

Paint is usually associated with walls finished in solid colors. However, paint can also be applied in a number of different textures and patterns to create a decorative finish on the wall. This special application of paint is called a *faux finish*, from the French word meaning "false or fictitious." Faux finishes can be achieved by applying paint to the wall with materials other than a common paintbrush. For example, to achieve the faux finish called *sponging*, a sponge is dipped in the paint and dabbed on the wall to add pattern. With the faux finish called *ragging*, paint is applied on pieces of cloth. See 14-12. A finishing technique called *marbleizing* creates a wall treatment that looks like marble stone. Many other faux finishes are available to create a unique look, 14-13.

Paint can also be applied to a wall in an artistic manner to create a scene or mural so lifelike that it "fools the eye." This technique is called *trompe l'oeil*, which means "illusion" in French. This technique can be used to turn a plain wall into a grand three-dimensional garden, complete with stone walls, fountains, and beautiful plants. See 14-14. The same technique can be used to paint the four walls of a child's playroom with beach scenes showing blue sky, sand, water, swimming fish, and dancing dolphins. Faux finishes and trompe l'oeil can create endless possibilities, but good results require patience and talent.

In addition, paint can be applied with a stenciling technique to add interest to a wall. *Stenciling* is applying paint by using a cutout form to

A                                                              B

C

**14-12**

*To create a faux finish, paint the wall a solid color and apply low-tack painter's tape to design a pattern (A). Use a rag to apply a contrasting paint color (B). The finished wall treatment is a diamond pattern called Harlequin (C).*

14-13

*This wall appears to be wallpapered, but the cross hatch and bold stripe are actually examples of another faux finish.*

14-14

*A faux finish was applied to this wall to create a trompe l'oeil illusion of a stone wall.*

outline a design or lettering. These stencil patterns can be either created or purchased. Paint is applied to the open area of the stencil, thereby transferring the design to the wall. The designs may vary from simple to complex and may entail one coat of paint or many to achieve the proper detail.

### Wallpaper

*Wallpaper* is decorative paper or vinyl applied to a wall with glue or paste. It can copy almost any surface, such as brick, stone, wood, and leather. Murals of outdoor scenes can be created from wallpaper. Because of the variety of patterns available, wallpaper can be used to enhance any room and create any style. See 14-15.

Wallpaper is practical as well as beautiful. Some wallpaper is coated or constructed with a thick layer of vinyl, which makes them durable and easy to clean. This type is often used in kitchens and bathrooms because it resists stains and water.

### Fabric

Fabric can be used to cover walls. It can be attached to the wall with glue, tape, or staples. Sometimes it is stretched over a frame and hung on the wall. At other times, it is stretched between curtain rods at the ceiling and floor. Fabric can add color, warmth, texture, and interest to a room.

Closely woven, medium-weight fabrics are the best choices for wall treatments. Look for fabric that will not fade, stain, shrink, or mildew. Fabric applied to walls can be difficult to clean and maintain.

### Cork

Cork makes a good wall treatment for rooms where sound insulation is needed. Cork also adds warmth and textural interest to a room.

### Ceramic Tile

Ceramic tile comes in a wide variety of sizes, shapes, and patterns. See 14-16. It can be used to create many different styles and designs. The tiles are durable and easy to maintain. A wall treated with decorative ceramic tiles can be the point of emphasis in a room.

### Mirrors, Glass, and Reflective Metals

Large mirrors, glass, and reflective metal tiles, or strips can be used on all or part of a wall. Mirrors make rooms look larger because the space is repeated in the reflection. If an entire wall is covered with mirrors, the room will look twice its actual size.

Large expanses of glass found in windows and glass doors also serve as a type of wall treatment. This is because they occupy wall space. Using glass extends the indoor space and brings the outdoors in. This creates the illusion of a larger space. Glass blocks may be used that allow light to enter a space but prevent a clear view into the space. Such an application could be used for a bathroom window area where light is desired but privacy is required.

Reflective metal tiles or strips can be applied to a wall to allow for the reflection of light into a space. The effect of mirrors, reflective metal, and glass as wall treatments can be dramatic. See 14-17. These types of wall

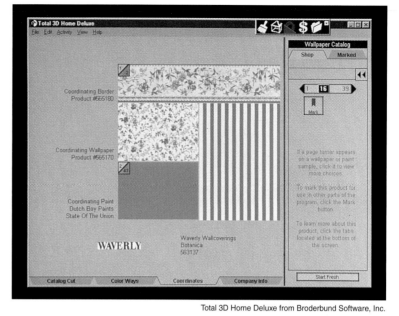

Total 3D Home Deluxe from Broderbund Software, Inc.

14-15 ——————

*Consumers can coordinate wallpaper selections with paint colors by using a CADD system.*

Laufen International

14-16 ——————

*Ceramic tile is installed on the walls and floor to create this sophisticated design.*

Ethan Allen, Inc.

14-17

*The reflective metal blocks installed on the
wall bring a sense of drama to this bedroom.*

Photo courtesy of Andersen Windows, Inc.

14-18

*The high ceiling and use of skylights give this kitchen a spacious,
airy appearance.*

treatment are especially popular in
spaces with a more modern or contemporary design. However, these
treatments are expensive when compared to other wall treatments such as
paint and wallpaper. Care must be
taken to assure that the reflected

image enhances the design of the
room.

As you have learned, the various
walls and wall treatments provide
many different looks. Each one has
its advantages and disadvantages.
Choose the one that fits the mood of
the room and best meets your needs
and wants.

# Ceiling Treatments

A *ceiling treatment* is a coating,
covering, or building material applied
to the ceiling area. The ceiling of a
room is often the least-noticed background, but it performs many tasks. It
holds and conceals insulating materials
that help control the temperature in the
house. It hides electrical wiring. Some
ceilings also hide water lines and gas
lines.

The height of the ceiling can help
create certain moods. Average ceilings
are 8 feet from the floor. Higher ceilings give a feeling of spaciousness and
usually create a formal atmosphere.
See 14-18. When painting a ceiling,
you will need an extension handle for
your paint roller. The extension handle
permits you to paint much of the ceiling without using a ladder, which is
safer. You can create the feeling of a
higher ceiling by painting it a light
color. You can also create the illusion
of height by using vertical lines on
the walls.

Lower ceilings make rooms seem
smaller and usually create an informal
mood. A ceiling will appear lower if
it is painted in a dark color or if patterned materials are added to the ceiling. Another way to make ceilings
look lower is to use horizontal lines
on the walls.

The four most common materials
used for ceilings are plaster, acoustical
plaster, acoustical tile, and gypsum

wallboard. *Acoustical* means that the material will reduce or absorb sound.

*Plaster* is one of earliest forms of ceiling treatments. It is seldom used today except in restorations of older houses. Its surface can be either smooth or rough. It is usually covered with a flat paint.

*Acoustical plaster* has a rough texture. It helps absorb sound and thus reduces the noise in a room. It is applied by spraying it onto the ceiling's surface. Acoustical plaster is difficult to paint, clean, and repair.

*Acoustical tile*, 14-19, is decorative and functional. It comes in many patterns and colors. It absorbs sound and is easy to clean.

Gypsum wallboard is frequently used today in ceiling treatments. It can be finished with a smooth surface or with a rough texture that resembles plaster. Paint is then applied as the final finish.

When planning backgrounds for your home, keep the goals of design in mind. This will help you achieve pleasing results in any room throughout the dwelling.

# Planning Your Background Treatments

The backgrounds in your decorating scheme set the stage for the furnishings you choose. Although they do not need to be costly, they do need to be planned carefully. This is especially important for floor and wall treatments.

## Planning Your Floors

Floor treatments receive more wear than other background treatments.

© Armstrong World Industries

14-19
*Acoustical tile absorbs sound and is easy to maintain.*

They are usually more expensive, too. Unless you plan to replace a floor covering within a couple years, choose one that is durable. Try to choose a color and style that is neutral enough to let you change your decorating scheme if you desire.

The floor treatment accents the entire room and helps tie the many parts of the room together. If a different floor treatment is chosen for each separate area of the house, the design will lack continuity and the spaces will not flow well. Using a single treatment such as carpeting or hardwood throughout some houses may be preferable. Doing so can make the house seem larger and more unified. This can be especially important if your house is small.

## Planning Your Walls

Classic wall treatments are those that continue to be in style year after

© Spiegel 1998

14-20 ———————————————

*Off-white paint is a classic wall treatment. It allows greater variety of design and makes rooms look more spacious.*

Permission granted by F. Schumacher & Co. to use copyrighted photographs. Designs and photograph © F. Schumacher & Co.

14-21 ———————————————

*Bold wallpaper and beautiful fabrics combine in this room to create an elegant design.*

year. When you choose a classic wall treatment, you will save the cost of changing your wall treatment as styles change. Off-white is a classic wall treatment color. As a background, it lets you use a great variety of colors and designs in a room. It also helps make rooms appear more spacious. See 14-20.

Bold, bright wall treatments can be used to give a room a dramatic look. Painted graphic designs, murals, and wallpaper with bold patterns make colorful focal points. Bold treatments tend to make rooms look smaller, so use them carefully. Be sure to choose wall treatments and furnishings that do not compete for attention.

The most common wall treatment is paint. It is important to choose the right paint for the room. Washable paints should be used in rooms that receive much use, such as kitchens and children's bedrooms. When painted surfaces can be cleaned, they do not need to be repainted as often. Enamel and semigloss paints are easier to clean than flat paints.

Wallpaper is available in a wide variety of types and designs. See 14-21. Hanging wallpaper yourself can save you money. If you hang your own wallpaper, think about using prepasted wallpaper. It often costs a little more money, but it is easier to use. The time and effort saved makes prepasted wallpaper a better bargain for most people.

## Planning Your Countertops

The same careful attention you give to your walls, floors, and ceilings should also be given to your countertops. Your countertops will impact the visual effect of your interior design decisions as much as any other background treatments. Countertops also have an important impact on how a space functions and how easy it is to maintain.

A *countertop* is a durable work surface installed on a base cabinet. Cabinets with countertops are found in kitchens, bathrooms, and play and work areas. Counter tops should be functional and attractive. They involve a substantial financial investment and cannot easily be changed. If you grow tired of your countertops, you cannot replace them as easily as the paint on a wall. Therefore, you should use special care when making countertop selections.

For the kitchen area, countertops should be stain-, scratch-, and heat-resistant. Perhaps no surfaces in your home will receive as much wear and tear as those in the kitchen. Common countertop materials include laminates, ceramic and porcelain tiles, and wood (such as butcher block). Newer countertop choices on the market today include solid surfaces, engineered quartz, stone such as granite, and metal.

### Laminate

One of the more affordable countertop choices is a laminate. See 14-22. The color, texture, and design are achieved by combining decorative surface papers with resins that are bonded under heat and pressure with other materials. This process forms a single unit with a decorative surface on a rigid base. Laminate countertops come in a wide range of colors and textures. Designs include solid colors, various patterns, and finishes that resemble metal, stone, or wood. As with other products, there are different grades of quality on the market. Less expensive laminates will not offer the durability of more expensive, name brand laminates.

Laminates are relatively easy to maintain by wiping with a damp cloth

Photography courtesy of Wilsonart International

**14-22**

*Quality laminate countertops are very attractive and affordable. There are hundreds of different colors and patterns from which to choose.*

or sponge. The product will show seams in the installation where sections are joined. Some textured laminate surfaces may be scratch-resistant. New products are available that are more resistant to stains than earlier laminate surfaces. If stains occur, you can apply a mild household cleaner to the area and gently rub it with a soft bristle brush. However, if the top surface is chipped or badly damaged, a repair will be difficult or impossible.

### Solid Surface Material

A *solid surface* is a durable countertop material that contains the color and pattern of the surface throughout. This product is constructed of an advanced blend of materials and minerals in an acrylic or polyester compound. Solid surface countertops are easy to clean and available in many colors, but much more expensive than laminates. When installed, the surface appears continuous, showing no seams.

**Activity:** List everywhere in your home that you have countertops or work surfaces.

Photography courtesy of Gibraltar Solid Surface® from Wilsonart

14-23 ──────────────

*This quality solid surface countertop is both beautiful and functional in this utility space.*

Florida Tile Industries, Inc.

14-24 ──────────────

*In this beautiful kitchen, tile was installed on the countertops. Tile was also used for the backsplash and floor.*

See 14-23. Also, solid surfaces can be made to blend seamlessly into sinks of the same material. Because the product can be shaped and molded, various customized edges are available.

Solid surfaces are scratch-, stain-, and heat-resistant. If damage does occur, these surfaces are repairable and renewable. They do not require sealing and are bacteria-resistant. Solid surfaces are available in many colors, and new additions to the market look like granite.

### Ceramic and Porcelain Tile

Tile can be expensive to apply due to the labor involved. Ceramic tiles come in many colors and patterns. They are easy to maintain and are heat- and scratch-resistant. The surface of the grout needs to be sealed to prevent staining. Ceramic tile is subject to chipping if struck by a heavy object.

Likewise, porcelain tiles are expensive to install and must be sealed. However, since the surface color usually penetrates porcelain tile, it will keep a like-new appearance in spite of physical damage. See 14-24.

### Natural Stone

Natural stone such as granite is elegant and expensive. Since stone is porous, it must be sealed, which makes it stain-resistant. In addition, stone countertops can be scratched and broken if struck with a heavy object. Due to the weight of stone, it should only be installed on very sturdy cabinet bases.

### Engineered Quartz

A new type of countertop that looks like natural granite or marble is *engineered quartz*. It is a stonelike material used for countertops that is made by combining quartz particles with a mixture of binders. The mixture is then subjected to a high-tech compression and heating process The surface has a polished granite or marble appearance and does not require a sealant as is needed with granite or marble.

Engineered quartz surfaces are gaining in popularity for several reasons. They are less costly than granite and marble; easy to maintain; and much more heat-, stain-, and scratch-resistant. These surfaces are usually guaranteed against defects by a limited warranty, which is not available with natural stone. See 14-25.

## Metal Surfaces

Metal surfaces are infrequently used for residential countertops, though they are common in commercial kitchens such as restaurants. The most common metal surface is stainless steel. Metal countertop surfaces are expensive. They scratch and dent easily, and are therefore less durable than other choices.

## Butcher Block

*Butcher block* is a work surface made by fusing a stack of long, thin hardwood strips. The exposed sides form the countertop surface. Butcher block is not heat- and stain-resistant and is less durable than most other countertops. Also, it can harbor any food bacteria that come in contact with it.

## Fiberglass

Bathroom countertops use many of the materials used in kitchens, but

Silestone® Photo courtesy of Consentino USA

14-25

*An engineered quartz countertop provides the homeowner with both a beautiful design and a warranty.*

there is an additional product to consider for that room. *Cultured marble* countertops are molded from fiberglass compounds. They are more expensive than laminates but less expensive than solid surface, tile, and stone countertops. As in the case of solid surface materials, you can obtain a bathroom sink and countertop all in one unit. Cultured marble countertops are scratch- and stain-resistant, easy to maintain, and durable if cared for properly. They come in solid colors, marblelike patterns, and polished or matte finishes.

As with all design decisions, countertop choices are made after considering the total appearance of the room. Walls, countertops, floors, and ceilings must all work well together to create a pleasing design that functions successfully.

**Discuss:** Which of the countertop materials discussed allow you to get a sink and countertop molded into one unit? (*solid surface and fiberglass*)

**Enrich:** Research the recommendations of the U.S. Department of Agriculture regarding how to sanitize butcher block surfaces and wooden cutting boards to prevent bacteria growth. Share your findings with the class.

## Summary

Floors, walls, and ceilings serve as backgrounds for the furnishings and accessories in a room. Floors may be treated with flooring materials or floor coverings. Flooring materials include hardwoods, softwoods, tile, natural stone, concrete, and brick. Floor coverings consist of soft floor coverings and resilient floor coverings.

Wall construction provides the basis for wall treatments. Walls can be constructed from gypsum wallboard, plastic wallboard, paneling, plaster, and masonry. Other wall treatments—those applied to walls—include paint, wallpaper, fabric, cork, ceramic tile, mirrors, glass, and reflective metals.

The height and the treatment of ceilings are important factors. High ceilings give the feeling of formality and openness. Low ceilings create an informal, close feeling. The illusion of higher or lower ceilings can be created by using different ceiling treatments. Common ceiling materials are plaster, acoustical plaster, acoustical tile, and gypsum wallboard.

Countertops are another consideration when designing background treatments. They should be functional, yet attractive and durable.

Your interior backgrounds will last for several years and involve considerable cost. You will want to select treatments for countertops, walls, floors, and ceilings so they set the stage for the furnishings and accessories that follow.

## To Review

1. Why are interior backgrounds important?
2. What is the major difference between flooring materials and floor coverings?
3. List two examples of each of the basic floor covering categories.
4. What makes up the largest surface area in a room?
5. Describe four wall treatments.
6. Explain how ceiling treatments can be used to make a ceiling appear lower than it actually is.
7. What is the benefit of using acoustical plaster or tile as a ceiling treatment in a room?
8. Why is it a good idea to use neutral backgrounds in a home?
9. What is the result of bold wall treatments in a room?
10. Name six choices available in countertop materials.

# In Your Community

1. Visit a store that sells flooring materials and floor coverings. Obtain brochures showing a variety of these products with information about their cost, warranties, and durability. Make two collages: one showing various flooring materials, and one showing several floor coverings. Display your collages to the class as you summarize your findings.

2. Visit a store that sells wall treatments. Obtain samples of six or more different wallpapers. Display these to the class, and explain the effect of each if it were installed in your classroom.

3. Locate samples from local stores that sell wall coverings, paint, tile, flooring, and countertops. Use a small box to make either a miniature kitchen or bathroom. Then, using the samples, create the interior backgrounds for the room. Show your room to your classmates and explain the principles of design you used to make your selections. (Review Chapter 12, "Using Principles of Design".)

# To Think About

1. The use of wall, floor, and ceiling treatments changed continually throughout history. Select a specific country and historical period, and research the types of interior backgrounds that were used. What social, environmental, historical, and geographical influences shaped the creation of these background treatments? Share your findings with the class.

2. Economics often influences the choices made for interior backgrounds. Imagine having the job of designing an affordable and durable interior for a new home built by Habitat for Humanity. The home will be occupied by a nuclear family with two daughters under age 10. What treatments would you select for the flooring, walls, ceilings, and countertops? Present your selections to your classmates and explain your decisions.

# Using Technology

1. Use a computer program to design an informative handout on wall treatments. Obtain photos of various wall treatments from online sources, or clip magazine photos and scan them into your document. Label the treatments and list one advantage and one disadvantage of each. Print the handout and share it with your class.

**Note:** For researching acoustical ceiling materials, have students explore *silentsource.com*.

2. Survey the floor treatments used in your school. Check the main office, the library or media center, stairways, a classroom, the gymnasium, and a student bathroom. Using a computer program, develop a spreadsheet listing the spaces surveyed and the various types of treatments used. Which floor treatments predominate? Explain why certain floor treatments and materials were used in one space but not any other.

3. Search the Internet for information on acoustical ceiling materials and the design options available to the consumer. Check at least three manufacturers to find the recommended uses of their ceiling materials and the effect of their products on controlling noise. Identify the Web sites you explore, and write a brief report on the information you find.

**Portfolio Project:** Students collect and mount samples of floor coverings, wall treatments, and ceiling treatments, labeling the samples and noting an appropriate use for each.

# CHAPTER 15
# Furniture Styles and Construction

## To Know

Casual style
Country style
Eclectic style
antiques
collectibles
reproductions
case goods
wood grain
deciduous
coniferous
solid wood
bonded wood
veneered wood
pressed wood
mortise-and-tenon joint
double-dowel joint
dovetail joint
tongue-and-groove joint
butt joint
corner blocks
coil springs
flat springs
innerspring mattress
foam mattress
waterbed
box springs

Ethan Allen, Inc.

## Objectives

After studying this chapter, you will be able to

- describe various furniture styles.
- identify ways to evaluate quality furniture construction.
- tell how consumers are protected when buying furniture.

Resource: *Furniture Styles*, Activity A, SAG. Students identify the styles of furniture illustrated and match each with its description.

**Research Activity:** Work in teams of four to document the important social and political events that took place in France during the periods associated with different furniture styles developed there. Share your findings with the class.

Once you create the interior backgrounds for your home, you continue the design process by deciding how to furnish it. The first two steps in furnishing your home are choosing furniture styles and evaluating furniture construction. The next step, selecting furniture for your home, will be discussed in Chapter 16, "Arranging and Selecting Furniture."

As discussed in earlier chapters, design has three characteristics: function, construction, and aesthetics. This chapter focuses on two of those characteristics as they relate to furniture—aesthetics and construction. By focusing on the aesthetics of furniture, you will learn to recognize the physical characteristics that make individual styles unique and appealing. In addition, you will learn about the history and evolution of different furniture styles. Then, by focusing on how furniture is made, you can evaluate the quality of the construction.

# Choosing Furniture Styles

Choosing furniture styles is a matter of taste, or personal preference. There is no right or wrong furniture—just furniture that is best for you. Studying the various styles can give you a good idea of which styles you like. Learning furniture styles will also help you use each piece of furniture to its best design advantage.

Furniture style refers to design only. It does not refer to the cost or the quality of construction. Any style, from Queen Anne to contemporary, can be made of good or poor materials using good or poor construction methods.

## Furniture Styles

The first documented fine furniture styles were those of the Ancient Egyptians in 3000 B.C. Fine quality Oriental furniture dates back to 300 B.C. Styles from Ancient Rome can be documented from 700 B.C., while styles from Ancient Greece date back to 1100 B.C.

For about 800 years (400 to 1200 A.D.), fine furniture making almost became a lost skill. It began its recovery in the 1200s with the emergence of Gothic art in Western Europe. Gothic art influenced both architecture and furniture design with the use of arches and columns. Many furniture styles used today date back to the traditional designs from the early 1600s.

## Traditional Furniture Styles

Traditional, or period, furniture styles were developed during different periods of history. Traditional furniture styles are designs created in the past that have survived the test of time and are still being used today. Traditional styles from France, England, and the United States are discussed in this chapter. A general time reference for some traditional and nontraditional furniture styles is shown in 15-1. Most furniture styles are named after the rulers of the era or the craftsmen who actually created them.

### Traditional Styles from France

While Louis XIII was King of France, 1610-1643, furniture styles were grand and formal. Rich inlays, carvings, and classical motifs were typical.

Louis XIV, the Sun King, ruled France from 1643–1715. He built the Palace of Versailles and filled it with

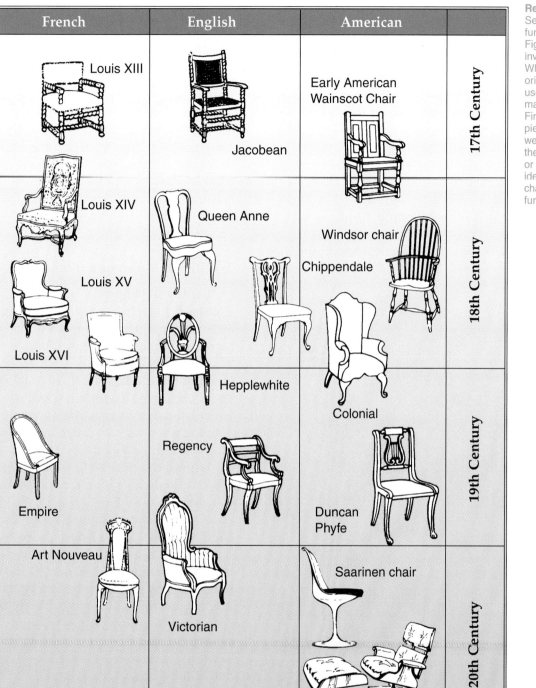

| French | English | American | |
|---|---|---|---|
| Louis XIII | Jacobean | Early American Wainscot Chair | 17th Century |
| Louis XIV<br>Louis XV<br>Louis XVI | Queen Anne<br>Hepplewhite | Windsor chair<br>Chippendale<br>Colonial | 18th Century |
| Empire<br>Art Nouveau | Regency<br>Victorian | Duncan Phyfe | 19th Century |
| | | Saarinen chair<br>Eames chair | 20th Century |

Ethan Allen, Inc.

15-1

*New styles of furniture are continually being designed.*

**Research Activity:** Select one of the furniture styles shown in Figure 15-1 and investigate its origin. Where was the style originally crafted and used? What local materials were used? Find pictures of two other pieces of furniture that were designed to go with the chair, such as a table or desk. Point out the identifying design characteristics of the furniture style.

**Discuss:** Name the chair styles with which you are familiar and rate them for comfort. Which is the most comfortable? least comfortable?

**Art Activity:** Create a unique design for an armless dining room chair that is both comfortable and functional.

extravagant furnishings. The furnishings had heavy ornamentation and gold overlays.

During the reign of Louis XV, 1715–1774, furniture styles had smaller proportions and became more delicate. Curved lines and soft colors were dominant.

Before the French Revolution, Louis XVI and Marie Antoinette ruled France, 1774–1792. Simple, straight lines and classic motifs, such as fluted columns, were popular in furniture.

When Napoleon ruled France, 1804–1815, he dominated everything—

Ethan Allen, Inc.

15-2

*Country French style of furniture is used frequently today. It is an interpretation of the French Provincial style.*

even furniture styles. The dignified style called *Empire* became popular. The furniture was large and heavy. It was decorated with his initial and military symbols. Egyptian, Greek, and Roman motifs were also used.

During the seventeenth and eighteenth centuries, craftspeople began copying styles that were popular in the court at Paris. The *French Provincial* style was practical, functional, and comfortable. Local wood was used to copy this style and decoration was simplified. See 15-2.

### Traditional Styles from England

During the reigns of James I and Charles I, 1603-1649, *Jacobean* furniture became popular. Turning and fluting were used on oak furniture. *Turning* is an ornamental detail used on furniture legs and other pieces made by rotating wood on a lathe to create a spiral effect. *Fluting* is another ornamental detail made by carving parallel grooves into the wood.

During the reign of Queen Anne, 1702–1714, there was an Oriental influence in furniture. The Chinese influence is represented in the *Queen Anne* style by the use of cabriole legs. A *cabriole leg* has a gentle S-shaped curve that ends in a decorative foot. Carved fans and shells are also characteristic of this graceful and comfortable style.

Several furniture styles became popular during the reigns of Kings George I, II, and III, 1714–1820. Sometimes these styles are called *Georgian*. Often they are labeled according to their designers— Thomas *Chippendale*, the *Adam* Brothers, George *Hepplewhite*, and Thomas *Sheraton*.

Thomas Chippendale was the first person to publish a book entirely about furniture designs, and his designs became popular around the world. Gothic and Chinese influences were part of the Chippendale design. Details such as the use of splat-back chairs and curved top edges on the backs of chairs and sofas were typical. Early Chippendale furniture has S-shaped legs with claw and ball feet, as shown in 15-3. Later, due to Chinese influence, his furniture had straight legs.

Furniture from the Adam Brothers, Robert and James, was designed to complement their architectural designs. The furniture was classic and symmetrical. The pieces had simple outlines, rectangular shapes, and tapered, straight legs.

George Hepplewhite is most famous for his graceful chair designs. The backs of the chairs had shield, oval, and heart shapes. See 15-4.

Thomas Sheraton designed furniture that had characteristic straight lines. He included motifs of urns, swags, and leaves. His furniture also included mechanical devices, such as disappearing drawers, folding tables, and secret compartments.

The *Regency* furniture style, 1810–1837, is named after the Prince of Wales who reigned as regent for nine years. The style reflects an interest in the ancient cultures of Greece, Rome, and Egypt. Bold, curved lines were dominant.

During the reign of Queen Victoria, 1837–1901, the *Victorian* furniture style became popular. Machines could make detailed pieces of furniture quickly and easily. This led to the excessive use of ornamentation that was typical of the style, as shown in 15-5. Other characteristics were massive proportions and dark colors.

### Traditional American Styles

The first European settlers in North America built sturdy, practical furniture. This furniture was a simplified version of the Jacobean style,

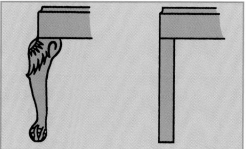

15-3 ———————————
*Curved legs with claw and ball feet were early Chippendale designs. His later designs had straight legs.*

Hickory Chair Co.

15-4 ———————————
*This chair has a shield back, which is characteristic of Hepplewhite.*

which was popular at that time in England. The colonists used native woods, such as maple, pine, and oak. They began making furniture with less massive proportions. Ladder-back chairs and canopy beds were common. Windsor chairs also became popular. See 15-6. These furnishings were generally called *Early American*.

Later the *Colonial* style became popular. It was based on England's

15-5 _____

*The American version of Victorian furniture is still found in homes today.*

Rea-Lynne Gilder

15-6 _____

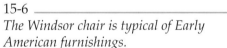

*The Windsor chair is typical of Early American furnishings.*

After the American Revolution, England's influence declined in all areas, including furniture styles. The *Federal* style became popular in the United States. It combined classic influences with patriotic symbols, such as eagles, stars, and stripes.

*Duncan Phyfe* was a major furniture designer of this period. He is noted for the lyre motif used for chair backs. Other characteristics of his designs are brass-tipped dog feet, curved legs, and rolled-top rails on chair and sofa backs.

In the early 1800s, a religious group known as the Shakers was recognized for their use of the circular saw in making furniture. *Shaker* furniture was very plain in design, but often painted in bright colors. Shakers were best known for their side chairs

**Enrich:** Visit an antique store to identify furniture styles of historical eras.

**Activity:** Draw examples of each of the different styles of furniture, labeling each.

Queen Anne and Georgian styles. The fully upholstered wingback chair became popular in the colonies during this period. It was designed to have a high back with sides, called wings, that provided protection from drafts. See 15-7. Graceful lines, S-shaped legs, and comfortable forms were characteristics of this period.

**Art / Research Activity:** Research the Federal furniture style and examine the shift away from England's influence toward a more patriotic appearance. Show or draw pictures of furniture reflecting that shift.

**Vocabulary:** Look up the term *lyre* in the dictionary, summarize its history in one sentence, and draw an example.

Ethan Allen, Inc.

15-7
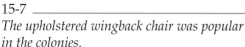
*The upholstered wingback chair was popular in the colonies.*

and rockers, although they did make other furniture. See 15-8.

## Twentieth Century Furniture Styles

At the beginning of the twentieth century, designers reacted against the cluttered look of the Victorian era. Instead, they wished to create furniture designs that represented a more modern lifestyle. They designed furniture with simpler lines and forms. The primary characteristic of Modern furniture was the use of abstract form. Furniture styles were also influenced by the ability of manufacturing companies to mass-produce pieces of furniture with automated machinery.

Also significant to the styles of this period was the influx of many architects into the field of furniture design. The leading architects included Gerrit Rietveld, Walter Gropius, and Frank Lloyd Wright. Twentieth century design also benefited from a vast international influence. Significant styles of the Modern period include Art Nouveau, De Stijl, Bauhaus, Organic, Art Deco, and Modern Scandinavian.

Photo by Paul Rocheleau, Hancock Shaker Village

15-8
*These Shaker rocking chairs face a Shaker sewing stand that has a drawer on each side.*

### Art Nouveau

The *Art Nouveau* style began as a revolt against historical revival styles. The term is French for *New Art*. The movement actually began in the 1800s and lasted until the early 1900s. The rejection of traditional styles by the Art Nouveau movement greatly influenced furniture design in the 1900s. The style was influenced by Japanese motifs and reflected a revived interest in the decorative arts. Characteristics include long, slightly curved lines that reflect natural growing forms of plants, such as blossoms, vines, and stalks. This line typically ends abruptly in a whiplike sharp curve. The curved lines were used in chair legs and backs. Pieces with this design are still popular today and may be found in modern homes and restaurants.

### De Stijl

*De Stijl*, which means *The Style*, began as an art movement around

**Writing Activity:** Research the religious beliefs of the Shakers and examine how their beliefs influenced their furniture designs. Write a report using pictures of furniture examples.

**Discuss:** Why do you think architects often had great influence on the furniture styles of their era?

**Research Activity:** Find a picture of a piece of furniture in the De Stijl style and share it with the class.

**Discuss:** What impressions are conveyed by very ornate, embellished, or intricately patterned furniture? What impressions do simple, plain designs convey? Which style do you prefer?

**Art / Research Activity:** Find out what motifs of blossoms, vines, and stalks were used by in Art Nouveau furniture styles. Draw the symbols on a piece of paper and label each.

**Example:** Two photos of Wright's Prairie style architecture are shown in previous chapters, in Figures 2-18 and 6-18.

**Writing Activity:** Write a paragraph describing your impression of Wright's Organic style furniture, as shown in Figure 15-9.

**Art / Research Activity:** Find out what motifs of trains, ocean liners, and cars were used in Art Deco furniture styles. Draw the symbols on a piece of paper.

1917 in the Netherlands. Gerrit Rietveld, a Dutch architect and furniture designer led the movement. The furniture style was influenced by abstract art and used geometric forms such as rectangles. The only colors Rietveld used were the three primary colors of yellow, blue, and red. His work influenced many later styles of furniture in the 1900s.

## Bauhaus

In the early 1900s, the German *Bauhaus* movement strongly influenced the direction of furniture design. Architect Walter Gropius established the Bauhaus school of design in Weimar, Germany in 1919. The Bauhaus philosophy was *form follows function.* In other words, if a furniture piece was intended for sitting (as in the example of a chair), it was given a form that made that function possible.

Typical Bauhaus furniture designs were very simple. Often chairs used chrome-plated steel tubing for support with seats and backs of canvas, wood, cane, or leather. Famous examples of this movement are the chair designs by Marcel Breuer and Mies Van der Rohe. Their designs eventually became known as the International style since they were popular worldwide. These designs are also referred to as Classic Modern style and continue to be produced and used today.

## Organic Design

*Organic* style is the name given to the furniture designed by American architect Frank Lloyd Wright, 1869-1959, and his followers. Wright was known for his Prairie style architecture. His homes and structures were designed to complement their natural surroundings. He positioned his houses to work within the natural

terrain of the land and take advantage of sunlight and prevailing breezes. Basic materials such as wood, masonry, and glass were used in these structures.

Wright believed that furniture should fit easily and naturally into its surroundings. His furniture designs were created specifically for the design of each house. While the furniture designs varied according to each specific house design, the furniture elements he commonly used were geometric shapes, flat surfaces, and slats. See 15-9.

## Art Deco

The most popular international decorative style in the 1920s and 1930s was *Art Deco*. Characteristics of this style were images suggesting the public's interest in speed, such as fast-moving trains, ocean liners, and cars. Art Deco pieces were constructed of unusual combinations of industrial materials and traditional luxury materials. For example, brushed steel was paired with exotic wood, ivory, or gilt bronzes. *Gilt* means applying gold or a material that looks like gold onto a surface. The furniture designs were influenced by other styles as diverse as mechanical design and Native American, ancient Egyptian, and African art.

## Modern Scandinavian

The *Modern Scandinavian* design began in Denmark, Norway, and Sweden in the late 1920s. Its influence on furniture design during the twentieth century is characterized by the use of chairs with molded wood seats or arms. The technique was first perfected in the construction of molded snow skis, made of many veneers of wood shaped by applying steam or

**Discuss:** What is meant by the term *form follows function* as it pertains to furniture? (*When a furniture piece is intended for a specific function, it is given a form that makes that function possible.*) What furniture style was linked to that term? (*Bauhaus*)

**Internet Activity:** Use the keywords *Frank Lloyd Wright* and *Prairie style* to find Web sites that describe and show Wright's architecture and furniture. List five of his most renowned examples, indicating where they are located.

heat. White birch was typically used because of its hard surface and firmness, but unusual pliability.

The style of the furniture featured natural wood in a simple clean line. Simple upholstery fabrics such as wool, cotton, or linen were used. The furniture style was very popular because it was warm, natural, and easy to maintain. It was considered functional and elegant. The smaller scale of the pieces worked well in apartments and smaller homes. See 15-10.

## Late Twentieth Century Styles

Later styles of furniture in the twentieth century included the Retro, Radical Modern, and Postmodern styles. The Retro style was popular in the 1950s and 1960s. This style used many of the same elements that were used in the early 1900s. The use of triangular, boomerang, and rhomboid shapes is characteristic of this style. (Recall from math that a rhombus is a slanted parallelogram.)

The single most important furniture design of this period was a simple chrome and molded plywood chair designed by the American designer Charles Eames. Because of the importance of this design, Eames is sometimes listed as a member of the Classic Modern group. His work, however, came many years after the Bauhaus and International style.

Some retro armchairs feature forms that hug the body. One such design was the *butterfly chair* by Harry Bertoi, an American sculptor and designer.

Modular furniture units also evolved during this period. These units were composed of separate seating pieces in standardized sizes. The

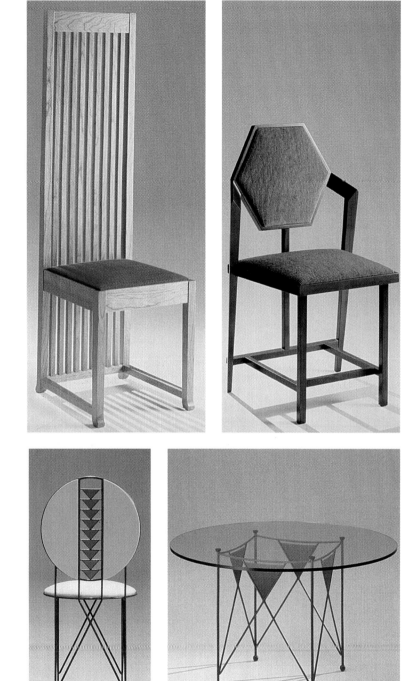

Courtesy of the Frank Lloyd Wright Foundation

15-9

*Frank Lloyd Wright designed his modern furniture to correspond to his Prairie style house designs.*

**Note:** Visit the Web at *scan-design.com/* for photos of Scandinavian style furniture.
**Internet Activity:** Search for a Web site that displays a butterfly chair. Share the address and a summary of the information provided with your classmates.

**Discuss:** Select houses shown in Chapter 6 in which the furniture pictured in Figure 15-9 would look appropriate.

**Discuss:** Name popular television programs that show Retro style furniture of the 1950s and 1960s.

Ethan Allen, Inc.

15-10

*The Swedish style furniture used in this room was inspired by styles from the Modern Scandinavian period.*

pieces offered great flexibility in space planning since they could be grouped together or separately in a variety of seating arrangements. Polyfoam was used in these pieces instead of the typical coil springs and webbing. By using the polyfoam, the modular units weighed less and were easier to move. Also, the polyfoam was less costly than the typical coils and webbing.

Radical Modern design was popular in the late 1960s. The characteristic of this style was inexpensive furniture that was made to be serviceable, but not long-lasting. One such style was

the *beanbag* chair. It was constructed of vinyl, leather, or cloth, and was filled with plastic beads. This chair was designed to conform to the body of the seated person.

The Postmodern design style of the late 1900s used traditional shapes from other styles of furniture, but constructed them in different materials and finishes. Examples of this are the chairs created by American architect Robert Venturi. He designed a Queen Anne Chair of bent plywood. He also created bent plywood versions of a Sheraton Chair and an Art Deco Chair. The results were artistic and light-hearted reinterpretations of historical design.

Other furniture designers of this period purposely designed furniture that could not be produced by machines. The goal of this movement was to remove furniture design from a factory manufacturing process and return it to the realm of art.

## Twenty-First Century Furniture Styles

Currently there are five dominant furniture styles popular in the United States. According to the American Furniture Manufacturers Association, the current styles are Contemporary, Traditional, Casual, Country, and Eclectic. See 15-11. Furniture in the five styles is available in many different price ranges and levels of construction quality.

### Contemporary

Contemporary furniture style is composed of designs that are the very latest introductions to the market. They take advantage of the newest materials and manufacturing methods. Many contemporary designs trace their origin to the Modern or International style designs created during the twentieth

Ethan Allen, Inc.

A

Ethan Allen, Inc.

B

Ethan Allen, Inc.

C

Ethan Allen, Inc.

D

**15-11**

*These rooms show examples of furniture styles that are currently popular in the United States. The furniture designs include Contemporary (A), Traditional (B), Casual (C), and Country styles (D).*

century, when function was such an important influence.

Plastics, metals, wood, and glass are often used to create an endless range of visual effects. Pieces of contemporary furniture have simple lines and forms. The feeling is streamlined and sleek. Geometric shapes such as circles, rectangles, triangles, cylinders, and cubes are often used. Colorful fabrics and accessories add beauty and variety to contemporary rooms by enhancing the furniture's simple lines.

In other settings, contemporary furniture may be used in a room design that appears very stark. In such a case, the use of color and accessories may be minimal.

### Traditional

The Traditional furniture made today continues to be inspired by the early designs of French, English, and American periods. This furniture style is characterized by symmetry and graceful, carved curves. The fabric colors are rich, and the wood finish tends to be dark with a polished sheen. Use of this style of furniture conveys a sense of elegance.

## Casual

*Casual style* furniture is a style that emphasizes comfort and informality. The feeling created by using this type of furniture is opposite the elegant mood created by traditional furniture. The emphasis is on comfort, and often the sofas and chairs have an overstuffed look. The fabrics are designed to be carefree in both look and function. Pine, ash, oak, and maple are the common types of wood used. This furniture style is an evolution of the American lifestyle. Its beginnings do not date back to any single historical period of design.

## Country

*Country style* furniture traces its origins to the lifestyles of rural areas. There are many subcategories of Country style furniture depending on the country that influenced the particular design. These styles include American, English, Italian, French, and Irish Country. Characteristics of the style may vary somewhat between countries.

In general, Country style furniture uses painted or distressed wood finishes that convey a feeling of age. Natural pine, cherry, and oak are also used. The chairs and sofas are plump and comfortable. The fabric is also designed to have a timeworn appearance.

## Eclectic

In the *Eclectic style*, furniture and fabrics cross over styles and periods. The style can be a mix of different ethnic, historical, and international influences as well as works by different artisans or manufacturers. Since a variety of styles are used in furnishing an eclectic room, consideration should be given to using the principles of design to help create a unified look. For example, the furnishings in an eclectic room should be in proportion to one another and somewhat related in mood. Careful consideration needs to be given to the combination of textures and colors.

## Antiques, Collectibles, and Reproductions

While Contemporary, Casual, Country, Traditional, and Eclectic are the dominant styles in furniture, antiques, collectibles, and reproductions continue to be popular choices. Such purchases can mix well with many styles of furniture.

### Antiques

*Antiques* are pieces of furniture made over 100 years ago in the style of the period. As furniture styles become outdated, good-quality pieces have become hard to find. Some antiques can be found at reasonable cost. However, furniture that is very old and reflects good construction can be quite costly. Fine antiques are those of good quality. The very finest antiques are museum quality, as in 15-12. Such pieces are very rare and expensive.

### Collectibles

*Collectibles* are highly valued furnishings less than 100 years old, but no longer made. If kept long enough, they will become antiques.

### Reproductions

*Reproductions* are copies of antique originals. Sometimes they

President Benjamin Harrison Memorial Home

15-12

*This fine antique Victorian bedroom set is museum quality.*

are made to look worn or used. For example, false wormholes may be added to the finish. The reproductions may or may not be accurate imitations. Careful inspection and research would be required to determine if the style is authentic or if it is a reproduction. See 15-13 for an example of an accurate and authentic reproduction.

# Evaluating Furniture Construction

Many furniture styles are constructed with wood, plastic, metal, wicker, or glass. The materials can be used alone or in combination with other materials. The furniture you select depends on the desires of your household, the mood of the room, and how much you can afford to spend.

Hickory Chair Co.

15-13

*This lowboy is a fine reproduction of an original antique. The original is found on the historic Tuckahoe Plantation along the James River in Virginia.*

Vocabulary: *Museum quality* furniture is shown in Figure 15-12. What does this term mean? (*the finest antiques*)

Vocabulary: Study Figure 15-13 and write a definition of what you think a *lowboy* is. Look it up in the dictionary and see if you are correct. If not, correct your definition. Contrast that term with *highboy*.

You will need to be able to evaluate the functional quality of the furniture for usefulness, convenience, and organization. You will also need to evaluate furniture's aesthetic value, such as its pleasing appearance or effect. (The design guidelines in Chapter 10, "Elements of Design," also apply to furniture.)

Knowing how to evaluate the quality of furniture construction is very important. The materials used in the construction of the furniture should meet industry standards and be the highest quality you can afford. Furniture should also be safe and durable. Understanding furniture construction can help you choose the

15-14
*If you buy furniture made by a well-known company, you can be assured that high quality wood was used.*

Ethan Allen, Inc.

highest-quality furniture for your money. See 15-14.

## Wood in Furniture

Wood is the most common material used in furniture construction. If it is the primary construction material used, the furniture piece is referred to as a case good. *Case goods* include tables, desks, dressers, headboards, and chests. You will also find wood used as the structural framework of furniture that is covered by another material, such as upholstery.

Wood used in furniture construction can be classified according to the following factors:

- type and quality of wood grain
- hardwood versus softwood
- solid versus bonded wood
- type of wood joints
- finished versus unfinished wood

These factors affect the quality of the piece. When looking at furniture, be sure to consider each factor to determine if the price reflects the quality.

### Grain

A *wood grain*, or pattern, is formed as a tree grows. See 15-15. The stump or base of a tree has a beautiful, irregular grain caused by the twisted and irregular growth of the tree's roots. Crotch wood has a special grain caused by branches growing out from the trunk of a tree. Burls, which are woody, flattened outgrowths on trees, have a unique and highly prized grain. It is very important to evaluate the appearance of the grain when you are selecting a case good.

Lumber is cut to show off the grain. The way it is cut can affect the appearance of wood grain in your furniture. Quarter slicing, rotary cuts, and flat cutting are methods that create different looks with the same kind of wood.

## Hardwood and Softwood

Furniture can be constructed entirely from hardwood, softwood, or a combination. Hardwood comes from *deciduous* trees, or trees that lose their leaves. The most popular hardwoods used for quality furniture include walnut, mahogany, pecan, cherry, maple, and oak. Hardwood does not dent easily. It is usually stronger than softwood and costs more.

Softwood comes from *coniferous* trees, or trees that do not shed their leaves. These trees are also called evergreen trees. Softwood does not have as beautiful a grain as hardwood, and it dents easily. Cedar, redwood, pine, fir, and spruce are the most common softwoods used for furniture. Some softwood is harder than some hardwood, so the names may be somewhat deceiving.

## Solid Wood and Bonded Wood

*Solid wood* means that all exposed parts of a piece of furniture are made of whole pieces of wood. Such furniture is usually expensive, especially if it is made of hardwood. The disadvantage of solid wood is that it has a tendency to warp, swell, and crack.

*Bonded wood* is wood that has been bonded by glue and pressure. Bonded woods include veneered wood and pressed wood.

*Veneered wood*, or plywood, is created by bonding three, five, or seven thin layers of wood to one another, to a solid wood core, or to a pressed wood core. See 15-16. Fine woods are used for the outside layers. Less expensive woods are used for the inside layers or core.

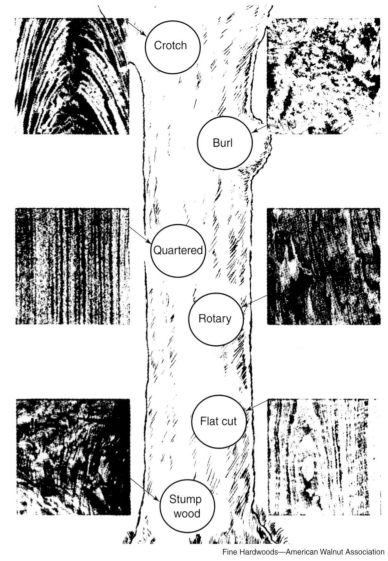

Fine Hardwoods—American Walnut Association

15-15

*Wood grain varies according to the part of the tree from which the lumber comes (crotch, burl, or stump-wood) or the way it is cut (quartered, rotary, flat).*

Since expensive woods are used only on the outside of veneered wood, veneering makes fine woods available at a moderate cost. Rare woods and beautiful grains are also available. Veneering permits the use of fragile woods, since the inside layers add strength. A disadvantage of veneered wood is the adhesive may not stick permanently, causing the veneer to loosen and chip.

**Activity:** Devise a rap or rhyme to highlight examples of hardwood and softwood.

**Discuss:** What type of bonded wood makes fine wood available at moderate prices? (*veneered wood*)

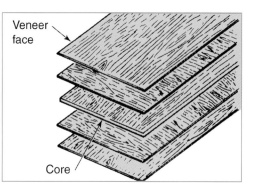

15-16

*In plywood, the grains of alternate veneers run at right angles to one another. This adds strength to the plywood.*

Most of the furniture made since 1900 is partly veneered. Today, veneered furniture is more common than solid wood furniture.

*Pressed wood* is made of shavings, veneer scraps, chips, and other small pieces of wood. These types of wood are less expensive than solid or veneered wood. Called *particleboard,*

*waferboard,* or *composite board,* the pressed wood is often used on parts of furniture that do not show. It may also be covered with a more expensive wood or with a plastic laminate, which is used on furnishings that need a tough, durable surface.

### Wood Joints

When selecting furniture, especially case goods, give particular attention to the how the wood pieces are fastened or joined. Wood pieces can be fastened in many different ways, including the use of wood joints. Common wood joints are pictured in 15-17. Glue should be used on all joints to add strength.

A *mortise-and-tenon joint* is one of the strongest joints used for furniture. The glued tenon fits tightly into the mortise, or hole. No nails or screws are used. Mortise-and-tenon joints are commonly used to join legs or rails to tables, chairs, and headboards.

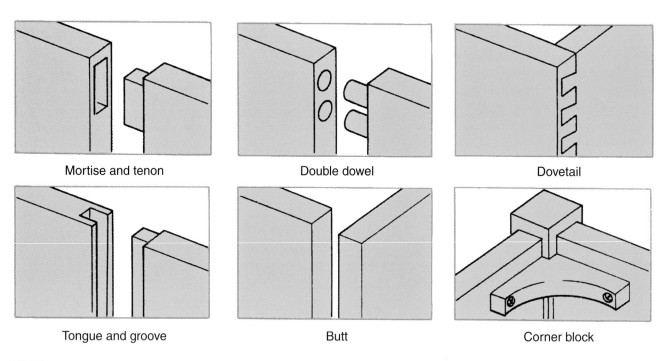

15-17

*Joints are an important factor in determining the quality of pieces of furniture.*

*Double-dowel joints* are very common and very strong. Glued wooden dowels fit into drilled holes in both pieces of wood.

*Dovetail joints* are used to fasten corner joints. They can be found in drawers of good-quality furniture.

*Tongue-and-groove joints* are created when a tongue is cut on one board and a matching groove is cut on another. These joints are invisible if they are made skillfully. They are used where several boards are joined lengthwise, such as in making tabletops.

*Butt joints* are the weakest of the joints. One board is simply glued or nailed flush to another board.

*Corner blocks* are small pieces of wood attached between corner boards. They support and reinforce the joint. They are used in the construction of chairs and tables. They keep one side from pulling away from the other.

### Finished and Unfinished Wood

Wood furniture may be purchased finished or unfinished. Most furniture pieces are already finished. Finished furniture has been treated in one or more ways to protect and improve the appearance of the wood surface. Some finishes include stains, sealers, waxes, and paints. Water-based stains and oil-based stains bring out the natural beauty of hardwoods and softwoods respectively. Sealers can be penetrating sealers or surface sealers. Plastic sealers resist moisture and are frequently used. Wax is used to preserve the wood and give it an attractive finish. Paint is sometimes used to hide a surface that is not attractive. It can also be used to enhance an existing furniture piece by applying decorative finishes.

With unfinished furniture, the wood is left in its natural state following construction. Untreated wood surfaces appeal to those who want to finish the furniture themselves, often to achieve a unique look. The initial cost of unfinished furniture is low. Therefore, before you buy, be sure to consider the cost of finishing the furniture yourself. It will cost you money, time, and effort.

You may choose to finish your furniture by applying a wood stain and a sealer or wax. Paint may also be used to finish the furniture. The paint could be applied in a solid color application or in a custom and novel application of a faux finish, such as sponging or ragging. Marbleizing a plain wooden table surface would create the impression of a marble stone top. Trompe l'oeil paint techniques could also be applied to unfinished furniture. For example, a plain wooden chest could be transformed into a seaside scene with a sailing ship. These paint treatments can turn a bargain piece of unfinished furniture into a custom work of art. For a description of these finishes, see Chapter 14, "Creating Interior Backgrounds."

When you buy wood furniture, check the points listed in 15-18. You should also read the labels carefully. They will tell you what finishes have been applied, the purpose of the finishes, and the care they should receive. It is important to understand all the terms on the labels. For instance, *solid walnut* means the exposed wood (in this case, walnut) is the same wood used throughout the entire piece. *Genuine walnut* means that walnut is the face veneer, but other woods form the core. *Walnut finish* means the piece of furniture has been finished to look like walnut.

## Plastic, Metal, Rattan, Wicker, Bamboo, and Glass Furniture

Plastic, metal, rattan, wicker, bamboo, and glass are other materials used

**Resource:** *Wood Furniture Joints,* transparency master 15-1, TR. Students examine various pieces of wood furniture to determine the types of joints used.
**Activity:** Examine wood furniture in your home to find out how many different types of joints are used. Report your findings to the class.
**Discuss:** Why do some people prefer to purchase unfinished furniture? (*lower cost, prefer to finish it themselves to achieve a unique look*)
**Activity:** Create a wallet or pocket card to use as a shopping checklist for buying wood furniture.
**Math Activity:** Research the price of an unfinished child's chair as well as the paint and paint supplies needed to paint it. Add all costs to get the total cost of the chair and all the materials needed. Compare the cost to that of a similar child's chair that is finished. What is the price difference? If you charged a fee for your labor and time, how would that affect the cost of the hand-painted chair?

**Example:** Have various types of wood samples, finished and unfinished, for students to view.    **Discuss:** What does the phrase *genuine cherry* mean? (*Cherry is the face veneer, but other woods form the core.*)

## Wood Furniture Shopping Checklist

___ Do doors shut tightly without sticking?

___ Have corner blocks been used for reinforcement?

___ Are dust panels provided between drawers?

___ Do drawers slide easily?

___ Are legs attached with mortise-and-tenon or dowel joints?

___ Do legs stand squarely on the floor?

___ Have insides of drawers, backs of chests, and undersides of tables and chairs been sanded and finished?

___ Are surfaces smooth?

___ Are surfaces solid, veneered, or laminated?

___ Has a protective plastic coating been used on surfaces that will receive hard wear?

___ Will the furniture piece fulfill your use, style, color, and size requirements?

___ Is the furniture within your budget?

15-18

*You may find this checklist useful when choosing wood furniture.*

© Spiegel 1998

15-19

*This set of clear plastic nesting tables gives this room a clean, contemporary look.*

**Discuss:** Why does the author recommend that plastic furniture not imitate other materials, but display its special properties instead?

in furniture construction. All should be evaluated for quality when buying furniture.

### Plastic

Plastic furniture is usually less expensive than wood. It is lightweight, sturdy, and easy to clean. Generally, it looks best in modern and contemporary settings. See 15-19.

Plastic used for furniture should not imitate other materials, such as wood. Instead, the furniture design should take advantage of the special properties of plastic. When shopping for plastic furniture, ask yourself the following questions:

■ Is the piece strong and durable?

■ Are the edges smooth and the surfaces flawless?

■ Are color and gloss uniform?

■ Are the reinforcement parts (that are not part of the design) hidden?

### Metal

Metal is popular for both indoor and outdoor furniture. Wrought iron, steel, cast aluminum, and chrome are all used for different furnishings. Metal is often combined with other materials, such as wood, fabric, or glass. See 15-20. When shopping for metal furniture, ask yourself the following questions:

■ Is the metal or metallic finish rustproof?

■ Is the surface smooth?

■ Are sharp edges coated or covered?

### Rattan, Wicker, and Bamboo

Rattan, wicker and bamboo furniture combine natural wood frames with woven stems or branches. Rattan furniture is made from the stringy, tough stems of different kinds of palm trees. These stems bend easily and are strong. Rattan furniture works well in casual or informal room settings. See 15-21.

Wicker furniture was originally used for outdoor furniture and has been popular since the 1800s. It is made by loosely weaving thin, flexible branches (often from willow trees) around a

**Discuss:** How do you think the cost of the tables in Figure 15-19 would be affected if they were made of metal or glass instead of plastic?

**Reflect:** Look around your home or your school and see how many different materials you can find in furniture.

**Discuss:** What type of furniture is constructed from the following: thin, flexible tree branches (*willow*); from the stringy stems of palm trees (*rattan*); and from woody tropical grasses (*bamboo*)?

frame. After the furniture is woven, it is usually varnished or painted. Wicker is lightweight and durable. It is also water resistant and has a natural gloss. Wicker furniture is now used in both indoor and outdoor settings.

Bamboo furniture is constructed of various woody, mostly tall tropical grasses including some with strong hollow stems. These stems or canes form the frame of the furniture. Bamboo and rattan can be combined in a chair by using the bamboo in the frame and rattan woven into the seat. Bamboo is most often used in casual room settings. When shopping for rattan, wicker, or bamboo furniture, ask yourself the following questions:

- Are the strands smooth and unbroken?

- Are the joints well wrapped and secure?

- Is the finish a high quality?

## Glass

Glass is usually combined with metal or wood. It is popular for tabletops and cabinet doors. When glass is a part of the furniture you are choosing, ask yourself the following questions:

- Is the glass tempered for safety and durability?

- Is the furniture designed to hold the glass firmly in place?

- Are glass surfaces free from bubbles, scratches, and other defects?

## Upholstered Furniture

Chairs, sofas, and other pieces of padded furniture are called upholstered furniture. Most or all exposed surfaces of a furniture piece are covered with fabric. See 15-22. This outer covering hides the inner construction details. Because these details are

Photography courtesy of Gibraltar® Solid Surface from Wilsonart

15-20

*Metal, plastic, wood, and glass furnishings are all included in the design of this room.*

Bruce® Hardwood Floors, glencove plank in toast

15-21

*Both rattan and bamboo furniture are popular for informal indoor settings.*

**Research Activity:** Find out when glass was first used in furniture, on what type of furniture piece, and in what type of application. Obtain a picture, if possible.

**Vocabulary:** Look up the term *tempered* as it applies to glass and use the term correctly in a sentence to demonstrate understanding.

**Resource:** *Upholstered Furniture Construction,* transparency master 15-2, TR. Students examine a picture showing the construction of upholstered furniture and explain the function of each part.

Hickory Chair, Co.

15-22

*Upholstered furniture may be completely covered in fabric or some wood may be exposed, as in this fine Sheraton style sofa.*

hidden, choosing good-quality upholstered furniture can be difficult. The information below will help you evaluate upholstered furniture.

### Upholstery Fabrics

Fabric is an important part of upholstered furniture. It is also a clue to the overall quality of a piece. Good-quality furniture has durable, well-tailored upholstery fabric.

Upholstery fabrics are made primarily of blends or combination yarns. The yarns can be woven to create fabrics with different patterns and designs. (Refer to Chapter 13, "Textiles in Today's Homes.") Upholstery fabrics come in many attractive colors and interesting textures. They can be heavy-, medium-, or lightweight, although lightweight fabrics do not wear as well as the others. When choosing upholstery fabrics, consider the following points:

- Woven fabrics with close, tight weaves are better quality than fabrics with open, loose weaves.
- Long floats, such as in the satin weave, tend to snag.
- Fabrics with equal number and size of warp and weft yarns are more durable.

- Flame-resistant fabrics are safer than untreated fabrics.
- Stain-resistant finishes make woven fabrics easier to clean.
- Colorfast materials are preferred.
- Medium to dark colors, patterned materials, tweeds, and textured fabrics do not show soil easily.
- Labels on fabric samples give content and care information.

### Upholstery Tailoring

When evaluating upholstered furniture, you need to look at the tailoring details. A quick way to check is to evaluate a cushion cover. If the cover can be removed, check the seams and filling material, and see if it has an inside casing.

For a more thorough evaluation, check the entire piece of furniture. Use the following checklist:

- Is expert sewing evident?
- Are threads secure and trimmed?
- Is the fabric smooth, tight, and free from puckers?
- Does the fabric pattern, such as stripes and plaids, match?
- Are curved shapes and corners smooth?
- Are skirts lined and do they hang straight?
- Are buttons and trims securely fastened?
- Are staples and tacks concealed?

The more *yes* answers you have, the better tailored the upholstery is. See 15-23.

### Frames, Springs, and Cushions

Upholstered furniture frames are made of wood or metal. As you evaluate the frames, keep in mind the points for choosing wood or metal furniture. You should choose a solid hardwood frame that is heavy and substantial.

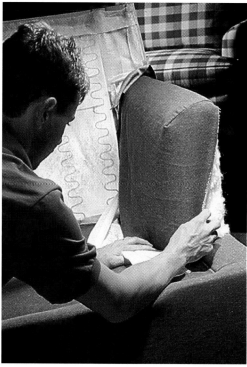

Ethan Allen, Inc.

15-23 —————————————

*This upholsterer was professionally trained by his company to ensure quality in the furniture he produces.*

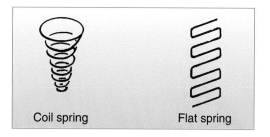

Coil spring          Flat spring

15-24 —————————————

*Coil springs are used in heavy furniture. Flat or zigzag springs are used when a minimum of bulk is desired.*

The joints should be secured with screws and corner blocks.

Springs are a part of the inner construction. The type and number of springs in a seat base help determine the quality. There are two types of springs: coil and flat, as shown in 15-24. *Coil springs* are spiral-shaped springs without padding and covering. They are used in heavier furniture. An average-size chair would generally have nine to twelve springs per seat. The springs are also attached to steel bands or webbing. They are tied as frequently as eight times per spring to provide support and enhance durability in a high-quality upholstered piece.

Lightweight pieces of furniture with sleek lines usually have flat or zigzag springs. *Flat springs* are flat, S-shaped springs that may have metal support strips banded across them. They offer firm comfort at lower cost.

Cushions need to be the proper size. They should fit snugly into the furniture. They need to give body support. Cushions are often made of urethane foam or foam rubber. These materials are durable, lightweight, and resilient. They can be molded into any shape and come in many sizes and degrees of firmness.

Covered or pocketed coils are sometimes used in cushions. They are usually covered with a thin layer of foam rubber and a layer of fabric. Other cushions are filled with down and feathers. These are very comfortable, but not as durable as foam. They are also more expensive.

Loose fill can also be used as cushion filling. Shredded foam, kapok, and polyester fiberfill are all types of loose fill. They are less expensive than the shaped fillers. However, because loose fill takes the shape of the casing, it may not retain its original shape. Loose fill is used for styles that have soft pillow cushions.

The cutaway illustration in 15-25 shows the inner construction of an upholstered chair. You can see how different materials are combined to provide seating comfort.

When choosing upholstered furniture, comfort is a very important factor to consider. For example, a sofa

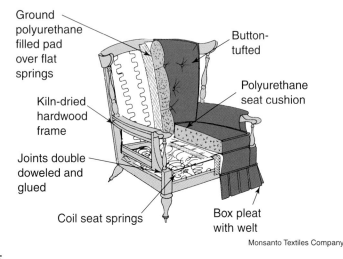

Ground polyurethane filled pad over flat springs

Button-tufted

Polyurethane seat cushion

Kiln-dried hardwood frame

Joints double doweled and glued

Coil seat springs

Box pleat with welt

Monsanto Textiles Company

**15-25** _____

*Several work steps are involved in making a chair durable, yet comfortable and attractive.*

**Upholstered Furniture Shopping Checklist**

___ Are the legs and joints securely attached?

___ What kinds of springs have been used?

___ Do you know the cushion materials and how they have been constructed?

___ Are the cushions reversible?

___ Does the outer covering have a well-tailored appearance?

___ Will the outer covering give good wearability for your purpose?

___ Does the outer covering have a stain-resistant finish?

___ Is it appropriate in style, design, and color for the room?

___ Is it within your budget?

**15-26** _____

*Check these points before you buy pieces of upholstered furniture.*

that does not feel comfortable is a poor buy. As you shop, sit on the sofa or chair as you would at home. Check the height and depth of the seat. Check the height of the back and arms. Be sure it fits your body's proportions. Other points to consider when shopping for upholstered furniture are listed in 15-26.

## Beds

About one-third of your life is spent sleeping. Therefore, you should choose the best bed you can afford. A bed includes a mattress, frame, and springs. Headboards and footboards may be added. See 15-27. Comfort is important when choosing a bed. Before you buy a bed, be sure to lie on it. That is the only way to check if it is comfortable for you.

Since you cannot see the inside construction of a mattress or box spring, you should choose a reliable brand. Many manufacturers have illustrations or miniature mattresses and box springs available for you to inspect when you visit a dealer. Check samples for support and durability.

### Mattresses

There are many types of mattresses available. The most popular type is the innerspring mattress. An *innerspring mattress* contains a series of springs covered with padding. See 15-28.

The springs vary in number, size, placement, wire thickness (gauge), and whether they are individually pocketed. These factors determine the firmness and comfort of the mattress. Manufacturers say a regular-size, good-quality innerspring mattress should have the following features:

- at least 300 firmly-anchored, heavy coils

- good padding and insulation placed over and between coils

- a tightly woven cover with a border that does not sag

*Foam mattresses* are made of latex or polyurethane foam. The foam is cut or molded to shape and is usually covered with a tightly woven cotton cloth. The mattress may be solid foam or the more-pliable molded foam. Foam mattresses are lightweight, less durable, and less expensive than innerspring mattresses. They vary in thickness, firmness, and quality. A good-quality mattress will be about 6 inches thick. It will have some holes or cores in it. The greater the number of cores, the softer the mattress will be. People with allergies often prefer foam mattresses.

A *waterbed* is a bed with a mattress that is a plastic bag filled with water. It conforms exactly to body curves and provides good, firm support. Waterbeds consist of a heavy-duty plastic water bag, a frame, a watertight liner between the mattress and frame to contain any leaks, and a water-heating device. Waterbeds range from full-motion to waveless types. When a standard-size waterbed is filled, it weighs about 1,600 pounds. Buildings must have strong foundations to support them. Waterbeds are often prohibited in rented dwellings.

Air mattresses are easy to fill and empty. When empty, they require very little storage space. For these reasons, they make good portable beds. They are primarily used for camping, but are handy for overnight guests.

## Springs

Most conventional beds have springs to support the mattress. Bedsprings have three basic forms: box, coil, and flat. Many people prefer box springs even though they are the most expensive. *Box springs* consist of a series of coils attached to a base and covered with padding. The coils may vary in number, size, placement, and gauge. Coil springs are between box springs and flat springs in terms of quality and cost. Flat springs are the least expensive.

© Spiegel 1998

15-27

*The use of a headboard and footboard add charm to the design of this bedroom.*

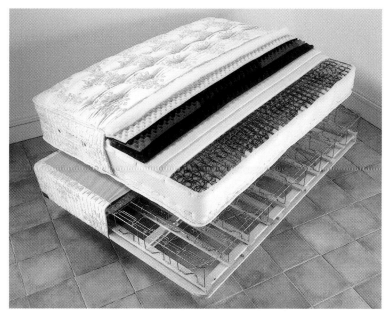

Image of Serta® Perfect Night® mattress provided by Serta, Inc., Itasca, IL

15-28

*When buying a mattress, it is important to check the quality of its construction, as shown in this high-quality mattress.*

When buying an innerspring mattress and springs, they should be bought in a matching set. When they are purchased as a set, the coils in the mattress line up with the coils in the springs. This makes the bed more comfortable.

### Frames

There are many types of bed frames. The most common type is a metal frame with a box spring and mattress placed on top. Sometimes springs, usually flat springs, are already built into the frame. An electric adjustable bed is like a metal frame bed, except the frame can be adjusted up and down according to the needs of the person sleeping in it. It is more expensive than a conventional metal frame.

Some bed frames, such as futons and sofa beds, can also be used for seating. A futon frame is a wooden bed frame that is low to the ground. A cotton mattress is placed on top of it to make a bed. Futons can be folded up to make a chair or sofa. In the case of a sofa bed, pulling out a concealed mattress converts a sofa into a bed.

# Consumer Protection

Buying furniture is a big investment. To help protect your investment, the government has agencies that protect consumers. The Federal Trade Commission (FTC) monitors advertising for truthfulness, while the Consumer Product Safety Commission (CPSC) oversees product safety.

Also, as discussed in Chapter 13, federal laws protect you. The Flammable Fabrics Act prohibits the sale of highly flammable fabrics for apparel and home furnishings. The Textile Fiber Products Identification Act requires that fibers be listed in their order of predominance by weight. It also requires generic names of fibers to appear on labels of all textile products, such as upholstery, carpets, and draperies.

Some fiber producers, fabric manufacturers, and furniture companies set their own high standards to surpass government requirements and industry standards. These companies guarantee the durability and performance of their products after you buy them. Information about guarantees and superior-quality materials appear on furniture labels. It is your responsibility as a smart consumer to read the labels before you buy so you will know what to expect from the product.

# Summary

Furniture styles are always changing. Many styles are identified with a certain country or historical period. The styles that have endured are known as Traditional designs. Furniture styles designed during the twentieth century in opposition to Traditional styles are known as Modern styles. Current furniture styles include Contemporary, Traditional, Casual, Country, and Eclectic.

Understanding furniture construction and materials can help you evaluate furniture and recognize good quality. Furniture can be made of wood and wood veneers that are held together with joints. Plastic, metal, rattan, wicker, and glass are other materials used to make furniture. Some furniture is upholstered. Knowledge of upholstery fabrics and construction details will help you make good choices.

Government agencies and federal laws concerning consumer goods and textiles protect your furniture investment. Some manufacturers set higher standards for their products.

**Activity:** Working with another student, alternate talking for 30 seconds apiece about what the chapter covered. Together, write a summary of the concepts in the chapter.

**Reflect:** Review the chapter objectives. Do you still need to review or research some topics to get the information you feel you need? If so, what topics?

# To Review

1. Name and describe three traditional styles of furniture.
2. Which following furniture style is *not* a Traditional style?
   A. Louis XV
   B. Chippendale
   C. Colonial
   D. Organic
3. What is the difference between a case good and an upholstered piece of furniture?
4. What is the difference between an antique and a collectible?
5. True or false. Veneered wood is more expensive than solid wood.
6. List four joints used to fasten the structural pieces of wood furniture.
7. What is the difference between solid wood and genuine wood?
8. A type of furniture that can be used both indoors and outdoors is:
   A. hardwood
   B. upholstered
   C. glass
   D. metal
9. What is the difference between coil springs and flat springs in terms of comfort and cost?
10. Name two government agencies that protect consumer interests when buying furniture, and briefly explain what each does.

**Answer Key**

1. (List three:) Louis XIII, Louis XIV, Louis XV, Louis XVI, Empire, French Provincial, Jacobean, Queen Anne, Georgian, Regency, Victorian, Early American, Colonial, Federal, Duncan Phyfe, Shaker (Descriptions are student response. See pages 332-337.)

2. D

3. Case goods are pieces of furniture made primarily of wood, such as dressers, chests, tables, and desks. Upholstered pieces of furniture are covered in padding and fabric, such as chairs and sofas.

4. Antiques are at least 100 years old. Collectibles are less than 100 years old, but become antiques if kept for 100 years.

5. false

6. (List four:) mortise-and-tenon, double-dowel, dovetail, tongue-and-groove, butt, corner

7. *Solid wood* means the entire piece is made from the same wood. *Genuine wood* means that the face veneer wood differs from the wood used in the core.

8. D

9. Flat springs offer firm support at lower cost. Coil springs are softer, more comfortable, and more costly.

10. The Federal Trade Commission (FTC) monitors the truthfulness of advertising. The Consumer Product Safety Commission (CPSC) monitors product safety.

## In Your Community

1. Plan a study trip to a local furniture store. Prepare a list of questions to ask your tour guide about the details of furniture construction in the products you are shown. Check the labels attached to three types of furniture. What consumer information is provided?

2. Visit a store that sells antique furniture or reproductions of antique furniture. With the help of the salesperson, identify as many different historical styles as you can. List the type of furniture it is, the country of origin or association, and the characteristics it possesses of the specific historical period. Share your findings with the class.

3. Arrange a trip to visit a lumberyard or building supply store. With the help of the salesperson, examine the various types of wood. Study the grain patterns in several pieces of wood and determine the part of the tree from which each was cut. Determine the characteristics of the wood: hardwood or softwood, solid or veneered, and finished or unfinished.

4. If possible, visit a large building supply store and examine the selection of wood stain available. Look for a store display that shows the same color stain applied to different types of wood. Note the variations in appearance. Can you make any generalizations about what you observe?

## To Think About

1. Imagine it is the year 2050, and you are designing furniture for use in a home. Sketch different pieces of furniture that might be used in this future period. Do you predict that the furniture will be completely different from anything ever designed before, or will it have components from earlier designs?

2. Different pieces of furniture require different considerations when selecting upholstery fabric. List the guidelines you would follow in selecting fabric for a family room sofa to be used by an active family with small children. How would this list differ from the guidelines you would follow for a retired couple selecting new fabric for a sofa in a formal living room? If possible, obtain samples of fabrics that you would recommend for each setting.

3. Select a historical period of furniture design and research how the design was influenced by social, economical, political, and artistic trends of the era. Include illustrations of the furniture design characteristics. Share your findings with the class.

# Using Technology

1. Select a furniture piece that you would like to buy now or in the future. Search Web sites for a company that sells this type of furniture. Find a style you like, and print one or more photos of it. Is the style Contemporary, Traditional, Casual, Country, or Eclectic? Make a brief report to the class.

2. Research the Federal Trade Commission to determine what laws and required labels protect you when buying a mattress. For instance, what does a white label represent? What does a red or yellow label mean? Use a computer to develop an attractive poster that provides guidelines for buying a mattress. If possible, incorporate photos from Web sites or artwork from a software design program.

3. Use a video or digital camera to take a close-up "tour" of a desk that you would like to own. Visit a local furniture store and ask permission to use your camera for the class project, or use a desk owned by a friend. Take images that focus on aspects of the desk that display good function, aesthetics, and construction. Identify the type of wood grain and joints used. Determine whether the piece is hardwood or softwood, solid versus bonded wood, and finished versus unfinished furniture. Create a video or pictorial presentation to show your information to the class.

4. Learn about your furniture-style preference by taking a quiz online. Search the Internet by entering the keyword *furniture quiz*. You will have several quizzes from which to choose. After taking a quiz, how would you describe your preference to a friend or salesperson? What did you learn about yourself? How can you use this information when you shop for furniture?

**Note:** For researching furniture styles, have students explore *meadowcraft.com*.

**Note:** For researching the Federal Trade Commission, have students explore *ftc.gov/bcp/menu-prod.htm*.

**Portfolio Project:** Cut pictures of different styles of furniture from magazines and catalogs to create a chronological timetable of furniture styles. Organize them according to their country of origin.

# CHAPTER 16

# Arranging and Selecting Furniture

## *To Know*

space planning
scale floor plan
template
interior wall elevation
clearance space
prioritize
ergonomics
sample board
comparison shopping
loss leader
seasonal sales
closeout sales
multipurpose furniture
unassembled furniture
recycle
restore
renew

Permission granted by F. Schumacher & Co. to use copyrighted photographs.
Designs and photograph © F. Schumacher & Co.

## *Objectives*

After studying this chapter, you will be able to

- describe how to use a scale floor plan to arrange furniture.
- explain the advantages of using computer-aided drafting and design (CADD).
- list factors to consider when arranging furniture.
- explain the steps to follow when selecting furniture.
- compare places to shop for furniture.
- determine ways to stretch your furniture dollars.

In the previous chapter, you learned about furniture styles and ways to choose quality furniture. This chapter explores the next steps in furnishing your home—arranging and selecting furniture. If you select furniture before considering its placement in the home, you may choose items that will not fit or result in good room design. Knowing how to properly arrange furniture will help you choose only the furniture you can really use. It will also help you get the most from your furniture budget.

# Arranging Furniture

Before you select the furniture for a room, you need to plan how you will arrange it. This first step in the design process is called space planning. **Space planning** is the process of placing furnishings for a well-functioning and visually pleasing area. To plan a space, you need to measure the dimensions of the room first. Room measurements let you know how much space is available in the room and how much furniture will fit in it. After taking measurements, several design tools can help you develop a space plan for a functional and attractive furniture arrangement.

## Developing a Scale Floor Plan

To begin your space planning, measure the length and width of each room. Then, measure and determine the location of all the existing features in the room, such as doors, windows, electrical outlets, heating and cooling vents, and air intakes. Any alcoves or other permanent features, such as fireplaces, cabinets, or built-in furniture

pieces, should be measured for dimensions, too. All measurements should include the floor placement of the features as well as their wall height.

Before arranging furniture, you need to develop a scale floor plan. A **scale floor plan** is a drawing that shows the size and shape of a space or room. A certain number of inches on the scale floor plan is equal to one foot. You can use a scale floor plan from house plans used to build a home, as described in Chapter 7, "Understanding House Plans."

If the house plans are not available, there are two ways to make your own scale floor plan. One way involves a manual process of using graph paper and templates. The second involves using a computer program to assist you. Whichever method you choose, use the scale of *¼ inch equals 1 foot*.

### Graph Paper and Templates

To begin, you will want to draw the room on graph paper and include the features and dimensions previously measured. Use the symbols from Figure 7-3 in Chapter 7 to indicate the doors, windows, electrical outlets, and other features.

After you create your scale floor plan, you can use furniture templates to represent the furniture in the room. A **template** is a small piece of paper or plastic scaled to the actual dimensions of the furniture piece it represents. Manufactured plastic templates allow you to simply trace the shape of the furniture onto your plan. If you do not have access to a manufactured template, you can create your own by cutting a small piece of paper scaled to the actual dimension of the furniture piece it represents. All templates must be the same scale as the floor plan, which usually is *¼-inch equals 1 foot*.

**Note:** Save unused templates and keep them in small envelopes or plastic bags for use in future years.

To create furniture templates, measure the length and width of the furniture you want to use. You may choose different colors for the different pieces of furniture. Cut them out and arrange the templates on the scale floor plan until you find the best arrangement.

See 16-1. Sometimes all the planned furniture pieces fit well. At other times, they may not. This is a much easier way to determine good furniture placement than actually moving heavy pieces of furniture back and forth.

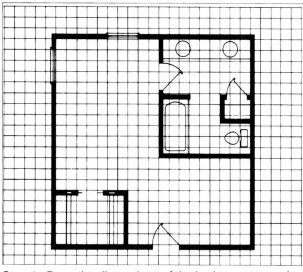

Step 1. Draw the dimensions of the bedroom on graph paper showing windows and doors in their correct positions.

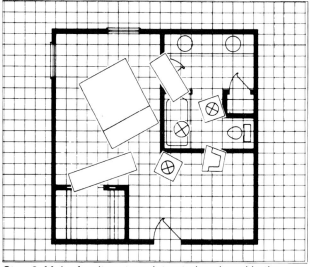

Step 2. Make furniture templates to be placed in the room, and cut them out.

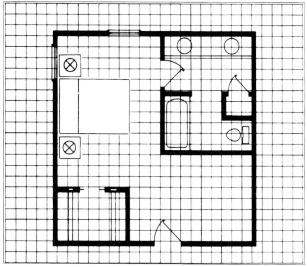

Step 3. Place the bed first.

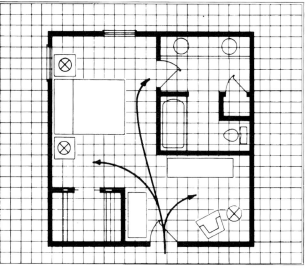

Step 4. Place the remaining furniture, keeping circulation paths clear.

16-1 _____

*Using a scale floor plan makes planning furniture arrangements easy.*

### Computer-Aided Drafting and Design (CADD)

You can use interior design software and a computer to create the scale floor plan. Computer graphics allow you to draw a room according to the dimensions needed. Usually, it saves time to generate the floor plans with a computer. Not only can you develop the plans more quickly, but you can also use other options to see the plan in many different ways.

Most people have difficulty visualizing from a floor plan how a finished room will actually look. With the assistance of a computer, you can place, or position, furniture in a room and move it around to consider different arrangements. Also, depending on the software, you can see interior wall elevations of the room. *Interior wall elevations* present a view of how a finished wall will look. Such images or drawings may illustrate bookcases, cabinets, interior trim, mantels, stairs, and furnishings.

With some programs, you can view the room from a *walk-through* perspective. A walk-through provides a more realistic picture that allows you to judge how well the furniture placement meets your expectations. For instance, it may seem more crowded in the walk-through view than it appears when only looking at the floor-scale drawing.

Learning how to use a computer software package may take some time, especially the more complicated programs. However, taking the time to learn how to use such a program can be worthwhile if you are planning several room arrangements or working with a very challenging floor plan.

## Factors to Consider When Arranging Furniture

Several questions will help you develop the best space plan for the furniture arrangement in your room. How will the furniture be used? What space does it need? How will room features and traffic flow affect furniture placement? You also need to consider the principles of design, discussed in Chapter 12, "Using the Principles of Design."

### Furniture and Room Use

How furniture is arranged depends on how it is used. Each piece of furniture has one or more specific uses and requires a certain amount of space as a result. For instance, a chest of drawers takes up floor space and wall space. Clearance space is also needed in front to open the drawers. *Clearance space* is a measurement term for the amount of space that needs to be left unobstructed around furniture to allow for ease of use and a good traffic pattern. See 16-2 for a list of clearance space requirements for furniture.

Furniture arrangement also depends on how the room is used. Before arranging furniture in a room, think about the activities that will take place there and the amount of space available. Then consider where within the room each activity will focus. List the basic furnishings needed for each activity area, and determine the amount of space the furniture will occupy.

For instance, you might want to create a conversation area in the living room. See 16-3. A grouping of chairs, sofas, tables, and lamps should be no more than 8 to 10 feet across. To encourage conversation, the area should form part or all of a circle. In the grouping, lamps and other accessories should be conveniently arranged in relation to their use. Attention should be given to the availability of electric outlets in planning the placement of lamps.

**Writing Activity:** Answer the questions in the first paragraph of the second column on this page concerning your room design and furniture placement.

.**Note:** If furniture is placed in a high-traffic area, experts advise increasing clearance spaces beyond the recommendations.

<br />

**Discuss:** Why is clearance space needed for some furniture? Name some pieces that require clearance space. (*Refer to Figure 16-2.*)

| Standard Clearance Spaces | |
| --- | --- |
| **Room** | **Clearance Space in Inches** |
| *Living Room* | |
| Around seating, such as chairs and sofas | 18–30 |
| Between sofa and coffee table | 15–30 |
| For minor traffic pattern area | 18–48 |
| For major traffic pattern area | 48–72 |
| *Dining Room* | |
| Between chair backs and wall or buffet (for diners remaining seated) | 18–24 |
| Between chair backs and wall or buffet (for self-service or host/hostess service) | 30–36 |
| Between table edge and wall or buffet (for self-service or host/hostess service) | 18–30 |
| For leg room in front of chair | 48 |
| *Kitchen* | |
| Between oven and opposite work space (opening door) | 40 minimum |
| Between refrigerator and opposite work space (opening door) | 36 minimum |
| Between dishwasher and opposite work space (opening door) | 40 minimum |
| For circulation space | 24 |
| For work zone space between counter and nearby obstacle | 48 |
| *Bath* | |
| For activity zone in front of sink | 18 |
| For circulation space | 24 |
| Between front of sink and opposite wall or obstacle | 40 minimum |
| *Bedroom* | |
| For activity zone in front of dresser to allow for work space and opening | 42–48 |
| For work zone space for making beds | 26–40 |
| For circulation space | 24 |
| Between twin beds | 24 |

16-2

*In the process of space planning you must maintain adequate clearance space for proper traffic circulation.*

**Activity:** Measure the spaces around furniture in your home and compare them to the recommended clearance spaces listed in Figure 16-2. How do they compare? Are any spaces so small that they present unsafe conditions? If so, discuss this with your parents.

**Enrich:** Visit a furnished model home. Study how the furniture is arranged and determine any changes you would recommend. Do the furniture placements incorporate the recommended minimum space allowances? Identify any that deviate and try to determine reasons for it.

**Resource:** *Evaluating Furniture Arrangements,* color transparency CT-21, TR. Students evaluate the furniture arrangements shown and their traffic patterns.

Photo Courtesy of Lindal Cedar Homes, Seattle, Washington

16-3

*The furniture in this grouping is arranged to encourage conversation.*

### Room Features

When developing your space plan, arrange furniture so it does not interfere with the features of the room such as windows, doors, outlets, and air vents. Do not place furniture where a door will hit it, and try not to block electrical outlets or air vents. Also, avoid placing furniture in front of a window, which makes opening and closing the window difficult.

Furniture arrangements also need to be planned around special architectural features. For example, furniture should not block a fireplace or built-in bookshelves.

By using a scale floor plan, either on graph paper or computer, you can see the placement of the features. If you have trouble visualizing how your furniture will be located in relation to the features, you can add walls to your plan and indicate the features. See 16-4. If you are using CADD, you can view interior wall elevations. By using CADD, you can also create a three-dimensional view of the furniture placement. See 16-5.

### Traffic Patterns

As you learned in Chapter 7, traffic patterns need to provide enough space for people to move about freely. Each piece of furniture should be placed so people can circulate easily throughout the room. To accomplish this, you

**Note:** Help students recognize the circle that is created by the furniture arrangement in Figure 16-3.

**Writing Activity:** Create a list of the furniture pieces that will be a priority in your first apartment and explain why each piece is needed.

**Math Activity:** Using Figure 16-4 as a guide, make walls for the social area you created earlier for SAG Activity B.

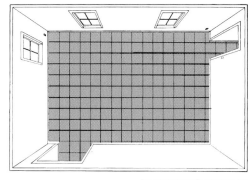

Drexel Heritage Furnishings Inc.

16-4

*A three-dimensional scale floor plan can be created by sketching doors and windows on walls drawn to scale. The walls can then be folded up, fastened at the corners, and placed on top of a scale floor plan.*

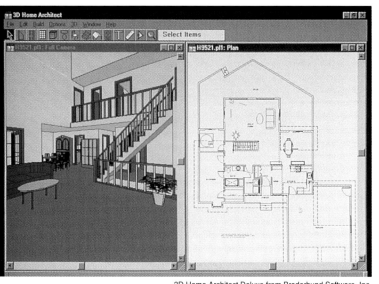

3D Home Architect Deluxe from Broderbund Software, Inc.

16-5

*When designing a room with a CADD program, you can create floor plans and elevations. You can also see how the room will look with furniture in place.*

must maintain proper clearance space around each piece of furniture. When furniture is placed in an area that receives high traffic, you need to consider increasing the clearance space. Your furniture placement should not create an obstacle course or block traffic patterns between rooms.

# Selecting Furniture

Once you know how much space you have and how you plan to use it, you can begin selecting furniture for your home. This process involves several steps. These steps include

- prioritizing your furniture needs
- determining how much you can afford to spend
- identifying your type of lifestyle
- identifying your furniture style
- determining your design preferences
- deciding where and how to shop
- choosing when to shop.

By following these steps, you can approach your furniture selection process in an organized manner. Such organization will help you make the experience both time efficient and enjoyable.

## Prioritizing Furniture Needs

Few people can afford to buy all the furniture they need at once. Consequently, the first step in selecting furniture is prioritizing your furniture needs. To *prioritize* means to rank goals in order of importance. This means deciding which pieces of furniture you need first and which can wait until later.

You should first buy the pieces you need most, such as furniture for sleeping, eating, seating, working, and storage. See 16-6. Later, you can buy the furniture used less often and accessories that accent the large furniture pieces.

When selecting home office furniture, for example, allow enough space for a continuous counter plus adequate cabinet and file storage. Most importantly, select a desk chair with ergonomic design. *Ergonomics* is the design of consumer products and

**Vocabulary:** Use the word *prioritize* correctly in three sentences; only one should deal with furniture selection.

**Vocabulary:** Examine the root words that make up the term *ergonomics* to determine its full meaning. Demonstrate your understanding of the term by using it correctly in a sentence.

environments to promote user comfort, efficiency, and safety. For example, an ergonomically designed chair has a tilting chair back and adjustable seat height and arm rests. All these features take the strain off your muscles when you work at a desk or computer.

Discuss furniture priorities with the other members of your family and ask for their input. This will allow you to make decisions that satisfy everyone. Listing all the ideas on paper will help prevent misunderstandings and make the priorities clear.

## Determining How Much You Can Afford

Once you have prioritized your furniture needs, the next step is deciding how much money you are able to spend. Identifying a specific dollar amount will clarify how many items on your list you can afford. All members of the household should express their views on this decision. Make a budget and be sure to follow it. Overspending is not likely to give the same satisfaction as spending only what you can afford. See 16-7.

Smart shoppers buy the best merchandise for the best price. Sometimes, however, trade-offs are made. For example, if you spend more money for a kitchen table than you budgeted, you will need to adjust your plans. You may cut back in other areas, wait longer than planned before the next purchase, or eliminate one or more items from your list.

## Identifying Your Lifestyle

You should choose furniture that fits the lifestyle of your household. If you are single, do you have plans to marry in the near future? If you are a young married couple, do you plan to have children? If so, you would want

Ethan Allen, Inc.

16-6

*The need for home office space is growing, and so is the variety of functional and stylish furniture choices available.*

to make selections that are durable and can withstand wear. The same emphasis on durability is also needed if you have pets. Are you a career person who will be subject to transfers and moves? If so, you would need to make furniture selections that are adaptable to many spaces.

Do you consider yourself formal or informal? If your household does not entertain with formal meals very often, having a formal dining room set is a waste of money and space. Furniture has little value if it is not used. All of these factors need to be considered so that the furniture selections you make will fit your lifestyle.

**Reflect:** Will you want your first home to have formal or informal furniture? Will you own a pet? Based on the lifestyle you foresee for yourself after graduation, what furniture decisions are you inclined to make?

**Math Activity:** Use catalog or Internet shopping to select furniture for your first home after graduation. With a budget of $5,000, identify the items you would buy new and their estimated prices. Also, identify the items you would try to buy secondhand and how much you would

budget. If you will inherit furniture pieces from your family, identify them. Add all prices to get a total.

**Discuss:** Which furniture pieces are so important to you that you might consider overspending to get them? To compensate for the overspending, on which items would you underspend?

Ethan Allen, Inc.

A

Ethan Allen, Inc.

B

Ethan Allen, Inc.

C

16-7

*Begin your selections by first prioritizing your needs (A). Gradually add more furnishings and accessories as time passes and as your budget allows (B). It may take years until the room is finished, but you will eventually have what you want—all within your budget (C).*

## Identifying Your Furniture Style

To begin, you may wish to review twenty-first century furniture styles, discussed in Chapter 15, "Furniture Styles and Construction." You can also look at magazines, store advertisements, and furniture brochures. In addition, you can use your computer to go online and actually look at product catalogues of name brand furniture. You may find it helpful to compile a notebook of pictures showing examples of furniture that you consider attractive.

Are you most comfortable with Casual, Contemporary, Country, Traditional, or Eclectic styles? Keep in mind that good design is timeless. However, the newest styles do not necessarily convey good design.

## Determining Your Design Preferences

As you identify your design preferences you apply the information studied in Chapters 10 through 15. Again, browse through home design magazines and assemble a notebook of pictures of fabrics, wallpapers, accessories, and other items that you find interesting. Make a list of your favorite colors, or go to a paint store and select sample color chips. What materials, patterns, and textures do you find appealing? See 16-8. Gathering samples from fabric and wallpaper stores can begin to give you a sense of your own personal design preferences.

You should make yourself familiar with decorating trends and be able to spot fads. Certain trends will have a lasting appeal, but fads do not. Ask yourself, how long you think you would enjoy your selections. You may wish to compare this to shopping for a new wardrobe of clothes. How often do you tire of the selections you have made from year to year? Furniture and design selections can be costly, and you will not be able to replace your selections with the same frequency that you change your wardrobe. Also, remember to gather input from all of the other members of the household. It is important that the design be one that everyone will enjoy.

If after doing research you desire more design guidance, you may wish to explore available resources and services. Interior designers, both in private design firms and as in-store consultants, are professionally trained to listen and direct you in your design process. They can draw your floor plan for you and create a sample board. A *sample board* is a design tool that includes samples of wall, floor, and ceiling treatments for a space. The board displays how the colors, patterns, and textures will combine in the completed room. The sample board includes your paint colors, fabric samples, and pictures of suggested furnishings and accessories. By assembling a sample board, you will be better able to visualize the finished project.

You may also wish to have the interior designer draw a picture or rendering of how the finished room will appear. Designers who are members of professional groups, such as the American Society of Interior Designers (ASID), are the most qualified sources for professional advice.

## Deciding Where and How to Shop

Furniture can be bought from many different types of stores. Generally, the more services a store provides, the higher the prices are. Before buying, therefore, you may want to do some comparison shopping. *Comparison shopping* is comparing the qualities, prices, and services linked to similar items in different stores. You can save time and energy by checking prices using your telephone or the Internet.

Ethan Allen, Inc.

16-8

*Can you tell that the person who designed this room enjoys nature?*

### Retail Stores

Retail stores, such as department or furniture stores, offer the most service to customers. For example, retail stores typically will deliver, unpack, and set up the merchandise in your home. However, the prices are usually higher to pay for these services. Some stores provide a decorating service. Decorating professionals will do a scale floor plan for you, visit your home, show you a wide selection of furniture, and take custom orders. Most custom-ordered furniture has to be ordered one to three months in advance.

Shop at retail stores with reliable service and buy furniture from manufacturers with good reputations. The good store will back up the merchandise it sells, and the manufacturer will replace defective products. See 16-9.

Furniture stores usually have a larger selection of furniture than department stores do. Both types of stores can order furniture they do not have in stock. Allow extra time for delivery of custom-made furniture.

Some retail stores offer their products at *discounted* prices. To be able to offer discounts, these stores may offer less service. You may need to wait for assistance in the store or for delivery of your purchase. Delivery services for larger items may be unavailable, or available only for an extra charge. If you later find a problem with the product, service may be limited. If you are willing to forego convenience for lower prices, you may be able to find bargains at these stores.

### Warehouse Showrooms

Generally, showrooms handle only a few brands of merchandise. In addition to brand names, they may also sell off-brands. Since the furniture is already made, you will have less choice of fabrics. The advantages of shopping in warehouse showrooms are savings and quick service. You can take the item with you or have it delivered in a few days.

### Catalogs and Computer Online Shopping

Catalogs let you shop by mail from anywhere. By shopping from catalogs or online, you can shop, purchase, and order furniture without ever leaving your room. You can find store brand merchandise as well as name brand merchandise. Some catalogs and online shopping sources may give you access to closeout items that have lower prices.

The main disadvantage of catalog shopping is not being able to inspect the furniture for quality or comfort. Also, the actual color of the wood and upholstery may look quite different from its picture. You should request actual fabric samples and finishes before you order.

Additionally, you should research the reputation of the supplier. What is the return policy and how helpful is the customer service department? Since the items will be shipped to you, they could become damaged in transit. If damage occurs, what is the company's responsibility and what would be expected of you? Also, keep in mind that shipping prices will add to the cost of the product. See 16-10.

### Other Furniture Sources

Salvage stores, garage sales, auctions, and flea markets can provide great bargains if you have time to shop carefully. Some items may need repairs or refinishing. You can decide whether a price is low enough to

Ethan Allen, Inc.

16-9

*When you select furniture from a manufacturer with a good reputation, you make a wise investment.*

Photography courtesy of JKB Photography

16-10

*Make sure you check the company's merchandise-return policy before you order furniture from any catalog or on-line computer site.*

make fix-up and freshen-up efforts worthwhile.

## Deciding When to Shop

*When* you shop is as important as *where* and *how* you shop. If you are hurried, tired, or shopping in crowded conditions, you may not make the best decisions. You may end up with purchases that you do not really want. Your choice of a time to shop will depend on your personal circumstances and desires. Budget your time just as you budget your money. Do you enjoy doing lots of research and browsing first, or do you recognize what you like as soon as you see it?

Shopping at certain times can save you money. Stores sometimes have high-quality furniture on sale. Some sales can significantly lower prices. There are many different types of sales, and understanding each can help you spend money more wisely.

### Loss-Leader Sales

*Loss leaders* are items priced well below normal cost to entice people into a store to buy them plus items not on sale. The store management hopes people who come for the sales will also buy several others items that are not on sale. If you shop this kind of sale, buy only those items offered at a good price. For instance, you may find a chair is on sale, but the matching sofa is not. If you want to buy only the chair, it may be a good bargain. However, if you want to buy a matching chair and sofa, you may be able to get a better deal somewhere else.

### Seasonal Sales

*Seasonal sales* are held so stores can get rid of stock to make room for new items. For instance, patio furniture is often on sale in August so the store can make room for furniture for college dorm rooms. Many high-quality products are discounted during seasonal sales. See 16-11.

### Closeout Sales

*Closeout sales* are held when a store is moving to another location or going out of business. It is better for the store to sell the merchandise at a low price or even at a loss than to move many heavy goods. It is even more important to sell all the merchandise if the store is closing.

If you buy furniture from a company that is going out of business, you should not expect any after-sale customer service. You will be on your own in dealing directly with the manufacturer of the product if a problem arises.

**Reflect:** Have you ever purchased something that you later regretted buying? Think back to how you felt when you bought it. Were you tired, rushed, or frustrated? Why do you sometimes make decisions you regret?

**Vocabulary:** Define *loss leader*. Find one example in a grocery ad and a second example in a furniture ad.

| Bargain Months | | |
|---|---|---|
| **January** | **February** | **March** |
| Appliances, blankets, carpets and rugs, furniture, home furnishings, housewares, and white goods | Air conditioners, carpets and rugs, curtains and draperies, furniture, home furnishings, housewares, and storm windows | Laundry appliances and storm windows |
| **April** | **May** | **June** |
| Gardening specials | Blankets, carpets and rugs, linens, and TV sets | Building materials, furniture, lumber, and TV sets |
| **July** | **August** | **September** |
| Air conditioners, appliances, carpets and rugs, fabrics, freezers and refrigerators, stereos, white goods | Air conditioners, bedding, carpets and rugs, curtains and draperies, fans, gardening equipment, home furnishings, housewares, summer furniture, and white goods | Appliances, paint, and TV sets |
| **October** | **November** | **December** |
| China and silverware | Blankets, housewares, and home improvement supplies | Blankets and housewares |

16-11

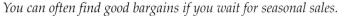

*You can often find good bargains if you wait for seasonal sales.*

## Sales of Damaged and Discontinued Items

Many stores mark down prices on items that are slightly damaged. Make sure you know where and how bad the damage is. A desk with a surface scratch may be a good bargain if the price is low. If the drawers do not open easily, the desk may not be a bargain.

Discontinued-item sales offer high-quality goods at low prices because the seller wants to get rid of items no longer in production. However, once the sale items are gone, you will not be able to purchase matching items. For example, you may find discontinued wallpaper on sale. If there is enough for you to wallpaper a complete area, it is a bargain.

As you shop at sales, keep in mind the saying, "Let the buyer beware."

When items are priced below their normal costs, there is always a reason. It is up to you, the buyer, to learn why and decide whether the lower price really represents a value to you. See 16-12.

## Information Sources

Before you make your final furniture selection, you should consult various sources for information on the furniture that interests you. These sources will provide information on the quality and reliability of the furniture. They will also help you become familiar with other furniture that is available. Begin by checking for important information at a library or online.

16-12
*Sometimes an advertised sale applies only to selected items. Always check whether the "sale" price is lower than the everyday price.*

### Books and Magazines

Home furnishing books and magazines can be found at the public library or can be purchased. Some books and articles tell how to refinish furniture. Some provide ideas on furniture selection and arrangement. Others give sources and costs for the merchandise featured. Money-saving ideas are often included.

### Product-Rating Organizations

*Consumer Reports* and *Consumer Guide* ® are publications from organizations that test and rate products. They provide information about quality, price, and other factors, such as warranty information. The reports are available as monthly magazines and annual buying guides. They and other product-rating reports can be found online, in a library, or at a bookstore.

### Advertisements

Advertisements in newspapers, magazines, radio, TV, and on the Internet often contain useful information. You can use advertisements to compare brand names, features, and prices.

### Labels

Labels found on furniture may contain information about the materials used, coverings, fillings, country of manufacture, and origin of style. For example, if the product is made in the United States, the label will state "Danish Style" rather than "Danish." The label may indicate that the materials used are *all new* or *partly made from used materials*. Labels also include care information.

### Better Business Bureau

The Better Business Bureau (BBB) is a nonprofit organization sponsored by private businesses. It publishes pamphlets and booklets on how to shop wisely for products and services. Your local BBB can give you information about stores and business people in the area. The BBB also maintains a record of consumer complaints against local businesses and tries to settle disputes.

## Stretching Your Furniture Dollars

Stretching your furniture dollars can help you acquire more furniture for your money. There are many reasons you may need to do this. For example, when you move into your first home, your take-home pay may not cover your many furniture needs. You may find it necessary to furnish your home with rented or used pieces until you can afford new furniture.

Another reason is the likelihood of increased housing costs as the size of your household increases. Consequently, finding ways to save money on furniture may become more important as you move through the life cycle.

You can stretch your furniture dollars by doing the following:

- shopping for bargains
- using multipurpose furniture
- buying unassembled furniture
- reusing old furniture
- creating an eclectic look

Ethan Allen, Inc.

16-13

*The detailed turning found in the legs of this table and chair set makes it more expensive than a set with simple, straight legs.*

## Shopping for Bargains

A good way to find furniture bargains is to buy furniture on sale. However, no matter how much the item costs on sale, it is not a bargain unless you need and can afford it. Also, the item is not a bargain if you would really rather have something else. A true bargain improves the quality of your life.

Sometimes what seems like a bargain may not be a bargain at all. One item may cost less than a similar item, but it may require more time or effort to acquire. For instance, carpeting at a store 50 miles away may cost 20 percent less than carpeting at a nearby store. This savings may be worth the long drive to some people, but not to others.

Although durable, simple furniture may not seem like a bargain, it really is. Complex furniture is often more expensive than simple furniture. Carving, latticework, turnings, and other extras add to the cost of furniture. See 16-13. The appearance of furniture with simple lines and colors can be updated easily by changing accessories.

## Using Multipurpose Furniture

*Multipurpose furniture* is furniture that can be used for more than one purpose. For example, a sofa bed can be used for sitting or sleeping. Flat-topped trunks and chests can be used as end tables and coffee tables while functioning as storage pieces.

### Unassembled Furniture

*Unassembled furniture*, which is furniture sold in parts that require assembly, may or may not be finished. It is often a lower quality than most assembled furniture. By assembling the furniture yourself, you save money. Since unassembled furniture is usually packaged very compactly, you can save delivery costs by hauling it home yourself.

You can creatively assemble pieces from items not normally considered furniture. For example, bricks and boards can be assembled into bookshelves. A round piece of board can be covered with a large circular cloth to make an attractive table. See 16 14.

Plastic or wooden cubes can be assembled in a wide variety of ways to create furniture. They can be used for shelves, tables, desks, and seats. See 16-15. Some cubes are divided to provide shelf space or accommodate drawers. Plastic cubes come in many colors, while wooden cubes can be painted to coordinate your decorating scheme.

## Reusing Furniture

After you acquire new furniture, you can still reuse your old furniture. This will help you stretch your home furniture dollars even more. To reuse your furniture, you can recycle, restore, or renew it.

### Recycling Furniture

To *recycle* means to adapt to a new use. Recycling furniture means using furniture for a new use after it no longer serves its original purpose. For instance, outdoor furniture can be used in your first living room, dining room, or family room. See 16-16. As your budget allows, you can replace the outdoor furniture with indoor furniture. The outdoor furniture can then be used to decorate your patio. Other outdoor furniture can be used indoors. For instance, patio benches can be used as coffee tables, end tables, or seating.

You can recycle furniture pieces in your own home or pass them on to

16-14
*A round board mounted on any kind of base can become a table.*

16-15
*These cubes can be arranged in many different ways to create shelves and storage space.*

**Reflect:** Could you use a round table such as pictured in 16-14? How could you make one inexpensively?

**Vocabulary:** Compare *recycling, restoring,* and *renewing* as the terms relate to furniture. Give their definitions.

**Internet Activity:** Search for Web sites that sell unassembled furniture. Make a list of their addresses and share it with the class. Determine if the stores have outlets in your area. If so, record their addresses.

**Discuss:** What is the advantage of using outdoor furniture for living room furniture in your first apartment? (*Later the outdoor furniture can be moved to a patio to make room for new indoor furniture.*)

Brown Jordan International Company, Designs by Rich Frinier

16-16

*This wrought iron patio furniture is effectively used as indoor furniture.*

someone else to use. You can also buy used furniture from other sources to recycle in your home. Garage sales, secondhand stores, and relatives are good sources of used furniture.

### Renovating Furniture

Often furniture can be renovated, which involves either restoring or renewing it. It usually costs less to renovate an old piece of furniture than to buy low-quality, new furniture. You can renovate furniture yourself, or you can hire a professional. If you choose to do it yourself, keep in mind that it takes time, patience, and work. It also takes money for supplies and equipment.

As you consider renovating a piece of used furniture, answer the following questions:

- Is it well designed?
- Will it blend well with the other furnishings?
- Is it well constructed and worth repairing?
- Can it be used "as is"?
- Do you have the time, patience, and energy to do a good job?
- Do you have the necessary equipment and supplies to do the job, or the money to buy them?
- Do you have a suitable place to work?

When you *restore* a piece of furniture, you return it to its original state as much as possible. There are several steps to restoring a piece of furniture, including repairing, refinishing, and possibly reupholstering. For example, you may want to restore an antique chair.

1. First, you would remove the paint and sand all the finish off the wood.

2. Then, you would make any necessary repairs, such as redoing the joints.

3. Finally, a finish as close to the original as possible would be applied.

4. Reupholstering would follow, if needed. Carefully remove the original upholstery fabric and use it as a pattern for the new upholstery. For a proper restoration, you should select an upholstery fabric pattern that is similar in design to the type of fabric that was originally used on the piece.

This process takes much time and skill. You must have a strong interest in restoring furniture to make it worthwhile.

Vocabulary: Define *eclectic* and use it in a sentence to define a specific piece of furniture.

Ethan Allen, Inc.

16-17

*This mixture of contemporary and traditional furnishings works well together to create an eclectic look.*

If the furniture is in good condition, but the upholstery is worn or dated, you can *renew* it. To renew furniture means to give it a new look. The steps in this process are similar to those followed in restoration, with one important difference. When you renew furniture, you update it and do not attempt to restore it to its original condition. Based on the fabric and/or paint finish you select, an old piece of furniture can take on a totally different appearance.

## Creating the Eclectic Look

Another way to stretch your furniture dollars is to create the eclectic look in your home. Eclectic is a type of decor based on a mixture of furnishings from different periods, styles, and countries. (Refer to Eclectic style as discussed in Chapter 15.) You can use this look while you are acquiring furniture piece by piece, or you can use it on a permanent basis. See 16-17.

Discuss: Why do you think the eclectic style of interior design appeals to so many young people your age?

Writing Activity: Write each letter of the alphabet on separate lines of a sheet of paper and work independently to write one term from the chapter that begins with each alphabet letter. After three minutes, pairs of students confer to fill in any blank lines. (If blanks still remain, discuss some possible choices with the class.)

**Resource:** *Furniture Arrangement*, reproducible master 16-2, TR. Students design a living area that includes dining for up to six people and a conversational grouping that seats at least six. They evaluate and rearrange the furniture as needed to meet guidelines and gather pictures of the furniture to be used in the room.

**Resource:** *Test Your Knowledge*, Activity F, SAG. Students write questions and answers for each of the topics listed.

# Summary

Using a scale floor plan aids in arranging furniture. It shows the dimensions and features of the room and allows you to move furniture templates around to create the best space plan. Good furniture arrangement is dependent on how the furniture and the room are used. Arrangements should provide for adequate clearance space to avoid interfering with room features and traffic patterns.

Selecting furniture involves several steps and begins with prioritizing furniture needs. Then you decide how much you can afford, what is your lifestyle, what are your furniture styles and design preferences, where and how to shop, and when to shop. Finally, you should consult information sources.

Stretching your furniture dollars results in acquiring more furniture for your money. This can be done by shopping for bargains, choosing multipurpose furniture, or buying furniture that needs to be finished or assembled. Reusing furniture can also save you money. Using the eclectic look in your rooms can be a design solution while you acquire furniture over a period of time or it may be a permanent style choice.

# To Review

1. How does a scale floor plan help in deciding furniture arrangements?
2. List three factors to consider when planning a furniture arrangement.
3. Explain the importance of prioritizing furniture needs.
4. Why should the amount of money that can be spent on furniture be decided before shopping begins?
5. List three places to shop for furniture and give one advantage of each.
6. Identify possible shopping drawbacks with each of the following sales:
   A. loss leader
   B. seasonal
   C. closeout
   D. damaged and discontinued items
7. List five sources of information useful for selecting furniture.
8. Name five ways to stretch furniture dollars.
9. List two ways to reuse furniture.
10. Identify the steps in restoring furniture.
11. Why does the eclectic look help people stretch their furniture dollars?

# In Your Community

1. Compare prices on identical pieces of furniture of the same brand name, company, such as a sofa or dining room table, by visiting two different stores. If the prices are different, try to determine why. A salesperson may be able to help you. Share your findings with the class.

2. Look through local newspapers to find advertisements representing each type of sale discussed in this chapter. Cut out the advertisements, mount them on separate pieces of paper, and label them. Bring them to class for discussion and display them in your classroom.

3. Select and measure one room in your house. Following the steps discussed in this chapter, draw a scale floor plan of the space. Make templates of either existing furniture or new furniture, and create two different furniture arrangements of your plan. Be careful to consider clearance space and allow for traffic patterns.

# To Think About

1. For you, what determines if a piece of furniture is a bargain? Explain your decision in a written, one-page paper. Be sure to use examples.

2. Make a list of the possible endings to this statement: "It is a bargain if..." Make another list of the possible ending to this statement: "It is *not* a bargain if…" Compare and discuss your lists with your classmates.

3. Suppose you were asked to design a combined living and dining room in a space measuring 20 by 26 feet. Since the space has windows overlooking spectacular views on two walls, your challenge is to avoid obstructing the view. The windows extend from the ceiling to three feet off the floor, and the room has one windowless wall. The fourth side of the space is open to the kitchen and a hallway leading to other rooms. Select and place furniture appropriate for a young couple that enjoys informally entertaining up to a dozen friends at a time. Identify the furniture pieces you would choose for the room. Also, create a floor plan showing the placement of the pieces. You may add electrical floor plugs for lamps and other electrical needs.

## Using Technology

1. Using a computer-aided design program, design a living room with dimensions of 20 by 18 feet. Show the placement of one door and three windows. Place furniture such as a sofa, two chairs, two side tables, and a coffee table in the room in three different arrangements. You may decide to add more furniture. Using the chart in Fig. 16-2, measure your designs to see if the recommended clearances are met. If not, redesign the arrangements as necessary to meet the recommended clearances. What can happen if clearances are too small?

**Note:** For researching furniture companies, have students explore *ethanallen.com*.

2. Search the Internet for a furniture company that sells furniture online. Determine if the customer service policies of the company are on the Web site. Specifically see if the following questions are answered:

   A. How does the company handle returned items?
   B. How does the company handle items damaged in shipping?
   C. What are the shipping costs?

   Based on what you find, how would you advise someone who is considering shopping for furniture online? If the policies are not explained online, how could a consumer get the information? Summarize your advice and recommendations in writing.

**Portfolio Project:** Review the floor plans you prepared in this chapter and "professionalize" their appearance. Redo them, if necessary, to create samples suitable for display.

# CHAPTER 17

# Addressing Windows, Lighting, and Accessories

## To Know

window treatment
draperies
curtains
shades
shutters
blinds
incandescent light
tungsten-halogen lights
electronic lamp (E-lamp)
fluorescent light
compact fluorescent bulb
fiber optics
light-emitting diode (LED)
reflected light
absorbed light
diffused light
general lighting
direct lighting
indirect lighting
local lighting
task lighting
wattage
lumen
foot-candle
accent lighting
structural light fixture
nonstructural lighting
accessories

Ethan Allen, Inc.

## Objectives

After studying this chapter, you will be able to

- describe types of window treatments.

- explain the differences between incandescent and fluorescent lighting.

- plan residential lighting for visual comfort, safety, and beauty.

- distinguish between structural and nonstructural lighting.

- list guidelines for the use, placement, and care of accessories.

**Resource:** *The Inside Story,* transparency master overlay IV-C, TR. Students look back at the topics covered in Chapters 1-16 by reviewing transparency master IV-A with overlay IV-B. Then, with the addition of overlay IV-C, they explore the "finishing touches" topics they will cover in Chapter 17.

**Discuss:** Dissect the phrase "Addressing Windows, Lighting, and Accessories" and determine what this chapter will cover.

**Vocabulary:** Review the chapter objectives, relating them to as many of the key terms as possible.

Some of the final steps for furnishing a room are selecting window treatments, providing good lighting, and choosing accessories that reflect your personality. You will continue to use the elements and principles of design that you learned in Chapters 10 and 12 as you add the finishing touches to your design.

# Window Treatments

*Window treatments* are applications added to window units either for helping control the home environment or for purely decorative purposes. The style, size, and location of windows need to be considered when choosing window treatments. Other very important considerations for selecting window treatments include the need to control sunlight and noise, and to provide the ventilation, privacy, and insulation for each room.

Some window treatments can help control the amount of natural light that enters a room by blocking all or part of the light from entering. For example, a treatment should provide both sun control and privacy in a sleeping area for adults or children. However, privacy and sun control may be less important for a child's playroom. For a sunroom, window treatments should allow as much light and air ventilation as possible. In contrast, a media room or home theater would require window treatments to regulate or block the amount of sunlight entering the room.

Window treatments include draperies, curtains, shades, shutters, blinds, and decorative top treatments. The right window treatments can enhance the appearance of a room. Certain treatments can camouflage windows that are not in proportion to the rest of the room.

Sometimes windows are left untreated, especially when privacy is not a concern. If the shape of the window is too difficult to treat or if the window itself is an important architectural focal point of the room, you may choose to leave it untreated. In 17-l, the uniquely shaped windows are left uncovered to give the room a dramatic look and let light enter freely. Furthermore, if windows provide a beautiful view of the outdoors, you may prefer having no window treatments.

Another consideration in the selection of the type of window treatment

Photo courtesy of Andersen Windows, Inc.

17-1

*These striking windows need no treatment.*

to be used is the feeling you wish to create in the room. Is the mood of the room to be formal or informal? Is the style of the space to be traditional or contemporary? Depending on the design of the window treatment, many different moods and effects can be created.

Other important considerations for the selection of window treatments deal with the initial cost of purchasing the treatments and the subsequent cost of maintaining them. (You may find it helpful to review this information in Chapter 13, "Textiles in Today's Homes.") Keep in mind that custom or made-to-measure window treatments are more costly than ready-made treatments that are mass-produced. In today's market, more and more attractive ready-made styles and options are available. Also, pattern companies offer many designs for creating your own window treatments or for hiring a seamstress to do so.

Whether you purchase or create your own window treatments, give careful consideration to the fabrics you select. Are they colorfast? Do they require dry cleaning or can they be laundered? Will you be able to maintain their appearance by simply dusting or vacuuming them? Do not invest in a window treatment that you have neither the time nor money to maintain.

## Draperies and Curtains

Draperies and curtains are the most common window treatments. They are extremely versatile and can fit into any decor. The type of draperies or curtains you choose depends on the room's decor and the function of the windows.

### Draperies

*Draperies* are pleated panels of fabric that cover windows completely or are pulled to the side. Depending on the design and type of fabric you select, a drapery can be used in any style decor. Draperies can be opaque or translucent. *Opaque* draperies block light, while *translucent* draperies permit the passage of light. They can be lined or unlined. Lining draperies blocks some sunlight from entering the room and protects the draperies from becoming faded by the sun. The lining also adds body, makes draperies hang or drape better, and increases their ability to insulate.

Draperies can be used alone or with other window treatments, such as curtains, shades, blinds, and decorative top treatments. In 17-2, center

Photograph courtesy of Waverly

17-2

*These drapery panels provide sunlight during the day and privacy at night. The swag top treatment is both decorative and functional since it hides hardware.*

**Reflect:** Of the windows in your home that have draperies, how many have stationary draperies? How many have draw draperies?

**Discuss:** What are some reasons for blocking sunlight from a room?

draw-drapery panels were selected for the French door. They can be opened during the day to allow light to enter the room. At night, they can be closed to provide complete privacy and help insulate the room. A decorative top treatment hides the drapery hardware.

The different types of draperies are named for how they operate. *Draw draperies* open and close from the center or side with a pull stick or cord on one end of the curtain rod. *Stationary draperies* cannot be opened and closed. Usually they are permanently positioned at one or both sides of a window.

### Curtains

*Curtains* are flat fabric panels that hang to the left and right of the

Kirsch

17-3

*These tab top curtains are hung on a decorative wrought iron rod. The roller shades control light and allow privacy in this home office.*

window and may be closed to cover the window. Like draperies, the design and fabric selected for the curtains will impact the style and mood of the room. Usually curtains have a pocket hem at the top, which is slipped onto a curtain rod and gathered to the desired fullness. Curtains may also be hung from the curtain rod with decorative drapery hardware or tabs of sewn fabric. The rod itself may be plain or decorative, such as a grooved wooden pole or a pole of brass or wrought iron, as in 17-3. Ruffles, bands of fabric, and trim may be added to the panels for interest. Tiebacks may also be used to pull the curtain panel away from the window, giving a curved shape to the drapery panel instead of simply a straight line.

The amount of light, insulation, or privacy curtains provide depends on the fabric. Curtains made of sheer fabric give a room a light, airy feeling. If more privacy is needed, heavier fabrics are used. However, this may make the room appear darker.

*Cafe curtains* are horizontal panels hung in tiers to cover part of a window. The top of each panel is joined to rings that slip over a curtain rod. Cafe curtains cannot be opened by pulling a cord as draw draperies are. However, you can open cafe curtains by pushing them to the sides. This lets you control air, light, and privacy. When using cafe curtains, one tier can be used to cover only the bottom half of the window. More than one tier can be used to completely cover a window. By changing the width or the number of tiers, a variety of looks can be achieved with cafe curtains. Cafe curtains are most often used in rooms that have an informal feeling.

The length of draperies and curtains should fall to *sill length*, *apron length*, or *floor length*, all pictured in 17-4. If the bottom edge of a window

**Vocabulary:** Compare and contrast the meanings of *decorative* and *functional* as they relate to window treatments. Give examples of each.

**Enrich:** Visit a model home and study the window treatments. Look at the fabrics and determine the function of each.

**Activity:** Examine various samples of curtain and drapery fabrics (borrowed from a drapery or fabric center). Discuss which is appropriate for various treatments. Talk about the qualities of each and the functions for which they are appropriate.

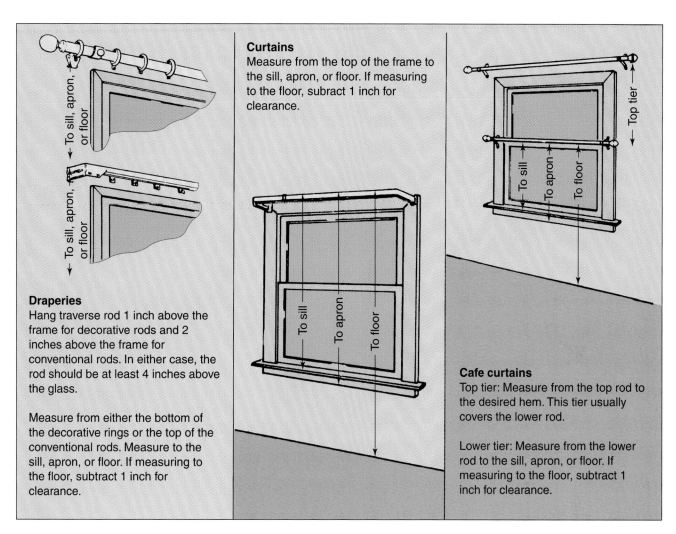

**Draperies**
Hang traverse rod 1 inch above the frame for decorative rods and 2 inches above the frame for conventional rods. In either case, the rod should be at least 4 inches above the glass.

Measure from either the bottom of the decorative rings or the top of the conventional rods. Measure to the sill, apron, or floor. If measuring to the floor, subtract 1 inch for clearance.

**Curtains**
Measure from the top of the frame to the sill, apron, or floor. If measuring to the floor, subtract 1 inch for clearance.

**Cafe curtains**
Top tier: Measure from the top rod to the desired hem. This tier usually covers the lower rod.

Lower tier: Measure from the lower rod to the sill, apron, or floor. If measuring to the floor, subtract 1 inch for clearance.

17-4

*Different methods are used to measure draperies, curtains, and cafe curtains.*

treatment falls at any other place, it will look either too short or too long. To correctly measure the length of draperies and curtains, use the methods shown in 17-4.

## Shades, Shutters, and Blinds

*Shades* block unwanted light, such as intense sunlight in the afternoon or streetlight at night. They are simple to operate and can cover all or part of a window. Shades vary in appearance to go with almost any decor. The fabric and other materials used in their construction affect the amount of light control, insulation, and privacy they provide.

- *Roller shades* come in various colors. They also come in various degrees of opaqueness. (A roller shade is shown in 17-3.) These shades tend to be used in informal rooms.

- *Roman shades* are constructed of fabric and are installed within the window molding. They fold into horizontal pleats when they are raised, but hang flat when they are closed. Depending on the fabric selected, they can adapt to many styles of design.

17-5 _____

*The weight of fabric selected for balloon shades determines the amount of sun control, insulation, and privacy.*

- *Balloon shades* are also constructed of fabric and are similar to Roman shades in their operation. They received their name from the balloon shape they take when they are raised. See 17-5. They are also very adaptable to different styles of design depending on the fabric and pattern selected.

- *Pleated shades* are very popular in today's market. They are

17-6 _____

*The pleated shades selected for this large window area are both beautiful and functional.*

constructed of synthetic materials and are available in accordion or honeycomb styles. See 17-6. Like Roman and balloon shades, pleated shades are raised and lowered with a cord. They are manufactured in many solid colors, patterns, and textures. They may be opaque, as in 17-7, or translucent. Certain pleated shades offer excellent insulation qualities. They work extremely well in contemporary settings.

Windows that are used for ventilation cannot be covered since air movement will be blocked. Shutters are appropriate choices for such windows. *Shutters* are vertical units that are hinged together to open and close much like a folding door. They are constructed of wood or synthetic materials. Built into the frame of the vertical panels are movable

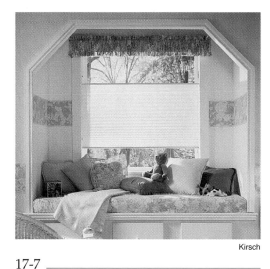

Kirsch

17-7 _____

*Pleated shades were selected for this child's room. A shirred fabric valance was added for interest.*

horizontal slats or louvers. The louvers may be adjusted to allow sunlight control, ventilation, and privacy. The width of wooden louvers in shutters may vary from 1½ to 4½ inches. They adapt well to both formal and informal room settings. See 17-8.

**Blinds** are window treatments made of slats that can be tilted, raised and lowered, or moved to the side. They are often made of wood, metal, plastic, or fabric. Blinds can be custom-made to fit windows with unusual shapes or placements. See 17-9. There are three basic styles of blinds.

- Horizontal blinds, often called *venetian blinds*, can be raised completely. The angle of the slats to the blinds can be adjusted to control the amount of air and light entering the room. See 17-10. They appear most often in informal settings.

- *Miniblinds* are horizontal blinds with narrow slats, as in 17-11. They can be adjusted and raised exactly like other horizontal

Weather Shield Windows & Doors

17-8 _____

*Shutter installations enhance formal as well as informal rooms.*

Velux-America, Inc.

17-9 _____

*Special miniblinds were installed between the panels of glass in these windows to control light.*

Permission granted by Hunter Douglas, Inc. to use copyrighted designs.
Designs © Hunter Douglas, Inc.

17-10 —————————————————————
*The wooden blinds installed in these windows are a*
*complement to the masculine feeling of the room. The arches*
*are left untreated to create a focal point.*

Permission granted by Hunter Douglas, Inc. to use copyrighted designs. Designs ©
Hunter Douglas, Inc.

17-12 —————————————————————
*These custom vertical blinds provide an excellent*
*solution to the treatment of this arched window.*

Kirsch

17-11 —————————————————————
*By adjusting these miniblinds, the person in this space*
*can enjoy a wonderful view of the city skyline.*

blinds. They also are most often used in informal rooms.

- *Vertical blinds* have slats that move to one side to leave a window uncovered. The angle of the slats also can be adjusted to control the amounts of air and light that enter a room. See 17-12. They tend to be used in more contemporary designs.

## Decorative Window-top Treatments

Decorative window-top treatments can be combined with draperies, curtains, shades, shutters, or blinds to add interest to the window installation. Such decorative top treatments include swags, valances, cornices, or lambrequins.

**Writing Activity:** Study the different styles of blinds pictured in Figures 17-10, 17-11, and 17-12. Select the one you think would work best in your room. Write a brief summary of your selection and why you chose it.

**Art Activity:** Draw illustrations of swags, valances, cornices, and lambrequins.

- A *swag treatment* has softly pleated fabric hanging in a curve across the top of the window. (Refer again to 17-2.)

- A *valance* is a horizontal treatment across the top of the window. It can be used to hide the drapery or curtain hardware. The many styles of valances depend on the cut and construction of the fabric, the degree of gathering, and the installation hardware used. (Refer again to 17-7.)

- A *cornice* is also a horizontal treatment that is usually constructed of wood. The wood is then padded and covered with fabric. Some formal cornices may actually be wood that has been carved in an attractive design. Other more informal cornices may have been painted or stenciled with a design.

- A *lambrequin* is constructed in the same manner as a cornice, but also extends down the left and right sides of the window.

Decorative window-top treatments may use either matching or complementary fabrics and designs to add interest to the treatment. Also, trims of decorative braid, tassels, and cording may be used to add a custom touch. They can be used in many different style rooms depending on the fabrics selected.

# Artificial Light

Natural light is not always available so artificial light is also needed. The two main kinds of artificial light used in homes are incandescent and fluorescent light. However, other types of light sources are becoming more available to consumers.

## Incandescent Light

*Incandescent light* is produced when an electric current passes through a fine tungsten filament inside a bulb. The electricity heats the filament until it glows and gives off light. See 17-13. Incandescent bulbs vary in shape and size, but they all work the same way.

Incandescent lightbulbs used in homes range from 15 to 300 watts. (See Chapter 9, "The Systems Within," for an explanation of watts.) When comparing two incandescent bulbs, the one with the higher wattage will give off more light. The chart in 17-14 lists the recommended wattage for some household activities.

Most incandescent bulbs used in homes have a *frost finish* that covers the entire inside surface of the bulb. The main purpose of the frost finish is to reduce glare and make shadows

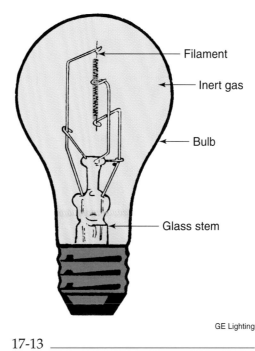

GE Lighting

17-13
*Inside an incandescent lightbulb, inert gas surrounds a filament. Electric current heats the filament and makes it glow.*

**Writing Activity:** Write a poem or rap to help recall the differences in swags, valances, cornices, and lambrequins.
**Discuss:** Name the two main types of artificial light. (*incandescent and fluorescent*)
**Research:** When an incandescent bulb burns out, what actually happens? Often the filament breaks, but what are some other reasons?

**Discuss:** What types of artificial light were used prior to the availability of electricity?

**Enrich:** Visit a lighting store or the lighting section of a home improvement center. Find examples of each type of lighting discussed in the chapter. Compare prices and how long each is expected to last. With this information, determine which is the best buy for you and explain why.

| Selection Guide for Incandescent Bulbs | |
| --- | --- |
| Activity | Minimum Recommended Wattage* |
| *Reading, writing, sewing*<br>Occasional periods<br>Prolonged periods | 150<br>200-300 |
| *Grooming*<br>Cup-type fixture over bathroom mirror<br>Other types of fixtures over bathroom mirror<br>Side fixtures by bathroom mirror<br>Bathroom ceiling fixture<br>Vanity table lamps, in pairs (person seated)<br>Dresser lamps, in pairs (person standing) | <br>100<br><br>150<br>one 50 or two 40s<br>150<br><br>100 each<br><br>150 each |
| *Kitchen work*<br>Ceiling fixture (2 or more in a large area)<br>Fixture over sink<br>Fixture for eating area (separate from work space) | <br>150 or 200<br>150<br><br>150 |
| *Shop/craft work*<br>Fixture over workbench (2 or more for long bench) | <br><br>150 |
| *white bulbs preferred | |

U.S. Department of Agriculture

17-14 _____

*Your activities determine the quantity of light you need.*

Discuss: What type of incandescent light would you choose for each of the following uses: garage door light, refrigerator light, oven light, and a three-way lamp?

Enrich: Check the Consumer Product Safety Commission (CPSC) for concerns about halogen lights in torchiere lamps. What safety issue is involved? What has the CPSC done? Write a brief summary of your findings.

appear softer. The frost finish also makes the bulb last longer because it keeps the surface of the bulb fairly cool. Because of the cooler temperature, a lampshade that accidentally touches this type of bulb is not likely to be scorched by it.

Bulbs without a frost finish produce a great deal of glare. They should be used only in fixtures that hide the bulbs completely from view.

Many kinds of special incandescent bulbs are available. One is the *three-way bulb*. Sets of filaments operate separately or together to produce different amounts of light, ranging from 30 to 250 watts.

Some bulbs have silver or aluminum coatings. These bulbs focus the light in certain directions. Other bulbs are coated with silicone rubber. This prevents the glass from shattering if the bulb breaks.

### Tungsten-Halogen Light

*Tungsten-halogen lights* are another form of incandescent lighting. In this type of bulb, a gas from the halogen family and tungsten molecules are combined to activate a filament. The special quartz bulb lights up instantly when the electric current is turned on.

Tungsten-halogen bulbs have many advantages over regular incandescent bulbs. They produce a better quality of light. The amount of light in an aging tungsten-halogen bulb does not decrease as much as in regular bulbs. Also, tungsten-halogen bulbs last up to three times longer than regular bulbs. Tungsten-halogen bulbs are less energy efficient than fluorescent lights, but more energy efficient than other types of incandescent lights.

### The Electronic 20-Year Lamp

The *electronic lamp*, or *E-lamp*, fits most sockets that use incandescent bulbs. It is sometimes called the 20-year lamp because it is expected to last up to 20,000 hours. This is based on an average use of 1,000 hours per year, or almost 3 hours daily. Incandescent bulbs, in comparison, are expected to last no more than 1,500 total hours.

## Fluorescent Light

*Fluorescent light* is produced in a glass tube by releasing electricity through a mercury vapor to make invisible ultraviolet rays. These rays are converted into visible light rays by a coating of fluorescent material on

Math Activity: Compare the cost of tungsten-halogen to incandescent bulbs. For a fixture that uses two 60-watt incandescent bulbs, what is the price of comparable tungsten-halogen bulbs? Since tungsten-halogen bulbs last three times as long as incandescent bulbs, how much would you pay for enough incandescent bulbs to equal their lifetime?

Activity: Using the chart in Figure 17-14, compare the wattage of lighting in your home to the suggestions for minimum wattage levels. Are any areas of your home too dimly lit? If so, discuss this with a parent.

the inside of the glass tube. There is a delay between the release of electric current and the production of light.

Fluorescent light is more energy efficient than incandescent light. A fluorescent tube produces about four times as much light as an incandescent bulb of the same wattage.

Fluorescent tubes are more expensive than incandescent bulbs, but they last longer and are less expensive to use. Fluorescent tubes can be expected to last up to 20,000 hours and use 40 watts or less of electricity.

Fluorescent tubes are straight or circular, and available in various sizes. Traditionally, the length of a straight tube or the diameter of a circular tube determines the wattage. See 17-15.

The color of light from a fluorescent tube varies by changing the coating of fluorescent material in the tube. Cool-white light is very efficient, blends well with sunlight, and makes colors look good. Warm-white light is cost efficient, but it is not flattering to some colors. Both types of lights are most often used in kitchens and bathrooms. Deluxe cool-white light closely imitates natural daylight. Full-spectrum fluorescent tubes now provide both cool and warm white light.

Due to provisions in the Energy Act of 1992, certain fluorescent lighting tubes are banned from production. The reason for being taken off the market is the low output of light per watt. Specifically banned from manufacture are cool-white and warm-white fluorescent lights. Some of these fluorescent lights may still remain in homes and on retail shelves, but none are being produced today.

## Compact Fluorescent Bulbs

A new type of fluorescent light is the *compact fluorescent bulb*. Compact fluorescent bulbs are a little larger than regular incandescent bulbs and

screw into regular lightbulb sockets. See 17-16. They save energy and operate for nearly 9,000 hours while using only 15 watts of electricity.

| Popular Sizes of Fluorescent Tubes | | |
|---|---|---|
| *Straight Tubes* | **Wattage** | **Length** |
| | 14 | 15 inches |
| | 15 | 18 inches |
| | 20 | 24 inches |
| | 30 | 36 inches |
| | 40 | 48 inches |
| *Circular* | **Wattage** | **Outside Diameter** |
| | 22 | 8 1/4 inches |
| | 32 | 12 inches |
| | 40 | 16 inches |

17-15 _____
*The wattage for fluorescent tubes depends on the length or diameter of the tubes.*

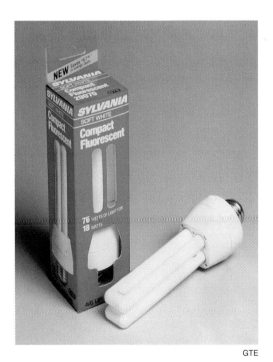
GTE

17-16 _____
*Although compact fluorescent bulbs look different from regular incandescent lightbulbs, they can be used in the same outlets.*

**Enrich:** Research the effects of lighting on people. Consider such topics as depression and hyperactivity.
**Discuss:** What is the difference in cool- and warm-white light on colors? (*Cool-white light makes all colors look good, while warm-white light is not flattering to some colors.*)
**Reflect:** Does your home use fluorescent lightbulbs? If so, are they straight tubes, circular tubes, or compact bulbs?

**Note:** The American Lighting Association at *americanlightingassoc.com* provides a wealth of information on types of new lighting and ideal uses.

**Internet Activity:** Search the Web to find out why the Energy Act of 1992 prohibited the manufacturing of certain types of fluorescent lights. Summarize your findings and report your sources.

Compact fluorescent bulbs help the environment. The electricity saved by replacing an incandescent bulb with a compact fluorescent one equals the energy produced by burning about 450 pounds of coal.

## Lighting from Fiber Optics

*Fiber optics* is a type of heatless light produced by passing an electric current through a cable containing very fine strands of glass. These cables are primarily used in communications, but also are being used for lighting. The lighting gives off no heat or ultraviolet rays that can distort colors. Currently, the lighting is used primarily in museums and for displays.

## Light-Emitting Diodes

Extremely long-lasting bulbs are being made from *light-emitting diodes (LED)*. LEDs are composed of crystals on silicon chips about the size of a grain of salt that produce light when a small electric current passes through them. An LED bulb can last 100,000 hours or more. In comparison with other bulbs, it will last about 10 times longer than compact fluorescent bulbs and over 100 times longer than incandescent bulbs.

# The Properties of Light

You can use light to achieve several different effects in your home. To do this, you first need to understand the various properties of light. Light can be reflected or absorbed. It can shine directly on a certain spot or lighten a whole room. By knowing the properties of light, you can make light work for you.

## Reflected Light

Light, color, and texture are closely related. Without light, there is no color. In turn, colors reflect and absorb various amounts of light. Surfaces with rough textures look dark because tiny shadows form where the light does not reach. Together, light, color, and texture greatly affect the appearance of rooms.

*Reflected light* is the light that bounces off surfaces. It seems to come from these surfaces as well as from its source. Light is reflected by light colors and smooth, shiny surfaces. Light is also reflected by background treatments in the home. See 17-17 to learn how much light can be reflected by various backgrounds.

## Absorbed Light

*Absorbed light* is light that is drawn in by a surface. Rough textures and dark colors absorb most of the available light rays. If light is absorbed, it cannot be reflected. In your home, use rough textures and dark colors in large areas. When light is absorbed, it makes the areas appear smaller.

| Reflected Light | | |
|---|---|---|
| **Background** | **Minimum** | **Maximum** |
| *Ceilings*<br>Pale color tints | 60% | 90% |
| *Walls*<br>Natural wood<br>Light colors<br>Medium colors<br>Dark colors | 5%<br>70%<br>35%<br>5% | 50%<br>80%<br>60%<br>25% |
| *Floors*<br>Carpeting, tiles, woods | 15% | 35% |

17-17
*This chart gives minimum and maximum amounts of reflected light.*

## Diffused Light

*Diffused light* is light that is scattered over a large area. It has no glare, which is the most troublesome aspect of lighting. Instead, it creates a soft appearance. Devices used to diffuse light are called *diffusers*. Diffusers spread the light evenly. An example of a diffuser is the frosted or white finish on incandescent and fluorescent bulbs. Other diffusers are more apparent, such as the covers for light fixtures. These diffusers are usually made of frosted or translucent glass.

# Functions of Lighting

Lighting is used for several reasons. It illuminates areas that may pose a safety hazard. Lighting is also used to focus attention on beautiful objects or attractive architectural features. The most common use of lighting, however, is to illuminate the environment so people can comfortably see.

## Lighting for Visual Comfort

To create visual comfort in your home, you need two basic types of lighting: general and local. The type and amount needed vary from room to room.

### General Lighting

*General lighting* provides a uniform level of light throughout a room. General lighting is achieved through the use of either direct or indirect lighting.

*Direct lighting* shines directly toward an object. It provides the most light possible to a specific area. See 17-18. If used alone, direct lighting creates a sharp contrast between light

Summitville Tiles, Inc.

17-18

*Direct lighting is used here to make food preparation and cooking easier and safer.*

and dark areas, which can cause eye fatigue. Therefore, if direct lighting is needed for a task, use other lights in the room as well.

General lighting can also be achieved through indirect lighting. *Indirect lighting* is directed toward a surface, such as a ceiling or wall, that reflects the light into the room. See 17-19. Indirect lighting may provide soft light for a large area. However, it does not provide enough light for detailed work.

General lighting should light a room well enough for occupants to see objects clearly and move about safely. The amount of general lighting needed depends on the shape, size, and use of the room.

**Vocabulary:** Use *reflected light, absorbed light*, and *diffused light* correctly in a paragraph explaining the light in your classroom, school library, or home.

**Discuss:** Why is glare so troublesome? With what types of artificial light have you experienced extreme glare?

**Discuss:** Why would a lampshade be considered a type of light diffuser?

**Vocabulary:** Create a Venn diagram comparing direct and indirect lighting. Draw overlapping circles, writing the qualities they share in the overlap. In the outer parts of the circles, write the qualities about them that differ. Use one side for direct lighting and the other for indirect lighting, labeling each.

**Reflect:** At home, is there adequate lighting for tasks such as cooking, sewing, and studying? Are improvements needed?

Randall Whitehead/Lighting Designer: Randall Whitehead, Light Source

17-19

*Indirect lighting is reflected on the wall and plant on the left side of this room. Direct lighting accents the floral arrangement on the center table.*

| Lighting for the Home | |
|---|---|
| **Task** | **Foot-Candles of Light** |
| *Dining* | 15 |
| *Grooming* | 50 |
| *Ironing* | 50 |
| *Kitchen duties* | |
| Food preparation and cleaning that involves difficult seeing tasks | 150 |
| Serving and other noncritical tasks | 50 |
| *Laundry tasks* | |
| Preparation, sorting, and hand washing | 50 |
| Washer and dryer areas | 30 |
| *Reading and writing* | |
| Reading reproductions and poor copies, and writing | 70 |
| Reading books, magazines, and newspapers | 30 |
| *Sewing* | |
| Dark fabrics | 200 |
| Medium fabrics | 100 |
| Light fabrics | 50 |
| Occasional sewing or high contrast fabrics | 30 |
| *Studying* | 70 |
| *Playing table games* | 30 |

U.S. Department of Agriculture

17-20

*Use this chart to determine the approximate amount of light needed for certain activities.*

## Local Lighting

General lighting does not always supply enough light for visual comfort. In these cases, it can be supplemented by local lighting. **Local lighting** is lighting used in specific areas where activities are done that require more light. Having the right amount of local lighting will prevent eyestrain. When it is used to help you see well enough to do a certain task, such as writing letters, carving wood, or sewing, it is called **task lighting**.

The amount of local lighting you need depends on the activity. The finer the detail or the faster the action taking place, the more light you need. For instance, playing table tennis requires more light than shooting pool.

Local lighting in one part of a room can serve as general lighting for another part. For instance, if you are reading in one corner of a family room, the lamp that you use for local lighting adds to the general lighting of the entire room.

To get the right amount of good quality light, combine general and local lighting. Together, they give adequate light without sharp contrast.

## Measuring Light

The following terms are used in the measurement of light. **Wattage** is the amount of electricity a bulb uses. **Lumen** is a measurement of the intensity of light coming from a source. One lumen is the amount of light produced by a source equaling the intensity of one standard candle. **Foot-candle** is a measure of how much light reaches an object. One foot-candle equals the amount of light a standard candle gives to an object one foot away. The amount of light needed or used can be measured with a light meter. Amounts of light needed for various activities are listed in 17-20.

As an example, if you plan to read a while, you need about 70 foot-candles of light over the reading area. A lamp with a 200-watt bulb can provide this amount of light when in the correct position. See 17-21.

## Lighting for Safety

Lighting for safety is very important. It can help prevent accidents and fires. Accidents can occur in dim and dark areas. To guard against accidents, plan lighting where it will work best for you. If you can answer "yes" to the following questions, you will know your lighting promotes safety. Can you

- light your way as you go from room to room?

- switch lights on or off from each doorway?

- turn on stairway lighting as you go up or down stairs?

- light entrances as you enter?

- control garage or carport lighting from the house?

- control outside lighting from inside the house?

Another aspect of lighting for safety concerns safe wiring. If wiring is unsafe, it can start fires in the home. To assure safety, the wiring used for lighting should meet standards set by various groups. For example, the National Electrical Code is a standard with which all wiring should comply. Often there are local requirements as well.

When you purchase electrical lighting fixtures, buy only those with a seal attached from a safety-testing organization such as Underwriters Laboratories (UL). See 17-22. The seal tells you that the light was manufactured according to safety standards. However, a safety seal does not guarantee that the parts

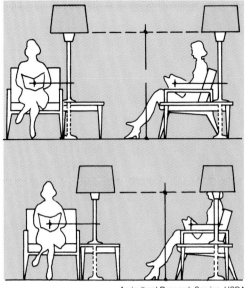

Agricultural Research Service, USDA

17-21 ————————————

*Lampshades above eye level should be farther behind you but closer to your side than lampshades at eye level.*

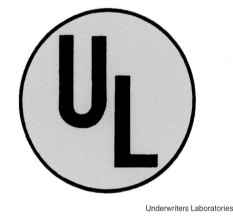

Underwriters Laboratories

17-22 ————————————

*A seal on a lamp showing UL or CSA assures you the lamp was made according to safety guidelines.*

will remain safe. You need to use lights safely and watch for possible dangers. Always read and follow the instructions for the use and care of the lights.

Electrical circuits should not be overloaded. Do not plug too many

Resource: *Lighting for Safety,* Activity D, SAG. Students indicate where light switches should be located for safety and identify statements that express good lighting plans.

Discuss: How can you prevent shadows with lighting? (*Prevent objects from going between you and the light source, watch the placement of lampshades, and make sure adequate light is available for diffusion.*)

Reflect: Have any accidents occurred at your home because of inadequate lighting? Was lighting part or all of the cause?

Discuss: Why is good outdoor lighting considered a safety issue? (*It helps prevent accidents and guards against crime.*)
Enrich: Talk with an electrician or visit Web sites to learn how electricians know what standards to meet as they wire buildings.

Enrich: Visit the Web site for the National Electrical Safety Foundation at *nesf.org* to learn how electrical safety results from the combined efforts of many companies and organizations in cooperation with the U.S. Consumer Product Safety Commission. Give a brief summary of the group's efforts and membership.

lights into one socket. The excess load could blow a fuse or trip a circuit breaker, leaving you without electric power in all or part of your home. Even worse, a fire could start.

## Lighting for Beauty

While all light can be decorative, some lighting is used for beauty alone. Soft light can create a quiet, restful mood. Sharp light can be used to highlight the focal point in a room. When lighting is used as a highlight, it is called *accent lighting*.

Photo courtesy of California Redwood Association

17-23

*Exterior lighting gives the redwood siding of this home a dramatic appearance.*

Decorative lighting can also be used outside the home, as in 17-23. Huge yard lights are often used in rural settings, while smaller ones are used in urban areas. Lights near entrances are also common. Patios can be lighted for night use. In such areas, the light should be attractive. Harsh and glaring light should be avoided. With the right choices, you can have pleasant, glowing light.

# Structural and Nonstructural Lighting

Lighting affects the appearance of a room. So does the means by which the light is delivered. The two ways of delivering light are through structural and nonstructural lighting.

## Structural Lighting

When a light fixture is permanently built in a home, it is called a *structural light fixture*. It is either included in the original plans or added during a remodeling project.

When you choose structural light fixtures, they should be in harmony with other aspects of the room's design. When choosing fixtures, consider the following points:

- Diffused light gives more visual comfort than exposed bulbs, which can produce glare.

- Fixtures that can change position are used in more than one way. Some fixtures may be raised or lowered. Others swing or swivel for a variety of effects.

- Fixtures that allow different light levels, such as three-way bulbs or dimmer switches, have more uses.

There are many types of structural lighting fixtures. Some are pictured in 17-24. *Valance lighting fixtures* are mounted over windows and hidden by the window valance. Since the window valance is open at the top and bottom, fluorescent light is directed upward and downward, giving both direct and indirect lighting. Valance lighting restores the daytime lighting balance to a room.

*Bracket lighting fixtures* are just like valance lighting fixtures, except they are used on walls or over work areas. Fluorescent light is directed both upward and downward. Bracket lighting can be used for general or accent lighting.

*Cornice lighting fixtures* are concealed sources of light that are mounted to the wall near the ceiling. Fluorescent light shines downward,

**Reflect:** Are any of the light fixtures in Figure 17-24 similar to something you have at home?

Wood-Mode, Inc.

Recessed wall washers

Wood-Mode, Inc.

Track lighting

The UltraCraft Co.

Cove and task lighting

The UltraCraft Co.

Combination of track, surface-mounted decorative, natural, and diffused natural lighting through glass bricks

17-24

*Structural lighting can create special effects in a room. It must be planned while the dwelling is being built or remodeled.*

**Math Activity:** Using a Web source such as *progresslighting.com/*, compare the cost of similar quality fixtures for each type of structural lighting discussed. List the prices from most expensive to least expensive.

**Art Activity:** Draw examples of each type of structural lighting fixture.

giving direct light only. Cornice lighting can be used on almost any wall for a variety of effects.

*Cove lighting fixtures* are also mounted near the ceiling. Fluorescent light is directed upward, giving indirect light only. Cove lighting is good general lighting, but it must be supplemented with local lighting. It also gives a room a feeling of height.

*Recessed downlights* are small, circular lights installed in the ceiling. When several are used together, they supply good general lighting. A few of them can be used for accent lighting. The typical scalloped pattern of light and shadow produced by recessed downlights gives a dramatic look to a wall.

*Surface-mounted downlights* are similar to recessed downlights. However, the housing cylinder or can is in plain view below the ceiling.

*Wall washers* are also installed in the ceiling. They have a contoured inner reflector that directs nearly uniform light on walls from ceiling to floor. This gives walls a smooth look.

*Soffit lighting fixtures* consist of an enclosed box attached to the ceiling. Often, a plastic panel at the bottom of the soffit box diffuses the light as it is directed downward. Soffit lighting is used where a large amount of local light is needed, such as over bathroom sinks.

*Luminous ceilings* are made of plastic panels that cover recessed fluorescent lights. They may cover part or all of a ceiling. They supply good general lighting and make a room feel spacious.

*Strip lighting* is a structure consisting of a strip of receptacles that hold a series of incandescent lightbulbs. It is often used around mirrors in a bathroom or dressing room to provide good task lighting.

*Track lighting* consists of several light fixtures mounted on a metal strip. The fixtures can be arranged in varying positions to shine in different directions and create different effects.

## Nonstructural Lighting

*Nonstructural lighting* is lighting that is not a structural part of the house. These lights can be moved, changed, and replaced more easily than any other form of lighting.

Lamps are the most common type of nonstructural lighting. They can be used for decorative purposes and to provide good lighting and safety. When choosing lamps, keep the following points in mind:

- A sturdy or heavy base prevents tipping.
- A diffusing bowl prevents glare.
- A harp makes it possible to change the height of the lampshade. A *harp* is a metal hoop or arch that supports a lampshade.
- The colors and textures of lamps and lampshades should harmonize.
- Light-colored, translucent lampshades give the most light.
- Lamps that can be adjusted are the most practical. Some can be raised and lowered, such as swag lamps. Some have swinging arms, and some use three-way bulbs.

Structural and nonstructural lighting can be combined in many different ways. See 17-25. The goal is always to achieve good lighting throughout the dwelling.

# Choosing Accessories

*Accessories* are items smaller than furnishings that accent the design of a room. An accessory should have a purpose in the room. It should not be used just to fill a space. Accessories can be used for decorative purposes or functional purposes. Some accessories serve both purposes. *Decorative accessories* add beauty to a room. Some

Activity: Working with a partner, look around your classroom and the school's library to identify nonstructural lighting sources.

Reflect: If windows were an attractive feature of a home and did not need window treatments for privacy, as is the case in Figure 17-25, would you add window treatments or not? Explain.

examples of decorative accessories are plants, floral arrangements, pictures, paintings, sculptures, wall hangings, and figurines. *Functional accessories* accent the room while serving another purpose. They may include such items as pillows, quilts, lamps, mirrors, books, bookends, candles, candlesticks, and clocks. Functional and decorative accessories are often used together. An example of an accessory that is both decorative and functional is a lampshade of a special design.

The accessories in your home reflect the personalities of the household members. They can show a preference for items such as pictures, clocks, antiques, or treasured objects from other countries or cultures. Some items may have sentimental value such as photographs, souvenirs, or trophies. Others may be parts of collections such as rare coins or antique porcelain plates.

Whether an accessory is chosen to be functional or decorative, it should blend with the style and period of the room. See 17-26. Sometimes an accessory may be useful, beautiful, or

American Lighting Association

17-25 _____

*Lamps, recessed downlights, and accent lighting provide artificial light for this room. A large window area provides natural light during the day.*

meaningful to you, but does not fit the purpose or scheme of the room. At that point, you should ask yourself if it really "belongs." If you feel that it brings a special statement of your individuality to the room, you may choose to include it.

**Reflect:** Locate the sources of the accent lighting evident in Figure 17-25.

Ethan Allen, Inc.

A

Ethan Allen, Inc.

B

Ethan Allen, Inc.

C

17-26 _____

*These lamps are good examples of accessories that are both functional and decorative. The styles shown are Modern (A), Contemporary (B), and Casual (C).*

**Discuss:** What categories of accessories exist? (*decorative, functional, and a blend of both*)
**Vocabulary:** Create a drawing of a lamp. Then, label each part and explain its purpose.

**Reflect:** Do you like to do homework using a favorite lamp? Identify the type and size of bulb it uses.

Ethan Allen, Inc.

A                                    B                                    C

17-27

*You can create different moods in a room by the accessories you choose. These accessories are examples of three different styles: Modern (A), Contemporary (B), and Casual (C).*

If an accessory detracts from the overall design of a room, you may decide that it should be placed some-where else in the home. For example, some people have a personal collec-tion of plaques, awarded for excel-lence in sports. This collection is obviously very important, but it does not fit the design of a formal living room. The plaques are more suited for display in a family or recreation room.

Accessories placed near one another should have something in common. The common factor may be color, texture, style, or purpose. This shared element will help tie the fur-nishings in the room together. See 17-27. Other decisions on the place-ment and arrangement of accessories are determined by applying the ele-ments and principles of design that you learned in previous chapters.

When you begin the process of acquiring and purchasing accessories, you will need to give thought to the price of the initial investment. You will need to set priorities concerning what you want and can afford. Accessories

that are both functional and decorative could be selected first. Also, consider accessories that are versatile and could be used in different rooms and spaces. Later, you may wish to start a collec-tion of accessories based more on their decorative value for a specific space, such as a collection of landscape pho-tographs to be used in a study or office.

In addition to cost, function, and versatility, you want to consider main-tenance of the accessories. A display of silver serving pieces may look lovely on a table in your dining room. How-ever, you must be certain that you want to dedicate the time it takes to dust, polish, and maintain the silver before you purchase such items.

Consideration also should be given to the replacement cost of the accessories. A collection of expensive, fragile, hand-painted figurines would not be a practical accessory to display within reach of small children. Such purchases should be stored safely out of reach. Otherwise, the investment should be postponed until the chil-dren are older.

# Summary

The finishing touches of furnishing a room are window treatments, lighting, and accessories. The style, size, and location of windows influence how they are treated. The amount of natural light you want to let in is also a factor. There is a variety of window treatments available. They include draperies, curtains, shades, shutters, and blinds. Decorative window-top treatments may be used in conjunction with most of these treatments. Window treatments can be made from a variety of fabrics and materials.

Artificial lighting is used to supplement natural light. You can choose between the two main types of artificial lighting—incandescent or fluorescent lighting. Each type has its advantages and disadvantages. Light can be used to achieve different effects. It can be used to create visual comfort through general and local lighting. As you work with light, you need to consider using it for safety and beauty.

Some lighting comes from structural fixtures, which are a part of the house. Other lighting comes from nonstructural items, which are separate from the house's structure. What you choose will depend on the type of lighting you need or desire.

Accessories are part of the design scheme. They can be decorative, functional, or a combination. They reflect the personality and lifestyle of the household. Successful placement and arrangement of accessories requires an understanding of the elements and principles of design.

**Activity:** Working with another student, alternate talking for 30 seconds apiece about what the chapter covered. Together, write a summary of the concepts in the chapter.

**Writing Activity:** Write each letter of the alphabet on separate lines of a sheet of paper and work independently to write one term from the chapter that begins with each alphabet letter. After three minutes, confer with a partner and fill in any blank lines. (If blanks still remain, discuss with the class some possible choices.)

# To Review

1. How do draperies differ from curtains?
2. Why are shutters and blinds appropriate for windows that are used for ventilation?
3. How do incandescent lights differ from fluorescent lights in terms of purchasing cost and operating cost?
4. List two energy-efficient types of lightbulbs.
5. List three properties of light, and give an example of each.
6. Why do homes need both general and local lighting?
7. List five structural light fixtures.
8. Explain the difference between functional and decorative accessories.
9. Why should accessories placed near one another have something in common?

**Answer Key**
1. Draperies are pleated panels of fabric. Curtains are flat fabric panels.
2. because they can easily be opened and still provide privacy and sunlight control
3. Incandescent lights are cheaper to install than fluorescent lights, but more costly to use.
4. E-lamp, compact fluorescent bulb
5. reflected light, absorbed light, diffused light (Examples are student response.)
6. to provide a low level of light to see objects clearly and maneuver safely as well as to provide higher levels of light to do tasks
7. (List five:) valance, bracket, cornice, cove, soffit, and track lighting; recessed and surface-mounted downlights; wall washers; luminous ceilings
8. Decorative accessories simply add beauty, but functional accessories add beauty and usefulness.
9. to help tie the furnishings together

## In Your Community

1. Identify the various types of window treatments used in your home and/or school. What function does each serve? Do the window treatments control light? provide privacy? provide insulation? Are they purely decorative, or both functional and decorative?

2. Take a tour of your school building and grounds. Determine which areas have lighting that is adequate for safety. Identify specific areas that you feel have inadequate lighting. What solutions would you recommend to improve the lighting for safety?

3. Research your local electrical wiring requirements. Find out who is responsible for inspection. What problems would you anticipate if there were no requirements or inspections?

4. Visit a local store that sells an assortment of home accessories. Make a list of the accessories you would buy if you had a budget of $200.00. Consider your lifestyle and interests as you make your selections. Would all of these accessories work together in the same room? If not, which rooms would you use them in? Now, assume that your budget has been cut in half and you have only $100.00 to spend. Which accessories would you eliminate and which would you keep?

## To Think About

1. Imagine you have just signed a lease for an apartment on the third floor of a five-story building, across a noisy street from a same-size apartment building. Suppose that all your windows face the street. Determine the types of window treatments you would select and prioritize a buying plan. Your new apartment has the following windows:
   - bedroom—large double-hung window
   - bathroom—small awning window
   - kitchen—jalousie window over the sink
   - living room—sliding patio doors leading to a balcony

2. Analyze one of the rooms in your home, and identify which surfaces reflect light and which absorb it. Under what circumstances is the reflected light helpful? When does it create problems? How does the light that is absorbed affect the look of the room?

# Using Technology

1. Search the Internet for companies that sell window treatments and observe their latest products. Find three types of window coverings or treatments that offer new designs, materials, or features. (You may need to search more than one company.) Make printouts of the products and bring them to class. Give a brief presentation, explaining each new product and reporting their price ranges.

2. Examine light from several different sources and compare them to sunlight. Obtain the following types of lighting: frosted bulb, colored bulb, cool-white fluorescent tube, warm-white fluorescent tube, halogen bulb, and fiber optic lighting. Shine all lights on a white surface, then on a colored surface, and observe the effects of each. Also, examine the effect of natural sunlight on the surfaces. Using a computer program, create a chart to display your findings. Share your information with the class.

**Portfolio Project:** Working from the floor plan prepared in Chapter 16's portfolio project, write or draw your recommendations for structural and nonstructural lighting. Explain the reasons for your selections.

CHAPTER 18

# Selecting Household Appliances

## To Know

appliance
EnergyGuide label
Energy Star label
ground fault circuit interrupter (GFCI)
warranty
full warranty
limited warranty
induction cooktop
self-cleaning oven
convection oven
microwave oven
horizontal-axis washer
dehumidifier
humidifier
software
hardware

Magic Chef Company

## Objectives

After studying this chapter, you will be able to

- list factors to consider when selecting household appliances.

- describe styles and features of various kitchen, laundry, and climate control appliances.

- choose household appliances to fit your needs.

**Resource:** *The Inside Story,* transparency master overlay IV-C, TR. Students look back at the topics covered in Chapters 1-17 by reviewing transparency master IV-A with overlays IV-B and IV-C. Overlay IV-C also shows the appliance topics they will cover in Chapter 18.

**Reflect:** How will the objectives of this chapter benefit you? What do you need to know about selecting household appliances?
**Vocabulary:** Working in pairs, write crossword puzzle hints for at least 10 terms in the "To Know" list as you go through the chapter.

Using a crossword puzzle computer program, create a crossword puzzle with the terms. Exchange puzzles with another student team and solve the new puzzle.

$M$aking a home attractive is only part of the inside story. To meet personal needs and priorities, a home must also be functional. Appliances greatly increase the usefulness of various areas in the home.

*Appliances* are household devices powered by gas or electricity. Large appliances, such as refrigerators and ranges, are called major appliances. Smaller appliances, such as toasters and hair dryers, are often called portable appliances. Appliances play a significant role in the kitchen and laundry room. They are also used in other areas throughout the home. Appliances help people meet their basic needs. Choosing appliances carefully can help create a home environment that is safe, comfortable, and efficient.

# Appliance Considerations

Most major appliances can be expected to last 10 years or more. When buying appliances, therefore, consider your future needs as well as your present needs. Will your household be expanding or compacting in the next decade? Will you be moving at some point? If you move, will you want to take your appliances with you?

Major appliances account for a large part of a housing budget. This is especially true when you completely equip a home, as in 18-1. If you rent a home that has appliances in it, part of your rent goes toward the cost of appliance maintenance. Because appliances are so costly, you need to consider their purchase carefully. Purchase and operating costs, features, size, safety, and quality are among the factors you should consider.

Laura B. Trujillo, ASID, Illinois Chapter

18-1

*A fully equipped kitchen is a convenient, but costly, part of housing.*

## Purchase Price

When considering a major appliance purchase, you must ask yourself if the appliance fits your budget. The cost of appliances can vary greatly from brand to brand and from model to model. Larger appliances with many features will cost more than smaller, more basic models. Prices also vary from one retailer to another. Consequently, smart consumers shop around and compare prices.

The purchase price of an appliance is only part of its true cost. When shopping, you should inquire about delivery and installation charges, and extra fees for hauling the old appliance away. If you pay for an appliance on an installment plan, you will also pay a finance charge.

## Energy Cost

Energy costs are another part of the expense of major appliances. Look for an *EnergyGuide label*, which states the average yearly energy use and operating cost of an appliance. These labels are required on new refrigerators, refrigerator-freezers, freezers, dishwashers, clothes washers, and water heaters. Room air conditioners and furnaces have an energy efficiency rating versus a label.

EnergyGuide labels enable you to compare average cost estimates for similar appliances, 18-2. This helps you determine which appliances are the most *energy efficient*, or use the least amount of energy. Of course, those that use the least energy are the least costly to operate.

In the past, purchase price was the only cost consideration when buying appliances. Today, however, the wise consumer also considers long-term operating costs. Purchase price plus operating cost reveals the true lifetime cost of an appliance.

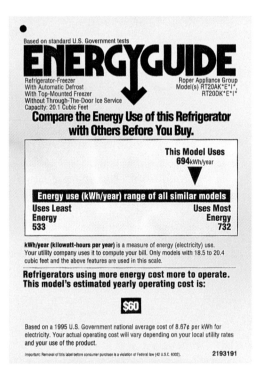

18-2

*EnergyGuide labels allow consumers to compare the average yearly energy costs of similar major appliances.*

To roughly estimate the cost of 10 years of operation, for example, multiply the operating cost figure on the EnergyGuide label by 10. You will notice that the inexpensive, "no-frills" appliances usually cost the most to operate. This means the money you save in purchase price may eventually be used to pay the extra energy costs needed over their lifetime.

You may find that an expensive appliance, with all the features you want, will cost less over time than a much cheaper model. A more expensive model will probably last longer, too. Of course, buying an energy-efficient appliance on sale represents even more savings. When buying appliances for the long term, therefore, consider both purchase price and operating costs.

When considering the energy usage of appliances, two labels are helpful to you as a consumer. The EnergyGuide label and the Energy Star label offer different information. An *Energy Star label* indicates that a product is at least 10 percent more energy efficient than similar products. The U.S. Environmental Protection Agency (EPA) and U.S. Department of Energy (DOE) sponsor the Energy Star program.

The Energy Star label makes it easy to identify energy-efficient products without sacrificing features, quality, or personal comfort. The label can be found on products in 30 different categories, including appliances, electronics, office equipment, lighting, heating and cooling equipment, windows, and even new homes. See 18-3. Consumers can save money monthly on their utility bills by choosing Energy Star products.

Clothes washers with the Energy Star label, for example, are at least 50 percent more efficient than minimum government standards. Dishwashers

SAVING THE EARTH. SAVING YOUR MONEY.

**18-3**

*The Energy Star label assures the consumer that the appliance is one of the most energy efficient models on the market.*

are 25 percent more efficient than the standards. Using products with Energy Star label not only saves you money in operating costs, but also promotes effective use of the environment. Effective environmental use focuses on reducing water use, promoting cleaner air, and using construction materials wisely.

## Features

Appliances are available with a wide range of features. Careful planning will help you choose the features that best meet your needs. When shopping, ask yourself some of the following questions: Is it available in the color you want? Will it coordinate with the other furnishings and appliances in the room? A particular design trend for consumer kitchens in recent years is the look of a "commercial kitchen." For appliances, this means selecting models with a stainless steel finish. See 18-4.

When deciding what appliance features you need, consider the people who will use it. Is the appliance easy to use? Does it perform all the tasks you want handled? Does it have extra features that will not be used? Extras add to the price.

Does anyone in your household have special needs? For instance,

Photo courtesy of Sub-Zero

**18-4**

*The sleek look of stainless steel is apparent in the background refrigerator and the two refrigerator drawers built into the island in the foreground.*

people in wheelchairs cannot reach as high or as far as others. Front-mounted controls would be ideal for these appliance buyers. People with difficulty grasping or turning knobs, for example, may find electronic touch pads easier to use.

After deciding which appliance features are needs, not just wants, consider the possibility of buying the extras at a later date. For example, you can buy a refrigerator-freezer and oven now, and get the icemaker and rotisserie unit later.

## Size

Size is another consideration when purchasing a major appliance. How large should the appliance be to meet the needs of your household? How many people will be using the appliance now and in the future? Do you need a large or extra-large model, or something more compact? Will the appliance fit the space planned for it? Does it fit through doorways and hallways?

## Safety

When purchasing a new appliance from a reputable dealer, you can be sure that it meets current safety standards. Flea markets, on the other hand, are common sites where appliances not meeting safety standards are sold. A bargain appliance with an unfamiliar brand name may mean that the appliance does not meet safety standards. The common safety symbols show the following marks:

- *UL* from Underwriter's Laboratory
- *ETL* from ETL SEMCO, a division of Intertek Testing Services Ltd.
- *CSA* from the Canadian Standards Association

Usually the first page of any installation or instruction guide addresses appliance safety. Look for a seal certifying that the appliance conforms to safety standards. Seals may be found on the back of major appliances and in their use and care material. On small electrical appliances, the seal is usually attached to the electric cord.

In addition, a ground fault circuit interrupter is being added to the cords on some small appliances for safety. A *ground fault circuit interrupter (GFCI)* is a safety device used in outlets or added to electrical cords to prevent shocks. It interrupts the unintentional flow of electricity to avoid shock, burns, and possible fatalities in the home. You'll learn more about GFCI in Chapter 20, "Keeping Your Home Safe and Secure."

Safety standards are developed through the joint efforts of many concerned organizations and individuals. Appliance manufacturers, safety-testing organizations, and the U.S. Consumer Product and Safety Commission lead the effort. Safety standards exist for each appliance category and undergo periodic review.

At home, appliance safety depends primarily on proper installation and use. See 18-5. The literature that accompanies the appliance identifies these requirements. Make sure you have the correct electrical or gas connections. A 120-volt, major electrical appliance should have a three-prong plug. The third (round) prong grounds the appliance. If a grounded appliance

Sharp Electronics Corporation

18-5

*An important safety issue with microwave ovens is using the right model for over-the-range installation. This model is designed specifically for that purpose.*

has damaged wiring, electric current will flow to the ground rather than through your body. The grounding prong, therefore, prevents electrical shock and should not be removed. Also, avoid overloading circuits by making sure your home has adequate electrical service for the appliance before it is installed.

Some appliances provide additional safety in the form of extra features. For example, some ranges provide childproof control locks, which prevent children from turning on the oven or burners. Some consumers regard such extra safety features as a need.

## Quality

The quality of an appliance is a key purchase consideration. Appliances that require frequent repairs are costly and troublesome to operate. You want appliances that will work dependably for many years.

Asking a few questions may help you evaluate quality. Is the appliance well constructed? Is it from a reputable manufacturer? Is the instruction book thorough and easy to understand? Is after-sale service offered?

Assessing quality also involves reading the warranty. A *warranty* is a manufacturer's written promise that a product will perform as described. A warranty may be full or limited. Under a *full warranty*, you may have the item repaired or replaced free of charge at the warrantor's option. Under a *limited warranty*, you can be charged for repairs. You may also be responsible for shipping the item back to the warrantor or taking other steps to get repairs.

When reading a warranty, be sure to find out how long the warranty lasts and what is covered—the entire product or only certain parts. Are labor fees included?

In addition to the full and limited warranties, one option to consider is the extended warranty. For an extra fee, you as a consumer can add several years to the manufacturer's warranty. Some home magazines also offer appliance warranties.

Resource: *Choosing Major Appliances*, Activity A, SAG. Students create an appliance checklist, select a pictured appliance, and evaluate it according to the checklist.

# Consumer Satisfaction

Satisfaction with your appliances will depend largely on the choices you make as a consumer. However, appliance manufacturers and retailers will also affect your satisfaction.

As a consumer, you have a responsibility to be informed about the appliances you buy. See 18-6. You need to know the various options that are available. These should be matched to the needs and desires of the people in

The Home Depot

18-6
*When consumers shop for appliances, they should be prepared to ask many questions.*

Vocabulary: Which would you prefer to receive with the purchase of a new appliance: a limited or full warranty? Explain why by contrasting the two types.

Discuss: What experiences have you or your family had with dissatisfaction over an appliance purchase? How did the retail business handle it? (This can be a cooperative learning discussion for teams or a class discussion question.)

Discuss: What do you think are essential appliances for a kitchen? Consider both large and portable appliances.

your household. You need to determine the amount of money you can afford to spend on an appliance. You will want to ask about warranties and service. You should read and understand use and care information before operating an appliance. Fulfilling these responsibilities will help improve your satisfaction with your appliances.

Manufacturers have a goal of preserving their reputation and keeping customers happy. When appliance buyers are content with their purchases, they become repeat buyers. Unsatisfied customers and returned merchandise can put a manufacturer out of business.

To assure your satisfaction, manufacturers strive to make appliances safe, dependable, and affordable. They provide a variety of models that meet varying consumer needs and preferences. Appliances generally conform to performance standards set by the American National Standards Institute (ANSI). Manufacturers give warranties and detailed instructions about the use of their appliances. Sometimes this information is made available on

free videotapes or CD-ROMs. Most manufacturers also offer free cookbooks, toll-free phone numbers, and helpful Web sites for more information about their products and how to use them.

The success of retail appliance businesses also relies on customer satisfaction. To meet the various needs of different consumers, retailers provide a selection of models. Responsible retailers train their salespeople to clearly explain the features of all models. Most retailers deliver and install appliances, and offer maintenance service, too. Some retailers give free classes and demonstrations. Reputable retailers serve as a go-between for you with the manufacturer to make sure the conditions of the warranty are met.

## Choosing Kitchen Appliances

Kitchen appliances are used for all aspects of food storage, preparation, and cleanup. See 18-7. The purchase

Magic Chef Company

18-7

*The tasks of storing food, cooking meals, and washing dishes are all made easier with the help of appliances.*

Reflect: Are there certain stores that your family avoids because of an unpleasant experience someone had?

Discuss: If you owned a business that sold goods or services to the public, what would you do to try to keep customers satisfied? Can all customers be satisfied?

considerations already discussed pertain to all these appliances. Use the following information to help select appliances wisely.

# Refrigerators

Refrigerators are a necessity for storing fresh foods. Perhaps that is why at least one refrigerator is used in nearly every home in the United States.

## Styles

Refrigerators are available in a few basic styles. A *one-door refrigerator* does not have a freezer. Instead, it has a frozen-food storage compartment. This compartment is colder than the rest of the refrigerator, but its use is limited. It is not designed to freeze foods. It provides only short-term storage for commercially frozen foods and keeps ice cubes.

A variation of the one-door refrigerator is the *compact refrigerator*. It is suitable for rooms in college residence halls, hotel rooms, and small apartments. It can be purchased or rented at a fairly low price. Compact models may be capable of freezing ice cubes, but they are not suitable for storing frozen foods.

Most refrigerators made today are *two-door refrigerator-freezers*. These models have a separate freezer section that freezes food. The temperature in the freezer section remains at about 0°F. The freezer section may be above, below, or at the side of the refrigerator. See 18-8.

The consumer can choose a built-in refrigerator or buy a refrigerator that can add panels to give a built-in look. A new option in refrigerators is a refrigerator drawer that saves floor space. It is installed in place of a cabinet and is convenient for small kitchens or efficiency apartments.

## Features

Refrigerators and refrigerator-freezers are generally sold in several basic colors to fit the wide range of decorating schemes. Special features include individual compartments for meat, produce, and dairy products with separate temperature controls. Adjustable shelves allow you to easily store large items. Another option is a reversible door that hinges on either side of the refrigerator. Being able to change the location of the hinges can allow better access to adjacent counter space. A reversible door is particularly helpful when a refrigerator may be

**Resource:** *Refrigerators,* Activity B, SAG. Students compare the features of four models of refrigerators.
**Enrich:** Using local newspapers, compare prices and features of refrigerators being sold in your area. Write a description of the refrigerator you want for your first home.

Whirlpool Home Appliances

18-8 _____

*Some refrigerator-freezer owners prefer having the refrigerator section on top and the less-used freezer at the bottom.*

**Enrich:** Find out how food was preserved before the era of refrigeration. When was food refrigeration perfected? Who developed the commercial freezing process?
**Discuss:** In your opinion, what are some advantages of having the refrigerator section above the freezer? What are some disadvantages?
**Enrich:** Find out whether top-mount refrigerator units, as shown in Figure 18-8, use more or less electricity than same-size models with the freezer unit on top. How wide is the difference in their energy use?

**Vocabulary:** Write a description of each of the three types of defrosting options available in today's refrigerators.
**Internet Activity:** Find a Web site that reports all the models of refrigerators available for sale and their cubic-foot size. Which size categories include the greatest number of models? What size is the smallest refrigerator? the largest? Report the address of the Web site you found.

moved to a new residence that may present different traffic patterns. Ice and water dispensers also are features that many people want.

The refrigerator's defrost system is a feature you will want to consider. In general, one-door models often require *manual defrosting*. This means that frost accumulates inside the refrigerator, reducing the efficiency of the appliance. When the frost becomes ¼-inch thick, the appliance must be turned off so the frost can melt. This usually requires emptying the appliance and drying the compartments before turning it on again.

Refrigerator-freezers may have either partial or full automatic defrosting. *Partial automatic defrosting* models do not accumulate frost in the refrigerator compartment. However, the freezer compartment must be defrosted manually. In *full automatic defrosting* models, no frost accumulates. These frostfree models are convenient, but they cost more. They also use more electricity.

Your storage space requirement is another important consideration. Space inside a refrigerator is measured in cubic feet. An 18-cubic-foot refrigerator-freezer may be the ideal size for a family that shops frequently or eats out often. On the other hand, the same appliance may be too small for a family that shops less frequently or buys food in bulk.

The amount of refrigerator versus freezer space you need is another important consideration. All 18-cubic-foot models, for example, do not have same-size refrigerator and freezer sections. Make sure both compartments provide the space you need. Check the interior dimensions and the size of the shelves. Will they accommodate the items you store? A range of sizes is available to meet the needs of various households.

Another consideration is the amount of kitchen space available for a refrigerator. Measure the height, width, and depth of the space you have. Take the measurements with you when you shop. A checklist for buying refrigerators is shown in 18-9.

| Checklist for Refrigerators |
|---|
| ___ Does the refrigerator require defrosting? |
| ___ Are interior and door shelves adjustable for more flexible use of space? |
| ___ Is space available for heavy and tall bottles? |
| ___ Is the interior well lighted? |
| ___ Is the refrigerator interior easy to clean? |
| ___ Are shelves made of strong, noncorroding, rust-resistant materials such as glass? |
| ___ Are all interior parts easily removable and/or accessible for cleaning? |
| ___ Is the fresh food section easy to reach, use, clean, and organize? |
| ___ Are door shelf retaining bars strong and securely attached? |
| ___ Is crisper space adequate? Is it designed to keep moisture inside? |
| ___ Is the freezer section easy to reach, use, clean, and organize? |
| ___ Is the refrigerator easy to move for cleaning? |
| ___ Does the refrigerator have a switch to turn off the anti-condensation heaters when not needed (that is, when there is no humid air to condense around the door)? |
| ___ Is the refrigerator's energy consumption, as shown on the EnergyGuide label, reasonable for its size and features? |

18-9 _____
*Consider these points before choosing a refrigerator.*

**Activity:** Examine your home refrigerator's temperature control and make a drawing. Do this by referring to your refrigerator's use and care guide or, if it's unavailable, look quickly into your refrigerator. Explain where your refrigerator's control is located and how to adjust temperature.

**Writing Activity:** Interview the person in your home who uses the refrigerator most often and find out what features he or she thinks are important in a refrigerator. You may use Figure 18-9 as a questionnaire. Write a summary of the refrigerator described and try to find one in the local ads.

# Freezers

When more freezer space is needed, you may want to buy a separate freezer. The size you need depends on how you will use it. Will it simply provide backup storage or will extra freezer space be needed regularly? People who preserve home-grown fruits and vegetables, buy food in bulk quantities, or freeze make-ahead meals usually need more freezer space.

## Styles

The two styles of freezers are chest and upright. Large, bulky packages are easier to store in a chest model, as in 18-10. Chest freezers use less electricity because less cold air escapes when the door is opened. One disadvantage of chest freezers is that they require more floor space. Another is that food must be lifted when it is removed. Chest freezers are defrosted manually.

Food is easier to see and remove in an upright freezer. Only a small amount of floor space is needed, but upright freezers cost more to operate.

You can choose an upright freezer with either a *manual defrost* or a *full automatic defrost* system. Full automatic defrost models are convenient, but purchase price and operating costs are higher. A checklist for freezers is shown in 18-11.

# Ranges

Many changes have been made in ranges. These changes have been due to advances in technology and growing concern about energy conservation. You will have several factors to consider when choosing a range.

Your first decision concerns fuel. Your choice of either electricity or gas

Whirlpool Home Appliances

18-10

*Chest freezers provide energy-efficient storage space for frozen foods.*

| Checklist for Freezers |
|---|
| ___ Will model fit your floor space and weight limitations? |
| ___ Will the type of door opening be convenient in its location? |
| ___ Are shelves and/or baskets adjustable? |
| ___ Are all sections readily accessible? |
| ___ Is the interior well lighted? |
| ___ Does it have a safety signal light to let you know that power is on? |
| ___ Is the freezer frostless? If not, does it have a fast-defrost system? |
| ___ Does it have easy-to-read and accessible controls? |
| ___ Does it have magnetic gaskets to seal cold air in more completely? |

**Reflect:** Do you know anyone who owns a freezer separate from the refrigerator? How do they use it?

18-11

*Consider these points before choosing a food freezer.*

**Enrich:** Research the latest trends in refrigerators and freezers by visiting a Web site such as *subzero.com* and examining news about the latest products.

**Vocabulary:** Create a list of words and phrases that are used to mean *range* in the "appliance" sense of the word.

**Discuss:** Which type of cooktop on an electric range provides the instant heat associated with gas ranges? (*glass-ceramic cooktop with halogen cartridges*)

**Note:** The ability to instantly turn heat on and off and adjust heat levels is the main reason that restaurants and chefs prefer gas ranges.

depends on the availability and cost of each as well as personal preference.

### Electric Ranges

Electric ranges offer several styles of cooking surfaces. The *conventional coil* cooktop has wires encased in coils. The electric current flows through the coils to produce heat, and the heat is transferred to cookware by conduction and radiation.

Some electric ranges feature a smooth *glass-ceramic* cooktop, which makes the range easy to clean. This surface may hide radiant coils, or *halogen cartridges* which provide

18-12
*Halogen cartridges use electricity but provide the instant heat of gas cooking.*

instant infrared heat. See 18-12. The heat travels mainly by radiation to the surface then by conduction or radiation to the cookware.

***Induction cooktops*** use a magnetic field to generate heat in the bottom of cooking utensils. Cookware must be magnetic. Cast iron or steel works well because they offer resistance to the passage of the magnetic waves, which generates heat. Heat from the cookware is then transferred to the food. No heat is created in the range surface. Cleanup is easy because spills do not burn and the coils are beneath a glass-ceramic surface.

### Gas Ranges

The combustion process between gas and oxygen in the air produces the heat in gas ranges. Regulating the flow of gas through a valve controls the heat. More gas causes a higher flame and hotter temperatures. In the past, a pilot light had to be lighted to use the burner. Currently, electronic ignitions are required on all new ranges powered by natural gas, except compact models for vacation homes.

Gas ranges are available with two types of burners—conventional and sealed. *Conventional burners* do not fit snugly into the cooktop, so spills can leak under the burners to cause a mess. No opening exists between *sealed burners* and the cooktop surface, which makes cleanup easier. The energy usage of gas burners is measured in British thermal units (Btu).

### Styles

Ranges come in several styles and sizes. Your choice depends on the capacity you need and the space you have. *Freestanding* models are the most common, with many size, color, and feature options. The oven is below the cooking surface. It may stand alone or

**Discuss:** Does your range at home use gas or electricity? Have you ever used a range that operates on a different type of fuel? Did you like it more or less than your range at home? Explain.

**Enrich:** Visit a large appliance store or research ranges on the Internet to learn the current trends in this appliance. Find out what types of technology are affecting the trends.

be placed between cabinets for a built-in look. See 18-13.

*Slide-in* and drop-in models either slide into a space or rest on a base cabinet. They fit snugly between kitchen cabinets and counters. Chrome strips are often used to cover the side edges and provide a built-in look.

*Built-in* models provide cooking surfaces separate from the oven. This allows flexible kitchen arrangements. The surface units are installed in a countertop, often a kitchen island. The oven is installed in a wall or custom-made cabinet. Some built-in ovens are double ovens. Many built-ins are single ovens installed above or below a microwave oven and/or a warming drawer. A *warming drawer* is used to keep hot food warm until serving time. Also, it warms-up dinner plates and serving pieces. Some warming drawers have humidity controls to keep selected foods moist. See 18-14.

## Features

Many consumers desire a self-cleaning feature for the oven. **Self-cleaning ovens** operate at extremely high temperatures to burn spatters and spills away. What remains is a small amount of ash that can easily be wiped away. Because very high temperatures are reached during cleaning, these ovens have extra insulation. This helps to save energy during normal baking periods. The self-cleaning feature adds to the price of the range, but the cost of operating the cleaning cycle is less than the cost of chemical oven cleaners. Generally, three to four kilowatt-hours of electricity are used during the self-cleaning cycle.

Another oven-cleaning option is the continuous-cleaning oven. *Continuous-cleaning ovens* have a special coating on the oven walls. Food spatters are oxidized gradually over a period of time during the normal baking process.

Photo courtesy of Sub-Zero/Wolf

18-13 ⎯⎯⎯⎯⎯⎯⎯⎯⎯
*This quality freestanding range becomes a focal point in the kitchen. Note that the refrigerator in the background has panels on the front to match the cabinets.*

Photo courtesy of Wolf Appliance

18-14 ⎯⎯⎯⎯⎯⎯⎯⎯⎯
*A warming drawer is an ideal appliance for someone who does a lot of baking or cooking.*

**Discuss:** Why is a self-cleaning oven an advantage even when the cleaning cycle is not being used? (*The extra insulation helps to save energy during normal baking.*)

**Art Activity:** Draw and label pictures that differentiate the three styles of ranges: freestanding, slide-in, and built-in.

Activity: Develop a plan for the purchase of a range to fit the needs of your first apartment or home. Which of the features listed in Figure 18-16 will you need? Why?

Models with this feature cost less than those with self-cleaning ovens. However, some owners are less satisfied with these because spatters and spills are not removed quickly. Also, continuous-cleaning ovens do not have extra insulation.

A surface-cooking option to consider is the ceramic cooktop. These cooktops have dual elements as well as warm and serve zones on the surface. Some ranges have thermostatically controlled surface units. Others have modular surface units that can be interchanged with a grill, griddle, or wok. See 18-15.

Other range features to consider include clocks, timers, and programmed cooking cycles. Delay and time-bake cycles allow you to start and stop the cooking process while away. Super hot ovens are a new type of oven available on electric models.

Although expensive, they rival the speed of microwave ovens while providing browning and crisping. Halogen lights and/or forced air create the intense heat that penetrates the food and cooks it rapidly. Study the checklist for ranges in 18-16.

## Convection Ovens

*Convection ovens* bake foods in a stream of heated air. Because heated air is continually forced directly onto the food, it browns and cooks faster at lower temperatures. Convection ovens require about two-thirds the time and half the energy of conventional cooking.

Separate convection ovens are available as built-in appliances or countertop models. Also, combination conventional/convection ovens are available. In the combination models,

Jenn-Air

18-15
*The modular surface units in this cooktop have been replaced with a grill.*

| Checklist for Ranges |
| --- |
| ___ Is the range suitable for cooking needs and kitchen space? |
| ___ Are cooktop burners or units an adequate size for the pans you will use? |
| ___ Is oven capacity adequate to meet regular cooking needs? |
| ___ Are controls placed for convenient and safe use? |
| ___ Are control settings and numbers easy to read? |
| ___ Is the range designed to simplify cleaning? Does it have a smooth backguard, an absence of grooves and crevices, removable burners or units, and a self-cleaning oven? |
| ___ Does the range offer features that are important to family needs and use? |

18-16
*Consider these points before choosing a range.*

Writing Activity: Write a short essay defending the features you prefer in a range. Look at printed materials or the Internet to get current prices to quote.

Enrich: Attend a presentation by a guest from the local electric company who discusses the energy cost of using different types of cooking appliances. Be prepared to ask questions. Summarize in one paragraph what you learned.

the cooking mode (conventional or convection) depends on whether the fan is on or off.

## Microwave Ovens

*Microwave ovens* cook food with high-frequency energy waves called *microwaves*. These appliances can cook, defrost, and reheat foods in a fraction of the time required for conventional ovens. Microwave cooking can also save up to 75 percent of the energy used by conventional ovens, depending on the type and amount of food cooked.

As food absorbs microwaves, the molecules within the food vibrate against one another. The friction produced creates the heat that cooks the food.

The time required to cook foods depends on the type of food it is and the power level used. Most microwave ovens have at least 10 power levels. Low power levels are needed for cooking protein foods, such as eggs, cheese, and meats, and for thickening sauces. Medium and high power levels can be used for most other foods.

Ovenproof glass, paper, and some plastics can be used as cooking containers because microwaves pass through them. Metal containers reflect microwaves, so heat is not created in the food.

### Styles

Several styles of microwave ovens are available. Countertop models are the most popular and offer the greatest choices of features. They can be placed on a countertop, table, or cart. See 18-17. Many sizes of microwave ovens are available, including very small models. Wattages on the ovens also vary.

Microwave ovens with ventilation hoods are attached to the wall and

cabinet above a range. These models are similar to countertop models. However, they may have less capacity. See 18-18.

Whirlpool Home Appliances

18-17 ———
*Countertop models of microwave ovens can be placed on carts, countertops, and tables.*

Mill's Pride

18-18 ———
*Microwave ovens built for over-the-range installation have vent systems, too.*

Reflect: Will a microwave be an adequate method of food preparation in your first apartment or home? If not, what other cooking appliances will you need?

Enrich: Find out whether range hoods or downdraft ventilation is required of local homebuilders in your community.

A microwave feature is sometimes built into convection ovens. The convection and microwave modes can be used alone or together in a cooking cycle.

## Features

Features available on microwave ovens include automatic programming, automatic settings, browning elements, temperature probes, and turntables.

A microwave oven with *automatic programming* automatically shifts power levels at preset times. This feature allows you to program the oven to do several operations in sequence. For instance, you can set this oven to defrost a food product, cook it, and then keep it warm. Pretimed settings, as for popping popcorn, are available on many microwave oven models.

*Automatic settings* are available on some microwave ovens. These settings determine cooking times and correct power levels for you. You just set the controls for the type and amount of food, and the oven does the rest.

*Browning elements* are electric heating coils on the top of some ovens. They add browning and crispness to food following microwave cooking.

A *temperature probe*, sometimes called a food sensor, helps you control cooking. It automatically turns off the oven or switches to a warm setting when food reaches a preset temperature. A checklist for microwave ovens is shown in 18-19.

## Range Hoods

Hoods are used over cooking appliances to help vent heat, moisture, grease, and odors from the kitchen. Hoods can be vented to the outside. Unvented models use a special screen and charcoal filter to collect odors and grease.

### Checklist for Microwave Ovens

____ Is the oven cavity the right size and shape for your needs?

____ Does it have the power settings and pretimed buttons you need?

____ Is there a signal when the microwave oven finishes cooking and shuts off?

____ Does it have a timer? If so, does the timer have enough minutes to allow you the flexibility you need?

____ Are the controls mechanical (knobs and push buttons) or electronic (touchpads)?

____ Are the controls easy to understand?

____ Does a cookbook come with the microwave oven?

18-19
*Consider these points before choosing a microwave oven.*

An alternative to a hood is a *downdraft ventilation* system. Fumes are pulled down by a fan located below the cooktop. The downdraft should be vented to the outside.

Quieter operation of the exhaust fans come with some of today's range hoods. You can also find remote fans so that the fan is not in the hood itself, but outside the house.

Many new style and size hoods are available. Some are designed to be a focal point of the kitchen and make a design statement.

## Dishwashers

A dishwasher can save the homeowner time, energy, and water. It also has the ability to clean dishes better than hand washing. It uses hotter water and stronger detergents. Also, dishes dry without being wiped with towels that may carry germs.

Note: For extensive information on how microwaves work, use the Web site *howstuffworks.com/microwave.htm*.

Activity: Make a list of all the appliances—major and portable—that your family owns to "cook" food in the broadest sense of that term. For example, a toaster, electric fry pan, and waffle maker would all be listed.

Most dishwashers are *built-in* styles, and many others are *portable/convertible* models. They are on casters, so they can be moved easily from storage to the sink. With casters removed, this model can be converted to a built-in. Other types include dishwasher drawers, as shown in 18-20, and compact countertop models.

### Features

Dishwashers often feature a variety of cycles to meet various cleaning needs. For instance, some models have special cycles for scrubbing pans, sterilizing baby bottles, or washing fine china. An adjustable upper rack makes it possible to wash large or odd-sized items. Small-item baskets, a continuous bottom rack for more capacity, and adjustable shelves and rack tines add convenience. Other features include top-rack only wash, hidden controls and heating elements, a preheater to heat water to the ideal temperature, a food disposer to eliminate food particles, and quite operation.

Many models offer energy-saving features, such as a nonheating cycle. This can save up to one-third the electricity used in a normal drying cycle, but dishes may not dry completely. See the checklist in 18-21 before choosing a dishwasher.

## Trash Compactors

Trash compactors compress household trash to a fraction of its original volume. The trash is placed into heavy-duty plastic bags or special paper bags lined with plastic. Compactors are available as freestanding and built-in models.

Trash compactors handle almost any kind of nonfood trash, including bottles, cans, and plastic containers. Some compactors feature separate compartments to help you separate

Photo courtesy of Fisher & Paykel

18-20

*This two-drawer design for a dishwasher allows faster cleaning of small loads of dishes.*

| Checklist for Dishwasher |
| --- |
| ___ Are the tub and door linings durable and stain resistant? |
| ___ Does the wash system have two or more levels? (A single system takes considerable loading care to get all the dishes clean.) |
| ___ Will it hold at least 10 place settings? Do your favorite pots and pans fit? |
| ___ Does it offer more than one cycle, such as rinse/hold or prerinse cycles? |
| ___ Is an automatic wetting agent dispenser provided? |
| ___ Is the dishwasher insulated to eliminate excessive noise and heat? |
| ___ Does it have an energy saver switch to turn the heating element partially or completely off during some cycles? |

18-21

*Consider these points before selecting a new dishwasher.*

**Discuss:** In your opinion, what are some reasons for household reluctance to buying dishwashers?
**Discuss:** What is the purpose of a trash compactor? (*to reduce the space taken by non-food trash*)

**Activity:** If you have a dishwasher at home, list the features it has. Which of these are used regularly? Would buying a model minus the unused features have saved a significant amount of money? Did you need to purchase a model with those features in order to get an energy-efficient model? Discuss the purchase with a parent.

**Enrich:** Research the difference between chute-fed and vertical trash compactors.

paper, plastic, glass, and metal for recycling.

Compactors are not intended for food scraps, due to the growth of bacteria and development of odors. Also, they should not be used to dispose highly flammable materials and aerosol cans. These items present safety concerns and should be discarded separately.

## Food Waste Disposers

A food waste disposer easily eliminates the smell and mess of food scraps. This appliance is installed below a sink to catch and grind most types of food scraps. It is connected to a sewer line or drained into a septic tank.

Both batch-feed and continuous-feed models are available. In *batch-feed* models, the food is scraped down the drain opening into the grinding chamber. Then cold water is turned on and the drain cover is put in place to start the disposer. When the scraps flush away, the water is turned off and the cover is removed. In *continuous-feed* models, scraps are added to the disposer while it runs. A stream of cold water is needed to help grind the scraps and flush them through the drain.

# Choosing Laundry Appliances

Doing laundry is a routine household task. Having an automatic washer and dryer in your home is highly convenient. You can do laundry whenever you want without the trouble and expense of taking it to self-service laundry.

## Automatic Washers

Size is one of the most important variables in automatic washers. Does

your household do frequent small loads of laundry, or fewer but bigger loads? Would you prefer a side-by-side or a stacked washer and dryer? Should they be full-size or compact, stationery or portable? If your home is small, it may be best to choose stacked laundry appliances. On the other hand, a portable washer can be stored in a closet and rolled to a nearby sink for use.

There are two basic types of automatic washers for the home: top-loading and front-loading models. Front-loading models are also called *horizontal-axis washers*. The tilted tub of the front-loader permits clothes to tumble through water no higher than the front opening, as shown in 18-22. While they cost more than traditional washers, front loaders use only half the water and save energy, too. Horizontal-axis machines have a faster spin speed that wrings out more water. They also use less detergent, but require special low-sudsing formulations. Generally, horizontal-axis machines use about one-third of the water of standard washing machines. New vertical-axis models are even more water conserving.

To suit a variety of fabrics, washers have cycles, such as normal, permanent press, and delicate. All cycles have the same basic steps: fill, wash, spin (drain), rinse, and spin again. Cycles vary in the length of time, speed of agitation, water temperature, and number of rinses.

### Features

Features on automatic washers include dispensers that release detergent, bleach, and fabric softener into the wash water at the right times. Other features include a control that lets you match water level to load size in top-loaders and a water temperature control for the wash and rinse water.

Porcelain-coated tubs are rust-resistant and smooth enough to

Maytag

18-22 —————————

*Front-loading automatic washers clean clothes with a small amount of water and tumbling action.*

protect fine fabrics. Stainless steel and plastic tubs are durable and rust-resistant, but may not be as smooth. See the checklist in 18-23 when buying an automatic washer.

## Dryers

Automatic clothes dryers are often bought at the same time as washers. They are usually available as a matching set. The dryer you choose should be large enough to dry a full load from your washer. An advantage of buying a matching pair is the dryer is designed to handle the same size load as the washer.

Dryers operate on gas or electricity. Compare installation and operating costs as well as purchase prices before you buy.

### Features

Basic clothes dryer models have a preset temperature that is safe for most fabrics. The drying time is the only variable. More expensive dryers have both time and temperature settings. A permanent press feature prevents wrinkles from forming by tumbling clothes without heat at the end of the drying time. An *air-dry*

---

### Checklist for Automatic Washers

___ Will the washer fit your space limitations?

___ Does the washer have a self-cleaning lint filter?

___ Is a water-level selector provided if the model is top-loading?

___ Is a water temperature selector provided?

___ Does it have a minimum of *regular, delicate,* and *permanent press* cycles?

___ Is a presoak cycle available? A permanent-press cycle? A knit cycle? A delicate cycle?

___ Does it have a control to stop the machine and signal when the load is unbalanced?

___ Are bleach, fabric softener, and detergent dispensers offered?

___ Is an optional second rinse selector provided?

___ Is the tub and lid made of porcelain enamel?

18-23 —————————

*Before buying an automatic washer, consider these points.*

option may be available to fluff items without using heat.

Most dryer models have a timer control or a *moisture-sensing* system, which shuts the dryer off when clothes reach a selected degree of dryness. Another feature of deluxe models guards against wrinkles. It tumbles dry clothes without heat for a few seconds every few minutes until they are unloaded. See the dryer checklist in 18-24 for other buying considerations.

## Choosing Climate-Control Appliances

Appliances can help control the climate in your home. They can maintain

---

Vocabulary: Analyze the
root word of the term
*dehumidifier* to deter-
mine its meaning.
Compare what you wrote
to the definition in the
text.

### Checklist for Dryers

\_\_\_ Is the lint trap conveniently placed
for ease in removing, cleaning,
and replacing?

\_\_\_ Is the control panel lighted? The
interior?

\_\_\_ Is there a signal (buzzer or bell) at
the end of the drying period?

\_\_\_ Is there a safety button to start the
dryer?

\_\_\_ Does the dryer offer one heat
setting or a choice?

\_\_\_ Does it have an automatic sensor
to prevent overdrying?

\_\_\_ Does it offer a wrinkle-guard
feature? An air-only, no-heat
setting?

\_\_\_ Does it have a touch-up cycle to
remove creases in dry clothes?

18-24

*Before choosing a dryer, consider these
questions.*

Whirlpool Home Appliances

18-25

*Room air conditioners come in different sizes to efficiently handle the
cooling requirements of different room sizes.*

humidity levels and temperatures that
increase the comfort of the indoor
environment.

## Dehumidifiers and Humidifiers

The humidity level of the air in
your home will determine your need
for a dehumidifier or a humidifier.
A *dehumidifier* is an appliance that
removes moisture from the air. Excess
humidity can cause discomfort as well
as mildew, musty odors, rust, and
other problems. A dehumidifier is
generally not needed if you have air
conditioning because that appliance
removes moisture as well as heat.

A *humidifier* performs the opposite function of a dehumidifier. It adds
moisture to the air. Dry air is a problem in some climates, especially during winter months when homes are
heated. Static electricity and splits in
wood floors and furniture are signs
the air is dry.

Dehumidifiers and humidifiers
can be built-in or portable. If you are
purchasing a new unit, your best bet
is to follow the recommendations of a
manufacturer that offers a wide variety. A type and size will be recommended for your situation.

## Room Air Conditioners

A room air conditioner is an appliance used for cooling a room or small
area. The air conditioner should be the
proper size for the area to be cooled.
It must also be the proper size for the
space in which it will be installed,
18-25. *Portable* room air conditioners
are designed for placement in window
openings. *Built-in* units are designed
for installation in exterior walls.

When you shop for room air
conditioners, you will need to know

Discuss: What regions of the country are likely to need dehumidifiers
most? least?

Enrich: Find out what level of humidity is recommended indoors.
Other than geography, what factors raise the humidity level in a
home? What lowers it? What is the effect of high humidity levels on a
home and the people in it? What is the effect of extremely dry air
indoors?

your cooling needs in detail. You can pick up a helpful form from a retailer that includes all the key questions to answer. For example, what direction does the room face? What are the size and the shape of the area to be cooled? How many people normally use the space at the same time? How much glass and insulation are in the area?

The answers to these and other questions help in calculating your cooling needs. A retailer will help you with this step. Cooling needs and the cooling capacity of room air conditioners are expressed in British thermal units (Btu). Once the Btu range you need is known, check the EnergyGuide labels of comparable models to compare energy efficiency ratings (EERs). Models with higher EERs use less energy and, therefore, cost less to operate.

Also check the controls. Are they easy to reach and use? Can you change the level of cooling to meet your needs? Can you program it to change cooling levels automatically? Check the louvers for air direction. Turn on the unit to check the noise level, if possible.

Many homes today have whole-house air conditioners as part of their HVAC system. For more information, refer to Chapter 9, "The Systems Within."

# Choosing Other Appliances

Many other appliances, both essential and optional, are available for home use. Water heaters, vacuum cleaners, personal computers, and a variety of portable appliances are among those that you might consider buying.

## Water Heaters

Hot water in a home is needed for bathing, laundry, and a variety of cooking and cleaning tasks. Water heaters are heated by either gas or electricity. The type of water heater you choose will depend on the heating system in your home.

If you are in the market for a water heater, you will need to consider the size you need. This will depend on the amount of hot water you use. The more people living in your home, the more hot water you are likely to use. Also consider whether you have other appliances that require large amounts of hot water, namely a dishwasher and an automatic washer.

Heating water adds to home energy costs. Therefore, it is wise to make sure your water heater is properly insulated. An insulating jacket can be wrapped around the water heater to provide added insulation. You may also wish to insulate hot water pipes to reduce heat loss. Set the thermostat at 120 degrees; however, if you have a dishwasher without a preheater, set the water heater thermostat at 140 degrees Fahrenheit. Most new water heaters are preset at 120 degrees at the factory and this cannot be adjusted. If so, you must have a preheater in the dishwasher. If possible, install the water heater near the kitchen and laundry areas. These steps will help save energy, too.

## Vacuum Cleaners

A vacuum cleaner is a useful appliance for removing loose dirt from rugs and carpets. It can also be used to clean hard-surface floors, draperies, and upholstery. Attachments allow vacuum cleaners to perform other cleaning tasks, too.

**Note:** You will need assistance to determine the ideal cooling capacity of a room air conditioner to buy. A retail dealer can provide a checklist to help you measure the room's heat load.

**Example:** Buying a room air conditioner with too little cooling capacity will leave your room too warm, while buying one with too much capacity will leave the room too humid, resulting in a cold, clammy feeling.

**Discuss:** Why is the placement of the water heater in the home so important? (*because the farther hot water must travel through cold pipes to get to where it's needed, the more it cools*)

Some vacuum cleaners use a High-Efficiency Particulate Arresting filter, called a HEPA filter. A HEPA filter removes additional allergens from the air before being recirculated into the room.

Your choice of a vacuum cleaner will depend on what you want it to do for you. There are many types available. These include canisters, uprights, minicanisters, and hand-held and wet/dry vacuums. Some people choose to own more than one type to meet their various needs.

### Canisters

Canister vacuums are easy to handle and do a good job of house cleaning. See 18-26. They are effective on bare floors, stairs, and upholstery. Canister cleaners, as well as other

Dirt Devil

18-26 ─────────────
*The lightweight vacuum cleaner can easily be carried throughout the home.*

types, may feature a power nozzle attachment that increases carpet cleaning capability with rotating beaters and brushes.

### Uprights

Upright cleaners are the choice of many people purchasing vacuum cleaners. They are made primarily to clean carpets. Most are adjustable for all types of carpet pile. Some adjust automatically, while others are set manually. Uprights are available in self-propelled models. Nearly all uprights have attachments for other house cleaning tasks, such as removing dust from furniture.

### Central Vacuum Systems

A central vacuum is a built-in system with a heavy motor that stays in one place, usually a garage or basement. A flexible, lightweight hose is carried from room to room and inserted into conveniently located outlets. The system can also have a power attachment and special cleaning attachments. The dirt is collected in a container usually located in a garage or basement. The air is filtered to the outside of the home. Some systems have a special filter for better filtering efficiency.

## Personal Computers

A versatile appliance that many people are purchasing for their homes is the personal computer (PC). PCs can be used to tutor students, entertain children, and organize entrepreneurs. They are commonly used to send and receive communications, and play games. PCs are also used to develop household budgets, pay bills, manage household records, control thermostats and alarm systems, and activate appliances. See 18-27.

When considering the purchase of a home computer, you must first decide what you want it to do for you. *Software* is a program of instructions that tells a computer what to do. Software can be purchased in disks or downloaded from the Internet. Programs are available for practically every subject, from establishing household budgets to analyzing the nutritional value of meals. Review the software programs designed for the tasks you want to perform. Then find out what type of computer system and how much computer memory you need to operate them.

*Hardware* refers to the components in a computer system. The components include *input devices*, such as keyboards, scanners, digital cameras, and video recorders. These devices are used to enter data into a computer. A *central processing unit (CPU)* is another hardware component. It follows built-in instructions as well as those on software programs. The CPU generally includes a disk drive, which reads the information on software programs and stores it. Information can be stored in a number of ways. An *output device*, such as a monitor, speakers, and a printer, allows a computer user to view and hear data.

When buying a computer, consider everyone in the household who might use it and all the ways it might be used. See 18-28. Find out if the computer's memory capacity can be expanded to meet future needs. Inquire about classes to help family members learn to use the computer. Ask whether telephone support service is available when questions arise. Investigating the purchase carefully will help you get the most use and value from this appliance.

Also, you need to consider how to set up the workspace where the computer will be located. When setting up

18-27
*Telecommuters frequently use the computer to contact coworkers through e-mail.*

the home office, the purpose and need of the office will determine what equipment and supportive wiring are needed. In addition to a powerful computer, perhaps many of the following items are required: a telephone, Internet connection, shredder, faxing machine, copier, scanner, and printer. Sometimes all or several of the faxing, copying, scanning, and

**Enrich:** Learn how technology is currently affecting the housing industry by visiting Web sites such as *smarthomeusa.com*.

**Activity:** Working with a partner, list the many ways a computer is used in the home. Pairs then pair to form teams, which exchange information with other teams until each student has a comprehensive list.

**Enrich:** Research the latest developments in laptop (notebook) computers. What is the smallest size available? What amount of memory does it have? What special features are available? Indicate the brands, model names/numbers, and prices of the computers you checked.

Ethan Allen, Inc.

18-28
*Placing a personal computer in a kitchen work area helps keep household records organized and allows children to play or do homework with a helpful parent nearby.*

appropriate electrical wiring, cable connections, and electrical outlets.

## Portable Appliances

*Portable appliances* can be moved easily from one area to another. They include everything from toasters to electric blankets to hair dryers.

In today's society, many major appliances are considered basic necessities. Living without a refrigerator or water heater, for instance, would require a big adjustment in lifestyle. The same is not true for portable appliances. These small appliances provide many conveniences, but are not considered necessities.

Portable appliances tend to be less costly than major appliances. However, the procedure for choosing them is much like choosing major appliances. The first step is determining your needs and resources. Then shop and compare. Portable appliances should be chosen to meet the specific needs of household members.

Check construction details, warranties, and prices. Decide which of the latest features you want and can afford. Look for recognized brands, and be sure appliances have a seal indicating that safety standards have been met. Read use and care information to help you select appliances that are easy to operate, clean, and maintain. As with other equipment in the home, you need to consider and plan for where and how to store the portable appliances. Important questions to ask yourself are whether the small appliance is a necessity and whether it can be used for various functions. Following these guidelines will help you make wise appliance choices. See 18-29.

printing functions can be combined in one piece of equipment. Multipurpose office equipment reduces the total surface space needed. Most importantly, attention should be given to getting an adequate surge protector as well as

Zojirushi America Corporation

T-Fal Corporation

Hamilton Beach

Hamilton Beach

**Discuss:** How would you define *kitchen clutter*? Do portable appliances contribute to it? What suggestions would you recommend to eliminate the buildup of clutter?

**Discuss:** Why do you think portable appliances make such popular gifts?

**Enrich:** Analyze a TV infomercial for a kitchen appliance. Examine what the appliance does and to whom it appeals. What is the total price (tax, shipping, and handling charges)? Would you want to own this appliance? Explain why or why not.

18-29

*Portable appliances are available for a wide range of personal care, food preparation, and cooking tasks.*

**Resource:** *Appliance Puzzler*, Activity E, SAG. Students complete statements about appliances.

**Reflect:** Review the chapter objectives. Do you still need to review or research some topics to get the information you feel you need? If so, what topics?

# Summary

Choosing household equipment, including major and portable appliances, is part of your housing decisions. If you want satisfactory performance from appliances, you must choose products that meet your needs. You should consider cost, features, size, safety, care, energy use, and quality when making appliance purchases.

Kitchen appliances include refrigerators, freezers, ranges, convection and microwave ovens, dishwashers, trash compactors, and food waste disposers. These appliances are available in a range of styles and features. Careful consideration will help you select those appliances that best meet your needs. Other appliances, including those used for laundry and climate control, must also be chosen with your needs in mind. Although they are a big investment, these appliances can improve the convenience, efficiency, comfort, and safety of your household.

## Answer Key

1. A full warranty provides free repair or replacement of an item. With a limited warranty, a consumer may be charged for repairs.
2. chest freezer
3. cast iron, steel, or other magnetic materials because they resist the electric current that causes the production of heat
4. because heated air is constantly forced onto the surface of the food
5. As food absorbs microwaves, the molecules vibrate within the food, causing the friction that produces the heat.
6. true
7. a setting on top-loading washers that adjusts the water level to match the load size, the tilted tub of the horizontal-axis washer that limits the water level to just below the front-door opening
8. A dehumidifier removes moisture from the air, but a humidifier adds it.
9. to prevent heat from escaping and thus reduce energy costs
10. Air is filtered to the outside of the home.
11. (List three. Student response. See pages 423-424.)

# To Review

1. Explain the difference between a full warranty and a limited warranty.
2. Which style of freezer is most energy efficient?
3. What type of material is used to make cookware for an induction cooktop? Why?
4. Explain why a convection oven cooks food faster and at a lower temperature than a conventional oven.
5. How is heat produced in a microwave oven?
6. True or false. A dishwasher cleans dishes better than washing them by hand.
7. Describe two water-saving features that are available on some automatic washers.
8. Explain the difference between a dehumidifier and a humidifier.
9. Why is insulation on a water heater important?
10. How does air filtering on a central vacuum system differ from that on most canister and upright vacuum cleaners?
11. List three questions you might ask before purchasing a personal computer.

# In Your Community

1. Visit a store that sells major appliances. Compare the prices, energy costs, performance features, size, safety features, warranties, and quality of two similar major appliances. Use the checklists given in this chapter to help you evaluate the two products. Share the findings of your comparison with your classmates.

**Writing Activity:** Students write each letter of the alphabet on separate lines of a sheet of paper and work independently to write one term from the chapter that begins with each alphabet letter. After three minutes, pairs of students confer to fill in any blank lines. If blanks still remain, discuss with the class some possible choices.

2. Locate a use and care manual for a major appliance. (Every home should have several.) List the kinds of information that it provides.

3. Find and read two magazine or newspaper articles on new types of appliances or new appliance features coming in the future. Report your findings to the class.

## To Think About

1. Suppose you found a small appliance (such as a toaster) for sale at a flea market or yard sale. It looked rather new, but it had no information about the use and care or warranty information. What are the potential risks of buying the small appliance?

2. A major appliance definitely has a major place in modern day homes. For instance, most American homes have a clothes washer, range, and refrigerator. These appliances are used daily and are part of everyday life. On the other hand, households tend to collect small appliances that are used infrequently. Give at least three reasons for this fact.

## Using Technology

1. Analyze a TV infomercial for a household appliance. (Infomercials are TV programs that present a commercial as an informative 30-minute program.) Summarize your observations by answering the following questions: What is the appliance's name and what does it do? According to the infomercial, why is it better than competing appliances on the market (if there are any)? How much does it cost? Do you think many people will be persuaded to buy one? Explain why or why not.

2. Locate a Web site that provides helpful comparisons of appliance features and prices for shoppers. Review the information for a vacuum cleaner or an appliance of your choice. Using a computer software program, write a brief description of the appliance review in chart form. Based on the information presented, which model would you buy? Explain your decision.

   **Note:** For researching consumer information, have students explore *consumerreports.org*.

3. Find the Web site for the Energy Star program and find out what appliances and other items are involved. What is the significance of the program to the nation's efforts to conserve energy? What conditions must a computer meet to earn the Energy Star label?

   **Note:** For researching the Energy Star label, have students explore *energystar.gov*.

**Portfolio Project:** Recommend a solution to a family trying to decide what new refrigerator to buy. The home currently has a 17 cubic-foot refrigerator/freezer that is much too small. Grocery shopping occurs once a week, and refrigerated items usually fill all available space. Few frozen foods are purchased. The family has two teenage children, one of whom uses a wheelchair. Everyone makes frequent trips for ice. Research the available options and make a recommendation.

# PART 5

# A Safe and Attractive Environment

C H A P T E R  19

# The Outdoor Living Space and Environment

## To Know

landscape
natural landscape elements
annuals
biennials
perennials
ground cover
hardscape
manufactured landscape elements
enclosure elements
landscape zones
conservation
water conservation
xeriscape
soil conservation
sunroom
landscape architect
American Society of Landscape
    Architects (ASLA)

The Long Cane Group, Inc. Atlanta, Georgia

## Objectives

After studying this chapter, you will be able to

- identify the goals of landscaping.
- list natural and manufactured landscape elements.
- determine zones in a landscape site.
- select furnishings for outdoor living.
- list conservation measures for landscaping.
- design an outdoor living space.

**Resource:** *A Safe and Attractive Environment,* transparency master V-A, TR. Students look back at the topics covered in Chapters 1-18 and review the new topics they will cover in Chapter 19.

**Activity:** Working in teams of four, cut a copy of the chapter objectives into separate strips, place the strips in an envelope, and give the envelope to another team. Empty the envelope you receive, place the strips of objectives into the most appropriate order, and compare your order to that in the text. Discuss the importance of each objective to the chapter.
**Discuss:** What are some reasons people are drawn to the outdoors?

The beauty of nature surrounds you. When making housing decisions, you should find ways to enhance and enjoy this beauty. People spend much of their time indoors—in schools, offices, and homes. The *landscape* is the outdoor living space. A beautifully landscaped area or even a small balcony in city housing can draw people outdoors. Everyone can find ways to enjoy the beauty of nature.

The natural surroundings are disrupted when a site is prepared for construction. The construction process often changes the layout of the land. If you leave the landscape alone after construction, it may never bring you pleasure. On the other hand, if you work in partnership with nature, you can have an outdoor living space that is psychologically rewarding. Note how the landscaping shown in 19-1 enhances the appearance of the home. A pleasing outdoor living space should encourage the positive development of each member of your household.

A

B

19-1

*After construction is complete, landscaping can make a site more attractive. Site A has been graded and is ready for landscaping. Site B is the finished landscape.*

## Planning the Landscape

The basic goal of landscaping is to create outdoor spaces to complement various activities. The landscape should be private, comfortable, attractive, safe, and convenient. If you are like most people, you will also want the area to be easy to maintain. Any or all of these qualities can be achieved in a well-planned landscape.

### Identify Your Goals

You will have more successful results if you identify your landscaping goals. Your goals may include some of the following:

- recreation and entertainment—including areas for playing and/or socializing
- privacy—attained by enclosures and screens that shield the space from the public
- comfort—which allows you to relax in an inviting space
- beauty—which highlights attractive areas and draws attention away from less interesting areas
- safety—which is achieved by installing landscaping elements correctly and providing adequate lighting

**Activity:** Before reading the chapter, talk with teammates to consider why people landscape a home. After a minute, write down your answers (no discussing) and initial them. One at a time, read a reason until all are read.

**Vocabulary:** Break the word *landscape* into root words to determine its meaning. Develop a definition and compare it to that shown in the text.

**Note:** Get additional information on outdoor living space on Web sites such as *rebeccasgarden.com* and *hgtv.com*.

**Art Activity:** Imagine being assigned the landscaping job for the top photo in Figure 19-1. How would your landscaping plan look? Draw a picture of the final results of the plan and attach a written description of its features.

**Activity:** If you could landscape your current home, what would be your goals? Review the goals listed and select those that apply to your circumstances, adding others as needed.

- creativity—evident in the ways that you use your landscape to express yourself
- ease of maintenance—which incorporates laborsaving ideas, such as raised planters, watering systems, and ground covers that require no mowing

A satisfying environment is created for your household when everyone's needs and personal priorities are considered in the planning process. Take time to identify your goals before you start your plan. As you formulate your goals, ask yourself these questions:

- What is the lifestyle of your household? Are there children and pets to consider?
- How much time, money, and effort are you willing to spend? See 19-2.
- If you are concentrating on one area of the site, how will it affect other areas? Will the addition of a patio, deck, or swimming pool reduce the lawn area too much?
- Do you know what types of materials to consider for your plans?

19-2

*Some people have the resources to landscape their site all at once. Others prefer to phase in steps over several growing seasons.*

- What activities are likely for the area?
- How much open space do you want to maintain?
- What measures can you take to save water and energy over the long term?

You should answer these and other questions before designing your outdoor living space.

# Landscape Elements

Before planning a landscape, become familiar with the various landscape elements. There are two basic types of landscape elements: natural elements and manufactured elements.

## Natural Landscape Elements

*Natural landscape elements* are those found in the natural environment. The terrain and soil are natural elements that are already on the site. Other natural elements include trees, shrubs, flowers, ground covers, boulders, stones, wood, bark, water, sun, and wind. Some elements, such as a natural stream, cannot be changed. Other elements can be altered to a certain degree. For instance, trees, shrubs, and large rocks can be added to or removed from the landscape.

### Topography

The topography, or contour of the land, is basic to the landscape. Level land is the easiest and the least expensive to landscape. The ideal topography is a gentle, rolling terrain with natural drainage.

### Soil

Good soil encourages plant growth and provides plants with the right nutrients. It has a proper balance of sand, silt, and clay. The soil must drain well, yet hold enough water to sustain plant life.

## Trees and Shrubs

Trees and shrubs range in size from small to large. Trees can provide shade as well as shelter from wind. *Coniferous* trees and shrubs remain green all year. *Deciduous* trees and shrubs, on the other hand, lose foliage in the fall and sprout new leaves in spring. See 19-3.

## Flowers

Flowers add fragrance and color to the landscape. They are divided into three types: annuals, biennials, and perennials. *Annuals* and *biennials* last one and two years respectively. Most of these flowers are planted yearly. *Perennials*, on the other hand, last for many years without replanting. Some perennials never need replanting. See 19-4. Many gardeners prefer perennials because they require less work than annuals or biennials.

Most flowers grow from seeds or bulbs. If you desire, however, you can plant seedlings. *Seedlings* are young plants started from seeds. You can start the seedlings yourself or purchase them from a nursery. With the right choices, you can have flowers blooming throughout the growing season. In some geographical areas, it is possible to develop landscape plans that provide year-round color.

## Ground Covers

A variety of ground covers are used in landscaping. *Ground covers* include grasses and various types of low-growing plants. *Grass* is the most common ground cover, and many types are available for lawns. Some are more appropriate for use in warm climates, while others thrive in

19-3 ───────────
*The leaves of deciduous trees change color in the fall.*

The Long Cane Group, Inc. Atlanta, Georgia

19-4 ───────────
*This professionally designed landscape combines coniferous and deciduous trees and shrubs with annual and perennial flowers.*

**Vocabulary:** Use *coniferous* and *deciduous* in sentences that demonstrate understanding.
**Science / Writing Activity:** Write an explanation of why leaves on deciduous trees change color in the fall and how this affects landscaping.

**Vocabulary:** Explore the meaning of *ground cover* by answering the following question: What are three examples and three purposes for using it?

cool climates. The growth cycle of grasses varies with the climate. Some grow well in the shade. Others need full sun. Some grasses can stand heavy traffic, while others will tolerate very little.

Other ground covers include *low-growing plants* that can be used in places where grass is not desired or cannot be maintained. Ground covers can be purchased in the form of vines, woody plants, or herb-like plants. Some are coniferous and others are deciduous, but all are perennials. Ground covers are commonly used when low maintenance is desired. They are also used in places that are difficult to maintain. Most ground covers are not suitable for high-traffic areas.

The Long Cane Group, Inc. Atlanta, Georgia

19-5

*A variety of manufactured landscape elements are used in this peaceful setting.*

### Boulders and Stones

Boulders and stones are available in various sizes and are commonly used for landscaping. Boulders with unusual forms, textures, or colors will add interest to any landscape. Such additions to the landscape plan are known as the hardscape of the plan. *Hardscape* is anything in the landscape other than vegetation and outdoor furniture.

### Water, Sun, and Wind

Water, sun, and wind will always be a part of the outdoors. They are considered natural landscape elements. Water is a basic need of any plant life, but high water levels can cause swampy yards, wet basements, and poor plant growth. Orientation to the sun and wind affect the use of outdoor living areas. At times, you need protection from these elements. At other times, you want to take advantage of them.

## Manufactured Landscape Elements

*Manufactured landscape elements* are those elements not found in the natural environment. They are, however, a common sight in most landscapes. These elements include hard surfaces, such as walks, driveways, steps, and various structures such as walls, fences, patios, and decks. These items are also referred to as hardscape. See 19-5. Numerous other items, such as lighting and outdoor furnishings, are landscape elements.

### Hard Surfaces

When hard surfaces are needed, they can be created with *brick* or *concrete*. See 19-6. Concrete can be made into bricklike blocks, steppingstones, and slabs. You can purchase

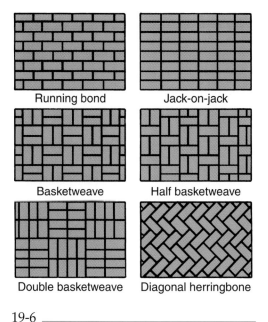

19-6 _____
*Bricks can be placed to form a variety of designs.*

19-7 _____
*This attractive walk is constructed of flagstone.*

these items ready to use, or you can make your own by placing the concrete into forms. *Asphalt paving* produces a hard surface and is relatively inexpensive to apply. In some cases, soil is compact enough to create a hard surface. *Flagstone*, shown in 19-7, is a flat stone found in certain areas of the country. It can be set in concrete or placed on a bed of sand. Such surfaces are also part of the hardscape in the landscape plan.

### Enclosure Elements

Walls and fences are *enclosure elements*, which means they enclose a space. They can be used to keep children or pets in. They can also be used to keep unwanted visitors out. Enclosure elements are constructed of various materials—wood, brick, stone, concrete, plastic, metal, or a combination of these.

*Freestanding walls* are often found on property lines. They give privacy and serve as a boundary, as in 19-8. *Retaining walls* have soil against one

Georgia-Pacific Corporation

19-8 _____
*A freestanding wall can provide privacy and beauty.*

**Discuss:** Which hard surface would you install for wheelchair traffic? Why?

**Art Activity:** Using strips of construction paper, create the designs of the fences in Figure 19-6.

**Reflect:** Observe the designs of the fences in your neighborhood. What are their purposes?

Anchor Wall Systems

19-9

*Retaining walls are used to hold soil in place.*

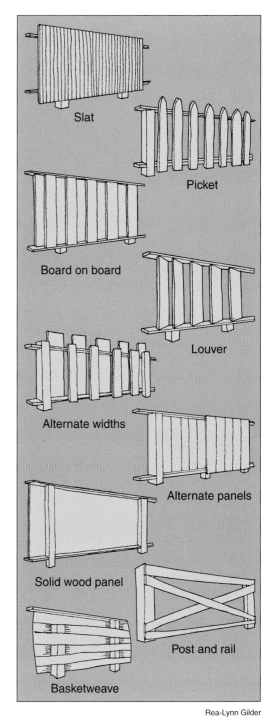

Slat

Picket

Board on board

Louver

Alternate widths

Alternate panels

Solid wood panel

Post and rail

Basketweave

Rea-Lynn Gilder

19-10

*Fences are available in a variety of designs. Nine popular styles are shown.*

**Discuss:** Would you consider a gazebo, such as that shown on the first page of this chapter, an enclosure? Why or why not?

**Activity:** Using Figures 19-8, 19-9, and 19-10, compare and contrast landscaping walls and fences.

side, as shown in 19-9. They are used for terracing and can form boundaries for yards and planting beds.

A *fence* is usually less expensive than a wall and is easy to construct. They are available in many styles and several heights. Several styles are shown in 19-10. Most fences do not provide as much privacy as walls.

Unlike a row of hedges or trees, enclosure elements do not need time to grow. Both walls and fences can be used immediately after construction or installation.

There are many other types of structures used in landscaping. You may build them or buy them ready to put in place. Courtyards, patios, decks, and terraces can enhance and extend your outdoor living space. Other structures you might consider include fountains, barbecue pits, gazebos, playhouses, and storage structures. You may also want to add plant containers to your landscape.

A variety of materials are available to build structures, including wood, brick, block, concrete, and flagstone. All of these materials are appropriate, and some are easy to use.

### Outdoor Furniture

Outdoor furniture is another manufactured landscape element. The furniture is usually constructed of metal,

**Social Studies Activity:** Research the origin of fences and outdoor walls. When did they first begin and for what purpose? What are some outstanding examples of outdoor walls built by different cultures and civilizations?

**Math Activity:** Visit a local store that provides fencing material. Select a fence you like. Compare the cost of having 50 feet installed versus installing it yourself. Consider the cost of tools you would need to buy or rent for the project.

wood, fiberglass, plastic, or glass. It is made from a single material or a combination. A variety of furniture styles is available to meet any need. Sometimes enclosure elements and other structures serve as furniture.

### Artificial Lighting

Another important element of the landscape is artificial lighting. Outdoor lighting should be functional, providing for safety and security. Lighting allows nighttime work or leisure activities. It can also add beauty to an outdoor setting. See 19-11.

Floodlights, spotlights, and underlighting can be used to accent a landscape site. *Automatic timers* are available for security lighting. These timers are designed to turn lighting on and off at predetermined times. *Photoelectric cells* are commonly used to turn lights on at dusk and off at dawn. *Motion detectors* activate lights when there is movement within a

given area. Some lights are designed to conserve energy. Many manufacturers produce low-voltage outdoor lighting kits that operate on 12 or 24 volts. Lights that use solar energy store it directly from the sun.

Some natural landscape elements are predetermined by the location of your property. Members of your household can choose other natural elements, as well as all manufactured elements. Recognizing the elements available to you can help you design an outdoor living space that meets your needs and goals.

# Designing the Outdoor Living Spaces

Designing a landscape is similar to designing the interior of a home. Think of the areas you are landscaping as outdoor rooms. Just as the inside of the house is divided according to certain activities, the grounds are divided into three *landscape zones*—public, private, and service. These zones were discussed in Chapter 4, "Choosing a Place to Live."

- The *public zone* is part of the site that can be seen from the street.

- The *private zone*, for recreation and relaxation, is generally separated from the public zone.

- The *service zone* includes sidewalks, driveways, and storage areas for tools, trash cans, lawn equipment, etc.

Only you can decide how much landscaping you want for each zone. The landscape plan should include backgrounds and accents. Be sure to allow for activities and traffic. You can be innovative in your use of the landscape elements as you plan the zones of the outdoor living space. See 19-12.

Photo courtesy of California Redwood Association

19-11

*The outdoor lighting plan of this redwood-sided home provides excellent safety and security.*

19-12

*This family's love of swimming convinced them to turn most of their small backyard into a beautiful, yet functional, swimming pool.*

Review the elements and principles of design and incorporate them into the rooms of your landscape. Recall the ways to use color effectively. You can apply what you have learned to the form, line, color, and texture of the landscape elements you choose. The landscaped space should have unity and balance. Landscape elements should be in proportion to one another and to the structures they surround.

## Landscape Backgrounds

Floors, walls, and ceilings serve as the backgrounds in your landscape. The topography and the soil are the floor. Hard surfaces and ground covers are the floor coverings.

You may not have good soil on the site. If not, with knowledge and effort, you can improve it. Soil can be improved by the use of compost and mulch. *Compost* is a decomposed or rotted natural material that is worked into the soil. *Mulch* is used to cover the soil, usually around plants, to prevent weed growth. It is an organic material, such as straw, peat moss, bark, or leaves. Both compost and mulch are important to building soil. They increase the penetration of water and air, help the soil hold water, and control soil temperatures. If you plan to include grass or any other plants in your landscape, the condition of the soil is important.

Grass is one of the most appealing parts of the landscape. It creates a pleasing floor covering for the landscape site and can provide recreational areas for the members of your household. It also prevents soil erosion and supplies oxygen to the air. When grass is mowed, the clippings produce organic matter for the soil. Grass is commonly used to unify or connect the other parts of the landscape.

Plantings other than grass may be used as ground cover in areas where there is no traffic. They typically do not need as much care as grass. See 19-13. A variety of plants can be used as ground cover. Local factors may limit your choices since some plants will grow only in certain soil, temperature, and sunlight conditions.

*Loose aggregate*, such as sand, gravel, cinders, wood chips, and bark, is suitable for sections of the site that have poor soil or are difficult to water. Loose aggregate is used when low maintenance is desired or water is scarce. Sometimes it is used as mulch in planting areas.

Sections of the landscape's floor will be paved or covered with other hard materials. For example, common surfaces include driveways and sidewalks. Hard surfaces on your lot should be sloped away from your house to provide proper water drainage. You do not want water standing or freezing on your driveway and sidewalks.

Walks are one of the easiest landscape elements to construct. They can be made of any durable material and are often used as borders. Walks divide the landscape site into separate areas and act as pathways to these areas. See 19-14. You should choose an attractive pattern for the walk. If the level of the ground varies, you can include steps in the route. Most walks are long-lasting. However, changes are sometimes necessary when plant life matures and becomes larger. If you anticipate changing the route at some point in the future, stepping-stones should be used to form the walk. They are easier to move than most other materials used for walk construction.

Trees, shrubs, walls, and fences create the walls of the landscape. Walls can act as a screen, giving visual privacy. See 19-15. They also curb noise and serve as a windbreak. You must decide which areas to enclose with walls. If you have a good view in one direction, you may want to take advantage of it by leaving it open.

The Long Cane Group, Inc. Atlanta, Georgia

19-13
*Native plants with colorful flowers or foliage can create a beautiful front yard requiring less care than grass.*

The Long Cane Group, Inc. Atlanta, Georgia

19-14
*A walk does not have to be placed in a straight line. This walk was designed to complement the landscape.*

**Discuss:** Why is it important to slope the hard surfaces in the landscape away from the house? (*to provide good water drainage away from the house and prevent water from pooling and freezing on the surfaces*)

**Discuss:** What functions do landscape walls perform? (*provide privacy, curb noise, block wind, provide decoration, and separate property*)

The Long Cane Group, Inc. Atlanta, Georgia

19-15

*The wall in this landscape acts as a screen to provide privacy.*

Photo courtesy of California Redwood Association

19-16

*A wrought iron gate can be attractive and functional.*

Suitable shrubs or evergreens can be planted close together to form a wall. If you want a dense grouping, combine trees with shrubs. Plant short shrubs among the tall trees. You could also plant two rows of trees, staggering the plantings to make a continuous barrier.

Walls were originally built to keep enemies away. Today, they serve different functions. They may be used to separate one property from another, provide privacy, and block wind. Many walls are decorative, using such materials as wood, stone, or concrete.

Fences are often used for the same purposes as walls. Some are solid, while others have openings. Fences that allow others to see into a private space are often covered with vines for more privacy.

Gates are part of the landscape's wall. They can add an interesting touch to the enclosure as in 19-16.

Reflect: Are there any walls in your yard? If so what purposes do they fulfill?

Reflect: Think about the nature parks in your area. Do you have a favorite spot in one of those parks? What forms the ceiling, floor, and walls of the outdoor space? Could you recreate a similar screen in your yard?

Gates must blend with the walls of the landscape.

The sky, with its clouds and color, is the ultimate ceiling of your landscape. Tall trees may frame the sky to create part of the ceiling. The spreading branches of some trees give a canopy effect. The trees may be located for the shade they produce. A *pergola* can also be constructed to add partial shade. See 19-17. If needed, shade can also be provided by an overhead structure. Ceilings can be constructed of canvas, bamboo, fiberglass, louvers, or lath.

## Accents

Accents in your landscape are the finishing touches. They are the colorful flowers, the interesting boulders, and the other special features you choose. Some accents become background elements for smaller accents. For example, a boulder may serve as a background for a cluster of flowering plants. You should include a variety of accents in your landscape plan.

Flowers are not a permanent landscape element. They die in dormant seasons, so they are considered an accent. When in bloom, they are spectacular in their color and showiness. There are many forms, heights, and colors of flowers from which to choose.

Flower plantings should be simple. Too many types or colors in a single bed will produce a disorganized appearance. Some flowers need full sunlight. Others do well in the shade or partial sunlight. Find out which flowers will do best in your landscaping project.

Planting beds are good choices for flowers. These beds are the spaces that are reserved for plants. Raised beds or planters are effective. They are ideal for older people or people who use

The Long Cane Group, Inc. Atlanta, Georgia

19-17

*A pergola may be included as a background in a landscape plan to provide partial shade.*

wheelchairs. Portable planters can be moved from one outside area to another, and then moved inside during the cold season.

Choices of materials for planters include wood, plastic, glass, metal, concrete, and glazed ceramics. See 19-18. Look for planters that are durable and decorative. In areas with freezing temperatures, avoid planters containing glass, ceramic, and other materials that shatter when the moisture in soil freezes.

Boulders and stones are often chosen as accent pieces. Sometimes they are placed informally in the landscape, as in 19-19. They have a more formal appearance when they serve as borders along paths and flowerbeds. Place boulders and stones to show

Savannah Hardscapes, Savannah, GA

19-18

*This ceramic planter is a beautiful accent to this garden area.*

19-19

*The boulders in this flowerbed serve as both an accent and a background.*

off their interesting features. Rock gardens are popular in landscaping.

Sculptures, murals, and mosaics can enhance your landscape design. The selection of these accents is very personal. In expressing your tastes, consider form, color, and texture. Usually a landscape will appear cluttered if you use too many of these accents. Most accents should be placed at eye level. Sculpture fits well against a background of foliage. You may, however, want to combine it with some type of structure.

## Other Landscape Features

Throughout your landscape, you can use many different features. You can have fun planning them and may even enjoy building some of them.

You might want a *gazebo* in your landscape. A gazebo is a raised platform that has four, six, or eight open sides. (One is shown on the first page of this chapter.) You can enjoy the landscape as you relax in a gazebo. It can double as a playhouse. Some gazebos have a protective roof. Others have lattice or vine-covered roofs. You can adapt a gazebo to fit your desires.

A water fountain is another popular landscape feature. Water projects can be very enjoyable. The sound and sight of running water has a soothing effect. Having water fall from a high level can produce sounds. Jets, bubbles, and sprays can also make soothing water sounds.

Water in motion has a special attraction. A small, inexpensive circulating pump may be installed to move the water. If you use water as a landscape element, it should be recycled. It can be used again in the landscape or used to water plant life.

You may want to attract birds to your property. You can do this by including a pool or pond in your landscape. The pool can be small or large. Small pools work best if they are near a group of plantings.

Birds will also be attracted to your yard if you hang feeders and birdhouses. If you enjoy watching birds, plan your landscape to attract them. See 19-20. Contact your local cooperative extension service office to learn what plants in your area attract birds. Be sure there are good places for nests in your landscape.

## Furnishing Your Outdoor Living Space

Outdoor furnishings can be used to extend your living space since they invite you outside. The furnishings can help make the landscape site enjoyable and functional for the entire household.

Outdoor furnishings generally include tables, chairs, accessories, and cooking equipment. Furnishings that are durable and weather resistant are best for outdoor use. They should have high-quality construction. Choose furnishings that resist the deterioration caused by temperature extremes, sunlight, wind, and water. The furnishings should also resist soilage.

See 19-21 for a description of materials commonly used in outdoor furniture. Many of these materials are also used for other outdoor accessories.

If you plan to move the outdoor furniture frequently, it should not be too heavy. When selecting furnishings, use what you have learned about organizing space and traffic patterns. The principles apply to outdoor living spaces as well as indoor spaces.

You may want to store the furniture during the off-season or use it in another location. Some furniture is appropriate for both indoor and outdoor use. If you want furniture for

19-20
*This birdbath will attract birds to the garden.*

dual-purpose use, keep this in mind when making your selection. See 19-22.

Carpeting is sometimes considered a part of the furnishings. It is best if outdoor carpeting is made of 100 percent synthetic fiber. Olefin, acrylic, and nylon are suitable fibers for outdoor use. The best outdoor carpeting is of needlepunched or tufted construction. The needlepunch process produces a feltlike carpeting. Tufting produces loops. The loops may or may not be cut. Either type of carpeting needs to be glued or taped down to a hard surface. For more information on carpet construction, see Chapter 13, "Textiles in Today's Homes."

Additional furnishings include decorative and functional accessories.

| Materials for Outdoor Furniture | | |
|---|---|---|
| Materials | Types | Descriptions |
| *Metal* | Aluminum | Lightweight and rustproof<br>Sometimes has a finish to prevent corrosion |
| | Wrought iron | Heavy and not very portable<br>Rusts without the proper finish |
| | Molded cast iron | Heavier than wrought iron<br>Brittle<br>Rust, cracks, and breaks easily |
| | Steel | Strong and durable<br>Weather resistant |
| *Wood and*<br>   *woody plants* | Cedar, cypress, and redwood | Needs a protective coating to prevent deterioration |
| | Rattan, wicker, and bamboo | Cannot be finished to withstand continuous<br>   outdoor conditions<br>Works well for sunroom furnishings |
| *Plastics* | Urethane | Durable<br>Requires minimal maintenace<br>Used for molded items |
| | Polyester and acrylic | Used for furniture tops |
| *Glass* | Fiberglass | Lightweight<br>Strong and durable<br>Weather resistant<br>Can be designed to fit contours |
| | Glass | Common for tabletops<br>Must be high quality |

19-21
*Outdoor furniture is made from a variety of materials.*

Brown Jordan International Company, Designs by Rich Frinier

19-22
*This attractive, lightweight furniture can be used for both exteriors and interiors.*

Accessories add the finishing touches to the furnished area. Common examples of decorative accessories include wind chimes, sculpture, driftwood, and urns. Examples of functional accessories include pillows and pads, cooking equipment, and waste containers.

Pillows and pads can be made of woven or knitted synthetic fibers. They must be filled with weather-resistant filler. This type of material can usually withstand moisture. Nevertheless, the pillows and pads should be protected from standing water.

Your outdoor living space may not seem complete unless you add cooking equipment. See 19-23. You

**Discuss:** If money were no object, identify the materials you would select for outdoor furniture. Refer to Figure 19-21.

**Enrich:** Tour a local store that sells patio or outdoor furniture, taking a copy of Figure 19-21 with you. Review the choice of materials. Find out what material seems to dominate in your area and why.

may choose a portable unit or a stationary one. A portable unit should be located so it does not interfere with the landscape. Position it in an area that is protected from strong winds and hot sun. You will not want the smoke from the unit to be a bother. Portable equipment can be stored when not in use.

If you choose stationary cooking equipment, place it in a convenient spot. However, do not allow it to detract from its surroundings. A well-planned unit can add pleasure to the landscape. Cooking equipment can be fueled by charcoal, natural gas, or propane. Cooking equipment that uses propane or natural gas is generally more convenient than equipment fueled by charcoal.

Accessories often set the mood for the landscape area. There is no end to the choices you have when you select accessories. Coordinate the style and color of your outdoor furnishings and accessories. Consider what is needed and determine where and how it will be used. When selecting furnishings and accessories, consider comfort, convenience, durability, portability, storability, quality, design, and maintenance.

## Lighting the Outdoor Living Space

Lighting can create a type of magic in the landscape. It can extend the use of the outdoor living space and invite you outside at night. Lights also enhance the view from inside the house. See 19-24.

Appropriate lighting is important for each area of your property. Outside lighting should illuminate the sidewalks and driveways. It should provide a clear view to and from your house. At the same time, lighting should discourage intruders. Lighting at entryways can help you see who is approaching.

Floodlights can be used for large areas, while spotlights are good for lighting specific features. You can highlight a garden sculpture or flowing water with a spotlight. Underlighting is especially appropriate for

**Discuss:** Would cooking equipment be a part of the public, private, or service zone? (*private zone*)

**Activity:** With a partner, create a list of themes for outdoor art, such as animals, cherubs, and whirligigs.

Photo courtesy of Wolf Appliance

19-23

*The addition of a grill enhances the usability of the exterior space.*

Photo Courtesy of Lindal Cedar Homes, Seattle, Washington

19-24

*Well-planned outdoor lighting can help extend the use of outdoor living spaces.*

**Discuss:** Why is outdoor lighting so important to the safety of the homeowners? *(It provides a clear view to and from the house, discourages intruders, and illuminates people who approach the house.)*

**Reflect:** Would you feel safe in an area as well lit as the outdoor living space of the house in Figure 19-24? Why?

small areas. *Underlighting* is the practice of directing the light upward from the ground level into plants or other landscape features. Uplighting a large tree, for example can create a spectacular focal point in a night landscape plan.

If possible, light fixtures should be situated so they are hidden from view. Ground-level lights can be placed behind plants or structures. Higher fixtures can be installed under eaves or on rooftops.

# Landscaping for Conservation

*Conservation* is the process of protecting or saving something. Your landscaping decisions can help to conserve soil, water, and energy.

Photography courtesy of Misty Michelle Brinkley

19-25
*The black and orange fencing material is used to prevent soil erosion during the construction of a new house.*

Efforts at conservation should begin when a house is being built. See 19-25. Disturbances to the soil occur during construction. If ground covers are planted at this time, erosion of the topsoil can be prevented. In steep areas, terraces can be built to prevent erosion. Builders should be encouraged to employ these and other conservation measures.

Once construction is complete, permanent conservation efforts can begin. Even if you have been in your home for some time, you can make a significant contribution to conservation. The lifestyle of the household is probably the most important factor in conservation. If you are environmentally conscious, you will want to conserve natural resources. If you consider economy to be important, you can conserve to save money, too.

Homeowners want their outdoor space to be comfortable and attractive. They can accomplish this and still conserve natural resources through landscaping.

## Water and Soil Conservation

Awareness is the first step in conserving water. *Water conservation* includes reducing water use and eliminating water waste. If you live in a dry part of the country, you realize how important it is to conserve water. People throughout the United States are becoming more aware of the need to conserve water. In many places, water prices have increased substantially while available water supplies have decreased. This is forcing consumers to review their water use habits.

Planning a water-efficient landscape design is one answer. *Xeriscape* is the term used to describe landscapes that are designed to tolerate drought and conserve water.

Xeriscaping involves grouping plants according to the amount of water they need. Then the plants are encouraged to develop deep roots by watering less often and deeper. Water retention is promoted by using mulches and adding more trees and grass.

Plan to use the most water in areas that receive the most use. These areas will include the lawn, play areas, and gardens. If you can use runoff water from roofs and gutters, you can reduce water costs.

Patios and similar areas need water only for accent plants. Areas near the property boundary may require little or no watering. If you use native plants, you should have low water use. Native plants are better adapted to the climate and usually need less watering than other plants, 19-26.

Watering, if needed, should supply plants with enough moisture to live. Too much water can lead to plant disease. Excess water also prevents plants from developing properly. It is better to water less often but deeply. Deep watering can help roots grow better and make plants more drought resistant.

The most effective watering method is trickle irrigation, known as *drip irrigation*. In this technique, water is delivered directly to the base of the plants, reducing evaporation and runoff. In some trickle irrigation systems, narrow tubing is routed under the ground. In other systems, water is delivered to the plants through a porous hose above ground.

The most common watering method involves the use of sprinklers. Sprinklers spray plants with water droplets or a fine mist. Portable sprinklers can be moved to various positions in the landscape. Built-in sprinkler systems have several stationary sprinkler heads located throughout the landscape. Built-in systems are generally more convenient than portable sprinklers because they do not have to be moved. A considerable amount of water is lost to evaporation when using sprinklers, particularly those that spray fine mists. If sprinklers are not controlled, water runoff can be excessive. See 19-27.

**Activity:** Contact your county cooperative extension office to obtain a list of plants native to your area. Consider sponsoring a school landscaping project using only native plants.
**Discuss:** What do you think the following quotation means: "When we heal the earth, we heal ourselves"?

19-26 —
*The native plants in this landscape require very little water.*

Melka Landscaping, Orland Park, Illinois

19-27 —
*The sprinklers in this built-in system are controlled to conserve water.*

**Science Activity.** Create a science experiment that shows the difference between a terrain shaped for gradual water drainage versus one that encourages the formation of streams. Level a one-inch layer of sand, peat moss, or loose dirt in two same-size, rectangular pans. Place a one-inch-high support under the shorter side of one pan and a 4-inch-high support under the other. At the raised edge of both pans, pour one cup of water slowly but steadily. Observe the difference in drainage patterns.

**Resource:** *Deciduous Trees,* transparency master 19-1, TR. Students discuss how landscape elements such as deciduous trees can be used to conserve energy.
**Activity:** Send a local soil sample to the county cooperative extension office to have it analyzed. Report the results of the analysis.
**Discuss:** Explain how timers can be used to conserve water in the landscape.

Irrigating at night saves water. However, some plants are susceptible to certain diseases if they are watered at night. Know the characteristics of your plants. Irrigating when the wind is calm will help reduce evaporation. A system controlled by a timer will also help save water. If possible, try to recycle water. You can use water from a pond to water grass or plants. Can you think of other ways to recycle water?

*Soil conservation* includes improving and maintaining the soil. Analyzing the soil is a very important part of soil conservation. Soil samples can be sent away for testing or analyzed on-site. The results of these tests will determine what should be done to improve the soil. Usually, soil improvement is a project most homeowners can handle with advice from an expert. However, for large or complex projects, a garden center or yard maintenance service can handle the job.

Soil can be improved by mixing organic matter with the native soil. The organic matter creates air space in the soil. It also retains moisture so less watering is needed. Improved soil increases the chances for good plant growth.

Soil conservation also includes taking steps to avoid erosion. The topography of the yard must encourage a natural drain pattern so water drains away from the house slowly. This gives moving water enough time to penetrate the earth, instead of eroding it. Improper grading and leveling of the lot encourages water to form streams, carry dirt off the lot, and create gullies.

Special care should be given to installing perforated plastic pipes to the ends of the downspouts. These pipes can be buried underground to direct the water away from the foundation of the house. One benefit of channeling water underground is soil conservation since water won't run off the downspouts to cause erosion and gullies. The second benefit is a reduced risk of flooding basements since the water is directed away from the house's foundation.

The plants you select for planting and the plan you develop for their placement can further prevent erosion and conserve the soil. To accomplish this, select plants and trees with good root systems and give careful consideration to their placement in the landscape plan. When planning a landscape, both water and soil conservation must be considered.

## Energy Conservation

Homeowner interest in conserving energy through landscaping is increasing. With the proper use of landscape elements, the climate in and around a home can be modified. Heat gains in the summer and heat losses in the winter, for example, can be reduced with good landscaping. In areas where air conditioning is used, cooling costs can be reduced as much as 75 percent. This is achieved by providing plenty of summer shade. In regions where air conditioning is not used, the home interior can be made more comfortable.

Properly placed vegetation and manufactured landscape elements can block prevailing winds. Windbreaks can save enough energy to lower heating bills by 10 to 15 percent.

Trees with high branches and many leaves provide summer cooling by blocking the sunlight. Tall trees provide less shade than those that are widespread. Since deciduous trees lose their leaves in the winter, they provide summer cooling and still allow you to benefit from the warmth of the winter sun. Deciduous trees are

**Science Activity:** Research the kinds of technology currently being used to improve water conservation. One Web site to study is *swcs.org/.*
**Enrich:** Check the county cooperative extension office to learn which plants in your area are susceptible to disease when watered at night.
**Example:** American gardeners are landscaping with native plants more because they are easy to maintain, drought-resistant, and a good food source for birds and butterflies.

a good choice for placement on the south and east sides of buildings. Coniferous trees are good as windbreaks on the north and west sides of buildings. The types of trees that do best vary from region to region.

Shrubs and vines provide good shade for the walls of a house. Most walls retain heat in the summer sun. Shrubs and vines act as insulation to reduce the heat reaching the walls. Coniferous shrubs and vines will also help prevent heat loss in the winter. If you plan enclosures to collect heat from the winter sun, use deciduous plantings.

Overhangs and roof extensions offer shade, too. They can be planned to shut out summer sun and take in winter sun.

A *sunroom*, or garden room, is another structure that can use energy more efficiently. A sunroom is a structure that uses energy from sunlight to heat a living space. Tile floors absorb energy from the sun, which is then released into the room. The room may be part of a house or entirely separate.

To ensure a sunroom conserves energy, it must be correctly positioned. For instance, it should face south, away from any shade cast by nearby trees or shrubs. In addition, window treatments can be used to regulate the amount of sunlight that enters the room during the day. They can act as insulation during the night to contain the heat, as in 19-28.

The conservation of natural resources for future generations should be everyone's concern. You can do your part, too. Information is available to help you make decisions about conservation. Before you decide which measures to include in your landscape, learn all you can. Since the role of landscaping varies from region to region and season to season, you need information specific to your area.

Permission granted by Hunter Douglas Inc. to use copyrighted designs. Designs © Hunter Douglas Inc.

19-28 _____

*The tile floor of this sunroom absorbs energy from the sun during the day and releases the heat during the night.*

Information about conservation measures is available from landscape dealers or the cooperative extension service in your county. Look for publications from the U.S. Department of Agriculture (USDA). Most large communities have at least one garden club. Members of these clubs can guide you to helpful conservation resources in your area. Libraries and the Internet are excellent sources of information, too.

# Completing a Scaled Plan

Being aware of what you have and how you want to use it is essential to developing a good outdoor plan. The needs, interests, and desires of your household must be considered. The site's climate, topography, soil conditions, and orientation to the sun must also be considered. What is attractive and what is unattractive about your outside environment? Determine the

**Discuss:** When an architect plans a house or an addition to a house, how important is it that his or her design takes into account the direction of the sun and wind as well as mature trees on the property? (*Windbreaks can save enough energy to lower heating bills by 15%. Trees with high branches and many leaves provide summer cooling by blocking the sunlight.*)

**Writing Activity:** Write a paragraph describing an ideal sunroom, including the types of plants to use there.

best natural resources on the site. Note the sunny and shady areas. See 19-29.

After compiling all the needed information, you are ready to develop a scaled plan for designing your landscaping. This plan is sometimes called a site plan. The northern edge of your site should be at the top of the plan. It is a good idea to begin your plan for the outdoor space with a map of the entire property. Your landscaping plan should include the following information:

- property boundaries
- location of the residence, showing windows and doors
- location of other structures
- orientation to the sun and wind
- location of the driveway and sidewalks
- position of both underground and aboveground utilities

- location of existing plant life, rocks, and other natural features

## Developing the Landscape Design

You can produce scaled plans of your site either manually or with the help of a computer program. Whichever method you use, draw the plan to scale. To show the greatest detail, use this scale: *¼ inch equals 1 foot*. When less detail is needed, sometimes the following scales are used: *1 inch equals 10 feet* or *1 inch equals 20 feet*.

### Drafting

Using graph paper, you can produce a drawing similar to Figure 19-30. You can also create several overlays to decide which plan you prefer. See 19-31. If plans are drawn entirely

Weather Shield Windows & Doors

19-29

*Thought was given to this well-designed landscape plan in that it provides enjoyment from the interior as well as the exterior.*

by hand, the drafting process can be very time-consuming. Some landscape planning kits have ready-made symbols that can be used to mark landscape elements.

## Computer-Aided Drafting and Design

With a computer and landscaping software, you can create scaled plans. The grounds area and all items on the premises can be drawn with computer graphics. Besides designing the landscape plan, a computer-aided drafting and design (CADD) program can create a realistic view of how your completed design will look. See 19-32. Some software programs allow you to view designs for the yard and outdoor living area from a walk-through perspective.

Some landscaping software can be learned in several hours. More complicated versions, usually used by landscape architects, will take longer. However, spending the time to learn a CADD program usually results in more designs and more views to help you better visualize possible results.

Regardless of which tool you use to create a design, feel free to experiment. Produce several designs and consider different placements for the features. Clearly mark spaces for specific uses. Complete the design by arranging the outdoor furnishings. Remember to allow for traffic and convenience when planning furnishing arrangements.

Once you have decided on a landscape plan, it is time to roll up your sleeves and go to work. You and the other members of your family may enjoy working together to create your outdoor living environment. On the other hand, you may choose to hire a landscape firm to carry out your entire plan or just the difficult parts. Many

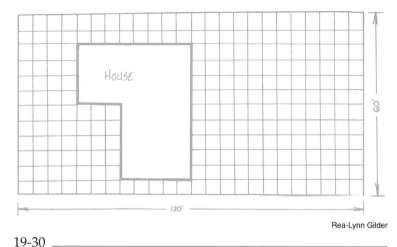

Rea-Lynn Gilder

19-30 _____

*Landscape plans should be drawn on graph paper.*

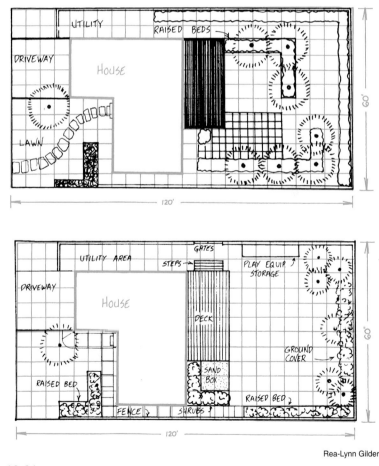

Rea-Lynn Gilder

19-31 _____

*Two alternate landscape designs are shown for the homesite in Figure 19-30.*

**Art Activity:** Use Figure 19-30 to create a landscaping plan that is completely different from the plans shown in Figure 19-31.

**Reflect:** If your home has a yard, what could be done inexpensively to improve it? Would moving a few plants make a difference?

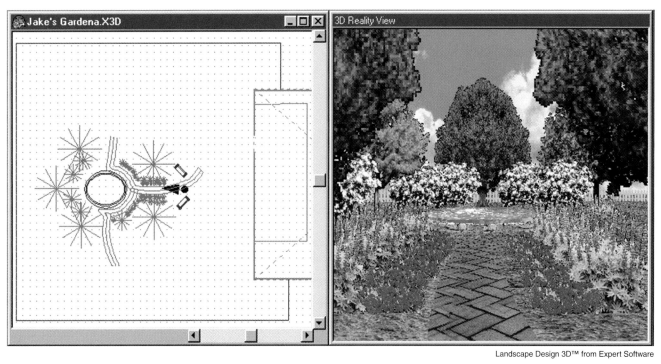

Landscape Design 3D™ from Expert Software

19-32
*The homeowner used a computer program to plan and visualize this private zone.*

The Service Master Company

19-33
*This lawn-care specialist is applying fertilizer to grassy areas.*

nursery owners are trained in landscape design. They are knowledgeable about plants and can help you with the planning.

Another alternative is to hire a landscape architect to design your plan. A ***landscape architect*** is professionally trained to create designs that function well and are aesthetically pleasing. Members of professional groups such as the ***American Society of Landscape Architects (ASLA)*** are the most qualified experts in this field. If you desire, you can hire specialists to care for your outdoor living area. Maintenance companies will establish a service contract with you to keep your lawn mowed, your flowers beds free of weeds, your shrubbery pruned, etc. They can provide periodic fertilizer applications to your lawn and garden as needed. See 19-33.

**Discuss:** What skills are needed to landscape the new private zone shown in Figure 19-32?

**Reflect:** How did the drawing on the left of Figure 19-32 help the designer more clearly imagine the resulting view, shown on the right?

# Summary

When planning the outdoor living area of your home, first identify your goals. These will depend on the lifestyle, needs, and desires of your household.

Recognizing the types of landscaping elements and their uses will help you make your plans. You must determine which natural elements are suitable for the site being landscaped. Then, you choose the manufactured elements that fit your situation.

Planning a landscape is much like planning the rooms inside your house. Just as a house is divided into several areas, the landscape site is divided into three zones—private, public, and service. Each zone is treated differently. When planning the landscape rooms, consider the floors, walls, ceilings, furnishings, and accents. Lighting should also be included so the outdoor living area is usable at night.

Knowing the topography and the soil condition of the site is important. This information helps you conserve soil and water. You should also plan the landscape to conserve energy.

Detailed plans of the outdoor rooms and landscape zones are needed to receive the satisfaction you want. For accuracy, plans must be drawn to scale. You can use various resources to help you make landscaping decisions and incorporate them into the site.

**Resource:** *Designing a Landscape*, Activity E, SAG. Students make landscape designs and list three goals they plan to achieve.

**Reflect:** Review the chapter objectives. Do you still need to review or research some topics to get the information you feel you need? If so, what topics?

**Writing Activity:** Write a one-paragraph summary in response to each of the chapter's objectives. Explain briefly what you learned.

# To Review

1. What is the basic goal of landscaping?
2. Name three examples of natural landscape elements.
3. Which of the following is not a ground cover?
   A. deciduous shrub
   B. grass
   C. loose aggregate
   D. low vines
4. List five manufactured landscape elements.
5. When landscaping a zone, a person should think of it as a _____.
6. Name three functions for the "walls" of a landscape design.
7. Name three accents used in landscaping.
8. List five factors to consider when selecting outdoor furniture.
9. List three reasons for including lighting in any landscape plan.
10. Explain the term *xeriscaping*.
11. For energy conservation, _____ trees should be located on the south side of a building.
12. Name five items to include on a site map.

**Answer Key**

1. to create pleasing outdoor spaces for various activities
2. (List three:) soil, terrain, topography, trees, shrubs, flowers, ground covers, boulders, stones, wood, bark, water, sun, wind
3. A
4. (List five:) driveways, walkways, pathways, steps, walls, fences, patios, decks, lighting, outdoor furnishings
5. room
6. privacy, noise reduction, windbreak
7. (List three:) flower beds, planters, boulders, stones, sculptures, murals, mosaics, gazebos, water fountains, pools, birdfeeders, birdhouses
8. (List five:) comfort, convenience, durability, portability, storability, quality, design, maintenance
9. (List three:) increase safety, discourage intruders, add beauty, highlight outdoor features, enhance view from the house, illuminate outdoor work, illuminate leisure activities
10. creating landscapes to conserve water
11. deciduous
12. (List five:) property boundaries, the residence with location of windows and doors marked, other structures, orientation to sun and wind, driveway, sidewalk, above- and under-ground utilities, existing plant life, hardscape elements

454    Part 5    A Safe and Attractive Environment

## In Your Community

1. Search several newspapers and magazines for gardening news. Report landscaping ideas that are suitable for your area.

2. At a local gardening store, look through their seed catalogs. Find five annuals and five perennials. Indicate how they can be purchased (seeds, bulbs, plants).

3. Consider directing a landscape beautification project in your community. Identify an area needing improvement. (It could be your school grounds, a community park, a government building, an assisted living home, the local library, or another well-known building.) Obtain the assistance of a local nursery to sponsor your project, or create fund-raising projects to meet your goal. Plan the area to be planted with a professional landscape designer serving as a volunteer. Use the principles of design discussed in this chapter along with conservation techniques. Encourage your classmates to roll up their sleeves and help with the planting.

## To Think About

1. Conserving natural resources such as water and energy are important for both present and future generations. What could happen if individuals and communities did not use wise conservation practices? What would it be like to live permanently in a drought-stricken environment? Do you think this could become a worldwide problem? Why or why not?

2. Imagine that you are a reporter for a local newspaper, and there is a water shortage in the area. You have been asked to interview people in the community who are practicing good water conservation practices. What questions would you ask them? What types of information would you report?

3. Suppose friends asked you to help them develop a private outdoor space around their home. How would you advise them on the following items: where to locate the space, what plants to install to block views from neighbors, and how to make the area easy to maintain? What resources would you use and suggest they review? What special considerations would you make if they lived in an apartment?

# Using Technology

1. Use a CADD program to complete the site plan of a house familiar to you. Draw a floor plan of the dwelling's ground level. Divide it into zones. Show how you would design the outdoor living space.

2. Search the Internet for two photos of houses that are nicely landscaped. Print out a copy of each. Determine the types of manufactured items used in the design and describe how they affect it. Do the items make the design more attractive, safer, more private, easier to maintain, and more conserving of resources? Write a brief report of your findings.

3. Survey the members of your household regarding the activities they would want a landscaping plan for the home to include. Using a word processing program, make a chart with the recommended activities in the first column. In the second column, list possible ways to incorporate these activities into a landscaping design for your dwelling.

4. Using a video recorder or camera, take pictures of the different types of fencing used at local schools, churches, libraries, and other public buildings. Show the results to your classmates. Discuss the likely goal of each and how well the goals are achieved.

**Note:** For researching landscaping, have students explore *hg.women.com/homeandgarden* and *southernliving.com.*

**Portfolio Project:** Using Figure 19-32 as a beginning point, plan an outdoor seating area for six people in this back yard. Assume that the blue rectangle at right is a ground-level screened porch, and the distance from dot to dot is one foot. You may add a patio, gazebo, or pergola. Also, add benches, furniture, or other seating options. Use a *1/4" equals 1'* scale to display your plan addition, and mark onto a copy of Figure 19-32 where the addition would fall. Include drawings or pictures of the new seating plans.

CHAPTER 20

# Keeping Your Home Safe and Secure

## To Know

precautions
electrical shock
toxic
carbon monoxide
radon
mold
lead paint
ventilation
asbestos
noise pollution
decibels (dB)
combustible
asphyxiation
smoke detector
escape plan
deadbolt locks
biometrics
vision disability
hearing disability
hand limitation
mobility limitation

G.E. Plastics

## Objectives

After studying this chapter, you will be able to

- list the types and causes of the most frequent home accidents.

- describe ways to keep the air in your home clean.

- explain how to make your home safe and secure.

- determine changes that can make the home safe and secure for those with special needs.

Resource: *A Safe and Attractive Environment*, transparency master overlay V-B, TR. Students look back at the topics covered in Chapters 1-19 by reviewing transparency master V-A. Then, with the addition of overlay V-B, they explore the topics they will cover in Chapter 20.

Activity: Have students review the chapter objectives, relating them to as many of the vocabulary words as possible.

Reflect: Read the objectives. What do you already know about these objectives? What do you need to know? How will they help you?

Y ou face a variety of risks as you go about your daily life. Using common sense and taking preventive measures may avoid other risks. The housing decisions you make can reduce the risk of accidents in your home. You can also make decisions that will help everyone in the home feel more secure.

# A Safe Home

You probably think of home as a safe place. Surprisingly, it is not. More injuries take place at home than anywhere else. Home accidents are a major cause of death and serious injury. Each year, accidents around the home hurt more people than traffic and work accidents combined. How safe is your home?

## Preventing Accidents

You should not wait until an accident happens to take safety measures. Survey your home for danger spots. Guard the members of your household against accidents that can have painful or even fatal results. Be sure that they know and follow safety rules.

### Preventing Falls

Falls are the most common type of home accidents. People of all ages suffer from falls, but the vast majority of those who suffer serious injury are older people. Children also experience falls, but they are caused by curiosity and usually are less serious.

Taking a few simple *precautions*, preventive actions, can help avoid many falls. Wet floors can cause people to slip and fall. Wipe up water or other spilled liquids immediately. Loose rugs also can cause falls. Choose rugs with a nonskid backing or place a nonskid pad under the rug. Remove tripping hazards by picking up toys, shoes, or other items left on floors or stairs.

When you use a ladder or stepladder, make sure it is securely in place before climbing. See 20-1. Whenever possible, a second person should support the ladder. After using a ladder, store it properly so that children will not be tempted to climb.

The bathroom can be especially dangerous because wet surfaces cause

**Resource:** *Causes of Accidents and Safety Measures*, Activity A, SAG. Students list five types of home accidents, their probable causes, and prevention measures.

Werner Ladder Co.

20-1

*Nonskid feet safely keep this ladder in position while in use.*

**Enrich:** Interview an emergency room worker in your town to determine the percentage of accidents the hospital handles that occurred in the home versus those that occurred in other locations.

**Writing Activity:** Create a flowchart of the steps of a process handled at home, such as preparing a meal. Identify any points in the process that are prone to accidents. Make a list of guidelines to increase accident awareness and prevention for these critical points.

many falls. Soap left in the bathtub creates a slippery, hazardous surface. You can reduce the danger of falling in the bathroom by using suction-type nonskid mats or safety strips in the shower and bathtub. Firmly attached grab bars can also help prevent falls.

The most dangerous room in the home, according to the National Safety Council, is the bedroom. Many falls take place in the bedroom, as do fires. One reason for the high rate of bedroom accidents is that people move around while half-asleep. Placing handy lamps next to the bed will help prevent falls caused by stumbling in the dark. A major reason for the high incidence of fires in the bedroom results from smoking in bed.

Stairways should have light switches at both the top and bottom, and a sturdy, secure handrail. When climbing or descending stairs, always keep one hand free to use the rail. Keeping stairs free of clutter will help prevent falls.

Falls also occur on the outside of the home, often as a result of slipping on wet leaves, snow, or ice. Promptly removing snow and ice from sidewalks will help prevent falls. Toys, garden tools, and other possible tripping hazards should be removed from walks.

### Preventing Burns

Burns are another major type of injury resulting from home accidents. Children under four years of age and elderly people are the most likely victims.

Hot cooking utensils can cause serious burns. See 20-2. Turn panhandles away from the edge of the range when cooking to avoid spills. Open steam-filled pans on the side away from your body. To move hot utensils, use potholders or oven mitts. Be sure the mitt or potholder is not damp because the heat from the cooking utensil could cause steam burns.

Scalding water can cause serious burns, too. Lowering the temperature of your home's hot water supply to 120°F can prevent scalding burns. Be careful of other household heat sources, such as toasters, hair dryers, steam irons, and portable room heaters.

### Preventing Electrical Shock

Electricity in our homes is convenient and makes possible a high standard of living. However, the home's electrical system must be properly designed, installed, and maintained to prevent it from being a safety hazard. An electrical shock can be fatal.

20-2

*Accidents often occur during busy periods when attention is focused somewhere else.*

*Electrical shock* is an electric current passing through your body.

Most electrical shocks result from the misuse of household appliances. Since water conducts electricity, electrical appliances must not be used near water or with wet hands. Dry your hands before using, connecting, or disconnecting electrical equipment. Do not stand on a damp floor while connecting or disconnecting an appliance's power cord. When disconnecting a power cord, grip the plug, not the cord. Pulling on the cord can weaken wires and eventually result in a shock or fire.

Use heavy-duty extension cords whenever possible. An extension cord should never be lighter than the appliance cord that is plugged into it. To avoid damage to electrical cords, do not tie knots in them or run them under rugs. Damaged or frayed cords and defective plugs must be replaced promptly. Do not plug too many tools or appliances into one outlet. Overloading circuits can cause electrical fires. See 20-3.

The National Electric Code requires safety grounding of all outlets. In kitchens, bathrooms, laundry rooms, and other locations near water, a special type of electrical outlet must be installed. The outlet includes a *ground fault circuit interrupter (GFCI)* to prevent shocks. Outlets on the exterior of your home should have weatherproof covers or caps. Circuit breakers and fuses are safety devices. They interrupt electrical power if too much current flows. Always replace a fuse with one having the same rating. Using a fuse with a higher rating could allow wires to overheat, causing a fire.

## Preventing Poisonings

Another major cause of home injuries and fatalities is poisoning. See 20-4. Swallowing common household products causes most such accidents. Laundry and cleaning aids, medicines, and cosmetics can be *toxic*, or poisonous. So are garden chemicals, materials used in the workshop, and many items found in the garage. The

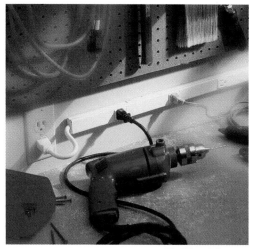

The Wiremold Company

20-3
*In areas where many electrical tools are used, install enough wiring and outlets to safely handle the electrical load.*

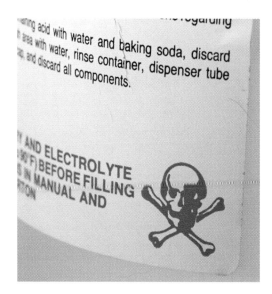

20-4
*The skull-and-crossbones symbol is a warning sign for poisonous materials. Many household and gardening products show this symbol on their labels.*

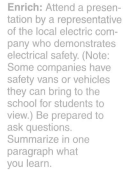

**Enrich:** Attend a presentation by a representative of the local electric company who demonstrates electrical safety. (Note: Some companies have safety vans or vehicles they can bring to the school for students to view.) Be prepared to ask questions. Summarize in one paragraph what you learn.

**Science Activity:** Research how GFCIs work and how they differ from standard outlets.

**Reflect:** Think about your home. Are you aware of any electrical problems that need to be addressed?

**Research:** Investigate how the symbol of a skull with crossed bones became a warning sign for poisonous materials. What was the original meaning of this symbol? How was it first used?

Research: Find out who to call when dealing with poisoning emergencies and what information you will need to provide.

Reflect: Can you recall a childhood accident you had that could have been prevented by a vigilant adult?

| Safety Checklist for Hazardous Materials | | |
|---|---|---|
| Yes | No | |
| ❑ | ❑ | Do you store the materials in locked cabinets that are well ventilated? |
| ❑ | ❑ | Do you store them in the original, labeled containers? |
| ❑ | ❑ | Do you keep them beyond the reach of children, pets, and strangers? |
| ❑ | ❑ | Do you always read the entire label before using them? |
| ❑ | ❑ | Do you follow directions carefully and use the materials only in the manner permitted by law? |
| ❑ | ❑ | Do you avoid inhaling hazardous materials? |
| ❑ | ❑ | Do you wear protective clothing and masks when directed to do so? |
| ❑ | ❑ | Do you protect your skin from exposure to accidental spills, and do you carefully clean spills up? |
| ❑ | ❑ | Do you wash your hands thoroughly after handling the materials and again before eating? |
| ❑ | ❑ | Do you wash contaminated clothing immediately after use when directed to do so? |
| ❑ | ❑ | Do you cover your pet's food and water containers when using the materials nearby or upwind? |
| ❑ | ❑ | Do you dispose the empty containers so they pose no hazards to humans, animals, wildlife, or valuable plants? |

20-5

*When handling a hazardous material, or any material unfamiliar to you, carefully follow these steps.*

leaves or other parts of some houseplants are poisonous, too, if eaten. The list of dangerous items is long. You can probably think of others.

To help prevent poisoning, always keep products in their original containers. Read and understand the product labels, and follow directions. Then, properly dispose the container and any leftover product. Use the safety checklist for hazardous materials in 20-5.

You may wish to use nontoxic alternatives for household products that contain potentially harmful ingredients. See 20-6.

## Keeping Children Safe in Your Home

Children are often the victims of home accidents. When they are present, extra precautions must be taken. To prevent falls, you should install gates, bars, railings, and other types of barriers. Keep children away from open windows, porches, and stairways. To help prevent falls in the dark, you can install night-lights.

Keep children away from electrical appliances and cords. Install safety covers on unused outlets to prevent possible electrical shocks. Guard against fire, and safely store matches and lighters out of sight. It is especially important to involve children in fire drills so they know what to do in case of a fire.

Children can learn to identify symbols that indicate poison, as shown earlier. Many products that can be dangerous to children, however, are not classified as poison. For example, how many laundry and cleaning products carry a warning label like the one shown in 20-7? Where are these products stored in your home? Too often, they are kept under the kitchen sink, where children can reach them easily. Dangerous products should be stored

Note: For good information on how to treat poisonings, refer to the Web site *aapcc.org/*.

Discuss: How can you be sure to recall the information in Figure 20-5 when you most need it? Recommend a plan for keeping this information at your fingertips.

| Safe Alternatives for Chemical Products | | |
|---|---|---|

You can substitute vinegar, baking soda, borax, and soap for most of the household products you use. To make an all-purpose cleaner with nontoxic ingredients, combine 1 gallon hot water, $^2/_3$ cup baking soda, and $^1/_4$ cup vinegar. For tough cleaning jobs, double the baking soda and vinegar. For specific household needs, use the following mixtures.

| Product | Hazardous Chemicals | Safe Alternative |
|---|---|---|
| *Abrasive cleaners or powders* | Ammonia, ethanol | Rub area with $^1/_2$ lemon dipped in borax; rinse and dry. |
| *Ammonia-based cleaners* | Ammonia, ethanol | Use a mixture of vinegar, salt, and water for most surfaces; for bathrooms, use baking soda and water. |
| *Bleach cleaners* | Sodium or potassium hydroxide, hydrogen peroxide, sodium or calcium hypochlorite | For laundry, use $^1/_2$ cup white vinegar, baking soda, or borax. |
| *Disinfectants* | Diethylene or methylene glycol, sodium hypochlorite, phenols | Mix $^1/_2$ cup borax in 1 gallon water. |
| *Drain cleaners* | Sodium or potassium hydroxide, sodium hypochlorite, hydrochloric acid, petroleum distillates | Flush with $^1/_2$ cup baking soda, $^1/_4$ cup vinegar, and boiling water. |
| *Enamel or oil-based paints* | Pigments, ethylene, aliphatic hydrocarbons, mineral spirits | Latex or water-based paints. |
| *Floor and furniture polish* | Diethylene glycol, petroleum distillates, nitrobenzene | Mix 1 part lemon juice with 2 parts olive or vegetable oil. |
| *House plant insecticide* | Methoprene, malathion, tetramethrin, carbaryl | Mix a few drops liquid soap and 1 cup water; spray on leaves. |
| *Roach and ant killers* | Organophosphates, carbamates, pyrethrins | To kill roaches, use traps or a mixture of baking soda and powdered sugar. For ants, use chili powder to hinder entry. |

20-6

*The alternatives listed here are less harmful to people and the environment than the well-known products.*

in a safe place, behind doors with safety latches or locks.

Keeping dangerous products out of sight is the best safety precaution to use with children. Simply moving them out of reach is no guarantee that children will not try to reach them anyway. Young children cannot judge the distance to an object and the length of their reach. Many serious childhood falls have occurred by climbing and stretching for distant objects that seemed reachable.

20-7

*This "Mr. Yuk" label was developed to warn children about products that may be dangerous to them.*

**Writing Activity:** Create a list of safety guidelines for children around swimming pools in your community. Include phone numbers to call in case of emergency.

**Science Activity:** Work in closely supervised teams to use one of the common household products listed in Figure 20-6 as well as its "safe alternative." Compare the results and write a report with recommendations.

**Discuss:** Have you seen the "Mr. Yuk" symbol in Figure 20-7 or something similar on products? Do you think children would pay more attention to this type of alert rather than the skull and crossbones? Explain.

A home swimming pool is another potential source of danger for children. For youngsters under five years of age, drowning is the second leading cause of accidental deaths around the home. Local codes usually specify the type and height of fences and other enclosures that must be installed around pools. In addition, pool owners should observe the following safety precautions:

- Supervise young children at all times.

- Keep a phone and emergency numbers handy. See 20-8.

- Learn cardiopulmonary resuscitation (CPR) procedures, a lifesaving technique to use in an emergency.

## Keeping the Air Safe and Clean

Clean air in the home is more of a concern now than it has been in the past. To save energy used for heating and cooling, houses have become more airtight. Such airtight houses, however, have increased the problem of indoor air pollution.

Few people realize that the air inside the average home may be badly polluted. Indoor pollution comes from many sources. Some insulating materials give off vapors that are pollutants. Tobacco smoke, dust, pet dander, and household cleaning and beauty products all add pollutants to the air in the home. Even stagnant water left in containers like vaporizers and humidifiers pollutes the air.

When these varied sources are allowed to create pollutants in an airtight house, problems may arise. The air can become polluted enough to affect health. People may develop allergies or feel tired and listless. Two pollutants—carbon monoxide and radon—can cause serious illness.

### Carbon Monoxide

Perhaps the most dangerous of all indoor pollutants is carbon monoxide. *Carbon monoxide* is a colorless, odorless, tasteless gas that is produced by the incomplete burning of fossil fuel. Fossil fuels include natural gas, propane, gasoline, coal, charcoal, and wood. Depending on how much gas is inhaled, symptoms can range from temporary headaches to permanent brain damage to even death.

Carbon monoxide gas is readily absorbed by the body's red blood cells. The primary job of red blood cells is carrying oxygen to all parts of the body. When these cells carry carbon monoxide instead, the body is starved of oxygen. The poisonous gas gradually invades every body cell. Nausea, coughing, and dizziness are the first signs of carbon monoxide poisoning. People are warned to call 911 or their local fire department immediately if one or more household members, and even pets, show the same flu-like symptoms.

20-8 ———————
*Tape emergency numbers directly to the phone so children can refer to them quickly.*

Most cases of carbon monoxide poisoning occur with the onset of cold weather. Furnaces that are restarted without a proper cleaning from the previous winter's use are a leading cause. Homes that are tightly caulked and weather-stripped prevent indoor air from escaping. These are ideal conditions for the creation and buildup of the poisonous gas. Entire households have been known to die within a few days of starting a poorly maintained gas furnace.

Regular maintenance of fuel-burning appliances is the best way to prevent the creation of carbon monoxide. Venting all fuel-burning appliances to the outdoors is another way.

### Radon

*Radon* is a natural radioactive gas. Radon is found in high concentrations in soils and rocks containing uranium and some other minerals. It is also found in soils with certain types of industrial wastes. Radon is believed to be a cause of lung cancer. Your risk of developing lung cancer from radon depends on the concentration and the length of time you are exposed to the gas.

You cannot see, smell, or taste radon. Federal and state governments are working to identify high-risk areas and provide information on dealing with the problem. The solution may be as simple as keeping the home well ventilated.

The federal government recommends that you measure the level of radon in your home. See 20-9. A radon test is the only way to know whether radon is present.

### Mold

Sometimes harmful mold (also commonly called mildew) can begin growing on surfaces in homes. A *mold* is a fungus that grows on damp or decaying matter. Some molds can be harmful to humans. These harmful molds can grow anywhere there is warmth and moisture, particularly in bathrooms, under carpeting, or in the cavities of walls, floors, and ceilings. Whenever there is flooding or water problems in a home, proper drying and ventilation is needed to avoid creating an environment for mold growth. Common causes of water problems include leaking pipes and emergencies such as an overflow from a clogged sink.

Health problems from harmful molds in the air include the development of allergies and other respiratory conditions. These reactions do not go away easily and are continually irritated by the harmful mold spores in

**Activity:** List all the fuel-burning appliances that affect your home's indoor air.

**Enrich:** Learn what types of radon test kits are available. Check the county cooperative extension office for information specific to your area. Do certain locations in the area have radon problems?

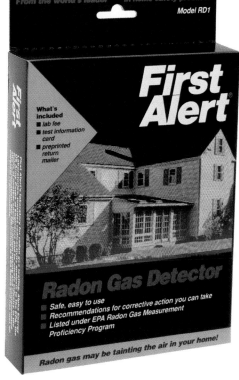

First Alert®

20-9 _____

*A radon monitoring device, like that shown above, is available from several companies. Radon detection services also are available.*

**Research:** Investigate black mold. Find out what causes it, where it grows, and how it can affect humans. Also, find out what must be done to eliminate its harmful effects in a home.

**Science /Art Activity:** Map the lifecycle of mold. Draw and label the various stages on poster board or transparencies to present the information to the class. Discuss each stage.

Resource: *Clean Air Puzzle,* Activity B, SAG. Students solve the word puzzle by filling the blanks in the given statements with terms from the chapter.

Research: Find out why lead was such a common ingredient in paint? What qualities does lead add to paint? What challenges did paint manufacturers overcome to make unleaded paint?

Example: A simple blood test can detect lead poisoning in the human body.

the air. If one or more household members suffer continuing difficulties with breathing and allergic reactions, a professional may be needed to inspect the house for mold. If mold is found, professional removal is often required.

## Lead Paint

*Lead paint* refers to lead-based paint, which was a common form of paint manufactured before 1978 that contained lead. When the hazards of lead poisoning became clear, the federal government banned the use of lead in paint in 1978. However, homes built or painted prior to that date often have paint that contains lead. Federal law also requires that individuals receive specific information regarding the presence of lead paint before renting, buying, or renovating pre-1978 housing.

The problem occurs when the paint chips, peels, or results in excessive amounts of lead-contaminated dust. Small children sometimes eat paint chips, mistaking them for candy. Lead can also be absorbed in the handling of some ceramics and other items containing lead.

Lead can be harmful, especially to young children, pregnant women, and senior citizens. In children, lead poisoning can cause damage to the brain and nervous system, which results in behavior and learning problems. Adults can also suffer many permanent physical difficulties.

A house can be tested for lead paint and airborne lead so the occupants know about any potential hazard. Also, steps can be taken to avoid the harmful effects of the paint. These include having the paint professionally removed from the walls and possibly replacing the windows. Also opening and closing windows with lead paint creates chips and dust,

thereby allowing the lead to become airborne.

## Ventilation

Proper *ventilation*, or air circulation, greatly reduces air pollution levels. The living spaces of the house need to be ventilated to exchange fresh air for stale air. Ventilation is also needed for the attic and a basement or any crawl space under the floor. If your house does not have built-in vents, they can be installed. Exhaust fans can be added to increase ventilation. If ventilation is planned, air will be exchanged at a good rate. See 20-10 for steps in diagnosing a too-tight house.

Eliminating or controlling the source of the pollutants can reduce air pollution. For example, ventilate the home well whenever painting, staining wood, or using chemicals that release vapors. Always follow manufacturer's instructions when using harsh chemicals. Become familiar with their negative health effects so you can recognize the symptoms if they occur.

Some types of pollutant must be professionally sealed or enclosed to prevent them from polluting the air. Asbestos is a prime example. *Asbestos* is a fireproof, cancer-causing mineral that can easily become airborne and inhaled. Because of its fireproof quality, asbestos was used prior to 1978 in insulation, linoleum flooring, and other building materials. When renovating an older home, any asbestos present needs to be professionally removed.

Two effective solutions for eliminating pollutants in the home are proper ventilation and elimination of their sources. Another solution you may want to consider is the use of an air cleaner. Such devices generally clean the air of particles, not vapors

Note: Since the 1980s, the federal government has phased out lead in gasoline, reduced lead levels in drinking water and industrial air pollution, and banned or limited lead in consumer products. For information on how to detect and prevent lead poisoning, search for the National Lead Information Center at *epa.gov.*

Vocabulary: Use the word *ventilation* accurately in a sentence.
Discuss: Do you consider air fresheners, perfumes, and colognes as air pollutants. Explain your view.

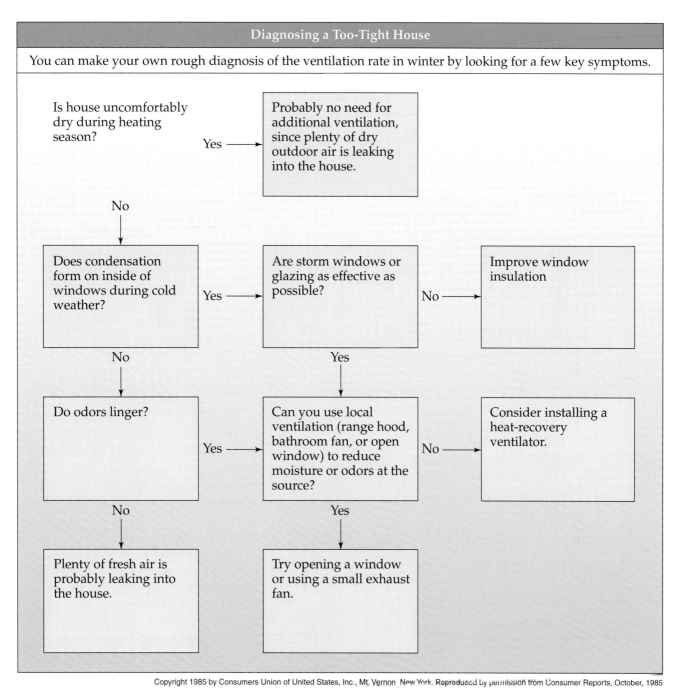

### Diagnosing a Too-Tight House

You can make your own rough diagnosis of the ventilation rate in winter by looking for a few key symptoms.

Is house uncomfortably dry during heating season?

→ Yes → Probably no need for additional ventilation, since plenty of dry outdoor air is leaking into the house.

↓ No

Does condensation form on inside of windows during cold weather?

→ Yes → Are storm windows or glazing as effective as possible?

→ No → Improve window insulation

↓ No (from condensation)

↓ Yes (from storm windows)

Do odors linger?

→ Yes → Can you use local ventilation (range hood, bathroom fan, or open window) to reduce moisture or odors at the source?

→ No → Consider installing a heat-recovery ventilator.

↓ No (from odors linger)

↓ Yes (from local ventilation)

Plenty of fresh air is probably leaking into the house.

Try opening a window or using a small exhaust fan.

20-10
*If you have problems with ventilation in your house, you may be able to correct them with a few simple steps.*

or gases. Before buying an air cleaner, carefully check its *clean air delivery rate (CADR)*. This is the industry measure by which air cleaner manufacturers test the performance of their appliances.

### Housecleaning

Housecleaning methods also affect the indoor pollution level. Indoor air quality is a growing concern across the nation. The federal agency responsible

**Research:** Find out what the test procedure is for determining the *clean air delivery rate (CADR)*, which measures the cleanability of air cleaners. What is the range of CADR ratings on various models of air cleaners? Does this or any industry test procedure measure vapor or gas removal?

**Activity:** Using the flow chart of Figure 20-10 as a guide, create a flowchart of your classroom or a room in your home. Determine what steps need to be taken to correct problems.

for this issue is the U.S. Environmental Protection Agency (EPA).

Using a feather duster, for instance, merely stirs dust around to later settle on another surface. A central vacuum system helps clean the air by filtering it and exhausting it to the outside. Indoor air cleaners with good airflow and sturdy filters can clean effectively, too. Some vacuum cleaners use a compartment of water to "filter" the air before it returns to the room. Cleaning services are another housecleaning alternative. See 20-11. They will handle any size job at times convenient to you and as often as you request.

## Controlling Noise Pollution

Noise is unwanted sound. *Noise pollution* is unwanted sound that spreads through the environment. According to government studies,

20-11

*Sawdust particles from remodeling settled throughout this house, so a professional cleaning service was called.*

noise is the leading cause of neighborhood dissatisfaction, which suggests it is a widespread nuisance. Medical research indicates that noise causes physical and psychological stress. It hampers concentration, slows work efficiency, and interferes with sleep. There may even be a link between noise and some harmful effects on unborn babies.

Sound is the sensation perceived by the sense of hearing. Sound is measured in units called *decibels*, abbreviated as *dB*. The quietest sound that can be heard is rated at 0 dB. Normal conversation is about 60 dB. The loudness of a sound and the length of time you are exposed to it determine its effect on you. Continued exposure to loud noise can cause permanent hearing loss.

### Reducing Noise

Listen to your house. Evaluate the noises you hear. Do they interfere with conversation? Are there sounds that invade privacy or cause distractions? Sound levels of some typical household appliances are listed in 20-12. Compare them to the level of normal conversation.

Solving some noise problems may be a simple matter. Solving others may take more effort. Indoors you can install sound-absorbing materials, such as acoustical ceiling panels. See 20-13. Carpets and draperies also help absorb sound. Pleasant sounds, such as music, can muffle unwanted sounds. You may want to consider closing off noisy rooms. When you buy new appliances, you may want to choose those that are designed for quieter operation.

Insulating exterior walls may control noise from outside the house. Storm windows or multiple-pane glass can keep out some of the noise. Landscaping techniques, such as building berms (earth mounds), erecting walls,

| Household Noisemakers | |
|---|---|
| **Appliance** | **Sound Level in Decibels** |
| Floor fan | 38 to 70 |
| Refrigerator | 40 |
| Automatic washer | 47 to 78 |
| Dishwasher | 54 to 85 |
| Clothes dryer | 55 |
| Hair dryer | 59 to 80 |
| Vacuum cleaner | 62 to 85 |
| Sewing machine | 64 to 74 |
| Food disposer | 67 to 93 |
| Electric shaver | 75 |
| Electric lawn edger | 81 |
| Home shop tools | 85 |
| Gasoline-powered mower | 87 to 92 |
| Gasoline-powered riding mower | 90 to 95 |
| Chain saw | 100 |
| Stereo | up to 120 |

20-12

*These are the sound levels heard by the person operating the appliance or someone standing nearby. Normal conversation level is about 60 dB.*

and planting shrubs, can also help reduce noise.

# A Secure Home

Your home should provide security, which is protection from physical harm. It should be a place where you can feel safe and sheltered from the unknown.

If you live in a well-built dwelling located in a relatively crimefree neighborhood, you are likely to feel safe. However, to more fully satisfy your need for security, you should include some protective devices in your home. Some of these devices

Cabinetry by St. Charles, products of Whirlpool Kitchens, Inc.

20-13

*Sound-absorbing ceiling tiles are stylish as well as effective in reducing noise levels, a requirement for this home office area.*

monitor the surrounding conditions to make sure the home stays safe.

## Security from Carbon Monoxide Poisoning

Any dwelling that burns a fossil fuel indoors should have a carbon monoxide detector. The chemical symbol for carbon monoxide is *CO*, so this device is also called a *CO detector*. Many local building codes require the installation of these detectors in new

**Reflect:** Study Figure 20-13 and think of additional ways to make the space quieter.

**Reflect:** Stop and listen carefully. Make a list of all the sounds that you hear—car horns, sirens, pets, people talking, motors running, and so forth. Where can you find total quiet?

**Enrich:** Attend a presentation by a firefighter or county cooperative extension agent to learn about carbon monoxide detectors. Summarize in one paragraph what you learn.

housing. Some cities require CO detectors in all housing.

This relatively inexpensive device sounds an alarm when low levels of the poisonous gas are present. It provides an early warning to occupants before harmful levels of carbon monoxide develop. See 20-14.

Since most carbon monoxide poisoning occurs when people are sleeping, CO detectors should be installed near bedrooms. The ideal location is on the hallway ceiling outside the rooms. If bedrooms are located on a second floor, the CO detector should be installed on the ceiling at the top of the stairs. For greater protection, carbon monoxide detectors may also be located in the kitchen and at the top of a basement stairway. If battery operated, it is important to check batteries and replace them on a regular basis.

20-14
*You can buy a combination carbon monoxide and smoke detector that mounts inconspicuously on the ceiling.*

# Security from Fire

Home fires are one of the most serious types of accidents, often claiming small children and the elderly as victims. Fires can cause not only bodily injury and death, but also costly damage to property. The leading causes of fire include:

- placing *combustible* (burnable) materials too close to a source of fire
- falling asleep while smoking
- being careless with flammable materials
- operating defective electrical or heating equipment

Fire department officials stress that fire prevention is a matter of common sense. You can help prevent a fire in your home by following these simple rules:

- Choose upholstered furniture constructed to resist a fire caused by smoldering material, such as cigarette ashes. Such furniture carries a gold-colored hangtag from the Upholstered Furniture Action Council (UFAC), as in 20-15.
- Store flammable liquids properly, using only approved containers.
- Keep matches in a safe place out of sight where children cannot reach them. Dispose used matches and cigarettes in a safe manner.
- Do not overload electrical wires.
- Dispose of trash regularly.
- Have your heating system inspected yearly by a professional.
- Burn only seasoned (dry) wood in wood-burning stoves and fireplaces. Do not use green wood, which can cause the build-up of a dark, flammable tar in the chimney.

Some fire deaths result from burns or injuries caused by panic. However,

UFAC

20-15 ―――――――――

*This label on upholstered furniture certifies the upholstery is resistant to sources of smoldering heat such as cigarettes.*

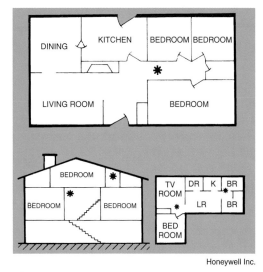

Honeywell Inc.

20-16 ―――――――――

*Smoke detectors should be placed on each floor of a dwelling, especially near bedrooms. They can be mounted on a ceiling or wall.*

the deadly smoke and gases released by a fire claim most fire victims through asphyxiation. *Asphyxiation* is the state of unconsciousness or death caused by inadequate oxygen or some other breathing obstruction. Some simple steps can help you escape injury. The best precaution, however, is having a fire emergency plan, which is discussed later in this chapter.

## Smoke Detectors

An inexpensive *smoke detector* will send a loud warning signal if a fire starts. The detectors are easy to install, and one should be placed on each floor of a building. The diagrams in 20-16 suggest good locations for smoke detectors. Most building codes for new homes require smoke detectors.

There are two basic types of smoke detectors: ionization and photoelectric. The ionization type responds more rapidly to fires where flames are present. The photoelectric detector is

quicker to detect a smoldering, slow-burning fire. Both types effectively provide an early fire warning. Most detectors are battery operated, but some are connected to the house's electrical current. As with other appliances, check for a safety seal before choosing a smoke detector.

If a smoke detector is battery operated, a fresh battery should be installed once a year. Most smoke detectors emit a sharp beep or have a flashing light to indicate that the battery needs replacing. It is a good idea to check smoke detectors for proper operation every month. Most units have a test button for this purpose.

## Fire Extinguishers

Fire extinguishers are classified according to the type of burning material they handle. The Class A extinguisher is for fires involving paper, wood, fabric, and other "ordinary combustibles." Class B extinguishers are used for liquids that combust into fire, such as overheated cooking oil in a skillet on the range.

Class C extinguishers are best for use on electrical fires.

The three classes are described in 20-17. In practice, many extinguishers available today can be used on fires of any type. They are marked ABC. Fire extinguishers should be located where they are easy to find and use. See 20-18.

### Plan for Fire Emergencies

The members of your household should have a plan of action, or *escape plan*, in case a fire occurs. Draw a scale floor plan of your home. On it, mark a main escape route and an alternate route from each room. Remember that children and older people will need special assistance in escaping from a fire. Make sure that all members of your household know the sound of the fire detector alarm

| Classes of Fires | |
|---|---|
| | **Class A Fires** Fire in ordinary combustible materials— involving paper, wood, cloth, and many plastics. |
| | **Class B Fires** Fire in flammable liquids, gases, and greases—a flash fire in your frying pan or oven—or in paint or solvents. |
| | **Class C Fires** Fires in electrical appliances and equipment— caused by faulty wiring, as in a TV. |

20-17 ⎯⎯⎯⎯⎯⎯⎯⎯⎯⎯⎯⎯⎯⎯⎯⎯⎯⎯
*Fire extinguishers are labeled for use on one, two, or all three classes of fires.*

and any other signal that might be used. For example, a loud whistle or a bell might be used to awaken and alert everyone in the home.

Everyone must understand that speed in leaving the burning building is essential. There is no time to waste getting dressed or collecting possessions. Be sure each person knows how to make the door test: If the knob or panels of the closed door are warm, do not open the door. Use an alternate escape route. If the doorknob or panels are not warm, open the door slowly. If no smoke or hot air blows in, it is probably safe to use that exit.

Part of your plan should include deciding on a place to meet once everyone is outside. After everyone is safely outside, go to the nearest telephone and call the fire department. In many areas, dialing 911 will connect you to an emergency services dispatcher. Some areas will have a local emergency number, instead. Report your name and address and describe the situation.

Once everyone knows the emergency plan, hold a practice drill. Repeat the drills periodically. Be sure to practice the use of alternate routes as well as main escape routes.

## Security from Home Intruders

Securing a home from burglary or unwanted intruders is important. Many security measures are merely common sense. For instance, do not publicize your absence when you are away from home. Most burglaries are committed during the day, while people are away at work or shopping. Take steps to make your home look lived-in, even when you are gone. The following will give a home that lived-in look:

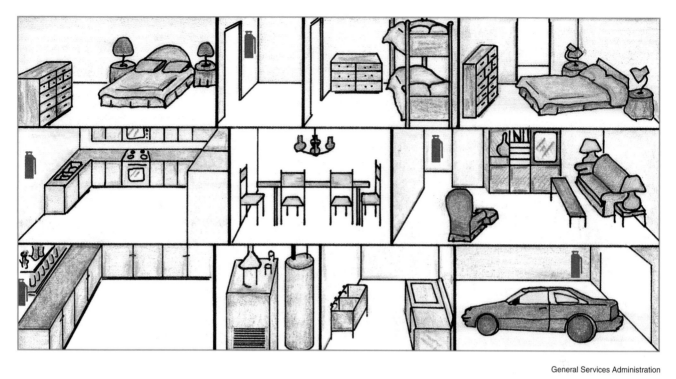

20-18

*Fire extinguishers should be installed in the garage, basement, kitchen, and easily reached locations on each floor. Ideally, they should be near exits, and no corner of the floor should be more than 75 feet away from an extinguisher.*

- leaving a vehicle in the driveway
- stopping delivery of newspapers and mail, or having a friend pick them up daily at the normal times
- returning emptied trash cans from the curb
- using a variable timer to turn lights, radio, or TV on and off
- keeping the yard mowed, or snow removed from walks
- opening drapes during the day and closing them at night
- keeping a dog that barks at strange noises

Do not let strangers into your home. You should have some way of knowing who is at the door without opening it. A peephole or a chain lock permits you to see who is there. Monitoring devices are available that permit you to see and hear the person at your door before that person sees you.

See 20-19. If a stranger asks to use your telephone, offer to make the call for him or her. Other security precautions include using outside lighting at every entrance to your home and installing secure locks on all doors and windows. You can also install a home security system with an alarm.

If a child is home alone, there are additional rules to be observed. The child should know how to use the phone, and important numbers should be available nearby. When answering the phone, no details should be given. For example, the caller should not be told the child is home alone or what time someone is expected back.

Make the exterior of your home as visible as possible. Install a system to light exterior doors and the yard. Use automatic timers so lights are on from dusk to dawn, 20-20. An alternate method is the use of motion-detecting

**Resource:** *Home Security*, reproducible master 20-2. Students learn how to protect their homes from burglars based on the information provided by a guest speaker.

**Enrich:** Determine the types of fire extinguishers needed for the rooms shown in Figure 20-18. Research the average cost of each at your local home improvement center.

**Discuss:** What are some side effects of feeling unsafe in your home?
**Note:** Most insurance companies have helpful brochures on how to prevent home invasions.

Nutone

20-19

*This video door-answering system lets you hear and see a caller at your door.*

lights that go on when anything moves near the house. Trim all shrubs so that doors and windows can be seen clearly from the street. If shrubs are growing under windows, make sure that they are thorny or cannot be used as a hiding place for an intruder.

### Locks and Other Security Devices

To make doors as secure as possible, install *deadbolt locks*, 20-21. This is a lock bolt that unlocks by turning a knob or key without action of a spring. Use the type that requires a key to unlock from the inside as well as the outside. This type is called a double-cylinder lock. When you move to a new residence, change lock cylinders to prevent entry by anyone who previously had a key to the door. Lock cylinders are less expensive than complete locks.

Keep all windows and exterior doors locked. If there is a door

**Research:** Explore the cost of video door-answering systems such as the one pictured in Figure 20-19. What is the price range?

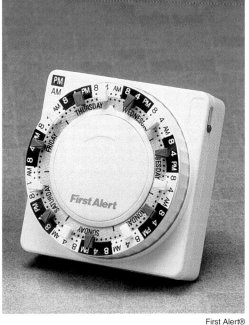

First Alert®

20-20

*A timer can be used to turn lights on at dusk and off at dawn.*

Kwikset Corporation

20-21

*A deadbolt lock makes entrances more secure. The type that requires a key to enter either side, as shown above, is best.*

**Enrich:** Observe a demonstration of a variety of locks demonstrated by a guest locksmith and write a summary of what you learned.

**Writing / Music Activity:** Work with teammates to write a rap that includes a list of ways to make a home look occupied when the family is away. Create a team presentation and perform it for a neighborhood or community organization.

between the garage and the house, keep it locked too. Never leave keys in the locks. Also, do not hide keys near entrances, such as under a mat. Intruders know the usual hiding places and can find them easily. Install extra locks or take other measures to make sliding doors and windows secure. See 20-22.

Install strong exterior doors that are made of metal or have solid wood cores. Many doors are so weak that they can be broken through with a strong kick. Hang the doors so the hinge pins are on the inside. If the pins are on the outside, a burglar can remove them and open the door. If you have a glass pane in the door, installing a rigid transparent panel is a good security measure. A panel of plastic, such as acrylic, is ideal for this purpose.

Another deterrent to burglary is to mark your valuables with an identification number. Your driver's license number is one that can be traced in any state. Marking valuables can deter a thief, since marked items are more

difficult to sell for quick cash than unmarked items. If your possessions are stolen, they are easier to trace and identify with an identification number. Keep valuable items, such as jewelry and savings bonds, safely locked away. You may wish to store them in a home safe, a private security vault, or a safe deposit box at your bank.

## Home Security Systems

Electronic home security systems are installed in many homes. The newest models use biometrics to determine who belongs in the home and who does not. *Biometrics* is identification of an individual by a unique physical characteristic. Safe, keyless entry into homes is possible with security systems that use biometric data. Fingerprints, the pattern of an eye's iris, and vein patterns in hands are some of the biometrics that can identify the members of a household.

The typical home security system, however, uses window and door sensors. The sensors trigger an alarm when someone forces open a door or window. Some systems also have sensors that are triggered by vibrations, body heat, or noise. Some also include smoke detectors or waterflow alarms, which signal a plumbing problem. Many home security systems will signal a burglary attempt with flashing lights, a siren, an alarm bell, or a combination. Other systems are connected to a monitoring station. If you are away, someone will know when the alarm goes off. The fire department or police will be notified. You can expect to pay a monthly fee for the monitoring service in addition to the installation charge.

Often the presence of a home security system will ward off intruders. Signs or stickers can be placed around the house and on doors and windows of the home to indicate the presence of

**Resource:** *Home Security Inspection Checklist,* Activity E, SAG. Students conduct a home security inspection based on a checklist and identify needed changes.
**Discuss:** Do you think you should change locks when you move into a new residence? Why or why not?
**Discuss:** Why does marking your valuable items with a drivers license number work well in deterring burglars? (*The number can be traced in any state.*)
**Vocabulary:** Examine the root words of the term *biometrics* to determine its meaning.

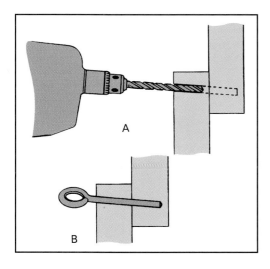

20-22
*To make windows and sliding doors more secure, drill through both frames at an overlapping point (A). Then place a pin in the hole (B).*

**Enrich:** At your local home improvement center, compare the costs of various types and styles of exterior doors. Do all of them look strong enough to withstand a forceful kick or punch with a heavy object? Decide which door you would choose, check its price, and report your choice to the class. If a sales brochure is available with a picture or description of the chosen door, pass it around for the class to view.
**Note:** Find more information about neighborhood watch programs at the Web site *nnwi.org/.*

the home security system. A barking dog may serve the same purpose. Some dogs are also trained to protect their owners. People who live on the same street may form a Neighborhood Watch program. People in such a program report any suspicious activities on their street to police. Some people prefer to live in a place that has security guards in stations or gatehouses.

Your personal needs and beliefs will affect the way you choose to keep your home secure. For instance, some people feel safe with a security guard nearby. Having a guard may make other people feel restrained or uncomfortable. No matter what your situation, you will probably want to take some security measures. Choose those that make you feel comfortable and safe within your home.

Whether you own or rent, you can take measures to prevent home accidents and safeguard your home against intruders. You will also want your home to be safe and secure for the other members of your household.

# Equipping a Home for People with Disabilities

Sometimes physical disabilities may make it necessary for a person to move from his or her home. However, if the present home can be modified, a move may be unnecessary. There are many ways that a home can be equipped to meet the needs of people with physical disabilities.

## Universal Design

Housing features that are nuisances or inconveniences to the average person can be significant barriers to people with physical disabilities.

One example is having no bathroom on the main level. Another example is a house with steps at every entrance.

Universal design refers to structural and nonstructural features that make a house easier for everyone to use. For example, a bathroom on the main level and a no-step entrance are *structural features*. These must be included in design plans during building or remodeling. Pull-out cabinet shelves, easy-to-grasp handles, and cold water dispensers on refrigerators are examples of nonstructural features. See 20-23. *Nonstructural features* are items that can be easily added to an existing house to make it more usable.

Universal design addresses the needs of everyone, not just one segment of the population. It was developed to make a house and all its components more usable. The design concept considers all household members, from

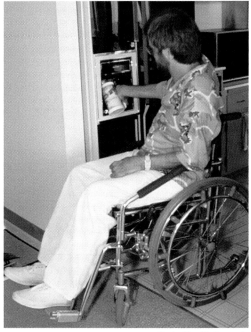

Barrier-Free Environments

20-23 ————————————————

*A refrigerator with through-the-door ice and water service was chosen for this home because family members include small children and adults with limited reach.*

the tallest to the shortest and the weakest to the strongest. Universal design addresses all the different stages in a person's life and the different personal needs they pose. With universal design, people can "age in place." Consequently, they do not need to find other housing during periods of temporary or permanent physical disability. Universal design is discussed in detail in Chapter 22, "Housing for Today and Tomorrow."

## Features for Special Needs

Few, if any, consumer products are designed specifically for people with physical disabilities. Consequently, the challenge for these consumers is finding products with features that complement their abilities. For example, various models of ranges are available with side, back, or front controls. People who can see objects close-up but not far away would benefit from a range with front controls, as shown in 20-24.

A person with a *vision disability* may have any degree of vision loss. For most people, changes in vision begin after the age of 40. These changes often become more severe after age 65. One in 20 people over the age of 85 are legally blind. People with vision disability live most comfortably and safely in familiar surroundings. Adapt living areas to the needs of a person with a vision disability with the following measures:

- Prominently mark changes in floor levels and countertop levels. Refer again to 20-24.

- Place furniture away from traffic lanes.

- Increase the amount of lighting and make sure it is evenly distributed.

- Use highly visible colors, such as yellow-orange and red.

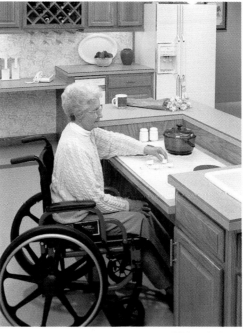

Whirlpool Appliances

20-24

*Front controls on the range are easier for people with physical disabilities to reach and operate.*

- Avoid using similar colors together. Instead, use contrasting colors to visually separate items.

- Keep a consistent light level in bedrooms and halls. Use nightlights.

- Where appropriate, use Braille or tactile markings in cookbooks and on controls, as in 20-25.

The checklist in 20-26 will help you analyze how well a home is adapted for the needs of people with vision disability.

The most common disability among older people is hearing loss. Hearing ability declines gradually, so a person with a *hearing disability* may have any degree of hearing loss. Hearing-impaired people need a communication system that complements their hearing ability. Amplifying devices on doorbells and phones may be sufficient. People with a total hearing

**Science Activity:** Investigate why hearing gradually decreases with age. What physiologically occurs to cause a diminished sense of hearing? What can accelerate poor hearing? How can people protect their sense of hearing?

**Activity:** Study Figures 20-23 and 20-24. List all the features obvious in the photos that assist a person with physical disabilities.

**Enrich:** Visit an assisted-living facility in your area that is designed with features intended for people with physical disabilities, such as vision, hearing, or mobility impairments. Identify each special feature and the function it performs.

**Research:** Find statistics regarding the prevalence of physical disabilities. On average, what percentage of Americans have a physical disability? What percentage has a temporary disability versus a permanent one? How long do temporary disabilities last? What is the average age of people with temporary disabilities? with permanent disabilities?

**Reflect:** How many people do you know who had a temporary physical disability? who have a permanent physical disability?

Writing Activity: Study Figure 20-26. Select another physical or mental disability and create a similar checklist for it.

loss will need visual signals, as in 20-27.

*Hand limitations* result from arthritis and other conditions limiting movement and gripping ability. Large lever-type controls on doors and faucets are needed for these individuals. Special faucets are also available with proximity sensors or electric eyes that turn them on and off. Electronic touch controls on appliances often are easier to use than knobs, which must

Whirlpool Appliances

20-25
*A Braille cookbook and Braille controls on the microwave help this visually impaired person make meals.*

### Checklist for Meeting the Needs of the Visually Impaired

☐ Are raised numbers or letters used on entrance doors, especially in apartment dwellings? (Note: They should be at least 3 feet above the floor.)

☐ Are hanging objects higher than the person with poor vision?

☐ Are obstructions removed from major traffic areas?

☐ Are sliding doors used on closets and elsewhere to eliminate walking into an edge of an opened door?

☐ Are handles treated with knurling (or a special adhesive) on doors that lead directly to steps or other potentially dangerous areas?

☐ Are push-button controls identifiable by touch?

☐ Are all control dials marked or shaped so fingers can feel different positions and know what settings they are? (In some cases, click stops may be substituted.)
The important controls to mark are
  ☐ range
  ☐ oven
  ☐ mixer
  ☐ faucets
  ☐ washer
  ☐ dryer

☐ Is storage adequate so items can be stored separately on adjustable shelves or similar items can be stacked without piling too high?

☐ Do water faucets always have hot water on the left and cold water on the right of the user?

20-26
*This checklist helps people adapt living spaces for people with vision loss.*

Activity: Analyze an area of your school, such as the library or cafeteria, for universally designed features. What improvements could be made?
Enrich: Attend a presentation by a county cooperative extension agent who discusses various inexpensive ways to help physically impaired individuals make better use of their existing homes. Be prepared to ask questions. Summarize in a paragraph what you learn.

be grasped and turned. Light switches that can be pressed are easier to use than those that must be moved up and down. On outside doors, keyless push-button locks are good.

A person who has a *mobility limitation* has difficulty walking. Living spaces that are all on one level will eliminate the need for using stairs. For climbing and descending stairs well, they must be easy to use. The stairway must have secure handrails and a nonskid surface on each step. Ideally, people with limited mobility should use stairways with shorter, wider steps. See 20-28.

Some mobility-impaired persons move well with the use of a walker. See 20-29. Others require a wheelchair. Accessibility requirements change drastically when the needs of a person using a walker or wheelchair must be taken into account. Determine if your house can provide a comfortable and convenient environment to a person with limited physical ability.

**Activity:** Study Figures 20-25, 20-27, and 20-29. List all the features obvious in the photos that assist a person with physical disabilities.

Axrock Industries, Inc., San Antonio Texas

20-28 _____
*Stairs used by a person with limited mobility should have a nonskid material, short risers, and wide treads.*

Nutone

20-27 _____
*A visual sign, such as a flashing lamp, signals the ringing of a telephone or doorbell to a deaf person.*

Whirlpool Appliances

20-29 _____
*Sometimes the use of a wheelchair or walker requires certain changes to the traditional placement of appliances.*

**Activity:** Study the accident-occurrence data of your school. Where have most accidents occurred? What could be done to make those locations safer? Consider a class project to address this concern.

**Reflect:** Think about the mobility-impaired people you know. Can they maneuver easily through their homes? What changes would improve their ability to use their homes more fully?

## Summary

A safe home provides freedom from accidents and offers security. Home accidents can occur to people of all ages. Special precautions should be taken to assure safety for older people, children, and people with disabilities. Preventive measures can eliminate many falls and other accidents. They also can lessen the possibility of injury as a result of fire, burns, and electrical shock.

A healthy home environment is free of air and noise pollution. You will want to know about pollutants and how to reduce them or control their sources. Proper ventilation and wise use of cleaning methods and materials are steps toward having a healthy home. Noise inside a home can be controlled in various ways.

Your home can be made more secure by using protection and warning devices. You can reduce the possibility of injury or death from fire by installing monitoring devices and fire extinguishers. An emergency plan is important in case of the need to evacuate. Good locks and an alarm system will help make your home more secure. Marking valuables help to deter theft and make stolen items easier to recover. Adjusting structural and adding certain nonstructural features can make a home safe and secure for those with special needs.

## To Review

1. List three types of home accidents. Give a possible cause for each and a precaution that could have prevented the accident.
2. Most victims of home accidents are the _____ and _____.
3. Name three health problems that may result from inside air pollution.
4. The unit of measure for sound is the _____.
5. Compare the terms *noise* and *sound*.
6. List three common products found in the home that may be hazardous.
7. Name three essentials every household should have to prevent fire injury.
8. List five ways to make a home appear occupied when everyone is away.
9. List two guidelines a child who is home alone should follow.
10. _____ locks should be used on exterior doors.
11. Name two monitoring devices that keep a home safe.
12. A good identifying number to use when marking valuables is a _____ _____ number.
13. Who in the household benefits when a home incorporates universal design?

14. List three types of home security systems.

15. List five areas to check for accessibility in a home.

14. (List three. See page 474.)

15. (List five. See pages 476-477.)

# In Your Community

1. Visit a local hardware store or a store that sells fire extinguishers. Note the different models available and their prices. Learn how to use a fire extinguisher. Explain its operation to the class.

2. Find an example of an accident (discussed in a newspaper article or TV program) that occurred locally. Explain how the accident could have been prevented.

3. Study the yellow pages of your local phone book. Make a list of companies that can be hired to detect the presence of radon, carbon monoxide, mold, lead paint, and asbestos in residences. You may need to call the companies to confirm that they offer the specific services. Share the list with your class. Consider asking a representative from one of these companies to give a presentation on how the pollutants are detected and removed.

# To Think About

1. The impact of lead poisoning can be severe on small children. Do you think the federal government should require the testing of older dwellings to determine the presence of lead paint before households with young children are allowed to move into the units? Why or why not?

2. How important is being aware of harmful molds in residences? Can people unknowingly expose themselves and their households to harmful indoor air quality? Who is responsible for investigating the presence of harmful mold: the current homeowner, the previous owner, or some government agency? Explain your position.

3. Instead of moving to a group-living arrangement, many senior citizens want to continue living in their own homes as long as possible. Yet, in their older years, getting around their homes grows more difficult. Do you think local building codes should require universal design features in new homes? Why or why not? Consider cost, aesthetics, and benefits in your analysis.

# Using Technology

1. Design a brochure titled "Safety for Children in the Home." Publish the brochure using a computer software program. Share the brochure with your classmates as well as household members.

2. Using a computer-assisted design program, produce a floor plan of your home that shows the location of smoke detectors, fire extinguishers, and routes for fire escape. Share the plan with your household members.

3. Search the Internet for information on radon, carbon monoxide, mold, lead paint, or asbestos. Produce a report on your findings and share the report with your class.

**Portfolio Project:** Develop a slide, transparency, or PowerPoint® presentation on safety and security in the home.

CHAPTER 21

# Maintaining Your Home

## To Know

disinfectant
plumbing plunger
closet auger
finish nail
box nail
short circuit
redecorating
interior designer
remodeling

**Resource:** *A Safe and Attractive Environment*, transparency master overlay V-C, TR. Students look back at the topics covered in Chapters 1-20 by reviewing transparency master V-A and overlay V-B. Then, with the addition of overlay V-C, they explore the topics they will cover in Chapter 21.

**Vocabulary:** Students work in pairs to select the four terms from the vocabulary list they know best as well as the four terms they know least. Each pair compares their words to another pair's. Which terms appear on both lists? Students check the glossary for the definition of words they do not know.

**Note:** Cartoons that deal with clutter, cleaning, and home maintenance may be used throughout the chapter.

## Objectives

After studying this chapter, you will be able to

- select the cleaning tools, products, and schedule needed to maintain your home.
- summarize how to properly maintain the landscape.
- explain how to use basic tools for common home repairs.
- list ways to improve storage and organize space.
- assess your redecorating choices.
- identify the pros and cons of remodeling.
- list resources for home maintenance.

Maintaining a home involves keeping it clean, safe and in good repair. It also involves making sure that equipment, electrical and plumbing systems, and other parts of the home are in proper working order. Maintenance is needed to keep the home environment secure and comfortable. You will use the decision-making process to choose how and to what level you maintain your home.

# Keeping the Home Clean and Well Maintained

Every house is different, and everyone has different standards of cleanliness. One person wants every part of a room spotless and each object in its place. See 21-1. Another person may not mind some clutter. When people share a home, they should come to an agreement on acceptable cleaning standards. The standards should be realistic. Everyone should be able to work together to meet the standards.

A certain minimum standard is needed for the health and safety of family members. Garbage must be contained and removed from the dwelling regularly. If garbage is uncovered or left for a period of time, it can attract animals and insects. In addition, any items that cause odors should be removed or properly stored. This helps to keep the air fresh.

## Interior Home Maintenance and Cleaning

It is important to decide how much time you can devote to cleaning. Your decision affects your choices in home furnishings. For instance, if you want to devote as little time as possible to cleaning, you would choose furnishings that do not show soil readily or contain fine woods. Also, you would avoid furniture and accessories that require frequent care. These include items that must be polished, shined, or frequently dusted.

Cleaning is easier if there is little or no clutter to maneuver around. Clutter can be eliminated in a number of ways. You can recycle items such as newspapers and cans. Items that are obviously junk should be discarded. If you are like most people, you will keep some items that you treasure, even though they produce clutter.

### Cleaning Tools

Cleaning the home is easier if you have the right equipment or cleaning tools. There are two main types of cleaning tools. The first type is used to remove loose dust and dirt. These tools include the following:

21-1 _____
*Cleanup is much quicker and easier when all household members help keep the home tidy.*

- a dust mop for picking up dust on hard floors
- a broom and dustpan for sweeping hard-surface floors and steps
- a vacuum cleaner with attachments for carpets, hard floors, woodwork, furniture, upholstery, and curtains
- cloths for dusting and polishing

The second type of cleaning tool removes soil that is stuck to surfaces. These cleaning tools include the following:

- sponges for washing walls, woodwork, and appliances
- a pail to hold cleaning solutions
- a wet mop for cleaning floors
- a toilet bowl brush
- a stepladder or stool for reaching high places

See 21-2 for a variety of cleaning tools.

### Cleaning Products

Cleaning products include the chemicals that aid you in your cleaning tasks. The basic cleaning products you should always have are:

- a glass cleaner for mirrors, bathroom fixtures, and the surfaces of kitchen appliances
- a grease-cutting liquid for fingerprints, oily stains, or soap residue
- a mild abrasive powder for stubborn stains on countertops and work surfaces

Some cleaning agents, waxes, and polishes are listed in 21-3. Many cleaning products also contain a *disinfectant*, which is a cleaning agent that destroys bacteria. Before you purchase any cleaning product, check your supplies. You may already have what you need. Look for those that can be used for more

21-2 _____
*These are some of the tools needed to get surfaces clean.*

Resource: *Comparing Cleaning Products*, reproducible master 21-1, TR. Working in groups, students test various cleaning products, record their procedures, and report their results.
**Discuss:** Do you think your family has far more cleaning tools and products than are actually needed to clean the home. Explain.

than one purpose. There are many multi-purpose cleaning products. Most are available in dry and liquid forms.

You must also be aware of dangers associated with many cleaning products. Check labels to see if the products are toxic. Many cleaning compounds are poisonous or flammable. In addition, always read labels on cleaning products to make sure they will not damage the surface you are cleaning. Follow directions carefully. Finally, do not mix different cleaning products. Some products create toxic gases when mixed with other cleaning agents.

To help make cleaning easier, keep all cleaning items in an organized area. See 21-4. Always store cleaning products out of the reach of children

**Discuss:** If there are toddlers and young children in the home, even as frequent guests, where should cleaning supplies be stored? (*out of their reach or in locked cabinets*)

**Reflect:** Does your family have a bucket or carrying tray to hold the cleaners you use on a regular basis?

| Cleaning Products | |
|---|---|
| **Cleaning Agents** | **Method of Action** |
| *Water* | Dilutes and flushes dirt away |
| *Alkalies*<br>• Soaps<br>• Washing soda<br>• Some general purpose cleaner | Breaks down surface tension of water, allowing the cleaning agent to penetrate dirt better |
| *Synthetic detergent* | Relieves surface tension to clean and cut grease better than soaps; does not react with minerals to form scum deposits as soap does |
| *Acid*<br>• Ammonia<br>• Vinegar<br>• Lemon juice | Cuts grease and acts as a mild bleach |
| *Fat solvent* | Dissolves soil held by grease |
| *Fat absorbent*<br>• Fuller's earth<br>• Talcum<br>• Bentonite<br>• Cornmeal | Absorbs oils in a dry form, then is brushed away with the soil |
| *Abrasive*<br>• Silver polish<br>• Scouring powder<br>• Steel wool<br>• Soap pads | Rubs dirt away in dry form or with water (depending on type) |
| **Waxes and Polishes** | **Method of Action** |
| *Solvent-base cleaning wax*<br>• Liquid wax<br>• Paste wax | Loosens soil on hard floors, removes old wax, and forms a new wax coating |
| *Water-base cleaning wax*<br>• Emulsion wax<br>• Solution wax | Loosens soil on hard floors other than wood and cork, and forms a new wax coating; won't remove old wax, which must be stripped with remover |
| *Furniture polish*<br>• Aerosol spray<br>• Creamy liquid<br>• Paste polishes | Lifts soil, removes old wax, and forms a new wax coating |
| *Multipurpose cleaner wax* | Lifts soil from countertops, tiles, appliances, cabinets, and furniture; removes old wax and forms a new wax coating |

21-3

*Using the proper cleaning agent for the job is important.*

Kraftmaid

21-4

*Storing cleaning supplies in one place helps make cleaning easier.*

or in locked cabinets. Keep cleaning products away from heat sources.

## Cleaning Schedule

Some people prefer to get their work done early in the day. Others like to sleep late and work at night. Some people like housework, while others do not. Whatever your energy level or your work pattern is, scheduling your cleaning tasks allows you to better use your cleaning time. A list of common tasks is shown in 21-5.

Your cleaning schedule may vary from day to day or week to week. It depends on the use of your facilities. The more often facilities are used, the greater the need for cleaning. Less use usually means less cleaning. The larger the household is, the greater the cleaning task. When making a cleaning schedule, include the name of the person

### Checklist for Cleaning Tasks

*Daily Tasks*
- ❑ Make bed.
- ❑ Straighten bedroom, bathroom, living area, and eating area.
- ❑ Wash dishes.
- ❑ Wipe kitchen counters and cooking surface.
- ❑ Sweep kitchen floor.
- ❑ Empty wastebaskets, ashtrays, and other garbage containers.

*Weekly Tasks*
- ❑ Change bed linens.
- ❑ Do laundry and mending.
- ❑ Wash kitchen garbage pail or change liner.
- ❑ Wash kitchen floor.
- ❑ Clean bathroom sink, tub, and toilet.
- ❑ Wash bathroom floor.
- ❑ Dust accessories.
- ❑ Dust and polish furniture.
- ❑ Vacuum lampshades.
- ❑ Vacuum carpet.
- ❑ Shake out small rugs.

*Monthly Tasks*
- ❑ Vacuum and turn mattress.
- ❑ Wash mattress pad.
- ❑ Remove old wax and rewax hard floors.
- ❑ Vacuum drapes and wipe blinds.
- ❑ Vacuum upholstered furniture.
- ❑ Clean kitchen shelves.
- ❑ Clean refrigerator, and defrost if needed.
- ❑ Clean range, including oven.
- ❑ Wash bathroom walls.

*Semiannual Tasks*
- ❑ Clean closets.
- ❑ Dry-clean or wash bedding.
- ❑ Clean drapes thoroughly.
- ❑ Wash seldom-used glasses and dinnerware.
- ❑ Clean silverware.
- ❑ Replace shelf liners.
- ❑ Wash walls.
- ❑ Clean woodwork.

21-5

*A checklist for cleaning tasks will help keep you on schedule.*

**Activity:** Working with teammates, determine what cleaning products from the list in Figure 21-3 could best be used for each task listed in Figure 21-5. Create a suggested list.

**Math Activity:** Imagine that you have $50 to spend on cleaning tools and products for your first apartment. Make a detailed list of all the items you would purchase, recording actual products and prices. Also, report the size and type of the cleaning product purchased, such as *12-oz. spray, 6-oz. paste,* or *16-oz. liquid.* Total the price of items on the list.

responsible for each task. Divide the tasks among household members.

Weekly cleaning tasks are easier if each family member helps with daily maintenance. For example, each person can be responsible for cleaning the bathtub or shower after bathing. An immediate wipe-down should leave it clean. Supply a sponge, brush, or towel. You may also need to use a glass cleaner. Keep everything needed for the task in the bathroom.

Techniques and procedures for regular and special cleaning of household items depend on their individual characteristics. There are many different types of furnishings on the market, requiring different cleaning approaches. See 21-6 for guidelines for furniture care and maintenance.

Over time, walls and woodwork will need more than cleaning. If the paint begins to chip or fade, you will want to repaint the surface. If wallpaper was installed, you may need to periodically reglue corners that begin to peel. If the wallpaper has become faded or damaged, you will need to strip the walls and select a new wall treatment. See 21-7.

## Exterior Home Maintenance and Cleaning

Just as it is necessary to clean and maintain the interior of your home, you need to establish a schedule for the house's exterior. A house represents one of the biggest investments of your lifetime. It is extremely important to keep the structure in good condition to avoid costly repairs and preserve its economic value. You will need to monitor all exterior areas.

### Roof, Gutters and Downspouts

Often homeowners do not realize the importance of keeping the roof,

gutters, and downspouts free of debris, such as leaves and branches. If the roof is constructed of shingles or metal, it is important to protect it from being scraped by moving branches that may scrape and damage the roof during a windstorm. Also, leaves and twigs should not accumulate on the roof as they contribute excess moisture that eventually causes damage.

Proper maintenance of gutters and downspouts also is essential. Gutters and downspouts should be kept clear of anything that may block the proper flow of water off the roof. Routine cleaning is recommended, and special attention is needed after storms and in autumn after heavy leaf-fall. See 21-8. If rainwater cannot flow off the roof, it will backup into the attic space and wall cavities. Water can cause extreme damage and eventually contribute to problems from mold, rot, and termites.

### Exterior Walls

The exterior walls of a house can be made of wood siding, manufactured siding, or masonry, such as brick or stucco. Wood siding needs to be monitored for rot and replaced as needed. Regular painting or staining is necessary to protect wood siding from the eroding effects of weather. See 21-9. Between paintings, the exterior siding should be pressure-washed to remove stains caused by mildew. Manufactured siding, such as fiberboard and fiber cement siding, also needs to be washed and painted on a regular basis.

If the house is constructed of brick, routine inspection of the mortar is important. Over time, the mortar between the bricks deteriorates and needs to be replaced. The term for this replacement procedure is *pointing up* the brick.

| Furniture Care and Maintenance | |
|---|---|
| Always observe the following general cautions: <br> • Save care labels that come with new furniture and follow instructions. <br> • When using commercial cleaning products, read and follow the manufacturer's label instructions. <br> • When using chemicals, protect your eyes with safety goggles or glasses. | |
| **Furniture Materials** | **Cleaning Procedures** |
| *Wood* <br> • Used indoors | Regular cleaning:  Vacuum and/or dust with a soft, dry cloth; do not use oiled or treated cloth. <br> Special cleaning: <br> • Use a liquid furniture wax or cream polish that gives the desired gloss. <br> • If dirty, clean with a cleaning or polishing furniture wax according to label directions, or with a solution of boiled linseed oil and mineral spirits in equal parts. Moisten a soft cloth with cleaner and rub briskly, changing the cloth when soiled. |
| *Upholstery* <br> • May be on furniture with or without springs <br> • Generally used indoors <br> • May have a stain-repellent finish | Regular cleaning:  Vacuum and check for any objects lodged in the folds of fabric or under cushions. <br> Special cleaning:  If heavily soiled, clean with a solution of two teaspoons of detergent to one pint of water. Test a small area on the back or underside for fading before proceeding with cleaning. Dip a brush or cloth in the solution and clean only small areas at a time. Rinse the cleaned area before moving to another and avoid wetting the furniture too much. |
| *Aluminum* <br> • Generally used outdoors | Regular cleaning:  Wash painted frames with mild soap and water. Coat the finish with auto wax to add protection. Do not use abrasive material or strong detergents. <br> Special cleaning: <br> • To brighten mildly discolored surfaces, wash with a solution of soap and water, and a small amount of a mild household acid, such as lemon juice, vinegar, or cream of tarter. (Aluminum used outdoors may darken) <br> • If the finish is pitted, polish with a soap-filled steel wool pot cleaner and rinse dry. All steel wool must be removed or it will rust and stain the aluminum. |
| *Painted metal furniture* <br> • Often used outdoors <br> • Also used indoors in children's rooms or casual settings | Regular cleaning: Wash surface with warm water and a heavy-duty liquid detergent. Rinse thoroughly with clean water to remove any detergent residue. Wipe dry or allow to air dry in a sunny or heated room. Apply automobile liquid or paste wax and polish. <br> Special care: To help clean tiny crevices, use a small brush, such as an old toothbrush. |
| *Wicker, rattan, and bamboo* <br> • Can be used throughout the home <br> • Is often used on enclosed porches <br> • Is not recommended for regular outdoor use | Regular cleaning: Vacuum, then wipe with a rag soaked in a mild detergent and warm water solution. Use a small brush to remove stubborn dirt. <br> Special cleaning: If mildew is a problem, wash the furniture with a solution of ¾ cup of chlorine bleach and one quart of water. Since bleach may lighten the surface, apply it to the entire piece of furniture. |

*(continued)*

21-6 _____

*For best results, always use the right cleaning agent and technique for each type of furniture surface.*

**Activity:** Working with teammates, solve puzzles made from Figure 21-6. Cut a copy of the double-column portion of the chart into two parts along the vertical line. (Eliminate the general information at the beginning. Note: the chart spans two pages.) Cut the left columns into 9 blocks of "Furniture Materials," following the horizontal lines. Place these in an envelope. Do the same with the right-hand column, placing the 9 descriptions of "Cleaning Procedures" into another envelope. Give both envelopes to another team. Take the envelopes you receive and sort the strips, matching each furniture material to its cleaning procedure.

| Furniture Care and Maintenance | |
| --- | --- |
| **Furniture Materials** | **Cleaning Procedures** |
| *Plastic resin*<br>• Used most often outdoors<br>• Also used in children's rooms | Regular cleaning:<br>• Use a nonabrasive all-purpose cleaner or a cleaner-polish and follow package directions.<br>• Wipe the surface with a solution made of hand dishwashing liquid and warm water. Rinse thoroughly and dry with a clean soft cloth. |
| *Slipcover*<br>• Adds a new look to old furniture<br>• Protects new furniture | Regular cleaning:  Vacuum while still on furniture, remove, and shake out loose dirt outdoors.<br>Special cleaning:  If washable, wash in warm water and laundry detergent. Do not overcrowd the washer. Smooth over furniture while still a little damp. Straighten seams and cording. Do not use furniture until the covers are completely dry. |
| *Cane*<br>• Used in the seats of dining room or occasional chairs | Regular cleaning:  Vacuum or dust regularly. Occasionally wipe with a damp cloth. |
| *Redwood*<br>• Used outdoors because of natural resistance to weathering and rot | Regular cleaning: Maintain a coating with a sealer to keep out moisture and thus retard cracks. Scrub with detergent and water. Rinse and dry thoroughly before sealing.<br>Special cleaning: Colored sealers restore redness to grayed redwood. |

21-6 _____

*(continued)*

**Writing Activity:** Recommend ways to preserve for future reference the furniture care labels and other information obtained at the time of a product's purchase.

© 2002 The Sherwin Williams Company

21-7 _____

*This couple decided to hang wallpaper to give a new look to the room.*

Stucco walls also require washing to eliminate the growth of mildew. However, special care must be used because the walls can be damaged by a high-pressure wash.

Regardless of your home's exterior, it is important to have the home inspected annually for termites. Termites are pale-colored insects that feed on wood, particularly wood that is holding moisture. Termites can destroy the structure of a house. Many companies offer service contracts that provide annual inspections and effective treatments, should any termites appear.

### Windows and Doors

Windows and doors are expensive investments in a house and should be treated with special attention. They require regular cleaning and careful

**Internet Activity:** Find Web sites that provide information about termites and carpenter ants native to your area. Summarize what you learn, explaining how to identify the insects and treat any spots where they are observed. Explain why homeowners should vigilantly watch for any signs of their presence.

21-8 _____
*One storm or windy fall day can fill gutters with enough leaves and twigs to prevent rainwater from reaching the downspouts.*

inspections to make sure they stay properly caulked and sealed. Use caulk and sealants to fill cracks and gaps that may appear over time. Caulking prevents air leakage, which is a cause of higher heating and cooling costs. Weather stripping that wears out over time should also be replaced. Inspect windows and doors made of wood for rot, too, and replace them as needed.

### Driveways, Patios, Terraces, Decks, and Porches

Driveways, patios, terraces, decks, and porches represent expensive components of the home's exterior environment. They, too, must be inspected routinely and well maintained.

Driveways may be constructed of concrete, asphalt, brick, or a variety of other materials. All are subject to heavy traffic, which eventually results

21-9 _____
*This siding can be corrected with a fresh coat of paint, but the surface must be scraped smooth and cleaned first. Installing maintenance-free siding may be more cost effective.*

in the need for repair. Driveway surfaces should be checked periodically for cracks and other signs of deterioration. Then, timely repairs should be made, filling cracks with a compatible product. When repairs become extensive, the driveway will need to be resurfaced or replaced.

Periodic pressure washing keeps the areas free of excess dirt and algae growth. You can also apply products called water sealants to the surface to repel moisture. These same steps should be taken to properly maintain patios and terraces.

**Discuss:** What piece of safety equipment does the worker have ready to use in Figure 21-9?

**Reflect:** Do you have specific daily, weekly, and monthly responsibilities regarding cleaning and maintaining areas in and around your home?

**Discuss:** What safety issues might arise from poorly maintained driveways, patios, decks, and porches?

**Reflect:** How is outside work taken care of at your home? Who is responsible for each task?

Decks and porches should be inspected for any signs of damage or rot. They, too, benefit from routine pressure washing, and painting or staining as needed. Careful inspection of handrails, steps, and railings is important to make sure they are safe and secure for use.

21-10 _____

*Many mowers shred the cut grass into fine pieces that sift to the soil and serve as mulch for the lawn.*

# Outdoor and Lawn Care

After you have spent time, money, and energy in making the outdoor living space attractive and inviting, you need to maintain it. You should make a maintenance schedule for that part of your environment. Some special tools will be needed to maintain the outdoor living space.

## Tools for Outdoor Tasks

If you have a lawn, a lawn mower is probably the most expensive and necessary outdoor tool. Most lawn mowers are powered by gasoline or electricity. The mower shown in 21-10 not only cuts grass, but also shreds it for mulch. Since landfills are filling up, people are being encouraged to use clippings as mulch throughout the landscape. Many communities charge extra to accept yard waste. Some areas will not accept it at all.

Other powered outdoor tools commonly used around a home are leaf blowers, lawn trimmers, and weed cutters. They are used for cutting down unwanted plants. Outdoor hand tools include pruning and lopping shears, shovels, rakes, and hoes. See 21-11.

Many yard tasks involve the use of tools that cut through plants or soil. This is true of all the tools mentioned thus far. The more frequently you sharpen these tools, the easier they are to use. In addition, sharp tools are safer and less likely to damage plants. You may want to sharpen your tools yourself, or you can have them sharpened professionally.

## Yard Maintenance

Yard maintenance should be scheduled according to the season.

The specific outdoor tasks will vary depending upon where you live. Plant life may need special care to withstand extremely hot or cold weather. During such periods, watering continues but fertilizing stops. Mulch is applied around the bases of trees, shrubs, and bushes. The mulch insulates the roots and helps to retain moisture and maintain a more moderate temperature. Sensitive plants may need to be wrapped for protection from extreme cold or wind.

Some summer-flowering bulbs, such as gladiolus, need to be dug up after the leaves have dried. These bulbs can be replanted in the spring. Bulbs that bloom in the spring need to be planted in the fall. Bulbs that bloom in the spring generally are not dug up and replanted.

If you live in an area where the ground freezes during winter, begin watering and fertilizing your landscape plants when the ground thaws. At the first sign of sprouting in the spring, roses and other plants that are covered during the winter in your area should be uncovered. Wait until the last frost to plant summer-blooming bulbs and flower seeds. You can divide perennials into smaller clumps at this time, and trim most trees and shrubs. Long-handled lopping shears are the best tool for shaping trees and shrubs and removing dead limbs.

Keeping mulch around plants will inhibit weed growth as well as retain the moisture in the ground. If plants begin to wilt, it is usually an indication that watering is needed. The age of the plants, the soil characteristics, and the weather are all factors in determining your watering schedule. Drip irrigation is especially useful for directing water straight to a plant's roots.

A lawn requires regular care during the growing season. When watering a

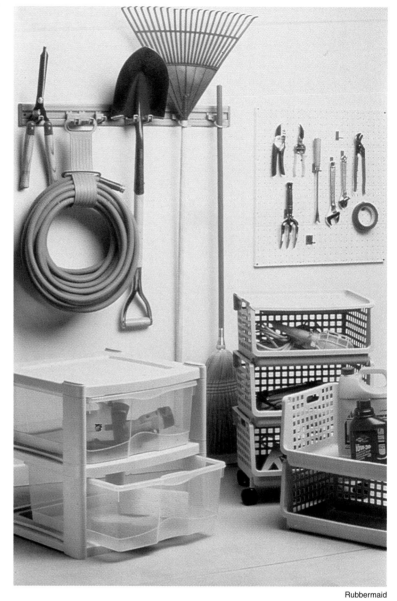

Rubbermaid

21-11

*Keeping the landscape well maintained often involves enough tools to merit their own storage center in the garage.*

lawn, it is better to water thoroughly and less often than to underwater often. Thorough watering encourages deeper root growth. The soil should remain moist between 8 and 12 inches under the ground. Weeds compete for space, moisture, and nutrients in the lawn. These unsightly plants can be eliminated by hand weeding or by chemical methods. Any products

**Research:** Investigate drip irrigation. Explain what it is and how it is installed. Where is it most often used? What is the main benefit of such a system?

**Math Activity:** Research the cost of professionally maintaining an average lawn in your community. Contact at least two lawn-service companies to find out the services offered and the costs. What is their definition of the average size lawn? Compare costs, and recommend the company you would select, explaining why.

**Research:** Investigate the various forms of mulch appropriate in your area and determine their effectiveness. How quickly does each break down and need to be replaced? Also, find out what one cubic foot of each costs.

**Resource:** *Repair Work,* Activity B, SAG. Students itemize the cost of assembling a home repair kit and answer related questions.
**Enrich:** Attend a presentation by a horticulturist from the county cooperative extension office to learn about proper care of lawns, trees, perennials, and other garden plants. Report what you learn.
**Discuss:** Why do you think good root growth is so important to plants?
**Enrich:** Visit a classroom used for career and technical education classes to observe various basic tools. Identify as many of the tools as possible.

applied to the yard should be handled carefully. Like household cleaning products, yard care products may be poisonous. Check to see how long after treatment it is safe for children and pets to play on the lawn. Use and store them according to directions.

Mowing the grass is a critical part of lawn care. If you mow the grass in a diagonal direction, you will prevent a striped look. Change directions each time you mow. Mowing the lawn too closely will prevent the development of a healthy root system. A general rule is to cut only the top third of the grass with each mowing, 21-12. Your mowing schedule will depend on the rate your grass grows.

# Making Common Home Repairs

Keeping a home safe and comfortable requires regular care and maintenance. Homeowner maintenance includes the inspection and repairs needed to keep the home safe and prolong its life. Often you can make the repairs yourself with the right

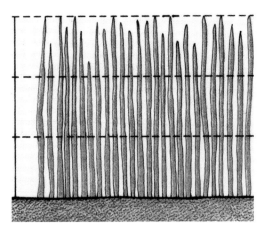

21-12

*Green grass is usually brown near its base. For a green lawn after mowing, never cut more than one-third off the top.*

tools and some basic knowledge of what to do.

When knowledge and experience is limited, you may want to hire a professional to do the work. This is especially important when safety is involved. Some utility companies have professional service people to handle electrical or gas repairs. Even the best do-it-yourself homeowner needs to call on a skilled professional from time to time.

## The Basic Tools

Tools can be expensive, but you should buy quality tools because they last longer. Consider shopping around or buying from discount stores. You can build your supply of tools by buying only what you need. To get the right tool for your job, ask for advice from people with experience. The following are basic tools, many of which are shown in 21-13.

### Hammer

A general purpose 16-ounce model with a curved claw is used primarily for driving and pulling nails. The curved claw provides leverage when pulling nails. The medium-weight head performs finish work as well as rough work.

### Screwdriver

A screwdriver is used for driving and removing screws. You need a straight blade screwdriver and a Phillips tip screwdriver. Both come in various sizes. The blade of the screwdriver must fit the slot(s) in the head of the screw to work.

### Adjustable Wrench

A wrench is used to tighten and loosen nuts and bolts. This tool is adjustable to fit nuts of different sizes.

**Social Studies Activity:** Interview people age 65 and older about how lawns and yards have changed since they were children. What has been the biggest change?

**Activity:** Working with a partner, create a list of exterior maintenance jobs around a home. Determine a schedule for how often they should be checked.

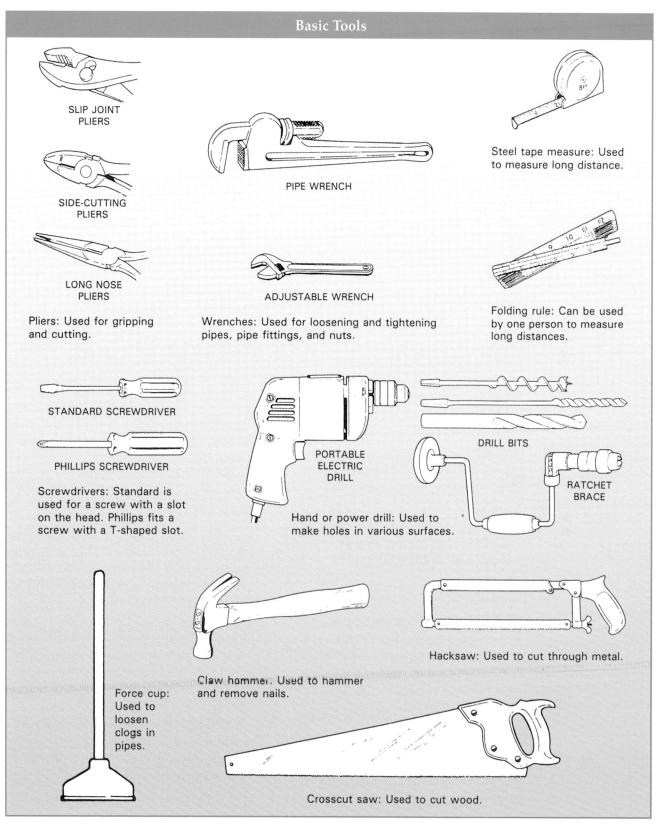

## Basic Tools

SLIP JOINT PLIERS

SIDE-CUTTING PLIERS

LONG NOSE PLIERS

Pliers: Used for gripping and cutting.

PIPE WRENCH

ADJUSTABLE WRENCH

Wrenches: Used for loosening and tightening pipes, pipe fittings, and nuts.

Steel tape measure: Used to measure long distance.

Folding rule: Can be used by one person to measure long distances.

STANDARD SCREWDRIVER

PHILLIPS SCREWDRIVER

Screwdrivers: Standard is used for a screw with a slot on the head. Phillips fits a screw with a T-shaped slot.

PORTABLE ELECTRIC DRILL

Hand or power drill: Used to make holes in various surfaces.

DRILL BITS

RATCHET BRACE

Force cup: Used to loosen clogs in pipes.

Claw hammer: Used to hammer and remove nails.

Hacksaw: Used to cut through metal.

Crosscut saw: Used to cut wood.

21-13

*These basic tools will help you handle many household maintenance tasks.*

**Reflect:** Which of the tools in Figure 21-13 does your family own?
**Discuss:** What tools do you think every person should own when they move to their first home?

**Enrich:** Have an agriculture teacher or county cooperative extension agent demonstrate how to sharpen a tool.

If a nut is hard to turn, apply a few drops of a lubricant. Let it soak for the recommend time period. If the wrench slips off the nut, turn the wrench over.

### Plumbing Plunger

A *plumbing plunger* is a device used to create a suction motion to clear a blocked drain. The plunger is also called a *force cup*. There are two types. A molded plunger is used for curved surfaces, such as the toilet bowl. The flat plunger is for level surfaces, such as sinks, showers, and tubs.

### Side-Cutting Pliers

This tool is used for cutting wire and stripping the insulation and plastic coating from electrical wire. Take care to not cut into the wire when removing the insulation.

### Long-Nose Pliers

These pliers are appropriate for bending wire and positioning small components into close and difficult work areas. This tool is not a substitute for a wrench and should not be used when objects must be securely gripped and tightened.

### Tape Measure

Choose a retractable tape measure that is at least 16 feet long and ¾-inch wide. There are many types of measuring tapes on the market. Some have a thumb lock to prevent the tape from retracting when in use.

### Channel-Lock Pliers

Sometimes called slip-joint pliers, this handy tool tightens nuts and bolts. This basic plumbing tool provides a secure grip on many common materials.

### Pipe Wrench

The pipe wrench is a holding tool for assembling fittings on pipe. Teeth are set at an angle in one direction. The teeth are designed to grip a curved surface firmly and produce a ratchet effect. This effect forces an ever-tighter grip and prevents the grip from loosening.

### Hacksaw

The hacksaw is a general-purpose tool for cutting metal. The teeth of the hacksaw can cut pipe when the tool is pushed forward. A hacksaw has no cutting action when it is pulled toward the body.

### Crosscut Saw

This saw, used to cut across the grain of wood, can also be used as a general purpose saw for sheet materials such as plywood. Many types work well for a variety of purposes. A ten-point crosscut, for example, has 10 teeth per inch of saw blade.

### Electric Drill

An electric drill is a light-duty tool to drill holes and drive or loosen nuts and screws. With a special attachment, it becomes a lightweight buffer or grinder. The size of a drill is determined by the drill chuck. The chuck is the clamping device that holds the drill bit. Common sizes are ¼-inch and ⅜-inch. For versatility, you need a ⅜-inch chuck, variable speed, and a reversible motor. You need a variety of drill bits, which are sized by diameter in one of three systems: fractional, decimal, and letters. Straight-shank drill bits will drill holes in metal and wood.

### Closet Auger

When there is blockage in the toilet caused by a washcloth or some item that can be retrieved, the closet auger is a useful tool. A *closet auger* is a device used to bore items to free blocked plumbing or wastewater lines. In some cases, the blockage is caused by a comb, pencil, or other object that cannot be retrieved. Usually the object can be forced through the pipe by alternately using the closet auger and plumbing plunger.

### Electricity Tester

Electrical circuits can be tested safely with an electrical tester, called a neon tester. Most hardware stores sell this item inexpensively. The tester is designed to light up in the presence of 110 volts and 220 volts. To use, firmly press each lead against the terminals. If the circuit has electricity, the light will go on.

### Flashlight

A two-cell unit is sufficient for most household needs. An industrial rated flashlight is brighter and more durable.

### Toolbox

One of the most overlooked yet vital components of a tool collection is a toolbox to hold your tools. Metal or plastic toolboxes are affordable and come in a variety of sizes and shapes. The main purpose of a toolbox is to keep your tools in the same location for use when repairs are necessary. See 21-14.

## Plumbing Repairs

Plumbing problems can occur in any home at any time. Some problems appear suddenly, such as when an item

Lasko Products

21-14

*When shopping for toolboxes, buy one that holds all the tools you use regularly.*

is accidentally dropped into a toilet. Other problems develop over time. Drains become sluggish or faucets and pipes begin to leak. Certain problems can result in water damage to parts of the home, adding to the repair costs. If you can handle minor plumbing repairs yourself, you can save the expense and inconvenience of hiring a plumber. One of the most common problems is a clogged drain. Pipes tend to clog when foreign matter finds its way into waste lines and accumulates.

**Activity:** Call three plumbers in your area. What is the charge just to come to your house? How much do they charge per hour or per job? Does the cost of the visit apply toward parts and labor? Create a chart comparing your findings.

**Enrich:** Compare the different styles and types of flashlights available by visiting a home improvement center or hardware store. What is your opinion of the most expensive flashlight and the least expensive one? Determine which of the types available is the best value for your needs and write a paragraph summarizing your decision.

**Discuss:** Why is a toolbox considered an important part of your tool supply?

**Vocabulary:** Demonstrate your understanding of the term *caustic* by using it correctly in a sentence.

**Note:** Some vapors can be caustic, resulting in damage to nasal passages, the throat, esophagus, and respiratory system. Be sure to have windows and doors open if the product's directions call for a well-ventilated area during use.

## Clogged Drains

The most common cause of a clogged drain is foreign matter, such as grease and hair, in the drainage system. Stoppages in the drainage system rarely occur in straight, horizontal, or vertical runs of piping. They usually occur where two pipes are joined together with a fitting, creating a change of direction. Stoppages may also occur in the trap, shown in 21-15.

If a drain is partially clogged, one cleaning method uses a chemical drain cleaner. Drain cleaners are available in liquid or crystal forms. Liquid drain cleaners are heavier than water and settle into the trap to dissolve grease, food, soap, and hair. Crystal cleaners in granular form begin the chemical cleaning process when they come in contact with the water in the trap.

Use these chemicals with caution because they are poisonous and caustic. A *caustic* substance will burn your skin. Wear protective gloves and keep your face away from the drain opening. Carefully read the directions on each container. Use acid drain cleaners to dissolve soap and hair. Alkalies cut grease. Never mix chemical cleaners because toxic gas may form.

If a drain is completely clogged, chemical cleaners may not work. The tool to use in this case is a flat plumbing plunger, as shown in 21-16. First remove the basket strainer in the sink waste outlet. If it is a double compartment sink, plug the other waste outlet with a rag to prevent loss of pressure in the drain. Place the flat force cup of the plunger directly over the drain opening. Two inches of standing water will provide the necessary seal for the force cup to take hold. Grip the plunger handle firmly with both hands and push down with a slow, even pressure. Pull up quickly and repeat the process several times. This will unstop most sink drains.

If the stoppage still exists, try a flexible spring cable. Place a container under the trap. Loosen two nuts on the trap and remove the J-bend. Use a small auger with a ¼-inch spring

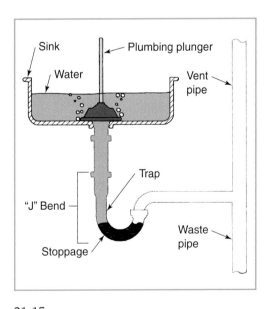

21-15 _____

*Since there is a curve in the trap, stoppage is likely to occur here.*

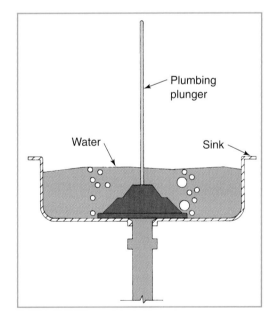

21-16 _____

*A plunger is pumped up and down to form a suction and surge in the drain.*

**Note:** The purpose of the trap in plumbing, shown in Figure 21-15, is to hold a small amount of water in the pipe to form a liquid barrier to sewer gases that would otherwise rise into the home.

**Writing Activity:** Create a flow chart that shows the steps to checking plumbing problems in a sink or toilet.

cable. Feed the cable slowly into the drainpipe. Rotate the cable as you feed it. Turn the handle until the obstruction is broken up. See 21-17. When finished, remove the cable, replace the J-bend, and tighten the nuts. Flush the drain with hot water and check for leaks.

When a toilet is clogged, try to determine the cause of the stoppage. If the substance will not cause additional blockage when forced into the drainage system, use the molded plunger. If material such as a diaper caused the stoppage, use the closet auger. Since an auger has a flexible spring cable, it can make sharp turns in a drain.

For some items, you may need to use the plunger and auger in alternating sequence. Compare the two methods in 21-18. Should these methods fail, the only solution is to shut off the water to the toilet, disconnect the toilet from the floor, and retrieve the object from the toilet's underside. Whenever the seal between the toilet and floor is broken, the rubber or wax ring that serves as the seal must be replaced. As you can see, this repair can become extensive. You may wish to hire a professional plumber to do this job.

Sewer lines can also be blocked by tree roots and debris growing into the lines. When this occurs, professional help is required to clean out or open the lines.

## Installing Nails and Screws

Nails and screws are fastening devices. Each has special uses in household repairs. Nails can be driven easily, but may be difficult to remove. Screws can be removed easily.

Nails come in two basic shapes. A *finish nail* has a very small head. You can drive it below the surface by using another nail or a tool called a nail set.

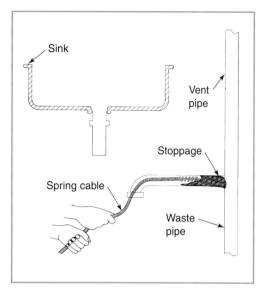

21-17
*The auger, which has a flexible spring cable, may need to be placed near the blockage to remove it.*

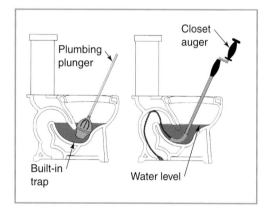

21-18
*Both the plumbing plunger and the auger may be needed for toilet blockage.*

Holes can be filled with wood filler or putty. Use finish nails when appearance is important. Installing paneling or shelves are two examples. A *box nail* has a large, flat head. Use it for rough work when appearance is less important.

When driving nails, hammer the head until it is seated on the surface,

**Reflect:** What precautions are taken at your home to prevent clogged drains? Is your home prepared for a plumbing emergency if one should occur?

**Vocabulary:** Compare and contrast nails and screws. Give an example of the proper time to use each.

**Writing Activity:** Referring to Figures 21-17 and 21-18, write instructions for using a closet auger.

but leave no mark on the surface. If you are placing nails or screws in walls, location is important. To secure heavy objects, place fasteners in line with a stud behind the wall surface. This allows the fastener to be driven into the wood of the stud for additional support. See 21-19.

You can find studs by tapping along the walls lightly. You will hear a lower tone when you tap the walls bordering hollow spaces between studs. When you tap a stud, you will hear a noticeably higher tone. You can also purchase inexpensive stud-sensing devices at hardware stores and home improvement centers. After you find one stud, you can usually

find adjacent studs by measuring 16-inch intervals to the left or right.

To install a wood screw, drill a pilot hole. Use the proper type of screwdriver, either a Phillips or a straight screwdriver. Try to match the size of the screwdriver to the head of the screw. Undersizing the screwdriver makes the task more difficult and can damage the screw head.

## Electrical Repairs

When electricity enters a house, the wires are connected into the service entrance panel. Service entrance panels contain either circuit breakers or fuses. Circuit breaker entrance panels are more common than panels with fuses, 21-20. If any circuit in your house is overloaded with appliances or other electrical items, the fuses or circuit breakers cut off the power. This prevents damage to wiring and possible electrical fires.

A *short circuit* is probably the most common cause of electrical problems. It is an undesirable current path that allows the electrical current to bypass the load of the circuit. Sometimes the short circuit occurs between

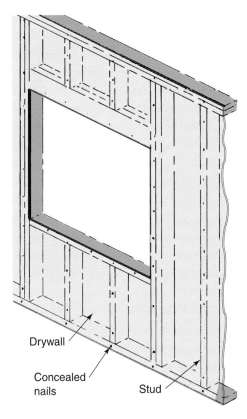

Drywall

Concealed nails

Stud

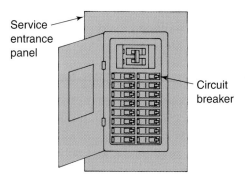

Service entrance panel

Circuit breaker

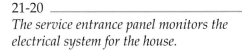

21-19

*Studs that are used to form walls are often placed 16 inches apart. Heavy objects that are hung on a wall should be fastened to a stud for best support.*

21-20

*The service entrance panel monitors the electrical system for the house.*

two wires due to faulty insulation. It can also occur between a wire and a grounded object, such as a metal frame on an appliance. Sometimes a black carbon deposit indicates where the short occurred. A short must be repaired before a breaker is reset or a fuse is replaced.

### Circuit Breakers

Usually a circuit breaker is activated when the circuit is overloaded. This happens when too many electrical appliances are used at one time. The switch on each breaker switches to the *off* position when a problem occurs. This interrupts the power.

Disconnect some appliances before restoring electricity to the circuit. To restore the electricity, move the handle of the circuit to the *reset* position, then to the *on* position. The *reset* position is usually on the opposite side of the *on* position.

### Fuses

You must replace a blown fuse to restore power. There are two types of fuses—plugs and cartridges. Plug fuses screw into the entrance panel like lightbulbs. A plug fuse has a clear window with a metal strip across it. The metal strip is called a fuse link. When current level exceeds the rating of the fuse, the link melts and a gap is formed. The result is a broken circuit with no flow of current.

To replace a plug fuse, remove the main fuse or turn off the connection switch. This will disconnect all power, so a flashlight may be needed. Locate the blown fuse. The window of a blown fuse is black or the fuse link is broken.

Cartridge fuses are held in place by spring clips. These fuses often show no sign of being blown. If the power is off, follow the same steps as

in replacing a plug fuse. Always replace the blown fuse with a new one of the exact size. To avoid electrical shock, stand on a dry surface and be sure your hands are dry.

### Wall Switches

All types of electrical switches can wear out as they get older. Do not attempt to replace a wall switch unless you know how to work with electrical wiring. Fatal electric shocks can occur. The illustration in 21-21 shows the black wires that are disconnected to remove a faulty switch.

### Power Cord Plugs

For the safety of members of the household, replace damaged or worn electric plugs before using them. When replacing a plug on a flat two-wire cord, use a snap-down plug.

To attach the snap-down plug, lift the top clamp. Slit the cord apart to ¼-inch from the end of the cord. Push the cord into the plug and tightly close the clamp. Test the cord to see that it works. Feel the plug to make sure it is not overheating.

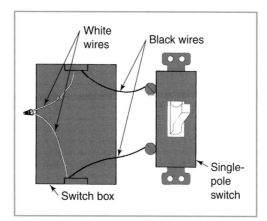

21-21 _____
*Extra precaution is needed when repairing electrical switches.*

## Making Replacements

Home maintenance includes more than making repairs. It includes replacing the parts of your house that wear out or become obsolete. It also includes replacing appliances that are no longer worth repairing.

When a quality item is purchased, it should perform well for many years before replacement becomes necessary. However, nothing lasts forever. A wise consumer, therefore, budgets for the repair and replacement costs that are certain to come. When repair parts become unavailable or costs become too high, it probably is time to make a replacement.

# Meeting Storage Needs

Whether your home is large or small, you need to make the most of your space. Organized storage helps to keep clutter out of your living spaces. Finding items is easier, too, when storage space is organized.

## Organize for Storage

You can reorganize closets in many ways using a variety of storage devices. Various types of storage components are available to help tailor the space to your storage needs. Many of these need not be nailed in place, so they can easily be moved. See 21-22.

Durable cardboard or plastic storage boxes come in many sizes, colors, and styles. Many have drawers or doors. Some fit under beds; others will fit in small spaces throughout the house. They can also be used to organize closet storage. Boxes can be painted, papered, or covered with fabric to match room decor.

Space under a stairway or at the end of a hall or room can often be converted to storage. You can buy ready-to-use shelves or other storage items for this space. They can be purchased in components and adapted to the space that exists. See 21-23. You can also build your own storage units.

Often utility rooms and garages have poorly organized storage space. Shelves and storage containers can make storage in these areas more efficient. Some types of shelves can be attached to the ceiling.

Shelves can also be placed in window nooks and over radiators. Shelf arrangements on bare walls provide open storage for displays. Racks can be attached to doors or walls. They can hold magazines, books, or supplies.

Hooks and poles can be used for some types of storage. They are popular for hanging coats. They can be used in bathrooms to hang towels and bathroom supplies. See 21-24. Also, supplies can be attractively placed in baskets or decorated buckets with handles.

## Space Savers

Many furniture pieces are designed to help save space. A sofa

Rubbermaid

21-22

*These organizer units can move to wherever they are needed most.*

© Spiegel 1998

21-23

*Some storage units made of wood can be artistically arranged to create dramatic furniture pieces.*

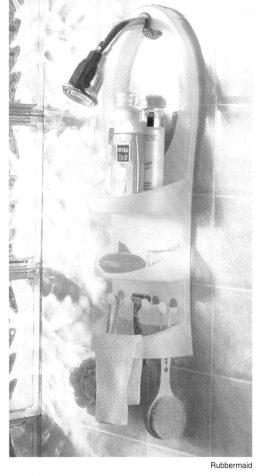

Rubbermaid

21-24

*Organizer units for the bathroom are available in many styles and colors.*

**Reflect:** Think about the furniture in your home. Which pieces are designed as space savers?

bed and a daybed are two such pieces. They double as sofas and beds. This saves room if you don't have space for both.

You can replace your regular bed frame with a platform that has drawers. This provides storage and sleeping space in the same area. You can also use stacking beds in a children's room to save space.

Stacking chairs and folding chairs are other types of space-saving furniture. Multipurpose storage and organizer units can double as small tables in the bedroom, living room, or home office. Padded chests used for seating, with storage underneath, also save space.

A drop-leaf table takes up little space when the leaves are down. It can easily be expanded when extra table-top space is needed. You can build a hinged table surface or desk that is attached to the wall. It can have legs that fold out or a hinged support that swings out from the wall. The table lies flat against the wall when it is not being used. Other household furniture and equipment can be mounted to the wall to save space.

In the kitchen, mounting small appliances on the wall or under kitchen cabinets can free valuable shelf space for other uses. Drawer trays, adjustable racks, hooks, and other shelving components keep food supplies, cooking equipment, and dinnerware orderly. See 21-25.

**Art Activity:** Draw a sketch of the way you would like your closet to look.

**Writing Activity:** If money were no concern, describe what you would do to transform your bedroom into a well-organized space.

Rubbermaid

21-25
*Storage organizers help make every bit of valuable kitchen space usable.*

Well-organized storage helps make living easier. It keeps your living spaces from becoming too cluttered. Having enough storage helps you make the most of your housing.

# Redecorating

Eventually you will probably want to change or update your decorating scheme. This is called *redecorating*. Parts of your home may look out of fashion. Some furnishings may be worn. Perhaps you may simply want a new look. As your life situation changes, so will your needs and values. In turn, you may redecorate part or all of your home accordingly.

Redecorating is different from decorating because you already have a base from which to start. If you decorated wisely the first time, there should be several items that you will want to keep when you redecorate. Old and new items do not need to match. They only need to complement each other.

Use the same steps in planning the redecoration that you used before

decorating. Planning is important when you blend the old with the new. Determine what you want to keep and what you want to replace. Evaluate why you want to eliminate certain items. Can you change any of them to fit your plan?

Sometimes what you already have can be redone to meet your needs. For instance, your sofa may be sturdy, but you may not like its color or pattern. Reupholstering may satisfy your decorating needs at a lower cost than replacing the sofa. This is especially true if you can do the work yourself.

You may redecorate in a single stage, or you can redecorate in a series of steps. Limited time and money may convince you to take the step approach. After you decide what you want to change, you can divide your project into phases. For instance, the steps to redecorating the living room may include painting the walls, replacing the carpet, and changing the window treatment. If you decide to repaint, do that step first since the room's new color may affect other redecorating decisions. See 21-26. As sales occur, some furniture and accessories can be replaced. Your priorities and budget will help you determine the order of the stages.

Professional services are available to help you decorate. An *interior designer* is a person who specializes in applying the principles and elements of design to interiors. An interior designer can plan your decorating, make purchases for you, and see that the work is done correctly. A designer will save you time and help you avoid costly mistakes. A designer also has contacts that you cannot make on your own, such as sources for the furnishings you want.

Only you can decide how much help you want from a designer and how much you want to do on your own. Most designers expect to do the bulk of the planning and let the client do some of the purchasing. Determine your needs, and then identify the work you want the designer to do.

You can also use the services of a decorator who is employed by a furniture store. No charges are made for this service, but you are expected to purchase some furniture from the store.

Knowing what you want will help you communicate your desires to a professional. You will be the one living with the decisions, so make your wishes known.

# Remodeling

*Remodeling* is usually more expensive than redecorating. This is because it involves changes to the structure, such as adding a wall or a room. There are times when remodeling is more of a bargain than moving or trying to live with the house's flaws.

Remodeling can extend livable space to existing areas, like a finished basement. Sometimes usable space is added to the structure, such as a family room addition or an attached garage. You may enclose a porch or build a patio. Some remodeling jobs, such as a more spacious and convenient kitchen, increase the market value of your home. See 21-27. Other projects may not increase the value of the home, but provide great comfort and satisfaction to your household.

The cost of remodeling is measured in many ways. You need to ask yourself if the cost of remodeling is a better value than moving or keeping your living space the same. Will remodeling increase the quality of life in your home? Will the process cause too many inconveniences for the members of your household? Adding a room is

21-26
*Here, the room's color stayed the same, but the homeowner chose to change window treatments as her first redecorating step.*

not likely to be as inconvenient as remodeling the kitchen or bathroom. Will you remodel, only to learn shortly thereafter that you need to move anyway?

You also need to decide whether to use professionals or do the work yourself. You can save about half the money by remodeling yourself. However, the work could take you twice as long or longer. If a project is simple and you know what to do, handling the remodeling yourself may be worthwhile. When tasks like rewiring and

Photo courtesy of Wolf Appliance

21-27 _____

*A more spacious and modern kitchen significantly increases a home's value.*

adding plumbing are involved, hiring a professional would be best. In fact, local building codes may require it. You may do some tasks yourself and hire people for others, or you may have a remodeling service do the whole job.

## Getting Your Money's Worth

Do your homework before you start a remodeling project. This will help you avoid making changes that cost you more than they are worth. Start by researching information about remodeling products, trends in design,

and financing. Get estimates on how much your remodeling project will cost. If you need a home improvement loan, shop to find the best rate. Consider whether you will regain the costs of remodeling when you sell your house. See 21-28.

Some contractors specialize in remodeling projects. If you do not want to do the work yourself, use a licensed contractor who will guarantee the work. Before choosing a contractor, learn the answers to the following questions:

- Is the contractor licensed? by whom?

- How long has the contractor been in business?

- Are former clients satisfied with the contractor's work? Ask the contractor for references or find names of clients at the local building department.

- Will the contractor show you a similar completed project?

- Does the contractor have insurance coverage for all workers?

- Will the contractor give you lien waivers to show that supplies and subcontractors used for the project have been paid? A *lien waiver* prevents you from being held liable if your contractor does not pay for items used to remodel your house.

Do not pay for the entire remodeling project until all the work is finished to your satisfaction. The best arrangement is to pay 25 percent of the total fee before work starts and the rest upon completion. Contractors are more likely to complete a project the way you want it if they are waiting to be paid.

As you make your remodeling plan, keep your neighborhood in mind. Keep your improvements in line with nearby houses. Try not to raise the value of your home more than 20 percent over the value of neighboring homes. If you do, you may not be able to get the full value when you sell your house.

Consider adding features that conserve energy when you remodel. Such features are bargains because they lower your monthly energy bills. They also increase the resale value of your home. You may remove a drafty window and replace it with a wall or with an insulating window. Insulating windows provide a good view and insulate better than standard windows. You may add insulation to your walls or replace old doors with insulating doors. You may also replace older appliances with energy-efficient models. Review Appendix B, "Energy Savers: Tips on Saving Energy and Money at Home," for more energy-saving tips.

# Resources for Home Care

There are resources for you to use if you need help in maintaining your home. Resource people can offer advice, or they can do the work for you. You might seek both advice and help with the work.

## Help with Home Maintenance

If you don't have the help you need in your family, or the time, you can hire people to do cleaning and maintenance for you. Service companies have employees who work by the hour, the day, or the job. You contract with the service, not with individuals. On the other hand, you can hire an individual who provides a specific service. Individuals set their own rates. See 21-29.

| Home Improvements and Increased Home Value | |
| --- | --- |

Projects that make a home more desirable often increase its value. A higher value means a better sales price when the owner sells the home. Sometimes the sales price is high enough to offset part or all of the improvement costs. The following figures show the average percentages of home improvement costs that are offset by a higher sales price.

| Project | Percentage of Costs Offset by Higher Sales Price |
| --- | --- |
| Fireplace addition | 100-125% |
| Kitchen remodeling | 75-125% |
| Solar greenhouse addition | 90-100% |
| Garage or patio addition | 75-100% |
| Bathroom remodeling | 75-100% |
| Bathroom addition | 50-100% |
| Room addition | 40-75% |
| Addition of energy saving measures (such as storm windows or more insulation) | 40-50% |
| Maintenance-free siding | 40-45% |

National Association of the Remodeling Industry

21-28
*Remodeling improves the usefulness and appearance of your home and often increases its sales value.*

The cost of the services varies with the job as well as the size and location of your house. For housecleaning, your cost is lower if you provide the cleaning products and tools. If you hire a cleaning service, it is important to learn what specific tasks are done at what costs. You may need to hire someone else or pay more for certain cleaning tasks. For instance, window washing is not usually part of a weekly cleaning service.

You can also hire someone to help with outside maintenance. You may have someone mow your lawn and trim the trees and shrubs. You can employ the services of a landscaping or yard maintenance company on a regular basis. They will provide complete maintenance or just do the specific projects you request.

**Discuss:** Why should people avoid making their homes more than 20% more valuable than other homes in the neighborhood? (*They may not be able to get the full value when they sell the house.*)
**Discuss:** Study Figure 21-28. Based on its data, what projects would you recommend to those wanting to improve their homes?
**Note:** The Web site of the National Association of the Remodeling Industry (NARI), is *nari.org.*

**Research:** Explore the remodeling industry. How big is it? What factors fuel the growth of the remodeling industry? Are they the same factors that fuel the homebuilding industry?

**Reflect:** Are there any areas of your home that could become more energy efficient if they were remodeled? What about replacing old appliances?

21-29

*Before hiring self-employed individuals, check their references and talk with former clients. You want to be sure the individual does good work and upholds his or her contracts.*

## Other Resources

You can learn more about how to maintain your home yourself. Home improvement centers offer free

The Home Depot

21-30

*Quality home improvement centers not only sell you a product, they offer classes to teach how to install it yourself.*

workshops and helpful literature. See 21-30. Free or inexpensive courses on home maintenance are offered at community colleges and technical schools. Decorating, remodeling, and home maintenance programs are common on TV stations. There are many Internet sites that can be explored by using *home improvement*, *landscaping*, and *gardening* as search words. You can buy videotapes and books, or borrow them from the local library. Newspapers and magazines often feature articles on home maintenance techniques and new products. Clip the articles and start your own resource file.

# Summary

The first step in maintaining your home is to keep it clean. The proper tools and cleaning products are important. A cleaning schedule for your household helps get the tasks done.

Yard maintenance also requires certain tools and products. Outdoor maintenance can be scheduled by the seasons. Maintenance needs are greatest in the fall and spring. Other tasks are done on a regular basis during the growing season.

The right tools can speed up home repairs. Basic tools and a knowledge of their use can help you make simple repairs. A professional should do repairs that pose safety risks or require expert knowledge. Repairs and replacements are part of home maintenance.

Creating and organizing storage space can simplify home maintenance. It can also increase living space. Many storage ideas are very affordable and easy to incorporate.

Redecorating and remodeling have their place in home maintenance. Both require careful planning. Many helpful resources exist for redecorating and remodeling as well as home maintenance. You can do the work yourself or hire a specialist.

**Resource:** *Basic Home Repairs,* color transparency CT-26, TR. Students explain how tools are used and review procedures for making basic home repairs.

**Discuss:** Review the chapter objectives. Do you still need to review or research some topics? If so, what topics?

**Activity:** Working with another student, alternate talking for 30 seconds apiece about what the chapter covered. Together, write a summary of the concepts in the chapter.

# To Review

1. True or false. Brooms and vacuum cleaners are the best tools for removing soil that is stuck to surfaces.
2. What are the three basic cleaning products every home should have?
3. What are two advantages of a cleaning schedule?
4. What is the danger in mowing a lawn too low?
5. True or false. Watering and fertilizing are elements of yard maintenance.
6. List five common home repairs.
7. Name five basic tools needed for home repairs and give their uses.
8. Name two methods of cleaning a clogged drain.
9. Describe the difference between finish nails and box nails.
10. What is an electrical short circuit?
11. Identify the two basic types of fuses.
12. True or false. When redecorating, all of the backgrounds, furnishings, and accessories in a room must be changed.
13. True or false. Remodeling is usually more expensive and complex than redecorating.
14. List three guidelines to follow when remodeling.
15. Name three resources that help homeowners maintain their homes.

**Answer Key**

1. false
2. glass cleaner, grease-cutting liquid, mild abrasive powder
3. (List two:) organizes a person's time, shows when each cleaning task needs to be done, divides tasks among members of the living unit
4. prevents the development of a healthy root system
5. true
6. (List five:) unclogging drains, fixing leaking faucets, installing fasteners, changing fuses, replacing wall switches, repairing power cord plugs
7. (List five. See Figure 21-13.)
8. (List two:) with a chemical drain cleaner, with a plumbing plunger, with a flexible spring cable, with the combined action of a plunger and a cable
9. Finish nails have a small head and can be driven below the surface with a nail set. Box nails have large flat heads and are used for rough work.
10. an undesirable current path that allows the electrical current to bypass the load of the circuit
11. plugs, cartridges
12. false
13. true
14. (List three. Student response. See pages 503-505.)
15. (List three:) cleaning services, outdoor maintenance services, interior designers, decorators, remodeling contractors, home improvement centers, local classes, publications, videotapes, TV programs, Internet sites

## In Your Community

1. Visit a hardware store. Have the manager or a knowledgeable salesperson describe some of the tools and supplies. Have the manager demonstrate how to use some basic tools.

2. Using the checklist in 21-5 to develop a cleaning schedule for your home. List the cleaning tools and supplies needed to perform the tasks on the schedule. Visit a local hardware and home store and determine the price of these items. What would be the range of cost for all these items new? Could most persons setting up a household be able to afford these items?

3. Survey properties in your neighborhood that show examples of exterior maintenance problems. Make a general list of the problems you see, but do not record the properties by name or address. As you identify each problem, also identify the solution or repair that you think should be used to remedy the problem.

4. Visit a home and garden shop that offers design assistance in remodeling kitchens and baths. Determine the size of the kitchen in your home (length by width) and ask a salesperson how much it usually costs to remodel a kitchen of that size. Does it cost a lot of money to remodel a kitchen? What steps are required to remodel a kitchen?

## To Think About

1. The idea of "easy maintenance" usually appeals to homebuyers looking for a home. What types of features would you seek in a home for it to deserve the title of "easy to maintain"? Make a list of both interior and exterior features. What features would be at the top of your list? Why?

2. Suppose you were setting up your first apartment. Using $100 to get started, what cleaning tools, cleaning products, and basic repair tools would you buy? Check prices at a local hardware store or home improvement center to current costs. What items would be on your list and why? What is the cost of each?

3. Cleaning and maintaining a home require human energy. Some people, particularly some senior citizens, are not physically able to complete heavy housework. They may hire someone to clean their home. Do you think that this represents a growing service because of the increasing number of senior citizens? Give your reasons.

# Using Technology

1. Using a computer-assisted design software program, make a redecorating plan for a living room, including a rough sketch of the final design. Develop a budget. Obtain samples of colors and designs that you plan to use. Put the items together in a binder and share the decorating plan with your class.

2. Develop a brochure of guidelines to follow when planning to decorate. Make a list of remodeling projects that you think are good do-it-yourself projects. Make a list of those you would recommend turning over to a professional. Print out the brochure and share it with your class.

**Portfolio Project:** Using Internet resources, develop a plan for organizing your personal closet space. (Use a *1" = 1'* scale.) Provide scale drawings to show the closet space as well as the placement and dimensions of new storage sections. Write a paper explaining the purpose of each section.

## PART 6

# Progress in Housing

C H A P T E R   22

# Housing for Today and Tomorrow

## To Know

automated houses
sustainable housing
photovoltaic (PV)
geothermal energy
graywater
renewable energy sources
nuclear energy
hydroelectric power
co-generation
fuel cell
microturbine
ecology
solid waste
hazardous waste
visual pollution
integrated waste management
green building
ecosystem

Photography courtesy of James Wilson

## Objectives

After studying this chapter, you will be able to

- explain the impact of technology on housing.
- identify ways to provide and conserve energy.
- summarize the importance of a clean environment.
- describe ways to maintain a clean environment.
- determine new housing solutions.

**Resource:** *Progress in Housing,* transparency master VI-A, TR. Students look back at the topics covered in Chapters 1-21 and review the new topics they will cover in Chapter 22.

**Vocabulary:** List the five objectives on the left side of a piece of paper. For each objective, write two terms that you believe relates to it from the "To Know" list. As you meet these 10 terms in the text, use each in a sentence that relates to it.

**Note:** Have a variety of housing magazines available for use during this chapter.

How can people have better housing for tomorrow? No one knows just what the future holds. However, by learning from the past and watching for new developments, people can make tomorrow's housing better.

# Recent Developments in Housing

As the needs of people have changed, so has their housing. Housing designs and construction are influenced by many factors. One factor having a great influence on developments in housing is new technology. Some people can remember when houses did not have electricity, indoor plumbing, refrigerators, or air conditioners. These are all related to advances in technology. New technology systems are continually being developed for use in homes today. New construction materials and methods of construction are being developed as well.

## Automated Houses

*Automated houses* are dwellings that have an integrated and centrally controlled system based on computer technology. This system controls all the systems in the home and focuses primarily on one or more of the following areas:

- convenience
- energy management
- entertainment
- safety

There are many versions and features of "smart" technology incorporated into homes being built today. The exterior of homes with automated

systems looks like any other house. See 22-1. However, the homes contain advanced systems, components, and materials—all the result of ongoing technological development.

### The SMART HOUSE

The SMART HOUSE is one type of home on the market that incorporates the concept of automated housing. These technologically superior houses are the result of a for-profit partnership that gives member manufacturers license to its technology. The leader in the development of SMART HOUSE technology is the National Association of Home Builders (NAHB).

SMART HOUSES feature a simple and easy-to-use home automation system based on computer technology. The main control system operates and manages the subsystems. These subsystems include security, lighting, entertainment, appliances, heating, and cooling. Telephones, programmable wall switches, sensors, and

SMART HOUSE, L.P. 400 Prince George's Blvd., Upper Marlboro, MD

22-1

*By looking at its exterior, you cannot identify this SMART HOUSE from any other house.*

hand-held and panel controls run the system.

The SMART HOUSE system begins with the *service center*. Electricity, telephone service, and cable television are brought into the house through the service center, as shown in 22-2.

A *system controller* is the main component in the SMART HOUSE system. It has two main functions. First, it is a network manager, routing the electronic signals that control the subsystems. To do the routing, the system controller must keep track of everything that is connected to the system. The controller functions from the database it has developed on the house.

Second, the system controller uses some logic and can manage different software to direct simple functions. For example, appliance manufacturers can install microprocessors in their appliances that are compatible with the SMART HOUSE system. These appliances can then be programmed for specific functions via the system controller. Such a program might operate a dishwasher at night in areas where the utility rate is lower than daytime rates.

The system controller operates continually, monitoring the various subsystems. It checks all the windows several times a second. It can tell if one has been forced open. Each room, as well as the outside area, is checked for security. The computer will take indoor and outdoor temperatures and adjust indoor heating or cooling needs accordingly. The computer senses when a person enters a room and turns lights on or off as needed. The system can monitor energy consumption, detect gas leaks, and even alert the fire department in case of fire. These are typical activities of the computerized system controller in the SMART HOUSE.

### Southface Energy and Environmental Resource Center

Another organization focused on housing technology is the Southface Energy Institute. Working with the Department of Energy and three of its national laboratories, the Southface Institute developed the Southface Energy and Environmental Resource Center. See 22-3. The Center includes an attractive home and office space that has a modern look. It also contains numerous innovative features for homes of the future. The building addresses energy efficiency, thermal comfort, indoor air quality, and

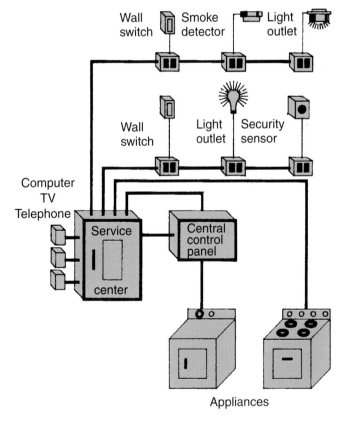

22-2
*This illustration shows the typical circuits for a SMART HOUSE.*

accessibility concerns. It also includes ways to reduce waste and use recycled materials.

Many of the features demonstrated in the home are used in sustainable housing. **Sustainable housing** is housing that is as self-sufficient as possible and uses minimum natural resources. This includes the building materials (such as recycled materials) as well as the utility operating activities (such as energy, water, and waste management).

Energy-related features include passive solar heating and cooling, solar water heating, and solar electric systems. A special component is a roof using solar electric shingles, shown in 22-4. These shingles are **photovoltaic (PV)**, which means they convert sunlight into electricity. The photovoltaic shingles resemble conventional fiberglass roofing shingles. The electricity they produce is used to supply part of the electrical needs of the house. Like other solar applications, the shingles perform best in full sun.

The living room of the Center has a well-planned passive solar design, shown in 22-5. The design takes advantage of sunlight as a heating source in winter. It also blocks the sun from directly hitting any surface in the summer. The living room stays comfortable in hot and cold weather and always looks sunny.

Other energy-saving measures at the Center include energy-efficient appliances and a geothermal heat pump. **Geothermal energy** is heat that is transmitted from the earth's center by steam, hot water, or hot rock. Southface also uses a solar-powered vehicle.

The landscape emphasizes the principles of *xeriscape*, or drought-tolerant landscaping. Also, the watering uses

Southface Energy Institute, Atlanta, GA

22-3

*The Southface Energy and Environmental Resource Center has many innovative features that can be applied to future homes.*

Southface Energy Institute, Atlanta, GA

22-4

*Photovoltaic shingles are installed on the roof of the Southface building to make electricity from the sun's rays for use in the house.*

**Note:** The Web site for the Southface Energy Institute is *southface.org*. It provides more information on the environmental benefits of "smart houses."

**Vocabulary:** Define *sustainable housing* by contrasting it to an average house in your area.

**Vocabulary:** Examine the root words of the term *geothermal* to identify what type of energy it describes.

Southface Energy Institute, Atlanta, GA

22-5 _____

*The living room of the Southface house is designed to block sunlight in the summer and let it enter in the winter.*

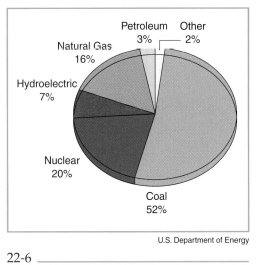

U.S. Department of Energy

22-6 _____

*The United States relies heavily on coal to fuel the generation of electricity for industrial use.*

graywater irrigation. ***Graywater*** is wastewater from washing machines, showers, and sinks. It is not contaminated with human waste. The landscaping also uses recycled materials, such as wood-chip mulch and concrete rubble for stepping-stones.

# Housing Concerns

Technology is causing changes in housing, and many result from the concerns of people. For example, there is concern regarding the affordability of housing. This has resulted in the development of new products that attempt to slow the increases in housing costs. The advanced technologies described here may someday make housing more affordable.

Energy usage is another concern. Some fear that fossil fuels are being depleted. Can alternate fuel sources be developed? Can recycling strategies be put in place to prevent the depletion of natural resources?

Another concern is for the health of the environment. What needs to be done to preserve a healthy environment for people today and all future generations?

## Sources of Energy

Fuel provides heat, and people need heat to live. Like all forms of energy, fuel begins as solar energy derived from the sun. Nature converts solar energy to raw materials such as oil and coal. The conversions take millions of years to complete. The raw materials are then refined and used as fuel for electricity. The chart in 22-6 shows that coal is the nation's main source of energy. Nuclear energy, hydroelectric power, natural gas, and petroleum are the other leading energy sources in the country.

The supplies of such common sources of fuel as oil and coal are being depleted. These sources of energy are *nonrenewable*. Researchers are working to find new sources that will supply enough fuel for the future. They are studying ***renewable energy sources***, which replenish themselves regularly. Renewable sources of energy include the sun, wind, water, and geothermal energy, all of which can be converted to electricity. The potential for converting solid waste to electricity is also being studied.

## Nuclear Energy

The discovery of nuclear energy marked the beginning of the atomic age. This was a monumental break-through for scientists and energy experts worldwide.

*Nuclear energy* is produced in a nuclear reactor by the breakup of Uranium-235. Heat is released when the nucleus of an atom *fissions*, or splits into two pieces. An abundance of energy is produced with only a small amount of fuel. One nuclear pellet the size of a miniature marshmallow equals the energy produced from 1,780 pounds of coal or 149 gallons of oil.

More than 100 nuclear energy plants provide nearly as much electricity as oil, natural gas, and hydroelectric power combined. Only coal produces more electricity than nuclear energy. In some states, nuclear energy is the leading source of electrical power. See 22-7. There are over 430 nuclear plants operating in the world.

Although the construction of new U. S. nuclear plants in the future is questionable, the current nuclear energy facilities will continue to play a major role in providing electric power. The benefits of nuclear power have been proven over the past decades. Nuclear energy does not pollute the air with gases or dust. However, there are concerns about the effects of nuclear energy on the environment. Though nuclear plants produce only a small amount of radioactive waste, the waste remains radioactive for hundreds of years. This waste must be carefully disposed to protect people

Arizona Public Service

22-7

*The Palo Verde nuclear plant in the Arizona desert is the largest in the world.*

from potential hazards. People also fear incidents at nuclear plants that might cause the accidental release of radioactive materials. Recent accidents occurred at Chernobyl in the Ukraine in 1986 and at Three Mile Island in Pennsylvania in 1979.

## Hydroelectric Power

Another important source of energy is *hydroelectric power*. This is electrical power that is generated by water moving through rivers and dams. Water as a source of energy is not new. Waterpower was first converted into electricity using water-wheels in the late 1800s.

Today's hydroelectric plants use turbines to drive electric generators. A *turbine* is a series of blades placed around a shaft. The turbine is powered by flowing water. The turbine's speed is determined by the swiftness of the water. The higher the speed of the turbine, the more electricity is generated. See 22-8 for an example of a hydroelectric system.

Most of the hydroelectric generating systems are located on major

**Resource:** *Nuclear Energy Around the World,* color transparency CT-27, TR. Students examine a chart showing the percentage of energy from nuclear power attributed to various countries in the world.
**Example:** The movie "China Syndrome" was based on incidents that occurred at Three Mile Island.
**Science Activity:** Explain with drawings how power results from a nuclear reaction. Make a presentation to the class.
**Discuss:** Does your community have a nuclear power plant nearby? What has been the reaction of the community to it? Does it have a good safety record? Would you be willing to live close to a nuclear generator?

**Activity:** Research the nuclear accident that occurred at Chernobyl or Three Mile Island. Report details of the incident, the extent of the damage, and the successfulness of clean-up efforts. What is the current status of that nuclear plant?

**Science Activity:** Examine the link between electric power plants and the formation of acid rain. Summarize your findings in a brief oral report.

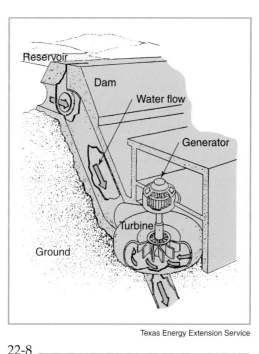

Texas Energy Extension Service

22-8
*This illustration shows how water flowing from a reservoir powers a hydroelectric generator.*

rivers. They are usually placed at dams, but small plants can be placed at any point along a river.

### Solar Energy

Many houses are being built to take advantage of the natural heating effect of solar energy. See 22-9. Solar energy could supply a majority of the energy needed to heat and cool buildings throughout the United States. Solar heating systems are expensive to install. A major part of the expense is the high cost of the component parts. Research is currently underway to develop less expensive components of solar systems.

Despite the high installation cost, utility bills are greatly reduced when solar energy is used. In the long run, solar heating systems usually cost less than conventional systems. The two types of solar heating systems, active and passive, were described in

Photo courtesy of Andersen Windows, Inc.

22-9
*This house has windows placed to take advantage of passive solar heating.*

Chapter 6, "The Evolution of Exteriors," and Chapter 9, "The Systems Within."

Active systems can be used to heat space, heat water, or produce electricity. An active solar system that converts sunlight into electricity is called a photovoltaic system. The sun shines on panels (called arrays) and converts this solar energy into electricity.

The downside of photovoltaic systems is they generate electricity only when the sun shines. The system's batteries can store enough electricity to power a house for several days, but persistent overcast weather can deplete it. Deluxe systems can match the reliability of power supplied by utility companies, but they are expensive. As the cost of solar electric systems declines, environmentally conscious homeowners will likely invest in this technology.

Some solar energy heating systems are designed to supply more energy than is needed. The excess can be sold to a utility company or stored in the lines until needed by the producer. It can also be stored in a bank of batteries. Two electric meters are needed. One measures incoming power from an outside source, such as a utility company. The other measures excess power produced by the homeowner that is sold. See 22-10.

## Geothermal Energy

The geothermal energy that comes from the earth's center creates volcanos, natural hot springs, and geysers. In certain locations, the heat is present near the surface. In others, it can be reached by drilling deep holes through lava, a type of volcanic rock. Reykjavik, Iceland, is the first city in the world to become almost entirely heated by geothermal energy. Approximately half a million people in California, Mexico's Baja Peninsula, and the Mexicali Valley meet their fuel needs with geothermal energy. Other geothermal projects are being developed in the United States.

Geothermal energy has advantages and disadvantages. One advantage is its low cost compared to other fuels. It also is a source of heat that does not emit harmful pollutants into the environment. A third advantage is that geothermal energy is a renewable resource.

There are some drawbacks, however, to geothermal energy. Some geothermal waters contain chemicals that require responsible disposal. A second disadvantage is that geothermal energy can be used only near the sites where it is produced. Hot water cannot be transported over long distances without losing heat and turning cold.

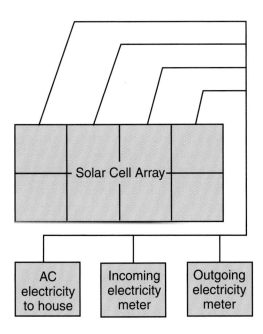

22-10
*In a photovoltaic system, silicon chips are joined by electrical wires to form solar cell arrays. The arrays collect different amounts of solar energy, depending on the season, time of day, and degree of cloudiness.*

## Wind as Energy

The use of wind as energy dates back to early civilizations when windmills were used to pump water and grind grain. Wind is experiencing a new popularity as an energy source and has been described by the U. S. National Renewable Energy Laboratory as the "renewable energy of the future." Although a wind energy system is relatively high in cost, wind is a clean and inexhaustible energy source. A minimum average annual wind speed of 10 miles per hour is necessary to run a wind generator. If the average is above 12 miles per hour, an excellent wind system can be developed.

Some regions of the United States have strong, shifting winds that can be used for power. Wind turbine generators grouped together to form wind farms can convert air motion to electrical current. See 22-11. The current that

**Enrich:** Contact your local electric company to learn if homeowners can sell them excess electrical power created through the conversion of solar energy with a photovoltaic system. Find out what it costs to install and operate the system. If the company provides fact sheets to interested homeowners, obtain copies to share with your class.

**Internet Research:** Search the U.S. National Park Service and your state's conservation department to find parks with hot springs, geysers, or another geothermal feature. Explain what the park closest to you contains that indicates the presence of geothermal energy.

**Example:** A windmill can convert a renewable energy source, the wind, into electrical energy.

**Discuss:** What are the advantages of geothermal energy? (*low cost, no harmful pollutants, and a renewable energy resource*) What are the disadvantages? (*can only be used locally, responsible disposal of some water may be needed*)

**Research:** Investigate one of the major projects being developed outside the United States to harness wind energy. Find out what the project costs and entails, when it will be finished, and how much energy it will provide when running at full capacity. Summarize your findings in a written report.

22-11
*This wind system converts the power from constant Pacific breezes to electricity for nearby California residents.*

developments will make residences less dependent on the electrical utility companies to provide electricity. This can be helpful especially in blackouts and during natural disasters when electric power may not be available.

## Conserving Energy

In the 1970s and 1980s when oil prices rose rapidly, laws were passed to encourage conservation of energy. See Appendix B, "Energy Savers: Tips on Saving Energy and Money at Home." for conservation tips that were developed as a result. Research on alternative energy sources, such as wind and solar power, was encouraged. Tax credits were given to homeowners and homebuilders for using energy-saving features and appliances in new homes. Many people took advantage of these laws and added energy-saving features to their houses.

Though the tax laws have changed, the general public is still encouraged to buy energy-efficient products. This advice applies to items as small as appliances or as large as a house. Every household has many opportunities each day to save energy and lower its utility bills. Using energy wisely and preserving it for the future is an increasing public concern.

One of the biggest decisions that will affect how much energy you use is the type of home you buy. Some houses have more energy-efficient features than others. These features not only save money in the long run, but also help make the house more comfortable. The checklist in 22-12 can help you choose an energy-efficient house.

## A Clean Environment

*Ecology* is the relationship between all living things and their surroundings. People harm the environment

**Discuss:** What three ways of generating electricity does a co-generation system include? (*photovoltaics, fuel cells, and microturbines*)

is produced is fed into utility lines or storage systems. The systems keep the power flowing even when the air is still.

### Co-Generation in Residences

A new way to produce most, and possibly all, the electrical energy a house requires is through a co-generation system. A *co-generation* system refers to distributed energy resources. This system is made possible through the development of new technologies that produce electricity. These developments include photovoltaics, fuel cells, and microturbines. Fuel cells and microturbines are being developed for possible use in residences.

- A *fuel cell* is an equipment system that produces electricity from the use of chemicals. Research is underway to handle the waste products of heat and water.

- A *microturbine* is a small turbine engine that produces electricity.

Homeowners of the future will be able to add these options to their list of possible home energy sources. These

**History Activity:** Interview your parents and grandparents to see if they recall the energy crisis of the 1970s. What memories do they have? How did it affect them?

**Vocabulary:** Explain the difference between the terms *ecology* and *environment*.

## Checklist for an Energy-Efficient House

Notice and evaluate these features for home energy efficiency.

*Orientation and Landscaping*

___ Orientation of long side of house (N, S, E, or W)

___ Windows facing east (Note number and compute area in square feet.)

___ Windows facing west (Note number and compute area in square feet.)

___ Shade from landscape features on east or west sides

___ Southern exposure unobstructed or shaded by deciduous trees

*Thermal Resistance*

___ Attic insulation (Note the type and thickness.)

___ Wall insulation

___ Under-floor insulation, especially in homes with crawl spaces, cold basements, and garages under living areas

___ Insulated ducts

___ Insulated hot water pipes

___ Insulated hot water heater

___ Double- or triple-glazed (paned) windows

___ Solid-core wood or metal door

___ Storm doors

*Lighting and Windows*

___ Fluorescent lighting in work areas

___ Windows or skylights over work areas

___ Windows occupying less than 10 percent of the total wall area (Measure the window area and calculate its percentage of total wall area.)

*Appliances*

___ Refrigerator located away from stove, dishwasher, and direct sunlight

*Ventilation*

___ Ceiling fans

___ Whole-house fan

___ Window/door placement appropriate for cross-ventilation

___ Attic vents near the roof ridge

___ Attic vents beneath the eaves

___ Air infiltration

___ Weatherstripping around doors

___ Weatherstripping around windows

___ Weatherstripping around attic entry door

___ Caulking around door frames

___ Caulking around window fames

___ Caulking around penetrations for pipes and wires

___ Tightly fitted windows

Texas Energy Extension Service

22-12 _____

*Use this checklist to compare houses for energy efficiency.*

**Discuss:** Do you feel that the average person could do a good job of using Figure 22-12's checklist to assess a home's energy efficiency? Explain.

**Reflect:** Of the items in Figure 22-12, on which would your home score lowest?

**Enrich:** Attend a demonstration on how to caulk, or learn by watching a how-to video.

each time they put undesirable items into their surroundings. This results in pollution. Look at 22-13 to see the many types of pollution that can harm your surroundings.

People have made many demands on the environment. Often they use it without regard to protecting and preserving it for future use. If the environment is to continue to satisfy so many needs, people must actively

preserve it. See 22-14. Solutions must be found for the growing pollution problem. Pollution not only destroys the environment, but also affects human health.

### Solid Waste

Every year people throw away tons of solid waste materials. *Solid waste* is any discarded material that is not a liquid or a gas. Much of the

New York State Department of Environmental Conservation

22-13

*This circle identifies many kinds of pollution. Notice that each kind can affect land, air, and water.*

**Reflect:** Which of the pollutants shown in Figure 22-13 affect your community? How do they affect you?

**Vocabulary:** How would you define *pollution*? How does your definition compare to that in the dictionary?

waste comes from our homes in the form of garbage. The total output of garbage is called the *solid waste stream*. Most solid waste is either dumped into sanitary landfills or incinerated. Both these methods have drawbacks.

Nearly 73 percent of solid waste is buried, but solid waste experts project that landfill space is filling up fast. Suitable sites are difficult to find because of the toxic substances that seep from landfills into groundwater despite safeguards.

With landfills becoming filled, incinerators are used more often. More than 14 percent of solid waste is incinerated. Incinerators do not pollute the groundwater, and they can generate energy. The downside is that incinerators can pollute the air, and they produce a highly toxic ash. For every 10 tons of waste burned in an incinerator, one ton of ash is produced.

Certain waste is particularly harmful. *Hazardous waste* is poisonous waste material that damages the environment and causes illness. The U.S. Environmental Protection Agency's (EPA's) definition of hazardous wastes includes all corrosive, ignitable, reactive, or toxic substances.

Modern industry produces many toxic substances that are hazardous to the environment. However, the average household also contains a variety of hazardous materials that require special disposal methods. Among the most common chemical hazards in the home are batteries, bleach, disinfectants, drain cleaners, insect sprays, medicines, and metal polishes. Certain lawn and home workshop products are also hazardous. Special ways of disposing of these toxic wastes are required. Most communities have developed waste management procedures for the disposal of household hazardous wastes.

Keep America Beautiful Association

22-14

*Many towns sponsor "community cleanup" days, when residents help remove trash to restore their environment.*

## Water Pollution

Half of all Americans use groundwater for drinking water, but it can become contaminated. This contamination occurs when hazardous chemical wastes, pesticides, or other agricultural chemicals seep down through the soil into underground water supplies.

Few people know the origin of their drinking water. Many people believe all toxins have been removed from drinking water before it reaches their homes. Generally, water is properly treated at municipal treatment plants. Federal and state laws require water suppliers to periodically sample and test their water supply. If tests show water standards are being violated, the supplier must correct the situation. Homes with private wells should have the water tested periodically.

Even if the water that enters your home is pure, your house can contribute to its pollution. Many homes built prior to 1988 contain plumbing systems that use lead-based solder in pipe connections. Older homes may even have lead pipes. In such systems, lead can enter drinking water as a corrosion byproduct. Some galvanized and plastic pipes may give off harmful chemicals to the water supply.

Modern technology can make a water supply safe. However, you will want to check to be sure you are not drinking polluted water. Samples of the water in your home can be easily tested.

## Other Types of Pollution

Air and noise pollutants exist outdoors as well as indoors. Safety and health issues related to air and noise pollution were discussed in Chapter 20, "Keeping Your Home Safe and Secure." *Visual pollution* is the harm done to the appearance of the environment as a result of human activities. Signboards, debris along roadsides, and the destruction of natural surroundings are examples of visual pollution.

Researchers continue to learn more about the effects of various pollutants on people. All pollutants are harmful in one way or another. People should welcome research and technology that helps them have a healthy environment. A healthy environment will help make tomorrow's housing better.

## Solving Environmental Concerns

The need for energy and the desire for a clean environment pose challenges for housing. One approach that tries to address all areas is a concept called *integrated waste management*. It is based on a hierarchy of preferred waste handling options developed by the EPA. See 22-15. The EPA is encouraging every community to use this approach when deciding how to

handle their trash. Beginning with the most preferred option, the hierarchy includes the following choices:

1. *source reduction*—avoiding excess that quickly becomes trash through the careful planning of a product or package from the very first step in development
2. *recycling and reuse*—finding useful roles for discarded materials
3. *incineration with resource recovery*—making use of the energy released by incineration
4. *incineration without resource recovery*—making no use of the energy released by incineration
5. *landfill*—burying the waste

Slowing the expanding volume of waste, the first option, offers the greatest opportunity for controlling environmental problems. Finding useful roles for trash and the energy released by incinerating it, the second and third options, also offer opportunities. The most wasteful methods of handling

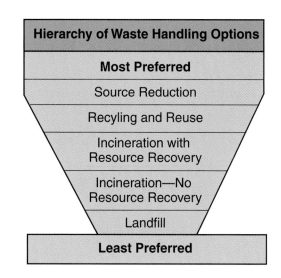

22-15 _____
*This illustration shows the five options for handling waste, ranked from most to least preferred.*

trash are the last two. In both cases, nothing is gained and something is lost, either energy or land.

## Source Reduction

As you can see, this hierarchy strongly supports careful planning as the best approach to waste management. Though industry plays the major role at this step, you can also play an important role.

Think about some of the ways your buying decisions can help the environment. Buy only those items that are the least environmentally harmful to produce. Also, buy those that are safe to use and less of a burden to dispose. Consider the amount and kind of packaging used on each item you buy. Some packaging is necessary for the protection and safety of the product. However, some packaging is excessive, adding to the solid waste problem. Finally, decide not to buy items excessively packaged or not really needed. This has the greatest environmental impact of all.

## Recycling and Reuse

The second level in the hierarchy is to recycle and reuse. Recycling means reprocessing resources for another use. EPA's goal is to increase the level of recycling in the United States. Many communities have recycling programs and waste disposal restrictions. You play a very important role in the total recycling effort.

Paper, cardboard, aluminum, glass, and plastic can all be recycled. See 22-16. Newspapers are made into many other products, such as newsprint, molded fiber packaging, home insulation, cereal boxes, and roofing felt. Aluminum is recycled into new beverage containers, storm doors, and gutters. Recycled glass is crushed, melted, and made into glass containers.

Some recycled glass is crushed and used for asphalt pavement mixes or permeable media in foundation drains.

When plastic products are disposed, they take hundreds of years to decompose. Thus, plastic recycling is becoming more important. A type of plastic that is successfully recycled from soda bottles is polyethylene terephthalate, called PET. It is used as a fiber in carpeting. A similar type of plastic is recycled into a material to make outdoor items, such as fences, decks, picnic tables, benches, and trash containers.

Many people believe the United States can recycle on a large scale. For example, recycled materials can be used to build new homes. Making products from recycled materials can often be more expensive than using customary materials. However, as the cost of natural materials increases, recycling becomes more affordable. Recycling also saves natural resources and landfill space.

Keep America Beautiful Association

22-16
*Most of the litter polluting roadsides consists of materials that can be recycled and reused.*

### Incineration with Resource Recovery

In this level of the hierarchy, some of the waste incineration is converted to energy. Waste-to-energy processes are still in the developing stages. Most involve incineration of solid waste and recovery of methane gas from landfills. The energy created from the incineration of garbage can be used to provide heat and electrical power for homes and businesses.

# Innovative Solutions in Housing

A shifting population, changes in lifestyles, and longer lifespan dictate attention to new alternatives. Housing designs of the future will reflect these and other considerations, such as the needs and personal priorities of people.

New solutions are being sought to meet their changing lifestyles, such as redesigning the space within a home. Recent research indicates that most new homeowners are less interested in having a separate, rarely used living room, such as that desired in past. Instead, many current house plans include great rooms. Will homes of the future eliminate separate living rooms? Will they instead have the increasingly popular entertainment rooms or home theaters? Lifestyle changes dictate the future direction for housing design.

Housing must accommodate the physical changes in people that take place naturally as they age. Housing should also take advantage of new technologies. Protecting the environment is another important goal of future housing. Housing designs that improve the quality of life of individuals and families while protecting the environment are discussed in this section.

## Universal Design

*Universal design* is a concept that makes houses and their contents easier for almost everyone to use. Ronald Mace at the Center for Universal Design at North Carolina State University developed the concept of universal design. Mace realized that, through careful design, products and environments could be usable by more people at little or no extra cost. Mace named the design concept *universal* since it simplified living for practically everyone.

The universal design concept targets the needs of all people, regardless of age, physical characteristics, or ability. By contrast, accessible or adaptable design is aimed at benefiting only certain people, such as persons with mobility limitations.

When universal design principles are used, every building and product within is developed to provide greater usefulness to as many people as possible. That includes every faucet, light fixture, shower stall, public telephone, entrance, and all other implements used in everyday life. The principles of universal design also apply to the spaces used in everyone's daily activities.

See 22-17 for a list of universal design features for entrances, kitchens, bathrooms, and the general interior. Some of these features are structural and must be built into the house. Nonstructural features are items that can easily be added after the house is built. Some universal design features are being built in homes of today, especially by request of the occupants. Innovation would involve the use of the features in all homes of the future so that the features are there already to make living easier for everyone.

### Universal Design Home of the Future

One group of people that benefit most from universal design is older, retired persons. Consequently, the American Association of Retired Persons (AARP) has cosponsored a model home, shown in 22-18, that incorporates universal design features. The project is called the Universal Design Home of the Future.

Other cosponsors of the project are ACCESS UNLIMITED, the Home Builders Association of Richmond, Virginia, the Industry Education Alliance (IEA), and Partners in American Vocational Education

(PAVE). In addition, 25 national building manufacturers and suppliers have joined the effort.

The model home demonstrates to builders how universal design can be incorporated in the houses they build. It also educates the general public about the housing features to seek when buying a home. The home is both aesthetic and functional. According to the sponsors, universal design features add about $2,000 to the cost of a $125,000 home.

| Universal Design Features in Housing | | |
|---|---|---|
| **Feature** | **Structural** | **Nonstructural** |
| *Entrances* | | |
| Accesible route from vehicle drop-off or parking space | X | |
| Covered entryway | X | |
| Full-length side window at entry door | X | |
| Maximum slope of 1:20 to entry door | X | |
| Minimum maneuvering space of 5 x 5 foot | X | |
| Package shelf or bench to hold parcels, groceries, and other items | | X |
| Movement-sensor light controls | | X |
| Ambient and focused lighting (at keyhole) | | X |
| High-visibility address numbers | | X |
| *Kitchen* | | |
| Knee space under sink and near cooktop | X | |
| Lever-type faucets | X | |
| Variable-height work surfaces (from 28 to 45 inches) | X | |
| Contrasting border treatment on countertops | | X |
| Pull-out shelves in base cabinets | | X |
| Full-height pantry cabinets for up and down storage | X | |
| Stretches of continuous counter for sliding heavy objects | X | |
| Full-extension pull-out drawers | | X |
| Adjustable-height shelves in wall cabinets | | X |
| 30 x 48-inch area of approach in front of all appliances | X | |
| Front-mounted controls on appliances | | X |
| Cooktops with staggered burners to eliminate dangerous reaching | | X |
| Glare-free task lighting | | X |

Center for Universal Design, School of Design, North Carolina State University, Raleigh, NC

22-17

*Universal design includes both structural and nonstructural features for entrances, kitchens, bathrooms, and the general interior.*

**Activity:** Compare your house to the universal design features listed in Figure 22-17. Identify the listed features that are reflected in your home.

**Vocabulary:** Identify the difference between the *Structural* and *Nonstructural* categories in Figure 22-17.

| Universal Design Features in Housing | | |
|---|:---:|:---:|
| **Feature** | **Structural** | **Nonstructural** |
| *Bathrooms* | | |
| Grab bars in tub or shower | | X |
| Adjustable-height shower head | | X |
| Mirror to backsplash at lavatory | X | |
| Toilet centered 18 inches from side wall | X | |
| 30 x 48-inch area of approach in front of all fixtures | X | |
| Grab bar in walls around toilet | X | |
| 32-inch minimum lavatory counter height | X | |
| Knee space under lavatory | X | |
| Lever-type faucets | | X |
| 18-inch maneuvering space at both ends of tub or shower | X | |
| Offset controls in tub or shower | X | |
| Built-in transfer seat in tub or shower | X | |
| Mixer valve with pressure balancing and hot water limiter | | X |
| *The General Interior* | | |
| 32-inch minimum clear door-opening width | X | |
| Lever-style door handles | | X |
| Adjustable-height closet rods and shelves | | X |
| "View" windows at 36-inch maximum sill height | X | |
| Electrical receptacles at 18-inch maximum height | X | |
| Maximum force of 5 pounds to open doors | | X |
| 18-inch minimum space at latch side of door | X | |
| Flush threshold (maximum of $1/2$-inch rise) | X | |
| Accessible route (42-inch minimum) throughout | X | |
| Light switches at 48-inch maximum height | X | |
| Crank-operated (casement) windows | X | |
| Loop-handle pulls on drawers and cabinets | | X |
| High-contrast, glare-free floor surfaces and trim | | X |
| Minimum maneuvering space of 5 x 5 foot | X | |

Center for Universal Design, School of Design, North Carolina State University, Raleigh, NC

22-17 ————————————————————————————————————————————
*(continued)*

The home is designed to be convenient, safe, and comfortable for persons of all ages, physical characteristics, and abilities. One feature that demonstrates usability by all ages is a seat that extends out from the bathtub, called a *cantilevered* seat. See 22-19. This seat makes it easier for an older person or someone with a temporary or permanent disability to use the tub. It allows a parent to sit closer when bathing a child. The tub has offset shower and tub controls that can be operated from outside the tub. The controls also have a thermostat to prevent scalding.

**Reflect:** Have any members of your immediate or extended family needed to move because their home lacked the universal design features they needed for living safely and comfortably?

**Writing Activity:** Of the universal design features listed on this page, which does your home need most? Write a paragraph explaining why.

## Benefits of Universal Design to All Users

The benefits of universal design to people with physical limitations are obvious. However, the benefits to others may not be as apparent. Here are some examples of how universal design benefits people who do not have physical limitations. These benefits focus on four areas: entrances, the kitchen, bathrooms, and the general interior.

### Entrances

*Level and accessible entrances*

- are easier to enter with groceries and packages.
- pose fewer hazards when wet or icy.
- are easier to repair and maintain than steps.
- are easier to clear of snow, ice, and leaves.
- provide more convenience for moving furniture, appliances, baby strollers, and bicycles in and out.

*Covered entries*

- provide less damage to the door's finish from the weather.
- offer sheltered space for receiving a package delivery or waiting for a school bus. See 22-20.

*Full-length side window at entry door*

- increases the natural light in the foyer.
- allows everyone to see who is at the door before opening it.

### Kitchen

*Knee space under sink and cooktop*

- provides a space to store a serving cart or recycling bins.

Universal Design Home of the Future, AARP

22-18 _____
*The Universal Design Home of the Future shows features that make this home usable by all people.*

Universal Design Home of the Future, AARP

22-19 _____
*A bathtub with a top edge extended for sitting makes it easier for all people to enter and exit the tub safely.*

- allows people to work while sitting on a stool.

*Lever-type water controls*

- permit easier adjustment of water temperature and volume.
- can be operated with use of a single hand or elbow.
- have fewer parts than other types of controls, so are less costly to repair.
- are easier to keep clean because of few crevices.

**Discuss:** Do you disagree with any of the listed benefits of universal design? Can you think of any features that you believe should be added to the list? Explain.

**Enrich:** Visit a historic home, one at least 100 years old. Observe all the features that conflict with the principles of universal design. Write an essay explaining how your family's life would differ if your housing resembled the historic home.

**Activity:** Search advertisements Tand the Internet for bathtubs with the top edge extended, as in Figure 22-19. Compare its price to the price of a standard bathtub.

Southface Energy Institute, Atlanta, GA

**22-20**
*This accessible entrance from the parking area is wide, level, and protected by an overhanging roof. Universal design requires one such entrance per house. Other entrances may have stairs, as shown in Figure 22-3.*

**Discuss:** Do you think a universally designed home is easier to keep clean and organized? Explain.

### Variable-height work surfaces

- make it easier to designate counter space for different functions.
- allow family members of all heights to help with meal preparation.

### Contrasting borders on countertops

- makes it easier to repair damaged edges without repairing the entire countertop.
- reduces the likelihood of spills because the ends of counters are easier to see.

### Pull-out shelves in cabinets

- make it possible to reach items stored in the back without stretching. See 22-21.
- permit easier maneuvering of large items in and out of the cabinet.

### Pantry cabinet with full-length shelves

- provides storage that can be reached from all heights.
- offers the maximum storage per square foot of floor space.

## Bathrooms

### Adjustable-height shower head

- can be adjusted to suit the height of different users.
- makes it possible to avoid wetting a bandage, cast, hairdo, or anything else that should remain dry.
- can be used for massaging one's back, rinsing hair, and washing the dog.

### Grab bars in tub or shower

- can double as a towel bar when hung horizontally.
- make it easier and safer to enter and exit a tub or shower.

### Over-sink mirror extending down to backslash

- allows children and seated adults to have a view of the mirror while using the sink.
- reduces water damage to the wall behind the sink.
- makes it easier to clean behind the faucet.
- makes the room seem more spacious.

## The General Interior

### Minimum door opening of 32 inches

- improves circulation throughout the house, especially when guests are visiting.

**Discuss:** What universal design features exist in this school?

**Discuss:** Study Figure 22-20. List reasons why this type of entrance would benefit homeowners more than the usual type of entryway with one or more steps.

A
Universal Design Home of the Future, AARP

B
Kraftmaid

22-21 _____

*Pull-down shelves (A) and roll-out trays in base cabinets (B) are handy for everyone, especially those with limited reach.*

- reduces damage to the doorframe when moving furniture or equipment through doorways.

### Lever-style door handles

- are easier for everyone to use.
- permit owners to open the doors with just an elbow or knee when hands are filled.
- adds an elegant touch, as in 22-22, at little or no extra cost.

### Adjustable-height closet rods

- make closets usable by children.
- increase storage by creating room for a second-tier closet rod or other types of organizers.
- tailor closets to individual wardrobe needs

Kwikset Corporation

22-22 _____

*Lever handles come in many styles from plain to fancy, like the one shown here.*

**Discuss:** Do you think universal design features could have any effect on a home's energy costs? Explain.

**Enrich:** Visit a home improvement center and search for ways to transform fixed cabinet shelves into the rollout type shown in Figure 22-21B.

*Tall windows placed low on the wall*

- provide a good view for everyone, especially children and seated adults, as in 22-23.

- add more natural light and elegance to the room.

- are easier for a child to open.

- require less reaching to open, close, and lock. **(24 to 36 inches from the floor)**

*Electrical receptacles 18 inches from the floor*

- are easier to find than those low to the floor and are easier to reach without bending.

- are located conveniently for electric cords to be removed correctly—by grasping the plug, not pulling on the cord. See 22-24.

These and other universal design features are gradually becoming standard features in all types of new housing.

## Green Buildings

A concept that is receiving attention is the idea of green buildings. A *green building* is not one that is "painted green" but instead refers to a structure that uses materials and techniques in all aspects of construction that conserves resources. These buildings can use one or more green products or measures in the structure.

Weather Shield Windows & Doors

22-23

*Tall windows extending close to the floor provide excellent views of the outdoors.*

Muscular Dystrophy Association

22-24

*Electrical outlets that are raised to 18 inches off the floor are much easier to use in both a standing and seated position.*

*Green products* are those that are used to conserve scarce resources and possibly were made from recyclable materials. An example is using steel construction to replace the use of wood, since wood is a limited commodity and thereby is costly. Although these homes conserve resources, today's "green-built" homes are virtually indistinguishable from other homes.

Most exterior doors are now insulated. Windows now have insulated glass and low-E glass to keep homes more comfortable and energy efficient. Vinyl siding and fiber cement siding have reduced the need for cedar, redwood, and other products usually used on exterior walls. Plastic lumber is used on decks. New energy-efficient dishwashers, refrigerators, and clothes washers are used. New toilets use less water to operate.

High-efficiency heating, cooling, and water heating have reduced the amount of energy used in the homes. Passive solar design takes advantage of the sun's energy to help heat homes through glass that is oriented toward a southern exposure.

More durable roof coverings such as metals and fiber-cement reduce the need for frequent roof replacement. Increased insulation in walls and attics make the home more resistant to energy loss. Steps taken to conserve energy also lower energy bills, reduce pollution related to energy production, and save precious resources.

## Planned Communities

Planned communities are one answer to today's housing problems. Instead of growing by one building at a time, these communities are designed to meet present and future needs. Careful consideration is given to the use of resources and the needs and values of the residents.

Planned communities are described as "one-stop living." They are made as self-sufficient as possible. Businesses, shops, recreation, and schools are included in the planning. Homes in these communities are an escape from the usually congested suburbs and high commuter traffic.

An example of a planned community is Columbia, Maryland. This is one of several communities planned by architect James W. Rouse. It is located on 15,000 acres of land between Baltimore and Washington, DC. About 3,200 acres are set aside for parks, lakes, and a golf course. The city of Columbia is really a group of seven villages built around an urban downtown. In this arrangement, the villages are called *satellite communities*. Columbia is planned as a racially and culturally diverse community. Homes are available in a wide range of prices and styles. Some can be purchased, and others can be rented.

Included in the planning of Columbia were specialists from many fields: architects, sociologists, educators, religious leaders, and doctors. They tried to answer the question, "What should be included in a well-planned community?" The factors they considered are listed in 22-25.

A community association is needed to govern a planned community. A well-run association can raise the quality of life as well as property values. The number of such associations is steadily increasing.

### New Urbanism

Recall from Chapter 2, "Influences on Housing," that new urbanism is a planned community. However, it has a different focus—houses in which people both live and work. For example, a person may have an art gallery on the first floor and live on the second and third floor. Many of these communities

**Resource:** *Planning a Community*, Activity C, SAG. Students plan and describe a community for 25,000 people.
**Reflect:** Would you like to live in a planned community?
**Discuss:** Identify an example of housing in your area that most closely resembles the trend of new urbanism.

**Enrich:** Research planned communities such as Celebration, Florida (a Disney community), and Columbia, Maryland. How were they planned? What are the benefits of living in these communities? What is the population of each? Search *celebrationfl.com/* and *columbia-md.com/*.

**Enrich:** Attend a presentation by a manager of a housing association or planned community to learn about using group participation to manage a living environment. Report what you learn.

Resource: *Future Housing,* Activity D, SAG. Students list current housing trends (regarding homeowners, the environment, building materials, and technology) and predict their future effects on housing.

Discuss: Do you think the factors listed in Figure 22-25 could occur in a community without central planning? Explain.

Enrich: Search newspapers for articles on three aspects of housing trends: materials, environments, and technology.

Discuss: Do you anticipate people living in outer space in your lifetime? Explain.

### Factors for Designing a Planned Community

- The lifestyles desired by the occupants
- Affordable housing
- Easy access to schools, health facilities, places of worship, stores, and goverment offices
- Recreational facilities that appeal to individuals and groups of all ages
- The use of parks, playgrounds, and green belts to separate space and create neighborhood zones
- Affordable public transportation
- Employment opportunities at all levels
- Education opportunities at all levels
- Effective and affodable health care facilities
- Effective communications about community events and activities

22-25

*These factors were considered when the planned community of Columbia, Maryland, was designed.*

are planned to make better use of land, especially near the central business district or community area that needs extensive renovation.

## New Living Spaces

Many of today's housing problems relate to space. About 75 percent of the people in the United States are living on less than 10 percent of the land, yet space for housing is difficult to find. It is also expensive. In just 40 years the cost of land has risen dramatically from about 10 to 25 percent of a home's purchase price. In some areas, the cost will be as much as 50 percent. To solve this problem, some new

sources of living space are being explored.

A possible "new frontier" is outer space. Although you may not be able to imagine it, living in a space colony is not impossible. For humans to exist for periods in outer space, extensive testing is needed to guide the development of life-support systems as well as new methods of food production and waste management.

Some preliminary research has been completed by having a community living under glass as though it were a space station. The Biosphere 2 project in Arizona has investigated human reactions to the controlled environment as well as ways to grow and harvest plants in climatic conditions similar to outer space. See 22-26. The Biosphere is a unique *ecosystem*, or a community of organisms within an environment functioning as a unit in nature. Currently the Biosphere is a nonprofit research and educational affiliate of Columbia University focusing on global climate change experiments.

Some people think living space could be extended downward into the earth. Earth-sheltered housing was discussed in Chapter 6. Caves, cellars, and basements all have had their place in the story of housing. However, the idea of building whole, modern communities underground has not attracted any interest.

Living space may be found on and in bodies of water. The SS United States, once the world's fastest oceanliner, has been converted into a seagoing condominium. However, the prices of its 282 housing units are extremely expensive.

Less costly living quarters on water are available. Some are on ocean sites, and others are on smaller bodies of water. Most of them are houseboats.

Discuss: Why do you think the idea of underground or underwater communities has not attracted much interest.

Discuss: Does the growing scarcity of land for housing point to an increased need for more high rises? Would more high rises in your community answer the land-scarcity problem or pose new problems?

Gill Kenny/Space Biosphere Ventures

A

C. Allan Morgan/Space Biosphere Ventures

B

22-26

*Biosphere 2 in Arizona is the largest and most complex ecosystem ever built (A). This area is devoted entirely to food production (B).*

However, the same idea may be used in the future to lessen the shortage of space for housing.

Some of these futuristic housing ideas may not become reality. Some may just be science fiction. It will be interesting to see which directions housing takes in the future. What do you expect to happen during your lifetime?

**Resource:** *Housing: Today and Tomorrow,* Activity E, SAG. Students complete the statements about concepts from the chapter by filling in the blanks.

**Writing Activity:** Create a crossword puzzle using the *To Know* terms and other key words from this chapter.

**Language Arts Activity:** Working with a partner, carry on a conversation about what was learned from this chapter, using as many key terms as possible. Ground rules are: one declarative sentence is spoken at a time, partners take turns speaking, and key terms cannot be used in questions.

## Summary

Of the greatest impacts on new housing is new technology. The SMART HOUSE is an example of housing that is based on new advances in technology. New materials continue to be developed for housing, as shown in the Southface Energy and Environmental Resource Center is another example.

Producing and conserving energy are present-day concerns related to housing. All forms of energy begin as energy from the sun. Nature converts it to raw materials that can be refined for fuel. Nuclear energy is a relatively new form of energy that has been harnessed. Generating power from the sun's rays, wind, and moving water is also possible.

An unhealthy environment affects housing as well as human health. Land, water, and air pollution are major concerns. The garbage in most communities is simply burned or buried. In places where garbage is recycled, it is sorted. The combustible materials are used as fuel for operating power plants or for heating. Metal cans, plastic, and glass can be reused. Scientists are trying to find more ways of recycling garbage.

Trends in housing offer new solutions to the concerns of people regarding their housing. Universal design makes housing more useful and comfortable to more people. It affects the housing structure as well as the interior components used in everyday life. Planned communities create a pleasant balance between housing and the surrounding environment. Planned communities now exist only on land, but future communities may exist below ground or in space.

## To Review

1. Give a brief description of a SMART HOUSE.
2. Name four housing concerns, other than energy use and conservation, addressed by the Southface Energy and Environmental Resource Center.
3. List the five major sources of energy in the U.S. today.
4. Identify one advantage and one disadvantage of nuclear energy.
5. Compare hydroelectric and geothermal energy.
6. How is wind used as an energy source?
7. List five features to look for when buying an energy-efficient house.
8. _____ is the relationship between all living things and their surroundings.

**Answer Key**

1. SMART HOUSE features a home automation system based on computer technology that controls the house's subsystems.
2. (List four:) thermal comfort, indoor air quality, accessibility, waste reduction, use of recycled materials, water conservation
3. coal, nuclear power, hydroelectric power, natural gas, petroleum
4. (List one of each:) advantages: no polluting dust, no polluting gas, abundant energy
   disadvantages: radioactive waste, challenges of disposing the waste, possible release of radioactivity
5. Hydroelectric energy is generated from running water in rivers and dams. Geothermal energy is heat carried by hot streams or rock heated by the intensely hot center of the earth.
6. With the use of generators, air motion is converted to electrical current.
7. (List five. See Figure 22-12.)
8. ecology

9. List the five waste-handling options for communities, from most preferred to least preferred, as recommended by the Environmental Protection Agency.

10. Name four features of universal design that would benefit a person with physical limitations. Describe how each would benefit other members of the household.

11. Describe a planned community.

9. source reduction, recycling and reuse, incineration with resource recovery, incineration without resource recovery, landfill

10. (List four. See Figure 22-17.)

11. Planned communities are carefully designed communities that meet the residents' current and future housing needs.

# In Your Community

1. Find out which waste products are accepted for recycling in your community. Share the findings with your classmates. What is the waste management plan in your community for hazardous materials?

2. Check with a homebuilder in your city to find out how he or she uses new technology in constructing houses. This should include building materials, construction techniques, and equipment. Ask if he or she has built a house with *SMART HOUSE* or *green buildings* technology. If so, how prevalent is this type of housing in your community?

3. Survey your neighbors and relatives regarding their ideas about future housing. Develop six questions about the types of housing they expect in the future. Share the survey results with your class. (Make sure not to reveal the source of any specific comment.)

# To Think About

1. Imagine you are a writer for a building technology magazine. Your assignment is to write a science fiction story about housing 100 years from now. What five items would you discuss in your article?

2. New uses for recycled materials are being determined daily. Make a list of three items that are not currently being recycled in your community and imagine how recycling them could benefit new housing. Some recent examples include converting old auto frames into steel beams and other building materials, and recycling worn auto tires into carpeting. What are your ideas?

# Using Technology

1. Using the Internet and magazines, collect photos and descriptions of new technology in housing. Select three interesting items. Print images off various Web sites or scan magazine photos, if necessary, into a computer. Develop a one-page, illustrated handout of the items and share the handout with your class.

2. Check the buildings in your community to see how many have solar heating systems. Using a digital or regular camera, photograph the visible solar collectors. Compile an inexpensive photo scrapbook, complete with written photo descriptions, to share with your class. What types of buildings (residential, commercial, or government) seem to use solar power most often?

**Portfolio Project:** Create a brochure that promotes housing with universal design and cites its benefits. Illustrate your brochure with drawings or photos from magazines or Web sites.

# CHAPTER 23

# Careers in Housing

## To Know

career
occupation
career cluster
bachelor's degree
master's degree
American Institute of Architects (AIA)
National Society of Professional
   Engineers (NSPE)
American Society of Interior Designers
   (ASID)
trade
apprenticeship
unskilled labor
semiskilled labor
skilled labor
entrepreneur
cooperative education
career ladder
career lattice
lifelong learning

## Objectives

After studying this chapter, you will be able to

- explain how to learn about careers related to housing.

- describe several careers within the housing field, including those held by entrepreneurs.

- list ways that computers are used to help professionals make housing decisions.

- determine the significance of a career ladder and lifelong learning to a successful housing career.

**Resource:** *Progress in Housing,* transparency master overlay VI-B, TR. Students look back at the topics covered in Chapters 1-22 by reviewing transparency master VI-A. Then, with the addition of overlay VI-B, they explore the topics they will cover in Chapter 23.

**Reading / Writing Activity:** Change the chapter objectives into questions and list them on the left side of a piece of paper. As you read the chapter, write the answers on the right half of the paper.

**Vocabulary:** Select 10 terms from the vocabulary list that are unknown or very unfamiliar. List them on a piece of paper, writing one term on every third or fourth line. When you reach each term in the text, write its definition and use it in a sentence.

The number of U.S. households is growing, requiring about two million new housing units each year. Providing housing and housing-related services for a growing population takes thousands of workers in various careers. Perhaps one of these careers will interest you.

# Who Provides Housing?

Many people associate construction workers with housing since they are obvious at home construction sites. Although they are an important part of housing, construction workers do not provide all that is needed for creating a good housing environment. See 23-1.

Before construction begins, urban planners and architects develop ideas for communities and buildings. Manufacturers develop building materials

23-1 _____

*Many people from different career areas were involved in planning, building, selling, designing, and furnishing this house.*

and a vast array of appliances, furnishings, and accessories to personalize a home. Designers, landscapers, and other professionals also contribute their expertise.

Many careers are involved with making housing environments more satisfying. A *career* is a series of related occupations that show progression in a field of work. Holding a series of related jobs or occupations is equivalent to having a career. The term *job* is commonly used to mean *occupation*. Strictly speaking, a *job* is a task, while an **occupation** is paid employment that involves handling one or more jobs.

Having a career means you will hold several occupations related by a common skill, purpose, or interest over your lifetime. An example of a career is the job path followed by some construction workers over a span of several years. They may enter the field doing one job well, learn to do others, and eventually supervise parts or all of various construction projects. As you move from one job to the next, you will gain new skills and knowledge.

## Career Clusters

Occupations or jobs that are closely related make up a *career cluster*. In 23-2, for example, you can see that landscaping involves the following five jobs:

- horticultural installations
- turf installations
- hardscape installations
- equipment operations
- equipment maintenance

In a small business, one or two people may divide the work and handle all the jobs. In a large business, however, five different individuals

Vocabulary: Compare and contrast the meanings of the terms *career, job,* and *occupation.*

Enrich: Read an inspirational story about a person who is happy in his or her job in the housing industry.

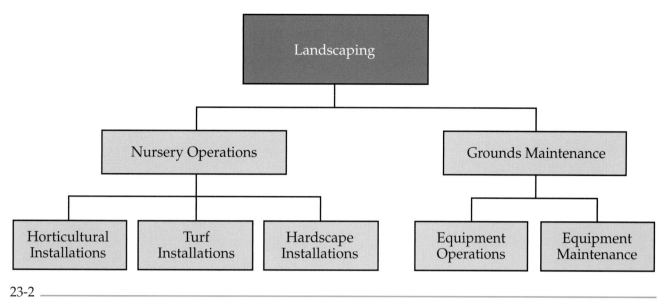

23-2

*All jobs in this career cluster are needed to provide a full-service landscaping business.*

would probably hold one job apiece and become specialists in their work.

Sometimes a career cluster is called a *career web.* Look at 23-3 to see why this name is appropriate. A career web groups the various jobs or occupations needed to get the work done. If one or two jobs in a career cluster or career web appeal to you, it is likely that others will, too. This is because the jobs grouped together share certain similarities. Remembering this relationship is helpful when researching information about careers.

## Career Information

Special skills and training are needed to carry out the assigned tasks of careers in the housing industry. When exploring different occupations, look carefully at what each involves and what is expected of the jobholder. Also, study the qualifications for entering that field.

Usually school counselors and teachers can direct you to helpful job information. Family members and neighbors can provide help, too. Good information is also available

in libraries and on the Internet. The U.S. Department of Labor is a particularly good source. It makes the following items available:

- The *Occupational Outlook Handbook* describes the major U.S. jobs and their working conditions, requirements, average salaries, and future outlook. This publication is available in most libraries and on the Department's Web site.

- The *Guide for Occupational Exploration* helps jobseekers understand what personal traits are required for various careers. It clusters jobs according to key worker traits. This approach lets you judge your suitability for various jobs based on how closely your abilities and interests match the job's requirements.

- The Occupational Information Network, called the O*Net, is the most complete online resource available. It provides tools for exploring careers, examining job trends, and assessing personal abilities and interests.

Enrich: Visit the school or community library and study how information in the *Dictionary of Occupational Titles* and the *Occupational Outlook Handbook* is arranged. Skim through each book and note the information provided about each career. (You could also complete this activity by using the Web sites for these two resources.)

Art Activity: Reorganize the information in Figure 23-2 into a web similar to the one in Figure 23-3. Be creative in designing your web.

Note: The Web site for the *Occupational Outlook Handbook* is *bls.gov/oco.* O*Net can be accessed at *doleta.gov/programs/onet.* The Web site for the *Dictionary of Occupational Titles* is *oalj.dol.gov/libdot.htm.*

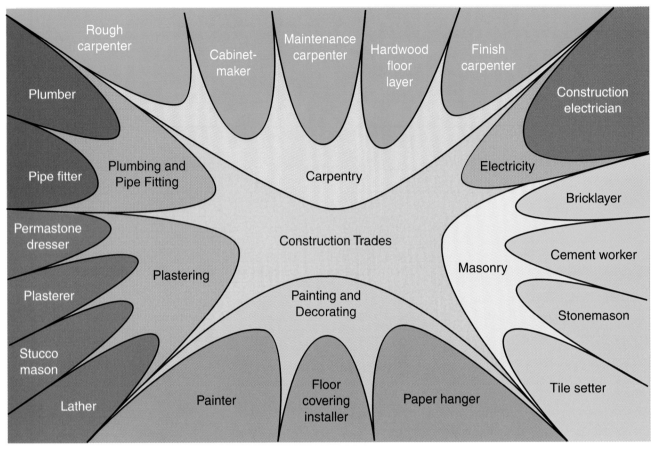

23-3

*A career web for construction trades shows the related areas of work and the types of skills needed.*

**Activity:** Working with teammates, develop a list of related careers for a specific housing career, such as interior designer, construction worker, or real estate agent.

As you explore various occupations, study their descriptions to get a clear picture of what each involves. See 23-4 for a list of the components of a complete job description. As you review each of these factors, consider the following questions:

### Job Duties and Responsibilities

What exactly does the job entail? Does the job involve working on tasks for more than one department? To which department does the jobholder report?

### Education, Training, and Experience

What educational level is considered minimum? How much training or experience is needed? Can people

### Components of Job Descriptions

- Job duties and areas of responsibility
- Required education, training, and experience
- Important personal traits
- Usual work environment
- Leading employers
- Minimum, average, and peak earnings
- Employment outlook
- Job rewards (if any)
- Related careers

23-4

*Examine all aspects of an occupation to decide whether it offers the best career path for you.*

**Enrich:** Attend a presentation by a school guidance counselor, vocational specialist, or community college representative to learn about training available locally for housing careers. Be prepared to ask questions related to your career goals. (The speaker may also discuss instruments available for helping students determine the types of jobs for which they are gifted.)

enter the field with less training and acquire expertise while working on the job? Are special certificates, licenses, or credentials needed?

### Personal Traits

Does the job need someone outgoing or reserved? someone who enjoys routines or constant change? a detail-minded person or one who likes to "think big"? Some people have personality traits that are in conflict with the requirements of certain jobs. This does not lead to career satisfaction or success.

### Workplace

Is the work environment a quiet office, a noisy factory, or the great outdoors? Are work hours during the daytime, Monday through Friday, or on evenings and weekends?

### Employer

What companies, government offices, schools, or other workplaces employ people with the expertise? Are these employers located where you plan to live?

### Earnings

What is the average beginning salary? What does it take to achieve higher earnings? Are additional degrees or training generally required?

### Employment Outlook

In 10 years, will the need for this career increase, stay the same, or decrease compared to average employment trends? Are too many people flocking to a field that is not growing? If the employment outlook for a job is poor, you will be faced with fewer job choices. It is best to focus on career areas that are growing. They will offer you greater job choices when you are ready to begin your career. See 23-5.

### Rewards

People have different ideas about what constitutes a "reward." For example, does the job involve frequent travel? Adventurous people would consider this job factor a reward. However, people who like to stay at home would be annoyed, perhaps irritated and angry, at so much traveling. Each situation brings other conditions that involve personal preferences.

**23-5**

*Interior design careers are expected to grow faster than the overall employment rate, but competition will be keen for most jobs.*

**Discuss:** Of the job factors described on this page, which would you rank as the most important for a person with long-term career goals to consider?

**History / Writing Activity:** Think of some character in history whose personal traits were perfect for the challenging job he or she handled. Write a paragraph explaining your choice.

**Reflect:** For what types of housing careers are your personal traits suited?

*Related Careers*

What other jobs closely match this one? Related jobs generally involve similar duties, responsibilities, and background requirements.

# Career Opportunities in Housing

Numerous job opportunities are available in housing. This chapter will examine the opportunities grouped according to the following fields:

- planning, engineering, and design
- construction
- sales and service
- entrepreneurship
- allied fields

As you study the job opportunities that exist in these housing fields, consider how they might apply to your own personal career choice.

## Housing Careers in Planning, Engineering, and Design

Attractive homes and neighborhoods do not happen automatically. They are the results of careful attention to planning, engineering, and design by many different professionals. Some of the key professionals and their contributions are discussed here.

### Urban Planners

Urban planners direct how land will be used in a community for growth or revitalization. They are sometimes called *regional* or *community planners*. These professionals work for community organizations, real estate developers, large construction firms, and branches of government.

Urban planners research a geographic area and propose long-range plans to benefit its social, economic, and environmental future. Their plans require a long review process by all interested parties. During that time, urban planners provide detailed facts for their decisions. The facts revolve around the estimated population growth and the infrastructure needed to support it.

Becoming an urban planner requires a bachelor's degree in architecture or engineering with an advanced degree in urban planning. A *bachelor's degree* is a college degree usually requiring four years of study. A *master's degree* requires another year or two of study beyond a bachelor's degree. A master's degree is also called a *graduate degree*. In addition, urban planners must take continuing education courses to maintain expertise.

### Architects

An architect's job is to design buildings that satisfy people. Such buildings must be safe, attractive, and useful. There is more to the job than design. Architects must be sure the proper materials are used and the builder follows the plans. See 23-6.

Established architects make a good salary, but becoming one takes considerable study and on-the-job practice. Five years are required to earn a bachelor's degree. A two-day examination must be passed to receive the license necessary to work as an architect. In most states, a college graduate needs three years of experience to become qualified to take the exam. The organization that promotes high professional standards among architects is the *American Institute of Architects (AIA)*. Its members must satisfy ongoing education and training requirements.

Architects may specialize in certain areas of architecture. Some choose to work only on residential jobs, while others may specialize in commercial fields. A growing career opportunity is the area of historical preservation. Architects who enter this field are called *preservationists*. They concentrate on how to identify, preserve, and restore buildings that have architectural or historical value. A combined degree in both architecture and history is ideal for this specialty.

Some architects specialize in planning housing designs that meet the requirements for universal design. They may create a new floor plan or update an existing design. With the aging of the population and a growing interest in universal design, demand for experts in this field will continue.

### Engineers

Engineers are educated in programs leading to degrees in science. Engineers whose work is related to housing take courses in mathematics, print reading, drafting, computer science, and physics. Four or five years are needed for a bachelor's degree, depending on the school. The organization that promotes high professional standards among engineers is the **National Society of Professional Engineers (NSPE)**. Its members are required to have a high level of preparation, service under a professional engineer, and ongoing continuing education and training.

*Civil engineers* are responsible for preparing the site. They level the land, design drainage and sewer systems, and lay out streets and sidewalks. Another part of their work is to study the soil of the site. They must know how much weight it will support without settling. See 23-7. Many civil engineers work for all levels of government. Housing developers employ others.

In many cases, an architect assumes the task of determining the

23-6
*Architects use computers to show every detail in the construction of a building.*

23-7
*This engineer is testing the soil for its suitability as a building site.*

**Discuss:** Do you think a person who is both creative and detail-oriented should consider a career in engineering or architecture? Explain your answer.

**Vocabulary:** Compare and contrast the work of structural engineers, mechanical engineers, civil engineers, and electrical engineers.

**Activity:** Check the *Occupational Outlook Handbook* for job opportunities for each of the engineering positions described.

**Enrich:** Observe a demonstration by a guest surveyor on the use of surveying instruments, such as the theodolite and rods or targets used to measure horizontal and vertical angles, distances, and elevations. If the surveyor permits, try using the instruments to sight measurements on the school grounds. Summarize what you learned from the demonstration.

ability of a building to withstand stresses. As structures become larger and more complex, the *structural engineer* advises the architect on the safety and strength of the design. He or she estimates the weight the building must carry and the pressures the structure and its foundation must withstand. Many structural engineers are self-employed, while others work for large engineering or architectural firms.

*Mechanical engineers* are concerned with the design of equipment for plumbing, heating, ventilating, and air conditioning. They plan the systems and equipment most appropriate for a building and oversee the installation.

*Electrical engineers* plan the electrical service needed for a household by calculating total lighting and equipment needs. They also plan the best layout for the electrical circuits and placement of switches. Their calculations and plans are included in the architectural drawings supplied to the builder.

Engineers who advise homeowners on how to stop unwanted water from entering a residence are *moisture migration specialists*. Because research links health concerns to mold growth, this area of expertise is increasing in importance. A moisture migration specialist identifies the source of the moisture problem and takes action to correct it. Moisture migration specialists may have a background in architecture.

### Surveyors

Using various tools, the surveyor locates corners and boundaries of tracts of land. Instrument findings are used to draw a map of the surveyed area. Several other workers assist.

- *Instrument workers* adjust and operate the surveying instruments.
- *Chain workers* measure distances between survey points.

- *Rod workers* use a level rod and range pole to help measure distance and angles.

Surveying involves outdoor work with much walking while carrying heavy instruments. Knowledge of mathematics is essential. A license is required in all states, but educational requirements for becoming a surveyor vary.

### Interior Designers

Interior designers plan and supervise the design and arrangement of building interiors and furnishings. Their goal is to enhance the interior's design and protect the health, safety, and welfare of the public. They prepare plans and documents for interior spaces to help their clients visualize how the rooms will look and function.

Interior designers must have specialized knowledge of basic housing principles, space planning, interior construction, building codes, equipment, materials, and furnishings. See 23-8. They should also have a strong sense of how to achieve an aesthetically pleasing look. Designers must excel at evaluating client needs and tastes, and transforming rooms to fulfill their wishes.

Interior designers work for individual clients, interior planning and design firms, or firms that sell furnishings. They select and estimate costs of furniture, floor and wall coverings, and accessories. When plans are approved, the designer may arrange the purchase of furnishings and hire or supervise various workers for delivery and installation.

Four years of training at the university level are required to become an interior designer. Courses include principles of design, history of art, computer-aided drafting and design (CADD), furniture design, lighting, acoustics, and textiles. Knowledge of

**Discuss:** Have you ever watched television programs that featured an interior designer? What characteristics are essential to become successful in that career? *(specialized knowledge of basic housing principles, space planning, interior construction, building codes, equipment, materials, and furnishings; a strong sense of aesthetics; an ability to evaluate client needs and tastes; skill in transforming rooms to fulfill client wishes)*

antiques, art pieces, and furnishings is also needed. Interior designers are paid for their knowledge, experience, and range of services. The organization that promotes high professional standards among interior designers is the *American Society of Interior Designers (ASID)*. Its members are required to have a high level of preparation and ongoing continuing education and training. Before using a designer's services, you will want to ask about his or her professional training and membership.

Some interior designers focus their careers in specialized areas such as kitchen and bath design. Others may concentrate specifically on lighting design. Specialty areas require additional education in a designer's chosen area of concentration.

### Landscape Architects

Landscape architects work with organizations, committees, government agencies, private firms, and individuals to beautify the land surrounding structures. Their work entails planning the placement of natural and manufactured landscape elements around buildings. See 23-9. They usually study four or five years in college. Required courses include surveying, sketching, horticulture, landscape construction, botany, science, and mathematics. About half the states require landscape architects to obtain a license. The organization that promotes high professional standards among landscape architects is the *American Society of Landscape Architects (ASLA)*. Its members are required to continually update their education and training.

### Drafters

From the sketches, plans, and instructions of an architect, designer, or engineer, a drafter prepares the detailed drawings used by the builder.

Judith Brinkley-Berry, ASID, Judith Brinkley-Berry Interior Design, Atlanta, GA, and Hilton Head Island, SC

23-8 _____

*Interior designers assist their clients with the selection of materials, equipment, and furnishings.*

The Long Cane Group, Inc., Atlanta, GA

23-9 _____

*Landscape architects work directly from their plans to place trees, shrubs, walkways, and other outdoor features.*

These drawings specify the materials to use, state exact dimensions, and identify the work the contractor or builder will do.

Drafters must be able to produce neat, accurate drawings using the tools of the trade and a computer.

**Internet Activity:** Look up the Web site for ASID to research the required training to remain active in this organization.

Knowledge of construction is needed as well as patience and good eyesight. Drafters may specialize in certain aspects of the job. One such specialist is the *architectural illustrator*. He or she prepares the presentation materials that are printed in brochures or shown to clients who want a picture of the building's finished look.

## Model Makers

To help clients visualize large projects, an architect or designer may have a scale model of the project built. See 23-10. A model maker will be hired to do this. Most model makers are self-employed. Necessary skills include being able to read and interpret prints, use scales, and visualize drawings in three dimensions. Model makers must do precision work while shaping materials in miniature.

North Carolina A&T State University, Greensboro, NC

23-10
*Model makers build three-dimensional models from an architect's drawings.*

## Ergonomics Designers

Ergonomics designers specialize in the science of ergonomics. They design consumer products and environments to promote user comfort, efficiency, and safety. These designers are also known as specialists in *human factors engineering* or *human engineering*. The science of ergonomics developed during the early 1900s when research focused on increasing worker comfort to boost productivity. Today the focus is on creating pleasing designs that enhance worker safety and long-term health.

An ergonomics designer may have an engineering degree or a degree in interior design with a concentration in furniture design. Examples of ergonomic design are desk chairs and computer keyboards that prevent hand and back muscle strain while working at a computer for long periods. Ergonomics designers also help incorporate universal design into homes, furniture, appliances, and consumer tools.

## Certified Industrial Hygienist

One specialized professional related to the removal of mold from buildings is the *certified industrial hygienist (CIH)*. This individual focuses on residential air quality problems that involve excess moisture. If mold has begun to grow, some of the mold spores may have contaminated the heating, ventilating, and air conditioning systems. These specialists can test air quality and recommend action to restore the "health" of the structure.

## Administrative Assistants

Today's office workers are usually called *administrative assistants*. No business can operate efficiently without the assistance of an office staff. The smaller the firm is, the more the employee duties vary. Some employees function as special assistants to architects, engineers, builders, interior designers, and contractors. Work may include keystroking documents onto a computer, filing, scheduling, preparing reports, bookkeeping, and handling visitors. Office assistants must know how to operate copiers, scanners, computers, printers, and complex telephones. See 23-11.

## Housing Careers in Construction

The homebuilder or contractor employs a variety of tradespeople to work on different stages of the construction. A *trade* is an occupation requiring manual or mechanical skill. Hiring tradespeople for construction projects is called *subcontracting.*

Tradespeople include the many jobs discussed here. Some local building codes require electricians, plumbers, roofers, or other specialists to have a current state license. Training for these jobs is available in schools that teach career and technical education, also known as *vocational schools.* Another way to receive this training is through an apprenticeship program. An *apprenticeship* involves learning a trade under the direction and guidance of an expert worker. After successful completion of a training program, some tradespeople become *self-employed.* This means they deal directly with employers, determining their own workloads and pay.

### Bricklayers and Stonemasons

These construction specialists build walls, partitions, fireplaces, and other structures. They use brick, block, and stone as well as other natural or manufactured materials. Bricklayers and stonemasons generally work with

23-11
*Administrative assistants manage the paperwork and details of running an office so the housing experts can focus on their specialties.*

hand tools. Understanding drawings, making accurate measurements, and working rapidly and neatly are among the important skills they must master. Bricklayers must be able to construct various patterns when laying bricks and blocks. Also, they must use accepted construction methods for safety and structural stability.

### Carpenters

Carpenters usually construct the framework of houses from wood, as in 23-12. Some houses are constructed of steel frames by installers who require special skills. Carpenters install windows, doors, cabinets, stairs, and paneling. They also lay hardwood floors, asphalt, and other types of rigid flooring materials. *Rough carpenters* build the basic framework or set the concrete forms. *Finish carpenters* install millwork, cabinets, custom staircases, and other detail work. Some carpenters learn their work on the job, while others prepare through special career and technical education programs.

**Example:** The careers shown in Figure 23-3 are some of the trades in the construction industry.
**Vocabulary:** What is an apprenticeship? How does a person become an apprentice?

**Enrich:** Visit a construction site under the supervision of the contractor. Ask questions about the skills of each worker and determine the different jobs needed to construct a home.

**Vocabulary:** Compare and contrast *rough carpenter* and *finish carpenter.*

23-12
*Carpenters build houses in freezing cold to sweltering temperatures. Only weather-related hazards, such as ice and rain, keep them off the job.*

Lowden, Lowden & Co.

23-13
*This electrician is wiring a circuit breaker panel in a large, multifamily structure.*

## Construction Machinery Operators

Handling heavy construction materials or volumes of dirt would be difficult and even impossible without special machinery. Unless carefully controlled, such equipment could endanger the lives of the operators and their coworkers.

Construction machinery is used to lift and carry tons of material under the control of skilled workers, often called *operating engineers*. They drive cranes, bulldozers, backhoes, forklifts, pavers, and trucks. Good eyesight, coordination, and safety-consciousness are required.

## Electricians

Electricians install wiring in new structures and repair older wiring systems. They read the electrical diagrams and symbols in the architectural drawing. In addition, knowledge of electrical codes and electrical loads is essential. See 23-13.

With the rapid advances in home technology, some electricians specialize in installing integrated wiring systems such as those used in "smart" homes. Electronic home systems specialists design the cable and wiring plan for the entire house so everything that uses electricity interacts. This system manages the televisions, sound systems, computers, appliances, and home theater as well as systems for heating, ventilating, air conditioning, and security.

## Estimators

These specialists study architectural drawings of a proposed project and determine how much it will cost to build. He or she examines the cost of materials, labor, and other expenses. In large construction projects, this person may be an expert in the engineering field. In such cases, he or she is called a *construction cost engineer* or a *cost analysis engineer*. Estimators must be thoroughly familiar with building materials, installation methods, and related costs. Some estimators have a background in construction work. Others enter the field through training programs after high school.

## Floor-Covering Installers

These specialists lay or replace resilient tile, vinyl flooring, and carpeting. Their work may include removing an old covering and sanding and cleaning the surface to be covered. They must be able to read architectural drawings and measure, mark, and cut accurately.

## Heating and Cooling System Installers

Ventilation experts and installers of heating and cooling equipment are responsible for the thermal comfort of the home. They must know how to correctly install the system to assure comfort and operating efficiency. Also, they know the proper test procedures to monitor efficiency and locate any air leaks. See 23-14.

## Masons and Cement Workers

The construction workers responsible for a building's footings, foundation walls, patios, and some floors are masons and cement workers. They set up the forms, mix and pour the concrete, and use various tools to smooth and finish it. They must know cement materials and how to work with them. They also must be familiar with cement additives that speed or retard the setting of concrete.

## Painters

Painters apply paint, varnish, and other finishes to decorate and protect

Advanced Energy, Raleigh, NC

23-14

*Technicians in heating and cooling use a blower-door test to check air leakage in a home.*

surfaces. Painting involves surface preparation by scraping, burning with a torch, sanding, washing, priming, and sealing. Then, a new painted surface is applied with brushes, rollers, pads, or sprayers.

## Paperhangers

These specialists attach wallpaper or cloth to walls and ceilings. Sometimes they must first remove old

**Reflect:** Have you ever hung wallpaper or assisted someone who was hanging wallpaper? What was the most difficult part?

**Reflect:** How many types of floor-covering installers would be needed to install the variety of flooring materials found in your school?

**Discuss:** Which of the construction careers described in the text require the ability to read architectural drawings? (*bricklayers, stonemasons, electricians, estimators, floor-covering installers*)

Vocabulary: What is the difference between plaster and drywall?

wallpaper by soaking or steaming it. Occasionally minor patching of plaster is done. They prepare surfaces by cleaning them and applying sizing to make them less porous. Workers measure, cut, and hang materials, applying paste as needed.

### Plasterers and Drywall Installers

Installers of plaster and drywall finish the framed walls of a structure. Whether they apply plaster or use sheets of drywall, the resulting walls look very similar. Plasterers apply wet, cementlike material to the wall in successive coats, using other hand tools to create a smooth, flat surface.

Drywallers use sheets of gypsum wallboard to create walls and ceilings. Installing drywall is a two-step task. First, installers nail, screw, or glue sheets of the drywall in place. Finishers then apply a pasty cement and perforated tape to conceal joints and nail heads. See 23-15.

23-15

*A drywaller fastens gypsum wallboard to the studs. Later, he conceals nail heads and joints with a thick paste and, after it hardens, sands it smooth.*

### Plumbers and Pipe Fitters

These construction specialists install pipe systems that carry water, steam, natural gas, and other liquids and gases. They also install plumbing fixtures and appliances that use natural gas or water. Plumbers and pipe fitters install piping between walls and under floors during early stages of construction. They return during final construction stages to attach fixtures and install appliances.

### Roofers

Roofers apply shingles and other protective materials to make roofs weatherproof. They may also apply waterproofing to walls and other parts of the building. Roofers must be proficient in applying the various roofing materials used, depending on the building type and geographical location.

## Housing Careers in Sales and Service

To achieve a satisfying housing environment, consumers buy many products and services. The house itself is the first purchase. Buying the many other products that go into a structure to turn it into a home follows.

Unlike most other occupations, the sales and service fields offer many opportunities for unskilled, semiskilled, and skilled workers. *Unskilled labor* describes workers who fill entry-level jobs that require no previous knowledge or experience. At the next level, *semiskilled labor* describes workers who have some experience and/or technical training. Positions that call for *skilled labor* refer to workers who have successfully completed a formal training program beyond high school, such as an

Enrich: Visit a home decorating center to learn about different types of paint and the variety of choices in wallpapers.

Research Activity: Determine the frequency of gas pipe installations compared to water pipe installations among plumbers and pipe fitters in your community.

apprenticeship. College degrees are helpful for some sales positions.

### Real Estate Agents

Careers in real estate include many kinds of tasks. *Real estate developers* specialize in planning and creating new housing developments, such as a townhouse subdivision. *Real estate managers* rent and manage property for clients. They may have the title of *resident manager*, in which case they live in the apartment complex and oversee the operation of the units. Consequently, they may receive free rent as part of their payment package.

The most common career in the field of real estate is the *real estate agent*. Real estate agents help people buy, sell, rent, and lease property. They also help appraise property and arrange loans for homebuyers. Real estate agents must be familiar with their communities, real estate law, banking laws, and building codes. A license, required by all states, is obtained after successful completion of a written test. Many real estate agents have a college background although it is not a requirement. Important personality traits include a pleasant disposition, honesty, neatness, and tact. A good memory for names, faces, and facts is very important.

### Salespeople and Consultants

Retailers of building materials, appliances, and home furnishings prefer to hire people with a background in housing and furnishings. Their job is to demonstrate and sell their employer's products. See 23-16. Larger stores often provide helpful publications on proper selection, use, and care of products.

Consultants or interior decorators who help customers select the right

23-16
*Knowledgeable salespeople help consumers recognize their options and determine the best choice for their particular need.*

furnishings, equipment, or materials usually work for the larger stores. Interior decorators do not have the extensive educational background and training that a professional interior designer has. However, they may offer helpful advice to customers on installation and use of certain products. Consultants and interior decorators need a basic understanding of design, materials, and methods of installation.

### Occupations with Utility Companies

Utility companies that supply electricity, gas, telephone, and cable and satellite TV services offer job opportunities in sales and service areas. *Consumer advisors* or *customer service representatives* acquaint consumers with various products and

**Discuss:** What personal traits do good salespeople have? What types of personal traits are not suited to a sales or consulting career?

**Writing Activity:** Interview people who have used real estate agents to sell or purchase a home. What characteristics did they like best about their agents? Write a description of the ideal real estate agent.

**Vocabulary:** What is the difference between an interior decorator and an interior designer? (*The decorator does not have the extensive training that an interior designer has.*)

**Reflect:** How do you anticipate technology will influence future careers with utility companies?

levels of service. They need knowledge of featured and competing products plus sales ability. In service jobs, employees install lines and equipment, make needed adjustments, and repair problems.

## Entrepreneurial Careers in Housing and Design

People who desire to work for themselves can build a business around most of the jobs discussed thus far. Workers who start and run their own business are called *entrepreneurs*. Entrepreneurial opportunities in housing exist in many planning, engineering, design, and construction areas. Additional entrepreneurial opportunities also exist in areas that address consumer needs for repair, remodeling, decorating, and landscaping help. See 23-17.

Strong skills and knowledge in a chosen career area are basic requirements for a career as an entrepreneur. The self-employed individual must take risks and be financially prepared to handle slow times in the business. Successful entrepreneurs also need the following skills and personal qualities:

- excellent communications skills
- strong self-motivation to do the best work possible every time
- enthusiasm for the unique product or service
- a nonstop desire to promote the business and look for opportunities for future work
- understanding of the legal and financial aspects of running a business
- ability to recognize when to seek advice from competent experts
- supervisory skills (if employees are hired)

Entrepreneurship is a good way to have a successful career that you can control. However, success is not guaranteed. People who want to become entrepreneurs need to be prepared for the risks and responsibilities of running their own businesses.

## Housing Careers in Allied Fields

The career areas discussed thus far account for the greatest number of occupational opportunities in the housing field. However, you'll find other professionals throughout the workplace who make significant contributions to housing. Here are two such career areas.

### Educators of Housing and Design

Teachers are needed at many levels of education in the field of housing

Texas Dept. of Transportation

23-17 _____

*This entrepreneur uses her creative skills to produce home accessories.*

and design. The levels include high schools, career and technical schools, community colleges, and universities. County cooperative extension offices also employ educators and specialists in the field of housing. In addition to teaching, some educators focus part or most of their time on researching issues important in the housing field.

### Positions with Government

Government positions related to housing exist at federal, state, and local levels. Some of the positions influence the passing, monitoring, and enforcing of laws concerning housing. People in government positions often deal with building codes, housing standards, and zoning.

Other government employees help with finances or money matters related to housing. They deal with appraisals, mortgages, and interest rates. Some workers help secure affordable housing for low- to middle-income households. Yet other government employees study housing facts and develop the government's statistical data on the housing industry.

# Effect of Technology on Housing Careers

Powerful information and communication tools are commonly used in the housing field. Construction crews and tradespeople can be seen carrying telephones, pagers, digital cameras, and lap top computers to their job sites. See 23-18. These tools allow a supervisor to manage several building sites and communicate instantly without actually visiting each site. The housing jobs involved in construction design and management tend to have the greatest need for high tech equipment.

## Computer Usage by Housing Professionals

Of all the high-tech tools available to housing professionals, the computer is the most important. Speed and accuracy in producing the desired plan or product are the greatest benefits of the computer. Also, designers and consumers can thoroughly evaluate designs before they are actually built. This avoids costly mistakes and prevents the building of structures that do not meet the needs of the intended users.

**Discuss:** What are some of the skills needed by teachers in the field of housing?

23-18

*Cell phones are standard equipment for those in housing careers who work outside an office.*

**Enrich:** Attend a presentation by a guest speaker from the local housing authority discussing careers available with the government. Be prepared to ask questions related to your career goals.

**History Activity:** Interview your grandparents or other older adults to learn how realtors, construction supervisors, and other people in housing-related businesses worked before computers, cell phones, and beepers were available.

A computer can modify designs quickly. Professionals can store designs easily and retrieve them for any redesign work the client may want in the future. Also, elements of successful designs can be incorporated into new designs. Computers reduce design work to a mere fraction of the time it takes to draft a plan to scale by hand.

Some computer programs can show designs from different views or elevations for a more realistic picture of the expected results. Certain programs even allow viewers to "see" a design from walk-through, fly-over, or fly-under perspectives. *Virtual reality* is the term used to describe the sensation of experiencing a computer image so completely that it seems real. Virtual reality research laboratories are advancing and refining this technology.

Architects, interior designers, landscape architects, and engineers often rely on CADD software programs. See 23-19. They use these programs as a work tool or as a

presentation tool when discussing plans with clients. Some of the jobs in housing that make frequent use of CADD are discussed here in more detail.

### Architects

Architectural firms use computers to produce plans showing every detail in the construction of a building. These plans show front elevations, side elevations, section views, and detail views of their structures. They also generate separate plans for electrical, plumbing, and heating and cooling systems of the building. See Chapter 7, "Understanding House Plans," for examples.

### Construction Engineers

Construction engineers and designers use computers in a variety of ways. These include analyzing and selecting structural components and managing the actual construction process. See Chapter 8, "House

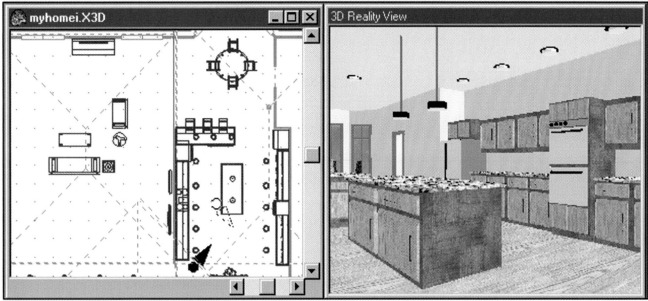

Home Design 3D™ from Expert Software

23-19

*With a CADD software program, both the kitchen floor plan and its elevation can be evaluated before installation begins.*

Construction," for a more complete description of how computers aid construction work.

## Interior Designers

Interior designers use computers to produce plans showing the locations of structural features, lighting, and plumbing fixtures. In addition, interior designers produce floor plans showing the furniture layout. They create specification sheets designating paint colors, wall treatments, floor coverings, and upholstery and drapery fabrics used in a home.

Interior designers use computers to create designs as well as present the designs to their clients. Examples of the opportunities to use CADD appear in Chapter 16, "Arranging and Selecting Furniture."

Efforts are underway to use virtual reality technology in interior design. The Computer Automated Virtual Environment (CAVE) at Virginia Polytechnic Institute in Blacksburg, Virginia, was the first university to explore this possibility. Designers are using it to give clients a glimpse of how they may experience particular designs. So far, this technology has been used in modeling, rendering, and animating plans for assisted-living residences and university buildings. See 23-20 for an explanation of how this technology works. See 23-21 for an idea of what a person standing in a computer-generated space might experience.

## Landscape Architects

Landscape architects use computers to create detailed plans and elevations of their proposed installations. These plans incorporate soil studies and show the exact placement of all plant materials, accent structures, and lighting. Landscape architects also use

computers to clearly present their ideas to clients. Examples of landscaping software appear in Chapter 19, "The Outdoor Living Space and Environment."

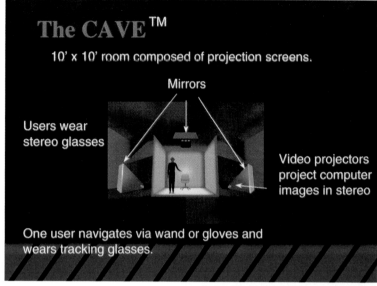

Design of Virginia Tech CAVE, by Joan McLain-Kark

23-20
*This diagram explains the technology that results in virtual reality.*

Virginia Tech, Rick Griffiths, Photographer/Imager

23-21
*The computer-enhanced photo shows the realistic environment a person sees when standing in this virtual-reality space.*

**Reflect:** Have you experienced virtual reality with computers? How did you feel? What are some common uses of this technology in the housing field?

**Writing Activity:** Think about the different ways you see computers used that influence housing. What are some factors that encourage people to use computers? Write a journal entry with your thoughts.

## Retailers

Retailers applied the power of the computer to every aspect of their businesses long before most other industries did. Today they use Web sites and in-store computer databases to help consumers see, compare, and easily order products for their homes.

23-22
*People who check coworkers' accuracy are in midlevel positions.*

Photo courtesy of Andersen Windows, Inc.

# Career Levels

Career opportunities in housing are sometimes grouped according to the qualifications and level of responsibility linked to each specific job. By these measures, work opportunities can be divided as follows:

- professional positions
- midlevel positions
- entry-level positions

## Professional Positions

Jobholders in professional positions make decisions that affect the lives of individuals, families, and whole communities. Engineers, planners, and designers are some of the people with professional-level positions. They work in both urban and rural areas. Generally, a bachelor's degree is required for these jobs. Special training and experience may also be required in addition to an advanced degree.

## Midlevel Positions

People in midlevel positions often work as *support personnel* to the professionals. They carry out the decisions of the professionals. Their job assignments often include supervising workers who have less authority and responsibility. See 23-22.

In housing construction, for example, one supervisor oversees the work of many laborers. Supervisors rarely do the wiring, plumbing, or roofing themselves, but know how to do these jobs well. Consequently, they are well qualified to evaluate workmanship and supervise those actually doing the job.

The middle level in a given career field may have sublevels. This is especially true on large or complex projects. As a result, midlevel supervisors report to a head manager with higher authority. The fact that midlevel supervisors are themselves supervised does not make their work any less important.

Those in midlevel positions are expected to have training beyond high school. Such training is available through career and technical schools, community and junior colleges, company training programs, apprenticeships, and military service. They also need good communication and teamwork skills to effectively manage the work of others.

## Entry Positions

People in entry-level positions follow the directions of those in professional and midlevel positions. The qualifications for entry-level positions in the housing industry are not high because they often involve easy, repetitive tasks. Usually you learn what you need to know on the job. Entry-level jobs may be found in administrative, construction, sales, and service areas. Some manufacturing jobs also use entry-level help, as in 23-23.

Often there is opportunity to move up if you do your job well. A few construction positions may not require a high school education. However, you are more likely to obtain a position if you graduate from high school and have some experience or knowledge in the field.

Does your school have a program in cooperative education? *Cooperative education* programs offer opportunities to work part-time and attend classes part-time. You may be able to secure a job through this kind of program. It will probably be an entry-level position that provides on-the-job training. You will also receive help from a counselor or career education teacher in your school.

Discuss: What cooperative education programs are in your school?

## Career Ladders

When the jobs in a career cluster are organized according to job qualifications, they form a career ladder or a career lattice.

A *career ladder* is a visual depicting career progress across related jobs, each requiring stricter qualifications than the previous one. The ladder shows the steps from entry-level work to midlevel jobs and professional positions. You can climb a career ladder by gaining more education, knowledge,

Photo courtesy of Andersen Windows, Inc.

23-23

*Entry-level workers are often trained to do specific, limited tasks.*

Vocabulary: Explain the phrase *career levels* to a classmate.

Reflect: Would you find doing easy, repetitive tasks in an entry-level position satisfying? Why or why not?

and experience. Study the career ladder shown in 23-24.

A variation of a career ladder is the career lattice. A *career lattice* is a chart of related career opportunities, organized from entry to professional levels. Unlike a career ladder, it may include jobs outside the career field being studied. The lattice shows you can move in more than one direction as you change jobs within a career cluster. See 23-25. You can move either up or across the lattice of jobs. You may even be able to move at an angle—both up and across at the same time.

The terms *open entry* and *open exit* are sometimes used to describe movement on a career lattice. They mean

you can enter any level and move to any position if qualified for the positions you choose to hold.

## Lifelong Learning

The computer has changed the workplace, causing employers to have higher expectations of their workers. In most cases, new employees are expected to know how to use the new tools of their field and access the information they need. No matter what career you enter, you will be expected to keep pace with the changes in your field. Speed is very important, but so is accuracy. There is no place for slow or wrong responses in today's high-tech environment.

**Career Ladder for Home Furnishings Service**

| High School Student | High School Graduate | Associate Degree Junior College | Bachelor's Degree College or University |
|---|---|---|---|
| 1. Window display aide<br>2. Home furnishings delivery assistant<br>3. Decorator's aide<br>4. Home lighting sales aide<br>5. Drapery or slipcover aide<br>6. Home funishings maintenance aide | 1. Window display assistant<br>2. Home furnishings delivery manager<br>3. Decorator's assistant<br>4. Home lighting sales assistant<br>5. Drapery estimator<br>6. Home furnishings maintenance specialist | 1. Window display designer<br>2. Home furnishings store manager<br>3. Interior decorator<br>4. Buyer for retail lighting store<br>5. Owner of an upholstery or drapery firm<br>6. Owner of home furnishings maintenance business | 1. Window display manager for a large retail store or chain<br>2. Regional manager of a home furnishings store chain<br>3. Interior designer<br>4. Lighting designer or consultant<br>5. Furniture designer for major company<br>6. Textile researcher |

23-24

*Education can help you climb a career ladder. As your skills and abilities increase, career opportunities with greater responsibilities will open to you.*

| Career Lattice for Housing Design and Interior Decoration | | | |
|---|---|---|---|
| **Professional** | | • Environmental designer<br>• Interior designer<br>• Housing specialist<br>• Home service advisor<br>• Home service director<br>• Textile researcher | |
| | | *Service positions:<br>care and renovation* | *Advisory and<br>design positions* | *Production positions:<br>construction* |

| | | *Service positions: care and renovation* | *Advisory and design positions* | *Production positions: construction* |
|---|---|---|---|---|
| **Middle Level** | **Supervisory** | • Home furnishings laboratory technician | • Home furnishings advisor<br>• Color coordinator<br>• Drapery advisor<br>• Home lighting advisor<br>• Florist<br>• Scenic arts supervisor<br>• Scenery designer<br>• Window display designer<br>• Household equipment advisor | • Home furnishings sewing specialist<br>• Drapery room supervisor<br>• Textile technician<br>• Laboratory tester<br>• Houshold products technician |
| | **Nonsupervisory** | • Home furnishings maintenance specialist<br>• Rug cleaner<br>• Upholstery cleaner<br>• Floor care specialist<br>• Maintenance specialist | • Decorator's assistant<br>• Drapery and slipcover aide<br>• Home lighting assistant<br>• Accessories assistant<br>• Floral assistant<br>• Decorative arts craftsperson | • Drapery and slipcover construction inspector<br>• Sewing specialist |
| **Entry Level** | | • Home furnishings maintenance aide<br>• Assistant upholstery cleaner<br>• Assistant rug cleaner | • Home furnishings aide<br>• Drapery and slipcover aide<br>• Appliance and equipment aide<br>• Home lighting aide<br>• Floral aide | • Drapery and slipcover construction aide |

23-25

*The career lattice shows horizontal and vertical changes you can make within related career areas.*

Employers usually provide some training. However, employees are often expected to use time outside the job to stay up-to-date in their field of expertise. Frequently updating one's knowledge and skills is known as *lifelong learning*. The term implies that your need for learning will never end. People who enjoy their work will view lifelong learning as an exciting challenge. Lifelong learning helps workers attain career success.

**Writing Activity:** Write a journal entry expressing how you feel about frequently updating your knowledge and skills throughout life to keep pace with changes in your career field.

**Reflect:** Do you know what type of career you want to hold? If so, is it in the housing field? If you are still undecided about a future career, what do you need to do to help your decision making?

# Summary

It takes the work of many people in various careers to create satisfying housing. Career clusters and career webs reveal how the various jobs within the industry interrelate.

Career opportunities in the housing field are widespread. Some professionals are involved with planning, engineering, and design work. Construction workers represent the most visible housing segment, representing a wide range of careers. Sales and service careers are part of the housing field, too. Many entrepreneurs work in the housing field in planning, engineering, design, construction, sales, and service jobs. In addition, utility companies, educational institutions, and branches of government offer jobs related to housing. All of these careers are affected by the increased use of computers and other high tech equipment.

Career ladders and lattices show careers existing at all job levels in the housing field. No matter what type or level of job a person holds, staying skilled and knowledgeable is important for career success and advancement.

# To Review

1. True or false. People who work in the construction industry provide everything needed for a good housing environment.

2. Grouping closely related occupations together creates a career _____.

3. Name three sources of career information.

4. List five components of a complete job description.

5. Name four career fields related to housing.

6. A bachelor's degree usually requires _____ years of study.

7. True or false. Many architects and engineers prepare for their occupations by completing an apprenticeship. Construction

8. True or false. Of all the jobs involved in the housing industry, the construction area offers the most opportunities for unskilled, semiskilled, and skilled workers. Sales/Service

9. Identify five characteristics of a successful entrepreneur.

10. The jobs involved in housing design and construction _____ tend to have the greatest need for high tech equipment.

11. In which career level do you find support personnel?

12. What is the main difference between a career ladder and a career lattice?

13. Why is lifelong learning important to a person striving for career success?

**Answer Key**

1. false
2. cluster
3. (List three:) school counselors, teachers, family members, friends, libraries, Internet, U.S. Department of Labor sources (*Occupational Outlook Handbook, Guide for Occupational Exploration,* and the Occupational Information Network)
4. (List five:) job duties and areas of responsibility; required education, training, and experience; important personal traits; usual work environment; leading employers; minimum, average, and peak earnings; employment outlook; job rewards (if any); related careers
5. (List four:) planning, engineering, design, construction, sales, service, entrepreneurship, education, government
6. four
7. false
8. false
9. (List five:) excellent communications skills, strong self-motivation to do the best work possible, enthusiasm for the product or service, nonstop desire to promote the business and look for future work, understanding of the legal and financial aspects of running a business, ability to recognize when to seek advice from experts, supervisory skills (if employees are hired)
10. management
11. midlevel
12. A career ladder includes opportunities within the field, while opportunities outside the field may appear in a career lattice.
13. It helps the person stay up-to-date in his or her field of expertise.

# In Your Community

1. Invite individuals to class who work in housing-related careers within your community. Ask them how they became interested in their fields, what educational routes they followed, what job duties they enjoy most, and which task they find least enjoyable. Prepare your questions in advance.

2. Ask your school counselor to administer an aptitude test and explain your results. Based on your test results, determine which types of jobs in the field of housing present the best opportunities for you to succeed. Determine whether any local employers offer these or similar jobs.

3. Look through a current edition of your local newspaper. What employment ads do you find for careers discussed in this chapter?

# To Think About

1. What type of job environment do you think best suits your abilities and interests? Do you think you would be more successful as a member of a team in an established company or as an entrepreneur? Compare and contrast the benefits and problems that each choice offers.

2. For various reasons, workers can no longer expect to work for one employer for an entire lifetime. Occasionally people find themselves out of work through no fault of their own. The ideal, of course, is steady employment. Review this chapter and identify the careers you believe would offer the greatest career stability. Report your conclusions and your reasoning to the class.

# Using Technology

1. Select a career from the chapter that interests you. Using a computer, construct a career ladder or career lattice. Begin with an entry-level position and progress all the way to professional-level positions. Print your results and share them with the class.

2. Use the Internet to examine the similarities and differences that exist in the educational requirements for an interior designer versus an architect. What is different about their job responsibilities and expertise? Find the answers by searching the Web sites of their respective professional associations. Share your findings with the class.

3. Search the Internet for three sources of information about the job requirements for a housing position you might pursue. Use at least one Department of Labor reference as a source. Investigate the salary potential of the profession. Is demand for the career increasing or declining? Summarize your findings and cite your sources.

**Portfolio Project:** Write a report on a housing career that interests you. Use the *Dictionary of Occupational Titles* and the *Occupational Outlook Handbook* as resources. You may interview a person who holds that career. Include pictures and art to enhance your project.

# CHAPTER 24
# Preparing for Career Success

## To Know

goals
shadowing
mentor
aptitude
abilities
internship
goal-setting process
short-term goals
long-term goals
networking
resume
reference
punctual
self-motivation
attitude
verbal communication
nonverbal communication
ethical behavior
team
negotiation
conflict
leadership
dual-career family

**Resource:** *Progress in Housing*, transparency master overlay VI-C, TR. Students look back at the topics covered in Chapters 1-23 by reviewing transparency master VI-A and overlay VI-B. Then, with the addition of overlay VI-C, they explore the topics they will cover in Chapter 24.

**Vocabulary:** Choose one of the words from the vocabulary list. Look up the definition in the glossary. On a 3" × 5"-card, write a tip for career success using the word. Post the card on a bulletin board titled *Suggestions for Success*.

## Objectives

After studying this chapter, you will be able to

- set career goals and make a career plan.
- know the steps to take to find a job in your career field.
- identify the skills, attitudes, and behaviors important for maintaining a job and attaining career success.
- describe the relationships between careers and personal and family life.

**Writing Activity:** Rewrite the chapter objectives in the form of headings on a worksheet. Draw lines for listing career goals; steps for finding a job; and skills, attitudes, and behaviors for job success. Leave space to make a career plan and describe the relationships between careers and personal and family life. Complete the various sections of the worksheet as you read through the chapter.

The actions you take now will lay the groundwork for the career you will have in the future. Preparing for your career may seem overwhelming at first, but doing a step at a time will make the process easier. If you have not started to think about your future, begin now. What would you like to do for a living? Whether your future will be in a housing field or not, this chapter presents guidelines that are useful for planning your career.

24-1

*For career inspiration, look to everyday activities you enjoy. Some can also open doors to moneymaking opportunities that will help pay for your education and training.*

# Setting Career Goals

After studying Chapter 23, "Careers in Housing," you may want to pursue some area of housing for your livelihood. To prepare yourself for a meaningful job in the workplace requires advance planning. This planning involves setting *goals*, which are aims or targets a person tries to achieve. Preparing yourself for the future involves setting goals today.

Before you can set career goals, you need to explore the real you. What are your personal priorities? Personal priorities were discussed in the first chapter of this text. You also need to know what your interests, abilities, and aptitudes are.

## Examining Career Interests

Few people your age know exactly what career they want. Sometimes adults who have prepared for one career decide they want to pursue another. As you grow older, you may notice that your interests change. This is perfectly normal. Active people are constantly developing new interests.

Usually a person's interests parallel his or her likes. If you enjoy mowing the lawn and keeping flowerbeds well maintained, you may enjoy a landscaping career. See 24-1. However, if you dislike that type of work, a landscaping job involving these tasks is definitely not for you.

Basically, interests involve people, data, or objects—and sometimes all three. In the case of the landscaping job, the focus was on objects—a beautiful lawn and flowerbed. By shifting the focus to people or data, different landscaping-related jobs come to mind. A person who likes to focus on data may enjoy designing landscaping plans. On the other hand, a person interested in people may enjoy a job teaching landscaping. By reviewing your likes and dislikes, you will get a better picture of the tasks you would enjoy in a career.

Before deciding on a specific career, you may wish to shadow someone who holds a similar job. *Shadowing* is the process of observing a person in the workplace to learn more about his or her job and its requirements. Also, you may seek to have a mentor assist you now and in the future with your career. A *mentor* is someone with greater experience and knowledge who guides you in your career, 24-2.

## Determining Abilities and Aptitudes

Career planning cannot take place until you know what you can do well. What are your *aptitudes*, or natural talents? An aptitude is an ability to learn something quickly and easily. Are some of your subjects in school much easier than others? Knowing this can help determine some of your talents. You may not be aware of all of your aptitudes if you have never been challenged to use them. A school counselor can give you an aptitude test to help reveal your strengths.

*Abilities* are skills you develop with practice. As you prepare to handle any job, you will learn that it requires certain skills. Suppose you own a lawnmower for cutting neighborhood lawns to earn money. Some of the job skills you will need to perform include the following:

- moving large objects out of the way and returning them when done
- adjusting the mower to the desired height
- refueling the mower engine
- operating the mower safely

Aldrich & Sons Builders, Hilton Head Island, SC

24-2

*This father is a builder of quality homes and a mentor to his two sons.*

- mowing the grass evenly
- catching or raking the grass clippings
- trimming and edging the lawn neatly
- disposing the yard waste in an environmentally sound manner, following local requirements

You can learn job skills by assisting someone who knows how to do the job tasks well, such as working in an internship or apprenticeship. You learned about *apprenticeships* in

**Vocabulary:** Look up *mentor* in a dictionary and compare the definition with the definition given in the text. Participate in a class discussion about people who have already served as mentors in your life.

**Discuss:** What are some of the job skills you would need to perform if you were going to paint home interiors?

Chapter 23. An *internship* is an arrangement with an educational institution whereby a student is supervised while working with a more experienced jobholder. In your entry-level job, you may work with someone quite skilled who can help you develop the necessary skills. Other places to learn job skills are schools and colleges, community organizations, employer training programs, and the military. See 24-3.

## The Goal-Setting Process

You can use the following process to help set goals. The *goal-setting process* is a set of steps to follow to achieve objectives. The steps are listed here and also appear in the example in Figure 24-4.

### 1. Identify a Goal.

State a specific goal with a deadline. For example, *to get a job* is not a well-stated goal because it is too vague. A better way to state the goal follows: *to get a job in my career area during summer vacation.* This states exactly what you desire and when.

### 2. Create a Plan

Develop a set of steps that will help you work progressively toward attaining your goal. Will you need to do, get, or learn something first? Be sure to work these steps into your overall plan.

### 3. Identify Available Resources

The resources needed to implement the plan need to be listed and evaluated. Do you need money, a computer, time, assistance from counselors and family members, or other resources? Make sure that your plan does not rely on resources that you do not have and cannot get.

### 4. Take Action

Be committed to your plan and follow through, meeting all deadlines.

Habitat for Humanity® International

24-3

*Volunteering offers other opportunities for learning new skills, as these young people are finding by helping the efforts of groups such as Habitat for Humanity.*

| Goal Setting—How to Achieve Your Plans | |
|---|---|
| **Steps** | **Example** |
| 1. Identify a specific goal. | **Goal**<br>• To get a job at the local home improvement center for the summer |
| 2. Determine a set of actions and deadlines for achieving the goal. | **The Plan**<br>• Call the store for information on getting a job application form.<br>• Go to the company's Web site to learn about its mission and goals.<br>• Write a letter of application and submit the form (if you can obtain it in advance).<br>• Request an interview. |
| 3. Identify what resources are needed to achieve the plan. | **Resources Needed**<br>• Computer to write the letter of application<br>• Transportation to interview<br>• Appropriate clothes for interview |
| 4. Follow through with action. | **Action Required**<br>• Prepare well for the interview, let your enthusiasm show, and focus on your commitment to get the job. |
| 5. Evaluate the results. | **Questions to Ask**<br>• Did I get the job? If not, why?<br>• What new plans do I make?<br>• What can I do differently next time? |

24-4

*Writing your goals down helps to show where your career plans are heading.*

### 5. Evaluate Results

Ask yourself, "Did I achieve what I set out to do?" Why or why not? If not, what can you change right now that will move you closer to your goal? What can you do next time to make a more realistic plan?

The goal-setting process can be used to achieve one objective or several. The example illustrates one fairly simply objective—getting a summer job. The process is also used for the more complex objective of entering a desired career.

## Making a Career Plan

Once a career goal is in mind, you can begin planning the steps to achieve it. Do not be fooled into

**Writing Activity:** Write an explanation of the saying "Failing to plan is planning to fail" as it relates to making a career plan.

**Discuss:** Why is the evaluation step such an important part of the goal-setting process? How could failure to complete this step affect your ability to reach future goals?

**Enrich:** Participate in a presentation by a guidance counselor discussing what tools and services your school offers to help students evaluate their interests and skills for career planning and job placement. Be prepared to ask questions related to your career goals.

thinking the right job will simply "come along." In today's highly competitive workplace, that is most unlikely. People who make no career plans usually find themselves left with jobs no one else wants.

Would you like to be an interior designer? See 24-5. Do you see yourself buying and selling real estate? Are you interested in teaching housing and design? Investigate what resources you need to achieve your goal and map out a plan. Begin by determining short-term versus long-term goals.

- *Short-term goals* are accomplished in several days or weeks.

- *Long-term goals* usually require six months or longer to achieve.

24-5

*While in high school, this interior designer took every art and design course possible and participated in extracurricular and volunteer activities that allowed her to apply her knowledge.*

Your master plan should document actions to take that will move you closer to your career goal in stages. What can you do now, next semester, next year, and so on to improve your chances of successfully entering the career of your choice? Will you need to get a degree? If so, do you need to take certain courses now to qualify later for entrance into college? Are you still trying to decide between two possible career choices? If so, you may need to talk to a counselor or find a job shadowing opportunity to help you decide. Do you need some career-related activities to mention in your resume? If so, consider working at a part-time job or volunteering at community or charitable organizations.

From time to time, review your plan to make sure you stay on course. Update it as needed. If you have difficulty putting your plan into action, talk with a teacher, family member, or trusted friend. Sometimes a small discussion will clear up your questions or concerns.

## Finding a Job

When you're ready to find a job, you can get job leads through a variety of sources. Start your search at the placement office of your school. Also, check the Internet, family, friends, newspaper want ads, and job fairs. The professional journals in your career field and the leading professional organizations often announce job openings, too.

Many jobs are found through networking. *Networking* is the exchange of information or services among individuals or groups. As a newcomer to the career field, the goal of your networking is to learn about possible job leads.

## Applying for a Job

When you find an employer or specific position that attracts your attention, quickly express your interest. You will need to apply for the job in writing. Then, if the employer wants to learn more about your qualifications, you will be invited for an interview.

### Developing Your Resume

You will need to develop a resume. A *resume* is a brief outline of your education, work experience, and other qualifications for work. A well-written resume can help you get a job interview.

An example of a resume appears in 24-6. Along with the resume, you need to develop a list of references. A *reference* is an individual who will provide important information about you to a prospective employer. A reference can be a teacher, school official, previous employer, or any other adult outside your family who knows you well.

You will need at least three references. Always get permission from each person to use his or her name as a reference before actually doing so. Your list of references, along with their titles, phone numbers, and addresses, should be kept private. Share this list only with an employer who has interviewed you and is considering you for the job.

### Your Portfolio

A well-developed, professional looking portfolio can help you get a job. A portfolio is a collection of items that show your special achievements and accomplishments. The portfolio includes examples of your work that emphasize your skills, talents, and knowledge.

Items to include in the portfolio are your resume, samples of your best work and letters of recommendation. If you have a news article about any of your accomplishments, be sure to highlight your name. Also, include reports of special projects you completed. The portfolio should be organized logically and placed in an attractive binder.

### Letter of Application

The letter of application is often the first contact you have with the potential employer. It can make a lasting impression. It should be neat and follow a standard form for business letters. The paper should be ivory, white, or a neutral color and free of smudges or mistakes. Create your letter on a computer to give it a professional look and to check spelling and punctuation. Have several people read the letter and offer advice for improving it. Your resume should be mailed with your letter of application.

A sample letter of application appears in 24-7. It is a good example to use in response to a job ad. The letter should be brief and to the point. It should include the following items:

- title of the job you seek
- where you heard about the job
- your strengths, skills, and abilities for the job
- reasons you should be considered for the job
- when you are available to begin work
- request for an interview

## Job Application Forms

You may be asked to complete a job application form before being interviewed. The job application form highlights the information the

**Reflect:** Who could you list as references if you were applying for a job? Why would these people make good references?

**Activity:** Make a list of all the items you might include in a portfolio as examples of your skills, talents, and knowledge.

**Reflect:** If you are preparing items for a portfolio for this course, would any be suitable to include in a job portfolio?

| Resume |
| --- |

**Sarah H. Johnston**
**328 Weston Boulevard**
**Greensboro, North Carolina 27405**

**EMPLOYMENT OBJECTIVE**
A position assisting an interior designer using my computer and art skills in a design studio

**EDUCATION**
Page High School, graduating May 2004
Followed the Design / Business programs
G.P.A.: 3.5 / 4.0

**Related Courses**

- Four years of art classes
- Family and consumer sciences course in housing and interior design
- Computer-assisted design (CAD) course from Guilford Technical Community College, Summer 2003. Received special permission to enroll.

**WORK HISTORY**
Framing specialist—September 2003 to present
The Art Shop, Greensboro, NC,

Sales clerk—May 2002 to August 2003
Amy's Upholstery Fabric Shop, Greensboro, NC

**HONORS AND ACTIVITIES**
Vice President, Family, Career, and Community Leaders of America local chapter, 2003-2004

Second place winner in School District's house plans design contest, November 2003

First place winner in School District's still art competition, April 2002

**COMMUNITY SERVICE**
Habitat for Humanity volunteer, Spring 2004

Arts and Craft Fair for Senior Citizens organizer, Greensboro Community Center, February 2003

School Literacy Program volunteer, October 2001 to March 2002

Youth Ministry soup kitchen volunteer, July 2000 to August 2002

**SPECIAL INTERESTS**
Interior design particularly kitchen design, computer design software, sketching

**REFERENCES**
Available upon request.

24-6 _____

*A resume provides a quick way for employers to learn about the applicant.*

## Letter of Application

328 Weston Boulevard
Greensboro, NC 27405
August 31, 2003

Ms. Cynthia Dawson
Interior Designer
Dawson Design Studio
1359 Lassiter Place
Greensboro, NC 27401

Dear Ms. Dawson:

Mrs. Julia McDowell of The Art Shop told me about your need for part-time employees with computer-assisted design (CAD) skills. I am both qualified and interested in securing a drafting position with your studio.

Having completed a course in housing and interior design at Page High School, I am familiar with floor plan design and arrangement. Also, I successfully finished a course in computer-assisted design at Guilford Technical Community College during the summer. As a result, I am skilled in using CAD and have a basic understanding of housing and interior design.

Attached is my resume for your consideration. I will be glad to supply further information and a portfolio of my work in an interview.

Until my graduation on June 5, I am available daily after 4:30 p.m. for an interview. After that, I am available anytime during the day at your convenience. I can be reached at home at 336/555-2952. I look forward to hearing from you.

Sincerely,

*Sarah H. Johnston*

Sarah H. Johnston

24-7

*Potential employers will know your interests and qualifications from your letter of application.*

**Writing Activity:** Write a letter of application to an employer, including all the items listed in the text. Be sure to use formal business style, proper grammar, and correct spelling. Exchange letters with a classmate and review each other's work.

**Activity:** Practice filling out a sample job application form, following the tips listed in Figure 24-8.
**Discuss:** What resources could be used to research local employers and jobs?

employer needs to know about you, your education, and prior work experience. It is often used for screening applicants for the skills needed on the job. You might complete a form in a personnel or employment office. Sometimes you may get the form by mail.

The appearance of the application form can give the employer his first opinion about you. Complete the form accurately, completely, and neatly. How well you accomplish that can determine whether you get the job. When asked about salary, write "open" or "negotiable." This means you are willing to consider offers.

Be sure to send or give the form to the correct person. The name of the correct person often appears on the form. Tips for completing the job application appear in 24-8.

## The Job Interview

The interview gives you the opportunity to learn more about a company and to convince the employer that you are the best person for the job. The employer wants to know if you have the skills needed for the job. Adequate preparation is essential for making a lasting, positive impression. Here are some ways to prepare for the interview.

- *Research the employer and the job.* Know the mission of the employer and specifics about the job. Also, try to learn what the company looks for when hiring new employees.

- *Be prepared to answer questions.* Go over the list in 24-9 and prepare answers for each.

- *List the questions you want answered.* For example, do you want to know if there is on-the-job training? opportunities for advancement?

- *List the materials you plan to take.* This seems simple enough. However, if you wait to grab items at the last minute, something is sure to be forgotten.

---

### Completing a Job Application Form

- Look over the form to see what information it seeks. How much space is there for writing responses? Which questions pertain to you?

- Read the directions and follow them carefully. Usually applicants are asked to print, using a pen with dark ink.

- Bring your resume, list of references, and other important data with you so you have all important information at your fingertips. Never write down guesses, only facts.

- Think through your responses first so you can write them concisely.

- When questions do not apply to you, write *N/A*, which means *not applicable*.

- Request a new form if you make a mess. There is no penalty for filling out another form, but you may be rejected if you turn in a sloppy one.

- Review the form one last time to make sure you replied to every question and filled every space.

24-8 _____

*Take your time when you fill out a job application form and follow these tips.*

**Enrich:** Attend a presentation by a human resources representative from a local business to learn what employers look for when interviewing job applicants. Be prepared to ask questions related to your career goals. (Note to teacher: Ask the speaker to bring an application form and distribute copies for student reference.)
**Reflect:** What items would you want to take with you to an interview?

- *Decide what to wear.* Dress appropriately, usually one step above what is worn by your future coworkers. For instance, casual clothing is acceptable for individuals who will do manual labor or wear a company uniform. If the job involves greeting the public in an office environment, a suit is more appropriate. Always appear neat and clean.

- *Practice the interview.* Have a friend or family member interview you in front of a mirror until you are happy with your responses.

- *Know where to go for the interview.* Verify the address of the interview location by checking the site beforehand, if possible. Plan to arrive ready for the interview at least 10 minutes early.

Being well prepared will make you feel more confident and comfortable during the interview. Be friendly and cheerful during the process. Use a firm handshake. Maintain eye contact at all times. Answer all questions carefully and as completely as you can.

You may be asked to take employee tests. Some employers administer tests to job candidates to measure their knowledge or skill level under stress. (Since all employers support a drugfree workplace, you will probably be asked to take a drug test if hired.) You can ask those who have completed similar tests what to expect.

After the interview, send a letter to the employer within 24 hours, thanking him or her for the interview. If you get a job offer, respond to it quickly. If you do not receive an offer after several interviews, evaluate your interview techniques and seek ways to improve them.

## Evaluating Job Offers

When considering a job offer or comparing two or more jobs, you should explore the following work factors:

**Resource:** *Interview Skills,* reproducible master 24-1, TR. Students use the handouts to practice preparing for a job interview with several employers invited to class to conduct mock interviews and evaluate student performance.

---

### Interview Questions

- What type of work do you prefer?
- What do you see yourself doing in 10 years?
- What in particular attracted you to this position?
- Why would you like to work for this organization?
- What accomplishments have you had that show your ability to handle this type of job?
- What are your greatest weaknesses?
- Do you believe your grades give a good indication of the type of work you do?
- What did you like most about your last job or work experience? least?
- Why did you leave your previous job?
- Is there any negative information in your past that would affect your employment with this company?
- Why do you feel you are the most qualified person for the job?

---

24-9

*Answer these questions to prepare yourself for a job interview.*

**Enrich:** Interview a friend or family member about a job interview experience he or she has had. Ask about aspects of the job interview that did and did not go well. Also ask for any advice the person might give you when you go for a job interview.

**Discuss:** What are some reasons an employer might not extend a job offer to an applicant?

- *Physical surroundings.* Where is your workspace located? Is the atmosphere conducive to your style of working?
- *Work schedule.* Will the workdays and work hours mesh with your lifestyle? Is occasional overtime work required?
- *Income and benefits.* Is the proposed salary fair? Will you receive benefits that are just as valuable as extra income? How much sick leave is granted during the year? Can unused sick leave be taken after year-end? Is personal or emergency leave available? Are there medical and life insurance benefits? What is the vacation leave policy? Is there a credit union? Will the company pay college tuition for courses related to your job? See 24-10. Is a cafeteria on the premises? Does it offer food to employees at reduced cost?
- *Job obligations.* Will you be expected to join a union or other organization? If so, what are the costs? Will you be expected to attend meetings after work?
- *Advancement potential.* Is there opportunity for advancement? After demonstrating good performance, how soon can you seek a position with more responsibilities? Before you can advance, are there special expectations such as a higher degree? Are training programs provided?

Talking about advancement requires considerable diplomacy. After all, you should not appear too eager to leave the job for which you are interviewing. Many employers would expect a new employee to remain at least one year at that job. If you place undue emphasis on advancing to another job, you will appear uninterested in the current opening.

You may also want to explore the transportation options to and from work. If you drive, determine the length of time and distance for the commute. Is parking provided? Is it free? Can you get to work in reasonable time by taking public transportation? How much effort it takes to get to work will greatly affect your satisfaction with the job.

## Maintaining the Job

After you get a job, adjusting to your new duties and responsibilities will occupy your first few weeks. Your supervisor and coworkers will help you learn the routine. You will probably be introduced to the company's policies and procedures along with special safety rules that all employees must know. See 24-11.

While your coworkers will be watching what you do, they will also

24-10
*If your goal is to obtain more education while working full-time, look for an employer that reimburses all or part of your higher education costs.*

24-11

*Remember and follow the directions you receive during the first few weeks. After this trial period, workers who do not show progress may be asked to leave.*

pay attention to "how you work." How to behave in the workplace is an important lesson all employees should learn. Making an effort to do your best will help you succeed.

## Work Habits

Employers want employees who are punctual, dependable, and responsible. They also want employees who take initiative and begin tasks on their own. In addition, an employee needs to be organized, accurate, and efficient.

A *punctual* employee is always prompt and on time. This means not only when the workday starts, but also when returning from breaks and lunches. Being dependable means that people can rely on you to fulfill your word and meet your deadlines. If you are not well, be sure to call in and let the employer know right away. If there are reasons that you cannot be at work, discuss this with your employer and work out an alternate arrangement.

Many people have lost jobs by not checking with their supervisor about time off.

Taking initiative means that you start activities on your own without being told. When you finish one task, you do not have to be told what to do next. Individuals who take initiative need much less supervision. They have *self-motivation,* or an inner urge to get things accomplished. Generally, this motivation will drive you to set goals and accomplish them.

You are expected to be as accurate and error-free as possible in all that you do. This is why you were hired. Complete your work and double-check it to assure accuracy. See 24-12. Your coworkers depend on the careful completion of your tasks.

## Attitude on the Job

Your attitude can often determine the success you have on your job. Your *attitude* is your outlook on life. It is reflected by how you react to the events and people around you. A

24-12

*Expect to have your work carefully scrutinized, especially during your first few months on the job.*

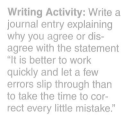

**Writing Activity:** Write a journal entry explaining why you agree or disagree with the statement "It is better to work quickly and let a few errors slip through than to take the time to correct every little mistake."

**Enrich:** Review the policies and procedures in an employee handbook. Make an outline of the categories under which policies and procedures seem to fall, such as attendance and benefits. Compare your outline with those of your classmates.

**Vocabulary:** The term *punctual* comes from a word meaning "having a sharp point." How does this meaning relate to the definition of *punctual* given in the text?

Reflect: How does it make you feel when someone seems genuinely interested in what you are saying? How do you feel when someone is barely listening to you?

smile and courteous behavior can make customers and fellow employees feel good about themselves and you. Clients and customers prefer to do business in friendly environments. Being friendly may take some effort on your part, but it does pay off.

Enthusiasm spreads easily from one person to another. Usually, enthusiasm means the person enjoys what he or she is doing. In a sales environment, enthusiasm increases sales. In an office, enthusiasm builds a team spirit for working together.

## Communication Skills on the Job

Being able to communicate effectively with others is important for job success. Communication is the process of exchanging ideas, thoughts, or information. Being a good communicator means that you can share information well with others. It also means you are a good listener.

Good communication is central to a smooth operation of any business. Poor communications is costly to an employer, as when time is lost because an order was entered incorrectly. Poor communication can result in lost customers, too.

### Types of Communication

The primary forms of communications are verbal and nonverbal. *Verbal communication* involves speaking, listening, and writing. *Nonverbal communication* is the sending and receiving of messages without the use of words. Nonverbal communication involves body language, which includes the expression on your face and your body posture.

Listening is an important part of communication. If you do not understand, be sure to ask questions. Also, give feedback to let others know you

understand them and are interested in what they have to say. Leaning forward while a person is talking signals interest and keen listening. Slouching back in a chair and yawning give the opposite signal—that you are bored and uninterested.

The message you convey in telephone communication involves your promptness, tone of voice, and attitude. Answering the phone quickly with a pleasant voice conveys a positive image for the company. Learning to obtain accurate information from the caller without interrupting that person's message is important. See 24-13.

Communication tools have advanced with the development of new technologies. To be an effective employee, you need to know how to

24-13

*When a caller leaves a message, be sure to repeat that person's request before hanging up to make sure you caught all the information.*

Vocabulary: Compare and contrast the terms *verbal communication* and *nonverbal communication*.

Enrich: Work with a partner to write a brief scenario about a challenging work situation. Role-play the scenario twice for the rest of the class. In the first scenario, show the worker reacting negatively to the situation. In the second scenario, show how the worker is able to use his or her attitude to react positively to the situation.

communicate well with the common tools of your workplace. For example, when sending e-mail communications, remember to think through each message as you would before sending a postal letter. Often messages are sent quickly without thought of how they may be interpreted by the recipient. The same is true of voicemail.

The development of good communication skills is an ongoing process. Attending communication workshops and practicing often can keep your skills sharp. You should periodically give yourself a communications checkup by asking your supervisor to suggest areas that need improvement.

## Ethical Behavior on the Job

*Ethical behavior* on the job means conforming to accepted standards of fairness and good conduct. It is based on a person's sense of what is right to do. Individuals and society as a whole regard ethical behavior as highly important. Integrity, confidentiality, and honesty are crucial aspects of ethical workplace behavior. Integrity is firmly following one's moral beliefs.

Unfortunately, employee theft is a major problem at some companies. The theft can range from carrying office supplies home to stealing money or expensive equipment. Company policies are in place to address these concerns. In cases of criminal or serious behavior, people may lose their jobs. If proven, the charge of criminal behavior stays on the employee's record. Such an employee will have a difficult time finding another job.

## Interpersonal Skills

Interpersonal skills involve interacting with others. Some workplace activities that involve these skills include teaching others, serving customers, leading, negotiating, and working as a member of a team. Getting along well with others can require great effort on your part, but it is essential for accomplishing your employer's goals.

### Teamwork

Employers seek employees who can effectively serve as good team members. Due to the nature of most work today, teamwork is necessary. A *team* is a small group of people working together for a common purpose. Often cooperation requires flexibility and willingness to try new ways to get things done. See 24-14. If someone is uncooperative, it takes longer to accomplish the tasks. When people do not get along, strained relationships may occur, which get in the way of finishing the tasks.

A big advantage of a team is its ability to develop plans and complete work faster than an individual working alone. On the other hand, a team usually takes longer to reach a decision

24-14
*When several people pool their ideas, the result is often better than any one person could accomplish.*

than an individual worker does. Team members need some time before they become comfortable with one another and function as a unit. Some people do not flourish in a team environment and become unhappy. Consideration should always be given to determining when the team approach is needed. You will be more desirable as an employee if you know how to be a team player.

Team development goes through various stages. In the beginning, people are excited about being on a team. Later, disagreements may replace harmony. The good result of this is people express themselves and learn to trust the other team members. Eventually leaders emerge and the team develops a unique pattern of interaction and goal attainment. Finally, the team

becomes very productive and performs at its highest level. It takes time, a genuine desire to work together, and incentives to build a strong team.

Creative ideas often develop from building on another person's idea. Being open and honest is essential. Also, trying to understand the ideas of others before trying to get others to understand your ideas is an effective skill to develop.

## Negotiation

Often there are times when employees and employers must negotiate on a task or work-related issue. *Negotiation* is the process of agreeing to an issue that requires all parties to give and take. The goal is a "win-win" solution in which both parties get some or all of what they are seeking.

Negotiation begins with trying to understand the other party's interests. Often a solution becomes clear when both parties have ample time to explain what they are trying to accomplish. Possible solutions that meet their mutual concerns can be developed. See 24-15.

## Conflict Management

When you work with others, disagreements are likely to occur. More serious disagreements are called conflict. *Conflict* is a hostile situation resulting from opposing views. It is important to know how to handle conflict to prevent it from becoming a destructive force in the workplace. This is called *conflict management*. A team leader has a special responsibility to prevent conflict among the team members. Several steps can be followed in managing conflict.

### Know When to Intervene

Many disagreements in the workplace can lead to productive change.

24-15

*To be able to negotiate well, you must know all the facts and present your view in a persuasive manner.*

The time to intervene is when the team's productivity slows, and one or more members are obviously unhappy.

### Address the Conflict

The next step is to acknowledge the conflict with those involved. Use an "I" approach rather than "you" approach in your communications. "You" statements tend to make people defensive. For example, do not say, "You are letting the team down by leaving the copier without paper." Instead say, "I fill the copier with paper when it's empty and so do the other team members. We would really appreciate it if you would, too."

Sometimes the cause of a conflict is not so simple or easily understood. Use a positive approach and try to understand the problem from the other's point of view. Treat others with respect and in the same way that you would like to be treated.

### Identify the Source of the Conflict

Try to state the problem as clearly as possible. Seek acceptance that there is a problem rather than a simple misunderstanding. Avoid jumping to conclusions and making snap judgments.

### Identify Possible Solutions

It is important that people involved in the conflict develop ideas for solving it. Individuals who are not involved should not participate in the discussion. Explore positive and negative aspects of each possible solution.

### Implement and Evaluate

The next step is to implement the agreed-upon solution. Once a solution is agreed and accepted, make sure everyone understands his and her role in carrying it out. Check periodically to monitor the progress of implementing

the solution and resuming normal teamwork. If progress falls short of expectations, bring the parties back together and repeat the process.

## Leadership Skills

Leadership skills are needed in all careers. *Leadership* can be defined as the ability to guide and motivate others to complete tasks or achieve goals. It involves communicating well with others, accepting responsibility, and making decisions with confidence. See 24-16.

Leadership roles are often part of midlevel and professional-level positions in the housing industry. People in these positions usually supervise work crews or staffs. However, people in entry-level positions often assume informal leadership roles by setting

24-16

*Leaders get along well with their coworkers and inspire them to perform better.*

**Resource:** *Leadership Practice*, reproducible master 24-2, TR. Working in small groups with a designated leader and an antagonist, students work through the following exercise: Worksheet strips are cut apart, placed folded in a container, and each group randomly selects one. The group discusses ways to solve its problem and agree on a course of action. After most groups have finished, students discuss their feelings about their group's leadership. (The exercise is repeated with new leaders, antagonists, and strips.)

examples and motivating fellow workers to do good jobs. Entry-level workers who show leadership ability have better chances of being promoted.

Being a leader may be easy for some people, but everyone can improve their leadership skills with practice. Becoming involved in a school club or organization can help. Taking a role as an officer or a committee chair will give you even more practice. A part-time job is another good place to gain leadership skills.

## Staying Safety Conscious

Safety on the job is everyone's responsibility. Many workplace accidents occur because of careless behavior on the job. Often poor attitudes can cause unsafe behavior, too. Common causes of accidents include the following:

- taking chances
- showing off
- forgetting safety details
- disobeying company rules
- daydreaming
- losing one's temper
- falling asleep

Practicing good safety habits is essential for preventing accidents and injuries on the job. A healthy worker is more alert and less likely to make accident-prone mistakes. Knowing how to use machines and tools properly is the responsibility of both the employer and employees. Wearing protective clothing and using safety equipment correctly helps keep workers safe. See 24-17. Your employer will emphasize the safety practices that must be followed in your workplace.

The government agency that promotes safety in the workplace is the Occupational Safety and Health Administration, referred to as OSHA.

You will be required to follow the specific OSHA regulations that apply to your workplace.

## Terminating the Job

More money, more responsibility, and better benefits are some of the reasons for leaving a job. There are others, too, but all job departures need to be handled in a way that is considerate of the employer. You should try not to leave your job with noticeable anger and hostility. Employers know that employees won't stay forever. However, they dislike a too-short notice, especially during a busy season.

When you make the decision to leave your job, let the employer know in writing by giving at least a three-week notice. It would be helpful to give a longer notice if you can. A letter of resignation should state your reason for leaving and the date you expect to leave. See 24-18. The letter allows the employer to begin looking for your replacement. Perhaps there

24-17 _____
*Because this surveyor works near construction and traffic, he must wear a hardhat and an orange-colored vest.*

**Reflect:** Think of a time when you or someone you know was involved in an accident. Did any of the factors listed in the text play a role in this accident? How might this accident have been prevented?

**Enrich:** Visit the OSHA Web site at *osha.gov* to investigate the types of information and resources available for workers.

## Letter of Resignation

118 Thompson Boulevard
Atlanta, Georgia 30303
June 1, 2004

Mr. John Alston
Alston Home Builders, Inc.
9923 Construction Avenue
Atlanta, Georgia 30303

Dear Mr. Alston:

I plan to leave Alston Home Builders, Inc., effective July 15, 2004. I thoroughly enjoyed my work here and thank you for the excellent training I received. I especially appreciate the opportunity you gave me to work "up the ranks" and demonstrate my ability as an assistant construction manager.

I now plan to further my education and enter the engineering program at Georgia Tech University this fall. Thank you in advance for helping me make a smooth transition in the coming weeks.

Sincerely,

*Rick Sampson*

24-18 _____

*A letter of resignation should state your reason for leaving and your last day of work.*

**Discuss:** If you were an employer, how would you feel if one of your best employees told you he or she was resigning? What actions on the part of the employee would make it easier for you to receive this news?

will be enough time to hire someone who can work with you during your final days. Many people have found that a past employer became their greatest ally when they needed a good reference for a future position.

# Careers and Lifestyle

Your success in a career will affect your satisfaction with your personal and family life. Likewise, your roles and responsibilities related to home life will affect your career. Balancing career and home life is important in any lifestyle.

The career you choose affects your lifestyle in many ways. It affects your income. For instance, most architects earn more money than drafters. Your income determines how much you can spend on housing, clothing, food, and luxury items. If you choose to be a drafter, you may need to live in a smaller, less elaborate home than an architect can afford. You may not be able to spend as much money on your family's needs and wants.

Your career choice may also affect where you live. If you choose a career in construction, you may need to live in a suburban or urban community where much new building is taking place. If you become an interior designer, you will want to live in a community that appreciates good design and professional design services. Whatever your career choice is, you will want to locate where the work is.

Your friendships are affected by your career choice, too. You are likely to become friends with some of your work associates. See 24-19. You may meet other friends through the people you know from work.

Your leisure time is affected by the hours and vacation policies of your job. If you choose to be a carpenter, you may spend evenings and weekends during good weather working. Vacations during the summer may be out of the question. If you start your own business, you may need to work as often as possible to keep your business running. You may not have as much leisure time as professionals who are established in their jobs.

## Career Satisfaction and Lifestyle

How you feel about your career affects your attitudes toward your personal and family life. If you are content in your work, you tend to be more relaxed and pleased with your personal life and relationships. If you feel stress and dissatisfaction because of your work, this may create personal and family problems.

Job success helps you feel good about yourself. This success might include mastering a new job skill or having one of your ideas accepted by

24-19
*Your coworkers may become lasting friends outside of work and good networking buddies.*

your manager. You may feel successful after completing a project to a client's satisfaction. Getting a promotion or raise is another form of success.

Satisfaction in your career helps your personal and family life. If you enjoy your work, you are less likely to bring problems and frustrations home at the end of the day. You will be able to focus on what is best for the family. See 24-20.

### Handling Stress

Working extra-long days or trying to meet several tight deadlines can lead to stress. Working at a job you dislike can cause stress and dissatisfaction, too. Not getting along with employers or fellow employees may also cause these problems.

When work becomes unpleasant, your personal and family life can be affected. Your concern about work may interfere with personal and family relationships. You may be too tired or busy to devote enough time to family and friends. Some people even allow workplace stress to damage their health.

You may need to make adjustments if work-related stress becomes too great. For instance, you may need to reduce overtime work so you can spend more time in activities you enjoy. You may need to resolve conflicts with coworkers so you can feel less tension from work. If you cannot solve or eliminate your work-related problems, you may need to find a different job.

## Balancing Family and Work

Belonging to a family involves many roles and responsibilities. Family roles might include spouse, parent, and homemaker. Spouses need to work together to have satisfying,

24-20

*When employees balance their careers with personal and family life, they are more energized and refreshed to handle all their responsibilities.*

loving relationships. Parents need to provide safe, loving environments for their children. They also need to keep home life orderly by managing the household tasks.

Career roles help people handle their family responsibilities by providing money to pay for various family needs. However, career roles and responsibilities may sometimes conflict with family roles. People with multiple roles—such as *wife, mother, interior designer*, and *community volunteer*—must balance their responsibilities to fully meet them all.

Sometimes family responsibilities will dictate the career decisions you make. For instance, you may be offered the chance to open a remodeling business with a partner. In such a case, you must consider the needs of family members as well as your own. Will the demands of a partnership interfere with the time you can spend with your family? Will you be able to meet the family's financial needs if the business does not go well? Can you handle

**Discuss:** Explain the meaning of the term *multiple roles.* Support or reject the statement "People who truly enjoy their work roles tend to be much happier in all their other roles in life."

**Vocabulary:** Define *stress* and give examples of situations that increase stress in your life.

**Reflect:** Think of a time when you had trouble mastering a new skill in sports, academics, music, or some other area. How did you feel? Did this difficulty affect other roles in your life?

**Vocabulary:** Dissect the phrase *dual-career family* to determine what it means. Compare your definition with the definition given in the text.
**Writing Activity:** Identify an employer in your area that provides days off for sick child care. Is this benefit offered to people in entry-level, midlevel, or professional jobs? Write a description of the policy and an explanation of how you think it could be improved.

the responsibility of managing a business and still devote time and energy to family members when they need you? These questions and many more will affect your final choice.

In many families, both parents are employed. These families are called *dual-career families*. When both parents work outside the home, meeting family needs can be challenging. See 24-21. Single parents who work have similar challenges in meeting family needs. Parents face many decisions about how child care and homemaking needs will be met.

Unless one or both parents work from the home, parents need to provide substitute care for their children. They must choose a child care service that best fits their needs and the needs of their children. Some employers offer benefits related to child care, such as on-site care or vouchers to help pay for child care. Employers may also offer days off with pay to be used when children are sick. Such benefits help lessen the strain on working parents.

Parents who work may also need to adjust their homemaking practices. Families may decide they cannot spend as much time on homemaking as they would like. They may hire a cleaning service, buy more convenience foods, or leave the less important homemaking tasks undone. All capable family members should contribute to caring for the home.

Dual-career families often need to make special efforts to keep communication open. Since family members may be away from home often, they must make the most of their time together. Families do not always need to plan special activities for family time. This can cause extra pressure when family members may already be tired from work. However, parents and children need to know they can talk with one another and share their feelings. See 24-22.

Some parents feel strain and guilt from trying to balance the responsibilities of family and work. Sometimes a parent may not be able to attend a school function because of work. This may cause feelings of guilt for the parent. It may even cause the child to feel resentment. Such feelings can cause problems at work due to lack of concentration.

24-21 _____
*Some working couples separate the household tasks into two separate to-do lists, while others like to accomplish tasks together.*

24-22

*Family members should take every opportunity to share news about their accomplishments and discuss their plans and dreams.*

From time to time, families need to make adjustments to keep responsibilities in balance. This may involve supporting one another so family members do not feel guilty or resentful about work responsibilities. Single parents may look to close friends and relatives for extra support. At other times, parents may adjust work responsibilities so they can spend more time with the family. These adjustments might include telecommuting, working less overtime, taking a part-time job, or starting a home-based business.

## Summary

Knowing the real you—your interests, abilities, and aptitudes—is the first step in career planning. The goal-setting process can help you set short-term and long-term goals to achieve a successful career.

Effective workplace practices are essential for getting, maintaining, and terminating a job. Getting the job involves finding an opening; developing a resume, portfolio, and letter of application; completing an application form; and interviewing. Maintaining the job involves having good work habits and a positive attitude. Terminating the job has procedures to follow, too, including notifying the employer in writing.

Balancing your career responsibilities with your other roles in life will influence your career satisfaction. How workers feel about their work directly affects their personal and family life. Attitudes about family life also carry over to their workplace roles. Keeping one's many roles and responsibilities in proper balance takes continuing effort.

## To Review

1. True or false. Mentoring is the process of observing a person in the workplace to learn more about his or her job and its requirements.
2. What are the steps of the goal-setting process?
3. Deciding what gift to buy for a friend's birthday next month is a _____-term goal.
4. Briefly identify the three categories of information that a resume outlines.
5. True or false. An uncle who is a schoolteacher would be a good reference for your job search.
6. By writing *negotiable* or _____, you indicate a willingness to consider salary offers.
7. List five steps to take to prepare for a successful interview.
8. Starting work without being told is called _____.
9. Integrity, confidentiality, and honesty are crucial aspects of _____ behavior in the workplace.
10. _____ management refers to managing serious differences of views before they cause disruption in the workplace.
11. Which federal agency is responsible for promoting a safe working environment?
12. List three ways in which career choices affect lifestyles.
13. True or false. Employer benefits can help reduce strain on dual-career families and single parents.

# In Your Community

1. Interview three employed people in your community whom you think have successful careers. Ask them how they obtained their jobs. Did they set goals? How much planning did they do? What advice would they give to individuals entering their fields who want to establish successful careers? Write a brief paper summarizing their ideas.

2. Choose a local employer that has jobs you might want to pursue as part of your career. Contact the company and ask if you could "shadow" one of the employees. Summarize to the class the employer's reaction to your request.

3. Interview five neighbors and friends regarding the effect of their job likes and dislikes on their personal and family lives. Record their responses in chart form, keeping their identities concealed.

# To Think About

1. Is it possible to talk to someone but not communicate? Explain your answer.

2. Think about a time when you had an informal communication and were misunderstood. How could the misunderstanding have been prevented?

3. Suppose you are a safety director who must report an accident that injured several employees to the company President. A grease fire started in the cafeteria's kitchen, causing serious burns to two cooks. You are to report what happened, why it happened, and to determine what actions could have been taken to prevent the accident. Make a list of specific questions to ask. Which agency would you call for more specific information about safety on the job?

# Using Technology

1. Using the computer, develop a chart or table for displaying a career goal involving some field of housing. Make sure your plan includes both short-term and long-term goals. Identify the steps you need to take to achieve your stated goals. Share your plan with a teacher or counselor for feedback on ways to improve it. Save this worksheet to work on later as you refine your career goal.

2. Using the Internet, locate at least six positions in your near community for a job in which you might be interested.

3. Search the Internet for opportunities to take interview quizzes free. Take the tests and analyze your answer with the recommended responses. Practice until your score reaches ninety percent.

4. Visit your school or local library to determine what resources they have to help you and your classmates get ready for job interviews. Maybe they have films or video. If so, check them out and review them for possible use in your class. Share the results of your search with your teacher.

**Portfolio Project:** Prepare a resume. Have a parent or teacher review it and make suggestions for improvement. Make all necessary corrections and adjustments and include a copy in your portfolio.

# APPENDIX A

# Housing and Related Legislation

Few items affect housing as much as government policy. The *what, where,* and *how* of buildings are legislated. Even the cost of housing is affected by government controls. Also, the federal government provides supervision and regulation to assure safety in environmental areas. These also affect housing and its occupants, particularly hazardous materials (such as lead-based paint), air and water quality, and conservation of natural resources. Several of the most significant actions that occurred at the federal level are listed here.

## 1901

The Tenement House Act was passed to improve conditions in tenement houses. It applied to houses already constructed and set standards for building new ones.

## 1918

The U.S. Housing Corporation was established to provide housing for veterans of war.

## 1932

President Hoover's Conference on Home Building and Home Ownership discussed the national decline in building and the shrinking availability of mortgage credit. As a result of the Conference, the Federal Home Loan Bank Act of 1932 was passed. This Act established 12 district Federal Home Loan Banks as the framework of a reserve credit organization for home-financing institutions. It failed in its purpose to provide an adequate volume of funds for mortgage credit.

## 1933

The Home Owners' Loan Act of 1933 established a corporation to refinance the mortgages of distressed homeowners. It financed over one million mortgages in three years, investing $3.5 billion in the process. It was considered quite successful.

## 1934

The Housing Act of 1934 created the Federal Housing Administration (FHA), an agency that still exists today. It also established the Federal Savings and Loan Insurance Corporation to protect deposits. FHA revolutionized home financing methods by making possible lower interest rates and longer amortized mortgage periods. Improvements in housing standards also resulted from the minimum physical property standards set as a basis for FHA participation.

## 1937

The Housing Act of 1937 started the public housing program with the objective of providing decent, sanitary housing for low-income families. The Act set the principle of basing rental payments on an individual family's ability to pay. It provided for annual subsidy contracts, whereby the federal government pays the difference between costs of managing the project, including debt amortization, and the rental revenues received.

## 1940

The Lanham Act provided for federal financing of housing for those involved in the war effort. Two million dwelling units were built under this Act during the war.

## 1942

The National Housing Agency created by executive order was the first attempt to coordinate all federal housing programs.

## 1946

The Veteran's Emergency Housing Act was passed. It established the VA program for mortgage insurance.

The Farmers Home Administration (now called Rural Development Administration) was created in 1946 in the U.S. Department of Agriculture This program offers assistance in rural areas to help families obtain housing. Programs include low interest loans and grants to limited-income households and the elderly.

## 1947

The President's "Reorganization Plan No. 3" created the Housing and Home Finance Agency. The Federal Housing Administration, the Public Housing Administration, and the Home Loan Bank were all brought under the supervision of the Housing Administrator.

## 1949

Many cities and states tried to deal with run-down, over-populated housing through various renewal efforts. These usually fell short of their goals for lack of money. As a result, the desire for federal assistance to the nation's major cities was posed to Congress. From this experience came the Housing Act of 1949. It developed the now well-known expression of a "decent home and suitable living environment for every American family."

For the first time, the Act permitted land cleared with federal aid to be sold or leased to private developers for residential development. It gave recognition to the fact that private financial resources must be attracted to the housing field to attain the goal of the Act. The 1949 Act became the symbol of the joint effort between public and private interests to decently house the low-income population and to clean and redevelop run-down buildings.

## 1953

President Eisenhower established a special committee on government housing policies and programs. This committee's efforts were reflected in the 1954 Housing Act. The objective was to create a total program to prevent housing blight. The committee concluded that federal assistance should be available only to communities willing to undertake a long-range program of slum prevention through sound planning and enforcement of housing and building codes. This became the basis for the "Workable Program."

## 1954

The Housing Act of 1954 incorporated the many recommendations of President Eisenhower's special committee, including the "Workable Program." It also established the Urban Planning Assistance Program, sometimes called the 701 Program. It added a great stimulus to public acceptance of the comprehensive plan and the planning process.

The Act also established the concept of rehabilitation, which is the retention and improvement of essentially sound structures in an urban renewal area. It recognized, for the first time, the need for nonresidential urban renewal projects to attack blight in business and industrial areas. This Housing Act also instituted the demonstration grant program, whereby the federal government participated in research-oriented projects.

The 1954 Housing Act was an extremely significant piece of legislation for urban renewal because it focused on the comprehensive goal of urban revitalization rather than the single goal of good housing.

## 1956

The Housing Act of 1956 established relocation payments for families and businesses, aid for housing for older people, and the General Neighborhood Renewal Program. That program was an urban renewal plan for areas too large for a single project.

## 1959

The Housing Act of 1959 further extended the urban renewal program and created the Community Renewal Program. This program grew out of the need for comprehensive, long-range planning of a city's renewal activities, both public and private, closely tied to capital financing and land economics. The Act also established special credits for college and university urban renewal projects.

## 1961

The Housing Act of 1961 shifted more of the financial burden from local communities to the federal government. In cities with populations below 50,000, the federal government paid 75 percent of the net project costs. This reduced the financial burden on cities willing to fight the problems of housing blight. The Act also established the Open-Space Program and the Mass Transportation Program. It greatly liberalized various programs of the Federal Housing Administration.

## 1964

The Housing Act of 1964 authorized code enforcement of urban renewal projects intended to attack the beginnings of blight in basically sound areas. To reinforce this effort, special low-interest loans for residential rehabilitation were also authorized. The Act also liberalized relocation procedures and aid.

## 1965

The Housing and Urban Development Act of 1965 authorized the formation of a cabinet-level federal agency, named the U.S. Department of Housing and Urban Development (HUD). The Act approved a variety of new approaches to urban improvement, including grants for the following: neighborhood facilities, public works and facilities, urban beautification, municipal open spaces, and rehabilitation loans to low-income homeowners. It set new public housing policies for rent supplements, leased private housing, and the purchase of existing units. The code enforcement "renewal project" of the 1964 Act, having proved unworkable, was revised as an "aid program."

The Older Americans Act of 1965 provided a number of services to aging persons, especially those at risk of losing their independence.

## 1966

The Demonstration Cities and Metropolitan Development Act of 1966 authorized the Model Cities Program to rebuild or restore extensive blighted areas. The Act stated that physical and social development programs should be coordinated, using local private and governmental resources. The original emphasis on renewal of housing was reasserted.

The Act required the provision of a substantial number of low- and moderate-cost standard housing units in the development of an urban renewal area. This rule did not apply to predominantly nonresidential uses. As incentives for the Model Cities Program and for coordinated metropolitan planning, it authorized supplemental federal funds. Other significant features of the Act included the following:

- "new town" development through FHA financing
- new FHA sales housing program for low-income families
- grants for surveys of structures and sites to determine historical value
- liberalized noncash policy permitting up to 25 percent of the cost of a public building
- authorization of air-rights projects for industrial development

## 1968

The Housing and Urban Development Act of 1968 was considered the most important piece of housing legislation since the 1949 Act. It added two new programs to house low- and moderate-income families whose incomes were above the level permitted by public housing.

Under the Homeownership for Lower Income Families Program, the government helped pay the home mortgage and mortgage interest of the housing project sponsor. This permitted the sponsor to charge lower rents. Other significant features included the following:

- provisions that relaxed mortgage insurance in urban neighborhoods
- special FHA risk fund for mortgages in deteriorating urban areas
- credit assistance to make low-income families eligible for mortgage insurance
- assistance to private developers of new towns
- creation of a new approach to renewal, known as the Neighborhood Development Program, which provided more flexibility in planning and permitted staged development on a one-year basis
- increased rehabilitation grants from $1,500 to $3,000
- authorization to close out a renewal project when only small parcels of land remain
- aid in alleviating harmful conditions in blighted areas where renewal action was programmed, but immediate action was needed before renewal could be started

## 1970

The Housing and Urban Development Act of 1970 extended and amended laws relating to housing and urban development. The Act authorized the establishment of a national urban growth policy to encourage and support orderly growth of populated areas. It gave emphasis to new community and inner city development, encouraging the coordinated effort of state and local governments. Some specific features of the Act include the following:

- provisions for parks, especially in low-income areas
- preservation and restoration of historic and architectural sites
- provisions for curbing urban sprawl and spread of urban blight

The Office of Fair Housing and Equal Opportunity established the Federal Equal Housing Opportunity Council. Representatives of 50 federal departments and agencies participated. They coordinated efforts to assure all persons, regardless of race, creed, sex, or national origin, equal and unhindered access to the housing of their choice.

The Clean Air Act was passed to control smoke pollution and provide environmentally sound treatment of solid waste.

## 1974

The Housing and Community Development Act provided funds that went directly to the general local government. These funds were in the form of community development block grants. They were provided to begin or continue urban renewal or neighborhood development programs. Benefits were directed mainly to low- and moderate-income families. They were assisted in securing decent, safe, and sanitary housing.

The Emergency Housing Act of 1974 authorized HUD to buy $7.75 billion in mortgage loans at below-market interest rates so lenders could offer mortgages at subsidized interest rates. The Act was extended in 1975.

The Real Estate Settlement Procedures Act was designed to give consumers more information about costs related to buying or selling a home.

The Solar Energy Research, Development, and Demonstration Act had two main goals. One was to pursue a vigorous program of research and resource assessment of solar energy as a major source of energy for the nation. The second goal was to provide for the development and demonstration of practical ways of using solar energy on a commercial basis.

The Safe Drinking Water Act of 1974 was enacted to protect public health by regulating the nation's public drinking water supply. Regulations protect against both naturally occurring and man-made contaminants that may be found in drinking water.

## 1975

The Energy Policy and Conservation Act mandated appliance labeling. The Department of Energy and the Federal Trade Commission jointly oversee the implementation of this Act.

The Emergency Homeowner's Relief Act of 1975 authorized temporary assistance to help defray mortgage payments on homes owned by persons who were temporarily unemployed or underemployed as the result of adverse economic conditions. The Act made it possible for unemployed persons to retain possession of their homes. It was passed because the nation was judged to be in a severe recession with reduced employment opportunities.

The National Housing Act was amended to increase the maximum loan amounts for the purchase of mobile homes.

## 1976

The Housing Authorization Act of 1976 amended and extended many laws relating to the fields of housing and commercial development.

The Energy Conservation and Production Act required states and localities to adopt Building Energy Performance Standards. Many new energy-saving ideas were encouraged.

An extension of the National Housing Act included $850 million for subsidized housing. Of that amount, $85 million was reserved for the construction of new public housing. The bill also provided a major increase in funding for a housing program for the elderly.

## 1977

The Housing and Community Development Act made it easier for people to buy and improve their dwellings. It revised many loan regulations that had become outdated because of inflation. It increased the ceiling for home loans made by federal savings and loan associations. It provided a new system whereby savings and loan associations would have more money available for larger loans. It increased the limit on FHA Title I home improvement loans. It also increased mortgage loan limits for purchases of manufactured houses.

The Department of Energy, the Community Service Act, and the Farmers Home Administration initiated programs for weatherization.

The amended Clean Water Act established a way to regulate discharges of pollutants into U.S. waters. The many important provisions of the Act include the following:

- gave the Environmental Protection Agency (EPA) authority to implement pollution control programs such as setting wastewater standards for industry
- continued EPA's requirement to set water quality standards for all contaminants in surface waters
- made it unlawful for any person to discharge a pollutant into navigable waters, unless a permit was obtained under its provisions
- funded the construction of sewage treatment plants under the construction grants program
- recognized the need for planning to address the critical problems posed by pollution from sources not located at the site

## 1978

The National Energy Conservation Policy Act was passed to require energy-saving measures nationwide and reduce the country's dependence on oil from other nations. The Act established the following provisions related to housing:

- creation of energy-saving information and services from utility companies to homeowners, including the financing of energy-saving improvements
- availability of energy conservation grants and loans for low- to moderate-income families, rural families, the elderly, and people with special needs

- income tax credits through 1984 for homeowners on weatherization items and on systems using renewable resources (such as solar, geothermal, and wind energy)
- energy efficiency standards for major home appliances
- increased regulation of electricity and gas rates as well as lower rates during periods of low usage

The Housing and Community Development Act amended and extended provisions for community projects, especially for people with special needs.

## 1979

The Housing and Community Development Act was revised to extend programs and appropriate funds to carry out the initial purpose of the Act. The Act was further revised and extended every year through 1986.

Congress authorized the Office of Technology Assessment to make a detailed study of the potential for conserving energy in homes. The study examined existing and promising technologies and their energy-saving potential.

The Energy Assistance Program provided money for low-income families to help pay winter home-heating bills.

## 1980

The Household Moving Bill was passed to allow movers to offer binding estimates of what a move would cost. This increased movers' freedom to raise or lower prices. It also established standards for informal dispute settlements. Panels were set up by movers to resolve conflicts.

## 1981

The Reagan administration agreed to increase subsidies to builders of low-income housing. The increase was granted in an attempt to revive construction, which had virtually halted due to high-financing costs.

## 1982

President Reagan presented the following measures to help people buy homes:

- eased regulations on mortgage revenue bonds, making lower-cost mortgage money available to some homebuyers
- increased money available for homebuyers
- revised Federal Housing Administration rules to permit more first-time homebuyers to qualify for loans
- reduced processing time for FHA loan applications
- relaxed government restrictions that limited real estate firms' participation in related businesses, such as providing title insurance

## 1983

A bill worth $760 million was passed to provide federal loans to homeowners facing foreclosure or falling far behind on mortgage payments because of the recession. Loans were made available to homeowners who had suffered "substantial loss" of income "through no fault of their own" and who were delinquent for at least 90 days or had received an intent-to-foreclose notice.

## 1985

The energy crisis laws and policies of the 1970s were dismantled, and tax credits for energy saving measures were stopped.

The Housing and Community Development Act was extended to provide emergency food and shelter to the homeless.

## 1986

Programs to clean hazardous waste sites were expanded. The EPA was mandated to study problems, set standards, and decide cleanup methods and timetables.

The Safe Drinking Water Act of 1974 was amended to include the protection of the water supply and focus on the prevention of contamination.

## 1987

Congress authorized funds for community development block grants. A permanent extension was made to insure home mortgage loans.

Inspection for and removal of lead-based paint in federally assisted housing became a requirement.

The Federal Omnibus Act included reforms in residents' rights and care standards in nursing homes.

The McKinney Homeless Assistance Act was created to protect and improve the lives and safety of the homeless. Special emphasis was on older people, people with disabilities, and families with children. Grants became available for shelters. Subsidies were provided for low-income renters. Child care programs became available in public housing. The Act was amended in 1988 and 1990 to provide transitional housing as well as permanent housing with supportive services, such as education for homeless children.

## 1988

The Fair Housing Act gave HUD the authority to penalize those practicing discrimination in housing sales and rentals. Discriminatory practices aimed at homebuyers and renters were outlawed in the following cases involving:

- race, color, religion, national origin, or family status
- occupants with physical or mental disabilities
- occupants with children under 18 years of age

The Act also provided architectural accessibility and adaptable design requirements in new multifamily housing.

The Indian Housing Act legally separated the federal government's efforts for Native Americans from other housing programs.

Money from the Community Development Block Grant and the Farmers Home Administration could be used to improve housing conditions along the Mexican border.

A program was begun to determine levels of radon in housing and remove it. Also, there was provision for screening drinking water for lead and for taking measures to reduce lead poisoning.

## 1990

The Cranston-Gonzalez National Affordable Housing Act was passed to help families purchase homes. Provision was made for the supply of affordable housing to be increased, especially for older people, the homeless, and people with disabilities. Financial assistance was provided for certain first-time homebuyers. Rental assistance was available for low-income families.

The Clean Air Act provided measures to reduce pollution for benefit to the health of the general public. These measures contribute to improving air quality both inside and outside the dwellings. Because so many homes have wood-stoves and fireplaces, this summary of the Act provides information on how these home-heating systems are affected by the Clean Air Act.

## 1991

The Cranston-Gonzalez Act was amended to include war veterans and residents of Indian Reservations.

## 1992

The Residential Lead-Based Paint Hazard Act of 1992 requires sellers, landlords, and agents to warn homebuyers and tenants of lead-based paint and its hazards in housing built prior to 1978.

The Energy Policy Act of 1992 required that states adopt a residential building code for energy efficiency that meets or exceeds the Council of American Building Officials (CABO) Model Energy Code. The Act also established thermal insulation and energy efficiency standards for manufactured housing similar to the standards of some site-built housing. In addition, pilot studies were authorized for five states on energy efficient mortgages. Also, energy efficiency labeling for window and window systems was required to assist consumers with making more informed choices.

## 1995

The Housing for Older Persons Act of 1995 was passed to exempt housing communities of older persons from the Fair Housing Act discrimination charges. In other words, senior housing communities could continue to limit their services to singles or couples age 55 years or older. They are not required by law to open their housing to younger people or those with different family arrangements.

## 1996

Federal law required regulation regarding the disclosure of lead-based paint in writing to renters and buyers of housing built prior to 1978.

Native Americans Housing Assistance and Self-Determination Act was passed to improve the delivery of housing assistance to Indian tribes in a manner that recognizes the right of tribal self-governance and other priorities.

The federal government amended the Safe Drinking Water Act of 1974 to go beyond just the treatment of water for safety. The law greatly enhanced existing law. It recognized source water protection and provided operator training, funding for water system improvements, and public information as important components of safe drinking-water strategy.

## 1997

The Housing Opportunity and Responsibility Act of 1997 reformed public housing. The Act provided for the demolition of deteriorating public housing and replacement with mixed-income housing through partnerships with the public sector.

Amendments to the Clean Air Act established air quality standards.

## 1998

Federal Housing Assistance was increased to Native Hawaiians.

## 1999

The Federal Omnibus Act of 1987 was amended and expanded to require skilled nursing facilities to provide services to meet the highest practical physical, medical, and psychological well-being of every resident.

## 2000

American Homeownership and Economic Opportunity Act of 2000 provides for removal of barriers to homeownership, including down payment provisions. Tribal housing, people with special needs, and others benefit from the law.

The federal government expanded the Energy Conservation and Production Act of 1976 to include a model program for weatherizing housing of low-income families. It provides grants for conservation and efficiency for affordable housing. This includes weatherization as a way to reduce energy operating costs and thus lower overall housing costs.

## 2001

Programs to assist vulnerable older persons are administered through the Administration on the Aging. These programs, federally mandated under various titles of the Older Americans Act of 1965, help vulnerable older persons remain in their own homes by providing support services. Attention was given to assuring these services were equally available to all groups including tribal communities.

# APPENDIX B

# Energy Savers: Tips on Saving Energy and Money at Home

Did you know the typical U.S. family spends close to $1,300 a year on the home's utility bills? Unfortunately, a large portion of that energy is wasted. By using inexpensive energy-efficient measures, you can reduce your energy bills by 10 to 50 percent and, at the same time, help reduce air pollution and the environment.

This appendix contains tips on saving energy throughout the home. As a first step, you will want to prevent any energy loss occurring in your home that is simple to correct. Your next step is to consider replacing old, inefficient items that are energy "gluttons" with newer, energy-saving models. According to the U.S. Department of Energy, the average home uses electricity, natural gas, and other forms of energy as follows:

- 44 percent for heating and cooling
- 33 percent for lighting, cooking, and other appliances
- 14 percent for water heating
- 9 percent for the refrigerator

You can see that heating and cooling your living space uses the most energy. This may be the area where you will want to focus your attention first.

## General Energy-Saving Tips

- **Energy Star and EnergyGuide labels**. The Energy Star label identifies the most energy efficient products and items available. The EnergyGuide helps you determine how much energy will be used.

- **Tighten up your home and save heating and cooling costs**. You could save 10 percent on your energy bill by reducing air leaks in your home. Use weather stripping to seal doors and windows. Use caulk and spray foam to seal cracks and gaps in ceilings, walls, and floors that let outside air in. If you're in the market for new windows, look for the Energy Star label for year-round comfort.

- **Change the air filters in the heating and cooling system**. This simple change will produce significant results for your family's annual energy bill and overall health.

- **Adjust your thermostat and turn up the savings**. During hot weather, set your thermostat as high as is comfortable while at home, and higher yet (around 85°F) when away. In cold weather, do just the opposite. This method can help save up to 20 percent in heating and cooling costs. Energy Star-labeled programmable thermostats make the adjustments automatically.

- **Consider replacing your central air conditioner**. If your central air conditioning system is more than seven years old, you may want to consider a replacement. Energy Star-qualified central air conditioners can save you up to 20 percent on cooling costs.

- **Keep cool in the shade**. Sunshine, even through a window, will increase the temperature in your home. Use shades—overhangs, awnings, trees, and other outside shading devices—to keep your house cool in the summer and save money. Interior curtains, shades, and blinds can also help.

- **Change a light and save a bundle**. Energy Star-qualified lightbulbs are 75 percent more efficient than standard incandescent bulbs and can outlast as many as 10 standard incandescent bulbs. Replacing just five of the most used bulbs in your home will save you time, replacement hassles, and money.

- **Set your water heater temperature at the "normal" 120°F setting.** This can save up to 11 percent of your water heating costs. Then, make a quick trip to the hardware store or home improvement center for a hot water insulation kit to wrap your water heater for preventing heat-loss.

- **Use hot wash water only when necessary**. Clothes washers use energy to both heat the water and clean the clothes. Highly soiled laundry needs hot water, but warm or cold water is preferred for most other loads. If you're in the market for a new washer, replace your old one with an Energy Star-qualified model. These models use 50 percent less energy and 30 to 40 percent less water per load. Average household savings could top $100 per year.

- **Run your clothes washer and dishwasher with full loads**. Try to operate them at night or during off-peak hours. Use as many energy-saving features on your appliances as possible. If you're in the market for a new dishwasher or clothes washer, look for the Energy Star label.

- **Old refrigerators use a lot of energy**. Freezers are big energy-users, too. If your refrigerator is 10 years old or older, it may be time for a replacement. A new Energy Star-qualified refrigerator uses less than half the energy of a 10-year-old conventional model.

- **Put your computer to sleep**. You could cut your computer's energy use up to 35 percent by making sure your monitor's "sleep" mode is on. Adjust the monitor to power down when not in use for more than a few minutes. A simple touch of the mouse will bring it back up. Note: Screen savers may be entertaining, but they use considerable amounts of electricity. Energy Star-labeled computers, monitors, printers, scanners, copiers, fax machines, and multifunctional office equipment have features that make them power down, or "sleep," when not in active use.

- **Pools and spas equal summer fun, but adjust your pump to save money**. Pool and spa filter pumps are often one of the largest seasonal users of electricity. Use your pool filter and sweeper in the late evening or early morning. Be sure to keep the cover on heated pools when not in use. For even more energy savings, consider replacing pool pumps and motors with updated, more efficient equipment.

# Protect Your Home From Outside Heat and Cold

## Insulation Tips

- Conduct an energy audit, or inspection, of your home. You can do this, or you can hire an independent contractor. The audit will determine which parts of your house use the most energy and suggest effective measures for reducing your energy costs.

- Check the insulation in your attic, ceilings, exterior and basement walls, floors, and crawl spaces to see if it meets the levels recommended for your area. (Insulation is measured in R-values. The higher the R-value, the better your walls and roof will resist the transfer of heat.)

- Consider factors such as your climate, building design, and budget when selecting insulation R-value. The easiest and most cost-effective way to insulate your home is to add insulation in the attic.

## Weatherization Tips

- First, test your home for air-tightness. On a windy day, hold a lit incense stick next to your windows, doors, electrical boxes, plumbing fixtures, electrical outlets, ceiling fixtures, attic hatches, and other locations where there is a possible air path to the outside. If the smoke stream travels horizontally, you have located an air leak that may need caulking, sealing, or weather stripping.

- Caulk and weather-strip doors and windows that leak air.
- Caulk and seal air leaks where plumbing, ducting, or electrical wiring penetrates through exterior walls, floors, ceilings, and soffits over cabinets.
- Install rubber gaskets behind outlet and switch plates on exterior walls.
- Look for dirty spots in your insulation, which often indicate holes where air leaks into and out of your house. You can seal the holes by stapling sheets of plastic over the holes and caulking the edges of the plastic.
- Install storm windows over single-pane windows or replace them with double-pane windows. Storm windows can double the R-value of single-pane windows, and they reduce drafts, water condensation, and frost formation. As a less costly and less permanent alternative, you can use a heavy-duty, clear plastic sheet on a frame or tape clear plastic film to the inside of your window frames during the cold winter months. Remember, the plastic must be sealed tightly to the frame to help reduce infiltration.
- When the fireplace is not in use, keep the flue damper tightly closed. A chimney is designed specifically for smoke to escape, so until you close it, warm air escapes—24 hours a day!
- For new construction, reduce exterior wall leaks by either installing house wrap, taping the joints of exterior sheathing, or comprehensively caulking and sealing the exterior walls.

## Warm-Climate Window Tips

- In the summertime, the sun shining through your windows heats up the room. Windows with spectrally selective coatings on the glass reflect some of the sunlight, keeping your rooms cooler.
- Install white window shades, drapes, or blinds to reflect heat away from the house.
- Close curtains on south- and west-facing windows during the day.
- Install awnings on windows facing south and west.
- Apply sun-control or other reflective films on south-facing windows to reduce solar gain.

## Cold-Climate Window Tips

- Double-pane windows with low-e coating on the glass reflect heat back into the room during the winter months.
- Install exterior or interior storm windows to reduce heat-loss through the windows by 25 to 50 percent. Storm windows should have weather stripping at all moveable joints. They should be made of strong, durable materials and have interlocking or overlapping joints. Low-e storm windows save even more energy.
- Repair and weatherize your current storm windows, if necessary.
- Install tight-fitting, insulating window shades on windows that still feel drafty, even after weatherizing.
- Close your curtains and shades at night, and open them during the day.
- Keep windows on the south side of your house clean to maximize solar gain.

## Duct Tips

- Check your ducts for air leaks. First look for sections that should be joined, but have separated, and look for obvious holes.
- If you use duct tape to repair and seal your ducts, look for tape with the Underwriters Laboratories (UL) seal to avoid tape that degrades, cracks, and loses its bond with age.
- Remember that insulating ducts in the basement will make the basement colder. If both the ducts and the basement walls are not insulated, consider insulating both.

- If your basement has been converted to a living area, install both supply and return registers in the basement rooms.
- Be sure a well-sealed vapor barrier exists on the outside of the insulation on cooling ducts to prevent moisture buildup.
- Get a professional to help you insulate and repair all ducts.

## Fireplace Tips

- If you never use your fireplace, plug and seal the chimney flue.
- Keep your fireplace damper closed unless a fire is going. Keeping the damper open is like keeping a 48-inch window wide open during the winter—it allows warm air to go right up the chimney.
- When you use the fireplace, reduce heat-loss by opening dampers in the bottom of the firebox (if provided). Otherwise, open the nearest window slightly, approximately an inch, and close doors leading into the room. Lower the thermostat setting to between 50°F and 55°F.
- Install tempered glass doors and a heat-air exchange system that blows warmed air back into the room.
- Check the seal on the flue damper and make it as snug as possible.
- Add caulking around the fireplace hearth.
- Use grates made of C-shaped metal tubes to draw cool room air into the fireplace and circulate warm air back into the room.

## Heat Pump Tips

- Do not set back the heat pump's thermostat manually if it causes the electric resistance heating to come on. This type of heating, which is often used as a backup to the heat pump, is more expensive.
- Clean or change filters once a month or as needed, and maintain the system according to manufacturer's instructions.

# Save Energy with Appliances

## Dishwasher Tips

- Check the manual that came with your dishwasher for the manufacturer's recommendations on water temperature; many have internal heating elements that allow you to set the water heater to a lower temperature.
- Scrape off, don't rinse, large food pieces and bones. Soaking or prewashing is generally only recommended in cases of burned-on or dried-on food.
- Be sure your dishwasher is full, but not overloaded.
- Do not use the "rinse hold" on your machine for just a few soiled dishes. It uses three to seven gallons of hot water each time you use it.
- Let your dishes air dry. If you don't have an automatic air-dry switch, turn off the control knob after the final rinse and prop the door open slightly so the dishes will dry faster.

## Refrigerator/Freezer Energy Tips

- Don't keep your refrigerator or freezer too cold. Recommended temperatures are 37° to 40°F for the fresh food compartment of the refrigerator/freezer. The temperature of the freezer compartment should be held near 0°F.
- To check refrigerator temperature, place an appliance thermometer in a glass of water in the center of the refrigerator. Read it after 24 hours. To check the freezer temperature, place a thermometer between frozen packages. Read it after 24 hours.
- Regularly defrost manual-defrost refrigerators and freezers. Frost buildup increases the amount of energy needed to keep the motor running. Don't allow frost to build up more than ¼-inch thick.

- Make sure your refrigerator door seals are airtight. Test them by closing the door over a piece of paper or a dollar bill so it is half inside and half outside of the refrigerator. If you can pull the paper or bill out easily, the latch may need adjustment or the seal may need replacing.

- Cover liquids and wrap foods stored in the refrigerator. Uncovered foods release moisture and make the compressor work harder.

- Move your refrigerator out from the wall and vacuum its condenser coils once a year unless you have a no-clean condenser model. Your refrigerator will run for shorter periods with clean coils.

## Laundry Tips

- Wash your clothes in cold water using cold-water detergents whenever possible.

- Wash and dry full loads. If you are washing a small load, use the appropriate water-level setting.

- Dry towels and heavier cottons in a load separate from lighter-weight clothes.

- Don't overdry your clothes. If your machine has a moisture sensor, use it.

- Clean the lint filter in the dryer after every load to improve air circulation.

- Use the cool-down cycle to allow the clothes to finish drying with the residual heat in the dryer.

- Periodically inspect your dryer vent to ensure it is not blocked. This will save energy and may prevent a fire. Manufacturers recommend using rigid venting material, not plastic vents that may collapse and cause blockages.

# Save Energy in Lighting

## Indoor Lighting Tips

- Turn off the lights in any room you're not using, or consider installing timers, photo-cells, or occupancy sensors to reduce the amount of time your lights are on.

- Use task lighting. Instead of brightly lighting an entire room, focus the light where you need it. For example, use fluorescent under-cabinet lighting for kitchen sinks and countertops under cabinets.

- Consider three-way lamps. They make it easier to keep lighting levels low when brighter light is not necessary.

- Use 4-foot fluorescent fixtures with reflective backing and electronic ballasts for your workroom, garage, and laundry areas.

- Consider using 4-watt mini-fluorescent or electro-luminescent nightlights Both lights are much more efficient than their incandescent counterparts. The luminescent lights are cool to the touch.

## Compact Fluorescent Bulbs

- These compact fluorescent bulbs (CFLs) are four times more energy efficient than incandescent bulbs and provide the same lighting.

- Use CFLs in all portable table and floor lamps in your home. Consider carefully the size and fit of these systems when you select them. Some home fixtures may not accommodate some of the larger CFLs.

- When shopping for new light fixtures, consider buying dedicated compact fluorescent fixtures with built-in ballasts that use pin-based replacement bulbs.

- For spot lighting, consider CFLs with reflectors. The lamps range in wattage from

13-watt to 32-watt and provide a very directed light using a reflector and lens system.

- Take advantage of daylight by using light-colored, loose-weave curtains on your windows to allow daylight to penetrate the room while preserving privacy. Also, decorate with lighter colors that reflect daylight.

## Torchiere Lamp

- If you have torchiere fixtures with halogen lamps, consider replacing them with compact fluorescent torchieres. Compact fluorescent torchieres use 60 to 80 percent less energy and can produce more light (lumens) than the halogen torchieres.

## Outdoor Lighting Tips

- Use outdoor lights with a photocell unit or a timer so they will turn off during the day.
- Turn off decorative outdoor gas lamps. Eight gas lamps burning year-round use as much natural gas as it takes to heat an average-size home during an entire winter.

- Exterior lighting is one of the best places to use CFLs because of their long life. If you live in a cold climate, be sure to buy a lamp with a cold-weather ballast.

# Landscaping Tips (Dependent on Geographic Area)

- Trees that lose their leaves in the fall are effective at reducing heating and cooling costs. When selectively placed around a house, they provide excellent protection from the summer sun, but permit winter sunlight to reach and warm your house. The height, growth rate, branch spread, and shape are all factors to consider in choosing a tree.
- Vines provide shading and cooling, too. Grown on trellises, vines can shade windows or the whole side of a house.
- Deflect winter winds by planting evergreen trees and shrubs on the north and west sides of your house. Deflect summer winds by planting on the south and west sides of your house.

# G L O S S A R Y

## A

**abilities.** Skills you develop with practice. (24)

**absorbed light.** Light that is drawn in by a surface and cannot be reflected. (17)

**abstract form.** The physical shape of an object that rearranges or stylizes a recognizable object. (10)

**abstract of title.** A copy of all public records concerning a property. (5)

**accent lighting.** Sharp lighting used for a highlight, especially to focus on a point of emphasis in a room. (17)

**accessories.** Items smaller than furnishings that accent the design of a room. They may be either decorative (such as pictures and figurines) or functional (such as ashtrays and lamps). (17)

**acoustical.** A common material used for ceilings that deadens or absorbs sound. (14)

**adjustable rate mortgage.** A payment contract in which the interest rate is adjusted up or down periodically according to a national interest rate index. (5)

**adobe.** Building material made of sun-dried earth and straw. (1)

**aesthetics.** A pleasing appearance or effect. (10)

**agrarian.** People who earn their living from the land. (2)

**agreement of sale.** A contract that states all specific terms and conditions of a sale. Also called a contract of purchase, purchase agreement, or sales agreement. (5)

**alcove.** A small recessed section of a room. (7)

**alphabet of lines.** Lines used on an architectural drawing that allow the drafter to communicate ideas clearly and accurately. (7)

**American Institute of Architects (AIA).** A professional organization that promotes architectural standards and requires members to have extensive education and training in designing and building structures. (23)

**American Society of Interior Designers (ASID).** A professional organization that requires members to have a high level of preparation and training in interior design. (23)

**American Society of Landscape Architects (ASLA).** A professional group of qualified experts in the field of landscape architecture. (19)

**ampere (amp).** The unit of current used to measure the amount of electricity passing through a conductor per unit of time. (9)

**analogous color harmony.** A color harmony made by combining related hues—those next to each other on the color wheel. (11)

**anchor bolts.** Bolts set about six feet apart into the concrete of the foundation walls. (8)

**annuals.** Flowers that must be replanted every year. (19)

**antiques.** Furniture made over one hundred years ago in the style popular at that time. (15)

**appliance.** Household device powered by gas or

electricity to help people meet their needs. (18)

**applied design.** Patterns that are printed onto the surface of a piece of fabric. (13)

**appraiser.** An expert who estimates the quality and value of a property. (5)

**apprenticeship.** Learning a trade under the direction and guidance of an expert worker. (23)

**aptitude.** An ability to learn something quickly and easily; natural talent. (24)

**archeologist.** Social scientist who studies ancient cultures by unearthing dwelling places of past civilizations. (1)

**architect.** A person who designs buildings and supervises their construction. (2)

**architectural drawings.** A house plan containing information about the size, shape, and location of all parts of the house. (7)

**asbestos.** A fireproof, cancer-causing mineral that can easily become airborne and inhaled. (20)

**asphyxiation.** The state of unconsciousness or death caused by inadequate oxygen or some other breathing obstruction. (20)

**assign.** To transfer the remaining portion of a lease to someone else and relinquish responsibility. (5)

**assisted-living facility.** A type of life-care housing for older people who need living assistance with certain daily routines, but not constant care. (4)

**asymmetrical.** A design in which one side of a center point is different from the other. (6)

**attached houses.** Housing designed for one household, but sharing a common wall with a house on one or both sides. (4)

**attitude.** A person's outlook on life. (24)

**automated houses.** Dwellings that have an integrated and centrally controlled system based on computer technology. (22)

## B

**baby boomers.** The adult population born during the period after World War II called the "baby boom," which lasted from 1946 through 1964. (2)

**bachelor's degree.** A college degree usually requiring four years of study. (23)

**balance.** A perception of the way arrangements are seen. It is the equilibrium among parts of a design. (12)

**beauty.** The quality or qualities that give pleasure to the senses. (1)

**bid.** A charge for construction that includes the cost of materials and labor. (5)

**biennials.** Flowers that must be replanted every other year. (19)

**bill of lading.** A receipt listing the goods shipped in a moving van. (4)

**biometrics.** Identification of an individual by a unique physical characteristic. (20)

**blend.** Yarn that is made of two or more types of fibers. (13)

**blinds.** Window treatments made of slats that can be raised up and down or moved to the side to control the amounts of air and light that enter a room. (17)

**bond.** The way that masonry units are arranged together in a pattern. (8)

**bonded.** Two layers of fabric that are permanently joined together with an adhesive. (13)

**bonded wood.** Wood that has been bonded by glue and pressure. (15)

**box nail.** A nail with a large, flat head. (21)

**box springs.** A series of coils attached to a base and covered with padding. (15)

**breach of contract.** A legal term for failure to meet all terms of a contract or agreement. (5)

**brick.** A block molded from moist clay and hardened with heat. (8)

**building codes.** Established minimum standards for materials and construction methods. (2)

**built-in storage.** Shelves and drawers built into a housing unit. (7)

**bungalow.** A one-story house with a low-pitched roof. (6)

**butcher block.** A work surface made by fusing a stack of long, thin hardwood strips. (14)

**butt joint.** A board that is glued or nailed flush to another board. (15)

## C

**Cape Cod.** A style of housing that is small, symmetrical, and one-and-one-half stories with a gable roof. (6)

**carbon monoxide.** A colorless, odorless gas produced by the incomplete burning of fossil fuel. (20)

**career.** A series of related occupations that show progression in a field of work. (23)

**career cluster.** A group of several careers that are closely related. (23)

**career ladder.** A progression of related careers, each one requiring more

qualifications than the previous one. (23)

**career lattice.** A chart showing related career opportunities, with careers in slightly different subject areas placed horizontally and careers requiring more qualifications placed above them. (23)

**case good.** A piece of furniture in which wood is the most common material used. (15)

**Casual style.** A twenty-first century furniture style that emphasizes comfort and informality. (15)

**ceiling treatment.** A coating, covering, or building material applied to the ceiling area. (14)

**cellulosic natural fiber.** Fiber made from the cellulose in plants. (13)

**census.** An official count of the population taken by the government. (2)

**central heat-pump system.** An electric refrigeration unit used to either heat or cool a house. (9)

**central-satellite decision.** A group of decisions consisting of a major decision that is surrounded by related, but independent, decisions. (3)

**ceramic tile.** A flat piece of fired clay coated with a protective glaze. (14)

**chain decision.** A sequence of decisions in which one decision triggers others. (3)

**childless family.** A family consisting of a husband and wife with no children. (1)

**circuit.** The path electrons follow from the source of the electricity to the device and back to the source. (9)

**circuit breaker.** A switch that automatically interrupts an electrical current in an abnormal condition. (9)

**Classic.** A housing style that represents the authentic repetition

of architecture with enduring excellence. (6)

**clearance space.** A measurement term for the amount of space that needs to be left unobstructed around furniture to allow for ease of use and a good traffic pattern. (16)

**climate.** Prevailing weather conditions of a region as determined by the temperature and meteorological changes over a period of years. (2)

**closed.** When the legal and financial matters of moving into a new home have been settled. (5)

**closeout sale.** A sale held when a store is moving to another location or going out of business. (16)

**closet auger.** A device used to bore items to free blocked plumbing or wastewater lines. (21)

**closing costs.** The fees for settling the legal and financial matters of buying and selling property. (5)

**co-generation.** A system that refers to distributed energy resources, made possible through the development of new technologies that produce electricity. (22)

**coil springs.** Spiral-shaped springs without padding and covering that are used in heavier furniture. (15)

**collectibles.** Highly valued furnishings that are less than one hundred years old but no longer made. (15)

**color.** An element or property of light. (11)

**color harmony.** A pleasing combination of colors based on their respective positions on the color wheel. (11)

**color scheme.** The combination of colors selected for the design of a room or house. (11)

**color spectrum.** The full range of all existing colors. (11)

**color wheel.** A particular circular arrangement of primary, secondary, and intermediate colors; the basis of all color relationships. (11)

**combination yarn.** A continuous strand of yarn made of two or more different yarns. (13)

**combustible.** The quality of being burnable. (20)

**comforter.** A filled bed covering that is often used as a bedspread. (13)

**common-use storage.** Storage used by all who live in a house, such as the storage for food, tools, and other shared items. (7)

**community.** A particular area that is smaller than a region, but larger than a neighborhood. Examples include a large city, small village, or rural area. (4)

**compact fluorescent bulb.** A lightbulb that uses only 15 watts of electricity and operates for 9,000 hours. (17)

**comparison shopping.** Comparing the qualities, prices, and services provided for similar items in different stores before buying. (16)

**complement.** A hue that is directly across from another hue on a color wheel. (11)

**complementary color harmony.** A color harmony made by combining complementary colors— those opposite each other on the color wheel. (11)

**composting toilet.** A self-contained, stand-alone toilet. (9)

**computer-aided drafting and design (CADD).** Software and hardware that creates designs with a computer. (2)

**concrete.** A hard building material made by combining cement, sand, and gravel with water. (8)

**condominium.** A type of ownership where the

buyer owns individual living space and has an undivided interest in the common areas and facilities of the multiunit building. (4)

**conductor.** Allows the flow of electricity; usually a wire. (9)

**conduit.** A metal or plastic pipe that surrounds and protects wires. (9)

**conflict.** A hostile situation resulting from opposing views. (24)

**coniferous.** Trees that do not lose their leaves. (15)

**con-ops.** A blend of condominium and cooperative units. In con-ops, the buyers own their individual living spaces as in condominium ownership, but common areas and facilities are owned cooperatively. (4)

**conservation.** The process of protecting or saving something from loss or waste. (19)

**construction.** A design characteristic that includes materials and structure. (10)

**Contemporary style.** A housing style in which the designs are surprising and often controversial; also refers to a twenty-first century furniture style composed of designs that are the very latest introductions to the market. (6)

**contractor.** A person who contracts or agrees to supply certain materials or to do certain work for a stipulated fee, especially one who contracts to build buildings. (4)

**convection oven.** A cooking appliance that forces a stream of heated air directly onto foods and cooks food faster at lower temperatures. (18)

**conventional mortgage.** A two-party contract between a borrower and a lending firm. This type of

mortgage is not insured by the government. Therefore, a greater risk is involved. (5)

**cool colors.** Blue, green, violet, and the colors near them in a color wheel. Also called receding colors. (11)

**cooperative.** A type of ownership where people buy shares of stock in a nonprofit corporation. These shares entitle them to occupy a unit in the cooperative building. (4)

**cooperative education.** Schooling that includes working part-time and attending classes part-time. (23)

**cork.** The woody bark tissue of a plant. (14)

**corner blocks.** Small pieces of wood attached between corner boards that support and reinforce the joint. (15)

**cost.** The amount of human and nonhuman resources used to achieve something. (5)

**countertop.** A durable work surface installed on a base cabinet. (14)

**Country style.** A twenty-first century furniture style that traces its origins to the lifestyles of rural areas. (15)

**creativity.** The ability to create imaginatively. (1)

**credit card.** An extension of money to the cardholder based on an agreement to repay. (5)

**culture.** Beliefs, social customs, and traits of a group of people. (2)

**curtains.** Flat fabric panels that cover windows. They have a pocket hem at the top, which slips onto a curtain rod. (17)

**curved line.** A line that is a part of a circle or an oval. (10)

### D

**deadbolt lock.** A lock bolt that unlocks by turning a

knob or key without action of a spring. (20)

**decibel (dB).** Unit of measure for the volume of sound. (20)

**deciduous.** Trees that lose their leaves. (15)

**declaration of ownership.** A legal document containing the conditions and restrictions of the sale, ownership, and use of the property. (5)

**deed.** The legal document by which the title is transferred from one person to another. It describes the property being sold. (5)

**dehumidifier.** A small appliance that removes excess moisture from the air. (18)

**demographics.** Statistical facts about the human population. (2)

**density.** The number of people in a given area. (2)

**design.** The entire process used to develop a specific project. It also refers to the product or result. (10)

**detail view.** An enlargement of a construction feature. (7)

**diagonal line.** A line that angles between a horizontal and a vertical line. (10)

**diffused light.** Light scattered over a large area. It has no glare and creates a soft appearance. (17)

**direct lighting.** Lighting that shines directly toward an object. It provides the most light possible to a specific area and very little is reflected from other surfaces. (17)

**disability.** An impairment or limit to a person's abilities. (2)

**disinfectant.** A cleaning agent that destroys bacteria. (21)

**double-complementary color harmony.** A color harmony consisting of two colors and their complements. (11)

**double-dowel joint.** Glued wooden dowels that fit into drilled holes in two pieces of wood. (15)

**dovetail joint.** Fastened corner joints in which tightly fitting teeth are carved on both pieces of wood. (15)

**down payment.** A partial payment that is made to secure a purchase. (5)

**downspout.** A vertical pipe that connects the gutter system to the ground to carry rainwater away from the house's foundation. (8)

**draperies.** Pleated panels of fabric that cover windows completely or are pulled to the side. (17)

**dual-career families.** Families in which both parents are employed. (24)

**dual-income family.** A family in which both the husband and wife are employed outside the home. (2)

**duct.** Large round tube or rectangular boxlike structure that delivers heated (and air-conditioned) air to distant rooms or spaces. (9)

**Dutch Colonial.** Houses built of fieldstone, brick, but sometimes wood. They feature gambrel roofs, central entrances, off-center chimneys, and dormer windows. (6)

**dysfunctional.** A behavioral environment that produces a negative effect on household members. (2)

### E

**Early English.** An architectural style built by English settlers in the United States beginning in the early 1600s. (6)

**earnest money.** A deposit the potential buyer pays to show that he or she is serious about buying the house. The money is held in trust until the closing of the transaction. (5)

**earth-sheltered.** Houses that are partially covered with soil. (6)

**Eclectic style.** A twenty-first century furniture style in which furniture and fabrics cross over styles and periods. (15)

**ecology.** The study of the relationship between living organisms and their surroundings. (22)

**ecosystem.** A community of organisms within an environment functioning as a unit in nature. (22)

**electrical shock.** An electric current that passes through one's body. (20)

**electric current.** Another name for electricity. (9)

**electricity.** The movement of electrons along a conductor. (9)

**electronic lamp (E-lamp).** A lamp that lasts up to 20,000 hours and fits most sockets that use incandescent bulbs. (17)

**electric radiant-heating system.** A heating system in which resistance wiring is used to produce heat. (9)

**elevation view.** The finished exterior appearance of a given side of the house. (7)

**emphasis.** A center of interest or focal point in a room. (12)

**enclosure elements.** Barriers that confine a space. (19)

**EnergyGuide label.** A label that states the average yearly energy cost of operating an appliance. (18)

**Energy Star label.** Indicates that a product is at least 10 percent more energy efficient than similar products. (18)

**engineered quartz.** A stone-like material used for countertops composed of stone particles and see-through binders. (14)

**entrepreneur.** A person who starts and runs his or her own business. (23)

**environment.** The total of all conditions, objects, places, and people that surround a living organism. (2)

**equity.** The money value of a house beyond what is owed on the house. (5)

**ergonomics.** The design of consumer products and environments to promote user comfort, efficiency, and safety. (16)

**escape plan.** A plan of action in case a fire occurs. (20)

**esteem.** A feeling of respect, admiration, and high regard from others. (1)

**ethical behavior.** Conforming to accepted standards of fairness and good conduct; based on a person's sense of what is right to do. (24)

**eviction.** A legal procedure that forces a lessee to leave the property before the rental agreement expires. (5)

**extended family.** A family that includes relatives, either several generations of people or several members of the same generation. (1)

**exterior elevations.** Architectural drawings that show the outside views of the house. (6)

## F

**factory-built housing.** Housing built either fully or partially in a plant and then placed or assembled on a site. The five types are modular, manufactured/mobile, panelized, precut, and kit. (4)

**Fair Housing Act.** A law that forbids discrimination in housing and requires multiunits to be accessible to the disabled. (4)

**family.** Two or more people living together who are related by birth, marriage, or adoption. (1)

**faux finish.** The application of paint in different textures and patterns to create a decorative finish; derives from the French word for *false* or *fictitious*. (14)

**Federal.** A style of housing that has a boxlike shape. It is at least two stories high and is symmetrical with a flat roof. (6)

**FHA-insured mortgage.** A three-party contract that involves the borrower, lending firm, and Federal Housing Administration (FHA). (5)

**fiber.** The raw material from which fabric is made. (13)

**fiber optics.** A type of heatless light produced by passing an electric current through a cable containing very fine strands of glass. (17)

**finance charge.** A fee paid for the privilege of using credit. It includes interest and carrying charges. (5)

**finishes.** Substances applied to fabric to improve its appearance, feel, or performance. (13)

**finish nail.** A nail with a very small head that can be driven below the surface. (21)

**fireplace insert.** A metal device that fits into an existing masonry fireplace and attaches to the chimney liner. (9)

**flammable.** Fabrics that burn quickly. (13)

**flashing.** Sheet metal used in waterproofing the roof. (8)

**flat springs.** Flat S-shaped springs that may have metal support strips banded across them. (15)

**float.** Segments of yarn that lie on the surface of the fabric. (13)

**floor coverings.** Flooring materials, such as carpets and rugs, that are placed over the structural floor. (14)

**flooring materials.** Materials that are used as the top surface of a floor, such as wood, ceramic tile, and brick. (14)

**floor plan.** A simplified drawing that shows the size and arrangement of rooms, hallways, doors, windows, and storage areas on one floor of a home. (7)

**floor treatment.** Flooring materials and floor coverings. (14)

**fluorescent light.** Light produced as electricity activates mercury vapor within a sealed tube to create invisible ultraviolet rays. These rays are converted into visible light rays by a fluorescent material that coats the inside of the glass tube. (17)

**foam mattress.** Latex or polyurethane foam that is cut or molded to shape and covered with a tightly woven cloth. (15)

**Folk.** A housing style originating from the common experiences of a group of people. (6)

**foot-candle.** A unit of measure for illumination. It is the amount of light a standard candle gives at a distance of one foot. (17)

**footing.** The bottom of the foundation, which supports the rest of the foundation and the house. (8)

**forced warm-air system.** A heating system in which the air is heated by a furnace and delivered to rooms through supply ducts. (9)

**foreclosure.** A legal proceeding in which a lending firm takes possession of the mortgaged property of a debtor who fails to live up to the terms of the contract. (5)

**form.** The physical shape of objects. It outlines the edges of a three-dimensional object and contains volume and mass. (10)

**formal balance.** The arrangement of identical objects on both sides of a center point; also called symmetrical balance. (12)

**fossil fuel.** A fuel formed in the earth from plant or animal remains; includes natural gas, propane, gasoline, coal, charcoal, and wood. (9)

**foundation.** The underlying base of the house composed of the footing and the foundation walls. (8)

**foundation wall.** The walls supporting the load of the house between the footing and the floor. (8)

**free form.** A shape that is random and flowing and communicates a feeling of freedom. It is found in nature. (10)

**freestanding houses.** Single-family houses that stand alone and are not connected to another unit. (4)

**French Manor.** A symmetrical house with wings on each side and a mansard roof on the main part of the house. (6)

**French Normandy.** Early French homes built by French Huguenot settlers; one-story structures with many narrow door and window openings and steeply pitched roofs. (6)

**French Plantation.** An architectural style built by French settlers in southern U.S. regions. (6)

**French Provincial.** A style of housing that has a delicate, dignified appearance and is usually symmetrical. The windows are a dominant part of the design, and the tops of the windows break into the eave line. (6)

**frost line.** The depth to which frost penetrates soil in a specific area. (8)

**fuel cell.** An equipment system that produces electricity from the use of chemicals. (22)

**full warranty.** A written agreement that allows a consumer to have a broken appliance repaired or replaced free of charge (at the warrantor's option). (18)

**function.** Purpose, usefulness, convenience, and organization of a designed object; the way in which a design works. (10)

**fuse.** Device used to open an electric current when an overload occurs. (9)

## G

**gable roof.** A roof that comes to a point in the center and slopes on both sides. (6)

**gambrel roof.** A two-pitched roof with the lower slope steeper than the upper slope. (6)

**garrison.** A style of housing in which an overhang allows extra space on the second floor. (6)

**general lighting.** Lighting that provides a soft, even level of light throughout a room or area. (17)

**general warranty deed.** Transfers the title of a property to the buyer. It guarantees the title is clear of any claims against it. (5)

**generic name.** A name describing a group of fibers with similar chemical composition. (13)

**geometric form.** The physical shape of an object that uses squares, rectangles, circles, and other geometric figures to create form. (10)

**Georgian.** A style of housing that has simple exterior lines, a dignified appearance, and is symmetrical. Georgian houses have windows with small panes of glass and either gable or hip roofs. (6)

**geothermal energy.** Energy coming from the heat of the earth's interior. (22)

**German.** A settler who traveled from the region called Germany today, arriving in North America in the late seventeenth century. (6)

**girder.** A large horizontal member in the floor that takes the end load of joists. (8)

**goals.** Aims or targets a person tries to achieve. (24)

**goal-setting process.** A set of steps to follow to achieve objectives. (24)

**golden mean.** The division of a line between one-half and one-third of its length, which creates a more pleasing look to the eye than an equal division. (12)

**golden rectangle.** A rectangle having sides in a ratio of 2:3. The short sides are two-thirds the length of the long sides. (12)

**golden section.** The division of a line or form in such a way the ratio of the smaller section to the larger section is equal to the ratio of the larger section to the whole. (12)

**gradation.** The type of rhythm created by a gradual increase or decrease of similar elements of design. (12)

**graduated-care facilities.** A life-care community for older people in which the residents move from their own apartments to a nursing home unit as needed. (4)

**grain.** The direction threads run in a woven fabric. (13)

**graywater.** Wastewater from washing machines, showers, and sinks, not contaminated with human waste. (22)

**Greek Revival.** Architecture imitating ancient Greece, where the main characteristic is a two-story portico. The portico is supported by columns and has a large triangular pediment. (6)

**green building.** Refers to a structure that uses materials and techniques in all aspects of construction that conserves resources. (22)

**gross domestic product (GDP).** The value of all goods and services produced within a country during a given time period, regardless of who owns the production facilities. (2)

**gross income.** Income before deductions. (5)

**ground cover.** Low-growing plants that cover the ground in place of sod. (19)

**ground fault circuit interrupter (GFCI).** Safety device used in outlets or added to electrical cords to help prevent shocks. (18)

**gutter.** A horizontal open trough located under the perimeter of the roof to channel water away. (8)

**gypsum wallboard.** A common building material used for interior walls and ceilings; also called *drywall* and *sheet rock*. (14)

## H

**Habitat for Humanity.** A partnership formed to help eliminate homelessness and substandard housing in the United States and other countries. (2)

**habitual behavior.** Actions that routinely occur without thought. (3)

**hand limitations.** Conditions that limit hand movement and gripping ability. (20)

**hardscape.** Anything in the landscape other than vegetation and outdoor furniture. (19)

**hardware.** The components in a computer system. (18)

**harmony.** Agreement among parts. It is created when the elements of design are effectively used according to the principles of design. (12)

**hazardous wastes.** Poisonous waste materials that damage the environment and cause illness. (22)

**header.** Small, built-up beams that carry the load of the structure over door and window openings. (8)

**hearing disability.** A degree of hearing loss. (20)

**high mass.** A space that is visually crowded. (10)

**high tech.** A high level of technology. (2)

**hip roof.** Roofs with sloping ends and sloping sides, sometimes topped by a flat area with a balustrade railing. (6)

**hogan.** Building made of logs and mud. (2)

**home.** Any place a person lives. (4)

**horizontal-axis washer.** A front-loading model of an automatic washer. (18)

**horizontal line.** A line that is parallel to the ground. (10)

**house.** Any building that serves as living quarters for one or more families. (4)

**household.** A group of people living together and sharing the same dwelling. (1)

**housing.** Any dwelling that provides shelter. (1)

**housing market.** The transfer of dwellings from the producers to the consumers. (2)

**hue.** The name of a color. It is the one characteristic that makes a color unique. (11)

**human ecology.** The study of people and their environment. (1)

**human resources.** Resources that are available from people, such as abilities, knowledge, attitudes, energy, and health. (3)

**humidifier.** A small appliance that adds the desired amount of moisture into the air. (18)

**HVAC.** A term referring to heating, ventilating and air-conditioning systems. (9)

**hydroelectric power.** Electrical power that is generated by water in dams and rivers. (22)

**hydronic heating system.** A circulating hot water system in which water is heated to a preset temperature and pumped through pipes to radiators. (9)

## I

**implement.** To put thoughts or plans into action. (3)

**incandescent light.** The light produced when an electric current heats a tungsten filament inside a bulb to make it glow with light. (17)

**indirect lighting.** Lighting that is directed mainly toward a ceiling or wall. It is reflected from these surfaces to produce soft, general lighting for a room. (17)

**induction cooktop.** A range that cooks food by using a magnetic field to generate heat in the bottom of cooking utensils. (18)

**informal balance.** The arrangement of different but equivalent objects on both sides of a center point; also called asymmetrical balance. (12)

**infrastructure.** The underlying foundation or basic framework. (2)

**innerspring mattress.** A series of springs covered with padding. (15)

**inspector.** A person who judges the construction and present condition of a house. (5)

**installment buying.** The process of buying something by making a series of payments during a given length of time. (5)

**insulation.** Material used to restrict the flow of heat between a house's interior and the outdoors. (9)

**integrated waste management.** A waste handling concept that conserves energy and cleans the environment. (22)

**intensity.** The brightness or dullness of a hue. (11)

**interest.** The price paid for the use of borrowed money. It is usually stated as an annual percentage rate of the amount borrowed. (5)

**interior designer.** A person who plans the decorating of an interior, makes the purchases, and sees the work is done correctly. (21)

**interior wall elevation.** Presents a view of how a finished wall will look. (16)

**intermediate colors.** Colors made by mixing equal amounts of a primary color and a secondary color; also called tertiary colors. (11)

**International style.** A modern style of architecture and furniture design beginning in the 1900s, influenced strongly by the Bauhaus, the German state school of design. (6)

**Internet.** The network linking thousands of computers from government agencies, businesses, educational institutions, groups, and individuals. (5)

**internship.** An arrangement with an educational institution whereby a student is supervised while working with a more experienced jobholder. (24)

## J

**joist.** Lightweight horizontal support member. (8)

## K

**kit house.** Housing shipped to the site in unassembled parts or as a finished shell from the factory. (4)

**knitting.** The process of looping yarns together. (13)

## L

**laminate.** A product made by uniting one or more different layers, usually a decorative surface to a sturdy core. (14)

**landlord.** A property owner; also called *lessor*. (5)

**landscape.** Outdoor living space. (19)

**landscape architect.** A person professionally trained to create designs that both function well and are aesthetically pleasing. (19)

**landscape zones.** The ground around a building that is divided into three areas—public zone, private zone, and service zone. (19)

**landscaping.** Altering the topography and adding decorative plantings to change the appearance of a site. (4)

**leadership.** The ability to guide and motivate others to complete tasks or achieve goals. (24)

**lead paint.** A term that refers to lead-based paint, which was a common form of paint manufactured before 1978 that contained lead. (20)

**lease.** A legal document listing the conditions under which the renter rents the property as well as the rights and responsibilities of both the owner and the renter. (5)

**lessee.** Another name for *renter*. (5)

**lessor.** Another name for *landlord*. (5)

**life cycle.** A series of stages through which an individual or family passes during a lifetime. (1)

**lifelong learning.** The frequent updating of knowledge and skills; implies that your need for learning will never end. (23)

**lifestyle.** A living pattern or way of life. (1)

**light-emitting diode (LED).** A source of light composed of crystals on silicon chips about the size of a grain of salt that produces light when a small electric current passes through it. (17)

**limited warranty.** A written agreement that obligates a warrantor to make no-charge repairs in specific cases or replace the product under certain conditions. (18)

**line.** The most basic element of design, created when two dots are connected. (10)

**local lighting.** Lighting that is used in specific areas requiring more light. (17)

**log cabin.** Originally a one-room house made from bulky pieces of unshaped lumber. (6)

**long-term goals.** Goals that usually require six months or longer to achieve. (24)

**loss leader.** An item priced well below normal cost to entice people into a store to buy it plus items not on sale. (16)

**low mass.** A space that is simple and sparse. (10)

**lumen.** A measurement of the intensity of light coming from a source. (17)

## M

**Mansard roof.** A variation of the gambrel roof designed by a French architect named Mansard. The low slopes of the roof encircle the house, and dormers often project from the steeply pitched part of the roof. (6)

**manufactured fiber.** Fiber made from wood cellulose, oil products, and other chemicals. (13)

**manufactured housing.** A factory-built, single-family dwelling that can be moved by attached wheels; called a mobile home if built before 1976. (4)

**manufactured landscape elements.** Landscape components that are not found in nature. (19)

**masonry.** A hard building material, such as brick, concrete block, and natural stone. (8)

**mass.** The amount of pattern or objects in a space; also the degree of crowding or openness in a space. (10)

**master's degree.** Requiring another year or two of study beyond a bachelor's degree; also called a *graduate degree*. (23)

**mentor.** Someone with greater experience and knowledge who guides you in your career. (24)

**meter.** A gauge that monitors electrical usage in the house. (9)

**microturbine.** A small turbine engine that produces electricity. (22)

**microwave oven.** An oven that cooks food with high-frequency energy waves called microwaves. (18)

**minimum property standards (MPS).** Standards set by the Federal Housing Administration (FHA) that regulate the size of lots. (4)

**mobile home.** A factory-built, single-family dwelling that can be moved by attached wheels; called manufactured housing if built before 1976. (4)

**mobility limitations.** Conditions that make it difficult for a person to walk from one place to another. (20)

**model.** A three-dimensional miniature of a house design. (7)

**Modern style.** The housing designs developed in the United States from the early 1900s into the 1960s; also refers to the twenty-first century furniture style that uses simpler lines and abstract forms to result in pieces that can be mass produced from automated machinery. (6)

**modular housing.** A type of factory-built housing that combines the wall, floor, ceiling, and roof panels into boxes called modules, complete with windows, doors, plumbing, and wiring before delivery to the site. Modules are joined at the site. (4)

**mold.** A fungus that grows on damp or decaying matter. (20)

**monochromatic color harmony.** The simplest color harmony, based on tints and shades of a single hue. (11)

**mortgage.** A pledge of property that a borrower gives to a lender as security for the payment of a debt. (5)

**mortise-and-tenon joint.** One of the strongest joints used for furniture. The glued tenon fits tightly into the mortise, or hole. (15)

**multifamily house.** A structure that provides housing for more than one household. (4)

**multipurpose furniture.** Furniture that can be used for more than one purpose. (16)

**multipurpose room.** A room used for many types of activities, such as reading, studying, watching TV, listening to music, and working on hobbies. (7)

## N

**nap.** A layer of fiber ends that stand up from the surface of a fabric. (13)

**National Society of Professional Engineers (NSPE).** A professional organization for engineers that requires members to have a high level of preparation and an apprenticeship under a professional engineer. (23)

**Native Americans.** American Indians. (6)

**natural landscape elements.** Landscape components found in the natural environment, such as trees and rocks. (19)

**natural stone.** Hardened earth or mineral matter. (8)

**near environment.** A small and distinct part of the total environment in which you live. (1)

**needlepunching.** The process of interlocking fibers with felting needles to produce a flat carpet that resembles felt. (13)

**needs.** The basic requirements that people must have filled in order to live. (1)

**negotiation.** The process of agreeing to an issue that requires all parties to give and take. (24)

**neighborhood.** A section of a community consisting of a group of houses and people. (4)

**networking.** The exchange of information or services among individuals or groups. (24)

**neutral color harmony.** A color harmony using combinations of black, white, and gray. Brown, tan, and beige can also be used. (11)

**New England.** The region of North America that now includes the states of Maine, New Hampshire, Vermont, Massachusetts, Connecticut, and Rhode Island. (6)

**new town.** An urban development consisting of a small to midsize city with a broad range of housing and planned industrial, commercial, and recreational facilities. (2)

**new urbanism.** Towns that encourage pedestrian traffic, are more in harmony with the environment, and are sustainable. (2)

**noise pollution.** An unwanted sound that spreads through the environment. (20)

**nonhuman resources.** Resources that are not directly supplied by people. Examples include money, property, and community resources. (3)

**nonstructural lighting.** Lights that are not permanently built into a home. They can be moved, changed, and replaced easily. (17)

**nonverbal communication.** The sending and receiving of messages without the use of words. (24)

**nuclear energy.** The heat released when uranium-235 is split in a nuclear reactor. (22)

**nuclear family.** A living unit consisting of parents and

their children; also, a childless married couple. (1)

## O

**occupation.** Paid employment that involves handling one or more jobs. (23)

**opposition.** Lines meeting to form right angles. (12)

**orientation.** placing a structure on a site in consideration of the location of the sun, prevailing winds, water sources, and scenic view. (4)

**overcurrent protection device.** A fuse or circuit breaker that stops the excessive flow of electrical current in a circuit if too much current is being drawn. (9)

**owner-built housing.** Housing constructed by the owner, although a contractor may be hired to put up the shell of the house. (4)

## P

**paint.** A mixture of a pigment and liquid that thinly coats and covers a surface. (14)

**paneling.** A building material that is usually made of plywood, but can be produced from a synthetic material. (14)

**panelized housing.** A form of factory-built housing in which panels of walls, floors, ceilings, or roofs can be ordered separately and assembled at the housing site. (4)

**pent roof.** Small roof ledges between the first and second floors. (6)

**perennials.** Flowers that bloom for several years without replanting. (19)

**personal priorities.** Strong beliefs or ideas about what is important. (1)

**photovoltaic (PV).** Solar cell that converts sunlight into electricity. (22)

**physical needs.** Basic survival essentials, including shelter, food, water, and rest. (1)

**physical neighborhood.** The actual dwellings, buildings, and land that make a neighborhood. (4)

**pigment.** Coloring agent. (11)

**planned neighborhood.** Determining the size and layout of individual lots before building begins. (4)

**plan view.** A view from the top of a building, as with an imaginary glass box. (7)

**plaster.** A paste used for coating walls and ceilings that hardens as it dries. (14)

**plastic wallboard.** A building material with a durable finish that is used on interior walls, usually kitchens and bathrooms. (14)

**plumbing plunger.** A device used to create a suction motion to clear a blocked drain. (21)

**Prairie style.** A style of housing designed by Frank Lloyd Wright with strong horizontal design that uses wood, stone, and materials found in the natural environment. (6)

**precautions.** Preventive actions that can help avoid accidents. (20)

**precut housing.** A type of factory assembly in which most lumber, finish materials, and other components are cut to exact size in the plant and delivered to the building site for assembly. (4)

**pressed wood.** A board made of shavings, veneer scraps, chips, and other small pieces of wood pressed together. Often used on unseen parts of furniture. (15)

**primary colors.** The colors of red, yellow, and blue. All other colors are made from these colors. (11)

**print.** A copy of an architectural drawing. (7)

**prioritize.** Ranking in order of importance. (16)

**private zone.** The part of a site hidden from public view that provides space for recreation and relaxation. (4)

**process.** The method used to accomplish a task. (5)

**proportion.** The relationship of parts of the same object, or the relationship between different objects in the same group. (12)

**protein natural fiber.** Fibers made from animal sources, such as silk and wool. (13)

**psychological needs.** Needs related to the mind, and feelings that must be met in order to live a satisfying life. (1)

**public zone.** The part of a site that can be seen from the street or road, usually the front of the house. (4)

**punctual.** A characteristic of being prompt and on time. (24)

## Q

**quality of life.** The degree of satisfaction obtained from life. (1)

**quiet area.** Space in a house provided for sleeping, resting, grooming, and dressing. (7)

## R

**radiation.** Lines flowing away from a central point. (12)

**radon.** A natural radioactive gas found in the earth. (20)

**rafter.** Any of a series of beams that support the roof. (8)

**ranch.** A style of housing characterized by a one-story structure at ground level that may have a basement. (6)

**rational decision.** A decision based on reasoning. (3)

**realistic form.** The design of an object that communicates a lifelike form and traditional feeling. (10)

**recycle.** Adapting to a new use. (16)

**redecorating.** A change of decorating scheme. (21)

**reference.** An individual who will provide important information about you to a prospective employer. (24)

**reflected light.** Light that bounces off a surface. (17)

**region.** A specific part of the world, country, or state. (4)

**remodeling.** Changing a structure, such as adding a wall or a room. (21)

**rendering.** A drawing with color to show a realistic view of how the completed house will look. (7)

**renegotiable rate mortgage.** A payment contract in which the interest rate and monthly payments are fixed for a stated length of time. When this length of time expires, interest rates are reviewed and may be changed according to the current rate of interest. Also called a rollover mortgage. (5)

**renew.** To give furniture a new look. (16)

**renewable energy sources.** Sources of fuel that replenish themselves regularly, including the sun, wind, water, and geothermal energy, all of which can be converted to electricity. (22)

**renter.** A person who agrees to pay rent for a place to live; also called *lessee*. (5)

**repetition.** Repeating an element of design. It is one of the easiest ways to achieve rhythm in design. (12)

**reproductions.** Copies of antique originals. (15)

**resiliency.** Ability to return to the original size and shape. (13)

**resilient floor covering.** A floor treatment that provides cushioning and is made of materials other than fiber. (14)

**resources.** Objects, qualities, and personal strengths that can be used to reach a goal. (2)

**restore.** Changing a piece of furniture back to its original state. (16)

**resume.** A brief outline of your education, work experience, and other qualifications for work. (24)

**reverse mortgage.** A payment plan designed for older people whereby a mortgage company converts the value of the house into income to the residents for as long as they continuously live in the house. Later the mortgage company assumes ownership of the dwelling. (4)

**rhythm.** A sense of movement that smoothly leads the eyes from one area to another in a design; the cause of an organized pattern. (12)

**ridge.** The horizontal line where the highest point of the roof frame meets. (8)

**roles.** Patterns of behavior that people display in their homes, the workplace, and their communities. (1)

**row houses.** A continuous group of dwellings connected by common side walls. (2)

**R-value.** A measure of how well a material insulates, or resists heat movement. (9)

## S

**saltbox.** A variation of the Cape Cod style of housing created by adding a lean-to section to the back of the house. (6)

**sample board.** A design tool that includes samples of wall, floor, and ceiling treatments for a space. (16)

**scale.** The size of an object on an architectural drawing, drawn proportionately to actual size. The relative size of an object in relation to other objects. (12)

**scale floor plan.** A drawing that shows the size and shape of a room. (16)

**Scandinavians.** Immigrants from Sweden, Finland, Norway, and Denmark. (6)

**seasonal sale.** A sale held at the end of a selling season to eliminate old stock and make room for new items. (16)

**secondary colors.** The colors of orange, green, and violet. These colors are made by mixing equal amounts of two primary colors. (11)

**section view.** A view taken from an imaginary cut through a part of the building, such as the walls. (7)

**security deposit.** A payment that insures the owner against financial loss caused by the renter. (5)

**self-actualization.** When a person develops to his or her full potential as a person. (1)

**self-cleaning oven.** An oven that can be set at extremely high temperatures to burn spills and spatters away. (18)

**self-esteem.** An awareness and appreciation of a person's own worth. (1)

**self-expression.** Showing a person's true personality and taste. (1)

**self-motivation.** An inner urge to get things accomplished. (24)

**semiskilled labor.** Describes workers who have some experience and/or technical training. (23)

**sensory design.** Applying design principles to complement the senses of sight, hearing, smell, and touch. (12)

**septic tank.** Underground tank that decomposes waste through the action of bacteria. (9)

**service drop.** The connecting wires from the pole transformer to the point of entry to the house. (9)

**service entrance panel.** A large metal box that receives power from the electric company's service drop or service lateral. It divides the power into individual circuits. (9)

**service zone.** The part of the site that is used for necessary activities. It includes sidewalks, driveways, and storage areas for such items as trash, tools, lawn equipment, and cars. (4)

**shade.** A value of a hue that is darker than the hue's normal value. (11)

**shades.** Screens that block unwanted light. (17)

**shadowing.** The process of observing a person in the workplace to learn more about his or her job and its requirements. (24)

**shingle.** A protective material installed in overlapping rows on roofs. (8)

**short circuit.** An undesirable current path that allows the electric current to bypass the load of the circuit. (21)

**short-term goals.** Goals that are accomplished in several days or weeks. (24)

**shutters.** Movable hinged screens that cover part or all of a window. (17)

**siding.** The material covering the exposed surface of outside walls of a house. (8)

**sill plate.** A piece of lumber bolted to the foundation wall with anchor bolts. (8)

**single-family house.** Housing designed for one family. (4)

**single-parent family.** A family with only a mother or a father. (1)

**single-person household.** A household consisting of one person living alone in the dwelling. (1)

**site.** The piece of land on which a dwelling is built. (4)

**site-built house.** Housing that is built on a site from the foundation up; also called a stick-built house. (4)

**skilled labor.** Refers to workers who have successfully completed a formal training program beyond high school, such as an apprenticeship. (23)

**smoke detector.** A small device that sounds a loud warning signal if a fire starts. (20)

**social area.** An area providing space for daily living, entertaining, and recreation. (7)

**soft floor covering.** A floor treatment made from fibers, such as carpet and rugs. (14)

**software.** A program of instructions that tells a computer what to do. (18)

**soil conservation.** The act of improving and taking care of the soil. (19)

**soil stack.** A vertical pipe that extends through the roof to vent gases outside. (9)

**solar energy.** Energy derived from the sun. (6)

**solid surface.** A durable countertop material that contains the color and pattern of the surface throughout. (14)

**solid waste.** Any discarded material that is not a liquid or a gas. (22)

**solid wood.** Furniture in which all exposed parts are made of whole pieces of wood. (15)

**Southern Colonial.** A style of housing that features a large two- or three-story frame with a symmetrical design. (6)

**space.** The area around and inside a form. (10)

**space planning.** The process of placing furnishings for a well-functioning and visually pleasing area. (16)

**Spanish.** A housing style from the south and southwest consisting of asymmetrical design with red tile roofs, enclosed patios, arch-shaped windows and doors, wrought iron exterior decor, and stucco walls. (6)

**specifications.** Written information about constructing a design that identifies the types and quality of materials to be used and gives directions for their use. (7)

**split-complementary color harmony.** A color harmony created by choosing one color and adding the two colors on each side of its complement. (11)

**spur-of-the-moment decision.** A decision that is made quickly and with little thought of possible consequences. (3)

**stenciling.** Applying paint by using a cutout form to outline a design or lettering. (14)

**stepfamily.** A blended family consisting of parents and children from previous marriages. (1)

**structural design.** The pattern created by varying the yarns of woven or knitted fabric. (13)

**structural light fixtures.** Fixtures that are permanently built into a home. (17)

**stucco.** A type of plaster applied to the exterior walls of a house. (6)

**stud.** Vertical 2 x 4-inch or 2 x 6-inch framing members. (8)

**subdivision.** A smaller version of the new town concept. (2)

**subflooring.** A covering of plywood sheets that is nailed directly to the floor joists. (8)

**sublet.** To transfer part of the unused portion of a lease to someone else and maintain responsibility. (5)

**substandard.** Houses that are built with inferior materials or workmanship or do not meet local building codes. (2)

**Sunbelt.** The southern and southwestern states of the United States. (2)

**sunroom.** A glass enclosed porch or living room with a sunny exposure. (19)

**sustainable housing.** Housing that is as self-sufficient as possible and uses minimum natural resources. (22)

**symbols.** Icons used on architectural drawings to represent plumbing and electrical fixtures, doors, windows, and other common objects in a house. (7)

**symmetrical.** A design in which identical objects are arranged on both sides of a center point. (6)

**synthetic.** A manufactured material made to imitate or replace another. (14)

**system.** An interacting or interdependent group of items forming a unified whole. (9)

## T

**tactile texture.** How the surface feels to the touch. (10)

**tanned.** Leather treated with tannin, a special acid that makes leather soft and resistant to stains, fading, and cracking. (13)

**task lighting.** Light that is used to help one see well enough to do a certain task, such as writing letters, carving wood, or sewing. (17)

**team.** A small group of people working together for a common purpose. (24)

**technology.** The practical application of knowledge. (2)

**telecommuting.** Working at home or another site through an electronic link to a central office's computer. (2)

**template.** Small piece of paper or plastic scaled to the actual dimensions of the furniture piece it represents. (16)

**tenement houses.** Early apartments. (2)

**textiles.** Any products made from fibers, including fabrics. (13)

**texture.** The way a surface feels or looks. (10)

**thermostat.** Device for regulating room temperature. (9)

**Tidewater South.** An architectural style built by early English settlers in U.S. southern coastal regions. (6)

**tile.** A flat piece of fired clay or natural stone that is available in a wide range of sizes, colors, finishes, and patterns. (14)

**tint.** A value of a hue that is lighter than the hue's normal value. (11)

**title.** A document that gives proof of the rights of ownership and possession of a particular property. (5)

**tongue-and-groove joint.** A joint created by matching a tongue cut on one board to a groove on another. (15)

**topography.** The physical features of the land, such as hills and rivers; the art of representing such features on maps and charts. (2)

**toxic.** Poisonous. (20)

**tract houses.** Groups of similarly designed houses built on a tract of land. (2)

**trade name.** Names used by companies to identify the specific fibers they develop. (13)

**Traditional style.** A housing design created in the past that has survived the test of time and is still being used today; also refers to furniture design. (6)

**traffic patterns.** The paths followed from room to room, or to the outdoors. (7)

**transition.** Drawing attention from one part of an object to another part. (12)

**trap.** A plumbing device that catches and holds a quantity of water. (9)

**triadic color harmony.** A color harmony using three colors that are spaced evenly around the color wheel. (11)

**truss rafters.** A group of members forming a rigid triangular framework for the roof. (8)

**tufted.** Yarn looped into backing material and secured with an adhesive to the backing and a second backing. (13)

**tungsten-halogen light.** The light produced when a gas from the halogen family and tungsten molecules are combined to activate a filament. (17)

## U

**unassembled furniture.** Furniture sold in parts that require assembly. (16)

**unity.** Repeating similar elements of design to relate all parts of a design to one idea. (12)

**universal design.** A concept that guides the design of housing for easier use by everyone. (4)

**unskilled labor.** Describes workers who fill entry-level jobs that require no previous knowledge or experience. (23)

**upholstery.** The fabric, padding, or other material used to make a soft covering for furniture. (13)

## V

**VA-guaranteed mortgage.** A three-party loan involving the borrower (a war veteran), lending firm, and the Veterans Administration (VA). (5)

**value.** The relative lightness or darkness of a hue. (11)

**veneer wall.** A nonsupporting wall tied to the wall frame that is covered with wallboard. (8)

**veneered wood.** Wood made by bonding three, five, or seven thin layers of wood to one another, to a solid wood core, or to a pressed wood core; often uses fine wood as the top layer. (15)

**ventilation.** The circulation of air. (20)

**verbal communication.** Communication that involves speaking, listening, and writing. (24)

**vertical line.** A line that is perpendicular to the ground. (10)

**Victorian.** A style of housing named after Queen Victoria of England that has an abundance of decorative trim. (6)

**virtual reality.** Experiencing a computer-generated image so completely that it seems real. (5)

**vision disability.** Any degree of vision loss. (20)

**visual imagery.** A type of nonverbal communication. It is the language of sight and communicates a certain personality or mood. (10)

**visual pollution.** The destruction of the appearance of the environment as a result of human activities. (22)

**visual texture.** The texture that is seen, but cannot be felt. (10)

**visual weight.** The perception that an object weighs more or less than it really does. (12)

**voltage.** A measure of the pressure used to push the electrical current along a conductor. (9)

## W

**wale.** The diagonal rib or cord pattern of yarn. (13)

**wall treatment.** A covering, such as paint or wallpaper, applied to an interior wall. (14)

**wallpaper.** Decorative paper or vinyl applied to a wall with glue. (14)

**wants.** Things you would like to have. (5)

**warm colors.** Red, yellow, orange, and the colors near them on a color wheel; also called advancing colors. (11)

**warp yarn.** Lengthwise strand that forms the lengthwise grain. (13)

**warranty.** A written guarantee of a product's performance and the maker's responsibilities concerning defective parts. (18)

**water conservation.** The act of reducing water use and stopping the wasting of water. (19)

**waterbed.** A bed with a mattress that is a plastic bag filled with water. (15)

**wattage.** The amount of electricity a bulb uses. (17)

**watts.** A measure of the electrical power used. (9)

**weather stripping.** A strip of material that covers the edges of a window or door to prevent moisture and air from entering the house. (9)

**weaving.** Two sets of yarns that are interlocked at right angles to each other. (13)

**weft yarn.** Crosswise filling yarns that form the crosswise grain. (13)

**window treatment.** An application added to a window unit either for helping control the home environment or for purely decorative purposes. (17)

**wood grain.** The natural decorative characteristics of wood. The pattern depends to a great extent on how the wood is cut from the log. (15)

**work area.** Parts of the house that are needed to maintain and service the other areas. (7)

**work triangle.** The imaginary lines connecting the food preparation and storage center, cleanup center, and cooking and serving centers of a kitchen. (7)

## X

**xeriscape.** Landscapes that are designed to tolerate drought and conserve water. (19)

## Y

**yarn.** A continuous strand made from fibers. (13)

**yurt.** A portable hut made of several layers of felt covered with canvas. (1)

## Z

**zoning regulation.** A government decision that controls land use and specifies the types of buildings and activities permitted in a certain area. (2)

# INDEX